Mass Communication Research

Mass Communication Research

CONTEMPORARY METHODS AND APPLICATIONS

Michael Singletary

University of Tennessee, Knoxville

Longman
New York & London

Mass Communication Research: Contemporary Methods and Applications

Longman, 10 Bank Street, White Plains, N.Y. 10606

Associated companies:
Longman Group Ltd., London
Longman Cheshire Pty., Melbourne
Longman Paul Pty., Auckland
Copp Clark Pitman, Toronto

Acquisitions editor: Kathleen Schurawich
Sponsoring editor: Gordon T. R. Anderson
Development editor: Susan Alkana
Production editor: Victoria Mifsud
Text design adaptation: David Levy
Cover design: David Levy
Cover photo: Wide World Photos, Inc.
Text art: Fine Line, Inc.
Production supervisor: Richard C. Bretan

Library of Congress Cataloging-in-Publication Data

Singletary, Michael W. Date.
　　Mass communication research : contemporary methods and
　applications / Michael W. Singletary.
　　　p. cm.
　　Includes bibliographical references and index.
　　ISBN 0–8013–0882–8
　　1. Mass media—Research—Methodology. I. Title.
　P91.3.S53 1993
　302.23′072—dc20　　　　　　　　　　　　　93–13973
　　　　　　　　　　　　　　　　　　　　　　　　　CIP

1 2 3 4 5 6 7 8 9 10-MA-9796959493

Contents

PART ONE
A Context for Applications
of the Social Science Research Method   1

PART TWO
The Rationale of the
Social Science Research Method   33

PART THREE
On Implementing the Principles
and Techniques of Social Science Research   103

PART FIVE
Some Additional Methods of Research   263

PART SIX
Applying Research Methods to Mass Media   305

PART SEVEN
The Research Literature   395

Preface

In today's marketplace, more than ever before, mass communication students must learn about research methods. Few will go on to become full-time researchers, but many will be in positions of staff or management in which they can use and evaluate research. The mass communication manager, for example, should be able to hire research services knowledgeably and judge the quality of the product. Reporters and writers should be able to make use of research methods for information gathering and data analysis. Advertising and public relations practitioners should be able to use research to plan effective campaigns. For students who do go on to work in survey research, marketing research, or academic research, a knowledge of research methods is essential.

Unfortunately, a first course in research methods can be taxing for both the instructor and the student because research methods are not easy to learn or to teach. Many instructors have seen students' eyes glaze at the mention of "normal distribution" and "threats to validity," and have seen students nod off during a brief discussion of the "exclusivity" requirement of content analysis. Instructors must work at making the material attractive. Students of research often do not respond well to a lecture format. But what is the alternative? How can the students' interest be enhanced? One way is to reduce the emphasis on lectures and increase the emphasis on activity. Another way is to describe the methods and principles of research in terms that the student can relate to. These ideas are the centerpieces of this text.

AUDIENCE FOR THE TEXT

This text is designed for a one- or two-semester course in research methods for undergraduate students and master's students of mass communication. It is written at a readable level, yet it does not avoid technical and difficult issues. Even doctoral students will find value in the straight forwardness in many of the explanations and statistical applications. The chapters on statistics are supported by a classroom research example—a survey of students' attitudes about the environment and their use of media in the formation of those attitudes.

FEATURES OF THE TEXT

Jargon-Free Language

Mass communicators, above all, appreciate the simple declarative sentence and active verb. With that in mind, this text uses "plain talk." It cuts through dense explanations to present topics in the plainest terms and to be "reader friendly."

Complete Coverage

At the same time, much of this material cannot be spoon-fed. For example, grasping the logic of statistics can be a strain, yet that logic is important to an understanding of research methods. This text maintains clarity, conciseness, and balance without watering down the substance.

Chapter Objectives

Objectives at the beginning of each chapter help you to select and focus on the most important features.

Chapter Summaries

Summaries end every chapter, helping you to absorb each chapter as a separate lesson.

Learn by Doing

Although reading is important, experience is the best teacher. The study of research methods should include as much illustrative activity as possible. On the strength of that principle, each chapter of this text offers exercises called Learning by Doing to illustrate the material. Most exercises can be done alone; some should be used in class.

Study Questions and Exercises

In addition to the exercises, each chapter offers study questions, many of which are also activity-centered. Finally, the text contains many illustrative examples.

TOPICS COVERED IN TEXT

The text covers all of the topics vital to learning mass communication research:

- The Logic and Method of Social Science
- Working with Samples
- Measurement of Social Science Variables
- Data Collection and Instrument Design
- Survey Research
- The Experimental Method
- Data Analysis
- Qualitative Research
- Content Analysis

In addition, the book offers other distinguishing topics:

Ethics

In today's research climate, the study of ethics is very important. Researchers have a moral obligation to protect both their subjects and the users of their data. This text highlights the importance of research ethics by devoting an entire early chapter to it.

History

Research methods should not be studied in isolation; the field has a history, a present, and a future. Chapter 2 provides a brief review and prospectus, and a context for understanding the kinds of research methods.

Computers

In the computer age, a research methods text should include a chapter about computer applications. Many of you will want to use computers in data analysis. Chapter 13 is designed to guide you from a questionanire to a computer printout. Computers can add excitement and a sense of accomplishment to what would otherwise be an abstract study.

Libraries

Most of a researcher's work begins in the library, yet few students know what information the library holds or how to find it. Chapter 20 provides the basic information for using the library effectively.

Applications

Four chapters present specific information about the practical application of research methods in the print media, broadcast media, public relations, and advertising.

ORGANIZATION OF THE TEXT

Although a great deal of thought went into the organization of this text, it is doubtful that any chapter organization would suit all users. Readers will ask: Should statistics come first, middle, or last? Should experiments precede surveys? Should computer applications precede data analysis? The questions suggest an analogy: In a cafeteria line, it matters not which items are selected first or last, but only that at the end of the line the plate is full. Knowledge of research methods is a full plate indeed, and the order of the items is less important than the fullness of the plate. Many of the chapters of this text can stand alone; the instructor can reorder them to suit personal style and the students' achievement level.

Part One: Context

Chapter 1 is a light, informative introduction that will pique young professionals' interest in the application of research to a variety of mass media career fields. Chapter 2 presents an overview of the history of social research as it relates to mass media.

Part Two: Rationale

Chapter 3 demonstrates the logic of social science and explains the rules of objective decision making. Chapter 4 shows how samples can be used to represent populations, and Chapter 5 describes the measurement of social science variables.

Part Three: Implementation

Chapter 6 examines research ethics. Chapter 7 presents questionnaire design and question-writing, and Chapters 8 and 9 discuss two of the principal methods of the field, surveys and experiments.

Part Four: Analysis

Chapter 10 describes summary and descriptive statistics; Chapter 11 includes t-tests, correlation, and analysis of variance; and Chapter 12 includes regression, factor analysis, and nonparametric statistics. An instructor can choose from among these according to need. Chapter 13 is designed to enable the student to input data and conduct elementary statistical analysis (if there is such a thing).

Part Five: Other Methods

Chapter 14 introduces qualitative research, and Chapter 15, content analysis. These chapters could be used with Part Three.

Part Six: Mass Media Applications

Although the methods of social science are generic, adaptations have been made for specific media: print, broadcast, public relations, and advertising. These chapters are contributed by persons who specialize in each area.

Part Seven: Library

Chapter 20 introduces the student to the library and the vast resources that it offers. Its placement in no way signifies the importance placed on the material. Instructors who prefer can simply direct students to the chapter at the proper time.

ACKNOWLEDGMENTS

The author would like to thank the following reviewers for their helpful comments and suggestions:

Susan Strohm, Pennsylvania State University
Michael Ryan, University of Houston
Jeremy Lipschultz, University of Nebraska, Omaha
Bruce Garrison, University of Miami
Charles Whitney, University of Illinois
Ardyth Sohn, University of Colorado

The author would also like to thank Joyce Wolburg for extensive reading and suggestions, and Don Cunningham for his help on the statistical chapters.

Contributors

Herbert H. Howard is professor of broadcasting and assistant Dean for graduate studies in the College of Communications, University of Tennessee, Knoxville. He holds a Ph.D. in mass communication from Ohio University and is co-author of textbooks on broadcast advertising and programming.

Mariea Grubbs Hoy is an assistant professor of advertising at the University of Tennessee, Knoxville. Dr. Hoy received her Ph.D. in business administration from Oklahoma State University. She teaches undergraduate and graduate courses in advertising research and advertising management.

Susan Lucarelli, formerly Susan Caudill, is an assistant professor in the School of Journalism, College of Communications, at the University of Tennesse, Knoxville. Dr. Lucarelli earned her doctoral degree in communications at the University of Tennessee, Knoxville, in 1989. She is the author of numerous refereed journal articles and is co-author of a book on the training and hiring of journalists.

Jane S. Row, M.L.S., is reference coordinator for the social sciences at the University of Tennessee, Knoxville.

Michael J. Stankey is an associate professor of advertising at the University of Tennessee, Knoxville. Dr. Stankey received his Ph.D in communications from the University of Illinois at Urbana-Champaign. He teaches undergraduate and graduate courses in advertising media planning, advertising management, and advertising campaigns.

Susan M. Strohm is an assistant professor in the School of Communications at Pennsylvania State University. She received her Ph.D. in mass communications from the University of Minnesota. Her research and teaching interests include the role of mass media in social conflict and social movements, advertising media planning and advertising ethics, and research methods.

Ronald E. Taylor is professor and head of the department of advertising at the University of Tennessee, Knoxville, where he teaches a doctoral studies course in qualitative research.

S. Paul Wright is an instructor of statistics, University of Tennessee, Knoxville.

Mass
Communication
Research

PART ONE

A Context for Applications of the Social Science Research Method

- Chapter 1: Research in the Field. Opening with a case study, Chapter 1 introduces you to applications of research in mass media. Also presented are an example of theoretical research and a discussion of the place of research in the field of mass communication today.
- Chapter 2: A Brief History of Mass Communication Research. In the belief that research methods should not be studied in isolation, Chapter 2 outlines the historical development of social science research from European roots to present practice. Milestones in research and some important researchers are discussed.

CHAPTER

1

Research in the Field

□
OBJECTIVES

After studying this chapter, you should be able to:

1. Identify some researchable problems in mass media.

2. Distinguish between applied and theoretical research.

3. Explain the need for "research literacy."

4. Explain the importance of research for society.

5. Describe several data-collection methods.

A CASE STUDY: USING RESEARCH IN PROFESSIONAL PRACTICE

In a recent presidential election, news editors of a Charlotte, N.C., newspaper and a TV station felt frustration with routine coverage of political news. Too often, they said, coverage of the news was managed or manipulated by political interests. For example, a politician would call a news conference and reporters would dutifully report what they were told, and little else. The news executives feared this kind of news reporting would not sufficiently inform the public. They reasoned that voters, to some extent, should lead politicians as well as be led by them.

The editors asked: If a politician says the most important issues of the day are X and Y, does the typical person on the street agree? In other words, does the political agenda of those who make the news match the political agenda of those who read or view the news? And if the person on the street agrees that the important issues are X and Y, is that person satisfied with the quantity and quality of information about the issues?

The editors of the Charlotte, N.C., *Observer* and the news director of Charlotte's WSOC-TV decided to do a little research. More precisely, they called on KPC Research, a subsidiary of the Knight Publishing Company, the parent company of the *Observer*, to do the research. They invited the Florida-based Poynter Institute, an academic institute for continuing journalism education, to lend a hand. The sponsors then initiated an impressive effort to improve the coverage of news in the Charlotte market.

The pairing of a newspaper and a TV station might seem strange because the two are sometimes viewed as competitors, but in this case it was not strange at all. Both wanted to know what the public felt were the issues, and how the issues were being covered. The news executives saw their roles in the news business as different enough to justify cooperation, and the joint effort also reduced the cost of the project for each sponsor.

KPC Research designed a questionnaire to identify the issues of the day and to measure the level of public satisfaction with political news in the market. They then conducted a telephone survey of 1,003 persons in the multicounty metro area. The survey provided baseline data on attitudes about political news.

During the interviews, respondents were asked if they would be willing to serve as part of an ongoing panel that could be contacted later about specific political issues. A **panel** is a sample of people who are surveyed at several different times. About 530 persons volunteered, and they were interviewed periodically during the 1992 political election. The results of the initial survey and the subsequent panel surveys led to many headlines and thousands of words of copy for the citizens of Charlotte.

Aside from serving an informational function, the *Observer*–WSOC-TV–Poynter research also served a promotional function. Promotion is important to media because, even when competition is minimal, media are entirely dependent on public support of their product. On the basis of this research, the sponsors were able to promote themselves to the audience as "going the extra mile," so to speak, to provide the best political information for the 1992 election.

For example, the *Observer* explained that its political coverage would be deeper than the usual "horse race" story in which candidate A leads candidate B by some number of percentage points. And the news would "go beyond political schemes and symbols" to focus on the facts underlying the issues. "We will seek to reduce the coverage of campaign strategy and candidates' manipulations, and increase the focus on voters' concerns. We will seek to distinguish between issues that merely influence an election's outcome, and those of governance that will be relevant after the election. We will link our coverage to the voters' agenda, and initiate more questions on behalf of the voters," the newspaper wrote under the headline: "We'll help you regain control of the issues" (Jan. 12, 1992).

The survey revealed that people in the market were "more and more upset with politics" and with politicians. They felt that politicians, once elected, tended to ignore constituents and that citizens had little ability to turn things around. The *Observer* noted that 58 percent of North Carolina adults failed to vote in the important Jesse Helms/Harvey Gantt Senate election of 1990 (Jan. 12, 1992). The survey further revealed that the leading issues in the community were the economy and taxes, followed by education, family values, crime, health care, and the environment.

Armed with the knowledge of what the Charlotte citizens felt was important, the *Observer* began to feature stories that addressed the issues. For example, on Jan. 23, 1992, the *Observer* juxtaposed survey results on health issues with a story about the U.S. Senate's consideration of a health insurance bill. From this, it was easy for the reader to see whether the Senate's direction was consonant with local wishes. Similarly, survey results were woven into stories on the economy (Jan. 26, 27), the State-of-the-Union speech (Jan. 28), college/university costs (Jan. 28), crime/drugs (Feb. 2), and other stories.

Although the most common kind of mass media research involves audience measurement and advertising, the *Observer*–WSOC–Poynter project is a good example of how research can be brought into other day-to-day workplace concerns of the mass media. Just 20 years ago, such a project was much less likely to happen. But today, managers, marketers, public relations personnel, and others are increasingly reliant on research to help in making decisions, and indications are that research will be used even more widely in the future. Moreover it will be used in a wide range of applications. Below are just a few more examples.

SOME OTHER RESEARCHABLE MASS MEDIA PROBLEMS

- Your news director assures you, the station manager, that the station's news team is "the best in the market," but you are unsure whether the news director's perception is shared by the audience. This is important, because the broadcaster who misjudges the audience risks losing big bucks in the ratings wars. How will you decide?

- You open a weekly newspaper in a small town in your state, and the paper becomes very successful. Now you want convert to a triweekly or even a five-day newspaper. You cannot afford to botch the expansion. How will you decide which move to make?

- You manage a radio station in a crowded market. Your station consistently ranks several places below the top rating. Should you lobby for a change in format (i.e., should you abandon your present playlist and adopt a new one)? Will your present audience stay on your frequency? How will you decide what to do?

- You are a public relations professional charged with maximizing public support for the work of a corporation. What is the present level of public support, and what are the corporation's strengths and weaknesses in the public's perception? How can you use research to improve the situation?

- You feel that your newspaper's *penetration* (defined as the proportion of subscribers to potential subscribers, or subscriber homes to total homes) is insufficient. Suppose there is a large audience that you are not reaching. Why are they not reading your newspaper, and what can you do to attract them?

Those are some problems the mass communication *manager* might face. Is research also relevant to the *staffer* (i.e., the reporter, advertising representative, or public relations person)? Consider these possibilities:

- The news reporter (any medium) wants to know if minorities and whites convicted of the same crime, are treated equally in the criminal court system of a city. How would the reporter decide? Would it be sufficient simply to look at raw percentages of the convicted or time sentenced? Social research methods give specific criteria and techniques for such decisions.

- The layout person for a magazine or a newspaper wants to know whether the color photograph that will sell the most copies of the periodical is of a pair of happy coeds washing a car on a sunny day, or an action/violence scene from the latest international crisis. This is a decision that can either support or damage a medium's competitiveness. How would one decide?
- The advertising representative needs to know which of several measures gives the best prediction of market success; or perhaps which kind of advertisement— "celebrity" or "slice-of-life"—will do the best job of moving customers to a product.

THEORETICAL RESEARCH

Although the most common kind of research in communication is **applied research,** especially audience studies, another kind of research is also very important to the field. It is called **pure research, basic research,** or **theoretical research,** and it typically is aimed at understanding and predicting communication *behavior* rather than at business issues. This is not to say that theoretical research is irrelevant to business, but that it usually has less urgency and more generality than applied research. Indeed, a *theory of news readership,* for instance, should be highly relevant to the business side of the media.

Applied research is sometimes called *administrative research* because it is used for administrative purposes. Theoretical research explores the relationships among phenomena, issues such as whether *A causes B* or whether *B* is largely explained by *C, D,* and *E.*

A Research Example

For example, Potter (1992, 392–405) conducted a study of how adolescents' perceptions of "television reality" change with maturity. "Television reality," or "TV reality" refers to the degree to which a viewer perceives what is seen on television as being the same as "real life." The nature of youthful "TV reality" is important if we are to study the kinds of things that children *learn* from television. It is important to know what and how they learn from television because these things sometimes are expressed in subsequent behavior. For example, children who are not taught otherwise might be more willing to resort to violence to solve real-life problems if that is the TV model they see.

Participants in Potter's research were students of a middle and high school affiliated with a large state university. The students were surveyed in 1983, 1985, and 1987. Four types of measures were obtained: the "reality" of television, the amount of TV viewing, some psychological measures, and some demographic (descriptive) measures. The plan was to compare levels of viewing and reality across age groups in order to track the changes in perceived reality that accompany maturity.

Although the interpretation was complex, Potter found, as expected, that the degree of reality attributed to television decreased as students moved through high school. Furthermore, he concluded that perceptions of reality have more than one dimension. For example, very young children tend to see television as a "magic window" with high correspondence to their life; but by the sixth grade, students begin to add a *probability* dimension. They say that certain things are possible, if not likely.

Potter suggested two other dimensions: utility and identity. *Identity* is the extent to which the person identifies with a TV character, and *utility* is the extent to which a TV presentation relates to the viewer's life.

What are the benefits of knowing the dimensions of reality for subsequent research? If you wanted to know, for example, whether persons who thought TV fiction was lifelike were more likely to be fearful of going outdoors, it would be important to study the fear in all of its aspects. This line of thought (measurement of dimensions) will be resumed in Chapter 5.

LEARN BY DOING

With the permission of your instructor, study the research practices of a local radio station, newspaper, TV station, or cable outlet. Learn how or whether the mass medium makes use of research, and the kind of research and the purpose of the research. Write a two-page report of what you find. Include a discussion of research that might be useful to the medium but that is not being conducted, if any. Describe management's attitude or orientation toward the use of research: Is research incidental, essential, a publicity gimmick, or a bona fide management tool? What research should the medium pursue?

Academicians and Theory

Most theoretical research, partly because it is slower to produce financial dividends, is conducted by academicians. Although complex and sometimes arduous, it nevertheless can be exciting as well as profound. Imagine the excitement, for example, when a researcher identifies an important relationship between variables that previously might not have been apparent to an observer; imagine creating a new and persuasive explanation for an aspect of behavior.

This kind of research amounts to *discovery*, and the social researchers are the Columbuses and Boones of the discipline. They blaze new trails and find new territories. The purpose of the discovery, of course, is to understand communication behavior.

On Research Literacy

The pages and chapters that follow describe research techniques that will help you to analyze problems of theory and practice. If media managers of the future are to compete successfully in an arena of intense competition, then they must learn to use the resources, such as the massive databases that are available today, and the techniques, such as social science research, that are available to them. They must learn to distinguish between good data and poor data, good research and bad research, and to recognize a research opportunity when they see one. In a phrase, they must become research literate.

For example, when a newspaper or broadcast station uses a sample of a few hundred, or even as many as 2,000, to represent a market that numbers in six, seven, or even eight figures, can the sample be trusted? Under certain conditions it can, as will be discussed in Chapter 4, and the critic will need to know those conditions. And what about how the survey questions are asked: Will the outcome of the research depend on the way the questions are written or presented? Will another researcher obtain the same results if two studies were conducted simultaneously? Many questions can be asked, and indeed they must be asked if a mass media person is to make good use of research.

Research as Management Style

Research should be part of the ongoing management style, not limited to miracle-cure applications introduced only at the eleventh hour of a management crisis. For example, if a newspaper or a radio station has suffered decline over a number of years and now has reached the crisis stage, then it is possible that the hour might be past when research would be useful. This is not an absolute, but a possibility. The insights from research might not reverse a decline that has been years in the making. A better management plan would be to keep a research finger on the pulse of the medium, and to make adjustments in the product as the pulse indicates.

THE IMPORTANCE OF RESEARCH FOR SOCIETY

Social research is important at three levels: the *personal* level, wherein we try to understand complex events and behaviors; the *economic* level, in which business decisions are made on the basis of data; and the *institutional* level, especially involving the interaction of mass media, individuals, and society.

Reliance on Media

The three levels probably overlap. DeFleur (1970) pointed out that in our society, where individuals may not have the support of an extended family to guide them, we are increasingly dependent on media sources of information. We rely on media for knowledge of current events and to prepare for business, education, entertainment, shopping, and so on. We rely on media to help us resolve political issues through public debate so that we don't have to resolve them by fighting in the streets. Donahue, Tichenor, and Olien (1972, 41–69), in an inspired essay on gatekeeping, discussed this function of the media in terms of "conflict resolution."

Media as Agenda Setters

But are the mass media passive and objective purveyors of information, or are they *leading* us as individuals and as societies? If they are leading us, then to where? and is their leadership proper and optimal? This line of inquiry implies a popular research area: agenda setting (McCombs and Shaw, 1972, 176–187). The principle of *agenda setting* is that the media may not be successful in telling us what to think, but they are quite successful in telling us what to think about (Cohen, 1963, 13). In other words, the media tend to set our agenda. Numerous research studies have examined and generally documented this tendency.

Agenda setting is an important issue. If the media tell us the recent fire, or hurricane, or explosion, or conflict is salient (as evidenced by placement and frequency of news stories)—but do not tell us about the nature, extent, and implications of water pollution, indigent care, education quality, or some other issue that lacks audience appeal—then it is possible that the media have not done us a proper service. Social research helps to explain who we are and where we are going. Research can help the media to function as surveyors of the environment.

The point here is that social research is important not just to administrative decision making, but even to survival of the species. Research provides a mirror with which we can see ourselves, and understand behaviors and events, and with which we can test the assumptions that drive society. Social research provides the power to correct the trajectory of the "Spaceship Earth."

WHO CAN DO RESEARCH?

Who Is a Researcher?

Writing survey questions and gathering data are easy; writing good questions and collecting useful data are not. Almost anyone can gather information and call it research, and a researcher might actually be self-trained, but a certain amount of formal training is desirable. Once trained in the general social science method and in data interpretation, the researcher might apply the method to any appropriate field, whether epidemiology, sociology, or mass communication.

Training in Research

How much training is required? For many research positions, the only hard rule is that the training be sufficient. This probably requires several university courses in research methods and research design, and several in statistics.

Also required is familiarity with statistical computer "packages," especially SAS, formerly known as the Statistical Analysis System, and SPSS, formerly known as the Statistical Package for the Social Sciences. For some research jobs, knowledge of formal computer languages is required. In general, the more extensive the person's training, the greater the research opportunity. Licensure of researchers is not required.

Mass media organizations occasionally publish handbooks on audience research methods (for example, the National Association of Broadcasters [1980] for many years distributed a primer of research methods), and some of the methods are easily applied. To a manager, the temptation of good data obtained cheaply is tantalizing; but discretion is advised. The most successful researchers—the ones least likely to reach beyond the data, and the ones least likely to err in interpretation—are the ones with the most training and experience. Much research is best left to trained and experienced researchers.

The Use of Statistics in Research

The study of *statistics* can be on either of two levels, theoretical or applied. *Theoretical* statistics includes the math that makes statistical hypothesis testing possible. *Applied* statistics, on the other hand, emphasizes applications. The study of statistics on an applied level is both an asset and a liability. As an asset, the applied approach moves math-phobic communicators quickly into complex data analysis. As a liability, the researcher who applies statistical tests without adequate comprehension risks embarrassment, misinterpretation, and poor decision making.

The best advice to the novice researcher is to learn as much as possible about statistics. Indeed, it is virtually impossible to read the behavioral journals in mass communication and the allied fields without a solid background in statistics.

INTRODUCTION TO SEVERAL DATA-COLLECTION METHODS

There are numerous approaches to data collection, and not all are quantitative. Surveys, secondary analyses, experiments, content analysis, and qualitative research will be covered in chapters that follow. Historiography and legal research, which are beyond the scope of this text, usually are taught in separate classes.

Survey Research

Surveys are the primary data-collection technique in mass media studies today. Survey research can be of two types, descriptive and analytical. Descriptive surveys are used to describe the characteristics of a population. For example, a newspaper publisher wants to know the characteristics of the newspaper reader. These might include demographics such as age, income, home ownership, education, and so on; or other qualities such as amount of time spent reading the paper, or level of interest in selected newspaper content.

Analytical surveys usually are more narrow in their focus, but not more narrow in their contribution to the understanding of behavior. For example, analytical surveys might be used to examine the strength of selected variables, such as membership in civic clubs, in explaining a behavioral phenomenon such as likelihood of voting in a local election. Analytical surveys are useful in prediction and in establishing the relationship among variables.

In the simplest form of descriptive survey research, the researcher draws a sample of respondents and asks them to fill out a questionnaire. Responses are tabulated in frequency form or converted to percentages. But surveys can be as simple or as complex as the researcher and the research question require. In more complex designs, the researcher's arsenal includes advanced techniques such as log linear analysis, factor analysis, and regression analysis. Truly, the extent of analysis that is possible through survey research is impressive.

How has the computer revolution impacted survey research? One direct impact is in the development of samples. For example, the computer can be programmed to produce random samples of telephone numbers. On a larger scale, the computer facilitates the generation of high-quality, national, cross-sectional samples—no mean feat.

Other direct impacts of the computer are related to data collection, data analysis, and word processing. Increasingly, researchers are relying on interviewers and respondents to input data on computers, with the obvious benefit of quicker analysis. Today, theoretical and applied researchers can accomplish in moments what in the previous generation would have taken more than a lifetime.

Secondary Analysis

An opportunity for research that escapes many is known as *secondary analysis*. The principle is simply that certain important data-collection agencies, for example the National Opinion Research Center at the University of Michigan, the bound volumes of Gallup and Roper studies, and the U.S. Census, make wonderful data sets available for anyone who has the skill to use them. The researcher needs only the research question to ask, or the hypothesis to test, to use these carefully drawn national random samples of adult Americans.

A recent example of secondary analysis involved a study of the influence of newspaper endorsements on election results (Hurd and Singletary, 1984). The authors analyzed the responses of some 3,000 Americans on how they used their newspaper and how their reading of newspaper endorsements affected their vote in the presidential election. They found that the influence of newspaper endorsements in a presidential election was very small, about 1 percent, but they noted that some elections are close enough that 1 percent can be crucial to the outcome. For instance, 1 percent of 50,000,000 is 500,000 votes, or more than the total cast in several western states.

Given the cost of survey research, most researchers are unlikely to be able to generate a comparable national sample from the population at large without financial support. Secondary data sources are a great resource that more often should be exploited.

Experimental Research

If you are new to research methods, then you might have the idea that the laboratory experiment is the most common kind of social research. Actually, in mass communication, the survey method is most common. But certainly, many experimental studies have been conducted and many have contributed to our understanding of "how things work." The strength of experimental research is in its environmental and statistical *control*.

Equivalence. For example, the influence of an experimental manipulation on one group of participants can be compared with its influence on another group; however, the groups must be equivalent from the outset by random or matched membership in the group. That is one kind of control.

Manipulation. Another kind of control has to do with experimental manipulation, whereby the researcher introduces as much of an experimental treatment as needed. For example, a researcher might show one group an essay with 10 errors, and a second group an essay with 20 errors, to learn whether the error level affects the credibility of the essay.

Environment. A third kind of control is in regard to the environment. If you are studying the effect of a variable on the performance of two groups, you certainly would want the two groups to have the same kind of environment. Otherwise, the differences in environment might cause some of the differences observed in the outcome of the study.

Content Analysis

 Content analysis involves "the objective, systematic, quantitative description of the manifest (or latent) content of communication" (Berelson, 1952, 18). In simplest terms, content analysis requires the analyst to count the occurrence or co-occurrence of variables. These variables can be themes, ideas, words, or styles—anything that can be objectively identified and counted. Content analysis can even be applied to photographs and advertisements, as well as to music lyrics, poetry, legal documents, books, political speeches, and so on.

Content analysis offers the researcher the opportunity to read between the lines of text, that is, to study not only manifest content but latent content. Even an author, for example, may be unaware that a text involves recurrent or subtle themes, but these themes can be objectively identified through content analysis. Content analysis has been used, for example, to identify the authors of some of the Federalist Papers, and to help decide if Francis Bacon or someone else wrote some of the plays attributed to William Shakespeare (see Chapter 13).

Historiography

Historiography is a kind of social science research method, although some scholars prefer to think of history as humanistic rather than scientific. Historical studies can be oral, traditional, or quantitative. *Oral histories* include extensive taped interviews with persons prominent in historical topics. For example, a historian studying the music of Appalachia might record interviews with individuals whose personal knowledge and experience contribute to an understanding of the music and the region.

Traditional historical studies are document based, usually relying heavily on primary and secondary library resources. Primary documents include items such as correspondence (e.g., the letters of President Andrew Jackson), financial ledgers, diaries, and autobiographies. Primary documents are important because they are closest to the reality and the context of the historical topic. Secondary sources risk filtration through other perspectives. For that reason, the scholarly journals in the field of mass communication generally avoid research that leans primarily on secondary sources.

Quantitative history is a nontraditional but important approach to the collection of data. The quantitative historian uses original and objective historical data, such as newspaper production costs, circulation figures, and census data, to investigate hypotheses about questions of history. For example, one historian compared the frequency of stories about the politics of slavery in Northern and Southern pre–Civil War newspapers to explain regional differences in political outlook (Shaw, 1984, 483–492). Another studied the extent to which the names of newspapers reflect the sociopolitical temper of the times (Caudill and Caudill, 1988, 16–25).

Although many traditional historians look with great suspicion on quantitative approaches to history (on the argument that numbers do not tell a sufficient story), quantitative approaches can add valuable insights to the people, events, and ideas of history.

Qualitative Research

Nonquantitative research sometimes is referred to as **qualitative research,** perhaps for want of a more descriptive term. The differences between quantitative and qualitative research are both subtle and profound. In general, qualitative research does not rely on quantitative hypothesis testing or the use of samples for inference to a population. Qualitative research relies more on observation, intuition, and personal insight.

Qualitative research involves several separate methods: traditional historiography, case studies, focus groups, observer studies (participant or unobtrusive), interviews, and what might be called reflective essays. Differences between qualitative research and quantitative research center on methods of data collection, kinds of data, sampling, reliability, conclusion drawing, and theory building. These are not trivial differences.

In some quarters today, it is being argued that the quantitative method has been insufficiently productive, and that the time has come to look for alternative methods. Although the author disagrees that communication research has become stagnant, or that the quantitative method has been insufficiently productive, the time is always right to look for alternative methods. Truth, after all, is where you find it, regardless of the source.

Legal Research

A hybrid area of mass media scholarship, legal research generally is neither quantitative nor qualitative, except marginally. Legal researchers examine cases and legal principles to gain an understanding of developments in law. For example,

McLean (1988, 152–157) studied the decisions of a federal judge elevated to the Supreme Court in order to anticipate directions the Court might take with his presence.

A few legal studies have involved quantitative approaches; others have been historical; but most are reviews of legal philosophy and case law on specific legal issues. You might ask: Shouldn't the legal scholar be a lawyer? The answer: not necessarily; a great deal of useful legal research can be accomplished by the non-lawyer academic legal scholar. For the nonquantitative researcher and the non-historian, legal research is an attractive alternative.

LEARN BY DOING

Select one or more research methods identified and discussed in this chapter and read an article on each that employs the research method. The articles can be found in any of the popular scholarly journals of the field, including *Journalism Quarterly, Journal of Broadcasting and Electronic Media, Journal of Communication,* or any other research journal representing the discipline of your interest. Write a one-page paper describing the method and the outcome of the research. What did you see as the strengths and weaknesses of the research?

SUMMARY

Research for mass media is not limited to audience analysis and opinion polling, but is also conducted for a broad range of day-to-day problem-solving applications. Problem-solving research is generally called *applied* research. One way of distinguishing between applied and theoretical research is to say that applied research has to do with behaviors or outcomes, and theoretical research is to say that applied research has to do with behaviors or outcomes, and theoretical research has to do with *explanations* of the behaviors or outcomes. Mass media managers should adopt research as an ongoing management style. Research is important not just for managers, but also for society. There are several broad categories of research, some of them requiring knowledge of statistics, others requiring archival or textual data.

STUDY QUESTIONS AND EXERCISES

1. Review the article titles of some recent editions of scholarly journals such as *Journalism Quarterly, Journal of Broadcasting and Electronic Media, Newspaper Research Journal,* and *Communication Research.* Select and scan a small number of articles, then report on the style and findings of the research.

2. Distinguish between applied and theoretical research. Give an example of each.

3. Chapter 1 suggested that the goal of communication research is in "understanding" communication behavior. But why is that important? What would be the benefit to society of having a good understanding of communication?

4. One of the research projects discussed in Chapter 1 was said to have a promotional benefit as well as a knowledge benefit. Should we be concerned about whether the use of research for promotion will undermine scholarly uses of research?

SOURCES

Berelson, Bernard. 1952. *Content Analysis in Communication Research.* New York: Free Press.

Caudill, Edward, and Susan Caudill. 1988. Nation and Section: Analysis of Key Symbols in the Antebellum Press. *Journalism History* 15(1):16–25.

Cohen, Bernard. 1963. *The Press and Foreign Policy.* Princeton, N.J.: Princeton University Press.

DeFleur, Melvin L. 1970. *Theories of Mass Communication.* 2d ed. New York: David McKay.

Donahue, George A., Phillip J. Tichenor, and Clarice N. Olien. 1972. Gatekeeping: Mass Media Systems and Information Control. In *Sage Annual Reviews of Communication Research.* Vol. 1, *Current Perspectives in Mass Communication Research,* ed. F. Gerald Kline and Phillip J. Tichenor. Beverly Hills, Calif.: Sage.

Hurd, Robert E., and Michael W. Singletary. 1984. Newspaper Endorsements in the 1980 Elections. *Journalism Quarterly* 61(2):332–339.

McCombs, Maxwell E., and Donald L. Shaw. 1972. The Agenda-Setting Function of the Mass Media. *Public Opinion Quarterly* 36(2): 176–187.

McLean, Deckle. 1988. Press May Find Scalia Frequent Foe but Impressive Adversary. *Journalism Quarterly* 65(1):152–157.

National Association of Broadcasters. 1980. *A Broadcast Research Primer.* 9th ed. Washington, D.C.

Potter, W. James. 1992. How Do Adolescents' Perceptions of Television Reality Change over Time? *Journalism Quarterly* 69(2):392–405.

Rubin, Rebecca B., Alan M. Rubin, and Linda J. Piele. 1993. *Communication Research: Strategies and Sources.* 3d ed. Belmont, Calif.: Wadsworth.

Shaw, Donald L. 1984. News about Slavery from 1820–1860 in Newspapers South, North and West, *Journalism Quarterly* 61(3):483–492.

2

A Brief History of Mass Communication Research

□

OBJECTIVES

After studying this chapter, you should be able to:

1. Outline the development of social science research in history.

2. Identify some of the principal mass communication theorists of the early twentieth century.

3. Describe mass communication research as the evolution of data from qualitative to quantitative.

4. Identify several important researchers of the 1940s, 1950s, and 1960s (e.g., Paul Lazarsfeld, Carl Hovland, Wilbur Schramm).

5. Identify Marshall McLuhan and his contribution to the effects tradition.

6. Identify a potentially important new juncture in the history of mass communication research methods.

Harold Innis, reflecting on his study of communication across the ages, told the story of two college graduates gabbing: "Literature?" asked one. "Sure; we took it in the senior year. It had a green cover" (Innis, 1973, 194).[1] The point is that students sometimes see the trees without seeing the forest, or the text without a context. Students of mass communication research need to see the big picture, the broad perspective, not just the cover.

Like literature, research methods should not be studied in isolation. The field has a history, a present, and a future. And whatever our consensus on research methods, our present circumstances didn't occur overnight or by fiat, but by increments of logic and experience across the years. The methods we have are a product of our history. A different history would produce different research outcomes, and perhaps even different techniques. You will need to know something of the history of social research in order to critique the method and to discover its place in the pursuit of truth and understanding.

THREE PERIODS IN THE HISTORY OF RESEARCH METHODS

Weaver and Gray have suggested that the history of mass communication research is roughly divided into three periods (Weaver and Gray, 1980, 124). Figure 2.1 lists the major research focuses of each period. Note that prior to about 1800, there was virtually no research devoted to the study of the press as a medium of communication (although not all agree[2]). That seems especially odd today, when so many people are concerned about the functions and the effects of media. Because Figure 2.1 was prepared in the late 1970s, more recent research topics are absent from it.

LEARN BY DOING

Recent Topics in Communications Research

Select one of the following journals: *Journalism Quarterly, Journal of Communication, Communication Research, Journal of Broadcasting and Electronic Media, Journal of Advertising, Public Relations Research Annual.* Beginning with about 1980, or as soon thereafter as practicable, review the contents page of each issue forward to the present. For each contents page, make notes about the kinds of topics or methods that you see. For example, do the prevailing topics focus on *interpersonal* aspects of communications, and if so, do they involve rhetorical style? persuasion? or what? Do the articles tend to be *descriptive* or *theoretical?* Does the research involve *policy issues? historical* issues? *legal* issues? Is the research focus on *processes* and *effects,* or is it of a more practical nature? Scan selected articles as needed to get a clearer notion of the journal's content. Write a one-page paper describing what you find. Keep in mind that Figure 2.1 was a broad review of research topics across many years, not limited to a single journal or a single decade.

The three periods of research might be conveniently called the period of *development,* the period of *transition,* and the *modern* period. The period of development was an extension of the Enlightenment. It reflected the broad interest in education and the pursuit of knowledge that grew during the latter part of the Industrial Revolution. Scholarship in this period included histories and biographies, but little or no study of the *effects* of media, or even the social context of the media, until at least very late in the period.

Why were thinkers of that day not moved to comment on the importance of media? Surely the written word was presumed to be powerful; in fact, power was

Development (Early 1800s–1930s)	**Transition** (1930s–1950s)	**Modern** (1950s to Present)
1. Mostly descriptive histories of printing, newspapers, and periodicals that focused on the lives and influence of major editors and publishers.	1. More interpretative histories of journalism, which looked at the interaction between societal forces and journalistic institutions.	1. Studies of TV's effects on various kinds of behavior, especially aggressive actions.
2. Philosophical writings on the role of the press in society and the nature of news by Walter Lippmann and others such as John Dewey, Robert Park, George Herbert Mead, and William Graham Sumner.	2. Studies of mass media content and propaganda messages by political scientist Harold Lasswell and others.	2. Studies of the impact of newspaper and TV coverage on riots and civil disorders.
	3. Studies of mass media effects on political attitudes and voting behavior by sociologist Paul Lazarsfield and others.	3. Studies of the effects of pornography on antisocial and criminal behavior.
	4. Studies of personal influence and communication within small groups by psychologist Kurt Lewin and others.	4. Studies of the effects of TV advertising on children.
	5. Studies of the effects of message characteristics (e.g., source credibility, one-sided vs. two-sided arguments) on people's attitudes and opinions by psychologist Carl Hovland and others.	5. Studies of media uses and effects in political campaigns, especially TV and newspaper uses and effects.
	6. Studies of people's use of radio and newspapers.	6. A major nationwide study of working journalists.
	7. Scattered studies of press coverage of legal cases, newspaper management, working journalists, media and popular culture, newspaper content, TV's effect on magazine circulation, and press coverage of election campaigns.	7. Numerous studies of newspaper readership and use.
	8. Studies of the freedoms and responsibilities of the press by the Hutchins Commission.	8. Several nationwide studies of newspaper managers.
		9. Co-orientation studies of interpersonal perception and communication, and mass media uses and effects.

FIGURE 2.1   Major Emphases of Journalism and Mass Communication Research (*Source:* Adapted from David H. Weaver and Richard G. Gray. 1979. *Journalism and Mass Communication Research in the United States: Past, Present and Future.* Bloomington: School of Journalism, Indiana University, p. 6. Reprinted by permission of David H. Weaver.)

the reason why authorities of the day tried to license the press and prohibit its free exercise. Did they simply take this importance as "given," self-evident, and too trivial for study? Were thinkers preoccupied with more fundamental issues? *Or did they lack the analytical structure later offered by empiricism?*

The latter question is appealing, for a person cannot build much of a house without tools, nor theories without logical structure. Empiricism is a logical structure with which to build theory.

The period of transition was pivotal in that mass communication research veered away from the humanities and philosophical approaches and into the camp of social science. It was here that the history of mass media research could have followed a different route; it was here that the American research system diverged from the European tradition. The transitional period was characterized by *interpretive* histories, studies of media content, and studies of the effects of mass media.

The modern period is characterized by the increasing use of quantitative methodologies and by sophisticated research designs. In effect, the history of American mass communication research is characterized by the transition of methods from historical to quantitative, from humanistic to social scientific. If one were to graph the frequency of quantitative social studies, the curve would begin as a low, long, horizontal line, then turn sharply upward near its end.

Research Roots

During the early 1800s and before, when social research as we know it did not exist, wisdom was derived in any of several ways: there were experiments, some of them raw by today's standards, such as Benjamin Franklin's experiments with a kite in an electrical storm; there were histories, such as Isaiah Thomas's *History of Printing in America;* and there were texts that mixed history and intuition or insight. But science was on the march, and before the end of the nineteenth century, the breakthroughs were becoming routinely spectacular. Science was becoming the model for "knowing" things.

As science advanced, as industry expanded, and as the world population grew, historians and philosophers—aware of the changing nature of society—looked increasingly for the explanation of social phenomena. Sociologists recognized, for example, that the movement of Americans from isolated farmsteads in the wilderness to villages and cities implied changed relationships among inhabitants. Scholars searched their minds for the keys to explain these relationships. Their data were largely the documentation of history and their personal intellectual insights.

During the latter nineteenth century, psychology and sociology began to develop as distinct disciplines and to adopt some of the principles of quantitative science. There is some evidence that journalists also began to follow the bandwagon of science: For example, they adopted the notion of "objectivity" in reporting. Objectivity implies aloof, impersonal, and clinical communication that purportedly would be more accurate, less debatable, more truthful, more scientific. (The counter argument is that objectivity might have been more a function of the need to sell news to multiple clients, or even to the possibility that the telegraph wire would break, than to any concern for scientism.) But there was no systematic study of the *effects* of communication, despite the newspapers' ubiquity and presumed importance to public discourse.

In fact, growth in the study of the effects of communication was very slow. Even the establishment of journalism schools after the Civil War and in the very early years of the twentieth century did little to promote the study of the effects of mass communication. Incidentally, the first journalism program apparently was offered by Washington and Lee University with General Robert E. Lee as its president soon after the Civil War. Kansas State College offered a printing program in

1873, and the University of Missouri offered one in 1878. The University of Pennsylvania entered the field in 1893. Usually, these early curricula were taught by former newspaper people (Weaver and Gray, 1980, 2).

Setting the Stage for Change

A number of conditions converged to set the stage for change in the conduct of mass communication research. These included the bitter experience of World War I and the use of propaganda as a war tool; growth in the number of newspapers until about the time of World War I, when the number began its slow decline; the development of communication technology; competition for advertising dollars; rapid growth of the population; rise of the middle class; growth of the cities; and universal education. There was also the popularity of Freudian and behavioral psychology, with their assumption of individuals' irrationality, their direction by unrecognized drives. Together these conditions led to a heightened awareness of the mass media and encouraged the systemic study of media effects.

For most purposes, the history of modern mass communication research, with its reliance on the social science method, dates from the 1920s and 1930s. It was in the 1920s that Harold Lasswell (1927) wrote the pioneer work, *Propaganda Technique in the World War*, and that journalist Walter Lippmann (1922) wrote *Public Opinion*, an influential text linking journalism and psychology. Lippmann conducted some of the first analyses of the American press: its operation, its economic base, the act of censorship, and the use of stereotypes in newspaper and motion picture content. In the 1930s, Alfred McClung Lee and Elizabeth Bryant Lee (1939) wrote *The Fine Art of Propaganda*. They and other writers, having asked key questions, opened the door for the development of research as we know it today.

European Roots

The American approach to research is not entirely unique. Part of its tradition is tied to the European schools of thought. Many of the early American media researchers received their training in European universities and were heavily influenced by European thinkers such as Gabriel Tarde and Georg Simmel. Tarde, a Frenchman, was a judge; he based many of his sociological theories on observations of behavior from the courtroom. In 1903, he offered a "theory of imitation" that now can be seen as a clear predecessor of American theories of social learning, diffusion of innovation, and opinion leadership (Rogers, 1986). These are important topics in the history of mass media research.

Simmel, a German, has been described as a father of social psychology (Rogers, 1986), and his work has had important implications for mass media research. His 1922 book, *The Web of Group Affiliations*, introduced to America the theory of communication networks "which consist of interconnected individuals who are linked by patterned flows of information" (quoted from Rogers, 1986). Years later, this idea formed the basis of a whole new line of "network" research that was put to test in the developing American system of empiricism with its emphasis on quantitative measures.

While Europeans retained their philosophical, critical, qualitative approach, Americans diverged into quantitative methods. (This is not to suggest that European research is devoid of quantitative approaches, but rather that quantitative methods might have not dominated European communication research as they have American research.) If both of these broad communities of scholars sought wisdom, then how could this divergence occur? One can speculate that it might have been the different continental histories (social and political), the subsequently different assumptions underlying judgments of truth, the different economic realities, and the different press systems.

The American approach to research might have been an extension of the intense interest in entrepreneurship and the tradition of Yankee-trader decision making. Surely, the entrepreneurial experience is more akin to the quantitative method than to the slow, thoughtful style of the European critical research. In any event, American research became increasingly quantitative and administrative.

The Early American Theorists

In the 1890s, four American sociologists began "the first comprehensive reckoning with modern communication" (Czitrom, 1982). George Herbert Mead, Charles Horton Cooley, John Dewey, and Robert Ezra Park found great importance in the function of the mass media, and they put the media center-forward in their thinking. They established an American agenda of communication as a field of study (Czitrom, 1982).

Dewey was deeply concerned with the notion of "mass" society, which implies a herd-like response to media on the part of the audience. He hoped that the media would "reconstitute community in a mass society" (Rogers, 1986). If the Industrial Revolution had transformed the social relationships among individuals—moving them from the close relationships of the village to the purely contractual relationships of the industrial mega-city—then perhaps the media through shared understandings could replace the loss.

It is interesting that Marshall McLuhan (1969) proposed a similar effect in the 1960s. He theorized that electronic communication among the populations of Earth would create a "global village," wherein aspects of the village tradition (suggesting communal interpersonal relationships and extended families) would be resumed.

Cooley studied political philosophy and ethics in the context of social problems under Dewey at the University of Michigan (Czitrom, 1982, 104). He made the first attempts to show how the media alter behavior and culture. But Park was the first American communication *theorist* (Rogers, 1986, 77). At the famed Chicago School, he was considered the most influential American sociologist between the two world wars (Czitrom, 1982, 113). Park pioneered the study of the press as a social and cultural institution.

Mead was heavily influenced by Dewey. He was the founder of the symbolic interactionist approach to social psychology, a field that contributed to the growth and definition of mass communication studies.

These prominent thinkers initiated the divergence with the European line of scholarship; subsequent generations of students and scholars extended their work and pushed forward the boundaries of empiricism.

LEARN BY DOING

The history of mass communication research, particularly in the twentieth century, is characterized by growth in the use of quantitative methods. To see this, turn to a research journal that has a long history of publication. For example, *Journalism Quarterly* has been published since the 1920s; *Public Opinion Quarterly* since the mid-1930s; numerous psychology and sociology journals have been published for many years. In such a journal, select a research article from the earliest days. Next, turn to about the midpoint in the life of the journal and select another article or two of interest. Finally, turn to a very recent edition and select an article or two.

Assignment

Review your selections in regard to methods and style across the years. Write a paper of two pages or more describing the research and tracing differences that you observed in one time period compared with another. Do you see any evidence of increased methodological sophistication across the years? Do you notice differences in the *topics* across the years? Include a brief synopsis of each article and its conclusion, along with a full bibliographic citation (author, date, article title, journal name, volume number, page numbers).

The Transition Period

Perhaps the most important writers of the transition period were Walter Lippmann, Harold Lasswell, Hadley Cantril, and Paul Lazarsfeld. Lippmann, the journalist and columnist who wrote *Public Opinion* (1922), was concerned with the influence of the press, especially as a propaganda tool—which had been a major issue during World War I. He was also concerned with the fact that people's knowledge of the world is colored by "the pictures in our head" and the "pseudo environments" communicated in the media.

Lasswell was a product of the Chicago School, but his methodology—different from his mentors'—was decidedly quantitative and empirical. Lasswell was a prolific writer, authoring or coauthoring 57 books. But he made a singular contribution to the field of communication that became an enduring paradigm of research: "Who says what to whom in what channel with what effect?" Disarmingly simple, the paradigm had the effect of sorting out the dominant variables in mass communication research. It permitted a clear view of numerous variables in the *process* of communication, one at a time. This was a major advance, unlike the earlier clouded and sweeping philosophical approaches.

Cantril became prominent in the late 1930s for his stewardship of the Institute for Propaganda Analysis, and for his analysis of the great Martian scare induced by Orson Welles' *War of the Worlds* radio broadcast. Lasswell and Cantril brought empirical and data-based approaches to the study of communication phenomena.

Also in the 1930s, W. W. Charters published the results of what were called the Payne Fund Studies, a series of examinations of the effect of films on children and youth. The results emphasized the need to consider the individual differences among viewers (Czitrom, 1982, 124–125).

George Gallup (1930), the noted pollster, was a young professor of journalism at the University of Iowa when he introduced what he called a "scientific method for determining reader interest." He observed that while allied fields were adopting the methods of science, journalists were still relying on hunches and instinct. For example, an editor who wanted to drop a feature would gauge from fan letters whether dropping it was a mistake. Gallup pointed out this was a poor measure. Although the usefulness of the method that he developed is qualified today, it was an important contribution for the time.[3]

A few years later at the University of Minnesota, Mitchell Charnley (1936, 394–401) offered a quantitative method of estimating the accuracy of newspaper reporting. It involved sending clips and survey forms to persons mentioned in the newspaper. For mass communication research, a field previously not noted for quantitative studies, this was a breakthrough.

Paul Lazarsfeld (Lazarsfeld, Berelson, and Gaudet, 1968) was among the dominant communication researchers in the 1940s. His study of the 1940 presidential election opened a line of communication research that dominated the field's research agenda for some 20 years. The most important concept from that research was "opinion leadership," the notion that individuals do not take their direction from the media, but rather filter information through influential others. Lazarsfeld's assertion was important because the press had always been presumed directly influential; it led to what has been called the era of "limited effects" because it placed the media at least second in the chain of influence.[4] The idea of opinion leadership never was resolved, but simply died out in the 1960s.

The final figure of the transition era was Carl Hovland (1953) of Yale University. Hovland's training was in psychology, and when he entered the army in the early 1940s, during World War II, he was assigned to help improve the will of the military to fight. He initiated experiments and surveys on the effectiveness of a series of army motivational films. Hovland's research was meticulous in both design and analysis. His attention to the details of design helped push forward the boundaries of methodology. He opened several lines of research, such as the nature of personal credibility, and he contributed massively to the development of communication research. He and a small number of other psychology researchers dominated the communication research of the 1950s.

In broad view, the work of Lasswell, Cantril, Lazarsfeld, and Hovland showed the way toward the paradigm of the *quantitative* method. Subsequent researchers have followed their lead, extending the methodology into elaborate mechanisms for making fine distinctions among quantitative measures. In sum, their work can be seen as another point of divergence, a point from which the modern research method clearly sprang. The remainder is the story of "more, bigger, and better."

On the history side of research, no account would be complete without recognition of Frank Luther Mott (1941), who produced a massive and lasting survey of history, and Edwin Emery (1954), who added interpretation and insight. Their histories of American journalism helped to educate many thousands of journalism students.

The Modern Era

From the 1950s forward, in particular, mass communication research has been characterized by increasing complexity, methodological sophistication, and theory building. Of the many important researchers and conceptual contributions, only a few can be highlighted in the paragraphs that follow.

Wilbur Schramm (1960), possibly more than anyone else, solidified the work of Lasswell, Lazarsfeld, Hovland, and others and shaped it into an academic discipline. Working first at Illinois and later at Stanford, Schramm was among the most prolific and influential mass communication researchers of his time. He combined methodological skill with perspective and insight. In dozens of books and countless articles, he made the greatest contribution to defining the modern social scientific study of communication.

Development of Statistical Methods

Not all the growth and change in communication research can be traced to the force of individuals. Certainly the concurrent development of statistics and later the advent of computers also precipitated change.

The modern study of statistics is often traced to Karl Pearson's studies at the turn of the century. He was concerned with how samples differ from populations, and how samples differ from other samples. His measures of correlation (coefficients of the systematic relationship between variables) have been applied to research in many disciplines. Over the years, insightful mathematicians have greatly extended the ability of researchers to make distinctions among the fine points of data.

From the late 1960s forward, the growth in statistics was more than equalled by the growth in the use of computers. Computers were first tested in the 1940s, but they became practicable only in the 1950s and 1960s. By 1970 most major academic institutions were equipped with computers, and by the late 1980s desktop computing was the norm. Computers have enabled analyses and simulations that in earlier years simply could not have been done. The computer can achieve in seconds what might take a large group of researchers months or years.

Today, researchers have at their desks more analytical power than earlier scholars would have imagined. The result is a deluge of published research. The challenge now for the research community is quality control; in many cases, the computer and statistics overmatch the researcher and the reader. The computer, of course, cannot by itself correct a faulty research design or poor implementation.

MODELS AND MEASURES

During the 1950s and 1960s, there was considerable interest in "models" of communication—graphic characterizations of how communication was said to work. For example, one influential model, by Claude Shannon and Warren Weaver (1972, 5th ed., 34), identified the principal elements in communication from the standpoint of mathematics and electric/electronic data transmission.

Information Theory

Shannon and Weaver identified the significant parts of the model as follows: information source, transmitter, message, noise source, receiver, and destination. This model constituted a useful analogy for the communication process. For example, the *information source* was a person, a reporter, a radio station, a newspaper, or whatever; the *transmitter* was the frequency generator, the press, the telephone line; the *message* was simply the information; and so on. The concept of *noise* was an important addition to previous research conceptions. Noise is any interference with a message.

The Westley-MacLean Model

Bruce Westley and Malcolm MacLean (1957, 31–38) offered another influential model a few years later. They added the concept of *feedback*, a term that—like noise, or distraction—we take for granted today. In addition, their model specifically addressed the process of *mass* communication. It might be noted that both Westley and MacLean were somewhat ahead of their time in the sophistication of their work, and in their contributions to communication theory.

The Semantic Differential

Charles Osgood, George Suci, and Percy Tannenbaum (1971, 8th ed.) were extremely influential for their studies of the "measurement of meaning." They introduced the concept of the **semantic differential,** a scale made of adjectives and their opposites. The semantic differential and the **Likert scale,** developed by Rensis Likert, are probably the two most widely used measures in communication research.

Ralph Nafziger and David Manning White (1958) were the editors of a mass communication research text that set the tone for a generation to follow. The text included chapters by Schramm, MacLean, Tannenbaum, and Westley, and others. Topics included statistical methods, research design, content analysis, and measurement—topics that seem routine today but were avant-garde in the 1950s.

THE McLUHAN PHENOMENON

"The Medium Is the Message"

From the mid-1960s, a substantial stir in communication research was created by a Canadian professor of English, Marshall McLuhan. Trained in electrical engineering and English literature, McLuhan coined the highly quotable and variably interpretable expression, "the medium is the message" (McLuhan, 1964, 21). This phrase suggested that electronic media were creating new ways of learning and perceiving. The implication is that the *medium* is what matters, perhaps more than what the medium presents. _or conveys_

The Volatile 1960s

McLuhan appeared at a time in American history when his ideas were bound to find a receptive audience; it was a time of race riots, civil disobedience, violence, and uncertainty—the volatile 1960s. His audience needed reassurance that what was happening was understandable, and he claimed to understand the importance of media. McLuhan was probably the most public scholar of the period; he was in extremely high demand. He was a machine gun of ideas about the effects of mass communication, but only a few of his ideas were testable by social science standards, and fewer won the support of objective research (Bennett, Swanson, and Wilkinson, 1992).

McLuhan's phrase "the medium is the message," seemed at the time to make great sense. But several of McLuhan's ideas lack the luster today that they had in the 1960s. Although undoubtedly he still has a following, today's young readers tend to have difficulty appreciating his conceptions. To one who recalls the period vividly, it seems odd that what passed for wisdom yesterday could be unattractive today, but that may be one of the profound effects or hazards of media: versions of "truth" arise and spread very quickly, not filtered through the correcting mechanisms of debate, persuasion, and time.

For example, McLuhan argued that written communication is linear, whereas he said television imagery is "mosaic," and that this creates a radical transformation in people's thought process. Loosely translated, this means that written communication is narrowly logical, while visual communication is "holistic"—the effect being that modern children learn things differently than earlier generations.

McLuhan also asserted that, partly because of the linear-to-mosaic transformation in thinking, the flow of information—which always had proceeded outward as from an exploding bomb—had reversed *inward*. He described this as *implosion*, saying that it would transform international cultures into a "global village."

Furthermore, McLuhan spoke of "hot" and "cool" media. Cartoons and caricatures were "cool" because they left a lot to be filled in by the viewer. Movies were "hot" because they did not. Television was "cool" because it did not require much of the viewer. In his conception, each medium was classifiable.

who say?

That is b/c
McLuhan's
conceptions
are
conveyed
via diff.
media
than in
60's
(Provingly
point)

Some of McLuhan's ideas were bound by the circumstances of the day. They were very persuasive in the 1960s because of the unsettled circumstances of the time. When the circumstances changed, the ideas lost some of their command. McLuhan's most enduring contribution thus seems to have been to tout the importance of media effects, and to spur interest in their study, rather than the substance of his hypotheses. That was no small contribution.

RESEARCHERS AND PRACTITIONERS

As schools of communication promoted the social science approach to knowledge and decision making, a gap grew between academics and the employees of the mass communication industries. The gap was symbolized as disagreement between the "green-eyeshades" (a reference to the stereotype of an old-time newspaper editor) and the "communicologists" or "chi squares" (the modern quantitative communication scholars).

A 1973 text by Philip Meyer helped to bridge this gap. The book was called *Precision Journalism,* and it tried to make social science, or at least its decision-making quantitative apparatus, relevant to practitioners in any field of mass communication. The book was very widely read and appreciated. Over time, Meyer's book will probably be seen as an important contribution in the growth of social science as it applies to mass communication.

Important Research Topics

In the modern era, several dominant strands of research can be identified. In the 1950s and into the 1960s, there was great interest in the study of attitudes, persuasion, and credibility. There was also great interest in the notion of "opinion leadership" described by Paul Lazarsfeld, Bernard Berelson, and Hazel Gaudet. Stephen Chaffee and Jack McLeod (1968, 661–690) articulated the notion of "co-orientation," a line of research that investigated the implications of shared experience.

In the early 1970s, a new line of research was sparked by an unassuming article in *Public Opinion Quarterly.* The article, by Maxwell McCombs and Donald Shaw (1972), proposed that one of the influences of the media was their setting of the issue agenda for the public. The idea generated hundreds of published research projects.

Also important was George Gerbner's "cultivation" research during the 1970s and 1980s (Gerbner and Gross, 1976, 173–179). "Cultivation" is the idea that what is seen on television as entertainment is translated into some version of reality in the mind of the audience.

Research during the 1980s and 1990s became more "micro," more complex, and more specialized. New journals were created. Research generally encompassed a very wide range of topics: mass media effects; interpersonal styles and outcomes; rhetorical techniques; cognition/perception/nonverbal studies; cultural studies; persuasion studies (elaboration likelihood); ethical/professional studies; risk communication; and special issue communication problems such as acquired immunodeficiency syndrome (AIDS) communication.

Many lines of research generally are known more for their concept than for their origin. But the point is that these research agendas have contributed to the growth of research. As researchers take on research projects, they add ingenuity and insight; they push the limits of what is known and how it is studied. These research topics, and their pursuit by hundreds of researchers, have contributed to the social science approach to mass communication studies that we have today.

SOME DATA ON METHODOLOGY AND FUNDING

The kind of research that characterizes a discipline is partly determined by the funding it receives. Research is expensive. In general, research in mass communication has not been funded at the same level as have the cousin disciplines of psychology, sociology, and political science (Weaver and Gray, 1980). Research is principally funded by universities, governments, and private sources.

A study by David Weaver and Richard Gray (1980, 124–151), with the support of the Gannett Foundation, estimated that 26 percent (32 of 122) of mass communication research projects published between 1954–1963 and 1968–1978 received external funding. Of the 32 funded projects, 87 percent were quantitative, 40 percent were one-time surveys, and 28 percent were historical/philosophical.

During the same period, funding was received by 45 percent of political science research projects, 63 percent of sociology research projects, 57 percent of psychology research projects. Data since 1979 are not available, but level of funding of mass communication research likely remains low. The reason is unclear. It might be that the discipline is too young to have earned credibility with funding sources; that mass communication researchers have failed to stake out a research agenda that demands support; or that persons responsible for funding have not yet been educated to the significance of mass communication in society.

Weaver and Gray concluded that mass communication research has been mostly "sporadic, disjointed and short-term." They suggested that where the research has been more systematic, long range, and therefore more conclusive, the funding has been more readily available. A brief review of recent titles suggests that the same critique applies today.

A Concluding Note

Schools of mass communication have granted the doctor of philosophy (Ph.D.) degree only since the 1950s. Even today, many faculties include scholars whose training was in allied fields, not mass communication. In fact, many faculties see great virtue in that. But in general, the transition to a field dominated by mass communication scholarship continues apace. Never mind that scholarly degrees in mass communication differ considerably from university to university. Eventually, the shared understandings promoted by study under the single concept of mass communication should militate toward a finer definition of the field and a clearer research agenda.

An important juncture in the history of research methods may be approaching. An increasing number of scholars are adding *qualitative* research to their repertoire of methodologies. They are using focus groups, case studies, interviews, and a variety of observational methods. Although these methods have long been available, the new interest represents a significant change in the direction of the previous 50 years.

Why the new direction? James Carey (1980) has argued for many years that research based on social science methods has become "stagnant," and that important breakthroughs in understanding communication behavior have been too few. Many would disagree with that, and in fact would point to the research record with pride. But Carey has contended it is time to try alternative approaches. Apparently, an increasing number of researchers are beginning to agree.[5] If present trends continue, mass communication historians of the future will add a new branch to the family tree of social science research.

Historians may see an analogy to Thomas Kuhn's (1970) paradigmatic approach to the history of science. A paradigm is a shared understanding of how knowledge will be generated. Kuhn observed that scientists develop conventional ways of researching and solving problems—that is, they develop paradigms—and that when these conventions no longer work, as when outcomes are not satisfactory, scientific revolutions begin and new paradigms evolve.

Knowingly, Kuhn observed that research is a "strenuous and devoted attempt to force nature into the conceptual boxes supplied by professional education." In other words, teachers provide a "normal" framework for generating knowledge and most students dutifully follow it; but eventually, the framework becomes inadequate to answer the questions that must be answered. When researchers no longer can evade "the anomalies that subvert the existing tradition," they begin the "extraordinary investigations that lead the profession to at least a new set of commitments, a new basis for the practice of science" (Kuhn, 1970, 5).

Time will tell whether the present juncture in mass communication research will lead to an altered paradigm or merely a minor adjustment in research conventions.

SUMMARY

Research methods should be studied in context, not in isolation. They are a part of our history. The history of mass communication research has three periods. The modern period is characterized by an increasing reliance on quantitative methods and elaborate research designs. The transition into the modern period in the history of mass communication research dates from the 1920s and 1930s. Some of the important writers of the period were Lippman, Cantril, Lasswell, and Charters. Among important researchers of the 1940s and 1950s were Lazarsfeld, Hovland,

and Schramm. The growth of quantitative research has continued unabated into the early 1990s, although some interest in alternative methods, especially qualitative, has emerged.

[handwritten margin note: hasn't it stagnated according to some?]

STUDY QUESTIONS AND EXERCISES

1. Visit your library to find publications by John Dewey, Charles Cooley, Robert Park, George Herbert Mead. Capsule in one to two pages some important notions that are revealed in their writing.

2. Review articles in three different scholarly journals, such as the *Journal of Communication, Journal of Human Communication Research,* and *Journal of Broadcasting and Electronic Media.* How are they similar or dissimilar? Do all make heavy use of tables and statistical tests? Do topics and research methods vary from journal to journal?

3. Read chapters 1 and 2 of Marshall McLuhan's (1964) famous book *Understanding Media,* or any of his published writing. Describe and discuss some of the key notions you find there.

4. Defend or condemn our reliance on numbers for judging wisdom. Do we give numbers more credit for accuracy in social science than they deserve, and intuition and insight too little credit? Or is the case more the opposite?

NOTES

The author would like to thank Dr. Eric Stilling, formerly a doctoral student at the University of Tennessee, Knoxville, for assistance in gathering the data and resources from which this chapter was written.

1. Innis attributed this quotation to H. W. Boynton. 1904. *Journalism and Literature and Other Essays.* Boston.

2. See James W. Carey. 1980. Comments on the Weaver-Gray Paper. In *Mass Communication Review Yearbook.* Vol. 1, ed. G. Cleveland Wilhoit and Harold de Bock. (Beverly Hills, Calif.: Sage, pp. 152–155. Carey disagrees with the conclusion of Weaver and Gray (1980) that little research had been done prior to 1800, stating: "First if you extend the word research to include scholarship it is not true that journalism and communication have been unstudied until recent times. Much of high intellectual quality has been written from the founding of the republic. Second, if one does a deeper analysis of the inherited tradition, one comes to quite a different view of the development of this scholarship." Another critique of the Weaver-Gray paper was offered by Stephen Chaffee, (Carey, 1980, 156–160). Chaffee observed that the lines of the history of communication research are clouded: Are we reporting the history of journalism, or mass communication, or simply communication research? He observed that a history of this type tends to drift from one sphere to another. He also argued that the kind of history reported here and in the Weaver-Gray paper gives "short shrift" to the spectacular growth of research in the modern era.

3. George Gallup said that his "Scientific Method for Determining Reader Interest" overcame most of the faults of other methods then in use. The method involved "going through copies of the newspaper column by column with a representative group of readers. . . . The paper is placed before the reader and within easy reading distance. The investigator marks with a pencil everything which has been read, a different copy being used for each person. The reader is asked to recall whether he read, in this particular issue, the feature, news story, or advertisement before him. The investigator gets from the reader a yes-or-no answer in the case of every item . . . making sure that nothing is overlooked" (Gallup, 1930, 6). Gallup called the reliability of the method "fully established."

4. As this chapter was being prepared, a classic recognition of opinion leadership occurred in national politics. It happened when former president Richard Nixon chose to make known his concern about American/Russian affairs by writing to 50 *selected opinion leaders* in the highest levels of industry and government, rather than addressing the mass media. Network newscasts openly referred to his technique as drawing from the notion of the "two-step flow of information." There was no indication whether his technique was purely intuitive, or whether it derived from previous knowledge of the literature of opinion leadership.

5. Carey, Comments on the Weaver-Gray Paper, pp. 152–155.

SOURCES

Bennett, Ellen M., Jill Dianne Swenson, and Jeff Wilkinson. 1992. Is the Medium the Message?: An Experimental Test with Morbid News. *Journalism Quarterly* 69(4):921–928.

Chaffee, Stephen H., and Jack M. McLeod 1968. Sensitization in Panel Design: A Coorientation Experiment. *Journalism Quarterly* 45(3):661–690.

Charnley, Mitchell V. 1936. Preliminary Notes on a Study of Newspaper Accuracy. *Journalism Quarterly* 13(3):394–401.

Czitrom, D. J. 1982. *Media and the American Mind: From the Time of Morse to McLuhan.* Chapel Hill: University of North Carolina Press.

Emery, Edwin. 1954. *The Press and America: An Interpretative History of Journalism.* Englewood Cliffs, N.J.: Prentice-Hall.

Ferment in the Field. 1983. A special edition of the *Journal of Communication* 33(3).

Gallup, George. 1930. A Scientific Method for Determining Reader Interest. *Journalism Quarterly* 7(1):1–13.

Gerbner, George, and Larry Gross. 1976. Living with Television: The Violence Profile. *Journal of Communication* 26(2):173–179.

Hovland, Carl I., Irving L. Janis, and H. H. Kelley. 1953. *Communication and Persuasion.* New Haven, Conn.: Yale University Press.

Innis, Harold A. 1973. *The Bias of Communication.* Toronto: University of Toronto Press.

Kuhn, Thomas S. 1970. *The Structure of Scientific Revolutions.* 2d ed. Chicago: University of Chicago Press.

Lasswell, Harold D. 1927. *Propaganda Technique in the World War* New York: Alfred A. Knopf.

Lazarsfeld, Paul F., Bernard R. Berelson, and Hazel Gaudet. 1968. *The People's Choice: How the Voter Makes Up His Mind in a Presidential Campaign.* 3d ed. New York: Columbia University Press.

Lee, Alfred McClung, and Elizabeth Bryant Lee, eds. 1939. *The Fine Art of Propaganda: A Study of Father Coughlin's Speeches*. Orlando, Fla.: Harcourt Brace Jovanovich.

Lippmann, Walter. 1922. *Public Opinion*. New York: Macmillan.

McCombs, Maxwell E., and Donald L. Shaw. 1972. The Agenda-Setting Function of Mass Media. *Public Opinion Quarterly* 36(2):176–187.

McLuhan, Marshall. 1964. *Understanding Media*. New York: Signet Books.

Meyer, Philip. 1973. *Precision Journalism*. Bloomington: Indiana University Press.

Mott, Frank Luther. 1941. *American Journalism A History of Newspapers in the United States through 260 Years: 1690 to 1950*. New York: Macmillan.

Nafziger, Ralph O., and David M. White, eds. 1958. *Introduction to Mass Communications Research*. Baton Rouge: Louisiana State University Press.

Osgood, Charles E., George J. Suci, and Percy H. Tannenbaum. [1957]. 1971. *The Measurement of Meaning*. 8th ed. Urbana: University of Illinois Press.

Rogers, Everett M. 1986. *Communication Technology*. New York: Free Press.

Schramm, Wilbur. ed. 1960. *Mass Communications*. Urbana: University of Illinois Press.

Shannon, Claude E., and Warren Weaver. [1949] 1972. *The Mathematical Theory of Communication*. 5th ed. Urbana: University of Illinois Press.

Weaver, David H., and Richard G. Gray. 1980. Journalism and Mass Communication Research in the United States: Past, Present and Future. In *Mass Communication Review Yearbook*, Vol. 1, ed. G. Cleveland Wilhoit and Harold de Bock. Beverly Hills, Calif.: Sage.

Westley, Bruce H., and Malcolm S. MacLean, Jr., 1957. A Conceptual Model for Communications Research. *Journalism Quarterly* 34(1):31–38.

The Rationale of the Social Science Research Method

- Chapter 3: The Logic and Method of Social Science.   An introduction to the empirical method, Chapter 3 provides a logical framework for accepting or rejecting evidence purporting to explain events. Emphasis is on the language and rules and some of the techniques of social science.
- Chapter 4: Working with Samples.   This chapter explains how to obtain a sample and when to attempt to generalize it to a population. Types of probability and nonprobability samples are described. Instruction on how to calculate sample error and sample size is provided.
- Chapter 5: Measurement of Social Science Variables.   Topics of discussion include measurement error, methods of measurement, and reliability and validity, are discussed. Characteristics and uses of the different levels of measurement are described.

CHAPTER

3

The Logic and Method
of Social Science

□
OBJECTIVES

After studying this chapter, you should be able to:

1. Define and explain empiricism and the logic of social science.
2. Describe the differences between natural science and social science.
3. Identify and discuss sources of error in social research.
4. Distinguish between private and public research; applied and theoretical research; and critical and administrative research.
5. Recognize and explain several assumptions that underlie the empirical method.
6. Identify some elements of prescience.
7. Identify the steps in the social research process.
8. Describe several kinds of hypotheses: null hypothesis, alternative hypothesis, working hypothesis, and research hypothesis.

Although the research applications discussed in Chapter 1 cover a broad range of purposes and methods, they all spring from the same line of reasoning—a logical structure that guides our definition and evaluation of *evidence* about behavior. No matter what kind of research (e.g., content analysis, survey research, experimental research), and no matter what purpose of the research (e.g., business decisions or theory), the rationale is the same. It is so fundamental that it is taken for granted; but if it were not accepted, and if different people used different criteria to evaluate evidence, we would have no common ground of understanding.

EMPIRICISM

The logic of social science helps us decide what to believe. For example, if you were told with great sincerity that chain ownership of newspapers reduces the editorial strength of a community newspaper, would you believe it? Even if it seemed plausible, wouldn't you need some hard evidence? If the assertion were true, then the effect of chain ownership should be *observable in the product*, not dependent on faith. There should be some evidence that others could agree on. This is known as **empiricism,** and it is the foundation of social science.

Evidence based on faith alone is not science; it is not empirical because it is personal. Personal wisdom is not subject to refutation. Scientific data must be open to inspection, and social science wisdom is always subject to challenge.

This calls to mind the story of the *Wizard of Oz*, the supposedly omniscient character who, when the curtain of secrecy was opened, is nothing more than a man, no better or worse than most of us. Dorothy uses her own brand of empiricism when she challenges his wisdom and exposes his deceit. Empiricism is the standard that says: If you claim to have evidence, then I'm willing to believe; but first, show me. *Empiricism is a protection against false wisdom.*

Some Assumptions of Empiricism

Empiricism suggests not just the criterion of observability, but a whole set of *assumptions* and *requirements* relating to the nature and cumulation of evidence. These are presented in the following list.

Some Assumptions of Social Science Research

The world is an orderly place.
There are individual and social regularities.
Behavioral regularities are observable and measurable.
Evidence does not require personal faith.
Behaviors have understandable causes.
Behaviors can be aggregated.
Aggregation is useful in social prediction.
Cross-sectional samples generalize to populations.
Prediction leads to principles or laws of behavior.

For example, if one is to make sense of things, one has to *assume* that the world is an orderly and predictable place (despite occasional events to the contrary) i.e., that there are social regularities. If it were not so, we would live in chaos. The assumption is made also that individual behavior is predictable, and that this predictability extends in good measure across society. Consider the opposite: If individual behaviors were truly unique, there would be no social science, only individual science.

Even when the reason for the behavior is not outwardly evident, the assumption is made that the reason is understandable, that behaviors have causes, and therefore that behavior can be explained and predicted. The assumption is made that the predictability of individual and social behavior will lead to broad principles of understanding of human behavior. Finally, the assumption is made that the predictability of samples can be generalized to populations.

Some Requirements of the Method

1. The first requirement of social science research is that it be *objective.* The scientific researcher must not have a personal interest in the outcome of the research, nor let a client's interest in the outcome guide the conduct of the research. The scrupulous researcher will avoid the client who, for example, wants research conducted to "prove" some point to the client's advantage. The researcher with a stake in the outcome of a research project might knowingly or unknowingly influence the outcome, and such an outcome would not be scientific.

don't turn around

LEARN BY DOING

As a simple study in social regularities, ride the elevator in an office building and observe the behavior of the riders. Are there observable social regularities? When individuals unknown to each other are placed in proximity, what are their identifiable behaviors? Do the riders speak, and if they speak, are their utterances hushed or self-conscious? Are people bothered by the closeness of a full elevator? Can any generalities of behavior be observed? Try this exercise, then discuss it in the context of aggregation of social regularities.

---

2. A second requirement is that the research be *systematic,* not selective, not rigged to achieve a given outcome. The ethical researcher does not pick and choose among the data that will be evaluated. To ensure integrity, the researcher typically describes in detail how the data were collected.

3. Third, research should be *hypothesis-guided.* **Hypotheses** precede data collection, and they stipulate what the outcome of the research should be. This discourages acceptance of things that happen by chance in the place of things that happen for cause.

4 Fourth, scientific research should be *cumulative;* it should add to what is already known. When research is isolated, it has no contextual meaning.

5 Fifth, scientific research should be *public.* Research may have been conducted on the basis of scientific principles; but if it is not public, then it is not fully subject to refutation and therefore is not science.

6 The sixth, and final, requirement is *refutation.* Social scientific research must be open to challenge and revision.

GUEST ESSAY

Some Philosophical Issues Related to Doing Social Science Research

Susan M. Strohm
Pennsylvania State University

Does "science" work as well for examining the social world as it does for studying the natural world? Can we examine social phenomena as "facts" in the same way physical scientists study physical objects? In doing social science and communication research, we are, as Earl Babbie (1986) noted, "observing ourselves." What special issues arise from being both observer and observed? *We are affected by observation*

These are issues of methodology, or the philosophy of the research process, rather than method, or the specific tools of research such as a survey, a tape recorder, or an electron microscope. To look at methodology is to examine our assumptions about the nature of "reality" and "truth." Those assumptions, in turn, have implications for what we choose to call "evidence," for the nature of accepted procedures and routine practices that make up the research process, and for the goals we set for our work.

What Is the Nature of the "Real World"?
What Does It Mean to "Understand" That World?

We do research in an attempt to make sense of the social world, but there are different assumptions among researchers about what constitutes the "real world," what "making sense" of it means, and how best to go about the task.

Two key issues arise. First, does an objective reality exist independently of us, out there somewhere and just waiting to be discovered? Or is reality only what you perceive? Second, does an "objective truth" exist? If so, how can we come to know it?

These issues imply much for the way we look at our tools and results. Is evidence something we "collect" as we might collect seashells on a beach? Or is our hand more evident, and evidence something we "manufacture" the way we might manufacture cake mix or automobiles? To what extent do the tools we create reflect our own views of reality and shape what we find? When we use our tools, are we discovering the singular truth about an observable world, or are we creating a subjective understanding of a subjective world?

These are intertwined questions and the answers researchers give tend to reflect two different ways of doing social research, the positivist and interpretative approaches. The *positivist approach* adapts the tools and rules of the physical sciences to the study of the social world and human experiences. Through observation and measurement of a physical, objective world, the positivist attempts to generate explanations for the way the world is and predictions about how it will be. The *interpretative approach*, on the other hand, assumes a subjective world and as a result, emphasizes understanding the way individuals construct meanings about their experiences. Each, in its own way, tells us what the world is like.

Positivism assumes that reality and facts exist separate from our observation of them, and that we can come to know reality empirically, through observation. There is a subject–object relationship between the researcher and what is being studied, in that the observed is external to and separate from the observer.

POSITIVISM

Truth is seen as located outside the observer. It corresponds to the external reality and can be identified and verified through careful observation. This verification, however, depends on an "objective" view, that is, taking a perspective that is somehow apart from or outside of the observer and his or her values and vested interests.

Verification occurs when objective observers, using common tools and methods, achieve common results. This agreement among researchers is a means of establishing what we "know," at least until a better idea comes along. Doing science is seen as a process of trying out a tentative solution to a problem, attempting to refute it, and, if refuted, trying to devise and refute a new solution to the puzzle.

Positivist

Emile Durkheim, a key figure in the history of sociology who is often associated with this view, argued that social phenomena, such as customs and morals, could be studied as "social facts," or things that are external to us and constrain the way we think, feel, and act. Because social facts are seen as "things," we can study them as if they had a physical reality using the tools and rules of the natural sciences. Social research, then, is a search for patterns in the social world—patterns that lead to the discovery of "laws," or cause-and-effect relationships, which are seen as determining much of human behavior.

To understand human behavior, positivists work toward explanation and prediction. *Explanation* involves the examination of causes and a search for the necessary and sufficient conditions under which an event will occur. (A necessary condition must always be present in order for an event to occur. A sufficient condition need not be there, but when it is, it alone is enough for the condition to occur.) *Prediction* looks at what might occur in the future and requires an understanding of the specific conditions under which laws might hold true.

vs
INTERP
or
QUAL.

The *interpretative approach* (sometimes referred to as *qualitative studies*) offers other answers to questions of the nature of reality and truth; therefore, it suggests another way of doing social research. In this approach, the social world is seen as existing as part of the human experience, not external to it. Reality is internal, as it is shaped (or even created) by our minds. Social reality is a symbolic world and cannot be examined or understood in the same way that we understand physical objects.

Research involves a subject–subject relationship, in that the researcher cannot be separated from what is being observed—the observer is part of the social world being studied. Because there is no external, independent reality that we can observe directly, we cannot tell what is objectively "true." What we call "facts" and what we "know" are intricately interwoven with our values and perceptions.

Without objective reality, there is no reason to search for laws to explain or predict human behavior. Wilhelm Dilthey, a prominent figure in the history of sociological thought, argued that "free will" was another reason to abandon the search for laws. Because human beings have free will, human behavior is not determined by laws and cannot be predicted. For Dilthey, the changing nature of the social world and the human spirit made prediction impossible.

To understand human behavior, interpretative researchers focus on the subjective experiences of the researched and the meanings they give their own actions and the actions of others. One means of creating this understanding was suggested by Max Weber, a founder of modern sociology. Weber argued that as both subject and object of research, we have a different relationship to that which we research than do physical scientists. This gives us a special opportunity to relate to what we study. Direct understanding, or *Verstehen*, comes when researchers have experiences similar to those of the researched and empathize with the people they are studying. In other words, the best way to understand someone is to "walk a mile in their shoes."

For researchers in either the positivistic or interpretative approach, the relationship between observers and observed is of central concern. Researchers wrestle with questions about their role in society. What should we do with our understandings? Is it enough to generate knowledge, or should we actively use our findings to make the world a better place?

Should Changing the Social World Be a Goal of Social Research?

Although we recognize that the dissemination of knowledge changes society, at issue is whether researchers should intentionally play an active role in shaping the nature of the change. Should we aim to be "objective" and work to determine "what is," or should we be "normative" and focus on "what should be"?

George Lundberg (1947) took a position of ethical neutrality and argued that our individual preferences should not lead us to taking sides on moral or ethical issues in our work. Researchers have no special right to direct society's use of scientific knowledge. Instead, researchers should use science to determine how to create the changes society decides it wants to make. From this perspective, the goal of working from a value-free perspective is what distinguishes social science from ethics and religion.

Others reject the notion that objectivity and ethical neutrality are possible, or even desirable, and might point out that even our choice of research topic says something about our values, in that it reflects what we think is important. Rather than trying in vain in suppress our values, some believe we should recognize and state our values in our research and, perhaps, use our research to change the world.

Patti Lather (1986, 257) argues that in an "unjust world," we should consider the benefits from doing value-based research with emancipatory goals. *Emancipatory research* attempts to critique the status quo and empower the researched by creating "emancipatory knowledge," through which the researched might better understand, and perhaps change, their own situations.

The differences in approach discussed here have sparked much debate in the communication field. Rather than being a negative sign, this diversity of approaches signals a vigorous field and can be a catalyst for innovation in communication research. Some observers see the field moving toward a deeper appreciation for the importance of understanding the meanings of communication, increased interest in communications and social contexts, and renewed concern about social relevance (Miller, 1983, 31–41). Each approach has room for creativity and the sense of wonder and discovery that comes from doing social research.

[handwritten margin note: somewhat patronizing that we can bestow empowerment (maybe facilitate)]

DIFFERENCES BETWEEN SOCIAL AND NATURAL SCIENCES

Science Defined

Is **social science,** and is the study of communication, really **science?** In popular imagery, the scientist wears a white lab coat and works with mice, monkeys, and microscopes. But the Latin meaning for the word *science* is "having knowledge." It comes from the past participle of the Latin *scire,* meaning "to know" (*Webster's New Collegiate Dictionary*).

Students of mass communication claim to have and to seek systematic knowledge of the processes and effects of the mass media. Ergo, social science research is science, and the study of mass communication is scientific, albeit different from the natural sciences.

Certainty of Knowledge

Social science research is modeled after research in the natural sciences, but differs in important regards. One major difference has to do with the certainty of knowledge. In social science research, outcomes are less certain because the precipitants of some social behaviors are not directly observable or measurable. For example, we cannot "see" the criteria by which a listener judges the credibility of a communicator. We cannot see, touch, or count an attitude that leads to race discrimination. Sometimes we can see evidence of the behavior, but we are left only to deduce the cause.

Variability of Samples

Another source of uncertainty in social research has to do with **reliance on samples** drawn from **populations.** There are two separate sources of uncertainty here. One is the fact that any **random** sample, no matter how carefully selected, can be unrepresentative of the population from which it is drawn. That may seem odd, because the so-called "random sample" is venerated. But "bad" samples (i.e., samples unrepresentative of the population) are always possible. For example, if you were to pick 3 persons in a group of 20 to estimate the average age of the group, it is possible that the average would be an accurate estimator. But it's also possible that it would be severely off the mark. That is simply within the nature of random selection.

To the extent possible, this weakness is offset in the application of statistics theory. Statisticians have developed estimates of the likely limits of sample variation; they call it **sampling error.** But even when the probabilities are taken into account, there is always doubt as to how well the sample represents the population. With random samples, 100-percent certainty just isn't possible.

The other source of sample variability is that truly random samples are seldom possible because nearly always some members of the population will be inaccessible to the researcher. They may be transient, noncooperative, incapacitated, or whatever. Their number varies in any community.

Since the extent of their inaccessibility most often is unknown, the magnitude of error also is unknown. And if the size of this error is unknown, how can we have confidence in our survey data? The answer is that we can't, at least not perfectly. But we can be *fairly sure,* within specifiable limits, and we can be exceptionally cautious about accepting the accuracy and significance of our results.

Natural scientists have to deal with hardships, but not usually such as described above. For example, the biologist drawing a sample of blood can be confident that any other blood sample from that individual (changes based on time passage and condition notwithstanding) will yield the same count. But the social scientist measuring the attitudes of a *sample of persons* cannot be perfectly confident that any other sample will yield precisely the same attitude score.

Blalock pointed out that some natural sciences (e.g., meteorology, geology, and medicine) also have problems stemming from inability to measure and explain properly. He said that social science is separated from natural science "by degree rather than by differences of a totally disparate nature" (Blalock and Blalock, 1982, 22).

LEARN BY DOING

Sample Error

To illustrate the error component of the random sample, write down the number for each month of the year: January = 1, February = 2 . . . December = 12. Next, select six classmates whose birth months are not already known. Calculate the average of their birth months. (Example: February, March, March, April, June, June = 2 + 3 + 3 + 4 + 6 + 6 = 24 ÷ 6 = 4; the six classmates have an average birth month of 4.) *If a person is about as likely to be born in one month as any other* (the assumption may not be perfectly correct), then the true average of a large enough group should be about 6.5. To check this, calculate the birth-month average for the entire class; then compare the average for the class with the average for the sample. The difference may be slight, but the two averages most often will not match. That is because the sample may include any combination of birth months, and one sample may be closer to the population average than another sample.

   If the birth-month test is not feasible, the same idea can be examined with a table of random numbers. A table of random numbers can be found in many statistics texts in your library. Start with a two-digit column of numbers. Select a few samples of 20 numbers and take the average of each. If any number in the table between 0 and 99 is as likely as another, the average should be 50. Indeed, if enough samples are drawn, the average will be 50; but in the first few samples, the averages are likely to be spread across a broad range. That is the nature of the random sample, and it is one of the problems for the social researcher in generalizing from the sample to a population.

STANDARDS FOR EVALUATING RESEARCH OUTCOMES

If samples are imperfect, then how is the social scientist to know whether to rely on outcomes generated by sample data? One standard is repeated outcomes, known as **replications.** If the researcher repeats a study, and gets more or less the same outcome, the outcome is more persuasive. Confidence in the data increases with repetitions. Another standard is based on *statistical significance,* which reflects the likelihood that a research finding might be the result of chance variations in the sample. This will be treated at length in Chapters 10 through 12.

How We "Know" Things

Charles Peirce (Kerlinger, 1973, 5) suggested that there are four methods of "knowing" things: with *tenacity,* a person feels something is so because it has always been so. With *authority,* something is so because the authorities have said it is so. With *intuition,* something is so because it seems right. Fourth is the method of *science,* of which social science is a part.

   Compared with natural science, social science research involves a unique conception of "knowing things." For example, a layperson may ask: What makes a voter a Democrat or a Republican? Another may answer: It is the person's *personal interest* that dictates party preference, and parties are expected to represent their members' interests; that is the nature of political parties. There are, however, other plausible explanations for party membership. There is the possibility, for example, that individuals join political parties for family tradition; for the sake of personal consistency; for hostility to another party; for some unstated behavioral purpose (such as the desire to run for office); or for other reasons entirely arbitrary. Surely, there are many reasons for voting, or for voting along party lines.

The social researcher anticipates these rival explanations and withholds a judgment of causality until sufficient data are at hand (Selltiz, Jahoda, Deutsch and Cook, 1959). The researcher's version of knowledge should be *data based*, and the data should be collected according to the principles of social science.

Intuition, Anecdotes, and Small-Sample Research. Intuition, anecdotes, hunches, and nonrandom samples can be considered elements of *prescience,* for they represent ways of "knowing" that do not include the rigor of science. But that is not to say *intuition* cannot represent wisdom, or that truth always is the product of a random sample, or that *anecdotes* are valueless. "Truth is where you find it," whether it be in anecdote, intuition, a sample of one person, or a more formal research design. The following list reviews the elements of prescience.

Some Elements of Prescience

- *intuition:* knowledge based on personal insight or revelation
- *anecdotes:* knowledge based on experience or lore
- *hunches:* hypotheses based on intuition or casual observation
- *nonrandom samples:* data that do not generalize to the larger population

There probably is truth in the *anecdote,* for instance, that "birds of a feather flock together." Certainly, cognitive consistency theory supports the idea that individuals prefer to associate with others who are like themselves to minimize the discomfort of interpersonal differences.

Likewise, there can be truth in *intuition,* the kind of casual wisdom that may lack the support of objective data. Granddad may have just "known" that the cow got sick after she ate a particular weed, or that a person's knees would get sore after a big rain.

On a more formal level, Ferdinand Tönnies was to some degree correct when he observed (intuited) the two kinds of societies: *gemeinschaft,* a village type society with close interpersonal relationships, and *gesellschaft,* a modern industrial society with impersonal, contractual relationships (Tönnies, 1957, 47). Each society has different needs for mass media, and his intuitive approach is useful in explaining our "dependency" on mass media for information (DeFleur, 1970).

Finally, there can be knowledge and wisdom in the sample of one, or **case study.** A well-known sample is the David Manning White (1950, 383–390) "gatekeeper" study of a single Illinois newspaper wire editor. The study showed clearly how one wire editor's choices in news selection could present a pattern of prejudice and bias. The editor systematically excluded minor stories that failed to support his mindset, such as his disdain for Roman Catholicism. If the news creates "pictures in our head" (Lippmann, 1922), and if the news is biased, then our "pictures" by definition are warped.

Gatekeeping is an important concept. The wisdom of White's one-man sample has stood the test of time, and the study is widely cited yet today. But intuitive, anecdotal, and small-sample explanations of phenomena present special problems. They make it hard for us to know when to believe. They do not follow rules that permit objective verification.

VALIDITY, RELIABILITY, AND OPERATIONAL DEFINITIONS

One goal of research is **internal validity,** defined as the extent to which a researcher measures what was intended to be measured. For example, if the researcher claims that TV violence increases viewers' fear of violence, then we need evidence that the fear is really caused by television, not by the neighborhood where the viewers live. We need internal validity.

Another goal of research is **external validity.** When data do not generalize to the larger population they are said to lack external validity. For a sample to have external validity, it must represent the whole population from which it is drawn.

A third goal of research is **reliability,** defined as the extent to which a measure obtains the same result with repeated uses. If a research outcome is internally valid, then it probably also is reliable, but the opposite is not necessarily the case. It is possible to have high reliability but low validity, as in the TV viewing fear-of-violence study discussed above. In that case, the researcher would see the same wrong data in repeated administrations. Several estimators of reliability and validity will be discussed in Chapter 5.

i.e. correlation w/o causation

A fourth goal is that researchers will clearly define the variables with which they work. For example, a researcher measuring media use might define *use* as "a self-report of attention to TV programming for any time greater than 15 minutes over a given period." Note that the definition stipulates the nature of attention and the kind of measure, in this case a self-report. Definitions based on the manner of the measurement are known as **operational definitions.** They are very important to the social research method, because they stipulate clearly to all how the data were gathered. For example, "liking" a political candidate could be *operationally defined* as "voting for the candidate."

SOURCES OF ERROR IN RESEARCH

The single biggest weakness of social research is its proneness to error at any of several levels. Errors can occur in conceptualization, definition, measurement, interpretation, and reporting.

Conceptualization

Errors in *conceptualization* occur as a result of clouded thinking. For example, let's say a researcher is studying the question of whether camera access to court has an impact on how television covers court news. (At this writing, numerous states were experimenting with the issue of whether cameras would disrupt the administration of justice.) To find the effect of access on coverage, the researcher might want to compare the amount of news coverage by some stations that have access with the coverage by some that do not. This probably seems a reasonable test. But is coverage of courts explained *solely* by permission to take cameras into court? Of course not.

There really may be several reasons for coverage or noncoverage of court news, such as the size of the news department, the professional orientation of its leadership, the size of the community, and the nature of the crimes covered. Access is just one of several possible explanations for differences in court coverage. Communication phenomena usually are not explained by a single variable (in the above case, *access*), but instead by some combination of variables. The successful researcher will define the issue clearly, and systematically account for all possible explanations. Research requires clear, systematic thought.

Definition

Errors of *definition* are often equivalent to errors of measurement and can imply faulty conceptualization or faulty data. For example, consider the definition of *media use* again. Suppose the researcher wishes to define media use as the number of hours spent with media on a typical day *times* the number of days spent with media per week. This would provide a measure of "total hours of use."

Although total hours seems a reasonable definition, the concept of media use may be defined in other ways. One popular method asks not how much time the respondent spends with media on a *typical* day, but rather the amount of time spent with media *yesterday*. The researcher would need to know whether one measure was indeed more accurate than another.

Measurement

Errors of *measurement* or instrumentation are even more difficult to overcome. For example, respondents may be unable to articulate the attitude that they hold, or if they can, articulation might make then uncomfortable. In either case, the attitude is not expressed. Sometimes, the respondent is not conscious of holding a given attitude. For example, suppose questions about sexual behavior made a respondent uncomfortable. The respondent might not want to admit, even to an interviewer, his or her true feelings, if indeed the respondent was conscious of them.

Interpretation

Errors of *interpretation* include: (a) faulty input of data (computer people refer to this as G-I-G-O: garbage in, garbage out); (b) failure to understand the statistical hypothesis test; and (c) overreaches of the data (e.g., when a researcher reaches a conclusion firmer than the data would support). Errors of interpretation lead to faulty conclusions and occasionally to faulty publications, although refereed journals screen submissions to avoid this.

HYPOTHESES EXPLAINED AND DEFINED

Social research is guided by hypotheses. A hypothesis can be general, in the sense that it can loosely guide the research, or specific, in the sense that it provides a testable relationship between phenomena. The former is sometimes called a **working hypothesis,** and the latter is called the **research hypothesis.** A working hypothesis broadly states an expected relationship; for example, that media cultivate certain perceptions among members of their audience. A research hypothesis is a precise statement of the relationship between variables.

A hypothesis that suggests *A* is not different from *B* is called the **null hypothesis** (H_0) or the hypothesis of no difference. The **alternative hypothesis** (H_1) stipulates that *A* is different from *B*. Hypotheses provide objective and precise decision points in the interpretation of data. For example, a hypothesis might state:

> H_1. Teens' perceptions of others' sexual behavior are positively and significantly correlated with their self-report data representing amount of time spent viewing visual media (TV, cable TV, etc.).

This hypothesis predicts a positive relationship between two variables: (a) perceptions and (b) amount of TV viewing. In this case, a negative relationship would suggest rejection of the hypothesis. Furthermore, a correlation must be stronger than would be expected by chance (i.e., through sampling error).

A hypothesis should specify the nature of the data; in the example above, the data are self-report estimates of how much time the respondents spend with visual media. Since self-reports are subject to error, the researcher might set a stringent "significance" level, that is, one in which an outcome would not likely be due to chance variations in the sample. The hypothesis in the example attempts to take personal judgment and error out of the decision about whether perception really is related to use of visual media.

Where Hypotheses Originate

Hypotheses can have either formal or informal origins. On the informal level, hypotheses can be thought of as extensions of hunches. A *hunch* is an informal expectation; it may be based on observation and reading, or it may be spur-of-the-moment intuition, but it is informal. The formal hypothesis of the type illustrated above typically grows out of a careful reading of the research literature.

For example, the researcher who wants to study the issue of whether media reportage of political and social conflict creates "malaise" (an attitude presumably induced by cynical, contentious reportage) in the audience would review the previous research at length before hypothesizing relationships (Robinson 1976, 409–432).[1]

Data Searching

Hypotheses also serve to avoid what is called **data searching.** Data searching exists, for example, when the researcher without good hypotheses correlates several variables in a data set, discovers unexpected relationships, and reports these as valid. The experienced researcher knows that such findings can lack substantive meaning. **Ex-post hypothesizing** can lead to wrong conclusions. The safest plan is to ignore relationships that are not hypothesized, and pursue them later on a more formal level. You may ask: Suppose the outcome was not hypothesized, but is nevertheless reasonable and important; must that be disregarded? The researcher who follows closely the rules of social science research will use such a **serendipitous** finding (defined as a valuable or agreeable thing not sought) as the basis for subsequent research, not for research reporting.

Serendipity and hunches have a place in research, but the scrupulous researcher will approach them with care to avoid wrongly accepting H_1 (the alternative hypothesis) when H_0 (the null hypothesis) is true. The researcher needs not only a relationship between data, but also a reason (i.e., a theory or hypothesis) to think the relationship is meaningful.

Hypothesis Significance

Significance in the context of hypothesis testing means that the obtained result was different than would have been expected by chance. Significance asks whether samples are drawn from the same population, and by inference whether some causal agent was at work in creating differences in outcomes.

Significance is the decision point for accepting or rejecting the hypothesis. By convention, researchers are willing to risk error—to accept the hypothesis of no difference when the opposite is true—5 times in 100 cases, depending on the importance of the research issue and the size of the sample. For some research, the significance level might be set at 1 in 1,000 ($p = .001$), or 1 in 10,000 ($p = .0001$). This accounts for the risk that sample variation, not the hypothesized relationship, might explain a research outcome.

Predicting Behavior

If social phenomena are orderly and systematic, then they should be predictable. The task for researchers is to identify the variables that make the prediction possible. If A is a function of B, C, and D, then do B, C, and D operate *equally* on A? One variable may contribute heavily to a relationship, while another may have a very slight impact.

In most social research, A is a function of many predictors, including many that escape detection. How would the researcher control for "peer pressure," for example, when peer pressure is subtle (it is not limited to conscious manipulation), cumulative (it occurs over long periods), and pervasive (it can hardly be avoided)? Nevertheless, if the researcher can identify the relevant variables, systematic relationships can be examined.

For example, suppose the researcher wants to study the "diffusion" of news to discover who talks to whom about which kinds of news. Imagine for yourself the variables that might dictate whether a person discusses news with others. You might select the following: a measure of news knowledge, on the assumption that people who know more about news are more likely to talk about news; a measure of personality characteristics such as extroversion, need for cognition, and dominance or passivity; a measure of the individual's specific knowledge of the topic at hand; and so on—plus the usual demographics such as age, education, political affiliation, and news sources. The researcher's goal is to *predict* diffusion; will those variables lead to an accurate prediction?

If the answer were yes, and if the researcher were to know the relative contribution of each, then the researcher would have the elements of a theory of news diffusion. This kind of theory and prediction can be expressed in the form of an equation:

$$Y = F(x_1 + x_2 + \ldots x_n)$$

where Y = likelihood of diffusion,
F = function of,
$x_1 \ldots x_n$ = variables that "explain" Y

If the independent variables (the ones that explain Y) can be identified and measured, and if the impact of each on Y can be measured, then we have a theory of news diffusion.

It has been said, "Nothing is so practical as a good theory," because theories suggest systematic relationships, and systematic relationships suggest prediction. Predictions make for efficiency of effort. Media managers can use theory to maximize the benefits of their decision making.

TYPES OF RESEARCH

Private and Public Research

Academics are not the only researchers using social science methods. Much research is done by marketers, advertising agencies, and consultants. However, if the research done by the private sector is not published and not held up for scrutiny, then it is not defined as *science*. Remember: Science must be public and open to challenge. **Private research** does not *cumulate* because it is private, and it is *not subject to refutation* by all researchers. It is sometimes called **proprietary research** because it is conducted strictly for purposes of the owner. **Public research** is published and open to examination and even refutation.

Theoretical and Applied Research

As indicated in Chapter 1, researchable topics fall into two broad categories, *theoretical research* and *applied research*. The lines between the two are not always clear, but applied research is generally thought of as problem-solving research.

Although mass media managers generally see the benefit of applied research, even if they don't always make optimal use of it, they do not always see the benefit of theoretical research. In this regard, the field of mass communication probably is different from some other professional fields. Engineers, for example, generally support or encourage theoretical research. The same might be said for chemists, psychologists, and political scientists. Certainly, some media managers do encourage and support theoretical research, but too many do not.

Failure to support theoretical research exists even among some mass media academic faculties, who divide into two camps, the media professionals and the research theorists. The media pros are persons whose teaching and scholarship is nonquantitative and founded on the *practice* of mass media; the research theorists rely more on social science and the research literature, usually with some emphasis on statistics.

You will come to your own conclusion about the reasons for this unhappy division of interests. The author observes that many mass media practitioners are for one reason or another averse to statistical interpretations, and theoretical issues often lack the readability, urgency, scope, and impact to attract the practitioner.

Whatever the source, this gulf between quantitative researchers and practitioners is a liability to the field and should be closed.[2] All mass media professionals should be trained in the methods of social research and in the principles of sampling and statistics. How else can managers be effective consumers of the benefits of social research? How can managers make the most of such research if they know little or nothing of what research can do? How can managers even read the research if they know nothing of the methods?

At the same time, researchers must learn to communicate the findings of their research more successfully. Too often, research reports rely excessively on numbers and jargon. These reports, like trees falling in the forest, will be "unheard" if unread. No matter how complex and how technical the methods of the research, the key points should be put into language that the professional in the field can understand.

Critical and Administrative Research

Another distinction in types of research is the distinction between administrative research and **critical research.** Here is the crux of the distinction:

> For the so-called empirical or administrative researcher, issues relating to the structure of economic and political institutions (and sometimes social and cultural institutions as well), the centralization of power, the characteristics of dominant–dependent relations and the incentives of vested interests, are excluded from analysis. The premises of critical research, by calling into question and focusing research efforts on changes in asymetrical political and economic relations—and concluding that they are preconditions of significant change—contradict and fundamentally threaten the administrative tradition. (Melody and Mansell, 1983, 104)

In other words, administrative researchers focus on narrow, problem-oriented topics to the exclusion of broader political and economic influences; critical researchers work at a system level and interpret phenomena from the standpoint of political and economic influences.[3]

Administrative research can be either applied or theoretical, but it is aimed at problem solving. For example, research undertaken to solve problems of staff credibility could be called administrative research, as could research undertaken to build the audience for a mass medium. Given the entrepreneurial, industrial, and technical nature of Western economies, an emphasis on administrative research is not surprising. But critics point out that such research is a bit like wearing blinders in the search for wisdom. When research has a commercial purpose, and when the researcher focuses narrowly on a topic, deeper truths might be overlooked.

Most of the criticism of administrative research comes from critical researchers, although not all critical researchers have the same scholarly orientation. Some are more interested in media content than in the social or economic forces that put it there.[4] They focus on qualities such as performance, writing, directing, political economy, film history, and aesthetics. Their work may be either quantitative or nonquantitative.

Other critical scholars, who might be distinguished as the European critical school, take the position that a microscope, figuratively speaking, misses the broader view of the social environment. Largely a Marxist approach to understanding, this critical technique is to examine "system level" or macro-variables rather than micro-variables.

Whereas the micro-researcher might study the kinds of news choices editors make, the macro-researcher might examine the economic and political circumstances of the industry that lead to predictable news choices. The capitalist would say news choices keep the public informed; the Marxist would say news choices exploit the public's base interests in order to maintain the wealth and power of those who control the media.

Critical research is typically nonquantitative. The data are more often logical, observational, and documentary. In the evolution of American social research, administrative research has clearly dominated; however, critical research is on the upswing. And there is room in American social research for both; researchers who wear blinders are not persuasive. They clearly need a broad perspective, an ability to see micro-variables on system level. The goal, after all, is wisdom, regardless of the research method.

SUMMARY

Social science research is built on a logical structure of assumptions, definitions, rules, and techniques that provide for the evaluation of evidence about behavior. The centerpiece of the structure is empiricism, the notion that evidence should be observable, not dependent on faith. Social science research is objective, systematic, hypothesis guided, cumulative, open to challenge, and replicable. Errors occur in conceptualization, definition of terms, measurement, interpretation of results, and reporting of results. To the extent possible, the rules and techniques of the method ensure the common understanding of data. Distinctions are made between private and public research; applied and theoretical research; and critical and administrative research.

STUDY QUESTIONS AND EXERCISES

1. Discuss: What is "empiricism," and why is the concept important in social science research?

   ■ Identify a belief that a person might have, for example the following: "There is more crime when the moon is full." Then discuss: Is this statement empirical? If not, can it be made so? How?

   ■ Consider the following assertion: "There are more automobile wrecks when the barometric pressure is low." Is this statement empirical? If not, can it be made so? How?

2. Social science research follows a kind of logic that begins with assumptions about the nature of phenomena. If these assumptions are invalid, then so is social science research. Identify the assumptions and discuss each: Are they irrefutable? For example, can research be truly "objective"? Is it truly possible to measure the depths of the human mind? Does empiricism set a higher standard than can be achieved?

3. The assumptions and logic of social science research are antithetical to intuition and anecdotes as sources of "truth." Does this mean intuition and anecdotes and nonrandom sample research have no merit in the search for wisdom? How can they be useful?

4. Identify two mass media problems that might be addressed through research. Describe how you would conduct the research. For example, one problem might be the question of whether a certain radio station should change its program format. How would the manager decide this difficult question?

5. Select and read a research report in *Journalism Quarterly*, the *Journal of Broadcasting and Electronic Media*, or the *Journal of Communication*; discuss the kind of research that you read about, its efforts to achieve accuracy, and the generalizability of its findings. Discuss the writing style and the data treatment. What kind of statistical manipulations did you see? How could researchers make their work more palatable to media practitioners? Would it be possible to simplify the methods and the data of social research to the point that an untrained reader could understand and appreciate research outcomes?

EXERCISES FOR GUEST ESSAY

1. Visit your library to learn more about the works of Wilhelm Dilthey, Emile Durkheim, and Max Weber. Use some of their original writings, as well as some secondary sources. You might want to begin your search with the *Encyclopedia of the Social Sciences* or *The Nature and Types of Sociological Theory* (Martindale, 1981). Develop a short summary of each of their thoughts on the philosophy of science issues. If they were producing communication research

today, what might each of their approaches be? In what ways would these approaches be similar? How would they be different?

2. Think about the last time you had a serious disagreement with an important person in your life. Write (a) a short description of the argument, (b) a short explanation of the event, and (c) a prediction about the conditions under which the event might recur. What do each of these short essays contribute to your understanding of what happened? What role does *Verstehen* play in this understanding?

3. Read the article "Research as Praxis" by Patti Lather (1986, 257–277) and the book *Can Science Save Us?* by George Lundberg (1947). (If Lundberg's book is unavailable, try the chapter entitled "Can Science Save Us?" in Cuzzort and King, 1980.) How would Lather and Lundberg each approach the issue of the creation and use of research with regard to pornography? How would *you* approach it? What do you see as the strengths and weaknesses of your choice?

NOTES

1. For a discussion of malaise, see Robinson, 1976, 409–432.
2. The distance and misapprehension between researchers and practitioners is perhaps well illustrated in comments by William L. McCorkle: "Weak journalism schools, in my opinion, where the emphasis may be too heavy on communicology and too little on skills taught by skilled people, are reluctant to invite top professionals because the theory-oriented and/or inadequately skilled faculty has too little in common all too often with real-world guests."
3. To pursue this topic, see the special issue of the *Journal of Communication,* Summer 1983, entitled "Ferment in the Field." It is an interesting critique of research.
4. For example, see the recent collection of essays by Avery and Eason (1991).

SOURCES

Avery, Robert K., and David Eason. 1991. *Critical Perspectives on Media and Society.* New York: Guilford Press.

Babbie, Earl. 1989. *The Practice of Social Research.* 5th ed. Belmont, Calif.: Wadsworth.

Blalock, H. M., and A. B. Blalock. 1982. *Introduction to Social Research.* 2d ed. Englewood Cliffs, N.J.: Prentice-Hall.

DeFleur, Melvin L. 1970. *Theories of Mass Communication.* 2d ed. New York: David McKay.

Kerlinger, Fred N. 1973. *Foundations in Behavioral Research.* 2d ed. New York: Holt, Rinehart and Winston.

Lippmann, Walter. 1922. *Public Opinion.* New York: Macmillan.

McCorkle, William L. 1991. Shop Talk at Thirty. *Editor and Publisher* (August 24).

Melody, William H., and Robin E. Mansell. 1983. The Debate Over Critical vs. Administrative Research: Circularity or Challenge. *Journal of Communication* 33(3):103–116.

Robinson, Michael J. 1976. Public Affairs Television and the Growth of Political Malaise: The Case of "The Selling of the Pentagon." *American Political Science Review* 70:409–432.

Selltiz, Claire, Marie Jahoda, Morton Deutsch, and Stuart W. Cook. 1959. *Research Methods in Social Relations.* New York: Holt, Rinehart and Winston.

Tönnies, Ferdinand. [1879] 1957. *Gemeinschaft und Gesellschaft* (Community and Society), trans. and ed. Charles P. Loomis. East Lansing: Michigan State University Press.

White, David Manning. 1950. The "Gate Keeper": A Case Study in the Selection of News. *Journalism Quarterly* 27(2):383–390.

SOURCES FOR GUEST ESSAY

Undergraduate Readings

Babbie, Earl. 1986. *Observing Ourselves: Essays in Social Research.* Belmont, Calif.: Wadsworth.

Cuzzort, Ray P. and Edith W. King. 1980. Can Science Save Us? In *20th Century Social Thought.* 3d ed., 114–130. New York: Holt, Rinehart & Winston.

International Encyclopedia of the Social Sciences. 1968–1971. ed. David L. Sills. New York: Macmillan.

Hughes, John. 1990. *The Philosophy of Social Research.* 2d ed. White Plains, N.Y.: Longman.

Lather, Patti. 1986. Research as Praxis. *Harvard Educational Review* 56(3):257–277.

Lundberg, George A. 1947. *Can Science Save Us?* New York: Longman, Green.

Martindale, Don. 1981. *The Nature and Types of Sociological Theory.* 2d ed. Boston: Houghton Mifflin.

Rogers, Everett M. 1982. The Empirical and the Critical Schools of Communication Research. In *Communication Yearbook 5,* 125–144, ed. M. Burgoon. New Brunswick, N.J.: Transaction Books.

Tichenor, Phillip J., and Douglas M. McLeod. 1989. The Logic of Social and Behavioral Science. *Research Methods in Mass Communication.* 2d ed., 10–29, ed. Guido H. Stempel, III, and Bruce H. Westley. Englewood Cliffs, N.J.: Prentice-Hall.

Additional Readings for Graduate Students

Diesing, Paul. 1971. *Patterns of Discovery in the Social Sciences.* Chicago: Aldine Atherton.

Kaplan, Abraham. 1964. *The Conduct of Inquiry: Methodology for Behavioral Science.* San Francisco: Chandler.

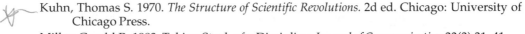Kuhn, Thomas S. 1970. *The Structure of Scientific Revolutions.* 2d ed. Chicago: University of Chicago Press.

Miller, Gerald R. 1983. Taking Stock of a Discipline. *Journal of Communication* 33(3):31–41.

4

Working with Samples

All scientific observation, whether statistical or not, is based on sampling. . . .
The earliest examples of sampling procedures are to be found in certain very
ordinary human activities. The common practice of taking a small part or
portion for tasting or testing to determine the characteristics of the whole
precedes recorded history and is one of the roots from which sampling
methodology stems . . .

F. F. Stephan, 1948

□
OBJECTIVES

After studying this chapter, you should be able to:

1. Describe some non-probability samples.

2. Describe some probability samples.

3. Describe exit polling.

4. Use a table of random numbers.

5. Create a list of random telephone numbers.

6. Create a multilevel area probability sample.

7. Calculate sample error and sample size.

8. Explain weighting and oversampling.

INTRODUCTION

An important portion of the logic of social science is based on random sampling,
the idea that a small subset of a population can be used to represent a whole population. For example, as was indicated in Chapter 3, the method asks us to assume

that individual behaviors are predictable, that they can be aggregated, and that they occur across society.

It is a nice assumption to make because we could not possibly conduct a **census** for every polling question that arises. If **samples** did not represent populations, every sample would be different and there would be few or no generalizations about social behavior. There would be no social science.

But there is a lot to know about samples; in fact whole books and university courses are devoted to the subject. There are several different kinds of samples— some random and some nonrandom—and several ways of obtaining them. Many issues must be addressed. For example, how large or small must the sample be? How are elements to be selected? How can sample bias be controlled? How do we recognize sample bias? How can we know when to have confidence in a sample? How is sample error calculated? This chapter will introduce some of the fundamentals of sampling and relate them to mass communication research.

In general, the selection of a sample is dictated by the needs of the researcher. If the intent is to generalize the sample to a population, such as when a TV station samples its audience's preferences, a **probability sample** is needed. Probability suggests that the sample is suited to statistical inference. If external validity (generalization to the population) is not an issue, such as when a newspaper or a TV station conducts a street-corner survey, then a **non-probability sample** might do. Several kinds of nonprobability and probability samples will be described below.

NON-PROBABILITY SAMPLES

Non-probability samples include the so-called **"person-on-the- street"** sample (or street-corner interviews), **telephone call-ins, convenience samples, purposive samples, focus groups, quota samples,** and **socio-samples,** among others. Each of these has an important research function, but none generalizes confidently to the population at-large. It is important to look at the strengths and weaknesses of each.

"Person-on-the-Street" Interviews

The news media often use this sample for news purposes. For example, the news editor or news producer, or perhaps the public relations person responsible for a company publication, will assign a reporter to learn several people's reaction to some event in the news.

An example involved a farm-news story (a legislative story on the Associated Press [AP] wire) and a newspaper reporter who was asked to interview 20 farmers to find out "what the local farmers think about this issue." The reporter called several prominent agricultural news sources, then some well-known local farmers. The result was a story that no doubt had merit per se, but not for its estimate of "what the local farmers think about the issue."

Why? The sample was not random; the questions were not uniform; the error margin was huge; and the persons in the sample were largely limited to persons of wealth and property. Those kinds of concerns signify the basic problem of the non-random sample: It might not be a good representation of the feelings of everyone in the population.

In another version of the person-on-the-street sample, a researcher will select an interview site such as a street corner, and then interview as many people as possible among those who pass by and agree to be interviewed. This might have the appearance of a good sample because it does not single out respondents but takes all who come. But it is seriously flawed. Why? The central problem is that not everyone in the population is able to be at that corner at the time of the interview. If the persons who do not pass that corner are different from those who do, then they won't be represented in the survey. This means that the sample might be biased in some way.

For example, the sample might overrepresent certain levels of education or training or social status—the kind of distinctions that permit some people, but not others, the freedom to be on the street at a given time. And so, again, the nonrandom sample carries a high risk of unrepresentativeness.

The problem here is not the person-on-the-street interview as a technique; it might be well suited to some uses. For example, it might be satisfactory for a *pilot study,* a study that is not by itself conclusive. Or it might be suited to some news purposes. Some media routinely run opinion surveys with photos of a half-dozen respondents to convey information and promote readership.

The person-on-the-street technique might also be appropriate for *mall intercepts,* a kind of research among the people who shop at selected malls. The person-on-the-street sample is not a reliable sample to represent a population, however, and it should not be reported in a way that gives a wrong impression of its merit.

subject to ballot stuffing B. Telephone Call-Ins

At the time of this writing, telephone call-in surveys were popular among both broadcasters and publishers. Here is how it worked: The sponsor would set up a "900" telephone number, announce the issue to be voted on, and invite members of the audience to call in their vote. Since the "900-" calls are billed to the caller, sometimes at a dollar or more per call, a popular topic would actually make money for the sponsor of the survey. It makes for good entertainment, but not good science.

Call-in surveys are easily abused. A newspaper in Norfolk, Va., for example, reported that after two days of telephone "voting" on an issue the count was close: 345 no votes and 304 yes votes. But then, as the newspaper reported, "somebody stacked the poll." In the next day and a half, the newspaper said, no votes increased almost 10 to 1. The newspaper concluded, "Someone somewhere wants to beat this [the issue of the vote] very badly" (*The Compass,* Norfolk, Va., August 4, 1991, p. 7). Had the change in the vote been more subtle, would the newspaper have known the vote was seriously biased? No, and that is a serious problem with this kind of poll. Since the nature of the sample is unknown, the usefulness of the survey is doubtful.

The same principle applies at the national level. When the CBS Television Network sponsored a call-in poll after President George Bush's State-of-the-Union address, 314,786 persons responded; but the result was substantially different from that of a more scientific poll conducted simultaneously. The polls were different by more than 20 percent on two of nine questions, and by more than 10 percent on five other questions (Morin, 1992, B3).

A final example: A call-in poll conducted by *USA Today* in June 1990 generated 6,406 responses, but it turned out that 72 percent of them came from two telephone numbers. In other words, the voting box was electronically stuffed (Morin, 1992, B2).

C. Convenience Samples

Another non-probability sample is the so-called convenience sample or available sample. The usefulness of this sample depends on the purpose of the research. Akin to the person-on-the-street sample, the *convenience sample* is a set of respondents who happen to be available to the researcher; the respondents are not selected at random.

The academic researcher, for example, who uses a classroom of students is using a convenience sample. This sample is widely used in social research, despite the fact that it risks poor external validity. It is used because many academic research projects require only that two groups of respondents be *comparable,* not representative of the population.

For example, if a researcher wanted to know whether watching "Sesame Street" improved language skill in children, it would be necessary to measure language acquisition of two or more *comparable groups.* (If the groups were not comparable, differences in language skill might be attributed to something other than "Sesame Street.") If the TV show had an impact on language, the test scores of the group that saw the show should be higher. Therefore, in this case, it would not matter whether the sample held external validity; it would matter only that the groups were comparable so that the question of language acquisition could be tested.

On the other hand, if the researcher wanted to know whether "Sesame Street" would improve language acquisition of all children of a population, that would require working with samples that described the population.

D. Purposive Samples

A fourth non-probability sample is the *purposive* sample, or simply a sample that fills a purpose. It can be a convenience sample, but more directed. For example, the researcher might purposely choose one classroom each of freshmen, sophomores, juniors, and seniors, rather than merely the first four classes available. Or, the researcher might solicit survey responses from members of certain civic clubs, such as Sertoma, Lions, Optimists, and Ruritans, because they generally have certain demographic characteristics. Like the convenience and person-on-the-street samples, the purposive sample has poor external validity, yet it may be justified by a research purpose.

Topics of the day

WHAT WENT WRONG WITH THE POLLS?

None of Straw Votes Got Exactly the Right Answer—Why?

In 1920, 1924, 1928 and 1932, THE LITER-
ARY DIGEST Polls were right. Not only
right in the sense that they showed the
winner; they forecast the *actual popular
vote* with such a small percentage of error
(less than 1 per cent. in 1932) that newspapers and individuals everywhere heaped
such phrases as "uncannily accurate" and
"amazingly right" upon us.

Four years ago, when the Poll was running his way, our very good friend Jim
Farley was saying that "no sane person
could escape the implication" of a sampling
"so fairly and correctly conducted."

Well, this year we used precisely the
same method that had scored four bull's-
eyes in four previous tries. And we were
far from correct. Why? We ask that question in all sincerity, because *we want to
know.*

"Reasons"—Oh, we've been flooded with
"reasons." Hosts of people who feel they
have learned more about polling in a few
months than we have learned in more
than a score of years have told us just
where we were off. Hundreds of astute
"second-guessers" have assured us, by telephone, by letter, in the newspapers, that
the reasons for our error were "obvious."
Were they?

Suppose we review a few of these "obvious reasons."

The one most often heard runs something like this: "This election was different.
Party lines were obliterated. For the first
time in more than a century, *all* the 'have-
nots' were on one side. THE DIGEST, polling names from telephone books and lists
of automobile owners, simply did not reach
the lower strata." And so on. . . .

"Have-nots"—Well, in the first place, the
'have-nots' did not reelect Mr. Roosevelt.
That they contributed to his astonishing
plurality, no one can doubt. But the fact
remains that a majority of farmers, doctors,
grocers and candlestick-makers *also* voted
for the President. As Dorothy Thompson
remarked in the New York *Herald Tribune,*
you could eliminate the straight labor vote,
the relief vote and the Negro vote, and
still Mr. Roosevelt would have a majority.
So that "reason" does not appear to hold
much water. Besides—

We *did* reach these so-called "have-not"
strata. In the city of Chicago, for example,
we polled *every third registered voter.* In
the city of Scranton, Pennsylvania, we
polled *every other registered voter.* And
in Allentown, Pennsylvania, likewise other
cities, we polled *every registered voter.*

Is that so? chorus the critics, a little
abashed, no doubt. Well, they come back,
you must have got the right answer in
those towns, anyway.

Well, we didn't. The fact is that we
were as badly off there as we were on the
national total.

Cities—In Allentown, for example, 10,753

out of the 30,811 who voted returned ballots to us showing a division of 53.32 per
cent. to 44.67 per cent. in favor of Mr.
Landon. What was the actual result? It
was 56.93 per cent. for Mr. Roosevelt, 41.17
per cent. for the Kansan.

In Chicago, the 100,929 voters who returned ballots to us showed a division of
48.63 per cent. to 47.56 per cent. in favor
of Mr. Landon. The 1,672,175 who voted
in the actual election gave the President
65.24 per cent., to 32.26 per cent. for the
Republican candidate.

What happened? Why did only one in
five voters in Chicago to whom THE DI-
GEST sent ballots take the trouble to reply?
And why was there a preponderance of
Republicans in the one-fifth that did reply?
Your guess is as good as ours. We'll go
into it a little more later. The important
thing in all the above is that all this con-
jecture about our "not reaching certain
strata" simply will not hold water.

Hoover Voters—Now for another "explanation" dinned into our ears: "You got too
many Hoover voters in your sample."

Well, the fact is that we've *always* got
too big a sampling of Republican voters.
That was true in 1920, in 1924, in 1928,
and even in 1932, when we *overestimated*
the Roosevelt popular vote by three-quar-
ters of 1 per cent.

In 1928 in Chicago, we underestimated
the Democratic vote by a little more than
5 per cent., overestimated the Republican
vote by the same margin.

We wondered then, as we had wondered
before and have wondered since, why we
were getting better cooperation in what we
have always regarded as a public service
from Republicans than we were getting
from Democrats. Do Republicans live
nearer mail-boxes? Do Democrats generally disapprove of straw polls?

We don't know that answer. All we know
is that in 1932, when the tide seemed to be
running away from Hoover, we were per-
turbed about the disproportion of Republican voters in our sampling. Republican
and Democratic chieftains from all points
in the country were at the telephones day
after day for reports of what the Democrats called our "correctly conducted" system. And then the result came along, and
it was so right, we were inclined to agree
that we had been concerned without reason, and this year, when it seemed logical
to suppose that the President's vote would
be lighter, even if he won (hadn't that been
the rule on reelections for more than a
hundred years?) we decided not to worry.

Figures—So the statisticians did our worry-
ing for us on that score, applying what they
called the "compensating-ratio" in some
cases, and the "switch-factor" in others.
Either way, for some of the figure experts,
it didn't matter; interpret our figures for
2,376,523 voters as they would, the answer
was still Landon. Then other statisticians
took our figures and so weighted, compensated, balanced, adjusted and interpreted
them that they showed Roosevelt.

We did not attempt to interpret the figures, because we had no stake in the result

The following telegram was received by The
Literary Digest: "With full and sympathetic
appreciation of the rather tough spot you now
find yourselves in, we offer the following suggestion as a piece of strategy to turn seem-
ing defeat into victory and put name of Literary Digest on every tongue in America in a
most favorable manner in your next issue—
print the front cover in red except for a small
circular space in the center; in this space print
the words 'And is our face red!' The people of
America like a good sport and will like you
accordingly." Signed: George Bennitt, A. C.
Johnston and Al Devore; 625 State Street,
El Centro, California.

[Editor's Note: We appreciate the suggestion,
which arrived when this issue's cover was on
the presses, so the above is offered.]

"LITERARY DIGEST? LEMME TALK TO
THE EDITOR!!!"
—Duffy in Baltimore Sun

In the 1936 U.S. presidential election, *Literary Digest,* a very popular national periodical of
the time, conducted a mail-in survey of voter preferences between Franklin D. Roosevelt
and Alf Landon. On the basis of millions of responses, the *Literary Digest* concluded Landon would win by a substantial margin. Of course, Landon did not win, and the *Digest*'s
error could not have been more severe. In fact, Roosevelt won by a large margin. With a
sample numbering in the millions, what went wrong? Very simply, the *Digest* got too
many responses from one segment of the voting population. The sample was biased. The
miscall was a severe embarrassment, and *Literary Digest* soon ceased publication.

FIGURE 4.1 Front Page of the November 14, 1936, *Literary Digest* (*Source:* Reprinted from Peverill
Squire, 1988. Why the 1936 *Literary Digest* poll failed. *Public Opinion Quarterly* 52:125–133.)

E . Focus Groups

The *focus group* consists of a small number of individuals who are brought together by the researcher to discuss a given topic. The focused discussion typically is unstructured, although some focus groups are required to complete a formal questionnaire. The focus group usually numbers fewer than 10 to 12 persons. The number is so small that it cannot reasonably be expected to represent a population. Since the group is nonrandom, and members often are recruited because they have some particular characteristic or demographic, it has low external validity.

However, despite the nonprobability nature of the focus group, it is extremely important in research today. The focus group sometimes brings to light ideas that a formal survey would miss. For example, focus groups were credited with finding an important new use for *Arm & Hammer* baking soda, opening up a whole new line of marketing. Here's how it happened:

Baking soda had long been used in cooking and in cleaning, but the Arm & Hammer company wanted to make better use of its name recognition and its public good will by expanding the uses of the product. They worked long and hard until finally they hit on something. Focus groups reported that baking soda could be used as an air freshener in refrigerators. When the marketers developed a campaign emphasizing this quality, the product "took off." The success of the campaign made it a *cause célèbre* in American marketing history (Honomichl, 1982, M-2, M-3, M-22).

In another example of the successful use of focus technique, Grusin and Stone (1992, 72–83) used focus groups to stimulate recall of detail about use of the newspaper in classroom activities. In other words, the free and open discussion of the focus group brought out recollections that would have been missed in a conventional survey.

The intent of a focus group is not to describe or represent populations of individuals, but rather to represent populations of opinions. The myriad opinions, feelings, and beliefs that focus group members bring with them are the population of opinions. They are fertile ground for insightful approaches to problem solving and discovery.

F. Quota Samples

The quota sample is widely used in media research when selected demographics are important. For such a sample, interviewers are instructed to obtain predetermined quotas of types of respondents. For example, if the researcher wanted to compare newspaper readers with nonreaders, a survey would require a quota of nonreaders proportional to their occurrence in the population.

G. Socio-Samples

In some research, such as the opinion leadership research of the 1950s and 1960s (described in Chapter 2), it is desirable to use respondents to identify other potential respondents. For example, the researcher interviewing anorexic high school students might use them to identify other persons similarly afflicted. You can think of it as **snowball sampling** because it starts with a smallish number and increases as the survey is conducted. Ethics dictate that the researcher be concerned about issues of privacy and disclosure in such sampling.

II. PROBABILITY SAMPLES

Probability samples are called **EPSEM samples**, meaning "equal probability of selection method." Equal probability suggests the essential nature of the random sample: that every element of the population must have an equal chance of being selected in a sample.

A. Simple Random Samples

The **simple random sample** (often abbreviated SRS) is an EPSEM sample, but the word *simple* can be deceiving: It is simple only in that it requires that every element in the population be given the opportunity to be included in the sample. This is a powerful notion; it underlies the principle of cross-sectional research because much is known about the properties of random occurrences. In sampling, it is the *nonrandom occurrences that cause greatest uncertainty, not the random ones.*

Simple random samples usually are selected without replacement. *Replacement* has to do with whether an element drawn from a population is subsequently put back into the pot, possibly to be selected again. For example, suppose you bought a raffle ticket, and your stub went into a bowl with a thousand others. The raffle promises several winners. If each winning stub is not put back into the bowl after being drawn, then your own number has an improved chance of selection. On the other hand, if the winning stubs are put back into the bowl, making it possible for each to win more than once, then your chances are the same from start to finish: 1 in 1,001.

If the population from which the sample is selected is large, or if the *sample* is large, then replacement is relatively unimportant. But if the population is small, say 5,000, then some correction may be necessary because small changes in the resulting statistics can be significant. When uncertain about the issue of correction for replacement, the sampler should seek technical advice or consult any of several texts on sampling theory (e.g., Kalton, 1983, 13.).

Probability samples are intended to estimate the distribution of a variable in population. A *variable* is any element that can vary, such as the length of time a person spends reading a newspaper, or one's political affiliation, or whatever.

Suppose a researcher wanted to know how many persons in your town of 15,000 read a daily newspaper every day. Being sure to spread the sample proportionately across the community, the researcher might select a number of citizens and telephone them to ask about their newspaper reading; the sample would then be used to estimate such occurrence in the population. If 52 percent of the *sample* said they read the newspaper every day, and if the sample were random, the researcher could assume that approximately 52 percent of the *population* also read every day.

When the population numbers in the millions and covers a very large area (i.e., when the boundaries are not as clear as city or county lines), the sampling principle is the same but somewhat more difficult to execute. How can the researcher go about obtaining a random sample? There are several popular methods, including the lottery method, the systematic interval method, or any of several special sampling methods discussed below—and a geography-based method that Wimmer and Dominick (1991) called a multi-level area-probability sample.

Lottery Method

The **lottery method** is a kind of random sample in which every element is given a number and every element has an equal chance of being selected. Selection is not biased in any known way. Unfortunately, for large populations the lottery method usually is not feasible. It would be virtually impossible to identify all of the people in a large community, number them, and then physically pull their numbers from a very large pile, or even from a table of random numbers. It can work when the numbers are small, but samplers usually look for alternatives.

Systematic Interval Method

In the absence of the lottery method, researchers often rely on the **systematic interval method.** This is the kind of sample that is drawn from an alphabetized directory such as a telephone book or city directory. The directories are called **sampling frames.**

From a random starting point on a page, the researcher selects each *n*th (e.g., the 9th, or 32nd, or 61st, or whatever) name or unit until the desired number of random selections is complete. The assumption is that because the names are spread throughout the frame, and because they are chosen by interval, not by some biasing characteristic, they should constitute a *random* selection.

Systematic random samples can be of high quality, but they naturally depend on the quality of the frame. For example, if the sampling frame is inaccurate or incomplete—it does not list all members of the population, which is customary with a telephone book—then the frame is of reduced merit. Elements missing from the sampling frame cannot be sampled, and so the sample cannot be represented as a cross-section.

Here is how the systematic interval sample is drawn from a telephone book:

1. Assume that you already know the size of the sample that you will need, say 250 persons. Divide the number of the sample into the number of names in the sampling frame. The result is your sampling *interval.* For example, if your sample is 250 and there are 15,000 names in the directory, your interval is 60. Selection of each 60th name in the directory will provide a sample of 250. However, you will need to pick a specific entry to start with, not necessarily the first one in the book. That is explained in step 2, below.

2. Next, use a table of random numbers (TON; use a table of random numbers in any statistics text in your library) to select any number between zero and the sampling interval (in this example, 60). That number will be the element

with which you begin your intervals. For example, suppose you drew the number 23; you would select the 23rd entry in the phone book, and each 60th thereafter (i.e., persons 83, 143, 203, and so on). Continue this until you have 250 persons. The result is a systematic random sample of 250.

The systematic interval method spreads the sample across the population; this avoids bunching respondents in any known way, such as overselecting the Smiths or Brzyzynsckis, or even overselecting neighborhoods. The systematic interval method is not strictly random, but it is considered sufficiently random to be acceptable. It is probably the most widely used method of sampling today, at least among all but the very large survey organizations.

The telephone book has important weaknesses, however. First, not all persons can be reached by phone; some have an unlisted number, some will not welcome the bother of a telephone interview, and some have no telephone. Second, the telephone book quickly becomes outdated as mobile Americans move from town to town and neighborhood to neighborhood. It's said that the telephone book decreases in usefulness by a small percentage each month of its existence. The reader can imagine that by its twelfth month, the telephone book is a weakened sampling frame.

"Weakness" in the sampling frame adds an element of uncertainty to the survey research process. Still, researchers generally feel that the telephone book is a fairly sufficient method of generating a sample to represent a population, especially if the persons not reached by the frame are not important to the purposes of the survey. In other words, if the persons who don't have phones are not likely to be voters, their nonresponse might not have a negative impact on a voting survey. This would be something for the researcher to consider.

The systematic sample has another complexity. Suppose, for example, that when you divide your sample size into the number of the sampling frame (population), the result is not a whole number. Should you *round* up, or down, or *alternate* up and down? It sounds like a small thing, but sometimes it matters. Suppose your sample size is 275 and your population 15,000; the sampling interval would be 54.54. If you were to round up, and select each 55th element (i.e., divide 15,000 by 55), you would obtain a sample of 272. If you were to round down to each 54th person, your sample would number 277. Would the difference of 5 respondents matter to the outcome of the research? In some cases, yes.

The point is more meaningful when the population is small. For example, suppose the population is not 15,000, but 2,900; a sample of 275 would require an interval of 10.54. If 10.54 were rounded down to 10, the sample would number 290; if rounded up to 11, it would number 263. Such a difference could be important.

This discussion has made the assumption that if you selected 275 persons you could interview all of them. Actually, that is unlikely in a systematic-interval telephone survey. An important percentage (i.e., 30 to 40 percent, depending on locale) will refuse to participate. Aside from outright refusals, another percentage of potential respondents will be unavailable for any number of *other* reasons, such as illness, an out-of-service telephone, or vacation. As a result, the entries in a systematic sample usually will number twice or more the expected completions. And then, if the persons not reached happen to be different from the persons reached, the completed survey may not accurately represent the population. This adds a large increment of uncertainty.

LEARN BY DOING

How to Use a Table of Random Numbers

In a table of random numbers (TON), any number is as likely as any other. Tables today are generated by computer and are believed to be without bias. If you were to try to make your own table of random numbers, you might introduce certain biases. For instance, you might put in too many 14s or 5s or whatever.

Suppose you wanted to select 10 numbers between 0 and 61: You could close your eyes and use your pencil tip to touch any one number in the table. Since 61 is a two-digit number, you would need two columns; take the number you selected and the next number to the right. If the two numbers are 61 or lower, they are your starting point. Next, examine the next consecutive two-digit numbers in the columns. Accept any two-digit number less than 61. Continue down the column, then start again at the top of the next two-digit column, if needed, until you have selected the 10 numbers. If you needed a three- or four-digit number, you would apply the same principle.

Practice using a TON by drawing a sample of counties in your state. Simply arrange the counties alphabetically and give each a number, or number them consecutively on a map. If the number of counties does not exceed 99, select any two consecutive columns in a TON and read down the columns until you have found and recorded 20 numbers between 0 and the number of counties in your state. Next, take the numbers to the map or the alphabetical listing and observe the distribution. Are the counties that you selected evenly distributed across the state? Were some important portions of the state underrepresented? Keep in mind that 20 is a very small sample; when you deal with larger numbers, the chance of smooth distribution is improved.

Random Number Generation. To get around some of these problems, researchers have learned to use computer programs for *random number generation.* For example, a researcher supplies the telephone prefixes (exchange numbers) and then programs the computer to generate a sample of *random* four-digit numbers. This makes it equally likely that *any* four-digit number will be selected, and anyone with a telephone can be called.

On the other hand, random numbers often identify phones that are not in use, which increases the labor required for interviewing. There is also the possibility that the remaining random numbers will oversample some geographic areas.

Use of this kind of sample is called *random digit dialing.* In another version of it, the *add-a-digit method,* researchers draw a *systematic* sample, for example from a telephone book, but each telephone number is increased or decreased by the number *1.* The owner of the new number therefore is unknown, and the calls can be sent *randomly* into the community. Because the telephone prefix is not changed, the telephone numbers remain proportional to their number in the telephone exchanges. Proportionality is important because neighborhoods tend to be homogeneous and because exchanges have unequal numbers of users.

Here is an example of the add-a-digit method. The number 555–1111 becomes either 555–1112 or 555–1110. Because the researcher has no idea whom the new number will reach, the procedure is random. In addition, it increases the likelihood of accessing unlisted numbers. All variations of random digit dialing are designed to increase access to the population and to distribute the responses across all sections of a community. On the negative side, the add-a-digit method some-times reaches unworking numbers and businesses.

To assure the validity of the sample, researchers often will examine the demo-graphics of persons who *do* respond, and compare those with some cross-sectional criterion such as *census* data, which include those who *don't* respond. If the demo-graphics of the *sample* closely correspond to the demographics of the *census*, then the researcher might argue that this is evidence to claim the survey is cross-sectional.

Stratified Sample

Another type of random sample is the **stratified sample.** The word *stratum* sug-gests layers, tiers, or levels. Sometimes it is useful to sample from a stratum rather than from a general population. For example, suppose you wondered whether uni-versity freshmen and seniors are equally concerned about First Amendment rights; you could consider all freshmen to be one population and draw a sample from that population, and all seniors to be another population, hence another sample. The key here is the element of random selection and the inference to a population. A stratified sample is also a probability sample if the sample is random.

Cluster Sample. The **cluster sample** is an extension of the stratified sample. Here is an example. A researcher wishes to conduct a statewide survey of grade school students. The researcher would first list all of the state's counties, or perhaps school districts; next, select specific schools within the districts; and, finally, select grade levels. The intent of a cluster sample is to make sampling possible when a proper sampling frame is not otherwise available.

Multi-Level Area-Probability Sample

Using a telephone book to select a local sample is one thing, but what if you are trying to generate a national sample? Most of us would leave the selection of a national sample to a professional sampling firm, but the student of research meth-ods would need to know something of the technique.

For a national sample, the **multi-level area-probability sample** (Wimmer and Dominick, 1991, 72) begins with the 50 states: Should each be included in the sample? If yes, should each state be represented by the same number of respon-dents? The answer to the second question is no. It would make no sense to have an equal number of respondents from both an unpopulous state (e.g., Wyoming) and a populous one (e.g., California). Instead, the sample should be proportional to the population of a state.

For example, if the state of New York accounts for 8 percent of the U.S. pop-ulation, it should account for that percentage of the sample. If the sample amounted to 1,500 persons, New York would have $1,500 \times .08 = 120$ respondents. If a sample of 1,500 were divided *equally* by the 50 states, each would be repre-sented by a mere 30 persons. Even if the number were 60 to 70 per state, it is a very small number to represent a populous area.

The next issue involves the distribution of the sample within each state. One state, for example, may have three cities and 100 counties, yet be allotted a mere 50 or so respondents in the sample of 1,500. Some counties will not be represented in the sample; others will be represented by fewer than a dozen people.

The researcher can use a table of random numbers (TON) to select counties that will be surveyed. At the same time, the researcher might ensure that each of the three cities is included; it probably would make no sense to exclude any one of them. In every case, responses would be made proportional to the population; larger population centers would be assigned more respondents than the smaller ones. In this way, each state could be sampled on a probability basis.

When the sampling reaches the city and county level, census data and telephone books can be used to make the final selections. Census areas, for example, have maps with numbered tracts and blocks. These tracts and blocks can be sampled (from a TON) right down to the city block. Alternatively, the researcher can conduct telephone interviews by using random telephone numbers proportional to area exchanges. This accomplishes essentially the same goal without reliance on geography.

You can see that using either telephone exchanges or census maps reduces the vast geography and population of the United States to a number of specific locations, telephone numbers, and people—to a cross-section that is remarkably efficient in portraying the likes and dislikes of the population. Professional sampling firms make an art of this, and their success rate is excellent. For example, national opinion polls by the best-known research organizations, including Gallup, Roper, and Harris, are seldom shown to be off the mark by more than a percentage point or two.

LEARN BY DOING

(optional exercise at the discretion of the instructor)

Building a Multi-Level Probability Sample

We want to draw a sample of voters in your state. Your instructor will tell you how many persons to include in the sample. When that is decided, visit your university library to find a map showing the counties. Next, number the counties and use a table of random numbers (TON) to select a random sample. Are any major population areas excluded? If yes, (i.e., if the sample is clearly irregular), adjustment must be made. Consider whether all counties should be included.

Next, visit the government documents section of the library. The U.S. Census reports should provide census maps of all the counties in your state. The maps will divide the counties into tracts and blocks. Use a TON to draw a sample of tracts. Within the tracts, draw a sample of blocks. Within blocks, stipulate the method of sampling (e.g., take each fourth residence after starting at a specified point).

If you need an in-person survey sample, select blocks and homes at which to interview. If you need a telephone survey, find the telephone exchanges for each of the counties in the sample. Use census data to learn populations for each county; make the number of respondents in each county proportional to the population of the state.

Write a report outlining your procedures and your decision points. Discuss what you found; is the sample defensible?

Exit Polling

In election forecasting, researchers have sometimes resorted to **exit polling** to learn hours ahead of poll-closing the probable winner of an election. In exit polling, people are interviewed about their choices as they leave the polls, and the reasons for them. Professional polls usually are systematic (i.e., they select each nth person to avoid selection bias). Exit polling in conjunction with other survey methods allows the pollsters to know the outcome before the vote compilers do.

Critics complain that voters leaving the polls may not be truthful about their vote, or that other biases may be at work and there is no way for the interviewer to be certain.[1] If the poll is wrong, and if the flawed results are reported before the polls close, then this might create a bandwagon for one candidate, or discourage voters for another, since it would appear that the outcome was out of late voters' hands.

An example of erroneous exit polling occurred during the 1992 New Hampshire presidential primary election. Exit polling throughout the afternoon and early evening of the vote "showed President Bush leading Patrick J. Buchanan by the narrow margin of four to eight percentage points" (unsigned story, *New York Times,* February 19, 1992). But when the official tally was complete, the margin of George Bush's lead in the Republican primary race was much more substantial: 16 percentage points. In opinion polling, where errors are seldom greater than 1 to 2 percent, the difference between 8 and 16 percent is huge. Peculiarly, the exit polls were highly accurate in regard to the Democratic candidates. The poll organizers were clearly puzzled by the failure of this exit poll.

How could it have happened? There are at least three possibilities. First and foremost in that voters leaving the polls were not frank about their choice; voting is private, and some people just don't like to say how they voted. Second, respondents may have voted for or against a candidate, yet retained doubts about their choice. Third, the outcome of the exit poll depended on the sample; if too many people decline to participate, or if certain kinds of voters were more likely to speak out, the poll could easily be biased.

But the weaknesses of exit polling should not be overemphasized; most often, exit polls by professional pollsters, whose work ultimately might be open to public inspection, are remarkably accurate. You are urged only to be aware of the strengths and weaknesses of the technique and as always to interpret cautiously.

Weighting

By virtue of its randomness, or by other circumstances, the sample sometimes will include too many or too few respondents of one type or another. For example, it frequently happens that women survey respondents greatly outnumber men, although they account for only a slightly larger percentage of the population. Women are more likely to answer the telephone, and men are less likely to be at home.

When responses are skewed—as when a sample has too many or too few ethnic group members—researchers can resort to a type of **weighting.** For example, if men account for 45 percent of a sample, instead of the proper 49 percent (of the general U.S. population), the researcher might divide 49 by 45 (49 ÷ 45 = 1.08) then multiply male frequencies by 1.08 to make them proportional to women's responses. Many polling organizations, including the well-known broadcasting and advertising audience research firms, use such "weights" to correct sample faults.

For example, an opinion poll story in *The Greenvile News* (South Carolina) on October 25, 1992, described the weighting of African American respondents: "Black participation in the survey is 20 percent, less than the 23.5 percent black turnout in the 1988 presidential election. Weighting the results to reflect a 23.5 percent black turnout would increase Bill Clinton's result from 30.7 to 32.4 percent; George Bush's percent would decrease from 38.5 to 37.4; and Ross Perot's number would decrease from 10.4 to 9.9 percent."

Weighting is not without controversy. Is it really helpful in representing nonrespondents (those who were not sampled), or is the change *cosmetic?* In some cases, weighting is artificial and therefore not useful in the calculation of an error margin. In other cases, weighting seems more justified. For example, if you wanted to know the average number of textbooks purchased by college students, you would have to control for the number of courses completed.

Oversampling

Another situation that calls for weighting is when a subgroup of the sample is **oversampled** to permit meaningful comparisons with another group. It would not do, for instance, to make comparisons between a group of 8 and a group of 354. Hence, the group of 8 might be oversampled by 100 or 150 or any number. For the purpose of comparison, this procedure is justified.

However, if the oversample is to be recombined with the remainder of the sample, the two portions must be returned to proportionality; otherwise the sample would be biased toward the oversampled group. A simple procedure is to calculate the ratio of the comparison groups to the total population. For example, if the group that is oversampled makes up 25 percent of the population and the other group makes up 75 percent (a 3:1 ratio), simply multiply the frequencies of the larger group by 3 to restore proportionality (see Babbie, 1989, 199). But again, an error margin calculated on the basis of a sample inflated threefold could be misleading.

Could you simply use a TON to extract the proper number of responses from the oversample (i.e., to reduce the oversample to its proper proportion in the population)? For example, if your sample included 150 persons and you needed only 25 to meet their known percentage in the population, could you randomly draw 25 from the 150? This would probably not be a good idea. Assuming the 150 were drawn randomly at the outset, and then sampled again, you would have increased your error margin by some number up to double what it would have been for the first selection. If you can live with such a margin, a random extraction might be useful.

A first line of defense against unequal frequencies is to convert subgroup responses to percentages. For example, if 25 percent of respondents within an ethnic group answered yes to a question and 35 percent of respondents outside the ethnic group answered yes, the percentages are comparable despite an unequal representation in the frequencies. The percentage of one group then will be comparable to the percentage of another, even if the actual frequencies in the sample are different.

SAMPLE ERROR

Sample Error for Percentages

You might expect that if a sample was properly selected, the sample would closely approximate the population from which it was drawn. Indeed, it should. But then again it might not; that is in the nature of sampling. When we pull 384 names from a hat, they can be any combination of names—perfectly matching the population average, or wildly different.

That is one reason why social researchers never claim to "prove" anything with a sample; there is always the possibility that the sample was unrepresentative. But if that's the case, when *can* we rely on a sample? The answer: It depends on the quality of the sample and the error level associated with it. The error level of a sample is described below.

Although sample averages can occur anywhere on a range of possible outcomes, statisticians have shown with the Central Limit Theorem that no sample properly drawn is likely to vary more than a given amount from the true mean of the population. The theorem says that in repeated samples, most averages will fall close to the middle of the distribution and a decreasing number will fall in the two ends of the distribution. The difference between the sample average and the population average is measured by *standard deviation*, a statistic that will be explained in Chapter 11.

For percentages, the standard error can be calculated very easily, and it is very useful to know (see Formula 4.1). For example, if someone tells you that 55 percent of the respondents favor candidate Smith, you can calculate the range in which the true percentage is likely to fall. Here are some examples:

$$\text{Standard error} = \sqrt{\frac{\% \times (100 - \%)}{n}}$$

Standard error of 55%, when $n = 50$:

$$\sqrt{\frac{55 \times (100 - 55)}{50}} = 7.0356$$

Standard error of 85%, when $n = 50$:

$$\sqrt{\frac{85 \times (100 - 85)}{50}} = 5.0497$$

Standard error of 55%, when $n = 250$:

$$\sqrt{\frac{55 \times (100 - 55)}{250}} = 3.146 \qquad \text{(Formula 4.1)}$$

From these calculations you can see two things happening. First, as the percentage moves away from the point of maximum uncertainty (the point at which about 50 percent of the sample says yes, and 50 percent says no), for example from 55 to 85 percent, the standard error decreases when the size of the sample remains the same. Second, as the size of the sample increases, the standard error decreases. It follows that when the sample size is largest, and the percentage response is larger or smaller than 50 percent, the error margin is smallest.

There is another important aspect of standard error: An increase of four times the sample size is required to reduce the error by half. That means that if you had a sample of 400 but were concerned about the error margin, you would need a sample of 1,600 to reduce the error by half (Myer, 1973, 118). The expense of a survey obviously would increase with sample size, however, and at some point a larger sample just wouldn't be prudent.

Sample Error for Means

Suppose you are working with sample *means* (averages), not percentages. How then might you calculate the error level? The standard error of a mean is the standard deviation (SD) divided by the square root of the number of persons in the sample (N). The standard deviation is the square root of the sum of the squared deviations divided by N. (This computation is not as imposing as it might seem; any standard statistical text will guide your calculations.) In formula form, these are expressed as:

$$\text{Standard deviation (SD)} = \sqrt{\frac{\Sigma(X - \overline{X})^2}{N}}$$

$$\text{Standard error of mean} = \frac{SD}{\sqrt{N}} \text{ or } \frac{SD}{\sqrt{N-1}}$$

(Formula 4.2)

 $N = n$?

And so, if the mean age of your sample was 25.3 years, and the standard deviation was 6.9, you could calculate the standard error. Let's say your sample size was 200. If we use the formula, we find that 6.9 divided by 14.14 (i.e., the square root of 200) equals 0.4873, the standard error of the mean. We could say, then, that the most likely true age of the population was 25.3 plus or minus 0.488 (Bruning and Kintz, 1987, 6).

Importance of the Error Margin

The error margin is very important in any survey research and especially in political polls involving the public interest. Suppose a news release from Senator Claghorne's office says that his recent scientific poll shows him leading candidate Deepthink by 52 to 48 percent in a sample of 150. To the untrained eye, this would look like a solid 4 percent difference. But if we calculate the error margin, a different outcome is possible. The error for a random sample of 150 is 4.07. In other words, Claghorne could be 2.035 points higher than reported, or 2.035 points lower; in the latter case the race would be a dead heat, too close to call.

Survey research scientists warn that the formulas for the standard error apply only to simple random samples with replacement. Other samples may produce overestimates or underestimates of the standard error. You are advised to refer to a sampling text in cases of substantial doubt (e.g., see Kalton, 1983, 78).

CALCULATING SAMPLE SIZE

One of the first questions asked of the survey researcher is: What size sample do I need in order to answer my research question? This is a very important question because the client will want to be confident of the data while keeping down the costs of research. The researcher will have to address three questions.

Confidence

The first question is: How confident must the client be that the sample can be trusted to represent the population? In some research situations, confidence is of the utmost importance; in others, a greater amount of risk is tolerable. Researchers most often want to feel at least 95-percent confident that a sample is like the population. That means that in 95 of 100 samples, a sample mean should not differ from the population mean by more than a given amount.

In some cases, however, the researcher or the client may wish to use an almost fail-safe criterion, say the 99.7-percent confidence level. That would mean that only 3 times in 1,000 would a sample fall outside the calculated error margin.

For purposes of calculating sample size, below, you need to know that the 68-percent confidence level, which is one standard deviation from the mean of the normal curve, has a "factor" of 1; 95-percent confidence has a "factor" of 2 (technically, 1.96), and 99.7-percent confidence has a "factor" of 3.[2]

Error Level

The second decision point is threefold: What error level can be tolerated? Would the client be seriously hurt by an error of plus-or-minus some percentage? And must the outcome be highly precise? For example, suppose you are willing to make major changes in your TV news operation if the audience is unsatisfied, but you don't want to make changes that will send your ratings even lower. What error level can you tolerate? If the sample is poor, how painful would be a wrong decision?

The error can be set at any level, but the researcher must keep in mind that the smaller the error level, the larger the sample and the greater the cost. Is the improved accuracy worth the cost? An error margin of 5 percent (i.e., 2.5 percent plus or minus) is commonly accepted as an appropriate error level.

Expected Outcome

The third question involves the *expected percentage outcome of the survey.* You no doubt will be perplexed by this because, if the outcome were known ahead of time, why would the survey be continued?

For most purposes, the outcome truly cannot be anticipated, and the researcher is advised to accept the most conservative standard, the 50–50 case. If 50 percent say yes and 50 percent say no, that's as uncertain as you can get. But occasionally we can say with reasonable certainty that a percentage outcome will be more or less than 50 percent. In general, the greater the distance from 50 percent, the smaller the error margin. This offers the advantage that, if an outcome can be roughly anticipated, the efficiency of the report can be improved.

From this discussion you can see that the answer to the question *How big a sample do I need?* depends on the confidence level (C), the error level (E), and the likely percentage response (P). Those three elements are combined in a formula to calculate sample size.

$$\frac{C^2}{E^2}(P \times 1 - P)$$

(Formula 4.3)

The Calculations

Take the square of the confidence factor (e.g., 1.96 × 1.96 = 3.8416). Next take the square of the error level (e.g., 5 × 5 = 25). Divide the square of the confidence factor by the square of the error (3.8416 ÷ 25 = 0.1536). Next, multiply 50 percent by 50 percent (50 × 50 = 2,500). Finally, multiply 2,500 by 0.1536 to arrive at your sample size: 384. That's all there is to it!

In order to set a 5-percent error margin with 95-percent confidence, when the outcome is most uncertain, a sample of 384 is required. If you had set the error level at 1.5, instead of 5, you would have needed a sample of 4,268.

Sample size increases with confidence level. Here is an example: Set the confidence level at 99.7 percent, a confidence factor of 3.0. The square of 3 equals 9; if the error level is 5 percent, its square is 25. Divide 9 by 25 = 0.36. Multiply 50 percent × (100 – 50) = 2,500, and then multiply 2,500 by 0.36 = 900. Clearly, the higher the confidence, the larger the sample. And of course, the larger the sample the greater the cost in time and labor.

Incidentally, a sample of 384 with 95-percent confidence and 5- percent error margin is appropriate for any population: theoretically, *sample size does not depend on population size.* That may seem counterintuitive; you would probably expect that a sample from, say, China, would have to be larger than a sample from your hometown of 100,000 persons. The size of the sample is not related to the size of the population. However, this notion hinges on the criterion that the sample must be *random.* Failing that, greater caution would be required. And in fact, the major pollsters don't usually rely on a sample as small as 384. They often use samples of 1,000 to 2,500.

LEARN BY DOING

Exercises

Practice calculating sample size. Below are some suggested confidence and error levels; others can easily be devised. Use these to see clearly how changes in one element of the formula affects another.

Sample size: $= (C^2/E^2) (\% \times \%) =$ sample size

---

1. Confidence level $(C) = 1.96$, error level $(E) = 10$, percentage response $(P) = 50\%$, $N = ?$
2. $C = 1.96$, $E = 2.5$, $P = 50\%$, $N = ?$
3. $C = 2.58$, $E = 5$, $P = 50\%$, $N = ?$
4. $C = 3.0$, $E = 2.5$, $P = 85–15\%$, $N = ?$

SUMMARY

An important portion of the logic of social science research is based on random sampling. Samples are described as either probability or nonprobability, depending on whether all elements of a population have equal opportunity to be included in the draw. Non-probability samples include street-corner samples, call-in samples, convenience samples, purposive samples, focus groups, and quota samples. Probability samples include simple random samples (SRS), systematic interval samples, stratified and cluster samples, multi-level area-probability samples, lotteries, and several kinds of random dialing techniques. Subsets of some samples are "weighted" to improve proportionality of responses. Some subsets are "oversampled" to provide greater comparability with other subsets. Sample size depends on the level of error that can be tolerated, the degree of confidence required, and the expected percentage outcome of the survey.

STUDY QUESTIONS AND EXERCISES

1. The Central Limit Theorem is a central element in the theory of statistics. But what is it? After reading about it in this text, use your library and other resources as you need them to develop your own articulation of the Central Limit Theorem.

2. What is a sampling frame, and how is it used in research?

3. What is a systematic random sample, and how is such a sample selected?

4. How does one use a table of random numbers (TON) in selecting a sample?

5. Explain random-digit dialing and add-a-digit dialing. How are these "better" than a telephone book sample?

6. Explain the multi-level area-probability sample. How is such a sample drawn?

7. Suppose an opinion poll in your state asked whether the people felt their chief executive was doing a good job; suppose 70 percent said yes and 30 percent said no. Calculate the standard error when the sample is number (N) equals 300.

8. Suppose your employer wants a survey with a high confidence factor and a low sample error—a very conservative approach. Set the confidence at 99.7 percent (a confidence factor of 3.0); set the error level at 3.0 (i.e., plus or minus 1.5). Assume a 50-percent yes, and 50-percent no response rate—the most conservative outcome. Calculate the sample that your employer would need to conduct this research. Then, recalculate using a 95-percent confidence level (1.96 or 2) and a 5-percent error level. Compare the two samples for feasibility.

9. Explain the benefit of sample comparability as discussed in this chapter. How is comparability different from randomness?

NOTES

1. Busch and Lieske (1985, 94–104) have pointed out that the time of day of the poll can influence its outcome. People employed on day shifts, for example, can only reach the polls at early hours and late hours; if their views differ from those of people who are not employed, the poll could be flawed.

2. The confidence level comes from the theoretical distribution of sample averages that makes up the normal distribution, the symmetrical bell-shaped curve—wherein most sample averages fall on and around the center of the curve, while others tail off to the ends of the curve. The distribution is divided into "standard deviations." Sixty-eight percent of the theoretical sample averages fall within one standard deviation, and 95 percent fall within two standard deviations. Nearly all of the sample averages fall within three standard deviations.

   By convention, most researchers are willing to accept the 95-percent confidence level, the one that says 95 percent of the time the sample will properly represent the population from which it was drawn. Occasionally, when the stakes are high, they require a 99.7-percent confidence level. The percentage confidence level converts to a confidence "factor": 68-percent confidence = a factor of 1; 95-percent confidence = a factor of 2 (actually, it is 1.96, but can be loosely calculated as 2); and 99.7-percent = a factor of 3. The confidence factor is used in the calculation of sample size and error.

SOURCES

Babbie, Earl. 1989. *The Practice of Social Research.* 5th ed. Belmont, Calif.: Wadsworth.

Bruning, James L., and B. L. Kintz. 1987. *Computational Handbook of Statistics.* 3d ed. Glenview, Ill.: Scott, Foresman.

Busch, Ronald J., and Joel A. Lieske. 1985. Does Time of Voting Affect Exit Poll Results? *Public Opinion Quarterly* 49:94–104.

Grusin, Elinor Kelley, and Gerald C. Stone. 1992. Using Focus Groups to Improve Survey Research. *Newspaper Research Journal* 13(1–2):72–83.

Honomichl, Jack J. 1982. The Ongoing Sage of "Mother Baking Soda." *Advertising Age* (Sept. 20), M2, M3, M22.

Kalton, Graham. 1983. *Introduction to Survey Sampling.* Beverly Hills, Calif.: Sage.

Meyer, Philip. 1973. *Precision Journalism.* Bloomington: Indiana University Press.

Morin, Richard. 1992. Numbers from Nowhere: The Hoax of the Call-In Polls." *Washington Post* (Feb. 15), B3.

Stephan, F. F. 1983. History of the Uses of Modern Sampling Procedures. *Journal of the American Statistical Association* 43, 12–39. Cited in Wright, T. ed. 1983. *Statistical Methods and the Improvement of Data Quality.* New York: Academic Press.

Wimmer, Roger D., and Joseph R. Dominick. 1991. *Mass Media Research: An Introduction.* 3d ed. Belmont, Calif.: Wadsworth.

5

Measurement of Social Science Variables

I often say that when you can measure what you are speaking about, and express it in numbers, you know something about it; but when you cannot express it in numbers, your knowledge is of a meager and unsatisfactory kind; it may be the beginning of knowledge, but you have scarcely, in your thoughts, advanced to the state of Science, whatever the matter may be.
Lord Kelvin, cited in Sears, Zemansky, and Young, 1980.

□
OBJECTIVES

After studying this chapter, you should be able to:

1. Describe three sources of error in social science measurement.

2. Describe and explain the four levels of measurement: nominal, ordinal, interval, and ratio.

3. Create and use Likert-type scales for attitude measurement.

4. Create and use semantic differential scales for attitude measurement.

5. Name and explain some threats to the internal and external validity of research outcomes.

6. Discuss the difference between true interval measures and ordinal measures used as interval measures, such as Likert scales.

7. Identify and describe several measures of reliability and validity.

INTRODUCTION

Measurement is the essence and the strength of the quantitative method. Without measurement, there would be no quantitative method. Indeed, measurement is routine: daily we see a variety of measures such as political opinion polls, TV ratings, the average cost of homes, public attitudes, the rank of athletic teams, scholastic aptitude scores, and so on.

Social measures are so ubiquitous, and trust in science so great, that most people not trained in social science research seem to take their accuracy more or less for granted. But such measurement is more fragile and error prone than most would expect. Measurement requires care, thoughtfulness, and skill. The intent of this chapter is to promote the proper use of measures and to identify their points of strength and weakness.

Most generally, measurement is the assignment of values to variables. Variables take a variety of forms including *physical*, such as the person's height in feet and inches; *behavioral*, such as the frequency of a person's voting or magazine buying; *conceptual*, such as a person's credibility; *psychological*, such as a person's anxiety level; or *spiritual*, such as a person's ethical orientation or religious faith. Each type of phenomenon offers special challenges and opportunities for measurement.

The values assigned to variables range from imprecise to highly precise; that is, they can be *semantic* or *numeric*. Consider this example of a semantic measurement: To say a person is in a "good mood" is a measure of sorts, but not very precise. Moods can range from deep depression to great elation, and "good" is simply somewhere on the continuum. As a *measure* it is not very precise because "good" to one person may be more or less so to another. But measurement of the number of times in a lifetime a person voted, a numeric measurement, could be highly precise.

The values we assign to *objects* can also be numeric, a higher order of evaluation—provided the numbers represent phenomena accurately. If we can say an object weighs 6.2 grams, or is 18 inches long, and if the measurement instruments are accurate, the measurement is relatively precise. The goal of measurement, after all, is precision. Different researchers should be able to weigh the same object and arrive at a very similar weight.

But herein lies the fundamental difficulty of social science measurement. Many of the phenomena, and certainly many of those in the study of communication, are concepts and constructs that can be neither seen nor touched, but only imagined and inferred. How are researchers to measure such things agreeably? How are they to know when they have measured accurately?

If the measure is of a behavior, such as the voting record of newspaper subscribers and nonsubscribers, the measurement is relatively direct and certain. But if the measure is of a *concept*, such as "morbid curiosity" about violence in the news, it enters an amorphous, cerebral area that hides confirmation. If the measure is of a **construct**—an idea formed from a combination of concepts, such as "ethical orientation"—the difficulty is compounded.

Sources of Measurement Error

Measurement errors have four sources: instrumentation, application, sampling, and random sources. **Instrument errors** occur when questions are poorly written or applied. Examples of poor questions will be given in Chapter 7.

Errors of *application* are typically errors of administration (e.g., failure to distribute instruments in the manner planned, or failure to provide comprehensive or comprehensible directions to participants). Errors of *sampling* are of two types. One type pertains to the incorrect drawing of a sample (e.g., failure to give all population elements the opportunity to be included). The other occurs when the sample is properly drawn, but its cases randomly fall outside the likely error margin. Such errors are unavoidable.

Random sources of measurement errors include carelessness on the part of respondents, misapprehension of purposes and options, or occurrences that disrupt the conduct of the research. It is the duty of the researcher to *control* random errors to the greatest extent possible.

Knowledge of the true error in a set of measures sometimes goes unknown because the variables are unseen. If researchers could clearly see or feel attitudes, motives, ethics, professionalism, or the effects of a host of variables (e.g., schools, television, violence, peers) on behavior, they could more accurately track and study them. But in addition to not being able to see certain variables, researchers often are hard-pressed to convince others that the variables even exist. For example, is there truly a "cultivation" effect of viewing television (i.e., the idea that people who watch a lot of television develop exaggerated views of reality), or is the observed effect a statistical artifact, an effect that would not exist except for poor measures and inadequate analysis?

THREATS TO THE VALIDITY OF MEASURES

Validity is of two types, internal and external. *Internal validity* asks: Have you measured what you thought you measured? *External validity* asks: Does the survey sample generalize to the population from which it was drawn?

Several threats to the validity of measures exist in all types of research. These were summarized by Campbell and Stanley (1963) in their classic text on research design. The first eight apply to the internal validity of a study.

Threats to Internal Validity

History.   Unexpected things, and sometimes undetected things, happen during the research to influence its outcome. This is especially true in longitudinal research. For example, suppose you are interested in the stability of an attitude over time. You conduct a measurement of the attitude at time 1 and again at time 2. But suppose something beyond your control happens between measures that increases your respondents' knowledge of the attitude object. This would alter the measures you would have obtained had the intervening variable not occurred.

Maturation.   This threat to validity is relevant to most age groups, for each of us is maturing daily, but it is of primary concern in studies of young people. For example, in the study of children, a certain amount of change in behavior could be the result of changes in maturity rather than the result of any independent variable.

There is also the problem of "short-term maturation." This refers to the onset of hunger, thirst, and fatigue. The comfort level of participants could easily affect the outcome of research.

Testing.   In a pretest and posttest in which the same test is used each time, the possibility exists that any change observed results from experience in completing the test rather than from the experimental variable. This is especially true in a timed test, where familiarity with the design of the instrument facilitates completion.

Instrumentation.   This threat to validity occurs when two observers use different "measuring sticks" to measure the same variable, or when the wording of a question is edited from the first administration to the second. More generally, this threat occurs when changes in a measure are due to the **instrument** rather than to a controlled independent variable.

Regression.   Statisticians point out that it is in the nature of extreme scores to *regress* toward the mean of a distribution in a subsequent measure. In other words, very high or low scores on a scale will tend to move toward the mean in subsequent tests. Hence, some of the change observed in a dependent variable may be explained by regression. When extreme scores qualify as **outliers**—scores that are more or less apart from others—statisticians will observe their effect on the data set very carefully and consider eliminating them entirely.

Selection.   This has to do with samples that are not properly drawn. For example, if a sample includes too many people of an ethnic, religious, or social group, the responses of these people may introduce bias to the data set. Similarly, if two groups are to be compared, but they are not equal in important characteristics, the difference is a threat to the validity of the comparison.

Mortality.   In any study that continues over time, it is possible that some participants will drop out. For example, one may move out of state; another may take a night job; another might become ill. When *mortality* impinges on a researcher's ability to compare two samples, or excessively reduces a sample size, it is a threat to the validity of the research.

Interaction. This occurs when two or more variables work together to produce an effect. Glass and Stanley (1970, 408) gave the following example: If boys and girls read equally well, but if boys read some kinds of text faster and girls read other kinds of text faster, text and sex are said to interact.

Threats to External Validity

The following were identified by Campbell and Stanley (1963) as threats to external validity. *Whenever you measure something, you change it.*

Reactive Effect of Testing. Campbell and Stanley pointed out that a pretested sample, having the experience of the pretest, might be unlike the population with which they are being compared, and hence a threat to external validity.

Interaction of Selection and Experimental Variable. Having the wrong respondents in a sample certainly will constitute a threat to the external validity of a study. In other words, a biased sample could create an interaction effect on levels of the experimental variable.

Reactive Effects of Experimental Arrangements. Experimental arrangements include the laboratory-type setting—a kind of surreal experience for participants, wherein "real life" may be suspended for the duration of the study. For example, when a participant is asked to use electrical shock to train a learner, it is not a "real life" exercise. Loosely contrived experimental "arrangements" clearly can have an impact on the outcome of an experiment.

Multiple Treatment Interference. It often happens that an experiment involves not one but several manipulations, the assumption being that each is isolated in its effect. Campbell and Stanley said this is especially a problem for "one-group" research designs, described below.

THE LEVELS OF MEASUREMENT

The values that can be assigned to objects or phenomena have four levels: nominal, ordinal, interval, and ratio.

noir

Nominal Measures

Nominal measurement has to do with "naming" and therefore with categorizing. If we say someone is a Democrat or a Republican, we have used a **nominal measure.** For convenience, we assign each Democrat and Republican a different number, such as 1 or 2, to distinguish between them symbolically. Note that this kind of measurement does not *evaluate* Democrats and Republicans, but merely counts them. In many cases this is sufficient. For instance, you might need to know the number of Democrats and the number of Republicans who responded to an advertisement.

But you can see that nominal measurement is a crude measure; every person who is counted has the *same value,* regardless of political status, experience, wisdom, money, gender, education, or whatever. Naming and categorizing units is sufficient as long as differentiation among elements is not required.

Ordinal Measures

Ordinal measures not only put responses in categories, but also rank, or order, them in some way. Suppose, for example, you saw five versions of an advertisement ranging from soft sell to hard sell, and a researcher wanted to know the advertisements' appeal to you. You could describe the most pleasing as 1, the second most pleasing as 2, and so on through 5. In effect, you could rank order them.

This is more information than just naming; this says that one response is more or less of some quality than another. However, notice that this ordering does not say how *much* 1 differs from 2, only that it is different. Some units could be different by relatively large or small amounts. Another example of rank ordering and unequal intervals is the finish of a horse race. The horses finish in the order 1, 2, 3, . . . *n*, but clearly not equal distances apart.

It may be useful to think of ordinal measures on a number line from 0 to *n*, in equal increments:

---

0   0.25   0.5   0.75   *1.0*   1.25   1.5   1.75   *2.0*   2.25   2.5   2.75   *3.0* etc.

Now suppose a respondent likes a particular advertisement and selects it as number 1 on the number line. But let's say it's a "weak" number 1 (not total enthusiasm), and so its true position on the number line is on the "2" side of 1, not the "0" side. So conceived, a given number 1 really could be anywhere on the number line between 0 and 1.50, in this example.

Similarly, a 2 could be between 1.5 and 2.5. And consider this possibility: One person could rank the advertisement 1.5 while another ranked it 1.75 (not much difference), but the whole numbers would be 1 and 2. In some cases the "true" rank of one respondent might be extremely close to the "true" rank of another, yet in their rank order, they would be one full unit apart.

The rank ordering of responses into whole numbers (e.g., ranks 1, 2, and 3) rounds off the error—suggesting equal intervals—and gives the impression of greater accuracy than probably exists. Nevertheless, rank ordering is widely used in social science research as a succinct way of organizing data and characterizing variables. And in fact, some statistical tests, for example the Spearman-Brown rank-order correlation, were specifically designed to test the differences between groups measured on the ordinal level. This matter of the ordering of data will be discussed again in the section below on the Likert and Semantic Differential scales.

LEARN BY DOING

Ask some of your classmates to *rank order* four issues of public affairs (e.g., environmental pollution, unemployment, taxation, and national defense), in terms of importance of the item to the respondent:

"Below are four issues of public affairs. Please consider each of these and assign the one that is most important to you the number *1*; the second most important the number *2*; and so on until you have ranked the four items."

Issue	Rank
environmental pollution	————
unemployment	————
taxation	————
national defense	————

To *summarize* the results, take the *average* of the ranks for each issue. Averaging most likely will require the use of decimals. Discuss the transformation of ranks to decimals: What, if anything, is lost or gained? Examine and interpret the quantitative distance between the averages of the four ranks.

Interval Measures

The third level of measurement is the interval level. **Interval measures** not only rank order variables, but also measure differences between ranks. Interval measures can indicate equal distances between units such that the difference between 2 and 3 is the same as that between 3 and 4 and between 4 and 5.

Furthermore, interval measures can be stated in decimals: A unit can be reported as 3.456, or whatever number, whereas an ordinal number should be reported in whole numbers. An example of interval measures is the hours spent by a person reading magazines or newspapers. A person could spend 0.15 hours, or 1.6 hours, or any other number. Decimals express clearly that the person who spends 0.30 hours reading spends twice as much time as the person spending 0.15 hours. This precision and proportionality is the strength of interval data.

Interval data are required for *parametric tests* (i.e., tests that estimate the population). However, many social scientists treat ordinal measures as if they were interval; this is a point of controversy that will be discussed below.

Ratio Measures

The fourth level of measurement is the **ratio measure.** A typical example of the ratio measure is the thermometer; it has equal intervals, and 40 degrees is twice as warm as 20. In addition, the ratio measure has an absolute zero, whereas interval measures may not. Statistical treatments are the same for ratio measures as they are for interval measures.

Other Distinctions among Measures

In addition to these four, there are other useful distinctions among measures. Nominal measures sometimes are called *categorical variables* because units can be categorized, as in Democrat and Republican, or male and female; and they are sometimes called **discrete variables** because they are distinct elements.

For example, an occupational category can be assigned the number 1, but not 1.536 or any other fractional number. Categorical data require nonparametric tests since they do not estimate the parameters of a population. Categorical variables are sometimes known as *frequency measures* to distinguish them from parametric measures.

Interval and ratio measures are described as **continuous variables** because they can take on any value. For example, a person can be 5.4352617 . . . feet tall; an infinite number of decimals could be added. Discrete and continuous numbers call for different kinds of statistical tests. Terms associated with different levels of measurement are shown in the following list:

Nominal	Ordinal[1]	Interval	Ratio
discrete	discrete		
categorical			
dichotomous			
frequency	continuous	continuous	continuous
nonparametric	frequency	frequency	frequency
	nonparametric		
	parametric	parametric	parametric

Nominal measures are either *forced choice,* meaning that response options are supplied and the respondent selects one, or dichotomous.

Dichotomous Measures.   A *dichotomy,* as the prefix suggests, is a two-choice measure. A respondent is either this or that, out or in, male or female, subscriber or nonsubscriber, yes or no. Dichotomous measures tell the frequency of a response, such as the number of readers and nonreaders, and not much else.

For some variables, such as gender, dichotomous measures are highly accurate. But in other cases, the simplicity of the measure works against accuracy. For example, suppose you were asked the following question:

> Please indicate whether you consider your political leaning to be
> _____ conservative _____ liberal.

It's possible you would have no trouble making a choice, but some would prefer to say: I'm neither of those; I'm not undecided, but I'm about halfway between being a conservative and being a liberal, sort of a moderate.

In that case, a dichotomy would force the respondent into a category that does not accurately measure a true position. The same goes for the common yes/no question: a respondent's position might not be captured by the options.

Forced-Choice Measures. The forced-choice measure gives respondents several (three or more) categories in which to place themselves. One benefit of the categories is that they give respondents a perspective (bench mark) on the range of responses. Another is that categories avoid the awkwardness of some demographic questions, such as age and income. Instead of asking the respondent "Please state your annual income," a figure that may have ego involvement for the respondent, a number of categories are provided and the respondent is merely asked to choose an appropriate one.

The number of options in the forced-choice measure is not fixed, but most often does not exceed five or six. A categorical measure with multiple response options carries more information than a dichotomy, but less than a continuous number. An example is the following:

Please indicate your annual household income:

1. up to $15,000
2. $15,001 to $30,000
3. $30,001 to $45,000
4. $45,001 to $60,000
5. $60,001 to over

(Indicate number of wage earners: _____)

If the annual income for the household was $45,176.55, or even $60,000, it would be categorized as a *4*. Statistical hypothesis testing would be based on the category numbers 1 to 5, not on the dollar amounts in the categories.

A respondent with an income of between $45,001 and $60,000 is a *4*. But is a family with a $60,000 income (category 4) substantively different from one with $60,001 (category 5)? You can see that the categories are rough measures, and therefore should be evaluated with caution and with statistical techniques that fit the measure.

On the positive side, if the survey is well planned, the sample will be large enough that each category will be well represented, and the average for each category will be about the midpoint for its value.

LIKERT SCALES

One of the most common measurement tools in social science is the *Likert scale,* usually a 5-point continuum with response options as follows: strongly agree = 5, agree = 4, undecided = 3, disagree = 2, and strongly disagree = 1. Note that the numbers could easily be reversed (i.e., strongly agree could = 1), depending on the needs of the researcher. The Likert scale and its variations are widely used today in measures of attitude and the effects of mass communication.

Likert scales were developed out of the knowledge that concepts are complex and that measures, like "smart bombs," should zero-in on aspects of the concept. The various aspects of the concept are known as **dimensions.** They can be thought of as components of measures.

Dimensionality of Measures

Multi-item scales usually are superior to single-item scales. For example, we might think naively that the person who wants to measure attitudes toward education should simply ask people their attitude. But attitudes toward education are probably multidimensional. One dimension might focus on the practicality of education; another on the liberalness of education; another on the universality of education, or the profitability of education, or whatever. Numerous *dimensions* of attitude toward education could be identified.

Now, if we asked only one question, "What is your attitude toward education?" which dimension would we be tapping? One respondent might respond to practicality, another to universality or profitability, and so on. It would make no sense for us to sum these disparate feelings, just as it would make no sense to add apples, oranges, and pears.

There are two ways to approach this problem. One is to create a measure *a priori* that is *focused on one dimension,* then use it in a measurement instrument. Another is to go into the survey without certainty about dimensionality, but attempting to measure all known aspects. In this case, the researcher would use statistical methods *post hoc* to identify the dimensions of the concept. The two approaches are different perspectives of the same task; the difference is in the orientation of the researcher.

Unidimensionality

The Likert scale was developed as an *a priori* method of establishing **unidimensionality** (McIver and Carmines, 1981, 9). Likert focused on the creation of a set of measures that tapped *one dimension* of a concept. Likert's technique was to write a large set of agree–disagree statements on a topic. For example, the topic might be "tax reform." The researcher would interview individuals or use personal intuition to derive a large enough set of statements to cover the range of likely responses. Likert-type statements were of the following style, wherein each numbered response represented a level of agreement:

America's middle class today carries an appropriate share of the national tax burden.

5   4   3   2   1

Taxes in America today are too low.

5   4   3   2   1

High taxes are necessary to support the range of social programs Americans admire.

5   4   3   2   1

The set of statements might number 50 to 100. Some would be written in the positive, some in the negative. They would touch on as many different aspects of taxation as possible. Then, a sample of respondents would rate each of the statements on a 5-point agree–disagree scale.

Next, the researcher would compute the correlations of all items. This item analysis was designed to show which of the items were scored similarly by respondents. If the marks for items were similar, and if the items were conceptually akin, then they were presumed to be measuring the same quality. Statements that could not be grouped were eliminated. This permitted the researcher *to narrow the large set of statements to a number that would measure a single dimension of a concept.* Likert's technique was an important contribution in the history of social measurement.

Multidimensionality

A person can also conceive of measurement on a *multidimensional* level. Complex concepts are not unidimensional. For example, suppose you wanted to measure "teacher effectiveness." A typical question is: Do you feel that this teacher is effective, ineffective, or are you undecided?

When the respondent rates effectiveness, what really is being measured? What are the *dimensions* of teacher effectiveness? Effectiveness can be critiqued in regard to presentational style (everyone dislikes a boring lecture), articulation (ability to conceive and express symbols), organization, presumed knowledge, fairness, voice quality, pace, warmth, consistency, and at least 20 other qualities. Clearly, teacher effectiveness is a multidimensional concept.

And so, a rule of thumb: Don't measure a complex notion with a single question; instead, use a *series* of questions that you have reason to believe will cover the important aspects. How can a person discover these important aspects? The thoughtful researcher often can generate measures on an intuitive level simply by imagining the likely concerns of the respondents. If that approach is insufficient, the researcher can ask a collection of individuals (who should be members of the same population from which the sample will be drawn) to discuss the topic and to identify its important aspects.

For example, in a study of source credibility, the author once asked a large group of students to name any highly believable newsperson, and then to list all of the words that suggested reasons for the person's believability (e.g., articulate, compassionate, knowledgeable). These were later sorted into factors that described "source credibility." The point is that if you are to measure a complex idea, such as source credibility, you must identify and measure its parts.

Suppose now that you have identified 25 possible dimensions of teacher effectiveness, and you have created several statements to measure each. The instrument numbers 75 to 100 statements—a large number, but not excessive. Suppose further that you obtain a random sample of persons to respond to the scales. You instruct the respondents to rate a teacher on each of the statements.

Whereas for Likert the analysis was very labor intensive, it can be done quickly today on the computer, even on many personal computers (PCs), through the use of a statistical technique called *factor analysis*. It is complex and conceptually challenging, but extremely useful for reducing large data sets to a smaller number of underlying dimensions. (Factor analysis will be discussed in Chapter 12).

In summary, dimensionality is vital to the measurement of complex ideas. Dimensions must be identified to the extent possible a priori, then confirmed through some objective technique, such as factor analysis. Armed with objective measures, the researcher can measure feelings about each of the dimensions, and cia hope to get a much better picture of feelings about the topic than a simpler measure would bring.[2]

Neutral Respondents

On the 5-point Likert scale, the midpoint is labeled either "don't know," "neutral," or "undecided." Since "undecided" and "don't know" are not very useful to us, can we leave them out? That would force respondents to make a choice they don't want to make. On the other hand, to leave them in is to facilitate nondecision. Social scientists have fretted about this at length. Although there is some evidence to support omitting the neutral response (Ryan, 1980), by far most social researchers simply overlook the issue or prefer to include it in the analysis.

Collapsing Data

If the researcher decides "don't know" responses are unneeded, they are easily excluded. This often is done when data are *collapsed* into fewer categories so that they can be cross-tabulated with another variable. For example, let's say you asked a sample of classmates to agree or disagree on a 5-point scale with a statement that TV news is trustworthy. The following data are fictional, and for illustration only:

1. strongly agree   35%
2. agree   35%
3. undecided   10%
4. disagree   10%
5. strongly disagree   10%

So there are five categories of response, and if the other variable has three categories, the cross-tabulation would involve 15 cells. This complicates interpretation of the relationship. Here is what the analyst sometimes would do: *collapse* the strongly agree and agree responses into *one* category called "agree," and the disagree and strongly disagree into one category called "disagree." The new table would read:

1. agree or strongly agree   70%
2. undecided   10%
3. disagree or strongly disagree   20%

You can see that the second table presents a sharper picture of the percentages on the positive and negative ends of the scale.

Next, the analyst would consider removing the undecided group. But that would leave us a table with only 90 percent of the respondents, and so we would have to account for the other 10 percent. We could handle this by saying: *Of those who had an opinion on the issue,* 77.7 percent agreed, and 22.2 percent disagreed. Such wording just puts the percentage on a proper base. The table then would read:

Agreement–Disagreement on the Trustworthiness of TV News among all who had an opinion:

agreed	77.7%	
disagreed	22.2%	(*Note:* Total is less than 100% due to rounding error.)

And so the five-category item would become two categories, and if it were cross-tabbed with a three-item variable the cells would number six. That makes it much more manageable and sometimes more revealing. Remember that the "don't knows" were excluded and that the percentages apply only for persons who voiced an opinion one way or the other.

Indexing

You will recall that the researcher should not hope to measure a complex idea with a single question, but should use a *series* of questions, sometimes called an index. An **index** is any supportable combination of measures that, taken together, measure a concept. An index could be a set of Likert-type statements, or a set of diverse measures, each with a different format, including behavioral measures such as "buying a newspaper."

For example, an index of interest in public affairs might be a set of four indicators as follows: voted in the last election; reads a daily newspaper; holds membership in a civic club; and gives importance to the concept of public service. The researcher could conclude *operationally* that any person responding affirmatively or positively to all four items was "public-affairs conscious," as differentiated from persons less so or not at all.

Notice that the items included *behavioral* measures (voting, reading a newspaper, membership in civic club) and an *attitudinal* measure (gives importance to public service). A mix of questions is usually desirable. The point of indexing is that a set of measures can be better than a single measure because they more nearly cover the range of meanings inherent in the concept.

Operational Definitions

The discussion of indexing gives rise to another important aspect of measurement, *operational definitions*. Recall from Chapter 3 that an operational definition is based on the concrete operations of the measurement.

Here is an example: To measure the attitudes of a sample of persons toward "broadcast advertising," the researcher would write several different questions, each addressing a different aspect of advertising, then *sum* the responses to the four questions for each respondent and use them as a *single* indicator of their attitude. The sum of the scores should be a better indicator than a single score. In this sense, a person's attitude toward broadcast advertising is *operationally defined* as the sum of the person's responses to the four questions.

Knowledge of this concept is important for both conducting research and critiquing research: If a person claims to have measured something, then we have to ask how it was measured. The adequacy of the measure will depend on the operational definition. For example, suppose a researcher claims to have found a significant relationship between "viewing horror movies" and "dysfunctional social behavior." Clearly, the measurement of both variables would be crucial.

But we have to ask: How is "viewing" *defined,* and how are "horror movies" *defined?* Is viewing horror movies monthly, or yearly, as likely to promote a behavioral effect as very frequent viewing? Would the *context* of the moving viewing matter? Many types of people watch horror movies, but do they *like* them equally? The answers to these questions could alter the measure.

And what is the measure of "dysfunctional behavior"? Could it be as benign as unwillingness to share a candy bar, or as sinister as personal injury? Would the supposed effect be found at few, several, or all levels of social behavior?

For any research, the *operational definitions* and the nature of the measurement instruments must be clearly stated and defensible. At the same time, operational definitions can complicate the research literature. If one researcher uses the measures *a, b, c,* and *d,* and another uses *a, b, c,* and *e* to study the same phenomenon, the interpretation could become either more clear or more cloudy, depending on the persuasiveness of the research report.

Equal-Appearing Intervals

It was noted earlier in this chapter that ordinal scales give the impression but not the fact of equal intervals, and that the absence of equal intervals introduces the possibility of error in rounding to whole numbers. This concept is very important because most social science measures are ordinal. Social scientists generally have taken the position that although Likert-type measures are ordinal, they are close enough to being interval to be analyzed with parametric statistics. They say that the assumptions of parametric statistics are "robust" enough to withstand the minor violations that Likert measures imply.

Furthermore, use of ordinal scales in some parametric statistical routines has been clearly validated by other measures. For example, factor analysis of Likert-type ordinal data routinely and reliably creates measurement indexes that are validated by subsequent measures. Kerlinger has addressed this issue:

> The lack of equal intervals is . . . serious since distances within a scale theoretically cannot be added without interval equality. Yet, though most psychological scales are basically ordinal, we can with considerable assurance often assume equality of interval. The argument is evidential. If we have, say, two or three

measures of the same variable, and these measures are all substantially and linearly related, then equal intervals can be assumed. This assumption is valid because the more nearly a relation approaches linearity, the more nearly equal are
the intervals of the scales. [The] results we get from using scales and assuming
equal intervals are quite satisfactory. (Kerlinger, 1973, 440)

However, Kerlinger went on to say, "Still, we are faced with a dilemma: if we use
ordinal measures as though they were interval or ratio measures, we *can* err in
interpreting data and the relations inferred from the data, though the danger is
probably not as grave as it has been made out to be" (Kerlinger, 1973, 440).

It appears that the difference between statisticians and social scientists comes
down to this: Social scientists feel that the power gained by the use of parametric
analysis, the robustness of the assumptions, and the favorable experience with ordinal scales outweigh the possibility of error introduced by the misapplication of
statistical tests. They feel that long years of successful experience are on their side.

The difference of view between statisticians and social scientists may also
have something to do with the significance of outcomes: If a scientist is working on
data that suggest a heavy personal, social, or physical impact, then greater caution
is advised.

Many social science investigations, although important, lack imminent impact; there is, therefore, greater tolerance of error. For example, the hypothesis test
in a study of news reading is probably not as impactive as the hypothesis test in a
study of AIDS susceptibility. Hence, social scientists are willing to bend the rules
just a bit in the expectation that a faulty decision will not be so detrimental, and
that it should be identified later in the course of replication.

They could, if they wished, use nonparametric tests that do not estimate parameters of a population; but nonparametric statistics are a less powerful order of
statistics. Parametric statistics are the most progressive methods available today. If
analysis of Likert-type measures or semantic differential measures were possible
only with nonparametric tests, social science would be somewhat closed out of
important modern methods.

SEMANTIC DIFFERENTIAL SCALES

Another ordinal measure that had a profound impact on communication studies is
the *semantic differential scale* developed by Osgood, Suci, and Tannenbaum (1957).
It was developed as a measure of the meaning of objects, then adapted by social
researchers to the study of attitudes and communication effects.

Here is how it worked. Osgood et al. collected large sets of adjectives such as
good, strong, and active (often 50 to 100 of these) and asked samples of people to
use them to rate an attitude object such as "police officer," or "desk," or virtually
any other object. Each adjective and its opposite formed a scale from 1 to 7. Each
response option had a number and a semantic meaning designed to represent approximately equal intervals.

Typically, respondents in this type of study are asked to indicate how closely the adjective or its opposite relates to their own feeling toward the attitude object. The scales are ordinal. Figure 5.1 is a brief example of an attitude object (i.e., "radio news") and a set of semantic differential scales. Each respondent made one mark per scale, and each mark was assigned a value from 1 to 7; the location of a mark on the line signified the respondent's feeling toward the attitude object.

The Components of Meaning

Osgood et al. (1957) used factor analysis to interpret the marks. They found that semantic meaning generally has three components: *activity*, *potency*, and *evaluation*. The feeling we bring to a concept can be generally categorized as involving an active dimension (activity), a strength dimension (potency), or an evaluative dimension (liking). The notion that the meaning of concepts has "components" is itself useful. It is consistent with the multivariable, multidimensional approach to explanations, and it points up the connotation that people bring to the meaning of words and concepts.

Relation to Attitude Measurement

But the evaluative aspect of meaning is also useful for another reason: It is consistent with theories of the nature of attitudes. Fishbein and Ajzen (1975) proposed that attitudes are made up of *cognitions* (bits of information), *affect* (evaluation, e.g., like–dislike), *conation* (behavioral *intentions*), and *behavior*. Note that *attitude* is defined partly as effect or evaluation. Hence, it is an easy step from measurement of meaning (Osgood et al., 1957) to the measurement of the affective component of an attitude.

Researchers began to use the *affective component* of meaning to represent attitude, and especially attitude change. From the 1950s through the 1960s, the measurement of persuasion and its attitudinal aspects was of overriding interest to communication scholars. This is true to a lesser extent today.

good	____	____	____	____	____	____	____	bad
weak	____	____	____	____	____	____	____	strong
nice	____	____	____	____	____	____	____	not nice
passive	____	____	____	____	____	____	____	active
heavy	____	____	____	____	____	____	____	light
worthless	____	____	____	____	____	____	____	valuable
hot	____	____	____	____	____	____	____	cold
cruel	____	____	____	____	____	____	____	kind
aggressive	____	____	____	____	____	____	____	meek
dull	____	____	____	____	____	____	____	sharp
formal	____	____	____	____	____	____	____	informal
stale	____	____	____	____	____	____	____	fresh
. . .	____	____	____	____	____	____	____	. . .

FIGURE 5.1 Radio News

LEARN BY DOING

Using Likert Scales

Select an issue of public affairs that is being discussed on your campus; for example, the crime rate, environmental pollution, U.S. involvements abroad. Write five Likert-type agree–disagree statements about the issue. Put them in the format of a brief but formal questionnaire: Give the survey a title, a brief introductory statement, and instructions for participants. Explain the response options. Administer the questionnaire to a small number of other students. When data are in, table them in the manner of the following:

	Statement Number				
Person Number	1	2	3	4	5
1	4	5	5	4	3
2	4	5	4	5	4
•					
•					
n	5	5	5	5	4

If some statements were prepared in the negative, be sure to convert the scoring. Calculate marginals for each item and each respondent (row and column sums). The marginals will tell you which items were responded to most and least favorably, and which individuals were most and least favorable to the issue.

Computer analysis probably will not be feasible for you at this point; at a proper time, use SPSS/PC+ to compute correlations for each pair of items, and to compute a Cronbach's alpha reliability measure. An alpha below about .70 will indicate that the scales are not sufficiently reliable.

Using Semantic Differential Scales

Select a public affairs attitude issue such as the crime rate or environmental pollution and construct a set of semantic differential scales. This will require you to select 8 or 10 adjectives that suggest qualities of liking or disliking; for example, good–bad, cruel–kind, sweet–sour, pretty–ugly. Put them in scale form in the manner suggested in Figure 5.1.

Response options can be numbered or left blank, but will eventually have to be numbered for purposes of analysis. In your instructions to the respondent, explain that the closer his or her mark to one end of the scale, the stronger the feeling toward the attitude object. For analysis, make all positive words 7, and all negatives 1.

Table the numbers in the manner of the above Likert-scale exercise. Next sort the responses by male/female, and compare. For each respondent, take the sum of the 10 scales; add the scores for men, and divide by the number of respondents; do the same for women. The data will look like this:

	Men	Women
person 1	35	48
2	42	40
n	•	•
	45	44
TOTALS/Averages	—	—

> The average for men and women will enable you to compare attitude scores; are men and women different on this question?
>
> In formal analysis, the scales would likely be factor analyzed, and the male/female comparison would be by t-test. You might wish to return to this example in a later session.

THERMOMETER SCALES

Another popular social science measure is the *thermometer scale* developed by the University of Michigan Survey Research Center (Wimmer and Dominick, 1991, 115). It typically caricatures a thermometer, and has gradations from 0 to 100, any of which may be selected by the respondent. Instructions typically suggest that if a respondent feels "warmer" and more positive toward an object, a number above 50 will be selected; if "colder" and more negative, a number below 50. Any whole number on the scale may be selected. As a graphic device, it is easy for respondents to relate to, and it provides a visual element in an otherwise "gray" instrument of ink on paper.

Interpreting Scores

The thermometer scale raises another interesting aspect in the discussion of equal intervals: The numbers are not defined by words. If a respondent picks the number 57, or 89, or any number from 0 to 100 (other than 50, which is "undecided" or "neutral"), what does the number *mean*? How is a 57 different from a 60 or a 43? If the number 57 or 89 or any other does not correspond to words, then what is its meaning?

There are really two parts to this issue: One has to do with the *absence of variation* in scores, and the other with *undefined variation*. Variation in scores is very important; it is the measure of deviation from the mean of the sample. If the analyst is to compare one group with another, an estimate of how they are different will be needed. Absence of variation would suggest no difference between the groups. Therefore, it is important to give the respondent sufficient opportunity to be unique (to agree, to disagree, or whatever). Three response options likely will produce less variance then five or seven, because there are fewer opportunities.

On the other hand, to increase the number of response options without defining them carefully may improve the *appearance* of the scale, not the *substance*. The opportunity exists for one respondent to be highly different from another because the response options are many; but is the difference real? In a sense, the 100-point thermometer merely magnifies whatever variance would have been observed with the briefer scale.

For example, if the 5-point Likert scale were parallel to a 100-point thermometer scale, then a 2 on the Likert scale might become a 25 on the thermometer. In the rules of math, adding or multiplying a number by a constant is permissible because the proportions remain constant. It would seem that the only "gain" in such a magnified measurement is in the realm of *random* variation. A certain amount of the variation will occur simply because the number of response options is greater.

Semantic Distinctions. Try the following for yourself: Create a 15-point scale and verbalize each of the points (e.g., very strongly agree). Can you make 15 such distinctions? Could you make the 100 that would be needed on the thermometer scale? Be aware that these are issues for which there are some uncertainties.

MAGNITUDE SCALING

Lodge (1981) has noted that category scaling (e.g., 2-, 3-, 5-, 7-, or 9-point) has serious weaknesses: (a) the forced-choice nature of the measure; (b) the ordinal nature of the measure; and, (c) the imposition of the *researcher's* categories on the data. To help resolve these weaknesses, some researchers have expanded the measurement arsenal by developing a technique called **magnitude estimation scaling.**

The nature of magnitude estimation is evident in the following "prototypical" instructions:

> You will be presented with a series of [light] stimuli in irregular order. Your task is to tell how intense they seem by assigning numbers to them. Let the first [light] stimulus be your reference. Give it any number that seems appropriate to you, keeping in mind that some of the stimuli will be [brighter] than the reference and others will be [dimmer] than the reference. Assign a number to each of the stimuli such that it reflects how much weaker or stronger it is compared to the first stimulus: The brighter it is compared to the reference, the bigger your number response; the [dimmer] it is compared to the reference, the smaller your number response. There is no limit to the range of numbers you may use. Try to make each number match the intensity [of light] as you see it. (Lodge, 1981, 7; adapted from Stephens, 1975, 30)

In other words, the respondent is given a reference point, then asked to use it to gauge the importance of other related items. For example, if an automobile parking offense is a 10 (it could be any number, but presumably small because relative to other violations it is minor), then what value would you assign to a violation of reckless driving? drunken driving? vehicular homicide?

Different respondents will propose different values. There is no upper limit, but most upper responses are in the thousands, not millions. Notice the qualities of the system: It provides interval data for parametric testing. The numbers do not have names, but they represent intensity of feelings. One response is proportional to another.

only 3 orders of magnitude!

Advantage of Magnitude Scaling

How do magnitude scales compare with category scales? Lodge (1981) said that when the scales are matched on metric stimuli (i.e., when they are given a comparable range of opportunities), the relationship is almost invariably curvilinear. He said that it represents a "law of human judgment":

> When . . . magnitude scales are compared to category scales in direct matches against a known metric, the relationship between scale types is characteristically curvilinear, typically concave downward—magnitude scales are almost invariably found to be superior in providing quantitative information about the intensity of people's judgments. (Lodge, 1981, 16)

Lodge concluded that magnitude scales are more accurate. He added that several comparison tests have shown that category scaling causes (a) loss of important information, (b) misclassification of stimuli and respondents, and (c) "because the number of categories and the assignment of numbers to categories are arbitrary, indeterminate regression coefficients." The latter is a reference to a correlation-based statistical test called *regression analysis;* Lodge is saying in effect that the correlation of categorical or ordinal scale items is problematical, if not faulty.

Bear in mind that this is the barest introduction to magnitude estimation scaling; application of the technique would require additional reading. However, if you are interested in this methodology, the opportunities are exciting. Magnitude scaling is being used in the context of survey research through the *Gallileo method.* In this technique, respondents are given magnitude estimation questions and their responses are clustered to identify types of interests represented in the sample.

ISSUES OF RELIABILITY

Writing questions, measuring dimensions, and creating indexes are important; but when the writing, creating, and indexing are done, how do we estimate the reliability and validity of what we have measured?

Defining Reliability

Reliability can be thought of as the extent to which a measure generates the same outcome in repeated administrations. It asks two important questions: First, if the variable is measured again and again, will the results be about the same? This is dependability, stability, and predictability. Second, what is the accuracy of the measure? How near is it to a "true" measure? The answer, of course, is an unknown, but it is estimated by the sample; and if the sample is random, it estimates the population. Mere consistency in a measure is insufficient. It is possible, for instance, to be highly consistent—to get the same results on repeated measures—but be inaccurate.

For example, does an "intelligence test" measure a genetic predisposition to learn, or does it measure personal interest, motivation, family support, or personal health? A test of intelligence might generate a consistent score in repeated measures, yet not really measure a person's ability to learn. Dyslexics might score poorly, but some just might not have received the right instruction.

Measuring Reliability

In practice, reliability is usually measured as a **correlation coefficient,** defined as the extent to which variables vary together. Correlation will be treated more fully in Chapters 10 through 12, but here is a brief explanation:

Correlation estimates the systematic relationship between variables. If scores on one variable rise, while on another they fall, the correlation is "negative." If scores on one variable rise, while on the other they also rise, the correlation is "positive." If there is no systematic relationship between the variables, then there is 0 correlation. Correlation can be as low as 0, or as great as +1 or –1. The larger the correlation coefficient, the stronger the relationship between the variables.

Test–Retest Reliability

One correlational test of reliability is the *test–retest method*. The principle is this: If you measured one sample and got the average score, and measured another sample and got a similar score, and you did this repeatedly, you would begin to believe that responses to your test were consistent; you could *rely* on the instrument. You could test the reliability with a measure of correlation. The extent to which the correlation coefficient departed from the perfect of +1 or –1 would be a measure of the reliability of the measure.

Split-Half Reliability

Another correlational measure of reliability is the *split-half method,* whereby half of the measure is correlated with the other half. If there is no reason to believe otherwise, then one half should be scored about the same as the other; hence again the correlation coefficient should be high.

Cronbach's Reliability

A final widely used measure is **Cronbach's alpha**—an inter-item correlation summary statistic that estimates the total variance of the set of scales and the individual contribution of each item. This measure is available on some statistical programs (including SPSS/PC+) and is very useful in establishing the reliability of an index or a set of measures.

Item Analysis in Reliability

The test–retest, split-half, and Cronbach measures are based on correlation. But correlation is not suited to every estimate of reliability. Some tests call for a kind of item analysis that can be interpreted either intuitively or by statistical test.

Here is an example. Let's say that you gave a sample of trainees a 10-item test and hoped that they, after instruction, would answer all 10 items correctly. In a perfect exam, each student would correctly answer each question. But let's say that did not happen, and that the scores were arrayed as given in Figure 5.2. Assign each correct answer a value of 1 and each wrong answer a value of 0. Set up a matrix such as the one given in the figure.

Simply by visual inspection you can see that all but one student (student #1) performed fairly well on the test, and that four of the test items—numbers 1, 2, 5, and 6—gave students the most trouble. It appears that despite some problems with the test, students performed pretty well.

But let's look at the analysis in another way. Let's start from the assumption that perfect *10*s by all students were unlikely from the outset; some variation in scores was expected because (a) not all students are of equal ability, (b) some students missed some lectures, (c) some lectures were poor, and (d) some variation was random, or simply beyond the control of the examiner. We won't be able to rule out all of those, but let's look at the latter, the element of *random variation.*

Could we say that the two items that were answered correctly by only six students were actually as good as the questions answered correctly by all, and that the difference in correct responses might have been due to random factors? There is a statistical test designed just for such a question. (It does seem sometimes that there is at least one statistical test for every conceivable situation.) It is called *nonparametric analysis of variance,* and in this case it measures the variation in the scoring of items. It estimates the likelihood that the observed variation occurred by chance rather than as a function of item quality.[3]

Student Number	1	2	3	4	5	6	7	8	9	10	Number Correct
1	0	1	1	1	0	0	1	1	0	1	6
2	0	1	1	1	1	1	1	1	1	1	9
3	1	1	1	1	1	1	1	0	1	1	9
4	1	1	1	1	1	1	1	1	1	1	10
5	1	0	1	1	1	1	1	1	1	1	9
6	1	0	1	1	1	0	1	1	1	1	8
7	0	1	1	1	0	1	1	1	1	1	8
8	1	1	1	1	0	1	1	1	1	1	9
9	1	0	1	1	1	1	1	1	1	1	9
10	0	1	1	1	0	1	1	1	1	1	8
	6	7	10	10	6	8	10	9	9	10	

Test Items

FIGURE 5.2 Example of Item Analysis (*Source:* Adapted from Bruning and Kintz, 1987, 223.)

ISSUES OF VALIDITY

Validity asks the question: Have you measured what you think you measured? If you meant to measure *X*, did you really measure it? Or did you measure *X* + *Y*, and perhaps *Z*, too? This of course is a fundamental question of measurement.

Suppose, for example, that you intended to measure "need for orientation," a variable sometimes used in mass media research operationalized as a measure of self-confidence, for "anchoring." But in fact you measured a kind of generalized anxiety; in other words, you tapped a notion that says the greater the anxiety level, the greater the need for orientation. One could easily confound the other. In that case, validity would be doubtful.

Measuring Validity

Statistical tests, indexes, and measures of reliability are no good at all without validity. But how can you know whether you have measured what you intended to measure when you cannot get into a person's head to assure measurement accuracy, or if you cannot get your hands on the things you hope to measure? Generally, validity is measured through the use of external or sometimes secondary criteria.

For example, suppose we asked a sample of people to describe their magazine reading as heavy, medium, or light, and subsequently we wanted to confirm their estimates, to establish validity. In another part of the survey we could ask them: Did you read a magazine of any kind *this week?* If yes, we might follow with: More than one? and Which one(s)? Now, with these specifics, we could check the accuracy of the respondents' earlier estimates of whether the magazine reading was heavy, medium, or light.

Types of Validity

Validity has several names. The preceding example could be called **predictive validity,** because the number of magazines read in a week predicted level of reading. Standardized college entrance tests, such as the American College Test (ACT) and the Scholastic Aptitude Test (SAT) are also believed to have predictive validity. Admissions officers use ACT/SAT scores as an indicator of likely success in college.

As an aside, standardized tests are useful but imperfect predictors of success in college; there are other important variables as well. At one major university, for example, SAT and ACT scores correlated only in the mid and upper .30s with university freshmen grades. If SAT and ACT results were stronger predictors, the correlation would be much higher. Apparently, ability to succeed on standard tests is only partly translated into success in college. No doubt other important variables would include maturity, motivation, peer group, personal finances, and others. However, in the same university sample, ACT scores correlated .82 with SAT scores; in other words, the person who scores well on one standardized test is likely to score well on the other.

Predictive validity is also sometimes called *criterion-related validity* (Kerlinger, 1973, 459). If something is evident on the face of it, it is said to have *face validity*. For example, if respondents reported watching television for up to 176 hours per week, we would be suspicious; the week has only 168 hours. The measure would lack face validity.

Researchers have also identified **construct validity** and **content validity.** The former is concerned with whether a hypothetical construct, probably a combination of concepts, is supported by external data. Content validity refers to "the degree to which a measure covers the range of meanings included within a concept." (Babbie, 1989, 125) For example, a measure of "news knowledge" might not be represented by newspaper reading alone, but a combination of all public affairs information sources.

SOME FINAL THOUGHTS

With so many opportunities for error in measurement, you might wonder how accuracy ever is achieved. But the point is not to dwell on the down side; rather, it is to elevate the critique—to raise your awareness of the strengths and weaknesses of the system, and to encourage ever more careful and precise measurement. Blalock made the point well:

> There is often a fine line between perfectionism and defeatism, as well as one between honesty in reporting measurement inadequacies and ignoring them, thus leaving research projects so wide open to criticism that they are not taken seriously. The only way out of the implied dilemmas seems to require a frank recognition of the inherent difficulties one may expect to encounter in both theory construction and empirical research. Once these difficulties are more adequately understood, both researchers and their potential critics may come to a more realistic understanding of the limitations that may be anticipated in any specific piece of research, as well as the difficulties encountered in "adding up" the results of diverse studies using different measuring instruments and appropriate to settings that are each somewhat unique. (Blalock, 1982, 13)

Measurement is a frontier in communication research; it is where big gains can be made and new opportunities created, as in the research being conducted in magnitude estimation scaling and Gallileo survey methodology. It is possible that the future will see greater reliance on physiological measures. Imagine research, for instance, in which the researcher exposes an advertisement, or a news story, or whatever to a willing participant and generates physiological or physical measures that can be shown to be precise, bias-free, reliable.

Actually, some impressive physiological measures are already in place: Researchers today are using brain wave analysis, special cameras to measure pupil dilation, autonomic measures such as galvanic skin response, and voice pitch analysis. However, these techniques are not without controversy.

For example, although the occurrence of a brain wave pattern is not disputed, its interpretation is. A brain wave can show that a response occurred, but not the kind of rational or behavior that accompanied it. Still, the possibilities for physiological research are exciting and as yet underused. Those of you interested in learning more about physiological measures are invited to review the work of Hansen (1981, 23–26) and Weinstein (1982, 59–63).

SUMMARY

Measurement is the essence, the strength, of the social science research method. Measurement is the assignment of values to variables. There are three sources of error in measurement: instrumentation, sampling, and random. Aside from such errors there are other "threats" to the internal and external validity of research.

There are four levels of measurement, each providing more information than the one before it: nominal, ordinal, interval, and ratio. Nominal data require nonparametric analysis; interval and ratio are suited to parametric analysis. Ordinal data, which present problems in regard to equal-appearing intervals, nevertheless can be analyzed as parametric or nonparametric. Some popular measures in social science are Likert-type scales; semantic differential scales; and magnitude estimation scales. Several tests of reliability and validity exist.

STUDY QUESTIONS AND EXERCISES

1. Identify the four "levels" of data; define and give an example of each.

2. Identify and explain three sources of error in measurement.

3. Errors of sampling are of two types. One occurs when the sample is poorly selected. Identify and explain the other.

4. Explain why *ordinal* data are unsuited to statistical tests that require *interval* data.

5. What is the typical social scientist's response to the problem you discussed in Question 4? Write a paragraph agreeing or disagreeing with that approach.

6. Explain the concept of "dimensionality" as discussed in the chapter. How are dimensions identified and measured?

7. In what ways is the semantic differential scale different from the Likert-type scale? Describe both scales in regard to number and type of response options and the style in which they are presented to a respondent.

8. Identify some methods of establishing the reliability of a measurement.

9. Measurement is one of the great challenges in social science. What is your view as to the adequacy of measurement and the likelihood of improvements in the future?

NOTES

1. Ordinal measures are treated either categorical or continuous, and either parametric or nonparametric. Nominal measures are nonparametric: They do not estimate the parameters (e.g., mean, standard deviation) of a population.

2. Advanced students of measurement are invited to read publications by Blalock, 1982; Cooper, 1974; Kruskal and Wish, 1978; and Lodge, 1981; in addition to standard sources such as Kerlinger, 1973.

3. Further description of nonparametric analysis of variance is beyond the intent of this text, but you are invited to see the *Computational Handbook of Statistics* (Bruning and Kintz, 1987) for a step-by-step description of how to conduct this test. If you are interested in further study of reliability and validity assessment, a number of excellent texts are available; for example, the succinct and readable text by Carmines and Zeller (1979).

SOURCES

Babbie, Earl. 1989. *The Practice of Social Research.* 5th ed. Belmont, Calif.: Wadsworth.

Blalock, Hubert M., Jr. 1982. *Conceptualization and Measurement in the Social Sciences.* Beverly Hills, Calif.: Sage.

Bruning, James L., and B. L. Kintz. 1987. *Computational Handbook of Statistics.* Glenview, Ill.: Scott, Foresman.

Carmines, Edward G., and Richard A. Zeller. 1979. *Reliability and Validity Assessment.* Beverly Hills, Calif.: Sage.

Cooper, John O. 1974. *Measurement and Analysis of Behavioral Techniques.* Columbus, Ohio: Charles E. Merrill.

Fishbein, Martin, and Icek Ajzen. 1975. *Belief, Attitude, Intention and Behavior: An Introduction to Theory and Research.* Reading, Mass.: Addison-Wesley.

Glass, Gene V., and Julian C. Stanley. 1970. Statistical Methods in Education and Psychology. Englewood Cliffs, N.J.: Prentice-Hall.

Hansen, F. 1981. Hemispherical Lateralization: Implications for Understanding Consumer Behavior. *Journal of Consumer Research* 8 (June): 23–36.

Kerlinger, Fred N. 1973. *Foundations of Behavioral Research.* 2d ed. New York: Holt, Rinehart and Winston.

Kruskal, Joseph B. and Myron Wish. 1978. *Multidimensional Scaling.* Beverly Hills, Calif.: Sage.

Lodge, Milton. 1981. *Magnitude Scaling: Quantitative Measurement of Opinions.* Beverly Hills, Calif.: Sage.

McIver, John P., and Edward G. Carmines. 1981. *Unidimensional Scaling.* (Beverly Hills, Calif.: Sage.

Osgood, Charles E., George J. Suci, and Percy H. Tannenbaum. 1957. *The Measurement of Meaning.* Urbana: University of Illinois Press.

Ryan, Michael. 1980. The Likert Scale's Mid-Point in Communications Research. *Journalism Quarterly* 57(2):305–313.

Sears, Francis W., Mark W. Zemansky, and Hugh D. Young. 1980. *University Physics.* 5th ed.

Reading Mass.: Addison-Wesley. Cited in Blalock, Hubert M., Jr., *Conceptualization and Measurement in the Social Sciences.*

Stephens, S. S. 1975. *Psychophysics: Introduction to Its Perceptual, Neural, and Social Prospects.* New York: Wiley. Cited in Lodge, Milton, *Magnitude Scaling.*

Weinstein, A. 1982. A Review of Brain Hemisphere Research. *Journal of Advertising Research* 22 (June/July), 59–63.

Wimmer, Roger D., and Joseph Dominick. 1991. *Mass Media Research: An Introduction.* Belmont, Calif.: Wadsworth.

On Implementing the Principles and Techniques of Social Science Research

- Chapter 6: Research Ethics.   This discussion of ethical requirements and failures in the treatment of data and research participants includes examples of human subjects research approval forms and an informed consent form. Disclosure, anonymity and confidentiality are discussed.

- Chapter 7: Data Collection and Instrument Design.   The focus here is on writing and laying out the questionnaire. Do's and Don'ts of question writing are presented. Preparation of the instrument for administration and coding is also described.

- Chapter 8: Survey Research.   This chapter describes some survey designs and guides the selection of the proper data collection method. Advantages and disadvantages of telephone, mail, and in-person interviews are discussed. Procedures for conducting survey research are described.

- Chapter 9: The Experimental Method.   Chapter 9 describes the purposes and techniques of the experimental method. Notational systems are described, and examples of experimental research are presented and critiqued.

CHAPTER

6

Research Ethics

□
OBJECTIVES

After studying this chapter, you should be able to:

1. Identify and discuss issues of ethics as they relate to treatment of data and treatment of research participants.

2. Explain informed consent and voluntary participation.

3. Explain the presence and duty of a human subjects research committee.

4. Discuss some research behaviors that are of doubtful ethicality.

Our word *ethics* is derived from the Greek *ethikos*, the Latin *ethice*, and the Middle English *ethik* (*Webster's New Collegiate Dictionary*). It suggests *character*, or ethos. The derivation and the meaning of the term are important because the significance of ethics sometimes is obscured by the vagueness of the term.

Just what is ethics? Ethics deals with what is right and wrong in behavior, and with moral duty and obligation. *Webster's New Collegiate Dictionary* defines it as "a set of moral principles or values." And so, in this chapter, we will be concerned with some of what is right and wrong—the moral principles or values— in the conduct of social science research.

Broadly speaking, we are concerned with two kinds of ethical issues or problems: the treatment of data and the treatment of research participants. Both are within the control of the researcher. Because researchers most often work more or less free of outside supervision, it is important that they recognize their responsibilities and adjust to their obligations. Researchers must be their own ethical police officers.

ETHICS IN THE TREATMENT OF DATA

Problems of ethics in the treatment of data can arise at any of several points in the research process: creating the measurement instrument, training interviewers, drawing the sample, inputting data, cleaning data, analyzing data, and writing the report.

Creating the Measurement

The researcher should avoid pressure to construct the measurement instrument so as to contrive an outcome. The pressure can be self-induced; for example, the researcher may need a certain outcome to make the work publishable. The pressure can also come from clients; a client might ask for a study that will "show up" the competition.

Research should not be wielded by the researcher—although it might by the client—as an offensive weapon. The researcher should just do the research and let the chips fall where they may. That is because of the potential for corruption of the research process; only the ethics of the researcher prevents it from happening.

Training Interviewers

The purpose of research is to generalize properly from a sample to a population, to distinguish accurately one experimental treatment from another, or to examine the nature of phenomena. Interviewers or other data gatherers (e.g., observers and content coders) are crucial to this process. If they are poorly trained, their data are suspect and the research outcome is in doubt.

For example, the interviewer who is poorly trained might ad-lib questions, offer personal explanations, or imagine answers not specifically given. These poor practices can influence the outcome of the research.

The researcher who certifies the usefulness of the finished report must ensure that the training of interviewers or data gatherers is simply the best that can be provided. Furthermore, the researcher is advised to acknowledge the nature of interviewee training in any written report and to concede failings where they were known to have occurred so that the reader can judge whether to accept the findings.

Drawing the Sample

If data are obtained from samples, and samples are used to represent populations, the samples must be drawn with great care. Unfortunately, good probability samples are not easily obtained, and a researcher will sometimes be faced with temptations. Some of those will be met with merely poor research methods, and others will constitute ethical violations.

For example, if the researcher needs a systematic random sample of 400 students, but for one reason or another obtains a lesser number, the temptation might be to "beef up" the sample by adding interviews from nearby classrooms. At best, this will be a poor practice because the non-probability nature of the convenient classrooms can subvert the probability aspects of the systematic random sample. But if the poor practice is not acknowledged—if the combined random and non-random samples are quietly treated as random—we probably would be justified in considering it a problem of ethics.

Inputting Data

The researcher in charge of the project will either personally enter data into the computer or supervise the work. In either case, guidelines will be required. For example, often an interviewer will observe an extraordinary response, such as when a respondent selects more than one response option. How should this be input when only one response is permitted? The researcher must have a consistent system for resolving irregularities.

Sometimes a question is unanswered by several respondents; these "missing data" can create problems for statistical analysis. For example, if the missing case is eliminated, the size of the sample will be reduced and the significance level will be affected.

To avoid that, the researcher might enter a substitute response; for example, the missing data could be assigned an *average* for the group, or the missing score could be treated as an "undecided," the neutral point on the scale. But each treatment could alter the outcome of the research, especially if the number of missing cases is large.

Entering an *average* in a blank response can affect the significance level of the outcome in two ways: It can reduce the variance that might have occurred naturally, and it can increase the sample size (N) that is used to calculate the significance level.

What if the respondent has answered a long questionnaire with the same response to every question (e.g., every question is scored 3: undecided, no opinion); does this indicate carelessness, and should the instrument be discarded? In some cases, yes; but the researcher must decide.

There is also the possibility that errors made in data entry will be undetected. If, for example, the scale is 1 to 5 and the entry is 7, error detection is easy, but if the error is within the 1 to 5 scale, it is not.

You can see that there are many important judgments and many possible failures in the inputting of data. The ethical researcher will approach the data set with professionalism and ethicality—ensuring that the input is as accurate, systematic, and objective as possible, favoring no particular outcome. Failures in the system should be recognized and reported as such.

Cleaning Data

It is important that the data be screened and cleaned. The input data should not be presumed accurate; in fact, it should be presumed inaccurate, and searched for confirmation. Screening a printout of the data matrix allows a quick visual inspection that will detect whether smaller or larger numbers or extraneous characters appear where they should not. This is not research esoterica; any large data set likely will contain numerous errors such as data entered out-of-column, the letter *l* mistakenly entered as the numeral *1*, and wrong numbers entered in haste. Some errors will be detected by the software; for example, unexpected characters will generate error messages. These errors are an issue of ethics because careless acceptance of faulty data can generate meaningless results. Careless handling of data is clearly unethical.

Finally, the ethical researcher is thorough in giving credit to others whose data, concepts, and publications formed the framework for a given project.

Analyzing Data

There are numerous opportunities for unethical behavior in the analysis of data; only a few will be mentioned here. One is the use of decision making to favor the outcome preferred by the researcher. For example, the researcher could elect to retain or reject a respondent whose responses arguably are careless, and the decision could have a bearing on the reported significance of the outcome. The ethical researcher should simply decide what is "right" (i.e., what will provide the most objective and accurate outcome), not anticipate the direction of the outcome.

Another issue is the establishment and acceptance of a significance level. By convention, a statistical test is significant if the probability value in a statistical test is less than 5 times in 100, usually stated as $p < .05$. But what if the probability is less than .059? The number .059 is not *less than* .05, and so it is not "significant" even though it is very nearly so. That small difference can determine whether the data are or are not publishable, or it can mean the acceptance or rejection of a hypothesis. The temptation to be generous is great, but generosity in such a case would not be ethical.

To complicate this issue further, perhaps the opposite point can also be made: It would be unethical to ignore such a probability, regardless of whether it satisfies an arbitrary standard. Ethical decision making is not always clear-cut.

A third issue is in regard to "post-hoc hypothesizing" and "data searching." Here is how it happens: The researcher collects a large set of data with a particular notion in mind, but fails to find evidence to support it. During the search, the analyst runs the correlation of all variables in the data set. In the correlation matrix, unexpectedly, there is a very interesting relationship. The researcher begins to construct reasons why the relationship probably occurred, and prepares a paper explaining the outcome. This is post-hoc hypothesizing and data searching. Why would it be an ethical problem?

The answer is complex, but it has to do with random occurrences. If we correlated the number of tiles in classroom floors with the number of visitors to the classrooms in a year, we might get a significant correlation, but would it be *meaningful* or just a matter of chance? Some correlations are specious, not supported by reason. Because of that, research should not proceed backward from conclusion-to-explanation-to-hypothesis-to-literature, but forward from literature-to-hypothesis-to-data-to-conclusion. Hypotheses and research questions should be stipulated from the outset, not constructed after the fact to fit the outcome that is observed.

Writing the Report

The final report should provide details of methodology, sampling, error margin, measurement, and analysis such that any competent researcher could repeat the study and obtain roughly the same outcome. (The word *roughly* is used to account for differences due to sampling.) Researchers generally are expected to retain data sets and documentation sufficient to reconstruct the research for 3 to 5 years. Such files will enable the researcher to defend an outcome, should any question arise (Wimmer and Dominick, 1991).

LEARN BY DOING

Experimental behavioral research is conducted in several social science disciplines (mass communication, sociology, political science, psychology) but is especially common in some departments emphasizing social psychology. Identify a faculty member in any social science discipline who is knowledgeable about the experimental method and conduct an interview. Learn about the person's ethical interests, concerns, and practices. Identify what the person sees as ethical abuses and the precautions that are taken to avoid them. If pertinent, give an example of the person's experimentation. Write a one- or two-page report for class, being careful to exercise ethical judgment about what is communicated.

Note that the interview is also pertinent to Chapter 9, The Experimental Method.

ETHICS IN THE TREATMENT OF RESEARCH PARTICIPANTS

When we speak of "treatment of research participants" as an issue of ethics, we are referring to the *abuse* of participants. Abuse can occur in experiments, surveys, or observational settings. The abuse can range from very mild to severe, and from physical to emotional harm. The researcher must be constantly aware that human research participants are *people,* not pawns to manipulate on a game board. Humans are fragile and precious, and must be treated with dignity and respect (Zimbardo, 1975).

Experimental Research

Over the years, experimentalists have produced some spectacular research successes, but perhaps at some cost to participants.

Solomon Asch (1951, 1956) conducted the famous "line drawing" experiment that has been cited in many books and articles. Here is how it worked: With a ruse for a purpose, he showed college students three lines of different lengths, and then a fourth line, and asked them to guess which of the three lines was the same length as the fourth. Under ordinary circumstances, this task would be no challenge for any of us. But Asch conducted the experiment in groups, and only one person—the naive subject—in each group was unaware of the nature of the research. One-by-one the group members made the same *wrong* guess until it was the turn of the naive participant.

Put yourself in that position. If you were in a group of eight, seven of whom made a consistent and simple judgment clearly different from yours, would you want to risk the possible embarrassment of being different? Would you want to risk ridicule for making a judgment clearly different by a ratio of 7 to 1? The answer of course is no, and in fact some of the naives simply went along with the group, giving their peers' wrong answer. That was one of the points of the research: to see how individuals subjugate judgment to their group affiliations.

It was a wonderful and intriguing experiment; it showed what might be a weakness in human nature, a susceptibility to be irrational for the sake of group norms. But was it sensitive to the feelings of participants? Blind adherence to group norms in the face of evidence is not admirable.

Suppose, for example, that you were one of the naive participants duped into acting in a way that you later would judge to be unsatisfactory; might you be angry? Might you use the experience in subsequent self-evaluation? Might you doubt yourself in light of the evidence of your naiveté? In other words, would there be a lasting and meaningful impact on your self-image? Could you shrug it all off and erase it from importance? If you had known your self-image was at risk, would you have participated? Does the researcher have any right to impose this burden on you? That is the ethical problem. Actually, the Asch experiment was mild compared with some others reported in the 1950s, 1960s, and 1970s.

Common in the period were studies of aggression; researchers wanted to know the circumstances and the variables that contributed to the ways one individual treated another. Typically, researchers gave one person an opportunity to aggress against another under different levels and types of frustration or reinforcement. The research was so common, in fact, that one popular measurement instrument was dubbed the "aggression machine." It was a console somewhat like a radio audio board labeled with fake outputs of electrical energy, usually in the 50- to 500-volt range. Experimental participants were encouraged to use the machine to deliver levels of shock to others under conditions of frustration or reinforcement.

Milgram (1974) conducted one of the classic projects of the type. He told participants they were to use the volt machine to help another person learn a long list of nonsense syllables. Each time the learner made a mistake, the participant was to deliver punishment (voltage), a higher jolt with each failure. The learner was a confederate of the researcher who was not really being shocked, but who pretended to be hurt by the voltage.

In the latter stages of each instructional session, the "learner" screamed in mock pain and pounded the room divider separating the learner from the voltage machine. The naive participant apparently thought the pain was genuine. Did that stop the person from delivering subsequent shock? In many cases, no.

And so, this is a powerful point: Individuals can be successfully directed by authorities to hurt others, even if it does not seem reasonable, and even if it could be harmful.

Put yourself in the position of the naive participant. When asked to deliver physical pain to another, what would you have done? Suppose you delivered what you knew to be lethal doses of electricity for so trivial a purpose; would you later think unkindly of yourself? Would you think of it as a weakness of character? Would you *thank* the experimenter for exposing this weakness in you? Not likely. If the researcher "debriefed" you, and explained that it was all a ruse, would that clean the slate for you?

Because social science research can leave a lasting and powerful impression, the ethical researcher will carefully consider the welfare of research participants.

REGULATIONS FOR HUMAN SUBJECTS RESEARCH

Since the mid-1960s to early 1970s, the use of human subjects in academic research has come under strict control, partly as an outgrowth of federal sponsorship. If universities accept federal research money, they must follow federal rules for its use. They are required to establish an Institutional Research Board to review and to approve all research involving human subjects. Not all academic institutions have the same policies regarding human subjects research, but all have policies, and all recognize the potential for abuse posed by unchecked research methods.

In the case of entrepreneurial researchers, federal control is minimal. It is largely left to the discretion of the researcher and the rule of law. That is one reason this discussion of ethics is important; persons conducting or using research must recognize for themselves the limits of acceptability in research practices involving human subjects.

Short Form, Long Form

To obtain IRB approval for human subjects research, the researcher submits either a short form or a long form (i.e., "expedited," or "Form A"). The short form (Figure 6.1) is for research that has no aspect that would be considered harmful to a human subject in any way (e.g., it would not involve psychological or physical trauma, personal intimacies, bodily functions, or other "sensitive" aspects of a person's being).

For any research judged sensitive, a much more thorough review is required. In no case can research begin before approval by the committee. This protects the university and the research participant, although the counter argument might be made that it tends to stifle creative and groundbreaking methodologies, or even politically sensitive proposals (Ceci, Peters, and Plotkin, 1985, 994–1010).

The Belmont Report

In 1979, the National Commission for the Protection of Human Subjects of Biomedical and Behavioral Research published *The Belmont Report,* which dealt with ethical principles and guidelines for the protection of human subjects of research. The report identified three basic ethical principles:

Form A

(This form is *Federally auditable* and **must be TYPED**.)

Certification of Exemption
from Review by Full Committee for Research
Involving Human Subjects

CRP # _____

Date received in RA _____

A. **PRINCIPAL INVESTIGATOR(s) and/or CO-PI(s)**: (For student projects, list both the student and the advisor.)

B. **DEPARTMENT:**

C. **COMPLETE MAILING ADDRESS AND PHONE NUMBER OF PI(s) AND CO-PI(s):**

D. **TITLE OF PROJECT:**

E. **EXTERNAL FUNDING AGENCY AND ID NUMBER** (if applicable):

F. **GRANT SUBMISSION DEADLINE** (if applicable):

G. **STARTING DATE:** Upon certification by Coordinator of Compliances. **(NO RESEARCH MAY BE INITIATED UNTIL CERTIFICATION IS GRANTED.)**

H. **ESTIMATED COMPLETION DATE** (Include all aspects of research and final write-up.):

    I. **Objective(s) of Project** (Use additional page, if needed.):

    II. **Subjects** (Use additional page, if needed.):

    III. **Methods or Procedures** (Use additional page, if needed.):

    IV. **CATEGORY(s) FOR EXEMPT RESEARCH PER 45 CFR 46** (see reverse side for categories):
    _____

CERTIFICATION: The research described herein is in compliance with 45 CFR 46 101(b) and presents subjects with no more than minimal risk as defined by applicable regulations.

Principal
Investigator   _____   _____   Date _____
                Name   Signature

Advisor   _____   _____   Date _____
                Name   Signature

Dept. Review
Comm. Chair   _____   _____   Date _____
                Name   Signature

Dept. Head   _____   _____   Date _____
                Name   Signature

APPROVED: Edith M. Szathmary   _____   Date _____
            Coordinator of Compliances   Signature
            Research Administration   Rev. 10/90

FIGURE 6.1   Example of Human Subjects Research Committee "Expedited Review" Form (*Source:* Reprinted by permission of Research Administration, University of Tennessee, Knoxville.)

INSTRUCTIONS FOR COMPLETING FORM A
PLEASE TYPE THE INFORMATION REQUESTED ON THE FRONT OF THIS FORM

Provide the required information in the space available if at all possible. If additional space is necessary, attach a separate sheet. Submit one copy of this form to the Coordinator of Compliances, 404 Andy Holt Tower.

ALL SIGNATURES MUST BE ORIGINAL on this form. When certified by the Coordinator of Compliances, a copy of the signed Form A will be returned to the Principal Investigator and a copy will be returned to the Department Head.

1. **OBJECTIVES:** Briefly state, in non-technical language, the purpose of the research, with special reference to human subjects involved.

2. **SUBJECTS:** Briefly describe the subjects by number to be used, criteria of selection or exclusion, the population from which they will be selected, duration of involvement, and any special characteristics necessary to the research.

3. **METHODS OR PROCEDURES:** Briefly enumerate, in non-technical language, the research methods which directly involve use of human subjects. List any potential risks, or lack of such, to subjects and any protection measures. Explain how anonymity of names and confidentiality of materials with names and/or data will be obtained and maintained. List the names of individuals who will have access to names and/or data.

4. **CATEGORY(s) FOR EXEMPT RESEARCH PER 45 CFR 46:** Referring to the extracts below from Federal regulations, cite the paragraphs which you deem entitle this research project to certification as exempt from review by the Committee on Research Participation.

45 CFR 46.101(B): Research activities in which the only involvement of human subjects will be in one or more of the following categories are exempt from these regulations.

(1) Research conducted in established or commonly accepted educational settings, involving normal educational practices, such as (i) research on regular and special education instructional strategies, or (ii) research on the effectiveness of, or the comparison among, instructional techniques, curricula, or classroom management methods.

(2) Research involving the use of educational tests (cognitive, diagnostic, aptitude, achievement), if information taken from these sources is recorded in such a manner that subjects cannot be identified directly or through identifiers linked to the subjects.

(3) Research involving survey or interview procedures, except where all of the following conditions exist: (i) responses are recorded in such a manner that the human subjects can be identified directly or through identifiers linked to the subjects, (ii) the subject's responses, if they became known outside the research, could reasonably place the subject at risk of criminal or civil liability or be damaging to the subject's financial standing or employability, and (iii) the research deals with sensitive aspects of the subject's own behavior, such as illegal conduct, drug use, sexual behavior, or use of alcohol. All research involving survey or interview procedures is exempt, without exception, when the respondents are elected or appointed public officials or candidates for public office.

(4) Research involving the observation (including observation by participants) or public behavior, except where all of the following conditions exist: (i) observations are recorded in such a manner that the human subjects can be identified directly or through identifiers linked to the subjects, (ii) the observations recorded about the individual, if they became known outside the research, could reasonably place the subject at risk of criminal or civil liability or be damaging to the subject's financial standing or employability, and (iii) the research deals with sensitive aspects of the subject's own behavior such as illegal conduct, drug use, sexual behavior, or use of alcohol.

(5) Research involving the collection or study of existing data, documents, records, pathological specimens, or diagnostic specimens, if these sources are publicly available or if the information is recorded by the investigator in such a manner that subjects cannot be identified directly or through identifiers linked to the subjects.

SEE 45 CFR 401(B) OR **FLYER #6** WHEN CHILDREN ARE THE SUBJECTS OF RESEARCH.

1. *Respect.* This principle suggests that individuals should be treated as autonomous (i.e., "capable of deliberation about personal goals and of acting under the direction of such deliberation"), and that persons whose autonomy is interrupted by research procedures should be protected.
2. *Beneficence.* This principle suggests that not only should individuals be treated with respect, but also that their well-being should be actively protected. "The Belmont Report" offered these general rules: Do no harm; maximize possible benefits; minimize *possible* harms.
3. *Justice.* This principle asks the question: Who ought to receive the benefits of research and bear its burdens? For example, if an experimenter wants to introduce a potentially beneficial product, and compare its outgrowth with a preexisting product, who should receive the new product and who the old? If one product really is better than another, it matters.

ISSUES IN THE APPLICATION OF ETHICAL PRINCIPLES

Application of these principles of ethics in the use of human subjects focuses largely on the following issues: privacy, informed consent, voluntary participation, disclosure, debriefing, anonymity, and confidentiality.

Privacy

In most cultures, privacy is very important, and violation of it is demeaning and degrading. Although this sensitivity to personal privacy inhibits some data collection, researchers must be respectful of it.

For example, suppose you felt it was important to understand the nature of graffiti and the people who write it, and suppose you hoped to observe graffiti writing in a public restroom. You are interested in both what is written, and who writes it. Your plan is to hang around the restroom and interview the writers. The problem, of course, is that writers of graffiti are rarely public; only their "work" is seen.

But if you cannot see who is writing, you cannot interview them. Suppose you decided to establish *camera surveillance* in the restroom stalls; would that be ethical? Clearly not. Even if you restricted it to above-waist shots? Forget it. Surveillance of individuals without their permission would be unappreciated, at best.[1]

Does that mean you just can't study graffiti? One enterprising researcher is reported to have used the following technique: With a freshly painted (i.e., free of graffiti) restroom, the researcher waited quietly outside until each user exited. The researcher then quickly entered to see if anything had been penned, and if so, ran to interview the person who must have done the writing.

Aside from the possibility that a researcher could get killed for the trouble, does an ethical question exist here? Is this interview merely a different kind of privacy invasion? It clearly puts the participant in an unwilling position. In the paragraphs that follow, we will discuss the principles of "informed consent" and "voluntary participation."

ℓ Informed Consent

Because research methods can have an impact on the life of participants, it is imperative that permission of participants be gained prior to the research. This is called *informed consent.* The term is said to have originated in the trials of Nazi physicians at Nuremberg after World War II (Wheeler, 1991).

Consent usually requires signing of a brief form prior to the research, particularly if the research participants are on-site. If the research is distant, such as by telephone or mail, different procedures are required. In the case of telephone research, participants' agreement to participate in the interview will constitute informed consent, assuming the research has been approved by a "human subjects research committee" (sometimes called a "research compliance office") prior to administration. For mail research, a brief statement expressing informed consent may be included in the instrument. Examples of on-site and mail-research informed consent statements are given in Figures 6.2 and 6.3

When research procedures involve the potential of harm to the individual, informed consent requirements are much more stringent. Following is a checklist suggesting the key elements of informed consent[2]:

1. Project title with sufficient description of project.
2. Description of benefits to participant or others.
3. Description of potential risks to participants, or if applicable, a statement that risks are minimal.
4. Disclosure of alternative procedures that may be advantageous to the participant in cases where research is combined with treatment or service.
5. Statement on confidentiality of records identifying participants, and the means of maintaining confidentiality.
6. Statement that participation is voluntary, and that refusal to participate will involve no penalty or loss of benefits, and that the subject may withdraw at any time.
7. Statement of whom to contact for more information.

Furthermore, the informed consent statement must be in ordinary language that participants can comprehend. It must not require participants to waive legal rights or claims. If young children are involved, it must require the permission of parents or guardians; and if prisoners, pregnant women, or mentally disturbed persons are involved, safeguards must be provided.

LEARN BY DOING

At the discretion of your instructor, plan a visit to the office or officer of your institution with responsibility for human-subjects research oversight. Learn the procedures required for use of human subjects. Is there a form to fill out? Who must sign it? What information is required? What research, if any, is exempt from review? How much time is needed for committee approval? Write a one- or two-page report on what you find about the supervision of human subjects research.

"We invite you to participate in the gathering of oral history about (a city) in the early 20th Century. Your participation will consist of one or more interviews that will be audiotaped. You will be identified on the tape and credited as the source of the information you provide. The tape will be donated to the (university) library which will make it accessible to scholars, students, and others studying (the city). A separate "Gift Form" from the library is attached to give them permission to control future use of our interview(s).

"Your participation will be voluntary, and you may decline or withdraw from participation at any time without penalty or prejudice. The interviewer or his/her research associates in this project will be happy to provide answers to any questions you may have about the project.

"Until transferred to the (university) library, your tape will be stored in a locked cabinet in Room (of the university library). If you have any follow-up questions on this project, please contact N. D. Good at this office, telephone number 555-4567.

* * * * * * * * * * * * * * * * * *

"I have read and understood this explanation of the oral history project and have had my questions about it answered satisfactorily. I voluntarily agree to participate."

_____   _____

Name   Date

_____

Participant Signature

_____

Researcher

FIGURE 6.2   An Example of "Informed Consent" when Research Is Conducted On-Site (*Source:* Working with Human Subjects, CRP Flyer #5, What Is Informed Consent? Research Administration, The University of Tennessee, Knoxville, p. 17. Reprinted by permission.)

Voluntary Participation

Informed consent naturally requires that research participation be *voluntary;* in other words, it should not be coerced. That is good common sense. To require anyone to participate in something that might be uncomfortable or even harmful is clearly wrong.

In seeking volunteers to participate in research, you will find it necessary to make major disclosure of the nature of the research. This unfortunately, sometimes

"The purpose of the attached questionnaire is to determine public attitudes toward local policies on school assignment. Please fill out and return the questionnaire in the return envelope. All of the questions are multiple choice and will involve only your marking the column that most closely reflects your view. Filling out the questionnaire should take you no more than ten to fifteen minutes.

"No questionnaire contains any questions or markings to identify you as a respondent. The results will be tabulated and analyzed only in aggregate form, so that anonymity is assured. Your return of the questionnaire will constitute your informed consent to participate in this study."

FIGURE 6.3   An Example of "Informed Consent" when Research Is by Mail (*Source:* Working with Human Subjects, CRP Flyer #5, What Is Informed Consent?, Research Administration, The University of Tennessee, Knoxville, p. 17. Reprinted by permission.)

reduces the validity of the research, but it nonetheless is necessary. Would you yourself volunteer for a research project that might make you look foolish? Not likely. When disclosure will defeat a research procedure, the researcher must simply find an alternative way to gather data. This is discussed further below.

Rather than using coercion, researchers sometimes will take the opposite approach: they will offer a reward for participation. The reward might be money, free time (such as a day away from work or a missed classroom lecture), or an academic grade. But is a reward proper? This is a grey area, not clearly ethical or unethical. One could argue that a reward constitutes coercion because it plays on the survival needs of participants rather than their preferences. A counter argument is that a reward does not physically coerce a participant, and so acceptance of the reward is sufficient to constitute voluntarism.

The position of the author is that a reward is "half a loaf"; it is not fully coercion, but it is not fully voluntarism either. Rewards are less problematical in the private sector where subjects are adult and the reward is monetary. In the academic setting, where young people are subject to exploitation, the problem is greater. Therefore it is ethically marginal to obtain research participation through rewards. For research participants under age 18, special local rules may apply.

Disclosure of Research Purpose

Disclosure is a serious problem for the validity of experimental research. Often, to disclose the nature of the research is to risk confounding the results. For example, if you were to tell participants you wanted to study them under conditions of frustration, their awareness of the task might influence their behavior. To see what this means, do a little role playing. Imagine first that you were randomly frustrated, then that you *knew* you were being *purposely* frustrated. Would you respond in the same way to each situation? Probably not, and that would affect the research outcome. But if participation is to be voluntary, some measure of disclosure is necessary; and if that is a problem, then the researcher has to work around it.

Experimentalists often get around this bothersome requirement by giving rough indication of the purpose of the research without disclosing the details. For example, the experimenter who wants to study awareness of a certain kind of advertisement embedded in a contrived "news" program might tell participants only that the research involved "how viewers respond to television." The technique is mildly deceptive, but probably harmless enough to be justified by the need for knowledge, provided the failure to disclose holds no threat of harm whatever to the participant. *Any* deceit is a challenge to ethicality, however, and must be approached with great care and responsibility.

Debriefing Research Participants

As a courtesy to participants, and in order to ease their concerns about the research, full debriefing of participants should follow any session. The debriefing explains the true nature of the research and the importance of the work. Often, the researcher will offer to send a copy of the research paper (a summary of the research) to participants. In any event, participants must be treated as fellow humans, not as discarded pieces of research paper.

Anonymity and Confidentiality

Several months after the author bought a new automobile, the manufacturer sent a questionnaire concerning the reliability of the vehicle and the quality of service. The return address was to the manufacturer in a distant city. In responding to the questionnaire I made a few complaints about workmanship, but was complimentary of the local service department. Unexpectedly, within a week, the local dealer called to verify that the complaints of workmanship were resolved. The questionnaire that was sent, presumably in confidence, to the distant city had been returned to the dealer for use as a promotional, customer-relations device.

There are two problems here: anonymity and confidentiality. If the instrument was a customer-relations device, it should have been labeled as such. A research participant should not be duped. The instrument implied anonymity and confidentiality, when in fact it provided neither. Such practice will discourage free response and future participation; it will obscure the truth of an issue.

If an instrument is presented as providing anonymity, then that anonymity should be absolute. The argument that respondent identity would be known only to one researcher or a select number of researchers is not sufficient. Identification implies the *possibility of disclosure,* and disclosure implies a different level of response. Research *confidentiality* means that the responses of individuals will not be disclosed in such a way as to identify them.

Anonymity is a special problem in mail research because it can greatly increase the cost. For example, in an anonymous survey, follow-up mailings must be sent to every person in the sample, even those who already responded. As a result, researchers have been known to resort to tricks such as code numbers, sometimes placed under the staple or hidden elsewhere in a multiple-page instrument, that will tell them who has or hasn't responded. But for ethical reasons the extra cost of the follow-up mailing should simply be budgeted into the project, and anonymity should be protected at all costs. Failure to uphold that principle will discourage full disclosure in subsequent research.

CONCLUSION

The importance of ethics in research cannot be overemphasized. Researchers must treat participants with respect and strive to secure their well-being. Furthermore, research procedures must account for issues of equity and justice for individuals. Researchers must inform participants of the nature of the research, explain any risks and benefits, and ask for their consent. Researchers must not abuse their positions of apparent authority and trust, especially in academic settings.

SUMMARY

Ethicality is implied at two broad levels of research: the treatment of data and the treatment of individuals. Treatment of data includes constructing the measurement instrument, training interviewers, drawing the sample, inputting data, cleaning data, analyzing data, and writing the report. Treatment of research participants must be fair, nonabusive, and respectful. Participation must be voluntary and with informed consent. Anonymity and confidentiality must be preserved, and regulations designed to protect individuals' rights must be met.

STUDY QUESTIONS AND EXERCISES

1. In 1971, Philip G. Zimbardo and three colleagues conducted an experiment on a university campus in which some student participants acted as prisoners and others acted as guards. The study was terminated early when many of the "prisoners" became seriously distressed and many of the "guards" brutalized and degraded their fellow subjects. The experiment generated a great deal of discussion of ethics and helped to usher in the current level of protection for experimental participants. In the journal *Cognition,* Zimbardo (1975, 243–256) reviewed the experiment and responded to criticisms of it. He and his associates also published an article on this experiment in the *New York Times Magazine* (April 8, 1973, 38–60). As a study in ethics, read one or both of these articles and write a one- or two-page paper supporting or condemning the research.

2. Select one of the following important sources and write a two-page review on its relevance to the debate about research ethics: Ceci, Peters, and Plotkin, 1985; Greenberg and Garramone, 1989; or Milgram, 1974.

NOTES

University of Tennessee–Knoxville. 1991. What Is Informed Consent? In *Working with Human Subjects: Understanding the UTK Review System.* CRP Flyer No. 5, revised May 1991. This is one of 10 flyers that describe many of the specifics of human subjects research in the University of Tennessee system. For more information, contact the Office of Research Compliance, University of Tennessee, Knoxville, TN 37996.

1. Surveillance in restrooms is not only unethical, but also illegal. The Michigan Appeals Court in 1983 called it "intrusion upon the seclusion of another." The owners of a skating rink had installed a camera over a restroom stall. A woman and her daughter filed suit, and the court ruled in their favor. See: *Harkey v. Abate* (346 N.W. 2d 74, Mich. App. 1983), cited in Fischer and Phillips (1989, 259–260).

2. These key ethical principles are adapted from *The Belmont Report* (National Commission for the Protection of Human Subjects of Biomedical and Behavioral Research, 1979).

SOURCES

Asch, Solomon E. 1951. Effects of Group Pressure on the Modification and Distortion of Judgments. In *Groups, Leadership, and Men,* ed. H. Geutzkwo. Pittsburgh: Carnegie.

Asch, Solomon, E. 1956. Studies of Independence and Conformity: A Minority of One Against a Unanimous Majority. *Psychological Monographs* 70(9).

Babbie, Earl. 1989. The Ethics and Politics of Social Research. In *The Practice of Social Research.* 5th ed. Belmont, Calif.: Wadsworth.

Ceci, Stephen J., Douglas Peters, and Jonathan Plotkin. 1985. Human Subjects Review, Personal Values, and the Regulation of Social Science Research. *American Psychologist* 40(9):994–1010.

Fischer, Bruce D., and Michael J. Phillips. 1989. *The Legal Environment of Business.* St. Paul, Minn.: West Publishing.

Greenberg, Bradley S., and Gina M. Garramone. 1989. Ethical Issues in Mass Communication Research. In *Research Methods in Mass Communication.* 2d ed., ed. Guido H. Stempel and Bruce H. Westley. Englewood Cliffs, N.J.: Prentice-Hall.

Milgram, Stanley. 1974. *Obedience to Authority: An Experimental View.* New York: Harper & Row.

Milgram, Stanley. 1965. Some Conditions of Obedience and Disobedience to Authority. In *Human Relations* 18(1):57–76.

National Commission for the Protection of Human Subjects of Biomedical and Behavioral Research. *The Belmont Report: Ethical Principles and Guidelines for the Protection of Human Subjects of Research.* April 18, 1979 (FR Doc. 79-12065).

Rubin, Zick. 1985. Deceiving Ourselves about Deception: Comment on Smith and Richardson's "Amelioration of Deception and Harm in Psychological Research." *Journal of Personality and Social Psychology* 48(1):252–253.

Sjoburg, Gideon, and Roger Nett. 1968. *A Methodology for Social Research.* New York: Harper & Row.

Smith, Stephen S., and Deborah Richardson. 1983. Amelioration of Deception and Harm in Psychological Research: The Important Role of Debriefing. *Journal of Personality and Social Psychology* 44(5):1075–1082.

West, Stephen G., and Stephen P. Gunn. 1978. Some Issues of Ethics and Social Psychology. *American Psychologist* 33(1):30–38.

Wheeler, David L. 1991. Informed Consent Questioned in Research Using Humans. *The Chronicle of Higher Education* (December 4):A-14.

Wimmer, Roger D., and Joseph R. Dominick. 1991. Research Reporting, Ethics, and Financial Support. In *Mass Media Research*. 3d ed. Belmont, Calif.: Wadsworth.

Zimbardo, Philip G. 1975. On the Ethics of Intervention in Human Psychological Research: With Special Reference to the Stanford Prison Experiment. *Cognition* 2(2):243–256.

CHAPTER

7

Data Collection
and Instrument Design

□
OBJECTIVES

After studying this chapter, you should be able to:

1. Write survey questions with clarity.

2. Lay out a survey questionnaire in such a way as to avoid offense and encourage response.

3. Format a one-fold legal-size questionnaire.

4. Recite some do's and don'ts of question writing.

5. Prepare a questionnaire for computer input and analysis.

INTRODUCTION

When the researcher knows the nature of the sample (e.g., telephone, mail, or in-person—Chapter 4), the kinds of measurements that will be taken (Chapter 5), and the hypotheses that will be tested (Chapter 3), the next step is to write and lay out the questionnaire, euphemistically called the "instrument" of data collection. Questionnaires must be written and designed to accomplish three objectives: comprehension, accuracy, and completion. If any of these objectives fails, the effort involved in producing the questionnaire can be for naught.

COMPREHENSION

The simplest of goals, comprehension is nevertheless difficult to ensure. The simplest of words and sentences can be construed differently from what was intended. That is not only to say *mis*construed, but *differently* construed, for the meaning of words, as David Berlo pointed out, is not in the words but in *us* (1960).

For example, think of the word *desk*. We all know what it means, yet we have different understandings of it. Some people see desks as heavy, secure, enduring, rich, colorful, arty, professional; others see them as stainless, clinical, cold, bare, cramped, or businesslike. Surely, desks have many styles and descriptions, any of which could make up an individual's understanding of *desk*. Desks have denotative meaning, the kind of meaning found in a dictionary; and connotative meaning, the kind of meaning that dwells largely within us (Osgood, Suci, Tannenbaum, 1957).

Furthermore, connotative meaning has at least three dimensions: *evaluation* (i.e., liking and disliking), *strength* or potency, and *activity* (e.g., mobility or busyness). The impressions or meanings conjured by one person for an object may be different from those conjured by another person, and this is the dominant problem facing the writer of a questionnaire.

Even if the meaning of a word is undisputed, the emphasis can affect the response to it. A favorite example is the sentence, "I never said John stole money." The emphasis in the sentence could be on any word, depending on the intent of the communicator. For example, the sentence could be interpreted: "I never *said* John stole money," or, "I *never* said John stole money." The difference is not profound, but it is real. One version implies indignation; the other version implies denial. Since the sentence can be read differently, interpretation of responses to it are open to question. The point is that the writer of questions not only must be good with words, but also must be able to project to the role of respondent, and to anticipate the myriad responses common to any diverse group of respondents.

Consider a seemingly simple question: "Is there a television in your home?" The words are simple enough, but the unique position of respondents has to be taken into account. One respondent might say, "Yes, but it doesn't work." Another might say, "Yes, but not here at the dorm." Both were yes answers, but neither contributed meaningfully to knowledge of the number of persons using television. If the intent was to measure the number of potential viewers, the answer yes could be misleading.

The problem here is that the purpose of the question was not apparent. What was the purpose? Was it to measure access to television, use of television, ownership of the primary receiver, or something else? Clear purposes can lead to clear questions and meaningful responses. To measure use of television, we might open with: "Did you happen to watch television yesterday?" We probably would also want to ask for the amount of viewing: "If you watched television yesterday, about how much time do you think you spent at it?" Alternatively, the question could be worded: "About how many different programs did you watch?"

A question on access might read: "If you happened to watch television yesterday, was that in your home, or elsewhere?" And finally: "In a routine or average day, about how many different TV shows do you watch?"

Even the use of several questions would yield only a sketchy estimate of the respondent's actual TV viewing. The point is that even a seemingly simple question, when seen from the perspective of a cross-section of people, can become a challenge to clarity.

ACCURACY

For accuracy, the questionnaire should be laid out in a manner that is efficient and attractive. *Attractive* here means pleasant enough to the eye and easy enough to follow that accuracy and completion will be easy to achieve. *Efficiency* means not stinginess with paper, or even brevity; rather, it means laying out the questions to encourage accurate and complete data.

For example, if the questions are presented in a typeface or type size that is difficult to read, respondents may be unwilling to complete the survey. Or if the questions seem to run together on the page, confusion may result. If the questions include "filter" questions (i.e., the type that tell the respondent, "If you answered no to Question 8, proceed to Question 10"), crowding the page may compound the confusion. These are problems of layout and design.

Questionnaire Layout

In general, a questionnaire should be laid out in a way that makes the respondent feel good about participating in the survey. The questionnaire should include ample white space; and graphic devices such as separation rules, box rules, pictures, and attractive typefaces should be used routinely. Questionnaires should look professional; they should give the appearance of thoughtfulness, thoroughness, and competency. Take the position of the respondent: If you received a questionnaire that was unattractive, boring, and lacking in gratification, would you complete it? But how would the writer make the instrument attractive?

A Do-It-Yourself Format

Although professional survey services will create attractive and expensive instruments, you might try this simple, do-it-yourself format—and make your own choice of paper, reproduction, visuals, and typefaces. Begin with 8½-by-14-inch (legal size) paper; fold the paper in half lengthwise; and use each 7-inch sheet as one page. For multiple pages, staple unobtrusively on the fold. On the cover page, use clip art, line drawings, or any appropriate artwork, and create a survey title. On the inside cover page, write a brief, cordial letter identifying the research sponsor and the purpose of the research and thanking the respondent for participating.

LEARN BY DOING

Questionnaire Design

Try your hand at laying out a four-page questionnaire of the type just described. This can be either a mock-up without actual questions, or a formal questionnaire written for a grade, at the discretion of your instructor. Visit your library for examples of questionnaires and for question samples.

Proceed as described in the text: Start with legal-size paper and fold two sheets in the middle so that you have four 8½-by-7-inch pages. Staple them neatly on the fold so that the staple is mostly unobtrusive. On the cover page write the title of the survey and the sponsor, and either sketch or suggest an attractive visual. On the first inside page, write a letter of about 7 to 10 lines introducing the survey and encouraging cooperation of respondents. On page three, either write or mock-up a variety of questions including forced-choice, Likert-type, dichotomous, checklists, semantic differential scales, and thermometer scales. Don't forget demographics and visuals.

The finished mock-up or questionnaire should reflect professionalism and thoughtfulness about layout and design.

Using Visuals

Visual elements will enhance the appearance of the instrument and subtly suggest that the sponsor approaches the work with thoughtfulness and responsibility. More than anything else, graphic devices are designed to promote clarity. For the adult respondent, graphics such as lines, boxes, and asterisks can make an instrument easier to follow and comprehend.

When graphics are used with younger respondents, special adaptations may be required. When respondents are very young, data should be gathered by personal interview, not the usual paper-and-pencil instrument. But with some young children, visuals can be useful.

For example, the designer might use a range of "smiley faces," from the broad grin to the heavy scowl, then convert these to a number system. The designer might also include "cute" visuals (e.g., clowns or bears) in the margins or white spaces of the instrument. The intent is to make the exercise attractive and interesting to children. For the fourth through sixth grades, paper-and-pencil instruments might be augmented with models and instruction. With young respondents, it is particularly important for response options to be appropriate to the age. Youngsters, for example, know nothing of percentages; they would be mystified by the semantic differential scale (i.e., a set of adjectives and their opposites aimed at measuring the affect a respondent has for an attitude object); and they might not understand the thermometer scale.

Rather than overreaching the ability of the young respondent, the researcher should conduct a pretest to evaluate comprehension, then pitch the questions and response options to the level of the respondent. If the age group responds well to animal characters and smiley faces, these can be incorporated into the response options. Before conducting a survey of high school students about their use of television, the author solicited the advice of a high school English teacher who knew the language skills of the survey population. She replaced a number of technically correct words with language commonly used by teenagers and thereby improved the comprehensibility of the instrument.

Using Incentives

A common practice is to tell respondents they can have a copy of the completed survey on request. Some sponsors include a modest financial inducement, such as a dollar bill, or even a pencil or other small reward. Some use expensive paper on the premise that a clearly superior product will command more respect. Research indicates that the choice of color is also important. For example, politicians surveying their constituents might use a heavy, brownish or ivory bond paper with a contrasting letterhead and margin line (Sabato, 1984, 38–43; this article includes a review of many of the techniques of successful mail communication) to connote the dignity and significance of government.

In addition, researchers use "live stamps" (not metered envelopes) and, when possible, individually typed or handwritten addresses or signatures, and different typefaces to separate instructions from questions. Finally, checklists and other multiple-response devices reduce the number of separate questions and increase the ratio of data to space. Such lists reduce the need for separate questions, scales, and spacing for repetitive items. They also save time for respondents because they require less reading and present a common context. Similar to the checklist is the matrix format (Babbie, 1989, 149); for an example see Figure 7.1.

COMPLETION

The goal of a questionnaire, of course, is completion by an appropriate respondent. Completion is promoted by both comprehensibility and appearance. But there are other factors as well. The questionnaire should be as brief as possible; it should be

	poor	so-so	don't know	good	excellent
a. availability of my adviser	1	2	3	4	5
b. willingness of my adviser to help	1	2	3	4	5
c. quality of courses in preparing me for employment	1	2	3	4	5
d. fairness in grading of my courses	1	2	3	4	5
e. quality of instruction in my courses	1	2	3	4	5
f. opportunities for interaction with faculty	1	2	3	4	5
g. quality of library holdings in my program	1	2	3	4	5
h. .	1	2	3	4	5
.	.	.	.	.	.
. etc.	.	.	.	.	.
o. .	1	2	3	4	5

The respondent is expected to circle the appropriate number.

FIGURE 7.1 Example of a Matrix

edited and re-edited to weed out needless questions and pointless verbiage. Most of us have a limited tolerance for questionnaires; the writer needs to make the best of the opportunity.

When complete, the instrument should be put aside for a few days, if possible, and then reread for overlooked problems. Has the writer used self as a standard, and is that standard shared by all other respondents? Has the writer made undue assumptions that might be resented by the respondents? The instrument should be prepared from a position of absolute tolerance and openness. Allowances should be made for respondents who have no feeling on the issue.

Avoiding Prestige Bias

Questions that invite prestige responses should be avoided. For example, consider the following question:

> About how many magazines do you read in a month?
> (Circle number)   0   1   2   3   4   5   +

Is there **prestige bias** in the question? The scale accounts for individuals who do not read, and others who read several magazines; therefore, a writer might conclude that the question is fair. On the other hand, the question is stated in the positive, as if people generally are expected to read magazines. If you were the respondent, would you want to report that you were somehow not doing what others were expected to be doing: reading magazines?

There are a couple of ways the researcher can handle this. One is to say, "About how many magazines do you read in a month, *if any?*" Another is to preface the question with a disclaimer such as: "Some people read magazines and some don't; *if* you sometimes read magazines, about how many would you say in a typical month? not any, 1, 2, 3, 4, 5?" This simply acknowledges that not all people read magazines; and it makes the response option "not any" less imputative.

Demand Characteristics

A related type of question embodies **demand characteristics.** It encourages the respondent to make the *expected* response rather than the *accurate* response. The question suggests to the respondent that a certain response is sought.

Response Options

Response options must be exclusive and exhaustive. That is, responses must include all the possibilities; and if a question has five response options, the respondent must answer only one, unless otherwise instructed. For example, suppose the question asked about your income, and gave five options, but none included you;

clearly, this would introduce error and uncertainty into the analysis. Here is an example:

> Please circle the number of the category that best represents your household income:
>
> **a.** $10,000 or under
> **b.** $11,000 to $25,000
> **c.** $26,000 to $50,000
> **d.** $50,000 or over

Looking closely, you can see that a person or family making between $10,000 and $11,000 would be unsure which category to mark; and the person making exactly $50,000 could be in category c *or* d. Another example is represented by the following categories of age:

> **a.** 18–35
> **b.** 35–49
> **c.** 49–55
> **d.** 55 and over

A 35-year-old respondent could mark either category a or b, and a 49-year-old either b or c.

Balanced Response Options

The options provided for a respondent should be **balanced response options,** containing an equal number of positives and negatives. For example, the following question is biased toward the positive because there are three or four positive answers, depending on how you rate "fair," and only one or two negatives.

> Given the president's first 100 days in office, what kind of a job would you say he is doing?
>
> _____ outstanding
> _____ very good
> _____ good
> _____ fair
> _____ poor

Balanced response options might be:

> _____ very good
> _____ mostly good
> _____ so-so, or undecided
> _____ mostly poor
> _____ very poor

Coding and Analysis

The design of questionnaires includes plans for data entry and analysis (Saris, 1991). Foremost, the instrument should include sufficient data to answer the research question. That will require the writer to think out the issue and plan how to test it. Planning the analysis should not be put off until the data are collected. On the questionnaire, column numbers are usually specified in parentheses in the right or left margin for the benefit of those who input the data. Typically, each questionnaire is assigned an *identification number* so that if a question arises about any response, the response can be located and investigated quickly.

LEARN BY DOING

Step 1: Write survey research questions that will establish a person's marital status, education, and income. *Step 2:* Visit your library to review questionnaires of some of the major pollsters such Gallup or Harris. Compare your questions with theirs; discuss the differences, if any.

Question Sequence

The instrument writer's job is to win the cooperation of the respondent and to encourage accurate completion of the instrument. To open the instrument with questions that are difficult, or embarrassing, or overly detailed would be to risk losing a respondent (Babbie, 1989, 150). Hence, the dictum: Open with something that sets the flow gently into more substantive issues. Win the cooperation and acquiescence of the respondent.

Next, organize the instrument in such a way that responses flow rather naturally. Cluster the questions for logical coherence. Decide whether a single question or a set of related questions best measures the topic. Avoid abrupt transitions. Put demographics at or near the end so that, if resistance develops to personal questions such as age and income, the substantive issues will already have been addressed.

Pilot Studies and Pretests

The pilot study is sometimes confused with the pretest. Even experienced researchers tend to lose the distinction between the terms. The **pilot study,** or preliminary study, is an exploration; it leads the way. It sometimes is conducted when the researcher needs knowledge of what can be accomplished by a fuller study. A pilot study uncovers questions and research directions that might not otherwise have been anticipated.

The **pretest,** on the other hand, has somewhat different uses in survey and experimental research. *Experimental researchers* use it most often as a benchmark in an experiment. For example, the experimentalist takes a measure of the respondent (pretest), then administers the experimental variable, then takes a posttest measure. The intent is to learn whether the experimental variable might have caused a change in score from the pretest to the posttest. Experimentalists also use the term pretest loosely to refer to a trial run of the experiment.

Survey researchers also might use a pretest/posttest design, but their most common use is in regard to the utility of an instrument. They use a pretest to see whether an instrument works. More specifically, they administer the instrument to a small sample of respondents primarily to learn whether the instrument presents problems that would confound subsequent analysis. The pretest should detect questions that are poorly written, or that fail to provide sufficient response options, or that do not contribute meaningfully to data analysis.

How many subjects are required for the pilot study and the pretest? If the researcher is concerned with external validity, the pilot study should be conducted with most of the same care and attention given any important study. The sample should be carefully chosen, and the size of the sample should reflect concern for confidence level and error level. The pilot study often is very much like a more formal study; it is exploratory, but it demands accuracy and external validity.

For the pretest, a much smaller sample might be appropriate. The researcher should select individuals who are representative of the population. There might be as few as 15 or 20 people in the pretest, depending on the level of risk that can be tolerated. Although there is no formula for the size of the pretest sample, confidence with an instrument increases with the size of the sample.

QUESTION WRITING

Anyone interested in a career in survey research would need a more thorough introduction to question writing than can be provided here; a university library is likely to have several texts devoted to question writing and questionnaire design. *Survey Questions: Handcrafting the Standardized Questionnaire,* by Jean M. Converse and Stanley Presser (1986), is an 80-page monograph that provides excellent insights into the techniques of question writing and design.

Double-Barreled Questions

One of the more obvious failures of question writing is the **double-barreled question.** For example, a course evaluation instrument asked students: "Is the instructor consistent and fair?" The problem is that an instructor might be highly consistent but at the same time highly unfair. It would be a mistake to think that "consistent and fair" were so closely related that to say yes to one would be to say yes to the other. To avoid this kind of error, a "double barrel," the question writer must constantly play the role of the respondent and consider every possible point of view.

Implicit Negatives

Converse and Presser (1986) have identified **implicit negatives,** or "restrictive" words that seem to have meaning beyond their face value and that confound measurement. An example of this is reported in the *General Social Survey,* conducted annually by the National Opinion Research Center, and sponsored by the University of Chicago and the Roper Center for Public Opinion Research at the University of Connecticut (1989).

One version of a question uses the expression "should allow," while the second version uses "should forbid." The reader might expect that the responses would simply be opposite, but it is not necessarily so. In fact, the different versions can generate strikingly different outcomes, even after correcting for positive–negative direction. Apparently, the expressions carry unequal meaning, connotative baggage that interferes with accurate measurement.

Misapprehension

Especially in the telephone interview, question writers must anticipate the possibility of misunderstood words. Broadcast news writers long have been cautious with sound-alikes: for example, the broadcaster writes *one million*, not *a million*, because *a* is too easily misunderstood for *eight*. Question writers must use the same caution.

Minimum Response Options

Also in the telephone interview, response *options* must be held to a minimum. Imagine, for example, that you have just asked a six-line question, and now ask the respondent: "Would you say that you very strongly agree, strongly agree, moderately agree, or are you undecided, or do you moderately disagree, strongly disagree, or very strongly disagree with the position given in the question?" Excessive response options overload the respondent. The point is to keep the questions and the responses as simple as will be sufficient to accomplish the research goal.

Hypothetical Questions

Suppose a question read: "If radio station WCQK were to change its format of light rock to a format of top-40 rock, would you continue to listen to the station's broadcasts?" The problem is that the question is hypothetical. **Hypothetical questions** may be unavoidable, but they must be evaluated with caution for several reasons. In an audience survey, some respondents may not want to seem disloyal; they do not want to abandon what was their favorite station. Saying yes is simply less stressful than saying no.

A well-known research example of this was published in the 1930s. In a study of attitudes toward race, LaPiere (1934, 230–237) wrote to a large number of hotels and asked if they would accept a certain race of foreigners as guests; a large percentage responded no. But when LaPiere and a foreign couple of that race visited the hotels in person, they encountered very little resistance. The point is that words don't always match behavior. A respondent might say "Yes, I'll listen to the new format," but then quietly drift to another station.

Often, survey questions will ask respondents to recall events or attitudes weeks, months, or even years earlier. Certainly we have good recollection of major events, but the routines of life can blur quickly. Can you recall, for instance, which TV programs you watched last week? Can you recall the number and identity of persons with whom you discussed public affairs in the past month? These are common questions for surveys that include measures of media use.

Converse and Presser (1986) offered five techniques for improving recall:

Bounded recall   gives the respondent a clear time frame, avoiding the tendency to make their response overly inclusive. Bounded recall gives the respondent a beginning and a cutoff time.

Narrowing the reference period   refers to the idea that the researcher should not try to require too much of the respondent's memory. The best strategy is to keep the reference period brief. For example, consider the question: "About how much television do you watch per week?" A better, more narrow alternative might be: "Did you watch television yesterday?" and, if yes, "About how much time did you spend yesterday watching television?" Of course, TV watching may vary from one week to another, and so the question writer might resort to an *average* for a more accurate estimate.

Landmarks   also can be helpful. Landmarks are reference points that help the respondent reconstruct an attitude or event. Suppose a public relations firm wants to know your feelings about oil spills. It might *mark* the question with a reference to the Exxon Valdez spill that dumped millions of gallons of crude oil on the pristine Alaskan shore.

Cues   provide another such strategy. The idea is that respondents' recollections may be improved if they are given cues that will remind them of relevant data. The writer, however, needs to be wary of the fine line between cueing and *leading* a respondent.

Open-Ended Questions

Questions are either *open ended* or *forced choice*. Here is an example of an **open-ended question:** "How do you feel about [raising, lowering] the drinking age in this state?" The question does not suggest response options; the respondent can answer in free form (i.e., the respondent is completely free to respond in a word or in a paragraph). The response might be written in longhand, or recorded on tape, or recorded in notes by the interviewer. Open-ended questions can be extremely useful, especially in exploratory research, but they present huge problems of analysis and interpretation since the responses cannot be readily added up.

How would you go about adding up dozens or hundreds of paragraph responses when the perspective of each individual is different? Regardless of the difficulty, analysis will have to be done. The answers will have to be categorized according to their apparent meaning, theme, direction, complexity, or whatever. This can be done with content analysis, discussed in Chapter 15; but the method is clearly more labor intensive than a simple yes, no, or undecided. Researchers generally avoid open-ended questions unless the conscious decision is made that free-form responses will contribute most importantly to the data.

Forced-Choice Questions

If not open-ended, questions most often are **forced-choice questions.** Typically, the respondent is given only a few options, such as yes–no, agree–disagree 5-point scale, Republican–Democrat. In many cases, those options are sufficient; but in others, the options may be less than clear. An answer may be partly yes, but also partly undecided, or even partly no. In such a case, the respondent is "forced" to choose an alternative that is partly if not wholly in error.

For example, suppose you were asked, "Do you support a state income tax to fund higher education?" Your answer might be, "Yes, but not more than a certain number of dollars per capita," or, "Yes, but only if the tax is certain to go to education." The forced-choice question elicits a response, but not an entirely accurate one, nor a highly informative one. As you can see, *the forced-choice question involves a trade of information and accuracy for ease of coding.*

Filter and Contingency Questions

Filter questions and contingency questions are closely related. The difference between the two is mostly one of perspective of the researcher. Let's say that an interviewee is to be asked a series of four questions on one topic; but clearly, if the respondent knows nothing of the topic, there is no point in continuing past the first question. Hence, we use a *filter question* that is something to this effect: "IF RESPONDENT ANSWERS 'NO' TO QUESTION 1, GO TO QUESTION 5 AND CONTINUE." The first question of the series has the effect of filtering out meaningless subsequent responses.

Contingency questions, on the other hand, are devised to make good use of a positive response. For example, if the interviewee says yes to a particular question, then the interviewer is encouraged to gather deeper data on the topic. For example, if the respondent answers yes, the interviewer is instructed: "IF 'YES,' FOLLOW WITH QUESTIONS 1A, 1B, AND 1C." Filter and contingency questions often are identified by bold lines and arrows. Such graphic devices help the researcher and the respondent follow the proper sequence of the questions.

Omitting "Don't Know" and "Undecided"

Forced-choice questions introduce errors into the data because the response options may not accurately capture the respondent's feelings. Similarly, there are some wins and losses in using the response option, "don't know," or "undecided"

(Ryan, 1980). To fail to include either of these as a response option would be to force some respondents prematurely into a decision; but to include one of them would encourage responses that have minimal value to the research question. Inclusion might also encourage respondents to avoid commitment to a point of view. Nevertheless, most researchers include the "don't know" or "no opinion" option.

Transitions

To create an orderly, even-paced questionnaire, the question writer groups questions for logical flow. If one part of the questionnaire is related to another, the transition can be easy. If the topics are unrelated, a transitional device is created. The device can be *semantic* (e.g., the respondent can be advised: "In Questions 3–7, we addressed the issues of so-and-so; now in the following four questions, it is important that we ask your feelings about this-and-that.")

The transitional device can also be *structural*. For example, the questionnaire might be organized into subsets, with each labeled by Roman numerals and perhaps a heading (e.g., PART I: POLITICAL ISSUES). The questionnaire can also be divided (structured) by bold lines and boxes, numerals, and headings, with the effect of separating the instrument into parts, and hence satisfying the need for clarity and organization.

WRAPPING UP

To this point we have discussed a number of the do's and don'ts of question writing. Now we need to step back and take a broad view of what we are trying to accomplish. The question writer will have to address several issues:

1. Does the questionnaire achieve a sufficient level of accuracy? — *internal validity*
2. Will respondents be encouraged to complete the instrument? — *motivation*
3. Do the questions satisfy the purposes of the research? - *what f(x)*
4. Do the questions and the data permit testing of hypotheses, if appropriate?

For example, in regard to the latter, consider the hypothesis: "Respondents' TV use is positively and significantly correlated with their estimate of the threat of danger in their community." A questionnaire testing this hypothesis must include questions about amount of TV use (including the *kinds* of programs watched) and questions about the presence of danger in the community (e.g., "How likely are you to be mugged while walking in your neighborhood?"). Such issues usually also require several demographic questions; for example, persons who live in high crime areas clearly are more likely to be concerned about muggings. Similarly, the gender of respondents may affect responses. Carpenters have a saying: "Measure twice, and cut once." That good advice can work for questionnaire writers, too; write twice, and measure once.

Here are some do's and don'ts of question writing:

Do

1. Prepare a persuasive introduction to the survey; make it brief and truthful. Level with respondents. Be sincere, tolerant, and pleasant; assure confidentiality, if appropriate. Be firm; don't equivocate. Reassure your respondents by your manner that you are the proper person to be asking these questions. For a mail survey, be clear on when the survey should be returned. Assure respondents of the importance of the issues addressed.
2. Make instructions for the interviewer, if telephone or in person, brief and clear. Assume that if either the interviewer or the respondent can be confused about what to do, he or she will be.
3. Begin the questionnaire with an interesting question; this will encourage respondents to continue.
4. Avoid initial questions that are overly complex or threatening to the self-esteem of respondents. Tough questions have to be entered gently. Collect demographic information at the end of the questionnaire.
5. Use terms and language that require little or no explanation. If a nickel word will replace a five-dollar word, use it.
6. Use closed-end questions. Limit responses to checkmarks, circles, or other simple marks.
7. Make response options exclusive and exhaustive. Respondents should not have to give more than one answer to any question.
8. Ask only one thing per question.
9. Be certain of the relevance of items; if items are irrelevant to some respondents, use filter questions to get around them.
10. Put questions in a logical sequence. Proceed from the general to the specific. George Gallup once addressed this as a "quintamensional" plan of question writing: Has the respondent thought of the issue at all? What are the general feelings on the issue? What are some specific feelings? What are some reasons for these feelings? And, how strongly are the views held?
11. Write clear instructions for filter or contingency items.
12. Use an attractive layout and design. Avoid clutter; be neat.
13. Allow no more than half an hour to complete the survey, preferably less. Assume that the shorter the questionnaire, the greater the completion rate.

Don't

1. Don't use "double-barreled" questions. For example, suppose the question asked: "Do you like dogs and cats?" And then suppose you like one, but not the other; what would you respond? Watch carefully for use of the word *and* in a question.
2. Don't use negatives; they tend to get lost in the reading. Some will confuse *not* with *now*.
3. Don't write leading questions.
4. Don't write questions that suggest prestige bias. For example: "How often do you watch public television?" The question makes the unfortunate assumption that the respondent watches public television at least some, when the opposite may be the case.

5. Don't write "Would you" questions if they can be avoided. Responses in the affirmative are easily given, but they may lack commitment. For example, the respondent might say yes to the question: "Would you listen to radio station WXXX if it changed its music format from Easy Listening to Country?" but the affirmative may only reflect congeniality, not commitment.

Finally, here are some examples of *poor* questions:

1. "What is your annual income?" Respondents may be offended by this invasion of personal data; income "brackets" may be more acceptable (e.g., $15,000–$25,000, $25,001–$35,000).

2. "How many hours in the past 30 days have you spent watching television?" The question has several deficiencies: The respondents probably do not recall their TV watching on all 30 days; even if they did, the arithmetic would be daunting. The question should be replaced: "Some people spend a lot of time watching television, and some don't spend much time at all; in a *typical day* during the past month, about how much time would you say you spent watching television, if any?"

3. "How much alcohol do you drink during the average week?" Questions with evaluative connotations must be handled gingerly, perhaps even approached obliquely rather than head-on.

4. "TV programming is filled with sex and violence. _____ agree _____ disagree." The statement is vague. What is meant by "filled"; how much is full? What is meant by "sex and violence"? Reasonable people can disagree on these terms, and so the terms must be defined carefully, and the respondents must be given a context for their responses.

5. "Do you ever go to the library to check out books?" The respondent may detect a social value implied here, and be inclined to fib to avoid a negative social implication. Furthermore, as a small point of semantics, a person might well spend a lot of time reading at the library without actually *checking out* books. There is also the problem of "ever." If someone checked out a book 18 years ago, is that relevant information for the current survey?

6. "How much time did you spend reading the newspaper yesterday?" The question seems to assume that all respondents read the newspaper yesterday, or should have—creating the imperative for a wrong answer by the respondent. This can be considered a matter of prestige bias, or demand characteristic.

7. "Did you vote in the last election?" Voting is a social value. Nearly all agree voting is important, but not nearly all vote. Don't put the respondent in the position of being embarrassed about this.

8. "How was the service you received from customer assistance?" The respondent may not have received assistance. In any event, the answer is open-ended; is that appropriate?

9. "Some people say that Senator Claghorne is doing an excellent job in office, and some people say he is doing a very good job; what kind of job do *you* think Senator Claghorne is doing? _____ excellent _____ good _____ poor _____ very poor." The question leads the respondent, because it does not suggest that the senator might be doing less well than very good. In addition,

the response options do not match the response suggestions in the body of the question.

10. "What is your religion?" Religious affiliation may be included in demographic data; usually the response options are specified, such as ____ Catholic ____ Jewish ____ Moslem, and so on.

11. "Do you support the president's stand on environmental and educational issues?" The question is double-barreled. A respondent might well support the president on one issue, but not the other; how then would the respondent answer? The question might also be criticized as vague, needing context.

12. "Hello, I'm conducting a poll for Senator Claghorne, a candidate for mayor of our town. If the election were held today, who would you vote for . . . Senator Claghorne, or one of the other candidates?" No explanation needed!

13. "State Attorney General Joe Schmoe is running for mayor of our town against Joe Smith. Which candidate, Schmoe or Smith, is better qualified to be mayor?" The question provides qualifications for Schmoe, but not for Smith, and so is unfair to Smith. This is an unbalanced question.

14. "Would you say you are a Democrat, Republican, or Independent?" The question really should be concerned with the issue of *registration* because the unregistered person *cannot vote*. There is also the problem of *would you* which is speculative and inconclusive.

15. "Do you think the government should spend any more of our tax money cleaning up slums in the United States?" The question is "loaded," or written to favor a response option. The words *any more* and *our tax money* suggest a negative response.

SUMMARY

A questionnaire is called the *instrument* of data collection. It must be written and designed to accomplish three goals: comprehension, accuracy, and completion. Instruments probably should open with questions of greatest interest to the respondent and least threat of offense. Response options must be exclusive and exhaustive. Graphic devices promote clarity. Pretests ensure an improved level of comprehension. Questions that include double meanings, double negatives, and implicit negatives should be avoided.

STUDY QUESTIONS AND EXERCISES

1. How is a pretest different from a pilot study?

2. Put yourself in the position of answering the following hypothetical question: "Radio station W–––– is considering increasing its news staff by five persons and adding 5-minute news summaries at the top of each hour. If we were to do this, do you think your use of the station would increase, decrease, or remain

about the same?" Critique the question and your response. Identify the problems, if any. How else could the question be handled?

3. Put yourself in the place of a respondent to the question: "What is your family income?" Should the question be worded differently? If so, write a proper question and briefly explain it.

NOTES

The author wishes to acknowledge Professor David Sumner, formerly a doctoral student at the University of Tennessee, for help in writing the do's and don'ts.

Thanks also to Constance Milbourn, formerly a Ph.D. student at the University of Tennessee, for help in writing the examples of poor questions.

SOURCES

Babbie, Earl. 1989. *The Practice of Social Research.* 5th ed. Belmont, Calif.: Wadsworth.

Berlo, David K. 1960. *The Process of Communication: An Introduction to Theory and Practice.* New York: Holt, Rinehart & Winston.

Converse, Jean M., and Stanley Presser. 1986. *Survey Questions: Handcrafting the Standardized Questionnaire.* Beverly Hills, Calif.: Sage.

Gallup, George. 1930. A Scientific Method for Determining Reader-Interest. *Journalism Quarterly* 7(1):1–13.

LaPiere, R. 1934. Attitudes vs. Actions. *Social Forces,* 13:230–237, 1934; cited in Tan, Alexis. 1981. *Mass Communication Theories and Research.* Columbus, Ohio: Grid Publishing.

Roper Center for Public Opinion Research, University of Connecticut. 1989. *General Social Surveys, 1972–1989: Cumulative Codebook.* National Opinion Research Center, University of Chicago.

Ryan, Michael. 1980. The Likert Scale's Midpoint in Communications Research. *Journalism Quarterly* 57:305–313.

Osgood, Charles E., George J. Suci, and Percy H. Tannenbaum. [1957] 1971. *The Measurement of Meaning.* Urbana: University of Illinois Press.

Sabato, Larry J. 1984. Mailing for Dollars: A Political Primer on the Subtle Art of Getting You, Dear Friend, to Send Money. *Psychology Today* (October 1984), 38–43.

Saris, William E. 1991. *Computer-Assisted Interviewing.* Beverly Hills, Calif.: Sage.

CHAPTER

8

Survey Research

□
OBJECTIVES

After studying this chapter, you should be able to:

1. Describe three main survey designs: cross-sectional, panel, and trend.

2. Decide which medium to use in collecting data: mail, telephone, or in-person interview.

3. Describe how to conduct a survey; discuss data collection, analysis, training, callbacks, unreached respondents, underage respondents, and proportionality for sex and age of respondents.

4. Explain the advantages and disadvantages of telephone, mail, and face-to-face surveys.

5. Explain how to improve the response rate of a survey.

6. Compare the costs of survey methods.

7. Describe the operation of a focus group.

INTRODUCTION

Definition of Survey Research

The word *survey* comes from the middle English *surveyen* (*Webster's New Collegiate Dictionary*) or the French *surveeir*, meaning "to look over or to see," as in: "She surveyed the horizon from her estate." In research, it means the collection of data from multiple respondents. A single respondent or a small number would be more akin to a case study. In simplest terms, **survey research** refers to the asking of questions and the collection of data.

Survey research is the workhorse of modern social science, enabling the researcher and the practitioner to collect massive amounts of data with speed and efficiency and to bring the data to bear on questions of either applied or theoretical research.

Versatility

Survey research is more versatile, sophisticated, and elegant than many would imagine. Although it does not make laboratory experiments obsolete, in many cases it achieves a level of statistical control that makes experimentation unnecessary. It can address questions of administrative decision making or issues of theoretical research.

How can a survey substitute for an experiment? A comparison of the methods will illustrate. In order to find whether men and women respond similarly to newspapers' letters to the editor, the experimenter would take one approach, the survey researcher another.

The experimenter in a laboratory setting might rely on observation, or measure pupil dilation, or perhaps gather paper-and-pencil responses. The drawback to the laboratory setting is the question of whether the respondents would respond differently in their natural setting. For example, in the laboratory, they are being instructed to read the paper; would they read it differently at home?

The survey researcher investigating the same question would use a mail questionnaire or an interview in a natural setting to learn whether respondents read the letters, how often, with what intensity, and whether they subsequently discussed the letters with others.[1]

The survey questionnaire might even include a behavioral item, such as whether the reader used the letters in initiating other social contact.

Survey responses provide information and control. As in an experiment, the survey researcher can investigate complex theoretical relationships while controlling for a variety of variables. For example, the survey researcher can ask whether reading letters to the editor is a function of (a) involvement in public affairs, (b) education, (c) wealth, (d) membership in civic clubs, (e) left-handedness, or (f) whatever. And all of these variables can be studied in one survey. This kind of control is powerful because it helps to rule out competing explanations without the contrived atmosphere of the laboratory.

THE SURVEY METHOD

The method of survey research is very straightforward. The researcher identifies a sample of elements or respondents, then collects data from each. If the survey *sample* is the same as the *population,* the survey is a *census.* Most often the sample is merely a small, representative subset of the larger population. For example, the researcher might identify a sample of 400 radio listeners in order to estimate the listening practices of the 50,000 residents of a community.

Survey Designs

There are three principal "designs" for survey research (Shoemaker and McCombs, 1989). One is the *cross-sectional survey*, in which all elements of the population are represented. Another is the *panel survey*, in which a sample, probably cross-sectional, is interviewed more than once in a given period. And the third is the *trend survey*, in which a research topic is tracked across different samples over time.

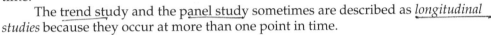

The trend study and the panel study sometimes are described as *longitudinal studies* because they occur at more than one point in time.

Data Collection

The two most common methods of collecting data are the mailed questionnaire and the telephone survey. Paper-and-pencil instruments are most often administered in person, such as in a classroom, or at the shopping mall, or by mail to the home or business of the respondent; telephone questionnaires are usually completed by the interviewer, either in pencil or on a computer screen.

Analysis

Survey data analysis can be very simple or very complex. At the simplest level, the analyst counts the responses to an item and reports the results in raw frequencies or in percentages. However, this level of analysis seldom is very satisfactory because it overlooks important relationships among variables.

For example, one item the analyst might report is the percentage of persons who read the paper daily; another item might be the average age of readers. But it would be more informational to see the two items tabulated together. This probably would show that readership is importantly related to age—that reading increases to a peak age and then diminishes. This *cross-tabulation*, for large samples is most easily done by computer. Survey analysis can become very complex with multiple variable cross-tabulations and sophisticated statistical procedures. Any analysis beyond the simplest level probably would be enhanced by informed use of the computer.

THE INFLUENCE OF OPINION POLLS

Mass media managers today are using surveys both for management and planning purposes, such as audience analysis; and for news purposes, such as political opinion polls. Most conspicuous are public opinion polls, the kind that show one candidate leading another by some margin or polls showing a percentage of Americans favoring some issue. News polls have become so common and so important that their influence in national policy-making is being debated. For example, as the nomination of Clarence Thomas to a seat on the U.S. Supreme Court was being presented to the Senate, a news story on the ABC Television Network (July 2, 1991) reported a national opinion poll that said only 54 percent of Americans believed the nominee was "a good choice," and 33 percent were undecided. The poll clearly said Thomas was not a consensus choice, and it cast a long shadow on the nomination. Since polls purport to represent voters and all citizens, this put considerable pressure on members of Congress and the president. Members of the Congress, of course, do not relish the opportunity to vote from positions of weakness. But as it turned out, Thomas was approved despite the weak public approval.

In other cases, special interest groups use survey data to support positions that they wish to promote to members of Congress. For example, an organization called U.S. English conducted a mail survey in 1991 that apparently was intended to convince Congress to put forward a constitutional amendment that would declare: "The English language shall be the official language of the United States Government." The survey asked: "Should your U.S. Senators and Representatives vote to pass this Amendment?" Clearly the intent was to take this measure of popular interest in the language issue to Congress as a persuasive device. Discussion of it here does not suggest support or disapproval of the topic, but merely makes the point that the survey is being used as a political instrument.

Government by Opinion Poll?

Some people probably see the influence of survey research in government as unsettling. For example, does America want or need "government by opinion poll"? But what could be more democratic than a popular survey? Why would anyone oppose political solutions based on the wishes of the majority? For one thing, there is the risk of error in sampling or in measurement, especially when opinions are closely divided and when issues are highly technical and complex. Such an error would risk wrongly promoting a less popular position. For another thing, Americans are not equally informed on all topics. How much sense would it make to survey individuals on a topic for which they are ill informed?

A third point is that the outcome of an opinion poll will depend on the time in the information stream that the survey occurred. A poll today might produce a different outcome than one two days from now, especially if the topic is of emerging interest.

What Are the Alternatives?

You probably can see that there is at least room for doubt about the wisdom of "government by opinion poll." On the other hand, what are the alternatives? Direct constituent contact? Since not all of us have easy or equal access to politicians, that could be a problem. Word-of-mouth estimates of public opinion? Same problem. Would it make sense for politicians to counsel only with people who consider themselves to be highly informed on a topic? Certainly not; anyone can have a stake in an issue, regardless of how much they know. I may know little about reforestation, but I certainly have a stake in the environmental health of the nation.

So, if political leaders are expected to represent broadly the interests and attitudes of their constituents, scientific survey research may be a godsend. It seems very likely that the nation's leaders will use survey research more and more. One can only hope the process will not be abused. The best defense against abuse is knowledge of the methods.

Mass Media Applications

Previous chapters provided a research context: the rules of sampling, the techniques of questionnaire design, and some rules of measurement. Now you are in a position to conduct a survey research project. Remember that the research can be either theoretical or applied, analytical or descriptive.

Suppose that you wanted to survey a newspaper audience, or a TV or radio audience, or the constituents of a political candidate; how would you proceed? Where would you even start?

Deciding the Survey Medium

One early decision would involve the question of whether to conduct the survey by mail, telephone, or face-to-face. Each method has important benefits and liabilities, and the researcher must weigh these carefully. The choice of interview method will depend on the size of the sample, the nature of the topic, the availability of labor and money to support the research, and the speed with which the research must be done.

For example, a topic that is complex might require a mail or face-to-face interview. An emphasis on speed of data collection might require a telephone interview. Having personnel on hand to conduct interviews might encourage a telephone survey rather than a mail survey. A topic that will require a long interview might be suited to face-to-face interviewing.

TELEPHONE INTERVIEWING

When to Use the Telephone

The telephone interview is appropriate to research situations that are relatively uncomplicated and demand quick turnaround.

For example, suppose you have a client who needs to know how many people watched a particular TV program, and you need a quick survey so that you can make some adjustments in the client's advertising strategy. You will not want to wait weeks for a mailed questionnaire to be returned; and face-to-face interviews will be slow and expensive, especially for this limited purpose. Your preference might be a telephone "callout" or telephone "coincidental" to identify persons tuned to the program at the time of the call. This would serve your limited purpose with speed and efficiency.

Telephone surveys are not well suited to survey issues that demand anonymity and confidentiality. For example, if the survey dealt with personal intimacy, or classroom cheating, or any especially sensitive topic, a live telephone interview would not encourage candor. There is also the possibility that the respondent will be suspicious about the authenticity of the interview. (Cases have been reported in which persons falsely claiming to be survey researchers asked sensitive questions for prurient interests.)

Interview Length

The telephone interview typically is brief, preferably not more than 5 to 10 minutes, although researchers have observed that some respondents who agree to cooperate are highly patient. They have been known to stay on the line as long as 30 to 40 minutes. Still, the researcher should not count on that.

When the telephone interview is very brief, topics either will be relatively uncomplicated or will not be explored fully. Most often, the interview will involve simple questions and simple responses. An experienced interviewer will conduct 5 to 7 interviews per hour. In contrast to that, if the interviews were conducted by traveling to a respondent's home, it is doubtful that the completion rate would exceed one per hour.

Some Interview Problems

The telephone interview includes some risk of *interviewer bias*. For example, the interviewer who disregards instructions, is bored or tired, or improvises questions can introduce unintended meanings. If questions are improvised (i.e., inconsistent from respondent to respondent), the responses cannot be properly summed.

There is also the occasional problem of *fictional interviews*—cases in which the interviewer calls a friend or relative and only pretends to have completed a bona fide interview. The research supervisor must be alert for this. Some telephone systems allow for *unobtrusive monitoring* (which means the research supervisor can listen to the interview without being noticed by the interviewer or the interviewee.) In addition, supervisors should make *random callbacks* to interviewees to verify that the interview proceeded properly.

The telephone interview is pervasive in today's market; but it is also *invasive.* It is projected into people's homes without their invitation. Some research firms are using computer-driven, prerecorded interview tapes. "Hello. This is Hal, the computer," says the obviously recorded message. What would be your response to a recorded interview? Cooperation or incredulity? Some respondents resent the recorded interview, while others respond to it with amusement.

People with unlisted numbers who are reached by random digit dialing can be querulous. "How did you get my number?" they sometimes will ask indignantly. And because most telephone interviews are completed between 6:00 and 9:30 P.M., the hours most people will be at home and awake, the interviewer risks further quarrel by interrupting dinner, the news, or whatever.

Sales under the Guise of Research. Respondents sometimes find that "survey research" is really a sales pitch in disguise. Such deceits create hardships for survey research. They damage legitimate survey research by association, and they build a resistance to subsequent cooperation.

The "Unreachables." Many would-be respondents cannot be reached with a reasonable amount of effort. For example, suppose Mr. Smith was called on successive evenings but was never reached. How many calls are enough? Interviewers usually make two or three callbacks (or up to four or five), on different days and at different times, but usually within two days; if no success, they move on to the next telephone number. In general, uncertainty about the validity of the sample increases with nonresponse. Nevertheless, a certain amount of nonresponse seems unavoidable.

Sex of Respondent. If women account for about 51 percent of a population, women should account for about 51 percent of the sample, but this does not often happen without special effort. Unless precautions are taken, women will be overrepresented in most telephone samples because women are somewhat more likely to answer the telephone.

The researcher can use one method or another to equalize the number of men, but each is problematical. The interviewer can ask: "May I speak to the man of the house, please?" only to find there is no man of the house, or that he just died, or that "he hasn't been seen in months." The respondent, not knowing the need for sample distribution, might resent that approach. To overcome this, some researchers resort to the question: "May I speak to the person age 18 or older at your house who had the most recent birthday?"

Assuming men and women are equally likely to have a birthday in any month, that approach should distribute responses from men and women evenly. There is some evidence that this results in the best sample distribution (Salmon and Nichols, 1983, 270–276). However, it also introduces an opportunity for confusion and delay. Imagine the respondent, unsure of the birthday order in the home, shouting to a cousin: "Yo! Betty Jean! When did you turn 18? Middle of last month, or the month before? Does your birthday come before Uncle Henry's? You don't know? When will Dad be home so I can ask?"

The author prefers a simple question that appeals to the respondent's fairness: "Ms. [respondent], where possible we are interviewing a woman at one house and a man at another, so that we can report an equal number of each; is there an adult male member of your household to whom I could speak?" If there is no man in the home, the interviewer thanks the person and hangs up, or completes the interview and hopes to balance it in a subsequent call. Unfortunately, although some researchers will argue the methods are robust enough to tolerate minor irregularities, uncertainties tend to defeat the strict principles of sampling.

IMPROVING THE RESPONSE RATE

Nonresponse can result from travel, hours of employment, illness, outright nonco-operation, or a host of other conditions. Although a certain amount of nonresponse is inevitable, some steps can be taken to minimize it.

Training Interviewers

For example, interviewers should be carefully *selected* and *trained*. Recruitment and selection of good interviewers is not a science, but it is clear that not all persons are equally good interviewers. A good interviewer is conscientious, bright, sensitive, careful, and thoughtful; encourages cooperation by tone or manner, and recognizes and corrects problems of understanding. Good interviewing minimizes the extraneous errors that can creep into a survey.

Once the interviewer is recruited and selected, training must be thorough. The interviewer needs to have a clear idea of what is to be accomplished, familiarity with the research instrument, knowledge of how to handle the unexpected responses that can crop up during an interview, sensitivity to the importance of errors, and sensitivity to the importance of congeniality.

 The interviewer should be instructed not to ad-lib interview questions. If explanations are permitted, then the interviewer needs to know the range of explanations. The risk exists that a single word change in a question can change a person's response.

Choosing the Interview Hours

Response rate can be improved by careful selection of the hour of the interview. For most telephone research, the hours of 6:00 to 9:30 P.M. are prime. Earlier calls might find the respondent not at home, or perhaps not yet "unwound" from the stress of the workday. After 9:30 P.M., respondents are increasingly likely to be settled for the evening, or to be irritated by a phone call awakening their youngsters.

Even the slot from 6:00 to 9:30 P.M. is problematical; a respondent who is busy frying chicken, or who is seated for dinner, or who is in the middle of a favored news program, can be a little resentful of the intrusion. But overall, early evening seems the best opportunity for successful telephone interviews.

With more women working outside the home, fewer face-to-face interviews are being completed in-home during working hours. Because so few adults are at home during the hours 8:00 A.M. to 5:00 P.M., the interviewer should secure advance permission and appointments for interviews. This will reduce the number of "not-at-homes." At the same time, evening interviews present special hazards; security is decreased, and working hours are fewer.

 Kalton (1983) proposed some other ways to encourage a good response rate (1983). First, convince the respondent of the *value of the survey*. For example, let the respondent know that the survey will contribute to public understanding of an issue. This kind of assurance will help the respondent feel that the time is well spent.

Identification of a *benevolent sponsor* can also be beneficial. For example, a survey by the university's communication research center will find less resistance than a survey by a retail or industrial source. Respondents should be reassured that their responses will be *anonymous and confidential,* especially if the survey deals with sensitive or controversial issues. Finally, failing to reach a respondent, the research supervisor should arrange for a given number of callbacks. Each of these practices should contribute to an improved response rate.

Age of Respondent

The older the respondent, the more likely the person will be at home to answer the telephone. This often results in a disproportionate number of respondents in the higher age brackets. It should be corrected by careful sampling, and if necessary, by weighting.

The age of the telephone respondent may not be evident to the interviewer, and to ask it can be a little awkward. To ask a 30-plus-year-old, for example, if he or she is over 18 can create some guffaws.

If age is an important criterion, and it usually is, then age probably should be stipulated in the brief introduction that precedes the interview. For example, the interviewer might say: [Company name] is interviewing persons between the ages of 19 and 91 in connection with . . . " This gives the person on the phone the opportunity to pass. Otherwise, the interview might be completed only to find at the end that the respondent is underage.

Introducing the Survey

Each telephone interview should be preceded by a brief introduction stating the purpose of the research and the sponsor. The introduction also asks permission of the respondent to be interviewed. The wording of the introduction is very important. For example, the introduction should indicate what the survey is about without leading the respondent in any direction. The request for permission to conduct the interview should be stated in a way that minimizes refusals. For example, the interviewer might say:

> Ms. Smith, my name is Mary and I am calling for the Five-Star Research and Design Company. We are conducting research on how newspaper subscribers feel about the recent changes in the *Daily Gazette. May I ask you just a few questions please?*

That polite introduction will win the hearts of some respondents, but others will say, "Well, I'd rather not participate." The interviewer might do better *not to invite refusal,* for example, by substituting the last sentence in our example with: "I would appreciate it if I could ask you just a few questions. First, do you think . . . ?" (and go on to ask the first interview question). This gives the respondent the option to continue or stop, but does not encourage refusal.

MAIL SURVEYS

Advantages

The mail survey has several advantages over the telephone interview:

1. The mail can reach a large number of people more or less simultaneously.
2. Since topics that involve some complexity can be addressed (so to speak) via the written word, respondents will have time to read and reflect on questions.
3. The mail sample frame is not constrained by geography, even by national boundaries.
4. Mail surveys do not require cumbersome administration, such as the hiring and training of interviewers and the maintenance of extensive work space.
5. Mail survey responses can be entirely anonymous, although anonymity can complicate follow-up mailings.
6. Unobtrusive mail surveys can be completed at a time, a pace, and a place that are convenient for the respondent.

Mail surveys are especially suited to small and specialized populations whose members are likely to be interested in the research and the outcome, assuming the mailing list is current and comprehensive.

Disadvantages

On the negative side, the return rate for mail questionnaires can be poor. Returns of 30 or 40 percent are common, and 60 percent can be considered good. With a poor return, the researcher again has the problem of uncertainty about whether nonrespondents are different from respondents, and therefore whether respondents are different from the population. In the absence of evidence to indicate external validity, the report of a mail survey with a poor return rate should be heavily qualified with disclaimers.

Disadvantages of the mail survey include the researcher's loss of control over *who* fills it out and *when* it is completed. A questionnaire aimed at a TV station manager, for example, might be passed to a promotion director (if completed at all). Furthermore, suppose the questionnaire is slow in being returned; the issues might have changed substantially in the time since the mailing. In addition, there is the risk that the questionnaire, in the absence of an authority figure, will not be taken seriously by the respondent. Finally, there is the risk that some questions will not be adequately comprehended by the respondent. (We would hope that a pretest would identify such a problem, but we could not be certain.)

On a positive note, Dillman (1978) has written that, if proper procedures are followed, mail return rates can reach 70 or 80 percent. Mail survey returns probably are best when motivated respondents are part of a smallish and cohesive population, such as members of a professional organization.

There is extensive literature on survey research that leads to the prescription of certain beneficial practices in mail research. One valuable resource for the career mail survey researcher is Dillman's book *Mail and Telephone Surveys.*

Some Mail Survey Techniques

The mail survey should be accompanied by a brief persuasive *letter* identifying the purpose and the sponsor and soliciting cooperation. In addition, the letter probably should give a *deadline.* That may seem odd, for the researcher has no control except goodwill; but without a deadline the responses may dribble in for months. At some point, they will have to be cut off. The researcher can gauge this by monitoring the returns; judgment will dictate the timing.

The mailing should be assembled with great care. Small points can make a big difference. For example, research has shown that the use of *real stamps* rather than a postage meter can be subtly influential; stamps suggest a personal touch. Similarly, a *personal signature* rather than a duplicated or stamped signature can be impressive. The style and tone of the cover letter can win or alienate other respondents. If possible, the letter should offer an *incentive* even if only the assurance that the results will be beneficial.

It is very important that the survey *not* be excessively *long.* Few respondents have the patience to spend longer than 15 to 20 minutes on a questionnaire that they might receive in the mail. Finally, the researcher should consider *prenotification* of respondents and a *follow-up* or reminder mailing, and should pay very close attention to the *appearance* of the survey instrument.

Anonymity and hence confidentiality are more easily protected in the mail survey than in the telephone survey. The researcher simply mails out questionnaires and awaits their return, not knowing the identity of the respondents. But this makes for some problems, and it raises ethical questions: Should the researcher keep some type of secret code to identify respondents? No. Should the researcher put a code under the staple so that it will not be seen? No. On a follow-up mailing, should the letter include another questionnaire? Only as a last resort, for there would then be no way to know whether a person completed more than one instrument. Not knowing who respondents are means that any follow-up mailing would have to go to respondents as well as nonrespondents; this increases the mail cost.

Abuses in Mail Survey Research

What abuses can be observed? A poorly trained researcher might flood the market with questionnaires whose intent is confused and whose interpretation would be impossible. Alternately, a survey source might send a "loaded" questionnaire to political constituents with the purpose of justifying a political position. In another scenario, a respondent's confidentiality might be compromised by a corporation that sends supposedly confidential answers to a third party for personal contact. To reduce the likelihood of abuse, surveys should be supervised by persons trained and knowledgeable in the techniques and ethics of the field.

Mail Survey Expenses

In the recent past, mail surveys were clearly cheaper than telephone surveys, but the cost difference today has decreased sharply. A two-page questionnaire, for example, would require one regular first-class stamp plus the cost of return mail. Questionnaires of several pages would require two or three stamps, dramatically increasing costs. Nonresponses would inflate the cost of the survey, since the researcher might have to send out twice as many surveys as would be expected back.

Here is the arithmetic of mail costs: If the researcher wants a return of 400, and expects a return rate of 40 percent, then a total of 1,000 questionnaires would have to be mailed. Multiply 1,000 times the cost of one stamp, then two, then three, depending on the number of pages in the survey instrument, to see the cost of the initial mailing. (At 1992 postal rates, this cost would range from $300 to $900.)

Each questionnaire must include a business-return envelope, and so each return would cost about the same as each questionnaire going out. Multiply the per-questionnaire cost by the number of returns. For 400 returns, this would amount to $120 or so at one stamp per return, or $360 for at three stamps per return.

Additional costs might include a presurvey postcard and a timely follow-up mailing. These could cost another several hundred dollars. Finally, there is the cost of writing the questionnaire, having it printed, and "stuffing" it into envelopes. These things require labor, and the labor must be compensated. You can see that a simple mail survey can become expensive.

Comparing Mail Costs with Telephone Costs

How does the cost of a mail questionnaire compare with the cost of a telephone interview? If telephone calls are local, then costs are primarily in regard to interviewer time. Long-distance or special line charges will increase the costs significantly, however. An interviewer might conduct five to seven interviews per hour, depending on questionnaire length and the number of incomplete calls.

To complete a telephone sample of 400 could require calling 750 or 800 numbers; if five interviews are completed per hour, it will take 80 hours to complete 400. If an interviewer is paid $6 to $8 per hour, the cost is $480 to $640. As with the mail survey, there are other expenses; telephone services, toll charges, monitoring systems, interviewer recruitment, training and supervision, insurance costs, and other overhead costs. Still, for a survey of about 400 respondents, the cost differences between mail and telephone have become smaller.

FACE-TO-FACE INTERVIEWS

As you can imagine, face-to-face (in-home) interviewing is expensive. An in-home interview typically will be lengthy, often running an hour or longer. With travel time, only a few interviews will be completed by a person in a workday. A rate of 6 completions per day for 400 completed interviews would amount to almost 67 *workdays* (i.e., 67×8 hours $\times$ hourly wage). And the costs are not limited to hourly wages; they include travel time, training, insurance, supervision, and office space. Because they are relatively slow and expensive, in-home interviews are typically reserved for projects with special purposes and special funding.

Advantages

There are, however, genuine benefits of the face-to-face interview. The interviewer can watch the respondent—gauging comprehension, following up where beneficial, filling in with explanations as needed, probing to uncover not just responses but *accurate* responses. The in-person interview might be beneficial when the research question is highly complex or technical. The telephone interviewee, for example, cannot be expected to remain on the line for 45 to 90 minutes, the amount of time a face-to-face interview might require.

The face-to-face interview is appropriate when the research topic is sensitive (i.e., highly personal, or perhaps likely to evoke avoidance). For example, telephone interviews about personal intimacies might meet resistance, even though the research is intellectually and scientifically warranted. On the other hand, a respondent might more readily commit personal information to an interviewer whose presence suggested confidence and understanding, but not embarrassment.

Disadvantages

At the same time, there are disadvantages to face-to-face interviews. At the time of this writing, liability insurance was becoming increasingly important but expensive. Suppose, for example, that your interviewer accidentally broke a precious item in the home of a respondent; worse, suppose the interviewer was accused of assault or theft, and your company was sued for negligence. In litigious America, you are expected to have insurance.

There is also the unfortunate fact that in some neighborhoods the interviewer's safety cannot be assured. In those neighborhoods, the telephone is a more efficient research technique. Although it is true that not all respondents can be reached by telephone, it is also true that not all respondents are available to the face-to-face interviewer.

Other Survey Designs

Although mentioned earlier in this chapter, the *panel study* deserves elaboration. It is a design in which the same individuals are surveyed at intervals, usually two or three times and possibly over a long period. The panel study is very useful in any research involving change. For example, a panel study would allow the researcher to trace changes in the electorate's attitudes toward candidates and issues, or toward media issues such as respect for the First Amendment. This kind of research can take place over months or years.

As might be expected, there are difficulties associated with the method. For example, gaining the cooperation of individuals is more difficult for repeated interviews than for the one-time interview, although some respondents take a certain enjoyment in being part of the panel. Another concern is *sample mortality*, the loss of members of the panel because of illness, relocation, or any of a host of other reasons. A survey panel that exists for several months almost certainly will lose a portion of its members. If the loss is excessive, then the validity of the survey will be in doubt.

Another special survey design is the *cohort study.* The cohort is a group of individuals having a statistical factor, such as age or social class or education, in common. For example, a cohort might be the persons who graduated from high school in 1966; the persons who attended a given university; or the persons who share any specified experience.

Some researchers have used a *sociometric design*; this might start with a small set of individuals chosen for known qualities, such as community involvement. Those individuals would be interviewed and then asked for the names of other individuals whom they also know to be active in the community. In this way, the researcher can find a special sample of individuals.

Computer-Assisted Surveys

Where does the computer fit into the modern scheme of survey research? Certainly the potential of the computer is great. It can reduce labor while increasing speed and accuracy. Reducing labor means possibly reducing costs. Increasing speed and accuracy and reducing costs means increasing user satisfaction.

What once was known as computer-assisted telephone interviewing (CATI) now has several monikers, all under the name computer-assisted data collection (CADAC; Saris, 1991). For example there are computer-assisted personal interviews (CAPI), computerized self-administered questionnaires (CSAQ), computer-assisted panel research (CAPAR), and touchtone data entry (TDE).

Since the 1970s, computerization has led to several survey interview innovations. For example, some respondents are asked to sit at a computer terminal and enter responses directly. Some researchers are experimenting with mail surveys by means of computer disks. More conventionally, the interviewer sits at a terminal and enters the telephoned responses as given. Each approach eliminates the paper questionnaire and subsequently the labor of analysis. Each also speeds the analysis.

One of the big problems in self-administered or other computer-assisted interviews, aside from the cost and maintenance of the technology, is in the organization of the computer program (Nicholls and Groves, 1986; Groves and Nicholls, 1986). Whereas the face-to-face interviewer can nimbly adjust the paper instrument to accommodate a variety of responses and problems, a computer screen full of written alternatives (called *branching and skipping*) can be a little messy. Every complication increases the risk of data loss.

But today these problems have largely been ironed out, and it now appears that professional polling firms are committing heavily to computer applications. No one software package dominates survey research, but a program called Questionnaire Programming Language (QPL) by National Technical Information Service is widely used in government research. Another popular program is Microcase Aggregate Analysis Program, put out by Cognitive Development (Bitter, 1992, 880).

A summary of the strengths and weaknesses of telephone, mail, and face-to-face surveys based on selected criteria is given in Table 8.1.

FOCUS GROUP RESEARCH

Chapter 4 introduced you to some success stories in focus group research and to the issue of sampling in focus group research. This section will briefly introduce the *method* of the focus group.

Focus groups are extremely popular in research today. Why? First, users point to success stories—the discovery of important insights that might have been missed by other research methods. Second, focus groups are intuitively appealing because they do not necessarily require the elaborate statistical and methodological designs that mystify and complexify interpretation. Finally, they can be efficient: They are quick, to the point, and insightful. Managers and investors find them understandable.

At the same time, the method is not flawless. The first of two principal concerns is in regard to external validity. As argued in Chapter 4, focus groups should not be generalized to populations. Nevertheless, the pressure to generalize findings is great, particularly when sampling is not fully understood. The opportunity for misuse of the data is clear.

The second concern is in regard to level of analysis. Most focus group data are qualitative, which means the interpretation tends to be subjective. The risk is

TABLE 8.1 A Comparison of Telephone, Mail, and Face-to-Face Surveys on Selected Criteria

	Mail	Telephone	Face to Face
Cost per response	low[a]	medium	high
Speed of initiation	medium	high	low
Speed of return	low	high	medium
Number of interviews completed	low	high	high
Design constraints	medium	high	low
Convenience for respondent	high	medium	low
Risk of interviewer bias	low	medium	medium
Interview intrusiveness	low	high	high
Administrative bother	low	low	high
Survey control	medium	high	high
Anonymity of response	high	medium[b]	low

[a]Recently, mail costs have risen to such an extent that the cost difference between mail and telephone today is small.
[b]In the case of random digit dialing, responses may actually by anonymous.

that enthusiastic researchers or managers will read meaning into the data that others would not share. In short, focus group research raises special challenges for reliability and internal validity.

Quantitative or Qualitative?

At the beginning of this chapter, *survey research* was defined as the collection of data from multiple respondents. Focus group research is an extension of survey research that diverges from conventional quantitative methods in regard to sampling and data analysis. Focus groups typically are very small, and their data are words and sentences, not numbers. Although some researchers convert the words to numbers, as in content analysis (Chapter 15), most focus group analysis is qualitative.

How a Focus Group Works

The focus group is initiated when a researcher or a service research firm identifies a small number of people to participate. The participants may be identified from mailing lists, the telephone book, or preferred grouping. The focus group typically is homogeneous; members share certain demographic characteristics, although they should not be related by birth or marriage. If members were widely different, discussion might be impaired.

Participants most often are paid a fee (e.g., $20). They are invited to appear at an office or conference location where they are treated to light refreshments before settling into the discussion. The atmosphere is comfortable and cozy, conducive to open and uninhibited talk. The room might be equipped with a one-way mirror; and the proceeding might be videotaped or audiotaped, and discreetly monitored by research sponsors. The researcher or a surrogate serves as moderator, gently leading the discussion from a prepared outline of questions or topics. The moderator should blend easily into the group, but not lead participants in any positive or negative comments.

The moderator has several important tasks. One is to keep participants talking about the topic at hand—usually a product or service. Another is to ensure that the discussion is not dominated or bullied by one or two participants. Another is to encourage all to participate freely. The moderator can prepare an agenda of questions to keep the discussion in the desired scope.

Often, the one- to two-hour session is taped and studied at length (Churchill, 1991; Wimmer and Dominick, 1991). Analysis of participants' comments may be entirely anecdotal or observational, or it may involve techniques of content analysis such as counting recurrent themes and assessing feeling intensity.

How many focus group sessions are needed? There is no one answer to this. Often the research will stop after two to four sessions, but some projects will require a dozen sessions or more. One rule of thumb might be that when replications no longer bring significant results, interviews should cease.

SUMMARY

Survey research is the workhorse of social science. Versatile in method, surveys permit analysis of complex theoretical relationships while controlling for numerous independent variables. Three principal survey designs are the cross-sectional, panel, and trend surveys. Each of the three media of survey presentation—telephone, mail, and face-to-face—has advantages and disadvantages. Women and older people are more likely to respond to telephone surveys. Abuses in survey research include sales under the guise of research, poorly written questions, and violation of anonymity or confidentiality. Computer-assisted telephone interviews are increasingly common among polling organizations, and focus group research is popular in industry and marketing today.

STUDY QUESTIONS AND EXERCISES

1. Argue one of the following positions: (a) Opinion polls are good news for democracy; at last, the political representatives of the people have the ability to solicit the points of view of people beyond their immediate circle of constituent advisers; (b) Opinion polls are a threat to democracy; opinion polls are not always accurate, and too few people are sufficiently informed on complex issues for opinion polls to be instruments of political decision making.

2. What are some advantages and disadvantages of mail, telephone, and face-to-face interviews?

3. Step back, now, and take the broad view: What are some uses of survey research? What are some strengths and weaknesses?

4. What are some ways to ensure a proper proportion of respondents by age and sex?

5. Explain how the survey outcome is affected when an interviewer ad-libs a question, or fails to use exactly the same question with each respondent.

6. The text says that surveys today are both pervasive and *invasive*. What is meant by that?

NOTE

1. As an aside, the letters section is usually a popular part of the newspaper. In conversation, people sometimes will ask: "Did you see the letter from [name of person] in the paper today?" There is considerable evidence that people read the letters and use them in forming their own opinions.

SOURCES

Bitter, Gary G. 1992. Social Science Applications of Computers. In *Encyclopedia of Computers.* Vol. 2. New York: Macmillan.

Churchill, Gilbert A., Jr. 1991. *Marketing Research: Methodological Foundations.* Chicago: Dryden Press.

Dillman, Don A. 1978. *Mail and Telephone Surveys: The Total Design Method.* New York: Wiley.

Frey, James H. 1983. *Survey Research by Telephone.* Beverly Hills, Calif.: Sage.

Groves, R. M., and W. L. Nicholls, II. 1986. The Status of Computer-Assisted Telephone Interviewing: Part II. Data Quality Issues. *Journal of Official Statistics* 2:117–134.

Kalton, Graham. 1983. *Introduction to Survey Sampling.* Beverly Hills, Calif.: Sage.

Nicholls, W. L., II, and R. M. Groves. 1986. The Status of Computer-Assisted Telephone Interviewing. *Journal of Official Statistics* 2:93–115.

Salmon, Charles T., and John Spicer Nichols. 1983. The Next-Birthday Method of Respondent Selection. *Public Opinion Quarterly* 47(2):270–276.

Saris, Willem E. 1991. *Computer-Assisted Interviewing.* Newbury Park, Calif.: Sage.

Shoemaker, Pamela J., and Maxwell E. McCombs. 1989. Survey Research. In *Research Methods in Mass Communication.* 2d ed. Ed. Guido H. Stempel III and Bruce H. Westley. Englewood Cliffs, N.J.: Prentice-Hall.

Wimmer, Roger D., and Joseph R. Dominick. 1991. *Mass Media Research: An Introduction.* Belmont, Calif.: Wadsworth.

U.S. English: 1991 National Opinion Survey. (818 Connecticut Avenue, N.W., Suite 200, Washington, D.C. 10006) (Questionnaire number 304#0006554).

9

The Experimental Method

After studying this chapter, you should be able to:

1. Describe four kinds of experimental control: variable, statistical, environmental, and sample.

2. Describe two notational systems of experimental design.

3. Apply a notational system to a description of an experimental research project.

4. Critique the validity of an experimental research project.

5. Recite some examples of experimental research.

A CASE STUDY

Anyone who regularly watches the evening TV news or who reads newspapers from several towns knows that there is great similarity in content from newscast to newscast and newspaper to newspaper. How does it happen? Does someone say, "OK, here's what's news today"? Is there a shared ethic for what constitutes news? Is the similarity a function of advertising revenue—the need to select stories that draw a crowd? Is it a matter of organizational policy, time of day, or the number of people on a news staff?

Some have suggested the similarity is partly due to the availability of wire copy (Associated Press [AP], United Press International [UPI], and other services). In effect, the wire services set the agenda for the newspapers. In most cases, newspaper editors know that certain national stories are important and that the only coverage they have is by the wires.

The wire services can also influence local newspaper or broadcast copy in another way. If they send a great deal of copy of one kind, and only a little of another, the implication is that one type deserves more attention. Thus, the wires clue editors in a general way to select news proportionately to what is received on the wire.

Whitney and Becker conducted a field experiment to investigate the effects of wire news availability on local newspaper content. Their working hypothesis was:

> Wire service editors' assignment of news items in various proportions to news categories influences other editors' selections of a subset of those items in similar proportions. (Whitney and Becker, 1982, 60–65)

To test the hypothesis, they created two wire service files (sets of news items) from which a small sample of editors was invited to make news selections. They went to considerable lengths to build *control* into the experiment (i.e., to account for all of the decision points that might matter).

File 1 held stories proportional to a routine run of the "A" wire. File 2 held stories of *equal number in each of seven categories of news.* Each file contained 98 stories in all, a typical morning's newspaper cycle. Sports, stocks, state and local items, and particularly important current interest items were omitted to preclude the influence of any overriding news judgment. Stories were of seven types: labor, accidents and disasters, crime and vice, human interest, national, political, and international.

Each category of news in file 2 included 14 stories. For file 1, proportions ranged from 5.1 to 24.5 percent, which was consistent with a routine wire cycle. The two files were about equal in overall "newsworthiness." The balanced and unbalanced files were presented alternatively to avoid a response bias.

The sample was 46 news persons responsible for wire news at selected Columbus and Dayton, Ohio, newspapers and TV stations. Sixty-three percent of the participants were newspaper personnel; others were TV personnel. Men made up 82 percent of the sample.

Participants were asked to select 21 stories—about the number of wire service items used by the largest newspaper in the two cities on an average day—from *each* file.

Results

Whitney and Becker (1982, 60–65) reported that the editors showed considerable variability in their selections of 21 stories from both decks; few stories were not selected by any participants. The most favored stories, however, were selected by 78 to 82 percent of the participants.

How did it happen? The researchers ruled out *response bias*. Table 9.1 shows that when the file mirrored what the editors expected from the AP wire budget, their news choices roughly followed the proportions of news sent in each category of news. In other words, if the wire sent 5 percent of news in one category, the

TABLE 9.1   Proportions in Wire File and Proportions Selected by Editors in "Balanced" and "Unbalanced" Conditions

	Balanced Condition		Unbalanced Condition	
	% in Wire File	% Selected by Editors	% in Wire File	% Selected by Editors
Labor	14.3	11.0	5.1	5.3
Accidents and disasters	14.3	20.7	7.1	7.3
Crime and vice	14.3	16.0	11.2	14.5
Human interest	14.3	11.7	14.2	17.9
National	14.3	22.2	16.3	19.8
Political	14.3	9.7	21.4	21.7
International	14.3	8.7	24.5	13.4

Note: In the balanced condition, editors were asked to select news from seven categories when each category held the some percentage of stories. In the unbalanced condition, editors selected the same number of stories when the stories in each category of news roughly mirrored the "A wire" output of the Associated Press. The table shows that the editors tended to select news roughly proportional to what was sent on the news wire.

SOURCE Adapted from Charles D. Whitney and Lee B. Becker, Keeping the Gates for Gatekeepers: The Effects of Wire News, Journalism Quarterly, Spring 1982. Used by permission of Journalism Quarterly.

editors selected about 5 percent. The one major exception was in regard to international news, which was selected at only about half the proportion sent.

Whitney and Becker (1982, 60–65) concluded that the data support the hypothesis that wire editors select stories proportional to their category, and that the local media are "influenced greatly" by the decisions of a "relatively few editors operating at the regional, national and international bureaus of the wire services." In other words, "The local media are hardly acting alone in shaping the political agenda."

Review

The case study illustrates many aspects of the experimental method that will be discussed in this chapter. For example, the researchers *controlled* for several possible explanations of the data; they wanted to be able to rule out extraneous influences. They *selected* the sample carefully; created the stories carefully; altered the presentation of the stories to avoid response bias; made the exercise as *realistic* as possible; and conducted the research *in the field,* at the respondents' place of work.

Furthermore, they had specific criteria with which to judge the outcome, and their careful planning made guesswork unnecessary. For example, they were able to compare the selection of labor stories when labor stories represented 14 percent of the file versus when labor stories represented 5 percent of the file.

The clear result was that when the file included a given percentage of items, a similar percentage was selected by the news personnel. This seemed to suggest that the wire services set the agenda for the newspaper, if in a rather indirect way. The corollary is that, if newspapers set the *public* agenda, then they are not alone in doing so, because the wires help set the *newspapers'* agenda.

THE GOALS OF EXPERIMENTAL RESEARCH

Experimental researchers want to *control conditions and variables of an analysis such that the influence of any experimental variable can be isolated and observed.* This is not always easy.

For example, suppose you studied individuals' "liking" for a specific new retail product, and you predicted "liking" would increase with the frequency of exposure to advertisements for the product. (This says that, very simply, the more the person sees the ads, the more they like the product.) It's possible—although by no means certain—that the prediction would be supported by the data; but does that mean the advertisements *caused* the increase in liking? Not necessarily.

There are probably several reasons for liking or not liking a product. One, for instance, might be that a person's peers like it. Another might be that it fills a need. Another might be that, yes, the advertising encourages liking. These are sometimes described as *competing explanations* of the change in the dependent variable. We will need some "controls" to account for them.

In *controlling* competing explanations, the experimenter tries to isolate the effect of one or more variables. Control is the centerpiece of the experimental method. It can be conceived in regard to variables, statistics, environments, or sampling.

Variable Control

In a study of the effect of advertising on a product's appeal, we would have to control the frequency with which the research participants see the advertisement. In other words, exposure to the advertisement is a *variable*. For experimental purposes, the researcher can *manipulate* the level of exposure to the advertisement.

For example, suppose one group of people saw the advertisement just once; another group saw it several times; and a third group saw it many times. A fourth group might not have seen the advertisement at all; such a comparison group is called a *control group*.

Variable control sometimes amounts to **experimental manipulation** because the researcher manipulates or controls the level of exposure to the variable.

Statistical Control

Statistical control can be thought of as attribute control (Kerlinger, 1973, 308). *Attributes* are characteristics that describe respondents, and they can be important in sorting out experimental effects. For example, if we are testing the effect of *B* on *A*, we would use attribute control to ensure that comparison groups are comparable in regard to qualities such as gender, IQ, home ownership, and age. Control in this sense means that the researcher has sorted out, or controlled for, some of the competing explanations of variation in the dependent variable.

Another type of statistical control has to do with the variation (or spread) of scores in a distribution. A researcher often will collapse ordinal scales into two or more classifications. By *collapsing*, we mean that all who scored below a given point are counted as though they scored alike, and all who scored above a point are also counted as though they scored alike.

For example, on a Likert-type scale, all who scored below 3 might be counted as "disagree" (despite the fact some were actually "strongly disagree") and all who scored above 3 might be counted as "agree" (regardless of whether some were actually "strongly agree"). This simplifies the analysis.

Environmental Control

Because the researcher is trying to isolate and study the systematic changes in a dependent variable, it is important to have **environmental control,** so that extraneous causes of change be screened out. *Extraneous causes of change* are potential causal agents that are not germane to the experiment.

For example, reading a newspaper might appear to improve the reading skills of a fourth-grade class in comparison with another class that didn't read the newspaper; but the difference *might* be the result of poor lighting conditions in the non-newspaper class, or some other variable extraneous to the point of the research. If groups are to be compared, they must be comparable in all significant variables, including environmental variables.

Sampling Control

The researcher also controls the experiment through *sampling*. For example, if a comparison is to be made between two or more groups to test the effect of an independent variable, then the groups have to be equivalent from the outset. If they are not, the observed difference might be the result of the inequivalency rather than of the experimental manipulation. For example, one group of respondents might unexpectedly be more experienced, or less capable, or more attitudinally inclined, or whatever.

How can the researcher ensure equivalence, or **sampling control?** One technique is the *random* assignment of participants to experimental groups. (Techniques of randomization are described in Chapter 4.) In large samples, **randomization** can be expected to distribute personal qualities evenly across the groups, although this is not a certainty. But in small samples, randomization presents a risk. Many researchers working with small groups will substitute **matching** for randomness. In other words, characteristics of participants will be identified, and participants will be assigned in approximately equal numbers in the comparison groups.

Threats to Validity

Threats to the validity of research were outlined in Chapter 5; the threats apply to all kinds of research, not just experiments. But experimental researchers are especially concerned with issues of validity because the strength of the method is in controlling for competing explanations of the research outcome. Researchers want to be able to rule out any explanation except the one being studied. For example, experimentalists want to be able to rule out an outcome resulting from unexpected occurrences, maturation of research participants, and testing and instrumentation (see Chapter 5).

RESEARCH DESIGNS

To maximize the control an experimenter has over the outcome of a study—and therefore to minimize the threats to the study's validity—a research design is carefully implemented. The **research design** is simply a plan of research that accounts for some of the competing explanations of the data (Zajonc, 1969). The plan can be described graphically by either of two systems of symbolic notation: the Campbell and Stanley notation, or the Haskins notation.

The Campbell and Stanley Notation

Best known is the system suggested by Campbell and Stanley (1963, 6; also see Cook and Campbell, 1979), wherein the letter R stands for "random assignment to groups," X stands for "experimental variable," and O stands for "observation" or measurement.

Here is how to use this simple system of notation. If you were to give a convenience sample of people a newspaper to read, then measure their knowledge of news, you could characterize the design as follows:

i e — non-random

$$X \quad O$$

where X = the variable, newspaper, and O = measurement

Notice that there was no randomization (the letter R does not precede X and O); it was a nonrandom convenience sample.

When you stop to think about it, you will see that this $X\,O$ design has serious flaws. Because the sample is nonrandom, it has low external validity. Because it has no pretest and no comparison group, it offers little confidence that the experimental variable had any effect at all.

What would an improved design look like? Try the following:

$$R \quad O \quad X \quad O$$

In this design, subjects are randomly assigned; that is an improvement. And there is a pretest (the first O); that, too, is an improvement. But there are problems. Could it be that some of the observed change from the pretest to the posttest is due to the respondents' *familiarity* with the test? After all, this is the second time they've seen it.

We could feel better about the outcome if we had something with which to compare. Try this:

Group 1.   R   O   X   O
Group 2.   R   O   O

We've added a comparison group (line 2), called the control group. Now we are beginning to control some of the threats to the validity of a study. For example, because we took a pretest, we know the a priori status of the sample on the experimental variable. And because we have a posttest, we can assess how much change could be attributed to the experimental variable, X. Furthermore, because we have a control group, we have a standard with which to compare. The control group, randomized, should be no different from the experimental group at the time of the pretest. Hence, any difference between the control posttest and the experimental posttest should be the result of the experimental variable.

There remains a problem. All of our respondents have completed the test twice; they may be sensitized to it. Their scores may be high because they have experience with the instrument. How can we deal with that? Try this:

1.   R   O   X   O
2.   R   O   O
3.   R   O

The third level in this design accounts for instrument sensitivity. The respondents in that level see neither the pretest nor the experimental variable; they see only the posttest. Hence, this level outcome can be compared with the second level; a significant difference might be attributable to the testing effect. It can also be compared with the experimental (first) level; if there is no sensitivity effect, and if the difference between the first and third levels is significant, then the difference might be due to the experimental variable.

There remains one level to add to this design:

1.   R   O   X   O
2.   R   O   O
3.   R   O
4.   R   X   O

This fourth level, finally, gets at the problem of test sensitivity and the question of the presumed effect of the experimental variable. Level 4 should be similar to level 1. Furthermore, we have controlled for selection bias (via randomization), testing, instrumentation, and mortality. The variable's history, maturation, and regression would be detected in a less formal way. But in all cases, the experimental researcher tries to control for extraneous causation, random effects, and systematic bias. This four-level design is called the "Solomon 4-Group design."

The Haskins Notation

The other important notational system was introduced by Haskins (1981). It is more complex, but at the same time more descriptive. Here is the Haskins notational system for the conventional pre–post–control design:

Laboratory Experiment

	t_1	t_2	t_3
Pa	M	$T1$ (fx)	M
Pb	M	(fn)	M

where:
$$Pa, Pb \ldots Pn = \text{randomized samples for experimental and control groups}$$
$$M = \text{measurement}$$
$$t_1, t_2, t_3 = \text{time of pretest, manipulation, posttest}$$
$$T1\ (fx) = \text{``forced'' exposure to experimental treatment}$$
$$(fn) = \text{nonexposure to experimental treatment}$$

To account for variations in the experimental procedure, Haskins suggested the following:

M = a measure, or dependent variable
P = a population
P_1a = randomized sample
T = treatment-stimulus
S = spontaneous-stimulus
t = a point in time
(ox) = opportunity for exposure to variable
(fx) = "forced" exposure to variable
(fn) = "forced" nonexposure to variable
(sx) = selective exposure to variable
(sn) = selective nonexposure to variable

In this notational system, a posttest-only, control-group design would look like this:

	t_1	t_2	t_3
$P1a$	—	(fx)	M
$P1b$	—	(fn)	M

The Haskins design would show (a) that the comparison groups were randomized; (b) that there was no pretest for either group; (c) that the experimental group was required to receive an experimental treatment of some sort; (d) that the other group was required not to receive the treatment; and (e) that both groups were given one measurement on the experimental topic.

The Haskins notational system encourages the researcher to *conceptualize clearly the organization* of a study. It requires the user to articulate clearly the timing and contribution of each portion of the research, and therefore to ponder the strengths and weaknesses of the design.

LEARN BY DOING

Critiquing an Experiment: Using a Notation System

1. Search any recent social science journal (not a trade journal) to find an example of experimental research. Read the article carefully and:
   a. Write a one-page description of the experiment and its conclusion.
   b. Use the R O X O Campbell and Stanley system to symbolize how the experiment was conducted.
   c. Include a full bibliographic citation (author name, date, article title, journal, volume, issue, pages).
2. For a second exercise, refer to the Learn by Doing exercise of Chapter 6, page 109; describe the experimental methods developed in that interview.

CRITIQUING THE EXPERIMENTAL METHOD

Win Some, Lose Some

The foregoing may have given the impression that the experimental method, with its ability to control variables, is the "end-all," the sine qua non, the ultimate method of research. Actually, the experimental method is not fail-safe. Despite a researcher's best effort, some variables are likely to escape control. In fact, *as we gain in control, we probably lose in internal validity*—a serious loss.

The Validity Issue

How could that be true? As the researcher tightens the grip on the research situation to control extraneous effects, the *context becomes increasingly unlike real life.* That is the major rap on the experimental method: it is artificial, unreal, and therefore of dubious validity.

Decide for yourself: A respondent travels to a specific location—a research room or social science "laboratory"—and is shown some number of commercials about a product. Is the person likely to feel the same way about the commercials as he or she would have under circumstances of casual viewing?

One counterpoint is that the reality or artificiality of the experiment varies; some experiments are more context-bound than others. In other words, some behaviors take place in conditions more akin to the lab setting.

Another point: A great deal of important research in other disciplines—medical, biological, and psychological—also takes place in the laboratory. The fact that the rats and monkeys used in such research are not human, that they lack the dimension of reality for the human condition, has not prevented their contribution to important research data. But communication research typically depends on human participants, and the lack of a natural setting can be a serious drawback to generalizing the findings.

Research with college freshmen and sophomores contributes to prediction of behavior despite the apparent absence of external validity. (Some argue that college students, especially those at large public universities, are a fair cross-sectional sample, given the broad range of income and ethnic groups they represent.) Mook (1983, 379–387) has argued: "A misplaced preoccupation with external validity can lead us to dismiss good research for which generalization to real life is not intended or meaningful."

Achilles had only one bad heel!

Experimenter Bias

But another Achilles' heel in the experimental method has to do with unintended **experimenter bias.** Volunteer research participants are instructed to appear at a given place and time. They tend to be at the command of the experimenter, knowing something is expected of them, but not knowing what that is. In this condition of expectancy, and possibly receptivity, they are asked to contribute something of themselves: a statement of attitude, a behavior, a tolerance of some sort. In this receptive state, the risk is that responses will represent what respondents think the experimenter wants, rather than what they really feel.

Invalidity may also result when the experimenter, working hard to make the experiment fruitful, unintentionally conveys to the participants a sense of direction that supports the notion being tested. The experimenter may even literally structure the exercise in a biasing way. This could be called a *demand characteristic.*

Peculiarly to social science, a finding is not necessarily accepted as true on the basis of a single study; the chances for a wrong conclusion are too great. And that is another strength of the experiment; it is highly *replicable.* In other words, if the outcome of an experiment is in doubt, the doubter is free to repeat it and either confirm or deny it.

Ethics and the Experimental Method

The study of ethics is especially important to the experimentalist because experiments typically involve administering or withholding a *treatment* (i.e., a manipulation of individuals). The researcher must be aware that individuals are fragile, and that experimental procedures can have long-term effects. For example, experiments that cause individuals to doubt their own judgment, or to lessen their self-esteem can be damaging. The experimenter cannot "erase" such manipulations by saying, "Never mind!" (i.e., by debriefing participants).

SOME EXAMPLES OF THE EXPERIMENTAL METHOD

Example 1

Gilbert and Schleuder (1990, 749–756) conducted an experiment on people's recall of color versus monochrome, and comprehension of complex print-media visuals versus simple. This research is of interest to professionals because editors generally believe color increases audience interest, and that complexity interferes with message reception. Is professional intuition correct?

Participants were 52 communication students at a major Southwestern University. A set of 40 photos from news and popular magazines was collected, of which 20 were judged relatively simple (e.g., a head-and-shoulders shot) and 20 were judged complex (e.g., a crowded street scene). The 40 photos then were videotaped for presentation in color or black and white. Twenty-six of the participants viewed the color photos, and twenty-six viewed the black-and-white version of the same photos.

After exposure to the photos, participants were given a task of recall. Did they recall the simple and complex, and color and black-and-white photos, equally well? Gilbert and Schleuder (1990) reported that the color photos were more readily recalled than the black and white, regardless of whether the content of the photos was simple or complex. Complexity did not seem to interfere with recall. "Contrary to popular belief," they said, "image simplicity did not reduce image processing time, nor improve image memorability. Complex images were, in fact, better remembered."

Gilbert and Schleuder's experiment was a posttest-only comparison group study. Comparison groups were created by *random* assignment. Validity of the outcome seemed to hang on the question of whether randomization ensured equality of the comparison groups. The experimental groups were small ($n = 26$); experimental groups typically *are* small, but the research design requires comparability among groups.

If, for example, the randomization resulted in one group having greater recall, or greater hand–eye skill on the computer used to record responses, then differences between the two groups might be due to something other than the experimental variable. Experimentalists often address this issue, as well as other threats to the validity of the research, by providing estimates of comparison group equivalency.

Example 2

Garramone, Atkin, Pinkleton, and Cole examined the effect of negative and positive advertising appeals on "five variables important to the political process: candidate image discrimination, candidate attitude polarization, involvement in the election, communication behavior regarding the election, and likelihood of turning out to vote" (1990, 302). These researchers observed that, in the 1988 presidential election, there was much talk about "mud-slinging" and the deleterious effects of "negative advertising." *Negative advertisements* could be defined as ads that attempt to denigrate the opposition rather than lionize the candidate.

Research participants in this experiment were 372 students in communication arts at a major research university. They were assigned to one of five experimental conditions or a control group. Participants in each experimental group were given different information regarding a pair of fictional political candidates.

Control-group participants saw only a biography of the two candidates; but participants in the other groups viewed one or two positive or negative political advertisements for the candidates. The advertisements were built around issues of college loan funds and environmental protection, presumably issues of interest to the experimental subjects. The positive and negative advertisements were kept as near alike as possible.

After confirming that the positive and negative advertisements were perceived as clearly different, the researchers examined the question of whether the type of advertisement affected the participants' responses on the five variables given above.

Results indicated the negative advertisements can lead to "greater candidate image discrimination" (i.e., they made the candidates more identifiable), and greater "attitude polarization" (i.e., a measure of liking or not liking a candidate), but not greater involvement in the election, communication behavior, or likelihood of voting.

The authors conceded that the sample had doubtful external validity; that the negative ads represented only one type of negative political advertising (issue based); and that the experimental setting was "artificial" in regard to context. They added that the "mud" slung in the experiment may not have reached a point sufficient to cause widespread concern in the electorate. They concluded that it may be necessary to conduct field experiments or survey research under campaign conditions to get a better handle on the effects of negative campaigning.

Example 3

Bennett, Swenson, and Wilkinson designed an experiment to address two related questions: Does the TV presentation of morbid news cause greater *interest* in such news than would newspaper or photographic presentations; and, in effect, is the medium the message? The latter question was posed as a test of Marshall McLuhan's famous expression of 25 years ago that it was the television medium itself, not necessarily its content, that mattered. Recall from Chapter 2 that McLuhan argued television was teaching or causing new ways of thinking and learning; hence, the dictum, "the medium is the message." Bennett, et al., pointed out that the expression seems to have slipped into conventional wisdom, yet "there is not a single study that directly tests" it (Bennett, Swenson, Wilkinson, 1992, 923).

To test the question, Bennett, et al., identified six news stories that were covered in three media: print, still photo, and television. One "good news" story and one negative but not morbid story accompanied four additional stories that were judged "morbid." The morbid stories involved a televised suicide, explosion of the *Challenger* space shuttle, the death of Jim Jones' cult members, and an airplane crash that killed many in an airlift of American women and Vietnamese orphans. The intent was to see whether morbid stories on television could be expected to generate more interest and curiosity than would happen with some other media.

The researchers' sample was 131 undergraduates in an introductory course in mass communication who received extra credit for participating. The experiment was designed as posttest only with three treatment groups. Method of assignment to groups was not indicated. Groups numbered 36 to 50. Each group saw all six stories: One group saw only print stories, another only photos, and another only TV stories.

Curiosity about these stories was measured *operationally* by an attraction-aversion "thermometer" scale of 100 points (see Chapter 5). A zero rating meant the respondents "couldn't stand the story," and would not want to learn more about it; a 50 meant respondents were not much interested in finding more about the story, and a 100 meant the respondents were extremely curious about the story. Respondents were instructed "to rate the news reports as if they were seeing them for the first time, even if they had seen or read these stories before." After the session, respondents were debriefed as to the nature and purpose of the study.

Analysis of variance was used to compare the three groups on each of the stories. Results showed that only one of the morbid stories, the *Challenger* disaster, was more interesting to respondents in the TV form than in the print or photo forms. The authors suggested that the shuttle explosion may have evoked overriding memories, such as the death of President Kennedy and the landing of The Eagle on the moon, and that there was insufficient evidence to support the hypothesis that interest or curiosity about events was greater for television than for the other media.

After acknowledging low external validity and the fact that most respondents knew of the stories before hand, the authors tentatively concluded that the medium is not the message. Television did not evoke significantly more interest in the stories than either photos or print stories.

Field Experiments

Laboratory experiments have the advantage of tight control, but the disadvantage of artificiality. The field experiment has the advantage of reality, but the disadvantage of loose control. Whereas the lab experiment emphasizes internal validity, the field experiment emphasizes external validity. **Field experiments** are simply experiments conducted in the field rather than in the lab. The case study that opened this chapter was a field experiment in the sense that it was conducted on the home turf of the participants.

In the typical field experiment, an experimental variable is introduced into an existing environment. For example, suppose the researcher wanted to compare *diffusion* (i.e., how news gets around) of a new product or service when the spread of information was by word of mouth or by radio. The researcher might identify two nearby towns matched closely for industry, income, education, and so on, then introduce the product by opinion leaders in one community and by radio in the other.

Introducing the two information campaigns at the same time would enable the researcher to compare and contrast the speed and accuracy of information-spread in the two communities. If this does not seem intuitive, consider this: The radio clearly would reach more people, more quickly, but it might not reach *the right people*. (Or maybe it would reach the right people, but the researcher would have to have a reason for expecting so.) The word-of-mouth spread, on the other hand, would involve fewer people, but each contact would be a direct hit. The researcher might also study the question of the accuracy of reception under conditions of radio broadcast and personal contact.

To track the information diffusion, the researcher probably would conduct a survey in the two towns and compare the spread of information to the relevant people. You can probably imagine some problems in this field experiment. For example, a person in one town may visit the other, and happen to hear the radio broadcast. Or a person in one town may telephone a person in the other. The point is that in such an open experiment, the researcher has little control. Thus, when the analysis is conducted, sources of invalidity must be considered.

Note that as in any experimental research, ethics is of great concern for the field experimenter. Citizens do not want to be manipulated without their knowledge, especially if the manipulation in any way puts them at disadvantage, whether financial, status, health, or whatever. In any field experiment, the researcher must weigh the ethics of the situation carefully.

SUMMARY   *— This is terrible*

The goal of experimental research is to control variables and conditions in order to isolate and observe the influence of an experimental variable. Control is the centerpiece of the method, and there are four types: variable, statistical, sampling, and environmental. To maximize research control, an experimenter employs a carefully devised design. The design can be presented in either of two styles of notation. Issues of ethics are especially important in experimentation, because typically respondents are either given a "treatment" or deprived of one. And although lab experiments strive for internal validity, field experiments are stronger on external validity.

STUDY QUESTIONS AND EXERCISES

1. Why is it that laboratory experiments are strong on internal validity, while field experiments are strong on external validity?

2. Apply the Campbell and Stanley (1963) notational system to the Whitney and Becker (1982) research that was presented in the chapter case study. Did Whitney and Becker conduct a pretest? Were respondents randomly assigned to groups? Which threats to validity are not accounted for by the design?

3. Many research projects use college or university students as participants; do you think samples of students have external validity? What are some arguments supporting or denying? Is external validity always necessary in experimental research?

NOTES

The experiments reviewed here were selected for their recency and their appearance in important mass communication research journals.

Students and researchers interested in further examination of this notational system are invited to consult Haskins (1981).

SOURCES

Bennett, Ellen M., Jill Dianne Swenson, and Jeff S. Wilkinson. 1992. Is the Medium the Message?: An Experimental Test with Morbid News. *Journalism Quarterly* 69(4):921–928.

Campbell, Donald T., and Julian C. Stanley. 1963. *Experimental and Quasi-Experimental Designs for Research.* Chicago: Rand McNally.

Cook, Thomas B., and Donald T. Campbell. 1979. *Quasi-Experimentation Design and Analysis: Issues for Field Settings.* Chicago: Rand McNally.

Garramone, Gina M., Charles K. Atkin, Bruce E. Pinkleton, and Richard T. Cole. 1990. Effects of Negative Political Advertising on the Political Process. *Journal of Broadcasting* 34(3):299–311.

Gilbert, Kathy, and Joan Schleuder. 1990. Efforts of Color and Complexity in Still Photographs on Mental Effort and Memory. *Journalism Quarterly* 67(4):749–756.

Glass, Gene V., and Julian C. Stanley. 1990. *Statistical Methods in Education and Psychology.* Englewood Cliffs, N.J.: Prentice-Hall.

Haskins, Jack B. 1981. A Precise Notational System for Planning and Analysis. *Evaluation Review* 5(1):33–50.

Kerlinger, Fred N. 1973. *Foundations of Behavioral Research.* 2d. ed. New York: Holt, Rinehart & Winston.

Mook, Douglas G. 1983. In Defense of External Invalidity. *American Psychologist* 38(4):379–387.

Whitney, D. Charles, and Lee B. Becker. 1982. "Keeping the Gates" for Gatekeepers: The Effects of Wire News. *Journalism Quarterly* 59(1):60–65.

Zajonc, Robert B. 1969. *Social Psychology: An Experimental Approach.* Belmont, Calif.: Brooks/Cole.

The Analysis of Data

- Chapter 10: Primary Data Analysis.   A case study example of one university's student attitudes toward environmental pollution sets up this chapter. Data reduction and descriptive statistics, especially cross-tabulations, are emphasized.
- Chapter 11: Intermediate Data Analysis.   This chapter explores central tendency, dispersion, and the sampling distribution, and how they are related to the t-test, correlation, and analysis of variance.
- Chapter 12: Advanced and Nonparametric Data Analysis.   This chapter explains how statistical procedures are related, for example, how correlation is related to analysis of variance. It also presents examples of regression analysis, factor analysis, and chi-square analysis.
- Chapter 13: Computer Analysis of Data.   Chapter 13 is designed to enable you, with little or no other guidance, to enter data in SPSS/PC+ and conduct elementary statistical analyses.

10

Primary Data Analysis

□
OBJECTIVES

After studying this chapter, you should be able to:

1. Recognize the following computer program elements:
   data list command
   variable list
   begin/end data command
   data matrix
   run command
   options

2. Explain the difference between fixed-format and free-format computer programs.

3. Detect "irregularities" (errors) in a data matrix.

4. Interpret descriptive statistics in a computer output.

5. Propose and interpret cross-tabulations.

6. "Collapse" (reduce) response frequencies to fewer categories.

7. Measure the association between nonparametric variables.

8. Select and explain significance level.

INTRODUCTION

The next logical step in the research process is data analysis. The tools of data analysis are statistical tests, which offer powerful detection and decision techniques and enable us to identify relationships among data that cannot be seen by visual inspection. Not all important research outcomes are readily apparent; the challenge for the analyst is to tease them to the fore with proper statistical methods. That will be the focus of this and the next two chapters.

Is this a sentence?!

Applied Statistics Are Not to Be Feared

Before going further, the author would like to address two points that might otherwise interfere. First is the matter of whether you are fearful of applied statistics. There *is* cause for concern if you have trouble with basic arithmetic—adding, subtracting, multiplying, and dividing—but not if you have a math deficiency at a higher level. Algebra and calculus provide the fundamental support for the assumptions and techniques of statistics, but *applied* statistics generally do not require computations beyond basic arithmetic.

This is not to undersell the importance of the mathematical approach to statistics; the best understanding comes through knowing how to handle the symbolism (notation) and the algebra underlying the formulas. In fact, the possibility that an untrained person will make judgments about data without proper respect for the logic and the assumptions of the method is a little scary; misapplications of statistics are easy to achieve and difficult to live down.

For example, an important "finding" that later proves *artifactual* (i.e., caused by something unexpected and nonsubstantive) might linger long after its denial. To avoid such a situation, the best analyst will be the most knowledgeable. But the point is simply that even the "math phobe" can and should learn quite a bit about statistics. The knowledge will be of benefit whether the user is a media pro or a research analyst. Furthermore, the person with even a little knowledge of statistics should know when to call for help; that in itself should be important.

Students have been heard to say in regard to career opportunities in research: "I can't see myself working with numbers all day, every day." For applied statisticians, different perhaps from accountants, working with numbers is not the point. Concepts—interesting ideas—are the point. Numbers are merely the tools with which to evaluate the interesting ideas.

For instance, does *A* cause *B*, or is *B* better explained by *C, D,* and *E, along with A?* Do people *learn* from media? What do they learn? Does what they learn affect their attitude, belief, value, or behavior structure? These are interesting questions, and statistics are merely the tools and techniques for trying to answer them.

Statistics Don't Lie   [*people lie*]

The second point is that the occasional uncomplimentary reference to the science of statistics should be disregarded. The idea, for example, that "statistics lie" is simply untrue. The problem is in the application, or the interpretation, not the statistics.

For example, if there are nine homes in a neighborhood valued at about $50,000, and one valued at $500,000, then the **mean** price, **average** price of a home in the neighborhood will be about $95,000—almost double the cost of the most likely figure. The disdainful will look at the figure and sneer that the statistics "lie," and do not accurately represent the "average" home in the neighborhood.

The *average* is not at fault; it is simply the wrong measure. The true average is not what's needed. What is needed is either the most *frequent* price (the **mode**) or the **median** price, the one that falls exactly in the middle of the distribution of prices. The "lying," if any, is on the part of the user, not the statistic. Most often, the problems of statistics involve ineptitude, not falsehood.

DATA ANALYSIS: AN EXAMPLE

An Environmental Survey

sentence?!

Now, back to making sense of the data. On the principle that examples are good teachers, second only to personal experience, let us begin with an example of data analysis. The example comes from a classroom project in which a group of students created a questionnaire, administered it, and conducted the computer analysis. If you wish, you may input the data and interpret it anew for first-hand experience. The full data set is reproduced in Appendix A.

The Research Question *(sub of)*

The topic of interest was "student attitudes about the environment." The research question was: What are student attitudes toward environmental pollution, and what are some variables that help to explain or predict those attitudes? The instrument appears in Figure 10.1.

compound Q

Dependent Variables

Remember, the **dependent variable** depends on or is influenced by another variable called the **independent variable.** The dependent measure is a measure of what *is,* and the independent measure is a measure of how it came to be. This study held numerous dependent variables, some of them paraphrased in the list below; for complete wording refer to the instrument in Figure 10.1.

1. Is pollution in America *severe, moderate, or mild?*
2. Is pollution in [your town, region] *severe, moderate, or mild?*
3. Rank the following five public matters by priority: *health care for all, homelessness, job opportunities, pollution of the environment, population control.*

In addition, the instrument offered numerous other possible dependent variables; for example, a measure of political-environmental activism, a measure of the urgency of action on pollution, and a measure of environmental behaviors.

STUDENT ATTITUDES TOWARD THE ENVIRONMENT: A SURVEY

As part of a classroom research project, we are surveying [local university] students' attitudes toward the environment. Please take just a few moments to complete this questionnaire.

Keep in mind that attitudes about the environment usually have one of two focuses: (1) problems of pollution, and (2) problems of ecology. For example, an oil spill is a problem of pollution, and its effect on wildlife is a problem of ecology. Also, it is important to distinguish between *local* and *national* pollution and ecology.

Please answer the following questions. *presumptive*

COLUMN
NUMBER

1. Some people feel that the pollution problem in America is severe; others think it is mild. What do you think? Using the following scale, please indicate the degree to which you think pollution in America is severe, moderate, or mild:

   7   6   5   4   3   2   1   *none?*   52

   severe   moderate   mild

2. What about pollution at the local level; for example, here in [local area], is pollution

   7   6   5   4   3   2   1   53

   severe   moderate   mild

3. For some students today, issues of pollution and the ecology are very high in their order of priorities; for others they are not high at all. Among the following items, which are arranged alphabetically, what is your own order of priority? Please choose the one that is most important to you today, and give it the number 1; next choose the second most important to you and give it the number 2; continue until you have ranked all five.

_____ health care for all	54
_____ homelessness	55
_____ job opportunities	56
_____ pollution of the environment	57
_____ population control	58

   Most of the remaining items in this questionnaire will take the following form, which will serve as an example:

   The environment is important to me.   4

   7   6   5   4   3   2   1

   If you agree somewhat with the statement, you might circle the numeral 5; if you strongly disagree with the statement, you would circle the number 1. If you strongly agree, you would circle the numeral 7. Remember only your opinion counts. This is not a test, and there is no right or wrong answer.

1. Fast-food restaurants should be forced to provide biodegradable containers for food even if it means raising prices.

   7   6   5   4   3   2   1   5

2. Many of the presumed environmental hazards are overstated.

   7   6   5   4   3   2   1   6

FIGURE 10.1 The Environmental Survey Instrument

3. Protests and demonstrations don't accomplish anything.

     7   6   5   4   3   2   1   7

4. The most important element in protecting the environment is the involvement of individual citizens.

     7   6   5   4   3   2   1   8

5. Stopping pesticide use on fruits and vegetables is necessary, even if it costs more money to buy them.

     7   6   5   4   3   2   1   9

6. In a democracy, the actions of individuals influence the actions of government.

     7   6   5   4   3   2   1   10

7. I would be willing to write to my elected local, state, or federal officials about environmental issues.

     7   6   5   4   3   2   1   11

8. I save recyclable products and place them in containers for recycling instead of throwing them in the trash.

     7   6   5   4   3   2   1   12

9. I feel that the environment is much safer today than it was 10 years ago.

     7   6   5   4   3   2   1   13

10. I listen to programs about the environment on public radio.

     7   6   5   4   3   2   1   14

11. Nuclear energy to provide electricity is a good idea because it helps keep my utility bill down.

     7   6   5   4   3   2   1   15

12. It is okay to boycott companies that pollute the environment.

     7   6   5   4   3   2   1   16

13. My own actions can make a difference in solving environmental problems.

     7   6   5   4   3   2   1   17

14. I read specialty magazines devoted primarily to environmental problems.

     7   6   5   4   3   2   1   18

15. When they are available, I buy products that are less damaging to the environment.

     7   6   5   4   3   2   1   19

16. Environmental pollution poses a threat to my health.

     7   6   5   4   3   2   1   20

17. Environmental problems will not reach a crisis point during my lifetime.

     7   6   5   4   3   2   1   21

18. New technologies will be developed to clean up existing environmental problems by the year 2000.

     7   6   5   4   3   2   1   22

(continued)

19. I get most of my information about the environment from the campus newspaper.

    7   6   5   4   3   2   1   23

20. If while walking across town I happened upon a group of people protesting an oil company responsible for pollution, I would stop to participate.

    7   6   5   4   3   2   1   24

21. I believe that the planet could be made uninhabitable by pollution.

    7   6   5   4   3   2   1   25

22. I get most of my information about the environment from television.

    7   6   5   4   3   2   1   26

23. If the city council were meeting to debate whether to allow a potentially hazardous waste disposal site in my community, I would contact a council member to voice my opinion.

    7   6   5   4   3   2   1   27

24. It is okay to "fight fire with fire" by dumping pollutants in the hallways and offices of companies that produced the pollution.

    /   6   5   4   3   2   1   28

25. Having separate trash and garbage pickups of glass, plastic, and paper is a good idea even if it costs me money.

    7   6   5   4   3   2   1   29

26. I get most of my information about the environment from a local newspaper.

    7   6   5   4   3   2   1   30

27. Good drinking water is so essential that I am willing to pay more taxes just to provide it.

    7   6   5   4   3   2   1   31

28. I get most of my information about the environment from a national newspaper.

    7   6   5   4   3   2   1   32

29. A new solid waste dump in my neighborhood would pose a threat to my health.

    7   6   5   4   3   2   1   33

30. There is no point in my speaking out against environmental hazards, because no one would pay attention to me anyway.

    7   6   5   4   3   2   1   34

31. I buy products made from recycled materials.

    7   6   5   4   3   2   1   35

32. Developing new energy sources should be a high priority.

    7   6   5   4   3   2   1   36

33. Nuclear generating plants pose little threat to my health.

    7   6   5   4   3   2   1   37

34. I take steps to conserve energy whenever possible.

    7   6   5   4   3   2   1   38

FIGURE 10.1 *(continued)*

35. I watch programs about the environment on public television.

      7   6   5   4   3   2   1   39

36. Human life is in danger of being destroyed by pollution.

      7   6   5   4   3   2   1   40

37. I get information about the environment from the library.

      7   6   5   4   3   2   1   41

38. I write on both sides of a sheet of paper to reduce waste.

      7   6   5   4   3   2   1   42

39. I make it a point to buy products that can be recycled.

      7   6   5   4   3   2   1   43

40. To conserve energy, I dress warmly when it gets cold instead of turning up the heat where I live.

      7   6   5   4   3   2   1   44

THE FOLLOWING QUESTIONS WILL HELP US TO CATEGORIZE YOUR RESPONSES.

41. Sex of respondent: _____ Male   _____ Female   45

42. Age in years: _____   46–47

43. Which of the following describes your political party affiliation?

    _____ Republican   48
    _____ Democrat
    _____ Independent
    _____ Other
    _____ None of the above

44. Which of the following best describes your political leaning?

    _____ Very liberal   49
    _____ Moderately liberal
    _____ Moderate
    _____ Moderately conservative
    _____ Very conservative

45. Which of the following best describes the income level of your family?

    _____ Less than $25,000   50
    _____ $25,000–$49,999
    _____ $50,000–$100,000
    _____ More than $100,000

46. Which of the following best describes the population of the community in which you spent most of your precollege years?

    _____ more than 300,000   51
    _____ 150,000 to 299,999
    _____ 50,000 to 149,999
    _____ 10,000 to 49,999
    _____ less than 10,000

Independent Variables

The principal independent variables were *mass media use, sex of respondent, age, political party, income, and population of home community.* For present purposes the mass media variable was very important. It asked respondents to indicate the extent to which they relied on radio news, TV news, newspapers, magazines, public radio, public television, and news magazines. Therefore it was possible to use an individual medium (such as TV news) as an independent variable, or to group several media as an *index* of media use.

The Measures

Except for demographics, questions in this instrument were of the modified Likert type; they were in the form of assertions or statements that could be answered on a 7-point agree–disagree scale.

The Sample

Respondents were 481 undergraduate engineering, mass communication, and liberal arts students at a major state research university. The sample could be described as a convenience sample; it was not strictly random. The instrument was administered by student researchers. Because the sample was not random, external validity is low. Still, the survey approximated the kinds of measures and analyses that often are undertaken, and it is readily extended to virtually any social science topic.

Program and Data Matrix

At this point, you have seen the instrument, named the dependent and independent variables, and are ready to set the data in machine-readable form. This will require a computer *program.* The program will include some *basic program language, variable names, column numbers, the data,* and *run commands.* The start of the program for the Environmental Survey appears in Figure 10.2.

The computer program used for this example was *SPSS/PC+* (the personal computer version of the program formerly called Statistical Package for the Social Sciences), version 4.0.1. An equally popular computer "package" is *SAS* (formerly, Statistical Analysis System). Social scientists traditionally have relied mostly on SPSS, because the package is targeted to their needs; but SAS has also made strong gains in social science. Most universities use either SPSS-X (the mainframe version), SPSS/PC+, or SAS—or all of these.

The program language includes the DATA LIST command, which simply tells the computer how the data are organized. It sets in motion the energy that will direct the program of analysis. Figure 10.2 also includes variable names, variable labels, and a few cases from the matrix of "raw" data. Review the figure carefully, because the text below will explain elements of it.

```
data list fixed/id 1-3 example 4 biodgrad 5 overstat 6 notacomp 7
  involve 8 pesticid 9 sinflgov 10 writreps 11 recycle 12 safeenv 13
  envpgmra 14 nuclgood 15 boycott 16 imakdiff 17 ireadmag 18 ibuyprod 19
  myhealth 20 nocrisis 21 newtechs 22 campus 23 joinprot 24 uninhabt 25
  iusetv 26 ccouncil 27 fitefire 28 seppikup 29 nsprinfo 30
  goodwatr 31 natlnews 32 dump 33 speakout 34 buyrecyc 35 priority 36
  nucgener 37 conserve 38 pbsonenv 39 deadlife 40 library 41 bothsids 42
  buycrecy 43 dreswarm 44 sex 45 age 46-47 party 48 leaning 49 income 50
  hompopul 51 USpollut 52 TNpollut 53 rhealth 54 rhomless 55 rjobopps 56
  rpollutn 57 rpopulat 58 group 59.
variable labels sex 'sex of respondent'/party 'political affiliation'/
  leaning 'respondents political leaning'/income 'your family income'/
  hompopul 'population of your hometown'/
  USpollut 'severity of pollution in the United States'/
  TNpollut 'severity of pollution in E TN region'/
  rhealth 'importance of health care for all'/
  rhomless 'importance of homelessness'/
  rjobopps 'priority of employment as an issue'/
  rpollutn 'priority of pollution as an issue'/
  rpopulat 'priority population control as an issue'.
value labels sex 1 'male' 2 'female'
  /party 1 'republican' 2 'democrat' 3 'independent' 4 'other' 5 'none'
  /leaning 1 'very liberal' 2 'moderately liberal' 3 'moderate'
   4 'moderately conservative' 5 'very conservative'
  /income 1 'less than 25k' 2 '25k to 49,999' 3 '50k to 100k' 4 '>100k'
  /hompopul 1 'greater than 300k' 2 '150k to 299,999' 3 '50k to 149,999'
   4 '10k to 49,999' 5 'less than 10k'
  /USpollut 1 'mild' 4 'moderate' 7 'severe'
  /TNpollut 1 'mild' 4 'moderate' 7 'severe'.
begin data.

001 5464254554464445533454211446342455524352119132267423151
002 5434455335443334443143214313564441333111122143256132451
003 5464456643443354533244443455253627725363124153134415321
004 717664672455666611545553655535235225555520 12144214351
005 4522264445453527443444545324475544442554622122266325141
006 7623535552166616534236541645275562656363555236465231451
007 6237457775327747714347663757341674737577521853136534 2151
008 7426274674777477154677417475717717474777221241474214351
009 7751765773317757731377371757352771737477622122317532451 51
010 7336655345466367132545636365726646552565221141366341251
011 5435564661555145342155566151645733155141120134354352411
012 534554353535 6366546546353535463535345365343123134456231451
013 7724652475146714725213732766163464623134212112132454421351
014 5223456522276267443465646352626662624365622122115624 3151
015 5662466557224642775464756435354377272426741201424553 52141
016 7623622761574657717226661765224477763413512554217735 1241
017 7553525663543566634124561454535563675365612314316535 1241
018 5326356631427176141252216525327527541175223142246341251
019 6557666716777567732272322762437777762436341777534734121
020 4444453533226554456655455336453554655512013214431 2451
021 5464653555444536444435534445355555445445122233154321451
022 7453772242165165521156216575635635141555221222143231451
023 5555444546555555554455455555554444544555221133133312451
024 5335616651176167161577467171736717172766121143354312451
025 6334653531446245335316342553333551142262122214332 1451
026 6226656624666566635666626365636636665666224213276214351
027 3553463331552123335125124453553333121324120144233321541
028 4434555532444345445455435353554445243343220232344312451
029 7721677777251775761426756573747177165656672253213641 43251
```

FIGURE 10.2 The Start of the Program for the Environmental Survey

The *variable name* is a very brief description of the variable. It is a unique set of symbols that identifies the data in a column. Program language limits the name to eight letters; an extra letter will cause the program to fail. For each variable named in the program shown in Figure 10.2, you will find a corresponding item in the questionnaire (Figure 10.1).

The *variable label* is simply a longer description of the variable—one that makes the printout easier to read. In SPSS-PC+, it can be up to 60 characters.

The *value label* tells the machine to give a number response a name. For example, the machine has been instructed in Figure 10.2 to print MALE beside the numeral 1, and FEMALE by the numeral 2. This makes the printout easier to read.

Variable names are followed by the number of the *column* where the variable can be found. For example, the variable named "id" (identification number or respondent number) is found in column 1–3. It requires three columns because the number in the sample requires three digits. Variable names and column numbers tell the computer where the variables are located.

The machine of course does not really understand that a variable such as "party" means the political affiliation of a respondent; "party" is simply a unique combination of symbols that distinguishes the variable from other variables. The machine does not think (although it might sometimes seem to, and perversely), but does only what it is told. Variable names are required for any computation.

Error Detection

Before beginning any statistical analysis, the researcher must *examine the data matrix* for irregularities. In any large data set, *input errors* can be expected, and these must be minimized.

Note that each *row* (a horizontal line of data) represents the responses of one *respondent.* Look at the beginning of the first row of data in Figure 10.2, and you will see the number 001, the identification (ID) number of the first respondent. The data were entered in order, but need not be. The origin of the data is not a factor, but each respondent has a unique identification number. The fact that some cases are out of order has no importance for the analysis.

Columns (vertical lines of data) are for *variables,* and *rows* are for cases (respondents). In Figure 10.2, *column* 45 is the variable "sex," and you will see in the data matrix that the column includes only the numbers 1 (male) and 2 (female).

Variable names are followed by a number that signifies the *column* in which the variable is found. The variable "age" is in columns 46 and 47; age requires *two* columns because it is given as a two-digit number. And so, the analyst can look at the matrix and identify any response, on any variable, by any respondent. These raw data are the basis for all subsequent analyses.

Note also that the data in Figure 10.2 represent a **fixed format input;** the *format* is the manner in which the data are entered. Each variable has one or more columns, and only that variable is described therein. If this were **free format input,** variables could occupy *any* column, provided only that the variables were entered in the same order and that the rules of spacing and language were followed. That is, in *free* format, variables must be in a regular order but not restricted to any special column. Figure 10.3 illustrates fixed and free format inputs.

The *fixed* format makes it easier for the analyst to examine the data. To see this, simply place a ruler beside the data matrix column. The ruler will guide your eyes in a straight line, making it possible for you quickly to scan the long list in search of data irregularities for the column. Examining the data in free form could be dizzyingly difficult.

How does one detect an irregularity in the matrix? Simply look for any number that does not seem appropriate. For example, if you know the proper responses to a question are 1 through 7, and you find a 9, then you can suspect an error, and you can correct it. On the other hand, on the same scale, if the response should have been 3 and the typist wrongly entered a 4, visual inspection will be of no help. But examining the input of a few questionnaires can bolster your confidence that input errors are minimal.

Missing Data

As you examine the numbers in the matrix in Figure 10.2, notice the occasional occurrence of blank spaces; these are *missing data,* items that were not answered by the respondent. The analyst cannot know whether the missed responses were caused by oversight, forgetfulness, misunderstanding, irritation with a question, ambivalence, or some other reason. In any event, missing data should always signal caution, for the computer has to be instructed on how to process the blanks. Some programs will convert the blank to a zero and then incorrectly include the zero in subsequent computations. A few zeros can radically affect a mean score (average) and thereby affect all subsequent analyses.

The computer can be programmed to deal with this in several ways. One is to recode a blank to an unused number, such as 9 or 99, then declare that legitimate numbers exclude 9 or 99. The program *manual* will tell you how to do that. If the

Note: Assume there are seven variables, A through G. In the fixed format, the machine will be instructed that variable A is in column 1 and that variable B is in column 2, and so on. In the free format, the machine is instructed only that variables A through G have been entered in that order, each occupies a unique column.

FIXED FORMAT

Variables	ABCDEFG
cases 1	2143534
2	1243546

FREE FORMAT

cases	1		2	143	53	4
	2	1	24	3	54 6	

FIGURE 10.3 An Illustration of Fixed and Free Format Inputs

number of missing cases is not too large, the analyst can consider substituting the *mean score* of all responses for that variable.

But suppose zero is a legitimate response option (e.g., if a respondent reads 0 newspapers per week); if blanks are converted to zero, how is the computer to distinguish between a legitimate zero and a blank? It can't. In that case, data might be recoded to exclude zero as a legitimate response.

In any event, missing data *must be accounted for,* lest they generate highly misleading outcomes for the research. Good statistical programs are accustomed to these problems; it is up to the researcher to know how they are to be resolved.

DATA REDUCTION

Having inspected the matrix and corrected it, you are ready to begin the analysis. Data analysis requires some form of *data reduction* or *data summary,* because most large sets of data offer more possibilities of analysis than the analyst can process by visual inspection. Efficiency is improved when the data are grouped in meaningful ways. These can include the mean, median, mode, range, standard deviation, variance, and a host of other descriptors.

Data reduction may involve counting, ordering, tabling, or graphing. All of these help to make a convincing presentation of the data. They are called *descriptive statistics* because they "describe" the sample and by inference the population. For some research, description is the whole purpose. For other research, descriptive statistics help to ensure that comparison groups really are comparable.

In SPSS/PC+, an analysis typically proceeds with a FREQUENCIES command. *Frequencies* are counts of the number of responses to each response option. For example, Table 10.1 shows the frequency of responses to a question of political party affiliation in the environmental survey data. The table is reproduced here very much as the output you would obtain in an actual run. The table shows, for example, that 212 respondents identified themselves as Republican, and that they accounted for 45.1 percent of the 470 usable responses. Look at Figure 10.4 to see for yourself the remaining percentages of persons calling themselves Democrat or Independent.

Notice that these political party data are strictly *nominal;* it would make no sense to treat the values 1 through 5 as *ordinal* (i.e., to say that being Republican is "more" or "less" than being Democrat), or as *interval* (i.e., that a mean of 2.04 persons identified themselves as having a political affiliation).

This type of frequency report could be conducted for every variable; it would help the analyst to identify problems in the data, and to see the *distribution* (spread) of responses. For example, if it happened that nearly every respondent selected the same response option, the analyst would need to know why. It might reflect reality or it might reflect a weakness in the question. (However, when the analysis is written up, the number of tables should be minimal. The ideal is to produce a small number of highly readable tables that *succinctly* capture the essential statistics of the study.)

Note also that the frequency table (Table 10.1) shows the valid percentage and the cumulative percentage. *Valid percentage* is calculated on a proper base. For example, 212 ÷ 481 = 44.1, but 212 ÷ 470 (deleting 11 missing cases) = 45.1. The *cumulative percentage* provides a quick summary of the types of responses to a variable. For example, in Table 10.1, the analyst can see quickly that 71.3 percent of respondents were Republican or Democrat, or conversely that 28.7 percent considered themselves neither Republican nor Democrat.

Graphical Representations

Some quantitative programs today include attractive graphics options, such as bar charts, pie charts, and frequency polygons. Examples of these can be seen in figures 10.4 through 10.6, which were prepared with the software package called Lotus 1-2-3. Graphic devices can be very helpful in summarizing data and in showing relationships between variables.

Statistical Representations

Table 10.1 is a frequency table that includes several statistics, such as mean, median, and mode. The *mean* is the average, and it is the most commonly used of the three. The *median* is simply the midpoint of a distribution. To see it in the present

TABLE 10.1   Political Affiliation in the Environmental Survey

Party			Political Affiliation		
Value Label	Value	Frequency	Percentage	Valid Percentage	Cumulative Percentage
Republican	1	212	44.1	45.1	45.1
Democrat	2	123	25.6	26.2	71.3
Independent	3	84	17.5	17.9	89.2
Other	4	6	1.2	1.3	90.5
None	5	45	9.4	9.6	100.1
MISSING	—	11	2.3	Missing	
	Total	481	100.0	100.0	

Party		Political Affiliation			
Mean	2.040	Standard error	.057	Median	2.000
Mode	1.000	Standard deviation	1.243	Variance	1.544
Kurtosis	.477	S E kurtosis	.225	Skewness	1.168
SE skew	.113	Range	4.000	Minimum	1.000
Maximum	5.000	Sum	959.000		
Valid cases	470	Missing cases	11		

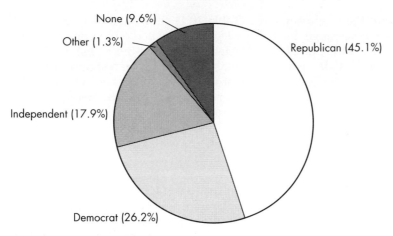

FIGURE 10.4 Political Affiliation Pie Chart

example, you would need to arrange the scores on any variable from low to high. If the number of scores is an odd number, the one in the middle is the median; if the number of scores is even, the average of the two in the middle is the median. The *mode* is the most frequent score in a distribution. For example, in Table 10.1, the mode was the response number 1, "Republican." The mode can be found by counting the frequency of each response.

   Kurtosis and **skew** describe the shape of the distribution. Kurtosis is the extent to which observations cluster around a point on a graph. If the data cluster in

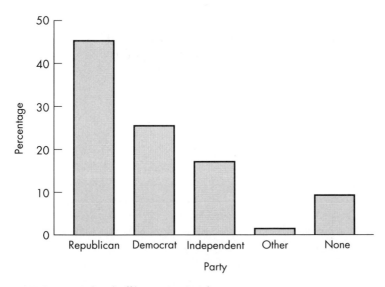

FIGURE 10.5 Political Affiliation Bar Graph

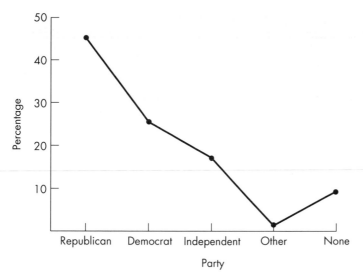

FIGURE 10.6   Political Affiliation Frequency Polygon

a narrow, tall band, they are said to be *leptokurtic*. If they cluster in a wide, short band, they are *normal* (see Figure 10.7).

If the data tend to cluster at one end of the graph, rather than at the center, they are said to be *skewed*. If the tail is toward the larger values, the skew is positive. If toward the smaller values, the skew is negative, or to the left.

Kurtosis is rarely reported in mass communication research, but it is used in economics and finance.[1] It is included here because it provides a useful *conception* of a distribution. If you have quantitative bent, you might pursue its calculation and implications for statistical analysis.

Here are some of the other properties presented in Table 10.1: The *maximum score* (the largest number in a response option) for any respondent was 5 and the *minimum* was 1. That is reassuring; had there been a 7 or 8, we would have been concerned about errors, since there were only 5 response options. The *range* was 4, the difference between the lowest score and the highest score.

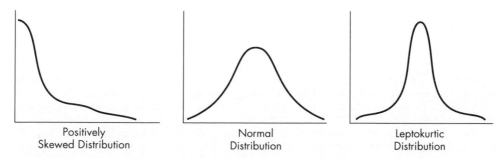

FIGURE 10.7   Illustration of Three Sample Distributions

CROSS-TABULATION

Tables

Frequencies and percentages permit the analyst to construct univariate tables (e.g., to say 30 percent said *A*, 25 percent said *B*, and so on). Such data are satisfactory to a point; for example, we may have genuine need to know the percentage of an audience that appreciates Wimbledon tennis broadcasts, or the letters to the editors column. But percentages in large volume are overwhelming, a jumble to the mind, and impossible to recall. Percentages need reduction to some other form. Furthermore, many percentages are not fully meaningful by themselves.

For example, to say that a respondent is college educated or that 29 percent of a sample are college educated is *useful*, but surely does not tell the whole story. Education contributes to most of a person's life and nearly everything in it, such as political affiliation, occupation, health, longevity, and lifestyle. All of this is to say that variables (data) become more meaningful when they are juxtaposed against other variables rather than viewed alone.

Suppose that we asked a sample of people how much time they spend watching television, and we plotted their estimates. Let's say that they averaged six hours per day, with some watching more and some less. Now, that would be interesting in itself. But what would happen if we examined amount of TV use in relation to education? Would we find that amount of viewing depended to any appreciable extent on a person's level of education? To find out, we could *cross-tabulate* the two variables. This important extension of statistical reporting is illustrated by the two fictional distributions in Figure 10.8.

Putting **cross-tabulation** in the context of our environmental study, consider the variables "sex" and "political party"; are men and women equally likely to be affiliated with the same political party? In our study, there were 244 men and 225 women; the small inequality can be easily corrected by use of percentages.

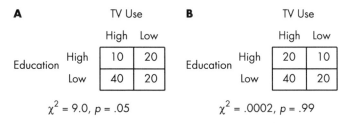

Figure **A** suggests that education is significantly related to amount of TV use. You can see that when education is high, TV use is 2:1 more likely to be low. Conversely, when education is low, TV use is 2:1 more likely to be high. A chi-square value as high as 9.0 is unlikely to happen by chance more than 5 times per 100.

But in figure **B**, education is not related to TV use. Respondents are twice as likely to be heavy TV viewers regardless of whether education level is high or low. The chi-square for such a distribution is very, very small and therefore highly nonsignificant.

FIGURE 10.8   Cross-Tabulating Education with Amount of TV Use

TABLE 10.2 Cross-Tabulation of Sex of Respondents with Political Affiliation

| | Political Affiliation | | | | | |
	Republican	Democrat	Independent	Other	None	Totals
Sex of respondent						
Male						
Frequency	131	40	46	2	25	244
Expected frequency	110	64	43	3	23	
row (%)	54	16	19	1	10	
column (%)	62	33	55	33	56	
total (%)	28	9	10	0	5	52
Female						
Frequency	81	83	37	4	20	225
Expected frequency	102	59	40	3	22	
row (%)	36	37	16	2	9	
column (%)	38	68	45	67	44	
total (%)	17	18	8	1	4	48
	212	123	83	6	45	469
	45%	26%	18%	1%	10%	

Chi-square (χ^2) = 28.29, *DF* = 4, *p* = .00001
Phi coefficient = .2456, *p* = .00001
Contingency coefficient = .2385, *p* = .00001
Note: All percentages are rounded.

Response options numbered five: Republican, Democrat, Independent, Other, and None. With two levels of gender and five of political party, we have a 2-by-5 table with 10 *cells.* Each respondent can be classified as belonging in one and only one cell.

The cross-tabulation, presented in Table 10.2, shows that the men are preponderantly Republican, and the women are slightly more likely to be Democrat. Men and women were about equally likely to be Independent or Other. You will want to verify these conclusions by studying the table.

From this you can see that a cross-tabulation provides more information than a simple percentage. Cross-tabulation is a staple of social science, especially when the analyst is working with nominal level data.

LEARN BY DOING

Cross-Tabulation

To help you understand cross-tabulation, you can learn to create a statistical table by hand.

Here is how to proceed. Look carefully at the Environmental Survey instrument (Figure 10.1) and then the computer program and partial data matrix (Figure 10.2). Find the name of two variables and their column number, then mark the column in which they are located. Values of variables are given in the "value labels" portion of the program.

Draw a contingency table that looks something like the following:

Variable: "LEANING"
Response Options

Variable: "SEX"
Response
Options   1   2   3   4   5

   Male   1

   Female 2

Next, look at the rows of data in Figure 10.2. Each row represents a different respondent. Study the first row, person 001, and find whether the respondent was male or female and then the number that represented the respondent's political "leaning." For example, a respondent might be a man (= 1) who is somewhat conservative (= 4). Find the portion of the table that represents that combination of "sex" and "leaning" and put a mark.

Do the same for respondent 002 and continue through all the rows of data in Figure 10.2. The complete data set is in Appendix A, so you can table as many or as few as is desired.

If your data analysis is limited to Figure 10.2, the frequencies will be small, but should be sufficient to illustrate the process.

Relationships among Variables. Typically the analyst looks for *relationships* among the variables (i.e., whether one variable is related to another in some systematic way). For example, do people who watch a lot of TV news think that they are more able, or less able, to have an impact on government than people who do not watch a lot? A person's estimate of his or her personal power to influence government has been dubbed *political efficacy.*

Let's test that question (see Table 10.3). For our purposes, efficacy will be measured by responses to a single item that states: "In a democracy, the actions of individuals influence the actions of government." The other variable, TV use, will be measured by the statement: "I get most of my information about the environment from television." Responses to both variables are measured by agreement or disagreement on a 7-point scale.

In cross-tabulation this would require 49 cells, too many for easy analysis. To make the analysis more manageable, we will *collapse* all the numbers on the low side of the midpoint of the variable into a new category called "agree," and all the numbers on the high side of the midpoint into "disagree." Responses at the midpoint (4) will remain separate. The result will be a 3×3 (read it "three-by-three") table with 9 cells. This type of cross-tabulation is shown in Table 10.3.

You can see that 242 of the 472 respondents have been classified into the lower right cell of the table, the intersection of high TV use and high political efficacy. Because these respondents feel politically effective, we would reject the hy-

TABLE 10.3   Collapsing Data for Cross-Tabulation: Use of Television by Feelings
of Political Effectiveness (Efficacy)

SINFLGOV (respondents' perceived influence on government)	IUSETV (respondent's use of television for news of the environment)			
	Low Use	Medium Use	High Use	Total
Low influence	14	14	66	94
	11.6	11.9	70.5	19.9%
	14.9%	14.9%	70.2%	
	24.1%	23.3%	18.6%	
Medium influence	7	10	46	63
	7.7	8.0	47.3	13.3%
	11.1%	15.9%	73.0%	
	12.1%	16.7%	13.0%	
High influence	37	36	242	315
	38.7	40.0	236.3	66.7%
	11.7%	11.4%	76.8%	
	63.8%	60.0%	51.3%	
Column total	58	60	354	472
	12.3%	12.7%	75.0%	100.0%

Chi-square (χ^2) = 2.381, DF = 4, p = .6660
Phi coefficient = .07, p = .6660
Contingency coefficient = .07, p = .6660

pothesis (implied in the research question) that high use of television leads to feelings of political ineffectiveness.

Now take another look at the cross-tabulation in Table 10.3. It tells you (a) how many persons are "low" (top *row*), "medium" (middle *row*) or "high" (bottom *row*) users of television for environmental news, *and* (b) how many think they can have a "low" (left *column*), "medium" (center *column*) or "high" (right *column*) impact on government (i.e., who feel politically effective).

Expected Values.   Look at the other data as well. Below the number *242,* the number of persons occupying the lower right cell, you can see the number *236.3;* this is the **expected value,** the value that would have been expected in that cell if the actual frequency were not known. In other words, if you didn't know the actual number was 242, and if you had to guess a number on the basis of probabilities, the best guess would be 236.3.

The expected value is computed as the product of the row total (here = 315) times the column total (here = 354) divided by the grand total (here = 472). In this case, 315 × 354 = 111,510; and 111, 510 ÷ 472 = 236.3. In other words, the expected value is the *row "marginal"* times the *column "marginal"* divided by the *grand total* for the table. In the same way, the expected value for the cell at the intersection of row 1 and column 2 is as follows: 94 × 60 = 5,640; 5,640/472 = 11.9.

The expected values are very important because they permit a test of the difference between the frequency that was *observed* and the frequency that was *expected*. This is the basis for the *chi-square test* that will be described in Chapter 12.

You might wonder: Why would we *expect* a number other than what was *observed*? The answer has to do with chance variation in the outcome. A certain amount of variance between the observed and the expected is always assumed; but if the difference is large, we begin to suspect that there is something going on here besides random variation (i.e., that one variable is *causing* a change in another, or varying systematically in relation to it).

Do not mistakenly think that the calculation of the expected percentage for a cell *predicts* the occurrence of a variable in a sample. For example, the calculation of the expected percentage does not predict the number of Republicans in a sample; it merely estimates the amount of variance, given the distribution that is *observed*.

Row Percentage.   Also below the number *242* in the lower right cell of Table 10.3 is the number *76.8*, the *row percentage*. The row percentages in the right-hand margin add up to 100% for each row. In row 1 of this illustration, 14.9% + 14.9% + 70.2% add up to 100%. In row 3, among respondents who said they get their environmental news from television, 76.8 percent considered themselves to have high political efficacy; 11.4 percent were undecided; and 11.7 percent considered themselves to have low political efficacy.

The same analysis could be repeated for people who are unsure whether they are high or low TV users, and for people who clearly are low TV users.

Column Percentage.   Table 10.3 also illustrates the *column percentage,* or the percentage of observations for each level of influence with each level of TV use. As with row percentages, the sum of all of the column percentages equals 100.

If you were conducting or using a survey of a newspaper audience, or a radio audience, or any audience, the same type of cross-tabulation could be meaningfully constructed. For example, suppose you wanted to know whether employment status (blue collar, white collar) predicted liking a certain TV program: "Employment status" would be the independent variable, and "liking a program" would be the dependent variable. The computer program would sort through the survey responses and tell you the number of respondents in each of the cells.

When Cross-Tabs Have More than Two Variables

Rather than sticking with a 2-variable cross-tabulation, it is possible to add other variables. Where we used two variables in a 3 × 3 table in the above example, the cross-tab could be programmed for three variables or even five—but usually not more than five, because the number of cells might be greater than the number of observations or some cells would be too small for analysis.

A five-variable cross-tabulation with two levels of each would require 32 cells, a very complex table. If any variable had more than two levels, the total number of cells would increase dramatically. Cells with fewer than five observations would present problems of analysis, especially if there were many of them. If any cell were to have fewer than five observations, the program manual would have to be consulted in regard to statistical treatment.

Cross-Tabulation and Elaboration Modeling

Cross-tabulation gives us great interpretive power, and should be widely used in mass media audience studies. Its power is illustrated in **elaboration modeling.** Babbie (1989, 416) credits Paul Lazarsfeld, the noted mass communication researcher, with developing the elaboration paradigm in the 1940s and 1950s. It is useful in explaining the supposed relationship between two variables by systematically adding other variables.

Here is an example of elaboration. Suppose we cross-tabulated two variables, A and B, and found that they were related; for example, that a young person's family income (A) is associated with the likelihood of his or her military service (B). (This is a fictional proposition for purposes of illustration.) More specifically, let us suppose that when family income is high, the likelihood of military service is low. Let's suppose further that the relationship is clear enough to be intuitively persuasive.

But is enlistment really *explained* by family income, or could there be another explanation? The elaboration paradigm would have you add another explanatory variable to the cross-tabulation in order to see if the same relationship holds. If the relationship between income and military enlistment were diminished by the new variable (i.e., if the new variable explains some of the previous relationship), then you would have improved your ability to predict enlistment and reduced dependence on income as the "cause" of enlistment.

Let's say the new variable is "attended college," and so now you cross-tabulate income by enlistment by whether or not the person attended college. (This is called a statistical *control* because it sorts out the influence of one variable under conditions of another.) Attending college probably has a lot to do with whether a person enlists in the military, and so the explanation of enlistments clearly is not *solely* the variable "family income."

If you knew of other good potential explanations for enlistment—such as military service by other members of the immediate family—you could probably improve the table even further. The important point is that you would be improving the quality of the *explanation* of enlistments. Notice that what seemed a persuasive set of numbers at the outset could be reduced to spuriousness. There is no statistical formula for this model; the analyst is simply required to *think* about the possible *causes* of phenomena, and not assume that A causes B or that B causes A without ruling out plausible rival explanations.

stop GO To 198

Proportional Reduction in Error

The paradigm relies on a principle called "proportional reduction in error," or **PRE.** The principle is that, if the addition of new variables improves the prediction of the relationship between A and B, then the improvement can be computed as a ratio of the error in one predictor variable to another. The PRE is always between 0 and 1.0, and the smaller the number the smaller the improvement in prediction by the new variable. The statistic, known by the Greek letter *lambda* (λ), provides an estimate of the amount of improvement of explanation provided by a variable.

The concept of PRE is also very important to other aspects of statistical analysis. For example, PRE is one of many *measures of association* between variables, which are among the most important techniques in statistics. You will need to have at least a passing knowledge of each. Not all are relevant to a particular comparison; therefore, you will need to choose from among them. Relevance depends on the *level* of measurement and the type of test.

For example, a measure of nominal data requires one measure of association, while a measure of ordinal data requires another. The kinds of association include tests of *independence* (i.e., tests of whether one variable depends on another), and tests of *correlation* (i.e., tests of whether one variable tends to increase or decrease in relation to another).

Tau

Gamma (γ) and Kendall's *tau* (τ) are measures of association for measures that are ordinal. Somers's *D* statistic is an extension of gamma, different only in regard to the treatment of "pairs not tied on the independent variable in the denominator" of the gamma formula. The *eta* (η) statistic is a measure of association when one variable is nominal or ordinal and the other is interval.

Chi-Square

The most common measure of the variation in a cross-tabulation is known as **chi-square.** It is designated by the Greek letter *chi* (χ) and in notation is followed by the superscript 2. Chi-square is commonly misconstrued as a measure of association, more or less akin to correlation; but statisticians point out it "is not a good measure of the degree of association between two variables" (Norusis, 1988. B-100). Rather, it is better used as a test of independence between variables. If a possible effect of one variable on another can only be attributed to the element of chance, then the variables are considered to be *independent*; that is, one does not depend on the other.

Independence versus Association

You may find the distinction between independence and association a little confusing. But consider them in this way: Correlation, one measure of association, is a dynamic measure; as one variable changes, another changes in relation to it. If the changes track closely, the correlation is high. Independence, on the other hand, is static; it is a test of whether the observed distribution in a table exceeds a level that could be attributed to chance. It has nothing to do with the dynamic relationship of the variables (Kerlinger 1973).

The use of chi-square as a test of independence led to development of other measures that *do* try to measure the association between variables. For example, *chi-square* may be accompanied by **phi coefficient.** Phi (φ) is the square root of the chi-square divided by the number of observations. This formula is expressed (Bruning and Kintz, 1987):

$$\text{Phi coefficient } (\varphi) = \sqrt{\frac{\chi^2}{N}} \qquad \text{(Formula 10.1)}$$

Phi as a measure of association can be satisfactory for 2×2 cross-tabs, but not for larger tables (e.g., 2×3) since the phi coefficient need not lie between 0 and 1; and in that case, with no upper limit, it is not interpretable.

Contingency Coefficient. For tables larger than 2×2, a **contingency coefficient** is preferred. This is computed as the square root of chi-square divided by chi-square plus the number of observations:

$$\text{Contingency coefficient } (C) = \sqrt{\frac{\chi^2}{\chi^2 + N}} \qquad \text{(Formula 10.2)}$$

Its value always lies between 0 and 1; the higher the number the greater the association. However, *the maximum value depends on the number of rows and columns;* therefore, the coefficient can be hard to interpret.

Cramer's V. Another extension of this is *Cramer's V.* It is computed as the square root of chi-square divided by the number of observations times $k - 1$ (where k = the smaller of the number of rows and columns:

$$\sqrt{\frac{\chi^2}{N(k-1)}} \qquad \text{(Formula 10.3)}$$

Cramer's V always lies between 0 and 1, and unlike the contingency coefficient, can reach a maximum of 1.

Because chi-square is hard to interpret, many social scientists turn to the PRE discussed above and its extensions, lambda, gamma, Somers's D, and Kendall's tau. You probably have detected a commonality to the method: Each coefficient is concerned with the degree to which one variable *depends* on another. Each formula simply adds an element that corrects for what might be a deficiency in another measure.

Correlation. A final measure of association is Pearson's r, the product–moment **correlation** coefficient. It is a measure of association between interval level variables. R always lies between -1 and $+1$; the greater the distance from zero, the greater the association. This is one of the most important measures of association in all of statistics and will be introduced at length in Chapter 11.

Significance Level

The final piece of information is *significance level,* an extremely important concept in research. It is reported as a coefficient between 0 and +1, and it is usually designated as a p value, short for probability. The smaller the p value, the greater the significance (Mohr, 1990).

Since the p value represents a probability, there is no single p value at which an outcome is "better," or more important, than another. A significance level of $p = .21$, for example, would mean that only 21 times in 100 would you wrongly conclude that a particular difference or outcome was not due to chance. A significance level of $p = .049$ would mean that fewer than 5 times in 100 would that happen.

How much risk of an erroneous decision would you be willing to tolerate? If the outcome were not profound, your p value could be generous; if life or health were at stake, your risk level would have to be very stringent. And so, the specification of a significance level is not fixed; it depends on the purpose of the research.

Nevertheless, there is a general standard to which most researchers subscribe. It is $p = .05$. If the researcher would risk error fewer than 5 times in 100 by concluding that an outcome is not due to chance, then that is the accepted level of significance. When the researcher wishes for greater certainty, or at least greater confidence, the significance level can be arbitrarily set at a lower number, such as $p = .01$, or $p = .001$, or even lower.

Notice that in Table 10.2 the significance of the chi-square statistic is $p = .00001$; that means the sex of the respondent is related to the choice of political affiliation. You can see that men were more likely Republican in this sample, and women were more likely Democrat. The significance estimate is so great that you could say with confidence that men and women students in this sample varied on this variable.

Nonsignificance

In statistical tables, *nonsignificance* is sometimes abbreviated n.s. *Significance* tells the researcher whether (a) a sample differs from its population, or (b) a sample differs from another sample. These are the bases of inferential statistics. The importance of significance cannot be overstated; it is the basis of statistical hypothesis testing.

An Example of Significance Testing. Let's say that you are an elementary teacher and you think that if children were encouraged to read a newspaper regularly it would improve their reading level in general. To test the idea you identify two classrooms of children whose abilities and home life are equivalent. (It would make no sense to compare groups that are known to be different.) You can demonstrate equivalence by administering a reading test (before giving newspapers to read) and taking the average for the classes.

After establishing equivalency, you provide newspapers for one of the classes to read for a period of weeks or months. The other class, of course, would not have the same emphasis on newspaper reading. Then, at the end of the study, you again administer a general reading skill test to see if the classes have remained equivalent, or whether one has moved ahead. Let's say the classroom with the newspaper averaged 8.7 on the reading test, and the classroom without it averaged 7.9; are the two scores different because of the newspaper or because of fundamental differences in the students?

As we saw in Chapter 4, perfect equivalence among samples is not expected. But if that is the case, when can we be sure that a difference is real, not related to chance occurrences or chance distributions in the sample? We never can be sure, but we can be *confident* at a given level.

In other words, we can know that certain differences are unlikely to happen by chance, and therefore probably have a cause; it is in that sense that we can be confident whether a reading score of 8.7 really is different from one of 7.9. The essence of significance is that it is a measure of the likelihood that a sample is or is not like another sample, or that a sample is or is not like its population.

In this example there is an extra clinker: Whatever difference was observed might have been the result of extra *instruction* that was required rather than reading the newspaper per se. In other words, reading *anything* might improve reading skills. The analyst will have to consider all such competing explanations of an outcome.

Multivariate Statistics

On reflection, you can see that this presentation has proceeded from the general to the specific and from the simple to the complex. First were the raw data, then simple frequencies and percentages; then two-variable tables, and finally multivariable tables.

Much of the growth of statistical analysis in the past few decades has been in the direction of multivariate analyses. The improvement has involved both *parametric* (estimating the parameters of a population) and *non-parametric* (frequency based) statistics. In multivariate statistics, we analyze one or more dependent variables with some number of independent variables, all in the same procedure—controlling in one procedure for the effect of each variable in relation to each other.

The array of techniques is awesome, and the subtlety and power of the methods is spectacular. These methods permit the assessment of numeric associations that simply cannot be observed intuitively or with lower level applications. But before going further into these techniques, we must stop to appreciate some fundamental calculations of statistics in Chapter 11.

SUMMARY

Knowledge of applied statistics is a requirement for the conduct of much social science research. However, some applied statistical methods do not require skill in higher mathematics. Contrary to a popular expression, statistics do not "lie"; the fault in statistical reporting generally is in misuse or misunderstanding.

In preparing the analysis of data, a researcher will identify dependent and independent variables; write a computer program to manipulate the variables; examine the input data matrix for errors; and compute frequencies on all or selected variables. Cross-tabulations often are useful in establishing the independence of variables. When the cells of a cross-tabulation are too numerous, responses are collapsed (reduced) into fewer categories. The theory of cross-tabulation includes proportional reduction in error (PRE) and elaboration modeling.

STUDY QUESTIONS AND EXERCISES

1. Find the variable called "IUSETV" in the computer program presented in Figure 10.2 and scan down the appropriate column in the data matrix. What numbers are most common for that column? Legitimate numbers are 1 through 7; does any number exceed 7? Select any other variable in the variable list and repeat the exercise.

2. In a chi-square computation the *observed* response is measured against the *expected* response; explain in your own words what the expected value is and how it is obtained.

3. Look at the Environmental Survey questionnaire (Figure 10.1). Think about how one variable in the survey might be related to another; then propose the cross-tabulation of two variables and illustrate it by making up a table of data to show the outcome you think might occur.

NOTE

1. Kurtosis describes a distribution that is not normal. If a leptokurtic distribution is superimposed on a normal distribution, the leptokurtic will be taller and thinner than normal in the middle, but fatter in the tails; researchers call it a "fat-tail distribution." With more elements than normal in the tails of the distribution, the risk of a type I error in statistical testing is increased. Financial researchers are concerned with this measure because, for example, in the case of the very large investor, small errors amount to big dollars.

SOURCES

Babbie, Earl. 1989. *The Practice of Social Research.* 5th ed. Belmont, Calif.: Wadsworth.

Bruning, James L., and B. L. Kintz. 1987. *Computational Handbook of Statistics.* 3d ed. Glenview, Ill.: Scott, Foresman.

Kerlinger, Fred N. 1973. *Foundations of Behavioral Research.* 2d ed. New York: Holt, Rinehart & Winston.

Mohr, Lawrence B. 1990. *Understanding Significance Testing.* Beverly Hills: Calif.: Sage.

Nie, Norman H., C. Hadlai Hull, Jean G. Jenkins, Karin Steinbrenner, and Dale H. Bent. 1979. *Statistical Package for the Social Sciences.* 2d ed. New York: McGraw-Hill.

Norusis, Marija J. 1988. *SPSS/PC + V2.0 Base Manual for the IBM PC/XT/ and PS/2* (SPSS Inc., 444 North Michigan Avenue, Chicago, IL 60611).

Stempel, Guido H., III, and Bruce H. Westley. 1991. *Research Methods in Mass Communication.* 2d ed. Englewood Cliffs, N.J.: Prentice-Hall.

11

Intermediate Data Analysis

□
OBJECTIVES

After studying this chapter, you should be able to:

1. Explain and calculate three measures of (a) central tendency and (b) dispersion.

2. Distinguish between three types of distribution: sample distribution, population distribution, and sampling distribution.

3. Describe or calculate three significance tests: t-test, correlation, and one-way analysis of variance.

Statistical calculations are a little like jazz music; they start out with the plausibility and comfort of a familiar melody, but quickly move into what seems abstraction. Often, the user loses sight of the *logic* of the extensive calculations: the averages, variances, standard deviations, sums of squares, squares of sums, and so on. Nevertheless, like jazz, the calculations come back to the familiar melody, via the significance test, which tells whether an observed outcome was different from what would have been expected by chance. At that point the statistical music is ended and the drumbeat of interpretation begins.

If you have any difficulty with statistics, it probably springs from inability to follow the logic of the calculations. The flow is so involved that it is a rare student who quickly and clearly grasps it all. The difficulty is entirely understandable, especially when a relatively simple procedure can require so many separate calculations that after a while the user is simply doing as told, not what is logical.

Even experienced and relatively sophisticated users have been known to describe the process as "magic," "hocus-pocus," and "whatever the machine says." In truth, the conceptual and computational logic of statistics is awesome, but can be learned. *You need only to find the logical structure* and keep an eye trained on it.

This chapter describes in the plainest language the logic and technique of several statistical tests. Emphasis is on the overarching themes, calculations, and concepts that are embedded directly or indirectly in every statistical technique—beginning with the notions of variance and standard deviation, and their role in deciding whether any proper sample is different from its population, or whether any proper sample is different from a comparable sample. Such decisions are the reasons why statistical tests exist, and you must have a firm grip on that purpose.

SUMMARY STATISTICS

Measures of Central Tendency and Dispersion

Data reduction, introduced in Chapter 10, often begins with a report of *summary statistics*, such as the mean, median, mode, range, standard deviation, and variance. The first three are measures of central tendency, and the second three of dispersion. Central tendency has to do with the midpoint of a distribution. The measure of central tendency or dispersion that is of interest to an analyst depends on the purpose of the research and the data distribution.

Central Tendency.   A measure of **central tendency** identifies a point in the distribution that best helps to describe the data set. The measure can be the mean (average), the median (the score in the middle of the distribution) or the mode (the most frequent score in the distribution). The mean is required for parametric statistics, which estimate the characteristics of a population.

Dispersion.   Measures of **dispersion** are measures of variation around the mean. They include **standard deviation, variance,** and range. The *range* is the difference between the highest score and the lowest score in a distribution. If the highest score and the lowest are the *same,* then there is no range, no standard deviation, no variance. If the highest and lowest scores are *not the same,* it is possible to calculate an average of the distribution, and the standard deviation and variance.

If we know the range, why would we need the standard deviation and variance? The range is a *rough* estimate of dispersion that takes into account only two scores, the highest and the lowest. In many situations such information is not adequate. Suppose you questioned 20 people on a 7-point scale, and all but two agreed on an issue, but the two who disagreed were at opposite extremes of the scale. In this case, the range would be a poor estimator of the variation around the mean. The range would show the difference between the extreme positions of the two, but not the similarity of the other 18 responses.

Another point about the range is that because it focuses on only two elements of a sample, the highest and the lowest, it fails to use information provided by the rest of the data. On the other hand the standard deviation and variance, measures of the difference between individual scores and the mean of a sample, are the viscera, so to speak, of statistical computations.

UNDERSTANDING THE MEAN, STANDARD DEVIATION (S OR SD), AND VARIANCE

It is important for you to learn about the mean and standard deviation. These are crucial to the mechanics and hence the concepts of hypothesis testing; they also are crucial to any description of sample characteristics. Once you are familiar with means and standard deviations, you will be able to move comfortably into a discussion of sampling distributions and classical inference and, finally statistical tests.

Calculating the Mean

Statistical calculations inevitably involve *notation* (symbols) and *formulas;* to the extent possible in the discussion that follows, these are simplified and verbalized so that you can convert the notation to language.

The mean of any set of continuous numbers (i.e., not categorical) is given as

$$\overline{X} = \frac{\Sigma X}{N}$$

$\overline{X}$ = mean
Σ = sigma (the sum of)
X = scores on any variable (e.g., family income)
N = number of observations in the sample   (Formula 11.1)

The formula reads: The mean equals the sum of the scores divided by the number of elements in the sample.

The mean, standard deviation, and variance are to statistical tests what concrete blocks are to masonry. They make tests possible, just as blocks make walls possible. Their purpose always is the same: to find whether a summary statistic in a set of scores is different from a standard.

Calculating the Standard Deviation

The *standard deviation* is a measure of how the scores in a sample are dispersed (spread) around the mean. For example, in some cases there is very little difference (very little spread, or variation) in scores; they cluster *near the mean* of the sample. This would be true of the average age in a university freshman class, where most students would be 18 or 19 years of old. In some other situations there would be greater variation. In a university *night class,* for example—where enrollment includes reentry students—the average age would be higher and the standard deviation greater.

Knowing the standard deviation, researchers are able to (a) examine the extent of the dispersion, and (b) compare the dispersion in one sample with that of another. Dispersion represented by standard deviation and its peer, variance, is very important. If you cannot picture it clearly after reading the section that follows, try it again.

Because the standard deviation involves the deviation of scores around the mean, the mean is involved in the calculation. The formula to calculate standard deviation is as follows:

$$S = \sqrt{\frac{\Sigma (X - \overline{X})^2}{N}}$$

(Formula 11.2)

The formula reads: The standard deviation equals the square root of the sum of the squared deviations of the scores around the mean, divided by N.

The symbol for the standard deviation of a sample is s.

Figure 11.1A illustrates the calculation of the standard deviation. Figure 11.1B provides a small practice example for you to try. (See page 206.)

Calculating the Variance

As suggested above, variance is the close cousin of standard deviation. What is the difference? The *variance* of a set of scores is the same as the standard deviation but minus the radical (square root). The attractiveness of the standard deviation is that it is in the same units as the input data. If you omitted the radical sign in the formula for the standard deviation, you would be working with the *squared* deviations, not real quantities. That by itself is not all bad, but it has one other disadvantage: The numbers are large. Working with squared numbers is not convenient. The formula to calculate variance is as follows:

$$S^2 = \frac{\Sigma (X - \overline{X})^2}{N}$$

(Formula 11.3)

There is more than one way to calculate the standard deviation and variance. The following formula accomplishes the same purpose as Formula 11.3.

$$S = \sqrt{\frac{\Sigma X^2 - \frac{(\Sigma X)^2}{N}}{N-1}}$$

(Formula 11.4)

But if the two formulas do the same job, why introduce the latter, more complex approach? It brings up a common theme in the computation of variance: the difference between "the square of the sum" and "the sum of squares." The latter formula uses the sums-of-squares approach to calculating the variance.

Scenario: Ten persons watched a movie and rated it on a 10-point scale, where 10 = "the greatest movie ever" and 1 = "the worst movie ever." Their ratings of the movie were as follows:

Person	Movie Rating
1	5
2	3
3	7
4	8
5	9
6	6
7	9
8	8
9	6
10	7

Calculation. To arrive at the standard deviation, symbolized as *S*:

1. Add the 10 scores and divide by the number of scores (to arrive at the mean):

$$5 + 3 + \ldots 7 = 68$$
$$68 \div 10 = 6.8$$

2. Subtract the mean from each score, and square the remainder:

$$5 - 6.8 = 1.8; 1.8^2 = 3.24$$
$$3 - 6.8 = 3.8; 3.8^2 = 14.44$$
$$\ldots$$
$$\ldots$$
$$7 - 6.8 = .2; .2^2 = .4$$

3. Add the squares.

$$3.24 + 14.44 \ldots + .4 =$$

4. Divide the sum of the squares by N = 10.
   That is the *variance*.

5. Take the square root of the variance.
   That is the *standard deviation*.

FIGURE 11.1A Calculation of Standard Deviation: An Example

Person	Movie Rating
1	6
2	6
3	7
4	9
5	8
6	8
7	8
8	7
9	9
10	7

FIGURE 11.1B Calculation of Standard Deviation: Practice Set

The uninitiated might think that the square of a sum of numbers $\div N$ would be the same as the sum of the numbers squared, but it is not, unless there is no variance whatever in the scores. For example, if there are four scores, each of them the number 2, then $\Sigma x^2 = (\Sigma x)^2 / N$ and there is no variance. But if any number in the set is different from the others, then Σx^2 does not equal $(\Sigma x)^2 / N$. The difference is a measure of dispersion.

When divided by N or $N-1$, the score is the variance of the set. If this is hard to follow, try it for yourself. Here is a very simple example, followed by a very short practice set:

1. Data: 2, 4, 2, 4
   The sum is: $2 + 4 + 2 + 4 = 12$
   The square of the sum is: $12 \times 12 = 144$
   The square of the sum divided by N is: $144 \div 4 = 36$
   The sum of the squares is: $(2 \times 2) + (4 \times 4) + (2 \times 2) + (4 \times 4) = 40$
   The difference is: $40 - 36 = 4$

2. Data: 3, 4, 3, 5
   The sum is: _____
   The square of the sum is: _____
   The square of the sum divided by N is: _____
   The sum of the square is: (___ × ___) + (___ × ___) + (___ × ___) + (___ × ___) = _____

   The difference is: _____

Again, the sum of squares and the square of the sum are not the same number, and the difference between them, when divided by N or $N-1$, *is the variance*. Specifically, $40 - 36 = 4$; $4/3 = 1.3 = $ variance. If you take the square root of the variance, 1.3, you will have the standard deviation, $SD = 1.14$. *The sum-of-squares approach is common to many statistical tests, especially correlation, regression, and analysis of variance*, all of which will be discussed in this and the following chapter.

Remember that the point of finding the variance is to learn the spread of scores around the mean, and ultimately to learn whether the variance of a sample is different from what would be expected in the population or another sample.

THE SAMPLING DISTRIBUTION

The mean, variance, and standard deviation are called *statistics*, and they are useful for describing a sample. When the mean, variance, and standard deviation are extended to a population, they are called **parameters.** Hence, statistics estimate the parameters of a population.

A random sample of sufficient size is expected to be largely like the population from which it is drawn. But if we don't take a *census* of the population, we cannot be sure. How is the fundamental problem resolved? The answer lies in a theoretical distribution called the *sampling distribution*. It is a connecting link between any random sample and the population from which it is drawn and it will be discussed below.

Sample, Population, and Sampling Distributions

We will be dealing with *several types of distributions*. First is the **sample distribution,** which is simply a description of how the people in the sample responded to a variable. For example, if the respondents gave you their "liking" for a TV program on a scale of 1 to 7, we might find that some would like it and some would dislike it and most would fall somewhere in between; subsequently, we could plot the frequency of each response option, then calculate a mean and a standard deviation for the scores. This is a sample distribution (see Figure 11.2).

The second type of distribution is the **population distribution.** The population is the set of elements (any collectivity, e.g., people, newspapers, animals) from which the sample is drawn. It could be "all the people residing within the city limits of [your town]," or "all the sophomores in state universities in America" or whatever.

A researcher hopes the random sample will be very much like the population on a given variable. And usually it will be, especially if $N = 100$ or greater. The population distribution is the distribution of responses of all elements in the population to the variable at issue (see Figure 11.2).

The third type of distribution is the **sampling distribution.** It is a theoretical distribution of the *averages of many samples* from a single population. It has known probabilities, which provide a way to estimate with confidence the extent to which a sample likely represents a population.

The logic of this is presented in Figure 11.3. Keep in mind that a researcher would never actually create a sampling distribution. It is a *theoretical* distribution, but one that can be described and predicted in mathematics. It amounts to a probability distribution of means. Knowledge of this distribution is what makes "significance testing" possible.

The sampling distribution of the means has a standard deviation. In fact, it is expected that, in the long run, about 68 percent of sample means will fall within plus-or-minus 1 standard deviation of the mean of the sampling distribution. Ninety-five percent will fall within plus-or-minus 2 standard deviations, and 99.7 percent within plus-or-minus 3 standard deviations.

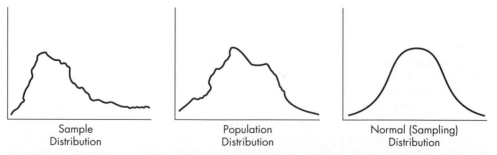

| Sample | Population | Normal (Sampling) |
| Distribution | Distribution | Distribution |

FIGURE 11.2   Illustration of Three Types of Distributions: Sample, Population, and Normal (Sampling)

The three types of distributions are illustrated in Figure 11.2. The *sampling* distribution will be shaped "normally" (bell-shaped), *regardless of the shape of the distribution from which it is drawn*. The *population* distribution will be unimodal, or bimodal, or irregular in virtually any fashion, yet repeated samples from the distribution will plot *normally*. This predictability is a source of power. And there is no one **normal distribution** curve, but many; there are infinite *sampling* distributions.

When the mean of a sample does not match the mean of a population, the difference is naturally called *error*. But if we do not know the mean of the population, because we are working only with a sample, how can we estimate the size of the error? The answer is the *standard error* of the statistic, calculated as the standard deviation divided by the square root of the sample size. The standard error estimates the likely range of difference between a sample mean and a population mean.

$$S_{error} = \frac{SD}{\sqrt{N}}$$

For example, if we know the mean of a random sample, we can say that it estimates the population. But as an estimate, it could be wrong by some amount.

1. Draw a random sample; the mean of the sample will *estimate* the mean of the population

2. If the population is approximately *normally distributed*, the population will approximate the theoretical sampling distribution.

3. The sampling distribution can be shown in mathematics to be normal (symmetric), with known probabilities at every point in the curve.

4. If the sampling distribution has a known mean and standard deviation, and if the sampling distribution is approximated by the population, which is estimated by the sample, then the population also has a known mean and standard deviation.

5. The standard deviation of the sampling distribution of means is the standard deviation of the population divided by the square root of the sample size. The coefficient is called the *standard error*.

6. The standard error (standard deviation of the sampling distribution) provides an *interval* within which the true mean of the population likely is found. For example, if the sample mean is 7.21 and the standard error is plus-or-minus 1.4, then the true mean of the population should be between (7.21 − 1.4) and (7.21 + 1.4).

7. Does that mean the standard error will always capture the true mean of the population? No. There is always the possibility that a sample will fall outside the standard error.

8. But, it is known from theory that 95 percent of all random samples from a population will fall within 2 standard deviations of the true population mean. Hence, if we multiply the standard error by 2 standard deviations (actually, it is 1.96 standard deviations), we will be able to claim with 95 percent confidence that the true (population) mean falls within a given interval of the sample mean.

9. In other words, the sample mean equals plus-or-minus 1.96 × the standard deviation divided by the square root of N.

10. This allows the analyst to make tests of two types: one to hypothesize that a sample mean will fall *within* the confidence interval; the other to hypothesize that it will fall *outside* the confidence interval.

FIGURE 11.3 A Capsule of the Sampling Distribution and Its Relation to Statistical Reasoning

We can't know precisely how much. But if we divide the sample standard deviation by the square root of the sample size, then add it to either side of the sample mean, we will have a range that should capture the true mean of the population.

The sampling distribution simply gives us the theory and the tools to work with. The sample is our best estimate, if it is properly drawn. The standard deviation of a sample divided by the square root of N provides an interval around the sample mean. If the true (population) mean is not the same as the sample mean, it probably is within the sample mean, plus or minus the standard error.

Confidence

If we want to be 95-percent *confident* that the error interval around our *sample* mean captures the true *population* mean, we can multiply the standard error by a factor of 1.96. But why 1.96? Recall that we said 95 percent of scores in the sampling distribution fall within plus-or-minus 2 standard deviations, but the more accurate figure is 1.96 standard deviations (see Figure 11.2). Two, or 1.96, is the confidence factor; it provides 95-percent confidence that the interval around the sample mean includes the population mean. A confidence factor of 3 provides even greater confidence.

The confidence level selected depends on the purpose of the research. There are times when we would want a stringent confidence level and time when we would not. The three-standard-deviation interval is so stringent that only an extreme score would technically qualify as "significant." That is the tradeoff: As confidence goes up, the ability to detect small but important differences goes down.

All of this assumes the sample is *random;* if it is not, all bets are off. This probably deserves further comment, because too often researchers are insensitive to the delicate nature of samples. Truly random samples for large populations are very difficult to obtain, especially in nonfunded research. As a result, researchers sometimes use loosely drawn samples and then nevertheless apply statistical techniques to the questionable samples—sometimes generating contrary or inexplicable findings.

Although one would like to suggest that a very stringent criterion of significance should be used to counter a poor sample, the truth is that *there is no correction for a poor sample.* The best approach is to get the best sample possible, then interpret it very cautiously. The use of external data such as census reports to gauge the degree to which the sample is like the population can be helpful.

At the same time, and this is important, experience has shown that technically nonrandom samples nevertheless can be satisfactory. For example, national pollsters cannot possibly draw a truly random national sample, nor even a truly systematic random sample (they simply cannot interview everyone designated in the set), yet they routinely have very good success. This is because their techniques *approximate* randomness, and they use fairly large samples, on the order of 1,500 to 2,500. The point is that the sample must be treated with great respect; statistical theory is based on random samples, and the more we violate randomness, the more we risk misusing the theory.

There are other complications. One is that the sampling distribution is understood in percentages of area under the curve. In other words, a given point on the normal curve represents a percentage of the total area of the curve. A sample, of course, has real scores, not percentages or areas. The percentage distribution on the normal curve is illustrated in Figure 11.4.

Other Distributions

To travel conceptually from the sampling distribution to a set of real scores, mathematicians and statisticians developed several other important distributions. The **Z-distribution** converts every point in the sampling distribution, and by inference the population distribution, to a *standard score* (Z-score). Any score can be converted to a Z-score by the following formula:

$$Z = \frac{X - \overline{X}}{S}$$

(Formula 11.5)

The formula reads: The Z-score equals the difference between a single score and the mean of scores in the sample divided by the standard deviation. In what probably seems an odd twist, this formula simply puts any score on a curve with a common base. It is a very important and useful concept. For example, if two teachers use different exams to measure comprehension, a Z-score can make the exams comparable.

The **T-distribution** was developed in 1908 by W. S. Gosset, who wrote under the pen name "Student." Student's T, as it is popularly called, is an extension of the Z-distribution; it is symmetrical, like the normal curve, but with another benefit. It

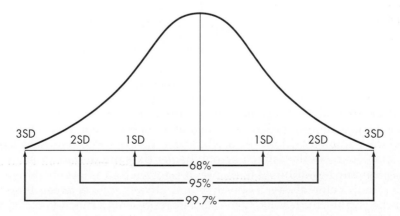

Note: 68 percent of sample means fall ± 1 SD of mean of sampling distribution.

FIGURE 11.4 Percentages of Area Under the Normal Curve

accounts for the number of sample units in the analysis, which are expressed as *degrees of freedom* (see below). The T- distribution, then, is a normal distribution of T-scores adjusted for sample size. For samples larger than 120, the effect of sample size is neutralized for this distribution.

Degrees of Freedom

Degrees of freedom is a complex notion, but think of it in this way: If there are 25 respondents in a survey, and if you know their total score, and if furthermore you know the score of 24 of the individuals, then the 25th score is *fixed*; it has no freedom to vary.

Degrees of freedom are the number of elements in a set that are "free" to vary (whose quantity is not known). Degrees of freedom (*df*) can be expressed as $df = N - 1$, or $df = (\text{row} - 1) \times (\text{column} - 1)$, or another such combination. For example, if there are 2 rows and 2 columns, than $df = 1 \times 1 = 1$.

Degrees of freedom are used when calculating the significance of a statistic. For example, in a T-distribution a probability table with degrees of freedom expresses the probability of a given score in the distribution.

Two other related distributions are the **F-distribution,** which with 1 and *N df*, is simply the square of the T- distribution with *N df*, and the Chi-square distribution, which is a frequency distribution for binominals. The point is that all of these distributions are related, and each fills a special need in statistical theory.

We have traveled, on the berm perhaps, from the *sample,* to the *population,* to the *sampling distribution,* to the *Z-distribution*, and finally to the *T- F- and Chi-square distributions,* as a way of estimating the closeness of the sample to the *population.* Everything that follows is simply a variation or extension of the principle: *The tests are designed to identify the systematic variation within and among variables, and to tell us when the variation reaches a level beyond what could be expected by chance.*

THE T-TEST

Tests of Significance

Confidence intervals help estimate a parameter (as represented by the statistic), but there is also another task here: to evaluate "specific claims about the magnitude" of the parameter (Mohr, 1990, 50). The testing of those claims, called *significance testing,* involves the estimation of whether the sample statistic exceeds what could reasonably be attributed to chance. It is referred to as a probability value, or *p* value. The *p* value always is positive and always falls between 0 and 1. The smaller the *p* value, the less likely the statistic represents a function of chance variation, and the greater the *significance* of the statistic.

If a score is significant (i.e. if it is not attributed to chance), *then it must have a cause.* Much of statistical application is designed to isolate such causes. When the *p* value falls below .05, it is said by convention to be significant.

The T-Test

The T-distribution bridges the sampling distribution and the sample by means of a test of significance, called a t-test. A t-test, or "means test," calculates whether a sample mean is different from a population mean, or from zero, or from another sample mean. The t-test is very widely used in social research.

T-Test: Sample versus Population

T-tests are of three types. First is the test of whether the sample mean is different from the population mean. Suppose, for example, you have selected a sample of TV viewers and are interested in the number of hours and minutes per day they spend watching television. From the sample, you calculate an average, and let's say it is 4 hours, 6 minutes (246 minutes). Now suppose you know from previous *national* TV surveys that the *average* time spent per person watching television is about 6 hours (360 minutes). Your question is this: Is the mean of your survey sample different from the mean of the population from which it was drawn?

The same question can be posed differently: Is the local sample from the same population as the national sample? Is the difference between the local mean and the national mean a difference that might be attributable to the sample, or is the local sample likely different from some other reason?

The t-test for such a question is as follows:

$$T = \frac{\overline{X} - \mu}{SEm}$$

$$\text{where } SEm = \frac{SD}{\sqrt{N}}$$

(Formula 11.6)

The formula reads: The t-score is the difference between the sample mean and the population mean divided by the standard error of the mean. Recall that the standard error of the mean is the standard deviation divided by the square root of N or N–1.

To test the significance of the question about TV use, we need only to subtract the sample mean from the population mean, and divide by the standard error, as calculated in the example of Figure 11.5 (which is based on fictional data). The simplicity and straightforwardness of the t-test makes it very popular as a research tool.

You are cautioned, however, that the t-test should not be used for multiple comparisons in one analysis. For example, if you were testing all combinations of TV use among five subgroups from one population, you would have 10 unique comparisons; but multiple t-tests would be ill-advised because each new application would increase the risk of error.

Think of it like this: for one test, at the 95-percent confidence level, there will be 5 chances of error in 100 applications. But if you conduct five tests, then clearly some of the outcomes have a higher than 5-in-100 chance of being wrong.

Variable: Number of hours per day watching television

Respondent	Hours
1	4.8
2	8.0
3	5.2
4	1.0
5	3.9
6	9.3
7	5.1
8	4.9
9	6.7
10	4.2
11	3.5
12	5.4
13	4.5
14	4.9
15	5.2
16	4.0
17	4.8
18	12.0
19	1.5
20	2.9
Total	101.8

Population mean = 6.0 hours
Sample mean = 4.1 (rounded) hours
Population mean minus sample mean = 1.9 hours
Standard deviation = 2.075 hours
Standard error = 2.075/4.472 (the square root of N) = .464
1.9/.464 (the standard error) = 4.095 = t-score

A t-score of 4.095 with 20–1 df has a probability value "beyond .001"; that is, a value as large as 4.095 would occur by chance only 1 in 1,000 times. Hence, we conclude that the sample was not within normal sample variation of the population. In other words, the sample was significantly different in the time spent watching television when compared with the national average. Notice that this says nothing about *why* the sample was different, only that it was different.

Note: Data are fictional.

FIGURE 11.5   Illustration of T-Test: Sample versus Population (*Source:* Bruning, James L., and B. L. Kintz. 1987. *Computational Handbook of Statistics.* Glenview, Ill.: Scott, Foresman.)

T-Test: Sample versus Sample

The second kind of t-test, more common than the previous, is whether the mean of one sample is different from the mean of another. Examples are given in Figures 11.6 and 11.7. The first, Figure 11.6, illustrates a scenario suggested in Chapter 10, a test of whether children's access to a newspaper improved their reading scores.

Variable: Score on reading skill.
Manipulation: Group 1 has classroom access to newspaper; group 2 does not.

Hypothesis: Reading score of group 1 is not different from reading score of group 2. (This is called the *null hypothesis,* because it indicates "no difference." It is a kind of strawman hypothesis because the analyst actually expects the opposite, that the two groups will be different. The opposite of the null hypothesis is the *alternative hypothesis,* dubbed H_1.)

Group 1 (newspaper)		Group 2 (no newspaper)	
Student	*Score*	*Student*	*Score*
1	7	1	7
2	8	2	5
3	7	3	5
4	9	4	8
5	5	5	7
6	8	6	4
7	9	7	6
8	8	8	7
9	8	9	6
10	7	10	6

T-Test (Output adapted from SPSS/PC+; Norusis, 1988):

	Number of Cases	Mean	Standard Deviation (SD)	Standard Error (SE)
Pupils in Group 1	10	7.6	1.174	.371
Pupils in Group 2	10	6.1	1.197	.379

Pooled Variance Estimate					Separate Variance Estimate			
F Value	2-Tail Probability	T Value	Degrees of Freedom (df)	2-Tail Probability	T Value	Degrees of Freedom (df)	2-Tail Probability
1.04	.954	2.83	18	.011	2.83	17.99	.011

Explanation of output: Students in group 1 had a higher reading score, and the difference between them and their peers in group 2 was significant at the level of p. = 011. In this fictional experiment, access to the newspaper *mattered.*

Note: Data are fictional.

FIGURE 11.6 An Illustration of the T-Test for the Difference between Independent Samples

The second, Figure 11.7, is from the Environmental Survey introduced in Chapter 10. It compares student attitudes on the environment at two points in time, October 1991 and October 1992.

The t-test for independent samples can be represented by either of the two following formulas: Formula 11.7, formidable in appearance, illustrates the role of variance in the calculations; Formula 11.8 is probably easier to conceptualize. The two formulas produce the same result.

Dependent variable: USPOLLUT (severity of pollution in the United States)
Independent variable: Time 1–2 (year of response to question)

	Number of Cases	Mean (M)	Standard Deviation (SD)	Standard Error (SE)
Time 1	234	5.42	1.01	.066
Time 2	235	5.37	1.01	.066

		Pooled Variance Estimate			Separate Variance Estimate		
F-Value	2-Tail Probability	T-Value	df	2-Tail Probability	T-Value	df	2-Tail Probability
1.01	.966	.57	467	.570	.57	466	.570

Interpretation: At time 1 (October 1991), the average student attitude toward environmental pollution as an issue was 5.42; after a year—time 2 (October 1992)—in which the environment was a political issue in the 1992 presidential campaign, the average student attitude score was 5.37. The F-value indicates that the variances of the two groups were not significantly different. The variances being equal, the pooled variance *estimate* was evaluated. The t-value of .57 was nonsignificant.

Conclusion: For these samples, attitudes toward environmental pollution were not significantly different from time 1 to time 2; apparently, the political campaign did not heighten students' concern about the environment.

FIGURE 11.7   A T-Test of Students' Attitude Change toward the Environment at Time 1 and Time 2. This output is adapted from the format used in SPSS/PC+.

$$t = \frac{\overline{X}_1 - \overline{X}_2}{\sqrt{\dfrac{\left\{\Sigma X_1^2 - \dfrac{(\Sigma X_1)^2}{N} + \Sigma X_2^2 - \dfrac{(\Sigma X_2)^2}{N}\right\}}{(N_1 + N_2) - 2}}} \times \left\{\dfrac{1}{N_1} + \dfrac{1}{N_2}\right\}$$ (Formula 11.7)

$$t = \frac{\overline{X}_1 - \overline{X}_2}{SE_{m1} - SE_{m2}} \quad \text{where}$$

$$SE_{m1} - SE_{m2} = \sqrt{SE_{m1}^2 + SE_{m2}^2}$$ (Formula 11.8)

Both formulas propose that the t-value is the difference between two means divided by the combined standard errors of the two means. The t-score is a ratio of the mean differences to the mean errors.

Notice that both formulas rely on sample *means, standard deviations,* and *standard errors.* A table of t-values (found in most basic statistics texts) will enable the researcher to find whether a t-score was likely to have occurred as a result of random variation. In the case of the fictional data in Figure 11.7, a t-value of 2.83 most often would occur as a function of random variation only 11 times in 1,000 (p. = .011). In other words, access to the newspaper in this fictional comparison significantly improved the reading scores of the young readers.

LEARN BY DOING

This exercise asks you to gather a small amount of data and to calculate a t-test. First, choose a topic. For example, you could ask whether men and women students are equal in their newspaper reading or TV news viewing. Write questions such as these: "About how many days in the past week, if any, did you read a newspaper (commercial newspaper, not campus newspaper)? About how many days in the same week, if any, did you watch either of the commercial network national news programs?" After deciding on your topic and your questions, interview about 10 men and 10 women. When you have their responses, array the data the following way:

	Days Read Newspaper		Days Watch TV News	
	Men	Women	Men	Women
person 1	3	4	4	3
2	4	3	4	4
•	•	•	•	•
10	5	4	3	4

Having collected and tabled the data, use Formula 11.8 to conduct a t-test to evaluate a hypothesis such as this: Men and women students at (your school) are equally likely to be (newspaper readers or TV news viewers).

When you have calculated a t-score, and figured the degrees of freedom (i.e., $N - 2$), check the t-score in the t- distribution in any book on statistics. Is the finding significant? Are men and women in your sample different in their use of these two media?

A T-Test from the Environmental Survey

Here is an example of the t-test as calculated from the Environmental Survey presented in Chapter 10. Data were collected in the fall semester of 1991 and the fall semester of 1992. This permitted a test of attitude change from time 1 to time 2. The year of the survey was also the year of the 1992 presidential election campaign, in which the environment was a major issue.

The groups in this test are identified in the variable called GROUP; group 1 = time 1, and group 2 = time 2. (You may need to review the computer program in Chapter 10 again.) The t-test will involve a comparisons of respondents in time 1 and time 2 on the following question from the survey: "Some people feel that the *pollution* problem in American is *severe;* others think it is *mild.* What do *you* think? Using the following scale, please indicate the degree to which you think pollution in America is severe, moderate, or mild . . . " (In the computer program, the question is identified as USPOLLUT.)

What outcomes are possible? Attitudes toward the environment could become *less favorable* if respondents rejected the political rhetoric of the campaign; they could *remain the same;* or they could become *more favorable.* But on the assumption that the increased attention to the environment should reach people not previously moved, we will hypothesize that attitudes toward the environment should reflect greater concern at time 2 than at time 1 (see Figure 11.7).

Figure 11.7 indicated that student attitudes toward the environment did not change significantly from 1991 to 1992, despite the rhetoric of the political campaign. Here is how to interpret the output. There were 234 respondents to the group 1 survey (conducted October 1991), and 235 respondents to the group 2 survey. The mean attitude scores for the groups were very similar, as were the standard deviations and the standard errors. In other words, there was little variation in the scores. The *F-value* tests whether the variances of the groups are equal. A small F-value denotes equal variances. The F-value in this test is very small and highly nonsignificant (significance would require a *p* value of less than .05). The heading "2-Tail Probability" simply provides for the possibility that the t-score was positive or negative. Notice that the variance estimate can be "pooled" or "separate"; if the F-value is large, and variances are unequal, then the pooled variance estimate is appropriate; otherwise, the separate estimate is sufficient (Norusis, 1988 B-122).

And now, the "main event" of the test, the decision point as to whether concern about the environment changed from time 1 to time 2. Under the heading "t-value" (Figure 11.7), you will see the t-score (or t-value) = .57, a very small t-score that is not significant. (It is merely coincidental that the probability value is also .57; that does not usually happen.) What the test shows is that when we compare the concern of group 1 with the concern of group 2, they are not different—or at least the differences could be attributed to chance.

The statistic in this case has given us a neat, clean, objective decision point—a clinical answer to what might otherwise have been a subjective question.

T-Test for Related Samples

A final note about the t-test: When the two groups being compared are *related* in some fashion—for example, one group of readers was tested at time 1 and again at time 2—a special form of the t-test may be needed, called the *t-test for related measures* (Bruning and Kintz, 1987). Bruning and Kintz suggest two formulas. The first subtracts the correlation of the groups from the variance. The second, much simpler to calculate, converts individual scores to *difference* scores and computes the variance on the basis of those scores. Both formulas can be found in many standard statistical texts.[1]

ANALYSIS OF VARIANCE

The t-tests suggested in formulas 11.7 and 11.8 are suitable for the comparison of two groups, but when an experiment involves several comparisons, the proper statistical technique is *analysis of variance,* often shortened to **ANOVA.** It is a natural extension of the means test, but places a greater emphasis on the variation within and among groups than on the means of the groups. ANOVA separates the variation that occurs on the dependent variable into variance that is contributed by the independent variable (called "explained" variance) and variance that is not otherwise explained (called "error" or "residual" variance). The "explained" variance is called the "main effect."

ANOVA employs an F-distribution, rather than a T-distribution. The F-ration is given in either of two formulas, which are equivalent (Weaver, 1989, 82–83; see also Nie, 1975).

There are two formulas for calculating the "F" statistic:

| **Formula 1** | **Formula 2** |

$$F = \frac{SS \text{ between}/(k-1)}{SS \text{ within}/(n-k)} = \frac{MS \text{ between or MS}_b}{MS \text{ within or MS}_w}$$

Where SS between = sum of squares for between-group variance
SS within = sum of squares for within-group variance
k = the number of samples or groups involved
n = the number of elements sampled for study
MSb = mean squares between groups
MSw = mean squares within groups   (Formula 11.8)

Example of One-Way ANOVA

The simplest kind of ANOVA is called *one-way ANOVA* because it examines the effect of only one factor on a dependent variable. Here is an example of one-way ANOVA: We will set up a simple experiment and use fictional data. Let's say that we have three small groups of respondents, and we want to find out whether a news story byline (which gives the author's name) influences respondents' estimates of the story's credibility. The samples are small for ease of calculation; but ANOVA typically uses small samples, of 30 or fewer, because the test is for *group* comparisons, not necessarily cross-sectional purposes. The emphasis therefore is on internal validity, which should be high, rather than on external validity, which might be low.

So that we can compare the three groups, let's assume they are comparable on important criteria—namely, that they are evenly represented by gender, age, and education; that they have similar reading skills; and that they have similar experience with news reading. Our goal is to control the research situation so that if the scores of one group are different from the scores of another, the difference must be attributable the experimental variable.

So let's say that we have prepared one news article, but we want to present it in either of three conditions: no byline, male byline, or female byline. The first hypothesis will be that the news story with a male byline and the news story with a female byline will *both* have significantly higher credibility than one without a byline. The second hypothesis will be that the credibility level of the byline story does not depend on the apparent gender of the writer.

To conduct this experiment, we select 30 persons and randomly assign them to three groups of 10 each. Group 1, for no reason other than convenience, will read the news story without a byline. Group 2 will read the story with a male byline; and group 3 will read the story with a female byline. Keep in mind that each group reads the same story; only the byline is different. If the byline is effective in enhancing the credibility of a story (our first hypothesis), then the scores of groups 2 and 3 should both be higher than the score of group 1. And according to our second hypothesis, the difference between groups 2 and 3 should be nonsignificant.

Now, let's create some numbers to represent these three conditions. (Remember that these are fictional data.) Scores are the respondents' estimates of the credibility of the news story that they read. Assume that the higher the number, on a scale from 1 to 7, the greater the believability.

	Group 1 (Control)	Group 2 (Male Byline)	Group 3 (Female Byline)
	5	5	6
	4	6	5
	4	5	4
	3	6	6
	4	4	5
	3	3	7
	5	5	5
	2	7	6
	4	5	5
	5	5	5
Total:	39	51	54
Mean:	3.9	5.1	5.4

Few people today would need or wish to calculate ANOVA by hand, because it is quickly done by computer. However, in the belief that hand calculation will enhance your understanding of the technique, the following description of the calculation is presented. Notice that the calculation will involve computation of the sum of squares and the square of the sum both for groups and for the entire table, in much the same manner as the earlier calculation of the simple variance of a set of scores (see Formula 11.3).

Our first goal is to calculate the "sum of squares between groups." This produces the so-called "main effect of the independent variable," and the "sum of squares within groups," which is the unexplained, error, or residual portion of the variance. Our second goal is to pose them as a ration that will generate an F-score. The method to meet those goals is as follows:

1. Take the sum of each group's scores, square the sum, and divide by the number of observations in the group. Add the results of the three computations: $(39 \times 39) / 10 + (51 \times 51) / 10 + (54 \times 54) / 10 = $ _____.
2. Add up all the scores in the table, square the sum, and divide by the total number of observations: $(5 + 4 + \ldots + 5 = $ _____$)^2/30$. Subtract this number from the number generated in step 1. The result is the sum of

squares between groups, or *SSb,* the variance attributable to being in a particular group in the set, the main effect.

3. Next, calculate the "sum of squares within," the portion of variation not accounted for by group membership, sometimes written as *SSerror,* or *SSwithin.* So, calculate the sum of the squares for each group, and subtract each sum from the square of the scores of the group divided by *N,* the number of observations in the group. The difference is the *SSw* for each group.

4. Add up the *SSw* values for the three groups. Now, position the *SSb* in ratio form over *SSw.* One additional piece of information is needed, however; that is a correction for the number of groups and individuals in the study. Divide *SSb* by *K* - 1, the number of groups minus 1. Divide *SSw* by *N* − *K,* the number of persons in the study minus the number of groups.

5. The division given in the preceding instruction results in what is called a "mean square between," or *MSb,* and a "mean square within," or *MSw.*

6. Now, divide *MSb* by *MSw* to arrive at an F- score. Take the F-score to an F-distribution table and learn whether the score is large enough to be significant. Significance would suggest that the F-score was too large to have been expected to occur as a matter of chance variation.

When you have completed the above calculations by hand, compare your results with the ANOVA table in Figure 11.8. The table was adapted from SPSS/PC+ computer output. Note that the "between groups" comparison, called the "main effect" or explained portion of the variance (which is the principal finding of the table), is "significant" at $p = .005$. This means that there was a byline effect, at least two of the groups were different, but we don't yet know for sure which ones.

The main effect has two degrees of freedom (*df*) because *df* is calculated as the number of groups minus 1. The sum of squares divided by the *df* equals 6.3, the *MSb,* or mean square between groups. Finally, the ratio of the main effect, or explained variance to the unexplained (*SSw,* residual, or error term) is 6.3/.97 = 6.49. In a table of F- scores, an *F* as large as 6.49 with two is not likely to occur by chance more than 5 times in 1,000; hence, the probability level is $p. = .005$.

There is one more step in analyzing this output. The ANOVA table tells us only that at least two of the groups are different; it does not say which ones. In other words, the significant F-score *might* reflect a difference between the male and female bylines, not the absence of a byline. It is up to us to use another test to decide which of the groups is different from which others. Several are available. The three most common are the *Scheffe test,* the *Tukey test,* and *Duncan's multiple-range test.* Each applies an objective statistical criterion to decide which groups are different. The reasons for selecting one test over another are more technical than can be described in this text, but for most purposes, the Duncan's multiple-range test or the Scheffe test will suffice.

We can see in Figure 11.8 that the mean credibility for the "no byline" group was lower than either of the byline groups; and since the F-score is significant, we have evidence that a byline contributes importantly to the credibility of the story.

Was the apparent sex of the byline also important? The multiple- range test, in Level 3 of Figure 11.8, indicates that it was not. The means of the male- and

LEVEL 1. Analysis of Variance

Dependent variable: Credibility owing to byline
Independent variable: Presence of byline; sex of writer

Source:	df	Sum of Squares	Mean Squares	F-Ratio	F-Probability
Between groups	2	12.6	6.3	6.49	.005
Within groups	27	26.2	.97		
Total	29	38.8			

Note: $MSb/MSw = 6.49/.97 = 6.49$ = F-ratio.

LEVEL 2. Summary Statistics and Confidence Intervals

Group	Count	M	SD	Standard Error	95-Percent Confidence Interval
1	10	3.9	.9944	.3145	3.18–4.61
2	10	5.1	1.1005	.3480	4.31–5.88
3	10	5.4	.8433	.2667	4.79–6.00

Group	Minimum	Maximum
1	2.0	5.0
2	3.0	7.0
3	4.0	7.0
Total	2.0	7.0

LEVEL 3. Multiple Range Test, $p = .05$.

	G r p 1	G r p 2	G r p 3
Mean	Group		
3.9	1		
5.1	2	a	
5.4	3	a	

[a]Pairs of groups significantly different at $p = .05$. How to interpret the multiple range test: Groups 2 and 3 are significantly different from group 1, but not from each other.

FIGURE 11.8   An Illustration of One-Way ANOVA

female-byline stories were not significantly different. So, we can conclude from this fictional set that having a byline significantly enhances credibility, but the apparent sex of the person named in the byline does not.

Is this better than intuition? It is, because an objective criterion was used, the mean and variance of the groups, and because we tested the magnitude of the variance against a theoretical distribution of F-scores. We cannot say for *certain* that the byline made the difference, or that the difference is real, but we can say that something other than chance probably led to the observed effect.

Factorial ANOVA

In our example, there was a single variable; hence the analysis was *one-way*. But in research, it often happens that multiple comparisons involve multiple independent variables, or factors. For example, most variables have not one but several "causes" or explanatory variables.

Suppose we said the credibility of a news story was explained not only by the presence or absence of a byline, but also by "the number of sources used to authenticate the story." The number of sources would then be a new variable in the analysis. If we were to categorize the number of sources into high, medium, and low, and analyze this variable in the context of the presence of a byline, we would have 3×3 *factorial* ANOVA. That is, we would have three levels of the byline variable (none, male, female) and three of the source variable (high, medium, low).

Any ANOVA with two or more independent variables can be a "factorial" ANOVA. It is conceived as such because an independent variable working alone in relation to a dependent variable may make a different contribution in relation to a second or later independent variable. The effect of factor A in relation to factor B or C on the dependent variable is called an *interaction effect*. The interaction effect can be thought of as the contribution of two variables together that would not be observed for the variables separately. If differences in the dependent variable are merely the same for one variable and another, then the interaction component of the analysis will tend to be zero (Nie et al., 1975, 402).

By analogy, you can see that the interaction effect contributes to the understanding of variation in much the same manner, but on a different calculation, the proportional reduction in error (PRE; see Chapter 10) and the partial correlation, which is discussed below.

Factorial ANOVA is *N*-way, as opposed to one-way. For example, factorial ANOVAs such as $2 \times 2 \times 2 \times 2 \times 2$ are fairly common. The calculations for an *N*-way analysis are similar in concept to what you have seen above for one-way ANOVAs, but are more appropriate to an advanced course in statistics and research methods.

TESTS OF CORRELATION

Whereas the t-test is a means test, correlation is a measure of "association." *Correlation* measures the extent to which scores on one variable change in relation to scores on another. The significance of the correlation tells whether the systematic variation is greater than could be attributed to chance; in other words, whether the correlation is significantly greater than zero.

The correlation of verbal and math Scholastic Achievement Test (SAT) scores, and the correlation of IQ and classroom performance for a sample of school children, are two typical correlations. Another very straightforward example is the relation between height and weight. We all know people who are relatively tall but light, and some who are short and heavy, but in general a person's weight presumably would be "related" to height: the taller the person, the heavier. To measure the correlation, we simply would select a sample of persons and record the height and weight of each. Our computations would then tell us the degree to which height and weight varied together.

The correlation between any two variables can be any number from minus 1 to plus 1. A zero correlation means there is no systematic relationship. Knowing that correlation cannot exceed 1.0 is very helpful. For example, a correlation of .31 has no particular meaning of its own, unless we know that such a correlation is roughly one-third as strong a correlation as is possible. And so, the proximity of the correlation to zero is very important in the interpretation of the coefficient.

Consider again the unknown correlation between height and weight. If every time a person grew in height by one unit the person also gained a unit of weight, then we could say that height and weight were perfectly, linearly related. If we were to *plot* the relation, our graph would be a straight line from the least height and weight to the most. But we know clearly that height and weight are not so neatly related, and so the correlation must be smaller than 1.0.

It is helpful to think of correlation in terms of a graph. The less linear the relationship, the more scattered the scores on the graph. The stronger the relationship, the more nearly the data will plot on a straight line. At the *zero-correlation point,* the graph would not have any of the characteristics of a straight line, and there would be no apparent relationship between the variables. But if the correlation were *moderate,* the graph of the distribution would begin to show signs of making a line from low to high, or from high to low.

In general, a low correlation is considered to be in the range 0 to .30 (absolute value); a moderate correlation, .31 to .60; and a high correlation, greater than .60. Perfect correlations in behavioral data are unlikely. However, when the sample size is very large or very small, these ranges can be deceiving. In a very large sample, a very small correlation may be significant; in a very small sample, significance might require a rather large correlation. Hence, any correlation must be evaluated in the context of the sample size.

Accounting for Variance

Many statisticians feel that the correlation coefficient by itself is insufficient, and that the *square of the correlation,* known as R-square, is a better indicator. R-square estimates the percentage of variance accounted for by the relationship between variables. In other words, the relationship between variables is conceived as having an "explained" portion of variance and an "unexplained," or error portion. The R-square describes the percentage of variation that would not likely be attributed to chance variation.

Suppose a correlation of +.31 is found between the purchase of a particular product and the frequency of exposure to an advertisement for that product. Nine percent of the purchase behavior is accounted for by exposure to the advertising. The other 91 percent of the variation (100 percent minus 9 percent) is unexplained:

Some people buy the product because of an attractive display; others because of the price; and others purely by chance. Keep in mind that the correlation of .31 does not tell us to what extent the ad *caused* the purchase behavior; it only estimates the systematic variation between the two variables.

Notice that the square of any less-than-perfect correlation is smaller than the correlation. For example, a correlation of .31 has an R-square of .31 × .31 = .09, or 9.6 percent. The small number is seen as a more realistic estimate of the relationship between variables, not because it is small but because it has eliminated variation that could be attributed to chance.

The concept of correlation is one of the most useful in research and you should think carefully about how it works. Figure 11.9 gives two examples that illustrate the method.

It is important to remember that correlations can be either positive or negative. If *increases in A* are associated with *increases in B*, the relationship is positive. If *decreases in A* are associated with *decreases in B*, the relationship also is positive. The variables vary together. But if one variable *increases* as the other *decreases*, the correlation is negative or inverse.

A straight line is not the only way to describe a correlation. For example, if we correlated a measure of news reading with a measure of age, we probably would get a *curved* line; reading would increase with age, but eventually would peak and then fall. Why? Reading by older people probably declines because of eyesight, health, and cost factors, among others.

A *curvilinear relationship* will not be properly represented by conventional measures of correlation. Instead, special forms, such as the *correlation ratio* (represented by the Greek letter *eta*, η), comparable to one-way ANOVA, should be used. The correlation ratio is described in numerous standard statistics texts.

The most common test of correlation is the *Pearson product-moment correlation coefficient* (R) It requires interval level measures for both variables. The formula is given as:

$$R = \frac{\Sigma(X - \overline{X})(Y - \overline{Y})}{\sqrt{[\Sigma(\overline{X} - X)^2][\Sigma(\overline{Y} - Y)^2]}} \quad \text{or}$$

$$R = \frac{N\Sigma XY - (\Sigma X)(\Sigma Y)}{\sqrt{[N\Sigma X^2 - (\Sigma X)^2][N\Sigma Y^2 - (\Sigma Y)^2]}} \qquad \text{(Formula 11.9)}$$

Imposing in appearance, the formula most simply involves the same quantities that we have discussed to this point, especially the variance and standard deviation and the ratio of the variances between the variables. The formula reads: Correlation (R) is equal to N times the sum of the cross-products of X and Y, minus the sum of X times the sum of Y, divided by the square root of the variance of the X variable times the Y variable.

Keep in mind that the intent of the formula is to estimate the common variance of X and Y, to give it a positive or negative sign, and to pose it as a ratio of the shared variance to the individual variance. The correlation ratio is a coefficient

Example A

Person	Score on Test 1	Score on Test 2
1	6	5
2	6	4
3	5	3
4	5	4
5	5	2
6	6	5
7	6	4
8	6	3
9	4	3
10	4	2

In this example, note that the scores in test 2 remain fairly consistent in relation to the scores on test 1; as scores on test 1 rise or fall scores on test 2 also rise or fall.

For this set of numbers, the correlation between test 1 and test 2 is $r = .6872$, significant at p .03.

Example B

Person	Score on Test 1	Score on Test 2
1	50	7
2	51	7
3	52	6
4	53	6
5	54	7
6	55	5
7	57	5
8	56	4
9	59	3
10	60	2

In this example as one set of scores rises, the other falls; this produces a *negative* correlation, and a high one.

For this set of numbers, the correlation between test 1 and test 2 is $r = -.9208$, a strong negative correlation.

Note: All data are fictional.

FIGURE 11.9   Examples of Correlation

whose significance is tabled in any standard statistical textbook in your library. As a result, the analyst can compute a correlation coefficient, decide the degrees of freedom, and go to a table to find the significance.

For example, if the sample were 100 pairs, and the correlation were .19, the analyst would find the correlation significant at $p = .05$. In other words, the table would show that such a correlation is unlikely to occur as a function of chance more than 5 times in 100. If the analyst wished to reduce the chance of error to $p = 0.1$ (1 in 100), a correlation of .25 would be required. But if, instead of 100 pairs, the analyst had only 25, a correlation of .38 would be required to meet the minimal .05 level.

In general, the larger the sample, the smaller the correlation required for significance. With very large samples, small correlations can be significant. Hence, many researchers opt to set very stringent significance levels.

The technique of correlation has several permutations. When the analyst has a continuous measure for one variable and a rank-ordered measure on another, the proper correlation coefficient is the *Spearman rank-order correlation,* designated by the Greek letter *rho.* It converts the continuous variable to a rank-ordered variable, then computes the difference between the ranks of the two variables. The formula is as follows (Bruning and Kintz, 1987):

$$\rho = 1 - \frac{6\Sigma D^2}{N(N^2 - 1)}$$

(Formula 11.10)

The formula reads: *Rho* equals 1 minus 6 times the sum of the squared difference scores divided by *N* times *N-* squared minus 1. In the formula, *D* is the difference score between a pair of ranks.

Extensions of Correlation

Here are some less frequent extensions of correlation; you will need to consult other texts for additional details on these.

1. Kendall's *Tau* is a measure of correlation used when the analyst has pairs of rank-ordered (not continuous) data.
2. The point-biserial correlation is appropriate when one variable is continuous (i.e., can take any value) and one is dichotomous (0–1, such as male–female, or yes–no).
3. The correlation ratio *eta* can be used when the relationship between two variables is curved.
4. Finally, correlation can be extended to three variables, either in multiple correlation or in partial correlation.

Partial Correlation.   *Partial correlation* tests the effect of two variables while the third is held constant. The procedure is roughly analogous to proportional reduction in error (PRE), which was discussed in regard to cross-tabulation (Chapter 10). In both cases, the intent is to identify the unique contribution of a variable to the explanation of a dependent variable.

Correlation Is Not Causation

It is important to recognize that correlation is not the same as causation. In other words, if two variables are correlated, it does not necessarily follow that one *causes* any change in the other. Correlations are merely numeric relationships; they can occur by chance.

For example, if you were to select a number of variables and measure them, and correlate them, there is a possibility that one or more correlations would be significant, even without apparent justification. Therefore, great caution is required. If two variables are correlated, the correlation must be plausible; preferably, it would have been *predicted* on the basis of previous research, and capable of some other form of corroboration.

To illustrate the point, the author correlated eight *apparently unrelated variables* in a survey of 2,389 freshmen at a major southeastern state university. The variables were (a) distance of the respondent from home (DISTHOME), (b) the number of schools to which the respondent applied (NUMAPPLY), (c) the respondent's self-estimate of emotional health (SLFRAT06), (d) estimated parental income (INCOME), (e) attitude about whether the government is protecting the consumer (VIEWS01), (f) number of hours per week watching television (HRSPWK09), and (g) having a goal of being well-off, financially (GOALS08).

Figure 11.10 shows the matrix of correlations. Notice that the distance a student travels to school is related to family income. That correlation was not expected, but it has some plausibility. We would have no reason to think distance traveled is related to several other of the variables. Yet, look at the correlation matrix in the figure: You can see that the student's distance from home is significantly related to the number of schools applied to. Do we have reason to expect that? In fact, look at all the p values, and identify the ones where $p < .05$; remember that

	DISTHOME	NUMAPPLY	SLFRAT06	INCOME	VIEWS01	HRSPWK09	GOALS08
DISTHOME	1.0000 (0) p =						
NUMAPPLY	.2624 (2389) p = .000	1.0000 (0) p =					
SLFRAT06	.0212 (2389) p = .301	.0240 (2389) p = .242	1.0000 (0) p =				
INCOME	.0518 (2389) p = .011	.0543 (2389) p = .008	.1300 (2389) p = .000	1.0000 (0) p =			
VIEWS01	.0041 (2389) p = .840	−.0094 (2389) p = .646	.0120 (2389) p = .557	.0480 (2389) p = .019	1.0000 (0) p =		
HRSPWK09	−.0015 (2389) p = .943	−.0487 (2389) p = .017	.0183 (2389) p = .370	.0273 (2389) p = .183	.0718 (2389) p = .000	1.0000 (0) p =	
GOALS08	.0028 (2389) p = .891	−.0108 (2389) p = .598	.1175 (2389) p = .000	.0559 (2389) p = .006	.0464 (2389) p = .023	.1129 (2389) p = .000	1.0000 (0) p =

FIGURE 11.10 An Illustration of Random Correlation: Seven Variables Selected at Whim

each of the variables was selected because it was unlikely to be related to any of the others.

Figure 11.10 indicates that, for some reason, maybe chance, the number of hours spent watching television is negatively correlated with the number of schools applied to. The post hoc analyst would say, "Well, that makes sense; if the person is watching television, he or she is unlikely to be simultaneously filling out a complicated application form." But this is speculation.

TV watching is also significantly correlated with concern that the government is not protecting consumers. Again, we might make a case to support this correlation; but suppose it had gone the other way? (Remember, we didn't know what to expect until the data were run.) The point of this illustration is that a test of correlation should be preceded by persuasive reasoning. We need a *reason* to correlate variables, and that reason should account for the variety of possibly rival explanations of the correlation.

SUMMARY

In this chapter the author has presented some of the logic of statistical reasoning. It began with summary statistics: the mean, variance, and standard deviation. These summary statistics are measures of "central tendency" and "dispersion," used to estimate the parameters of the population. They are the foundation of all parametric statistical tests. The population is approximated by the theoretical sampling distribution.

The t-test, also called a "means test," tests the difference between two means divided by the standard error. Analysis of variance (ANOVA) is an extension of the means test that focuses on the ratio of variances among groups.

Correlation is a test of association between variables. It is a ratio, the covariance of two variables divided by the product of the two variances. Most figuratively, it is the extent to which two variables "vary together." The t-test, ANOVA and correlation are integral parametric statistical hypothesis testing.

STUDY QUESTIONS AND EXERCISES

1. What is the purpose of measuring the variance of a sample? Refer back to the text to answer this question.

2. Construct a situation that would call for correlation and another situation that would call for a t-test; make up a very small data set to represent each. Calculate the t-test only.

3. Under what conditions would a person use ANOVA rather than a t-test?

4. Why do researchers typically rely on the .05 significance level? When should it be altered?

NOTE

1. Sandler (see Bruning and Kintz, 1987) extended this notion with the *A statistic,* ratio of the sum of the squared difference scores to the sum of the difference scores squared. But these rarer uses of the t-test are beyond the scope of this introductory text. If you are interested, consult any of several standard statistics texts for examples of how to apply the formulas.

SOURCES

Babbie, Earl. 1989. *The Practice of Social Research.* 5th ed. Belmont, Calif.: Wadsworth.

Bruning, James L., and B. L. Kintz. 1987. *Computational Handbook of Statistics.* Glenview, Ill: Scott, Foresman.

Glass, Gene V., and Julian C. Stanley. 1970. *Statistical Methods in Education and Psychology.* Englewood Cliffs, N.J.: Prentice-Hall.

Kerlinger, Fred N. 1973. *Foundations of Behavioral Research.* 2d ed. New York: Holt, Rinehart & Winston.

Mohr, Lawrence B. 1990. *Understanding Significance Testing.* Newbury Park, Calif.: Sage.

Nie, Norman H., C. Hadlai Hull, Jean G. Jenkins, Karin Steinbrenner, and Dale H. Bent. 1975. *Statistical Package for the Social Sciences.* New York: McGraw Hill.

Norusis, Marija J. 1988. *SPSS/PC+ V2.0 Base Manual for the IBM PC/XT/AT and PS/2* (SPSS Inc., 444 North Michigan Avenue, Chicago, IL 60611).

Weaver David. 1989. Basic Statistical Tools. In *Research Methods in Mass Communications Research,* ed. Guido H. Stempel, III, and Bruce H. Westley. Englewood Cliffs, N.J.: Prentice-Hall.

12

231-242

Advanced and Nonparametric Data Analysis

□

OBJECTIVES

After studying this chapter, you should be able to:

1. Express the relationship between correlation and analysis of variance.

2. Distinguish between two types of regression analysis.

3. Interpret aspects of a multiple-regression computer printout.

4. Interpret aspects of factor-analysis computer printout.

5. Distinguish between parametric and nonparametric tests.

6. Compute simple chi-square tests.

INTRODUCTION

"Close examination shows the conceptual bases underlying different approaches to data analysis to be the same or similar" (Kerlinger, 1973, 632). Kerlinger's words are meaningful. Despite the awesome range of square-roots, squares, *N* minus 1, and so forth, the fundamental purpose and method of statistics is repetitive. *Statis-*

not same thing

tical tests examine the extent of differences in central tendency or variance, and estimate whether the observed statistics could be attributable to chance.

Furthermore, it is possible to swing from one statistical test to another on a "common thread," like the vine—forgive the simile— that carried Tarzan from tree to tree across the jungle. For example, we have said that the t-test is the difference between two means divided by the standard error; the standard error, of course, is the standard deviation divided by the square root of *N* minus 1. The standard deviation without the radical is the variance. The test known as analysis of variance (ANOVA) focuses on the variance, but simply uses a sum-of-squares approach to the calculation. The F-score in ANOVA is merely the square of the T-score when df are equivalent.

ANOVA is akin to correlation; ANOVA determines whether a relationship exists between variables, and correlation estimates its extent. For example, ANOVA tests whether the dependent variable, *Y*, is affected by the independent variable, *X*. The effect is represented in a F-statistic. An ANOVA relationship can be roughly converted to correlation by taking the square root of the ratio of the "sums of squares between groups" to the "sums of squares total"; both measures are available in conventional ANOVA computer output (Kerlinger, 1986). The correlation of an ANOVA can be important, because the F-score indicates only whether the variation is greater than would be expected by chance, not the extent of the relationship. The formula for the correlation of two variables in an ANOVA is:

$$\eta = \sqrt{\frac{SSb}{SSt}}$$

Where $SSt = SSb + SSw$ (Formula 12.1)

How is such a correlation interpreted? If SSb happens to be exactly the same as SSt, which is unlikely, then the coefficient is zero and there is no relationship between the variables. But if a relationship exists, and if the F-score for the relationship is significant, as indicated by the F-table, then the correlation between the variables is significant. *Eta* can also be evaluated in terms of r-squared; if the correlation ratio is squared, it provides the amount of shared variance between the variables (Kerlinger, 1973).

The point is, if you can keep an eye on the logic of the process, you will discover that parametric statistical tests are closely related, both conceptually and in calculation. The choice of test depends on (a) the level of the data (nominal, ordinal, or interval/ratio), (b) more specifically, whether the data are categorical or continuous, (c) the number of independent variables, (d) whether variables must be tested for "interaction," and (e) whether the percentage of variance explained is central to the idea being tested.

This chapter will continue the text's mission of explaining the range of statistical testing while focusing on the commonalities of the methods. The three principal foci of the chapter will be regression analysis, factor analysis, and nonparametric tests.

REGRESSION ANALYSIS

Regression analysis, one of the most important tools in the practice of social science research, is an extension of correlation and is also fundamentally related to ANOVA. Whereas correlation describes the extent to which variables vary together, regression adds an estimate of the unit of change in Y associated with each unit of X. The regression formula calculates a "weight" for the independent variable, X, such that the correlation line drawn through the data has the minimum amount of error. The line is called the *least squares* line because it minimizes the squared deviations from the mean.

Simple Regression

Regression analysis is of two types, *simple* and *multiple*. **Simple regression** is used to predict an outcome on one variable on the basis of another.

Here is an example. Let's say that we need to predict a high school student's GPA, and we have reason to believe that the student's knowledge of current events will help us to do that. Clearly the prediction would be imperfect: Some students with limited knowledge of current events would grade well, while others with extensive knowledge might grade poorly; but overall, we would expect that high school grades would be related to knowledge of current events.

For example, look at the following fictional data showing the supposed relationship between high school GPA (the Y variable) and a measure of News Knowledge (the X variable) for 10 students.

person	Y variable: High School GPA	X variable: News Knowledge
1	2.9	3.1
2	3.2	3.2
3	2.5	2.9
4	3.5	3.7
5	3.0	3.2
6	2.8	3.4
7	2.5	3.0
8	2.8	2.8
9	2.9	3.5
10	2.8	3.0

This is a very small sample for purposes of the illustration; prediction should be improved by increasing the sample size. In looking at the data, can you see any relationship between the variables? The relationship can be seen more clearly if we plot the pairs on a graph as in Figure 12.1.

Had the relationship been perfect, every increment of increase in news

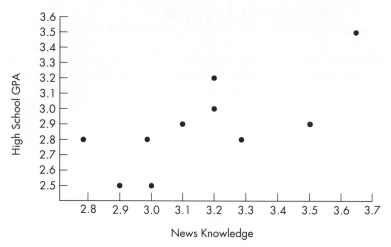

FIGURE 12.1 Plotting the Relationship between Variables

knowledge would have been accompanied by an increment of increase in GPA. The 1's in the graph would have formed a straight, diagonal line. In the absence of a perfectly straight line, a perfect correlation between the variables, we use what is called the "line of least squares." This is the line that would be formed by subtracting each score from the mean so that the best possible line is formed from the existing data.

The formula for predicting the Y variable from the X variable is:

$Y = BX + A$ where, in our example

X = the news knowledge score
A = the score at which the regression line crosses vertical axis of graph
B = a measure of the slope of the line   (Formula 12.2)

Measures of A and B each also have formulas:

$$B = \frac{N\, \Sigma XY - (\Sigma X)(\Sigma Y)}{N\Sigma X^2 - (\Sigma X)^2}$$ (Formula 12.3)

$$A = Y - BX$$ (Formula 12.4)

Following are the calculations required by these formulas. Calculate each statistic for yourself, and compare with the following data.

1. The sum of the X scores _____28.9_____
2. The sum of the Y scores _____31.8_____
3. The mean of the X scores _____2.89_____
4. The mean of the Y scores _____3.18_____
5. The sum of the squares of the X scores _____84.33_____
6. The sum of the squares of the Y scores _____101.84_____
7. N times the sum of the XY scores _____924.4_____
8. The sum of X times the sum of Y _____919.02_____
9. B (see Formula 12.3) _____.6650_____
10. A (see Formula 12.4) _____1.258_____

Now, with these calculations and the fictional data, the GPA for Student 1 can be predicted. Remember, the formula is $BX + A$. Student 1's X score is 3.1; B is .6650 and A is 1.258

$$.6650 \text{ times } 3.1 + 1.258 = 3.319$$

Although the predicted GPA for student 1 was 3.319, the actual GPA was 2.9; the formula overestimated performance, or the student did not live up to expectations. Some other students in the group will fit the model more neatly. But the point is that regression provides an objective method of estimating an outcome on one variable based on another. When the sample is large, and when the relationship between variables is strong, simple regression can be very useful as a management and decision-making tool.

Remember, the point of all this is (a) to draw the best line through the data, (b) to estimate the change on Y due to X, and (c) in effect, to predict Y on the basis of X. In the example in Figure 12.1, the calculations identified a *constant*, or beginning point on the regression line, and a *weight* with which to multiply each student's high school GPA. The calculations permit us to predict the GPA on the basis of news knowledge, not just for any student in the study, but also for any in the population.

The linear relationship between the Y and X variables can be described by the shared variance of Y and X represented as an F-score on the F-distribution. F-scores are conveniently tabled in many statistics books; the user merely calculates the F-score and then checks the table to see if an F- score of a given size is likely at a given level of probability. If the data are analyzed by computer, the probability of an F- value will be given in the regression table printout.

Multiple Regression

Multiple regression analysis is very common in social science research (Ache, 1982; Berry, 1985). It is powerful because it allows simultaneous examination of *several* independent variables against a dependent variable (Shroeder, Sjoquist, and Stephan, 1986). This reveals how each of the variables contributes to the variance and whether the contribution is unique or in combination with another variable.

When several variables are used to "explain" the variation in a dependent variation, the formulation—called a **statistical model**—takes the form of an equation: $Y = bo + b1x + b2x + b3x + e$, where Y = the dependent variable, bo = a starting point on the regression line, $b1x$ to $b2x$ = independent variables, and e = error. The intent of regression analysis is to fit the best model (i.e., to explain the most variance with the fewest variables).[1]

An Example. For the Environmental Survey in Chapter 10, respondents ranked several important issues, including environmental pollution, on a scale of 1 to 5. Of course, not all respondents gave it the same rank, but what would explain the variation? Multiple regression can help us find certain relationships.

What variables do you think would influence a person's priority for environmental pollution? A person's sex, politics, and income? For this exercise, the author regressed these against the dependent variable but found only a very slight relationship, with regard to political leaning. But that variable accounted for only 1 percent of the variance in the model—too little to be impressive.

Stronger explanations were needed, and so the author cast a new model that was likely to do a better job of explaining the dependent variable. Variables were:

1. RPOLLUTN—the dependent measure, the rank of environmental pollution for each respondent.
2. USPOLLUT—a measure of how severe the respondent perceives pollution in the United States.
3. BUYRECYC—a behavioral measure, an indication of concern for the environment expressed in the need to buy recyclable products.
4. IUSETV—a measure of whether the respondent gets most environmental news from TV news.
5. IREADMAG—a measure of whether the respondent gets most environmental news from news magazines.
6. NSPRINFO—a measure of whether the respondent gets most environmental news from newspapers.

Why was the model likely to explain more of the variance? A person who thinks environmental pollution is severe will tend to rank it higher than someone who does not; and surely someone who is committed to buying recyclable products ranks pollution high among issues. The mass media questions were included to identify whether one medium more than another might influence a person's perception of the importance of the pollution.

Computer Output

The data were analyzed with the SPSS/PC+ program, and the results are given in Figure 12.2. The figure is a model of the type of output that would be obtained in formal research. In order to examine it fully, you will need to understand some important terms.

Dependent variable: RPOLLUTN—rank of pollution among five major issues.

Independent variables:

1. USPOLLUT—perceived severity of pollution in the United States.
2. BUYRECYC—extent that respondent would buy recyclable products in deference to concern for pollution.
3. IREADMAG—extent that respondent gets environmental information from special publications.
4. NSPRINFO—extent that respondent gets environmental news from newspapers.
5. IUSETV—extent that respondent gets environmental news from TV news.

Variable entered at step 1: USPOLLUT

Multiple R	.281
R-Square	.079
Adjusted R-Square	.077
Standard Error	1.100

ANOVA

	df	Sum of Squares	Mean Square
Regression	1	47.589	47.589
Residual	458	554.608	1.210

F = 39.299   Significance: .0000

Variable entered at step 2: IREADMAG

Multiple R	.335
R-Square	.112
Adjusted R-Square	.109
Standard Error	1.081

ANOVA

	df	Sum of Squares	Mean Square
Regression	2	67.864	33.932
Residual	457	534.333	1.169

F = 29.021   Significance: .0000

Variable Entered at Step Number 3: BUYRECYC

Multiple R	.363
R-Square	.132
Adjusted R-Square	.126
Standard Error	1.070

ANOVA

	df	Sum of Squares	Mean Square
Regression	3	79.526	26.508
Residual	456	522.671	1.146

F = 23.127   Significance: .0000

FIGURE 12.2 An Example of Multiple Regression Analysis: "Explaining" Variance in Students' Ranking of Environmental Pollution

(continued)

Variables in the Equation:

Variables	B	SE B	Beta	T	Sig T
USPOLLUT	−.231	.053	−.20	−4.32	.0000
IREADMAG	−.108	.029	−.163	−3.62	.0000
BUYRECYC	−.131	.041	−.148	−3.19	.0015
(constant)	5.067	.306		16.50	.0000

Variables not in the equation:

IUSETV	.07	1.69	.0906	(n.s.)
NSPRINFO	.01	.41	.6784	(n.s.)

Interpretation: This model proposed that the dependent variable, RPOLLUTN (rank of pollution) was "explained" by five independent variables. Three of the variables, USPOLLUT, IREADMAG and BUYRECYC contributed 33 percent of the explained variance; IUSETV and NSPRINFO were nonsignificant.

Note: This example is adapted from the typical regression report of SPSS/PC+.

FIGURE 12.2 (*continued*)

The **multiple R** is the correlation for the model. It is the square root of the *R-square,* which is the percentage of variance accounted for by the model. The **adjusted R-square** is simply a more conservative estimate of the variance accounted for. The *standard error* can be thought of as plus-or-minus error in the obtained score due to chance.

In Figure 12.2, notice also the brief ANOVA tables. Variability in the dependent variable can be divided into two components, the part attributed to the regression, called **regression sum of squares,** and the part that is not, called **residual sum of squares** (Norusis, 1988, B-202). When the *regression mean square* is divided by the *residual mean square,* much as would occur in ANOVA, an F-score is the result. Here, the F-score equals 39.299, which is highly significant, $p = .0000$.

Regression Coefficient. The column labeled *B* is the regression coefficient; in a complex model it may not be useful because items may not be measured in the same units. More useful is the *beta* (β) which is a standardized regression coefficient. Beta is to *B* as a Z-score (standardized score) is to two different test scores. The beta for USPOLLUT equals .20, which is the strongest in the model. Notice that beta values for NSPRINFO and IUSETV are nonsignificant. In other words, those two variables contribute little to explaining the dependent variable, the rank priority of pollution.

Now, back to the *Multiple R.* R = .281 is not a strong correlation, and when it is squared (see *R-square*), it accounts for only .079 percent of the variance in the model. But that is with only one variable, USPOLLUT, the perceived severity of the problem. What happens when we add other variables? The variable IREADMAG (gets environment news from magazines) contributes importantly to the model; it increases the R-square by about 4 points. Finally, the variable BUYRECYC (buys recyclable products) adds another 2 points, for a total of 13.2 percent of the variance accounted for. Theoretically, we could keep adding variables until all of the variance was accounted for.

Recapping. What has the printout told us? First, in this model, the most important variable was the perceived severity of pollution. Second, respondents in this survey apparently relied heavily on news magazines for their environmental news. Furthermore, their behavior toward the environment (buying recyclables) reinforced their priorities. Contrary to what might have been expected, newspaper and TV news coverage, often criticized for sensationalism, seemed to play little part in the dependent variable.

FACTOR ANALYSIS

Factor analysis is a powerful statistical tool that can be useful either for *discovering* relationships among measured items or for *confirming* such relationships (Kim, 1978; Kim and Mueller, 1978; McKeown and Thomas, 1988). It tells us which variables have been marked similarly by the respondents, and therefore which variables apparently "belong together." Typically, it is described as involving the identification of underlying mathematical relationships. Any set of continuous measures can be factor analyzed.

The calculations begin with the intercorrelation of all items and the development of linear equations to represent the relationships. Items that are correlated are presumed to share commonality and are called factors or dimensions. Following are two brief examples from the Environmental Survey (Figure 10.1).

Factor Example 1

The survey instrument included several items designed to represent environmental "activism":

7. WRITREPS—I would be willing to write to my elected local, state, or federal officials about environmental issues.
12. BOYCOTT—It is okay to boycott companies that pollute the environment.
20. JOINPROT—If while walking across town I happened upon a group of people protesting an oil company responsible for pollution, I would stop to participate.
23. CCOUNCIL—If the city council were meeting to debate whether to allow a potentially hazardous waste disposal site in my community, I would contact a council member to voice my opinion.
24. FITEFIRE—It is okay to "fight fire with fire" by dumping pollutants in the hallways and offices of companies that produce pollution.

Now, if these items were intended to measure activism, could we add up the responses to the five items of any respondent and call the sum of "activism score?" In other words, could the five questions be used as an index of activism? Factor analysis can tell us. Only the items that cluster together—that seem to have similarity—should be summed. Summing dissimilar clusters would be like adding apples and oranges.

In any factor analysis, it is helpful to examine the correlation matrix. Figure 12.3 shows that, for the five activism items, all correlations are low, but that FITEFIRE (dumping pollutants in office hallways) correlates very poorly with three of the four other variables. FITEFIRE correlated slightly but significantly with JOINPROT (willingness to join a protest). This gives us a clue as to what to expect in the subsequent factor analysis: FITEFIRE should be a separate factor.

Computer output for factor analysis usually includes a principal components analysis. It is the program's attempt to find a single best fit for the data. Typically, the one factor accounts for the preponderance of variance. Some researchers and statisticians find useful applications for the principal components approach, but in general it is difficult to interpret. For most purposes, the researcher will find the rotated factor matrix more informative and more useful.

Rotated Factor Matrix. Whereas the principal components procedure draws one principal line through the data, the rotation procedure examines all combinations of variables until the several best subsets have been identified. The output is called a **rotated factor matrix.** There are several methods of rotation, each focusing a dif-

Variable	Cases	Mean	SD
JOINPROT	475	3.06	1.81
FITEFIRE	474	2.46	1.84
WRITREPS	473	4.85	1.56
BOYCOTT	472	5.37	1.60
CCOUNCIL	475	4.71	1.79

	JOINPROT	FITEFIRE	WRITREPS	BOYCOTT	CCOUNCIL
JOINPROT	1.0 •	.24 $p = .000$	.43 $p = .000$	.27 $p = .000$	.35 $p = .000$
FITEFIRE	.24 $p = .000$	1.0 •	.05 $p = .23$	.08 $p = .05$	.04 $p = .33$
WRITREPS	.43 $p = .000$	.05 $p = .23$	1.0 •	.29 $p = .000$	.40 $p = .000$
BOYCOTT	.27 $p = .000$	.08 $p = .052$	.29 $p = .000$	1.0 •	.25 $p = .000$
CCOUNCIL	.35 $p = .000$	.04 $p = .05$	.40 $p = .000$	.25 $p = .000$	1.0 •

Note: SPSS/PC+ uses "•" to denote where a coefficient cannot be computed.

Interpretation: Although all correlations in the matrix are low to moderate, correlation of FITEFIRE is particularly low on all other variables except JOINPROT. This suggests that we should look for this relationship in the subsequent factor analysis.

FIGURE 12.3 Correlation Matrix of Variables in a Factor Analysis

Factor	Eigenvalue	Percentage of Variance	Cumulative Percentage
1	2.06	41.3	41.3
2	1.01	20.2	20.2
3	.77	15.6	77.1
4	.61	12.3	89.5
5	.52	10.5	100.0

Using the "minimum eigenvalue criterion" (see page 242), wherein factors are significant if they are greater than 1.0, this factor analysis identified two factors.

Varimax Rotation

	Factor 1	Factor 2
JOINPROT	.67	.39
FITEFIRE	.01	.96
WRITREPS	.79	−.002
BOYCOTT	.59	.08
CCOUNCIL	.74	−.05

Interpretation: The factor analysis identified two factors, or two levels of environmental activism. Items characterizing each factor are underlined. Items in factor 1 might be interpreted as mild or moderate activism, while factor 2 represents a stronger activism.

FIGURE 12.4 Rotated Factor Matrix: Factor Analysis of Items Measuring Environmental Activism

ferent statistical principle, but probably the most usual rotation is called varimax. It optimizes the variance accounted for.

An example of a factor matrix with varimax rotation is given in Figure 12.4. Coefficients called **factor loadings** represent the extent to which an item correlates with its factor. Notice that each survey item has a loading on both factors, but each is higher on one factor than another. Technically, any factor loading is meaningful, but typically, a loading of .45 or higher is considered to be important if it is not exceeded by the same variable's loading on another factor.

Items that loaded heavily on factor 1 are JOINPROT, WRITREPS, BOYCOTT, and CCOUNCIL. Factor 1 accounts for 41.3 percent of the variance. The only item with an important loading on factor 2 is FITEFIRE. Factor 2 accounts for 20 percent of the variance.

What does the analysis tell us? Look at the difference in the factors: Factor 1 represents moderate activism, and factor 2 is extreme. Many respondents apparently drew the line on FITEFIRE— they were not willing to dump on a company floor to protest pollution. This tells us that if we want to combine items in a common set, we might be justified in combining four of them, but not five. That is an important, objective skill for the analysis of data.

Factor Example 2

The Environmental Survey instrument (Figure 10.1) asked respondents where they usually get environmental *news*.

10. PBSONENV—I listen to programs about the environment on public radio.

14. IREADMAG—I read specialty magazines devoted primarily to environmental issues.

22. IVSETV—I get most of my information about the environment from television.

26. NSPRINFO—I get most of my information about the environment from a local newspaper.

28. NATLNEWS—I get most of my information about the environment from a national newspaper.

35. PBSONENV—I watch programs about the environment on public television.

37. LIBRARY—I get information about the environment from the library.

Can respondents be grouped in regard to when they get their environmental news? Factor analysis can help us find out. First, as before, let's examine the correlation matrix of these variables (see Fig. 12.5). A close look will reveal that the variables NSPRINFO, IUSETV, and NATLNEWS correlate consistently among themselves, but not with the other variables. That is confirmed in the rotated factor matrix in Figure 12.6 (page 244), which shows two primary factors. Factor 1 accounts for 40.7 percent of the variance. The items that load well on Factor 1 are ENVPGMRA (public radio), IREADMAG(magazines), PBSONENV (Public television), and LIBRARY. Items that load well on factor 2 are IUSETV, NSPRINFO, and NATLNEWS—the principal commercial news media.

Factor analysis has made the distinction clear: One set of respondents was inclined to rely on public and literary sources, and one set was inclined to rely on commercial media sources. A possible follow-up would be to separate respondents into the two types of media users, and use that as a control variable in further tests.

Eigenvalues. How do we know when a factor is important enough to be included in the analysis? We use an **eigenvalue** criterion. The eigenvalue is the sum of the squared loadings in a factor. If an eigenvalue is 1.0 or larger, it is conventionally considered significant. Any factor with an eigenvalue of less than 1.0 is disregarded.

NONPARAMETRIC TESTS

Recall that in parametric statistics, samples are used to estimate the parameters of the population. But parametric tests, such as the t-test, correlation, and ANOVA, require the researcher to make certain *assumptions* about the population. The first assumption is that the sample is drawn from a population whose distribution is "normal." But in real life, could the population ever be anything but normal? Yes.

For example, suppose you were sampling a population to study liking for a product advertised on television. Now if the product was attractive to a very young set of buyers, was less popular among young adults, but then was more popular among mature adults with money to spend. Such a curve would be bimodal and therefore *nonnormal*.

Variable	Cases	Mean	SD
ENVPGMRA	472	2.87	1.79
IREADMAG	475	2.70	1.73
IUSETV	475	5.19	1.41
NSPRINFO	475	4.01	1.51
NATLNEWS	472	3.77	1.67
PBSONENV	475	3.79	1.88
LIBRARY	471	2.77	1.60

	ENVPGMAR	IREADMAG	IUSETV	NSPRINFO	NATLNEWS	PBSONENV
ENVPGMRA	1.0 •	.63 $p = .000$	−.04 $p = .32$	.21 $p = .000$	.28 $p = .000$	.49 $p = .000$
IREADMAG	.63 $p = .000$	1.0 •	−.10 $p = .01$	.15 $p = .001$	.28 $p = .000$	.48 $p = .000$
IUSETV	−.04 $p = .32$	−.10 $p = .01$	1.0 •	.19 $p = .000$	.01 $p = .83$	−.03 $p = .52$
NSPRINFO	.21 $p = .000$	.15 $p = .001$	.19 $p = .000$	1.0 •	.44 $p = .000$	.14 $p = .001$
NATLNEWS	.28 $p = .000$	.28 $p = .000$	.01 $p = .83$	.44 $p = .000$	1.0 •	.25 $p = .000$
PBSONENV	.49 $p = .000$	.48 $p = .000$	−.02 $p = .52$	.14 $p = .001$	.25 $p = .000$	1.0 •
LIBRARY	.42 $p = .000$	.52 $p = .000$	−.21 $p = .000$	.12 $p = .005$	.30 $p = .000$	.46 $p = .000$

Note: "•" denotes where a p value cannot be computed.

Interpretation: This correlation matrix shows that media use roughly formed two types, commercial and noncommercial. This division is further confirmed via the rotated factor matrix in Figure 12.6.

FIGURE 12.5 Correlating Media Use

The second assumption involves *homogeneity of variance.* This means that if N samples are drawn from the same population, their variances *should* be similar, although sometimes they are not. This is especially important in ANOVA because within-group variance is calculated as an average of the group variances (Kerlinger, 1973, 287). Computer programs provide for F-tests of homogeneity of variance.

The third assumption is that measures should be continuous in nature and should have equal intervals. How strictly should you rely on these assumptions? "The evidence to date," Kerlinger has argued, "is that the importance of normality and homogeneity is overrated." He cites several major studies showing that parametric tests are robust against violations of these assumptions. Nevertheless, caution is urged, and many researchers today will suggest that when the assumptions of parametric statistics are in doubt, the researcher should revert to a nonparametric test.

Factor	Eigenvalue	Percentage of Variance	Cumulative Percent
1	2.84	40.7	40.7
2	1.32	18.9	59.6
3	.90	12.9	72.4
4	.58	8.3	80.8
5	.50	7.3	88.0
6	.50	7.2	95.2
7	.33	4.8	100.0

According to the minimum eigenvalue criterion in which a factor is significant if its eivenvalue is greater than 1.0, this analysis developed two factors.

Varimax Rotation

	Factor 1	Factor 2
ENVPGMRA	.77	.13
IREADMAG	.82	.04
IUSETV	−.29	.64
NSPRINFO	.19	.80
NATLNEWS	.43	.57
PBSONENV	.72	.09
LIBRARY	.77	.06

Interpretation: The factor analysis developed two factors. Factor 1 is characterized by literary and noncommercial sources of environmental news. Factor 2 is characterized by commercial sources of environmental news. The two factors combined account for 59.6 percent of the explained variance in the set.

FIGURE 12.6   Second Example of Factor Analysis: Media Use for Information about the Environment

The Chi-Square Test

The most common of the many nonparametric (or "distribution free") tests is *chi-square*. It is extremely common in mass communication research and is relatively easy to apply. Some chi-square statistics can be calculated comfortably by hand. One use of chi-square is the "goodness of fit" test, which measures the frequency with which an event was observed against what was expected. If the observed outcome fits the expected outcome, the null hypothesis is not rejected.

An Example of Chi-Square.   Siegel illustrated the method with an example involving horse racing (Siegel, 1956, 45). His question was: Does the starting gate number of a horse affect the number of wins? Stated differently: Is winning a horse race independent of the starting gate position of the horse? There were eight gates. Gate 1 had 29 wins; gate 8 had 11. The win-record of other gates varied, some toward the high end of the scale, others toward the low end. There were a total of 144 wins. *If wins were independent of starting position, then the number of wins per gate should be relatively even.* With eight gates, each starting position should have roughly 18 wins

(144/8 = 18). The test, then, was whether the number of *observed* wins per gate was significantly different from the number of *expected* wins.

The formula to calculate chi-square is:

$$\chi^2 = \Sigma \frac{(O - E)^2}{E}$$ (Formula 12.5)

The formula reads: Chi-square equals the sum of the observed minus the expected, squared, and divided by the expected. To calculate the horse race data, simply subtract the *expected* number of wins in each gate from the *observed* number in each gate, square the remainder, then divide by the expected value for that gate. The *sum of the chi-squares for all of the gates* is the total chi-square. The greater the chi-square, the less likely it is attributable to chance. A table of chi-square values, available in most research texts, will help to decide whether the chi-square score is significant. Because chi-square is sensitive to sample size, tests involving large samples should use stringent significance levels.

Two Mass Media Examples. This example and straightforward technique is available to the mass media manager when needed. For example, suppose the TV news director is concerned about the number of errors in reports coming from the newsroom and wants to know if such errors were randomly distributed among the news staff, or whether they were significantly attributable to a smaller number of people. Paralleling the race horse example, and assuming the errors were properly identified and verified, the manager could quickly test the question.

How? Count the number of errors during a time period, and identify the writer involved in each. Divide the number of errors by the number of writers; call that the *expected* number of errors per writer. Then compute a chi-square for each writer using Formula 12.5. If the sum of the chi-squares suggests the errors exceed the variation that could be expected by chance (i.e., if someone is contributing disproportionately to the number of errors), then the chi-square test will show it.

Another example might be a test of the question of whether radio sales personnel are more or less equal in ability to generate sales of a certain type. The station manager would simply count the number of sales per person, take the average as the *expected* value, and compute the chi-square. Remember that the test centers on the question of whether the difference between the observed and expected is larger than would reasonably be attributed to chance.

Chi-Square for Two Variables. When chi-square involves two variables (Figure 12.7), the calculation is a little more complex, but still is manageable. Bruning and Kintz (1987) call the 2×2 chi-square a "simple chi-square" with the following formula:

$$\chi^2 = \frac{N (AD - BC)^2}{(A + B)(C + D)(A + C)(B + D)}$$ (Formula 12.6)

Political Leaning   Sex of Respondent

                                   Male   Female

	A 59	B 92

Liberal ... 151 (51.7%)

	C 90	D 51

Conservative ... 141 (48.3%)

Total   149   143   292
           (51.0%)   (49.0%)

	Value	df	Significance
Pearson chi-square	17.883	1	.00002
Phi	.247		.00002
Cramer's V	.247		.00002

Legend: "Liberal" = either "very liberal" or "moderately liberal"; "conservative" = either "very conservative" or "moderately conservative."

Note: Persons responding *undecided* or *neutral* have been omitted.

FIGURE 12.7   An Example of a 2 × 2 Chi-Square: Cross-Tabulation of "Political Leaning" with "Sex of Respondent" (*Source:* Adapted from Bruning and Kintz, 1987.)

The numerator of the formula reads: N times the cross-product of one diagonal minus the other, squared. For clarity, the cells of the table are labeled A through D, as in Figure 12.8 (adapted from Bruning and Kintz, 1987). The denominator is the product of the two row sums and the two column sums. And so, the chi-square value is fundamentally an estimate of whether the variance from the expected value is greater than could be attributed to chance, just as it is conceived in many other tests. It is a test of the independence of the two variables. If they are independent, then the only variation should be random. If they are not, then additional variation is possible. That is the test.

When chi-square is calculated on a table larger than 2 × 2, the expected values are calculated from the original chi-square formula: The observed minus the expected, squared, divided by the expected. But the expected scores are generated from the marginals, rather than from an average. *Marginals* are the row and column sums and the grand total.

Here is how to calculate the expected value for a table of 2 × 3 cells or larger: The expected value for any cell is its *row sum* times its *column sum* divided by the *grand total* for the table. Figure 12.8 is an example of such a chi-square table. Look at the cell at the top left of the cross-tabulation; observe the frequency and the

Political Leaning		Sex of Respondent		
		Male	Female	
Liberal		59	92	152 (32%)
Moderate or undecided		96	84	180 (38.1%)
Conservative		90	51	141 (29.9%)
Total		245 (51.9%)	227 (48.1%)	472

	Value	df	Significance
Pearson chi-square	18.139	2	.00012
Phi	.196		.00012
Cramer's V	.196		.00012

Legend: "Liberal" = "Very Liberal" or "Moderately Liberal"; "Conservative" = "Very Conservative" or "Moderately Conservative."

FIGURE 12.8 An Example of a 2 × 2 Chi-Square: Cross-Tabulation of "Political Leaning" by "Sex of Respondent"

expected frequency. Now, calculate the expected frequency for that cell for your self: Look to the end of the *row* in which the cell is located and find the total; multiply it by the *column* total in which the cell is located; and divide by the *grand total.*

The expected values for each cell are then subtracted from the observed, and squared, and divided by the expected. The result is a chi-square score for each cell. When the chi-squares for each cell are added, the sum is applied to the chi-square distribution tabled in many statistics books. The table will tell whether the chi-square is larger than a chance distribution would likely produce, and hence whether the variables are independent.

There are many other nonparametric tests. In fact, there are nonparametric one-way and two-way ANOVAs, several types of nonparametric correlations, and a variety of tests for one- and two-sample research situations. Siegel's 1956 text on nonparametric methods is considered a classic; it is a valuable reference text. The computer program manuals (e.g., *SPSS-X, SPSS/PC+, SAS/STAT Guide*) also offer excellent descriptions and explanations of both parametric and nonparametric methods.

Nonparametric tests are too often overlooked in favor of parametric methods. Remember, simplicity is a virtue. In fact, graduate student lore has an expression for it—KISS ("keep it simple, stupid"). Always use the simplest statistical test that is sufficient for the research circumstances you face. Excessive complexity is nonproductive.

SUMMARY *Terrible*

Statistical testing has a common thread, and the user who understands that thread can travel comfortably from technique to technique. Regression analysis can be viewed as an extension of correlation and analysis of variance; factor analysis can be viewed as an extension of correlation and regression. *like what?*

Parametric statistics require several important assumptions by the user; violation of these can threaten the validity of the research. Nonparametric statistics are considered a bit less powerful, but they do not require stringent assumptions. They are called "distribution free" (Siegel, 1956, 3).

Nonparametric statistical tests are needed when there are substantial doubts about the normality of a population. The appropriate statistical test is the least complex that will accomplish a given purpose.

STUDY QUESTIONS AND EXERCISES

1. If computer support is available, use the data provided in the Environmental Survey to compute a multiple regression model. For example, use the variable called USPOLLUT as the dependent variable and select any other three variables as independent variables. The SPSS/PC+ computer language is:

   ```
   . . .
   END DATA.
   REGRESSION VARIABLES = USPOLLUT (plus other three)
   /DEPENDENT = USPOLLUT
   /METHOD = STEPWISE.
   ```

2. Review mass communication research journal articles to find and report on applications of regression analysis and chi-square. Describe the research design and the kinds of data reported in the research.

3. Using the formula: (expected − observed)^2/expected, calculate a chi-square where the expected equals 25 and the observed equals 35. How many *df* would you have? Check the chi-square value for significance in a chi-square table.

NOTE

1. Many books have been written about regression analysis and its complex variations and subtleties. The material presented here is obviously only the barest introduction. If you are interested in applying such techniques, the author urges you to take advantage of reference sources and advanced academic courses.

SOURCES

Achen, Christopher H. 1982. *Interpreting and Using Regression.* Beverly Hills, Calif.: Sage.

Berry, William D., and Stanley Feldman. 1985. *Multiple Regression in Practice.* Beverly Hills, Calif.: Sage.

Bruning, James L., and B. L. Kintz. 1987. *Computational Handbook of Statistics.* 3d ed. Glenview, Ill.: Scott, Foresman.

Kerlinger, Fred N. *Foundations of Behavioral Research.* 2d ed. New York: Holt, Rinehart & Winston.

Kerlinger, Fred N. 1986. *Foundations of Behavioral Research.* 3rd ed. New York: Holt, Rinehart & Winston.

Kim, Jae-on. 1978. *Factor Analysis: Statistical Methods and Practical Issues.* Beverly Hills, Calif.: Sage.

Kim, Jae-on, and Charles W. Mueller. 1978. *Introduction to Factor Analysis: What It Is and How to Do It.* Beverly Hills, Calif.: Sage.

Lewis-Beck, Michael. 1980. *Applied Regression: An Introduction.* Beverly Hills, Calif.: Sage.

McKeown, Bruce, and Dan Thomas. 1988. *Q Methodology.* Beverly Hills, Calif.: Sage.

Marija J. Norusis. 1988. SPSS/PC+ V2.0 Base Manual (SPSS Inc., 444 North Michigan Avenue, Chicago, Ill. 60611).

Schroeder, Larry D., David L. Sjoquist, and Paula E. Stephan. 1986. *Understanding Regression Analysis: An Introductory Guide.* Beverly Hills, Calif.: Sage.

Siegel, Sidney. 1956. *Nonparametric Statistics for the Behavioral Sciences.* New York: McGraw-Hill.

13

Computer Analysis of Data

□

OBJECTIVES

After studying this chapter, you should be able to:

1. Enter SPSS/PC+.
2. Enter data in machine readable form.
3. Write program language to identify and locate variables.
4. Write program language to perform basic statistical runs.
5. Print statistical output.

INTRODUCTION

Challenging the Computer

Although word processing by personal computer (PC) is wonderful, it does not begin to challenge the technology. The computer's real potential is in its speed and ease of data storage and retrieval, especially in the *simulation* of complex phenomena and in *complex calculations*. Of special interest for this text is the matter of complex calculations. The computer facilitates calculations that just a few years ago simply would not have been feasible—and it does them with blinding speed. The importance of this in the history of human knowledge will best be seen in retrospect; today we probably are too close to the issue for a clear view. But the impact must surely be profound. The PC is being used profitably not just for word processing, but also for a range of applications in education, business, agriculture, law, medicine, architectural design, real estate, and in other fields (Madron, Tate, and Brookshire, 1985).

The computer does not ask whether its output is "reasonable"; it simply does what it is programmed to do. The correctness of the output will remain for the ethical analyst to decide, because the machine does not have independent judgment. Thus, computer use calls for personal integrity, analytical skill, and knowledge.

A research assistant once announced excitedly that two variables in a survey of college students had correlated very highly, $r = .89$. But a more experienced analyst knew that correlations of that magnitude in such a study are rare, and examination revealed that the high correlation was caused by an error in programming. The point is that data should not be believed just because they are processed by computer.

Assuming the legitimacy of computer output, think of the power that the computer puts into the hands of individuals: It permits access to vast data bases. It works with speed and accuracy, accomplishing in milliseconds what a task force would need days, or months, or longer to do. It permits decision-making where intuition might be foiled. The technology is available, and its use is improving, but even today few people are able to extend its use beyond word processing.

HOW THE COMPUTER WORKS

To understand how the computer works, you might think of electricity as a stream of water flowing from point A to point B. If a dam is put in the path, the flow is diverted. In the computer, the dams are a series of **chips,** tiny conductors that replaced vacuum tubes. Chips and transistors send the electricity back and forth, on and off. The on–off process is extremely quick, and each occurrence is a meaningful operation with an outcome. The process is "logical" or successive: If A, then B; if B, then C.

Computer Logic

In computer language, a problem is broken into its parts, and the parts are put into their proper order. For example, if $C = A + B$, it would make no sense to ask the computer to calculate C before defining it as $A + B$. In the same way, it would make no sense to install a chain on a bicycle before you installed a sprocket wheel. Seen in this way, a **computer program** is simply a set of instructions that breaks a problem into its logical parts, then puts the parts in proper order. When the program is in place, the machine can be instructed to begin a "routine"—that is, to follow **computer logic.**

The Binary Code. How does the machine know to follow this process? In digital computer language, all *information* (defined as numbers, codes, symbols, and words) can be defined by zeros and ones (this is called the **binary code**). A *zero* causes the electricity to do something, and a *one* something else; hence, each *combination* of zeros and ones is meaningful. These ons and offs make a series that leads to an outcome. In other words, each combination of ons and offs (bits) can generate a product. A series of such products becomes the output seen on the computer screen. Once activated, a computer program simply permits the electric current to proceed from the beginning to the end of a routine in an orderly fashion.

The evolution of computing has been awesome, and it continues apace. There is much to know and learn. More detail about the technical operation of the computer, is provided in Appendix B of this text, "An Introduction to Computers for Data Analysts," by S. Paul Wright.

STATISTICAL PACKAGES

For media managers or staffers who want to use statistical tests in decision-making, some important tests can be calculated by hand, although such work is laborious, sometimes tedious, and error-prone. Analysts today are more likely to use computers programmed with **statistical packages,** which offer a comprehensive assortment of statistical tools. Since the machine and the program do the calculations, the analyst's main job involves conceptualizing the problem to be tested, programming to set the computer in motion, and analyzing the machine's output.

There are several comprehensive statistical packages, including StatGraph and JMP (popularly called *JUMP*); but the two principal packages for social scientists are SAS, once known as Statistical Analysis System, and SPSS-X, once known as Statistical Package for the Social Sciences. SAS and SPSS-X **mainframe packages** are designed to run on central or "super" computers, which do some things that most PCs cannot do, such as handle immense volumes of data quickly. PCs will suffice for the vast majority of social research data sets, however.

Both SAS and SPSS-X have PC versions, and PCs that will do most of what social science researchers will be called upon to do. This chapter will focus on the PC version. The author prefers the PC version because the job control language remains constant as long as a given program is in operation. Furthermore, the PC is not subject to the periodic backlogs and frequent general shutdowns that plague university mainframe computers.

SPSSX and SAS

SAS seems to be preferred among theoretical statisticians. It promotes a generic approach to statistical analysis called the "general linear model." SAS is also increasing in popularity among *social scientists,* but at the time of this writing, SPSS-X and its PC version remain the preferred package for social science. SPSS was *designed* for social science: It performs tests that are called for by research journals, and it arrays data in typical journal format. Furthermore, its program language is easy to use and interpret.

For anyone hoping to build a career in social science research—for example, an analyst at a major advertising firm or a contract survey researcher—knowledge of these packages is a must. In short, anyone responsible for data analysis should be familiar with statistical programs.

Introducing SPSS/PC+

The program that will be presented in this chapter is the PC version of SPSS-X, called SPSS/PC+. SPSS/PC+ has been published in several versions, each expanding the scope of offerings and ironing out problems of calculation and interpretation. The version discussed here is version 4.0, and knowledge of it should help with any subsequent version. The intent of the chapter is to present the logic of the system and the commands necessary for a novice researcher to enter data and conduct elementary analyses.

GETTING STARTED

On the assumption that you may know nothing at all about personal computers, and much less about statistical packages, we will begin with the instruction to "boot up" the machine (i.e., load the computer's operating system). We will assume you are working with an IBM (International Business Machines) or IBM-Compatible PC that is already loaded with MS/DOS (Microsoft Disk Operating System). But be forewarned that this presentation will barely scratch the surface of what SPSS/PC+ has to offer. SPSS-X and SPSS/PC+ represent a vast collection of statistical, graphical, file management, and editing procedures. In fact, the chapter will cover only the barest routines. After working with this chapter, however, once equipped with an IBM or compatible as described and loaded with SPSS/PC+, you should be able to input a data set and conduct simple analyses.

Loading SPSS/PC+

Before a statistical package can be used with a PC, it must be loaded into its memory. Since SPSS/PC+ is too large for a single floppy disk (it requires some 12 megabytes of disk space), it is transported on several of them. Before attempting to load the program, make sure that you have at least 20 megabytes of space available on your hard drive. Once loaded, the program will remain on the computer's hard drive even when the machine is turned off.

In the PC analysis of data, speed is important. With old, slow machines, the analyst can spend long idle seconds and minutes awaiting calculations. Ironically, the machines are so good that we become impatient with even a few seconds of delay, forgetting that even slow computer calculations make huge savings in time and tedium compared with hand calculations.

PC Processing Speed

Mainframe computers are very fast, and they can handle mountains of calculations with ease. PCs can do much of what a mainframe can do, but often much more slowly. An IBM PS/2 with 286 processing and 10 megahertz (MHz) speed, for example, might require 30 minutes to run a large correlation matrix, while a modern mainframe would do it in a flash. A 386 processor with a 25 MHz speed would be considerably faster than a 286 with 10 MHz, but since machine speed depends on more than MHz, we cannot say confidently that 25 MHz is two-and-a-half times faster than 10 MHz; still, it should be faster to some extent. IBM PCs with 486 processing and 66 MHz speed are four to six times faster than most 286 machines. The numbers 286, 386, and 486, refer to the "generation" of the chip that is used in the computer.

SPSS/PC+ was developed for IBM PCs and compatibles, but recently it was also made available to Apple and Macintosh users as well. It includes a *tutorial disk* that describes how to use the program. The user simply loads the tutorial disk into the machine, strikes *Enter*, and follows the detailed *menu* of instructions.

Calling up SPSS/PC+ from the Hard Drive

Once SPSS/PC+ has been loaded onto the hard drive, it will remain there even when the machine is turned off. To bring the program to the screen, first boot up (turn on) the machine and wait for the system prompt, usually the symbol >, C> or A>. On reaching the system prompt, you must enter the SPSS directory. To do this, type

    cd\spss

(read it cd-backslash-spss; *cd* means "change directory"), and
press the *Enter* key. Having entered the SPSS directory, now type

    spsspc

and press *Enter*.

The program will be activated and a brief screen will display the version number and the owner of the program. Then the program will generate a screen of two halves, upper and lower. The upper half holds a menu system for using SPSS/PC+. The lower half is called the *scratch pad* because that is where the data will be entered or *pasted* into the program.

The Menu System

To paste a menu item onto the scratch pad, use the keyboard arrows to send the cursor to the appropriate menu item and press the *Enter* key. The item will be pasted onto the scratch pad, the lower half of the screen. The menu board also *defines* and explains each of the menu items. Note that in the menu mode, when the cursor flashes square, word editing is not possible. The *edit* mode, signified by a hyphen, will be discussed below.

Although there is some merit in knowing the menu system of SPSS/PC+, you will quickly outgrow it. Faster and less clumsy *freeform* commands can be obtained from the menu card appropriate to the version of the program and manual that you are using. To understand them, you will need access to a user's manual. Recent versions of these are given in the reference section at the end of this chapter. The manuals will familiarize you with the analytical possibilities and the commands necessary for programming a given set of data.

The Edit Mode

If you wish to work in SPSS/PC+ without having to rely on the menu system, it will be necessary for you to enter the *edit* mode by typing *Alt e;* the letter *e* can be upper or lower case. You will see that the cursor changes from the form of a square to a hyphen. In the edit mode, you can simply type whatever commands or data that you have.

If your program is fairly complex, or if your data set is large, the fact that you are limited to the lower half of the computer screen may be inconvenient; you may wish to use the whole screen. To get rid of the manu, simply type *Alt z.* The menu will disappear and you will have a full empty screen. It is also possible to rid the screen of the menu by pressing *Alt m,* but *Alt m* does not increase the size of the scratch pad. Reverse the unwanted *Alt m* by pressing *Alt e.*

At this point, you should be able to write your program and enter your data directly onto the screen. In some cases, the procedure is extremely simple. For example, let's say that you interviewed 20 people to learn their attitude on a controversial issue, and you recorded the gender of the respondent and gave every respondent an identification number. Here is how to write the program. In the edit mode, type

    data list fixed/

in the upper left-hand corner of the screen. Having done that, give each of your three variables (identification number, gender, and attitude) a unique name of eight or fewer characters and write the column number in which each can be found. The identification number will require two columns because there were 20 respondents; the first is 01, the second is 02, and so on. Gender will require one column, and attitude will require one column. The program will appear thus:

    data list fixed/identifi 1–2 sex 3 attitude 4.

This tells the machine the *data* are in *fixed form,* and that the variables are *identification, sex,* and *attitude.* The numbers tell the column location of the data. It is important to note that every complete command ends with a period. If a command has a subcommand, it is preceded by a slash line.

When you have typed the data list command and the variable names and columns, go to the next line and type

    begin data.

After typing the *begin data.* command (be sure to include a period), type the data. Since the designation of "male" and "female" are not convenient for data analysis, we need to assign each sex a number. Arbitrarily, we will say that a male is the number 1 in column 3, and a female is the number 2. If respondent number 01 is a male whose attitude is represented by a 4, and respondent number 02 is a female whose attitude is a 5, and so on, for the 20 respondents, then the data and the beginning of the program would look like this:

data list fixed/identifi 1–2 sex 3 attitude 4.

begin data.
0114
0225
0314
0413
0525
0624
0713
0825
0914
1023
1112
1223
1325
1414
1524
1615
1724
1813
1924
2013

When all data are entered, the next command—naturally enough—is *end data.*

. . .
1924
2013
end data.

The T-Test Commands

The next part of the program is the beginning of the analysis. Suppose we want to know whether men's attitude toward the controversial issue is different from women's. Strictly speaking, our attitude data are ordinal, 1 to 5, but we will treat them as interval. Because we want to compare the mean score of the men with the mean score of the women, the proper test is a t-test (see Chapter 11). In SPSS/PC+ language, the program would be written as follows, immediately after the *end data.* command:

t-test groups = sex (1,2)
/ variables = attitude.

The t-test in this comparison requires two groups, which will be men and women. The program tells the machine that the sex variable will form two groups, and that the dependent variable will be an attitude score. Each male respondent and each female respondent will have an attitude score. The machine will run a statistical test to see whether the scores are significantly different. To activate the run, type *F10* and press *Enter*.

Figure 13.1 shows the output of the t-test much as it came from the computer. The test groups were formed on the basis of sex of respondent, and the dependent variable was an attitude. Group 1 comprised men, and group 2 comprised women. There were 10 men and 10 women in the comparison, and the mean score was 3.5 for men and 4.2 for women.

Relying on the "pooled variance estimate," because the variances for the

data list fixed/ identifi 1–2 sex 3 attitude 4.
begin data.
end data.

t-test grups = sex (1, 2)
variables = attitude.

Independent samples of SEX

Group 1: SEX = 1   Group 2: SEX = 2

t-test for: ATTITUDE

	Number of Cases	M	SD	Standard Error
Group 1	10	3.500	.850	.269
Group 2	10	4.200	.789	.249

		Pooled Variance Estimate			Separate Variance Estimate		
F-Value	2-Tail Probability	T-Value	df	2-Tail Probability	T-Value	df	2-Tail Probability
1.16	.828	−1.91	18	.072	−1.91	17.90	.072

Explanation: This test helps us decide whether the attitude scores of men [SEX EQ 1] in this sample are different from attitude scores of women [SEX EQ 2]. The *mean* scores for men and women are different, but the score of greatest interest is the *2-tail probability*: It represents the number of times in 100 that a researcher would risk being wrong in concluding that, in this case, attitudes of men and women are different. If the researcher used the conventional probability value of <.05 for "significance," the conclusion would have to be that the attitudes of men and women are not statistically different.

FIGURE 13.1 Example of a T-Test Computer Output (*Source:* Adapted from SPSS/PC+.)

groups were equivalent with 18 degrees of freedom, the t-value is negative 1.91; the probability of a t-score this large by chance is .072 (A t-score of 1.96 is required for the .05 significance level.) In other words, about 7 times in 100 different tests a difference as large as suggested by the mean scores of the respondents could be obtained as a matter of sample variation rather than as a real difference between the sexes.

Because .07 is very close to .05, the conventional level of significance, the decision on whether the attitudes of men and women were different remains a little ambiguous. But at least we have an objective criterion on which to base a decision. For most purposes, when the probability is greater than 5 times in 100, we say that the difference is nonsignificant, and we decline to rely on it.

No Room for Error

Be aware that any misplaced period or comma, any misspelled word, or any misplaced datum will cause the program to abort. There is absolutely no room for error—a hard truth that must be accepted.

Saving a File

When the analysis cannot be completed in a single sitting, the file must be *saved* for future work. In the SPSS/PC+ program, a file can be saved by pressing *F9* and *Enter* (in the Alt E mode). *F9* will produce a menu item at the bottom of the screen called *write whole file*. At that prompt, press *Enter*. The next prompt will be *name the file*. You can give the file any name of eight or fewer characters followed by a period and three more characters, such as *.dat* or *.fil*. Having named the file, press *Enter*. For example, a file name might be:

    survey.dat

If the file is to be saved or filed on (i.e., *written to*) a floppy disk, the file name would be preceded by the designation of the disk drive that contains the disk:

    a:survey.dat

That means the file would be written to the floppy disk in drive A, not to the SPSS directory on the hard drive.

The data are easiest to retrieve when they have been written to a file on the SPSS/PC+ directory (not on the floppy disk). Simply press *F3* and *Enter*. The menu at the bottom of the screen will prompt you to edit or insert a file. Move the cursor to the *insert* command and press *Enter*. The next prompt will ask for the file name. Write in the name, such as

    survey.dat (or)
    a:survey.dat

and press *Enter;* your file will appear on screen exactly as you left it.

When the data you want to work with are located on a floppy disk, the *data list* command will take the following form (with your own file name):

data list file = "a:survey.dat"/

This will tell the machine that the data are in a file in the A drive, and that the file is named "survey.dat" or other file name.

When you have completed your data entry and your program, or whenever you intend to leave the full-screen edit mode, it is imperative that you *write the file to memory*. Do this by pressing *F9*, following the prompt, and pressing *Enter*. Once you have saved the data, you can run it without fear of losing it. For example, you might input and edit a file in the whole-screen mode, then write it to memory, but *run* it from the split-screen mode so it will return to the screen after being run.

Regardless of whether you prefer the full screen or the split screen, when you wish to end the program and go to the system prompt, type *finish.* at the bottom of the program. *Remember: The program will not be entered in permanent memory without a specific command.*

Some Editing Functions

In the *Alt e* mode, editing is easy: deletions are made with the *Delete* key or the *Backspace* key. To go to the bottom (the end) of the file by pressing either *Page Down* or *Control End.* To go to the top of a file, press *Page Up* or *Control Home.* To move the cursor quickly from one end of a line of data to another, press *Control* and the *arrow key.* Advanced methods of marking, moving, and editing data are also available.

Cases and Cards

There is virtually no limit to the number of *cases* (i.e., respondents) or even the amount of data that can be entered and analyzed. The author has worked with files of up to 25,000 cases. Data are entered in terms of lines or "cards," a throwback to the days when numbers were punched on computer cards. No more than 80 columns of data can be entered per line.

Suppose, for example that one case requires 120 columns. The final 40 columns, on line 2, must be preceded by one forward slash mark (/). Likewise, each case requiring additional cards would be preceded by a slash mark.

Printing the Output

Once a job has been run, you will probably want "hard copy." There are two ways to get it. The easiest is to press the *Print Screen* key while the statistical report is on the screen. Press the space bar for page two and press *Print Screen* again, and so on.

It is important to know that a file can only be scrolled from beginning to end, not the other way. If you accidentally scroll beyond a desired page, the job must be rerun. Fortunately, the run is usually quick and virtually cost-free.

The second way to obtain hard copy of a PC run in SPSS/PC+ is to type

Print SPSS.LIS

when you have the C:\ SPSS prompt, and press *Enter*. This command will print all of the analyses that you have produced in the sitting. If you have made many runs and don't really want all of them, this will generate a lot of unwanted paper.

OTHER STATISTICAL RUNS

Most often, an analysis of data will require several runs. Aside from the t-test, illustrated above, the most frequent and useful applications are *correlations, factor analysis,* and *cross-tabulations.* Program language for each will be presented briefly. Although you likely will have special needs that require special commands, the examples below are a staring point.

Correlation

Recall that correlation asks whether one variable changes systematically in relation to another. In the t-test, above, we had one variable called "attitude"; for purposes of this example, we will add a second attitude variable, "attitwo." Hence, the data set would be amended as follows:

```
data list fixed/identifi 1–2 sex 3 attitude 4 attitwo 5.
01145
02255
03145
04134
05254
06245
07134
08254
09145
10234
11123
12235
13254
14144
15245
16155
17244
18134
19245
201350
end data.
```

To correlate the variables "attitude" and "attitwo," type the following commands on the line below *end data.*

```
correlation variables = attitude with attitwo
    /options 2 3 4 5
    /statistics = all.
```

The *options* command instructs the computer as to what kind of information is needed; for example, exclude missing values pairwise, report two-tailed probability, provide a correlation matrix, and display count and probability. There are many variations in this program, and not all can be covered here. You are encouraged to rely on the SPSS/PC+ user's manual and to tailor the program to your needs.

Factor Analysis

The following commands would be typed on the line below *end data.*

```
factor variables = identifi sex attitude attitwo
    /criteria = mineigen
    /rotation = varimax.
```

The four variables are not reasonably factor analyzed; they were included merely to illustrate the grouping. The *mineigen* command stipulates that an eigenvalue of 1.0 is required for factor significance. *Varimax* is the type of rotation of the factor matrix.

Cross-Tabulation

The following commands for cross-tabulation of variables follow the *end data.* command:

```
crosstabs tables = attitude by attitwo by sex
    /options = 18
    /statistics = all.
```

The *option* 18 provides all cell information: for example, cell counts, row and column percentages, and expected values. As before, you are encouraged to experiment with the program to see firsthand what it provides.

SUMMARY

To run an SPSS/PC+ program, you must first enter the SPSS Directory: At the prompt, type *cd\spss* and press *Enter,* then type *spsspc* and press *Enter.* In SPSS/PC+, type *Alt e* to get into the freeform edit mode, and then *Alt z* to work in full screen rather than split screen. All SPSS/PC+ programs begin with a *data list* command followed by a forward slash mark (/) and a list of variables. Data can be entered directly onto the screen, or called from an external source. Use the *F3* function key to insert a file into the SPSS/PC+ program; use *data list file = "a:survey.dat"/* (use your own file name) when data are to be analyzed but will remain external to SPSS/PC+. Use the *F9* function key to write the file to memory. Use *Print Screen* or *Print SPSS.LIS* to print output.

STUDY QUESTIONS AND EXERCISES

1. For practice with SPSS/PC+, make up a small data set, using examples in this chapter as a model. Make up three attitude variables and two demographic variables. Give each case an identification number. With this fictional data set, run several statistical procedures:
   correlation
   t-test
   cross-tabs

SOURCES

Madron, Thomas Wm., C. Neal Tate, and Robert G. Brookshire. 1985. *Using Micro Computers in Research.* Beverly Hills, Calif.: Sage.

Norusis, Marija J. 1988. *SPSS/PC+ Base Manual for the IBM PC/XT/AT and PS/2* (SPSS Inc., 444 North Michigan Avenue, Chicago, IL 60611).

Norusis, Marija J. 1988. *SPSS/PC+ Advanced Statistics for the IBM PC/XT/AT and PS/2* (SPSS Inc., 444 North Michigan Avenue, Chicago, IL 60611).

PART FIVE

Some Additional Methods of Research

- Chapter 14: Qualitative Research.   After explaining some differences between qualitative and quantitative research, this chapter introduces three qualitative techniques.
- Chapter 15: Content Analysis.   This chapter describes the methods of content analysis through examples and discusses computer analysis of text. It also describes a hypothetical research project.

14

Qualitative Research

RONALD E. TAYLOR

University of Tennessee, Knoxville

□
OBJECTIVES

After studying this chapter, you should be able to:

1. Discuss the nature and purpose of qualitative research.

2. Explain some of the differences between qualitative and quantitative research approaches.

3. Briefly describe three methods for gathering qualitative data.

4. Understand how researchers approach the coding and analysis of qualitative data.

5. Suggest appropriate uses of qualitative research in mass media studies.

A daily newspaper means different things to different people. To the publisher it may represent an investment in which to reap a sizable profit. To an editor or writer it may represent a way of earning a fulfilling life. To an advertiser the newspaper represents a way to reach an audience. To one reader it may represent a way to find out what is going on in the community; to another its comics and advice columns may be a welcome diversion at the end of the day; to yet another reader the newspaper may be a way to find solace from the family through ritualized reading. To the newspaper carrier it may represent a way to earn money for college or a way to help pay household bills. To the nonsubscriber, it may be just another bundle of paper lying in the driveways and under the shrubbery in the neighborhood.

All forms of mass media could be characterized in much the same way: What they mean varies from individual to individual. Yet there will likely be some common, or shared, meanings within groups of people. The observation that things mean different things to different people is a basic tenet of qualitative research. *Qualitative research is any systematic investigation that attempts to understand the meanings that things have for individuals from their own perspectives.* There has been much debate over the years about the merits of qualitative research versus the merits of quantitative research. The mass communication researcher who understands the differing assumptions that underlie the two approaches and who knows something about how each is practiced will fare better in the long run than the researcher who holds blind allegiance to one research approach. Although the two approaches often are not compatible, each offers insight into how people think and behave.

The word *qualitative* is sometimes loosely used to refer to all research methods that are not quantitative, but this is a misnomer. For example, a particular form of market research that uses focus groups is often labeled "qualitative." In this approach, consumers are invited to a research site (laboratory) where a moderator leads a discussion about a new product concept or a proposed advertising campaign. Respondents are asked to comment on and to give opinions about the moderator's item of interest. Often this artificially constituted group is observed through a one-way mirror and videotaped. This is an interesting and sometimes useful way to answer market-driven administrative-type questions, but it is not truly qualitative research as the term is used here because (a) the research is not performed in a natural setting, (b) the object of discussion and comment is of great importance and meaning to the marketer but possibly of little importance to the constituted group, and (c) the research does very little to *advance* our understanding of human behavior.

A second mislabeling of qualitative research occurs when quantitative researchers conduct a few open-ended interviews with respondents before writing a structured questionnaire or include an open-ended question on a structured questionnaire to cover items the researcher may have overlooked. Both of these techniques certainly improve the quality of quantitative approaches, but neither is qualitative research.

CHARACTERISTICS OF QUALITATIVE RESEARCH

Qualitative research begins with the assumption that human behavior is made up of thoughtful, meaningful responses to stimuli in the world. What something means to someone affects how the person will respond to it. Meaning is not static; rather meaning itself is always in a process of interpretation and refinement. Meaning may change as time passes, when objects appear in different settings, or as individuals themselves change. The world, then, is dynamic and changing, as people constantly interpret, reinterpret, and make meaningful responses to it. Yet there is order and pattern to be found in people's behavior because ordering and patterning the world is an innate human characteristic. Thus, truth is regarded as relative and specific: What is true today may not be true tomorrow or 10 years from now; and what is true for one group of people in one setting may not be true for another group in a different setting.

Herbert Blumer (1969) argued that human beings act toward things on the basis of the meanings that the things have for them. "Things" in this sense refers to everything that human beings note in their worlds: physical objects, other human beings, institutions, guiding ideals, situations. According to Blumer, *meaning* comes out of the interaction that individuals have with others and through self-reflection. *Thus*, meaning is not inherent in an object or simply a matter of human psychological perception. Rather, it is developed and modified through an interpretive process used by people in dealing with the things they encounter. Blumer's view of meaning is called *symbolic interactionism.*

The way in which qualitative researchers go about their investigations is guided by the assertions that meaning is both individual and shared, that it comes from interaction with others, and that it is contextual.

As much as possible, qualitative researchers attempt to study and capture meaning in a natural setting. Since what it means to read a newspaper, for example, may change from person to person and from place of reading to place of reading, qualitative researchers seek to study and capture those various meanings and to identify shared meanings. Reading a newspaper in the morning may be qualitatively different from reading it in the evening. It may be that morning readers are preparing for the day and evening readers are reflecting on the day or catching up on things that occurred while they were at work. People may read the newspaper at the breakfast table, in a commuter pool on the way to work, while watching or listening to a morning news show, or in front of the television in the evening. Some readers may prefer to find a comfortable chair and read in perfect quiet. Some people may read the front page first; others may begin with the sports section; still others with the financial section. Some may discard the advertising inserts before they begin any reading at all. To the qualitative researcher, a simple dichotomous question such as, "Did you read the newspaper yesterday? Please check 'Yes' or 'No,'" fails to address the individual meanings and contextual nuances associated with the act of newspaper reading.

Many college students like to watch soap operas on television. Such viewing often takes place in a dorm or student lounge, where student conversations occur about the actors or the plot. Certainly viewing in a group setting is very much different from viewing alone in one's room or apartment.

Thus, to understand the meanings that things have in varying contexts, qualitative researchers conduct their investigations in natural settings such as homes, lounges, club meetings, offices, bars, libraries, theaters, video arcades, street corners, neighborhood markets—in short, wherever the behavior being studied occurs *naturally.*

A goal of qualitative research is to understand the world from the perspective of the people being studied. Qualitative researchers believe that they themselves hold a particular view of the world that may be very different from the views held by the groups they wish to study. For that reason, qualitative researchers must be able to suspend their own interpretations of what things mean and rely instead on sustained observation, conversations, and interviews with their research participants. Rather than distance themselves from the people and their behavior, qualitative researchers get as close to the phenomenon as they can. They commonly regard the people who are studied as *participants* in the research process rather than as *subjects*. Qualitative researchers feel that formalized questionnaires and rating scales depict a world seen by the researcher, not the one seen by the participants. Hence, understanding of the participants' worlds can come about only by collecting and observing data in the forms that are natural to the participants. Rather than seeking the hard, replicable numbers that survey and experimental researchers gather, qualitative researchers gather primarily verbal and visual data that is said to be "valid, real, rich, deep, and thick." This is not to say that qualitative researchers are necessarily opposed to numbers, to counting, or even to statistics; they are not. However, the meaningful worlds of everyday people are usually not constituted through statistical analysis.

Rather than relying on statistical analysis of numbers, qualitative researchers use human insight to find order and pattern in the data that they collect. One check on the accuracy of a researcher's interpretations is to present them to the research participants to see if they agree. In this sense, the qualitative researcher becomes the research instrument, with all of the inherent powers and weaknesses of the human mind.

To review:

e.g. Jap. exchange student

Some Characteristics of Qualitative Research

- Assumes human behavior is based on interpretation of things encountered.
- Meaning is always a central concept.
- Meaning arises out of social interaction.
- Meaning changes over time and with context.
- Meaning is both individual and shared.
- Human behavior exhibits pattern and order. *(: can be used to predict future behavior*

PROCESS OF QUALITATIVE RESEARCH

In its very purest form, qualitative research begins with the question, What is going on here? and nothing more. No formal hypotheses are stated and little structure is imposed on the research process. Often what the qualitative researcher thinks is going on isn't going on at all, and too much rigidity in the research process could cause the researcher to miss totally what was important to the participants.

Within the qualitative approach, the word *theory* has a meaning very different from its meaning in other approaches. In other approaches, *theory* is posited before data collection and data are collected to test the researcher's theory. In the qualitative approach, data collection precedes theory and theory becomes a way of organizing the data. Nonqualitative theory is often cast at a very wide level to apply to many situations and contexts; qualitative theory is "grounded" in its data (Glaser and Strauss, 1967) and although it may apply to similar contexts, there is no assumption that it should. Generalization itself is not a goal. Theory that can be applied to one setting only is called *substantive*. Theory that has application across more than one setting or context is called *formal*. Qualitative researchers do sometimes discover that their findings help to explain behavior in more than one setting, for example, "gatekeeping," which refers to personal bias in the news selection process.

Commonly, mass communication qualitative researchers do have general notions about which aspects of human behavior they wish to study, such as newspaper reading, TV viewing, interpretations of advertising, and videotape renting and viewing; therefore, they begin their study with questions related to the proposed area of study. Nonetheless, researchers must be careful not to impart great significance and meaning to the area of study just because it is important to themselves. For example, a researcher who wanted to study the meaning of network TV advertising to a segment of the elderly population was somewhat dismayed to find through her interviews with senior citizens that they cared very little for and paid little attention to such advertising. It just wasn't a very important aspect of their lives. Because her research approach was flexible, the researcher learned through her interviews that retail advertising and in particular store-advertised discounts were more important to the group.

Once a researcher has decided on a general area of interest, access to a group of participants and to a site must be negotiated. This may be as simple as gaining permission to observe and interact with students in a classroom or as complicated as gaining permission to observe the staff meetings of an important community or national organization. In either case, the researcher knows that at first his or her presence may cause participants to act differently and that only through repeated and sustained observation will people be likely to return to their usual patterns of behavior. The researcher begins the process open-minded and must put aside personal notions and interpretations of what things mean. The goal is to capture and understand the meanings from the perspectives of the participants.

Early on, the researcher may discover that what to study has been misjudged or that there are more interesting research questions than the ones originally asked. Here the flexibility of the qualitative approach becomes important. Because the researcher decides what data to collect next after initial entry into the setting, it is quite possible for the focus of the study to shift as more meaningful things are discovered. The researcher, as data are collected, moves back and forth from collection to interpretation, testing all possible explanations for the data. Researchers make copious notes to themselves before, during, and after data collection. When data collection becomes redundant (i.e., no new information appears to be forthcoming), the qualitative researcher has finished the collection task. How long this takes depends, of course, on the thoroughness of the research, the scope of the research study, and the shared patterns among the participants.

One of the worst things that can happen to a qualitative researcher is to end up with a huge stack of field notes, observations, and interviews with no real sense of the connections among the data. It is quite common for novices to feel somewhat overwhelmed with the quantity of field notes they collect. If a systematic procedure is followed and insight is used along the way, however, such disasters will be avoided.

The dynamic nature of qualitative research precludes step-by-step instruction in the same way that the steps of survey research or experimental research can be articulated. However, there are a number of qualitative methods that guide the researcher.

Comparison of Qualitative and Nonqualitative Approaches to Resarch

Qualitative Approach	*Nonqualitative Approach*
Meaning is a central concept.	Limited or no role for meaning.
Assumes multiple and dynamic realities.	Assumes single, stable reality.
Dynamic nature of research precludes step-by-step instruction.	Research methods are well documented and structured.
Data collection precedes theory. Research moves from specific to general (*inductive approach*).	Theory precedes data collection. Research moves from general to specific (*deductive approach*).
Data are primarily verbal and visual: "real, rich, valid."	Data are primarily numbers and assigned numerical values: "hard, replicable, reliable."
Works with "participants" in a natural setting.	Recruits research "subjects," often to laboratories for controlled observation and experimentation.
Researcher is the instrument.	Researcher creates an instrument such as a questionnaire or attitude scale.
Relies on human insight.	Relies on statistical measures and tests.
Generalizability is not usually claimed for findings.	Generalizability is claimed.
Counting is okay, but often not very useful.	Counting is okay and very useful.

LEARN BY DOING

1. Ask 10 acquaintances to tell you about when, where, why, and how they read your campus newspaper.
2. Make a note of all the instances of reading the campus newspaper that you observe in a day, such as reading in class, reading in the library, reading in a dorm room, reading in a TV lounge, reading in the cafeteria.
3. From this very limited research, what can you tentatively conclude about the "meaning" of reading? Can you find both individual and shared meanings?
4. Which procedure gave you greater insight: talking with people or observing? How do you suppose reading the newspaper is different from all the other types of reading that college students do?

QUALITATIVE RESEARCH METHODS

Qualitative researchers rely on a variety of methods in their attempt to understand the world as their participants do. The most common methods include participant observation, interviewing, and document analysis.

Participant Observation

Participant observation is often regarded as the purest form of qualitative research because it occurs in the natural setting and requires the researcher to do and to understand things as the research participants do. In this approach, the researcher enters the research site and—by observing, talking with, and participating in the same activities as the research participants—tries to understand the world as they do.

Participant observation requires a sustained and long-term commitment from the researcher and may extend from as little as a few months to several years. Many think of the archetypal participant observer as the anthropologist who says goodbye to family and sails away to spend several years on some faraway island studying native culture. This is probably the best-known form of participant observation, but it is possible to participate and observe in group activities on a more restricted and more convenient basis.

For example, if you wanted to study what TV soap operas mean to college students in group-based viewing situations, you might choose to join such a group with the intent of participating in and observing their behavior. You would make notes about the arrangement of furniture in the setting, who sat where, and who watched what shows and when. You would observe the interactions among viewers and record their comments to one another. You would probably interview many of the participants. You would need to observe over several weeks to ensure that you were observing typical behavior, and would observe to the point of redundancy (i.e., until nothing new or novel appeared to be happening). Your first observation period, which might last an hour or two, would suggest to you the types of observations and kinds of data that would be useful to collect. Participant observation is time consuming and often inconvenient, but if you really wish to understand a phenomenon in all its shapes and textures, the advantages outweigh any disadvantages.

Gaining access for a participant/observer study can be a problem simply because many people are suspicious of the researcher's motives. Why would someone want to observe if not to look for wrongdoing? Who has access to the information gathered and for what purposes? The researcher must be prepared to answer such questions satisfactorily before being granted access. Powerful groups such as corporate boards of directors or U.S. Senate committees, for example, may have no interest at all in being observed or in risking that their agenda and decision making processes be made public. In other cases, participants may choose not to grant access because they see no benefit for themselves. Although each situation is different, generally the qualitative researcher gives participants an opportunity to review and to benefit from the study. Through insight, the researcher hopes to go beyond what any individual participant sees, to see things that the participants do not always see: processes, patterns, and other common elements among group members. By suspending his or her own meanings and interpretations to understand those of others, and by making a long-term commitment to the study, the participant/observer does stand in some danger of *going native,* that is, of forming a strong identification with the group under study. The best safeguard against going native is the researcher's own journal and field notes that help to track personal feelings and discoveries on a daily basis.

An Example of Participant Observation

One of the author's students was interested in studying the phenomenon of marketing fads. She chose as an example Cabbage Patch dolls and decided to explore the meaning of the dolls to children. In addition to the university's human subjects review board, the student had to negotiate permission and access to children at after-school care sites through a school superintendent, two school principals, a program director, two site directors, and finally the parents of the children. Gaining access took about six weeks.

The student chose interviewing and participant observation as her research methods. For two days in each of six weeks, she joined the children's play groups, tape-recorded interviews and conversations about Cabbage Patch dolls, observed and made notes about how they played with the dolls. In all, she produced about 200 pages of transcripts and notes as the data for her study.

By choosing participant observation and interviewing in a natural setting, she learned many things that would have gone undiscovered had she used a structured questionnaire. Among the delightful surprises of the study were the researcher's observations that (a) dolls were sometimes used as baseball bats; (b) both boys and girls owned this particular brand of doll; (c) children took the dolls as companions to many public places, such as restaurants, theaters, football stadiums, and shopping malls; and (d) in these public places strangers often reacted to the dolls as if they were human.

The student's work focused on the meaning to children. When we presented the findings in several campus symposia, we discovered another group of owners—faculty members—for whom the dolls had very different meanings.

Interviewing

When participant observation is too time consuming or too costly, when site access can not be negotiated, or when the behavior does not lend itself to observation, the researcher may choose to gather data through **in-depth interviews** with participants. In this method, the researcher typically selects a sample of 15 to 30 individuals and conducts interviews about the phenomenon of interest. The researcher may do repeated interviewing with each participant over several days or several months. Interviews are typically tape-recorded, transcribed to written form, and analyzed. Because the goal is always to capture the participant's understanding and meaning of things, the researcher typically prepares only a few general questions and some suggested topic areas. Interviewers must be careful not to lead participants too much or to direct the conversation in particular ways. The goal is to make participants relaxed and comfortable in the interviewing situation and to allow them to talk freely about their lives.

An Example of Interviewing

The "conventional wisdom" of advertising-effects research has held that there is no direct relationship between alcoholic-beverage advertising and overall alcoholic-beverage consumption, and that such advertising is directed at brand-switching behavior. The author and two of his students wondered what the meaning of such advertising was for a particularly vulnerable group: alcoholics in recovery. Twenty participants were recruited from drug treatment centers and interviewed from one-and-one half to two hours about their experiences in recovery.

The interview typically began with the statement: Tell me about your recovery. Participants talked about many things that they saw as important to being able to recover from alcoholism, one of which was negating and reinterpreting the messages and promotions of alcoholic-beverage advertisers. But they talked about many other strategies and behavior changes as well. It was only by understanding the other things that impeded the recovery process for alcoholics that the researchers could understand the relative importance of advertising. Interviewing was a more effective and efficient way of gathering the information than was participant observation, which would have taken years. Nevertheless, the researchers have no way of knowing what they may have missed or failed to uncover because of the method selected. In the analysis of the data the researchers sought to find common themes and patterns among the responses of the 20 participants.

Document Analysis

Document analysis is another way in which qualitative researchers seek to understand the meanings that objects have for others. It allows researchers to gain insight into the ways in which things in the past may have been interpreted or understood. Personal diaries, committee reports, transcripts, memos, and all forms of mass media content are rich veins for studying what things mean.

Because meanings change over time and within context, the researcher should never assume that there is a single "meaning" to a document. The researcher might be interested in discovering what the document meant to the people who produced it, to the people to whom it was directed, to the people who read it when it was produced, or to the people who read it today. Combined with historical study, document analysis can help to explain why people act toward objects in certain ways today based on the movement of beliefs and ideas from one generation to another.

──────────── *An Example of Document Analysis* ────────────

As a graduate student the author was curious as to why members of the legal profession were so adamantly opposed to advertising by lawyers. A first attempt at understanding the meaning of advertising for lawyers by conducting interviews led to nothing more than discovery of a shared belief among lawyers that lawyers were professional, advertising was unprofessional, and, therefore, lawyers did not advertise. To understand why the legal profession was opposed to advertising it was necessary to read the documents of the legal profession, which included 100 years of committee reports, ethics opinions, essays, relevant state and U.S. Supreme Court decisions, and books on ethics. Eventually a pattern emerged that revealed that the anti-advertising sentiment was deeply rooted in the American Bar Association's desire to control the professional behavior of lawyers in the United States during the early part of this century, a pattern that was not evident to practicing lawyers in the latter half of this century. Such sentiment had passed from one generation of lawyers to another, had been formalized within legal education and disciplinary proceedings, and had become part of the professional culture. Present-day lawyers regarded it as a "taken-for-granted" aspect of being a lawyer.

Few qualitative investigations rely on a single method of research. Commonly, the qualitative researcher will combine participant observation, interviews, and document analysis in a single study.

ANALYSIS OF QUALITATIVE DATA

Because experimental and survey approaches deal with explicit problem statements and more formal ways of collecting data, these nonqualitative research approaches can, prior to data collection, determine how the data will be analyzed. Experimental and survey approaches lend themselves to a clear, step-by-step progression for specifying the research hypothesis, collecting data to test the hypothesis, and then analyzing the data with procedures articulated in advance. Qualitative researchers, on the other hand, follow a more flexible procedure—trying to make sense of their data as they collect it, and sometimes deciding what to collect or who to interview next on the basis of what has just been collected. Such flexibility makes a priori specification of data analysis somewhat problematic because the researchers are never quite sure what the final data are going to look like.

Data analysis actually begins when the study begins. The researcher asks himself constantly, What do the data mean? He or she is constantly looking for pattern and connection among concepts and words, among actions and words, among conditions and consequences of behaving in certain ways. The researcher must be cautious not to form conclusions prematurely but rather to think in terms of working hypotheses. He or she asks whether a particular observation can be related or extended to a broader concept or category. For example, in the study of alcoholics these specific observations were coded under the broader term "impulses to drink": everyday stress, social occasions, anger at one's spouse, a particular song played on the radio, beer commercials.

Careful researchers organize as much as possible the data as they are collected. Recorded interviews are dated and labeled. Memos in the field are typed and dated. More and more qualitative researchers are putting aside their paper, pencils, scissors, and glue and entering their texts into computer programs to aid in the data management task. A program like The Ethnograph (Seidel, Kjolseth, and Seymour, 1988) for example, allows researchers to produce numbered lines of text, to create codes within codes, and to print out the data in various coded categories. With this program, the text can be manipulated in a variety of ways (e.g., all comments that deal with a single concept can be printed together).

The very careful, meticulous, and thoughtful examination of the collected text is called *data coding*. Each qualitative researcher codes in a slightly different way. For each collected comment or note, the researcher asks if a logical connection exists between it and any other comment or note. This is where the researcher's insight comes into play. Sometimes connections are not immediately obvious and it may take several weeks or years to identify all of the connections. Sometimes a researcher will go back to field notes after having already published work from them and see relationships that were not apparent in the first analysis. The creativity of the human mind cannot be managed in the same way that statistical output can be.

One of the best ways to develop your insight is to read the books and research articles of other qualitative researchers and study how they have coded and demonstrated the relationships in the data for their studies. Another way is to take existing coding schemes and analyze whether they help you to see relationships in your data. For example, Strauss (1987) suggests a coding paradigm that consists of conditions, interaction among actors, strategies and tactics, and consequences. Bogdan and Biklen (1982) suggest a coding scheme that includes setting/context, definition of the situation, perspectives, ways of thinking, process, activity, event, strategy, relationships and social structure, and methods. Whatever coding scheme you use or develop, the task is to take specific instances of behavior and demonstrate how they relate to broader concepts.

LEARN BY DOING

Here is a small part of a transcript from the study of alcoholics referenced in the previous example of interviewing. A middle-aged woman is talking about her recovery process. How would you code the text? What connections do you see among your codes? What would you look for in other transcripts to determine if there is a common pattern between two or more of the research participants? Do you think there might be a relationship between social isolation and alcoholic-beverage consumption?

> . . . I watch sports. I've always loved sports. Do you know what they show during the games? They show Bud Dry and Michelob and Coors Light and mountains and everyone in this attractive Size 5; there's no fat on them and they're happy and they have beer. It's a beautiful day outside or they're on the lake or. . . . That's why I wanted that . . . I was a bookworm in school.

> A straight "A" student. My best friends were. One was salutatorian and the other was valedictorian, and I graduated third. We were the nerds of the school. Guys didn't ask me out, but when I started drinking I became popular because I wanted to fit in. I've always wanted to fit in so bad that I have done anything to [fit in] and the commercials remind me of that sometimes . . . . I wanted those friends. I didn't have a care in the world. But they don't show it when you're by yourself. They don't show you sitting watching television . . . with a six-pack or with a case because you can't deal with it anymore. They don't show when you'd do anything for a drink. They don't show it when you're beat up because your boyfriend got drunk. They don't show, it's kind of like Al Bundy . . . sitting in his easy chair with the house a mess. There's empty beer cans. The place isn't picked up, the kids are crying, the dog is barking, your hair is a mess, and he's sitting here with his T-shirt on and his hand stuck down in his pants belching. That's a part of it, too.

Pattern: Discovered or Imposed?

One haunting question that good qualitative researchers always worry about is whether a pattern has been discovered or if one has been imposed. To reduce their self-doubts, they test their patterns against other plausible explanations for the data—by making sure that they have gathered data to the point of redundancy, by asking others to follow their trail of evidence, and by checking their interpretations with the study participants.

WRITING THE QUALITATIVE REPORT

There is no single format for writing a qualitative report. Because of its richness and depth, much qualitative research is presented in books and monographs rather than through journal articles. Regardless of format, qualitative researchers are obligated (a) to demonstrate how the study was conducted and how the concepts used to organize the data were developed; (b) to illustrate those concepts with sufficient observations and comments; and (c) to show the connection of the report to other research, or to show that there is no connection. Often, beginning qualitative researchers will want to share everything that they have discovered, but space limitations usually preclude that. There is also a tendency to want to include every observation that illustrates a concept, but this is hardly necessary. Keep in mind that the report is intended to demonstrate the relationships among various concepts, not to present an exhaustive list of every instance uncovered.

Qualitative writers use literature reviews in different ways. Some use them in standard report formats (i.e., early on in the work to establish importance and to provide background). Others prefer to weave the literature review into their own analysis, to demonstrate how their findings relate to other work. Some researchers prefer not to do a literature review until they have finished their own study, because knowing the concepts written about by others may suppress their own abilities to see what is going on in a particular situation.

SUMMARY

Qualitative research is any systematic investigation that attempts to understand the meanings that things have for individuals from their own perspectives. Qualitative researchers assume that human behavior is made up of thoughtful, meaningful responses to objects in the world. The meaning of things comes from the social interaction among individuals and through self-reflection. Meaning may change over time, with context, as individuals change, and as patterns of social interaction change. The primary methods of qualitative research are participant observation, interviewing, and document analysis; and the primary data for qualitative research are usually verbal and visual. Qualitative researchers seek to understand the order and pattern in the lives of their research participants.

STUDY QUESTIONS AND EXERCISES

1. What do you consider the most important characteristics of qualitative research?

2. Young and Rubicam, the advertising agency that prepares the advertising for the U.S. Postal Service, assigned qualitative researchers to study the interactions between letter carriers and residents on mail routes. The researchers found that in rural areas letter carriers are seen as a contact with society and as a respite to loneliness. The research led to a creative strategy that emphasized the human aspect of the postal service with the theme "We deliver for you." Would the meaning of the postal service likely be the same in urban areas?

3. A particular research approach suggests certain kinds of questions and information that can be gathered and also constrains other types of questions and information. For what kinds of questions would qualitative research not be appropriate?

4. How can the qualitative researcher guard against imposing a pattern on his or her data rather than discovering the ones that are there?

5. Some students note the similarities between what journalists do and what qualitative researchers do: interviewing, taking notes, and writing. What intellectual demands and research expectations are placed on the qualitative researcher that are not placed on the practicing journalist?

6. The rhetoric of quantitative research often includes a goal of "prediction and

control," and the rhetoric of qualitative research often includes a goal of "understanding." If you wanted to predict the likely winner of a national election, which research method would you choose? If you wanted to predict how the U.S. Supreme Court was likely to rule in a particular case, which research method would you choose?

7. Do you think there are any individual characteristics that make some people better qualitative researchers than others?

8. Would you expect that separate qualitative researchers studying the same phenomenon in different settings would arrive at the same or similar conclusions about its meaning? Why or why not?

9. Some theorists argue for combining quantitative and qualitative approaches within a single study. What advantages and disadvantages do you see in this?

10. Focus groups are not advocated as a form of qualitative research in this chapter. Can you think of situations or conditions under which focus groups would be appropriate for qualitative research?

SOURCES

Blumer, H. 1969. *Symbolic Interactionism: Perspective and Method.* Englewood Cliffs, N.J.: Prentice-Hall.

Bogdan, R., and S. Biklen. 1982. *Qualitative Research for Education.* Boston: Allyn & Bacon.

Glaser, B., and A. Strauss. 1967. *The Discovery of Grounded Theory.* Chicago: Aldine.

Hicks, D. 1986. The Meaning of the Cabbage Patch Doll to Children. M.S. thesis, University of Tennessee, Knoxville.

Seidel, J., R. Kjolseth, and E. Seymour. 1988. *The Ethnograph.* Corvallis, OR: Qualis Research Associates.

Strauss, A. 1987. *Qualitative Analysis for Social Scientists.* New York: Cambridge University Press.

Taylor, R. 1983. For Advertising by Lawyers, a Verdict Is at Hand. *Advertising Age* (July 18): M-26.

Treise, D., R. Taylor, and L. Wells. 1992. A Qualitative Study of Alcoholics in Recovery and Alcoholic-Beverage Advertising. *Proceedings of the American Academy of Advertising.* San Antonio, Texas. April 1992.

SUGGESTED READING

Bogdan, R., and S. Taylor. 1975. *Introduction to Qualitative Research Methods.* New York: Wiley.

Cook, T., and C. Reichardt. 1979. *Qualitative and Quantitative Methods in Evaluation Research.* Beverly Hills, Calif.: Sage.

Denzin, N. 1978. *The Research Act: A Theoretical Introduction to Sociological Methods.* New York: McGraw-Hill.

Filstead, W., ed. 1970. *Qualitative Methodology.* Chicago: Markham.

Lindlof, T., ed. 1987. *Natural Audiences: Qualitative Research of Media Uses and Effects.* Norwood, N.J.: Ablex.

Lofland, J. 1976. *Doing Social Life: The Qualitative Study of Human Interaction in Natural Settings.* New York: Wiley.

Marshall, C., and G. Rossman. 1989. *Designing Qualitative Research.* Beverly Hills, Calif.: Sage.

Van Maanen, J., J. Dabbs, and R. Faulkner. 1982. *Varieties of Qualitative Research.* Beverly Hills, Calif.: Sage.

15

Content Analysis

□
OBJECTIVES

After studying this chapter, you should be able to:

1. Define content analysis.

2. Describe the techniques of conducting content analysis.

3. Create exclusive and exhaustive coding categories.

4. Prepare a coding form for the collection of data.

5. Train coders.

6. Estimate intercoder reliability and validity.

INTRODUCTION

Although it is used primarily in academic research, **content analysis** can also serve research-minded mass communication managers and practitioners. For example, a TV news manager might study the news program of a leading competitor to learn its audience appeal. An advertising executive might study the opposition's creative efforts for style and appeal. And an interested consumer might use content analysis for a relatively objective accounting of media content. In fact, the potential of content analysis is very great for practitioners, managers, and researchers who know the technique.

Content analysis is something that most of us do almost daily, albeit on a very casual level. We do it when we pose new information against whatever else we know; we look for generalities, regularities, and patterns in the information.

We read between the lines. We test the consistency of the information. For example, when President George Bush spoke glowingly of domestic initiatives and accomplishments during his term in office, some people recalled his previous speeches and emphases; some concluded perhaps that his executive contribution had been more in the area of foreign policy than in domestic and national economic programs. No doubt this was reflected in the outcome of the 1992 presidential election.

And when we read a novel, we sometimes conclude that the fiction is, or is not, an author's self-portrait. In some cases, we ask whether the meaning exceeds the plot (i.e., whether the words say one thing, but mean another). Such observations amount to "reading between the lines," which is rather like literary detective work. We use content analysis to find things in the text that are or are not apparent. And although these things can be done on a casual basis, they can be done more objectively, more accurately, and more persuasively by use of formal techniques.

Content analysis is simply a method reducing text to numbers. It amounts to counting the occurrence of elements that appear in text. For example, a content analyst might study the frequency or percentage of robbery and wreck stories in the local newspaper. This requires some careful definitions. What constitutes a "wreck" or a "robbery story"? Is a lawsuit that results from a wreck a "wreck story" or a "law story"? Is a million-dollar embezzlement a "robbery story"? Is any white-collar crime story a "robbery story"? When the definitions are worked out, the analyst simply counts and compares the number of stories involving "wrecks," "robberies," and "other" (i.e., everything else). You can see that the system hangs on the quality of the definitions and the integrity of the researcher.

CONTENT ANALYSIS DEFINED

Bernard Berelson wrote the most widely cited definition of content analysis: "Content analysis is a research technique for the objective, systematic, and quantitative description of the manifest content of communication" (1952, 18). Although not necessarily comprehensive (other researchers have defined *content analysis* differently), the definition identifies several crucial aspects of the method. It is useful to examine each.

Objective

Objectivity is an essential requirement of science, and therefore of content analysis. Failure to meet this requirement will reduce the research to the level of personal belief, a very hard sell. As in any research, the researcher should have no vested interest in its outcome, nor even the *appearance* of a vested interest.

For example, the researcher investigating the supposed "liberal bias" of a network news program should not accept financial support from an organization dedicated to opposing network news. The research method may or may not be legitimate, but how will skeptics perceive it? The principle of objectivity demands that the researcher be disinterested and open to any research outcome, not working toward a specific outcome.

Systematic

Content analysis must also be systematic. A logical extension of objectivity, being systematic means that the researcher does not pick and choose among the text elements that will be counted. Furthermore, it means that the researcher will not omit sections of text that would contribute importantly to the research outcome. For example, impetuousness evidenced in a single correspondence from President Andrew Jackson, written in a moment of frustration, may not be a good indicator of his presidential temperament. Failure to be systematic would amount to bias. Remember, the intent is to give truth the opportunity to emerge.

Students sometimes think learning about research is dull stuff, but it need not be. One classroom of students had some fun with content analysis by converting it to "rap" music (Figure 15.1). Try writing your own lyrics; pick a topic and rap a while!

What?

Quantitative

Content analysis is a quantitative method. It converts text to numbers. But quantitative does not necessarily mean complex; that depends on the researcher and the text. One quantitative analyst might report only frequencies and percentages, for example, that among 45 references to incidents of violence, 20 involved rape ($20/45 = 44\%$) and 25 involved theft ($25/45 = 56\%$). Another analyst might introduce much greater complexity to the analysis. Although most content analysts rely on frequencies, percentages, and chi-squares, some use parametric statistics such as t-tests, regression, and factor analysis. The level of quantitative application depends also on the measurement employed and the question that is asked.

Descriptive

Berelson's (1952) definition says that content analysis describes the content of communication. The description, of course, is quantitative (e.g., "there are 20 of these and 25 of those," and all of them characterize the communication). The description is accurate only if the definitions are accurate.

Manifest

Berelson's (1952) definition also suggests that what is counted in text should be manifest (i.e., not a matter of faith). The word *manifest* means apparent. The implication is that the analyst should objectively examine a text and single-mindedly count the elements that are of interest, not be driven by some vague, unstated agenda. The content "must be coded as it appears rather than as the content analyst feels it is intended" (Stempel and Westley, 1989, 126). That is an important point.

(With apologies to Hammer, 2-Live Crew, and poets and rappers everywhere.)

Today we're gonna talk about analysis.
But a kind of research ain't all it is.
It's a thing that we all routinely do,
That tells what is or isn't true.

We use it to find recurrent themes,
To read-between-the-lines, or so it seems.
What we study is manifest content;
And what we want to know is what it meant.

We study because the meaning lies
Not always right between the eyes.
It often lies a tad below
The surface of the radio.

The meaning's not just what we say,
But what seems natural each day.
Meaning can be found in television;
Laugh tracks are not the only derision.

TV's message is sometimes serious,
Problem is, it's not always clear to us.
Is there any dark conspiracy?
Or is someone barking up the wrong tree?

So we do our analysis with two laments,
Where one is manifest, the other latent.
We think we're learnin' names and games;
If there's other stuff, then who's to blame?

Do you know? Do you know? Do you know?
Well, content analysis helps us define
The true, true nature of what's below
Or above or between the printed line.

Content analysis needs definitions,
Some tools and rules we have to follow,
And these require some recognition,
If we're to know what to allow.

One of the tools we use is "counting,"
To add the frequencies amounting.
Counting calls for common sense,
But meanings can have eloquence.

Objectivity is another requirement,
You call it like it is, without relent.
Your personal bias must be avoided,
If truth to tell will be exploited.

The things you count are systematic,
Not things that happen, whims erratic.
They are things that help to tell you whether
What you heard is what you'd rather.

(continued)

FIGURE 15.1 A "Rap" Lecture on Content Analysis

So before you count the things you see,
Repeated in the news, endlessly,
You should with care and calm define,
The things you'll count on the printed line.

You can't just count the things that strike you,
'Cause others might not see it like you.
And if your definitions are loose, you're liable
To reach a conclusion that's not viable.

Then you wouldn't have shown a doggone thing,
'Cept the counts that a wrong definition can bring!

FIGURE 15.1   (*continued*)

But there is also a "latent" aspect of communication. When the data have been coded and interpreted, the analyst sometimes can find not only what is manifest, but also what is *latent* (i.e., what was not previously evident). Latency suggests something beneath the surface. For example, an analysis of song lyrics could reveal not only the number of times a performer used certain words, but also the relative "contentedness" that the words represent. Contentedness might be implied by the use of certain symbols or by the implication of the words. In other words, the analyst could detect not only what was intended, but also what might not have been intended. It is not always the words that matter; it might be the context, or even the logic suggested by the juxtaposition of important symbols.

What Can Be Analyzed?

Any text or any communication that can be converted to text is amenable to content analysis. This includes photographs, advertisements of all kinds, presidential speeches (McDiarmid, 1937), newscasts, poetry, song lyrics, historical papers, legal opinions, literature (Albrecht, 1956; Martin, 1930), TV programs, and on and on. There is virtually nothing that can't be put into the form of text or subjected to counting.

THE PROCEDURES OF CONTENT ANALYSIS

Here are the steps typically followed in content analysis:

1. select topic
2. decide sample or census
3. define concepts or units to be counted
4. construct categories
5. create coding form

6. train coders
7. collect data
8. measure intercoder reliability
9. analyze data
10. report results

Demystifying the Method

To demystify and illustrate the method, let's go through a hypothetical project (we don't really expect to carry it out) from start to finish. Although we will work with only one research question, remember that the same techniques would apply to virtually any topic, provided adjustments are made to meet the peculiarities of the particular project. In other words, this project will represent many others in outline form.

Selecting the Topic

Most content analyses are descriptive. For example, a popular project among students is an investigation of how women, minorities, or the elderly are characterized in TV commercials (Seggar, Hafen, and Hannonen-Gladden, 1981, 277–288). The advertisements are thought to be important because they are believed to define the role or status of the person in society. The typical procedure is to count the number of advertisements in which a person from the group appears, and to count what activities involve that person in the advertisement.

For example, suppose the elderly are shown in only one in eight advertisements (fewer than might be expected from their proportion in the population), and that their portrayal is largely of "inactivity" or "dependency." The portrayal can then be considered in relation to what an individual thinks should be the "proper" role or context.

Unfortunately, many descriptive content analyses are faulted for "shallowness and lack of meaning" (Stempel and Westley, 1989, 126). Too often, content analysis research "doesn't go anywhere" (Luebke, 1992, 2–9). It lacks generality; it adds little to the body of knowledge that explains how things work. It is simply a snapshot at a point in time—a snapshot that might be different a month from now, unconnected to any other social phenomena. As argued elsewhere in this text, social phenomena don't exist in isolation; social behavior is a long string of connected experiences. A snapshot lacks explanatory power. In fact, the critic could easily argue as historians often do that a straightforward documentary analysis would do as well; couldn't a narrative description be more informative than a percentage?

The power of content analysis might be improved if research topics were theoretical instead of simply descriptive. For example, suppose you had a content analysis of the portrayal of the elderly in advertisements, and suppose you could study their portrayal in relation to elderly self-esteem. In other words, you would be studying the effect of advertisement characterizations on the self-esteem of elderly who see the advertisements. This would add a bit of complexity and subtlety—a bit of theory—to the analysis. The counterpoint would be that univariate explanations (e.g., one-variable explanations of self-esteem) are also deficient; but it would be up to the researcher to make that determination and to add other explanatory variables as feasible.

An Example of Theoretical Content Analysis

Rossow and Dunwoody (1991) studied the relationship between the plurality (complexity) of a community and news coverage of a controversy. Generally speaking, newspapers of small and large circulation are a little different in the way they present the news. For example, smaller newspapers—located in towns where "everyone knows everyone"—are more likely to support consensus. Community pressure is toward good news and maintenance of order. Larger newspapers, however, with a very diverse (pluralistic) community, have less pressure for consensus. They are more ready to present conflict as news. Consensus is not an issue because the proportion of persons unknown to others is very high.

Here is a simple illustration of the point. If you were to move to a large community previously unknown to you, and in which you knew virtually no one, you would tend to be unconcerned about what strangers thought of you. What would you care if they disliked your ragged jeans and unmown grass if you would never see them again? But if you were move to a community where you were already well known, and where social relationships were reciprocal, you would be more careful. In effect, the social pressure of the small community is toward consensus. The relationship between community structure and news coverage has been documented by Olien, Donohue, and Tichenor (1978) over a period of 20 years of research.

And so, small communities don't want to hear bad news. But in a case where they can't avoid it, such as when the federal government wants to establish a nuclear waste dump nearby, do they react similarly to their more pluralistic counterparts? The research took place in and around two communities in Wisconsin, where the U.S. Department of Energy targeted two possible repository sites for nuclear waste.

Rossow and Dunwoody (1991, 86–100) devised hypotheses to investigate the matter. One was that in such a situation the newspaper in the smaller town would present more "enabling information," the kind that permits but does not require the reader to act in response to the news. In other words, confronted with a threat, the small (consensus) community would provide more specific information to deal with it. The researchers further hypothesized that when the editor of a newspaper was personally concerned about the waste dump issue, the frequency of enabling information would be even higher.

For a sample, the researchers identified 33 communities that would be affected by the repository. Each was served by a daily or weekly newspaper. The 33 were ranked on a pluralism scale. Next, the four most pluralistic, the four least pluralistic, and the four nearest the middle of the continuum were selected for study. Newspaper circulations ranged from 1,500 to 58,000. Newspaper stories about the repository were studied from the time of the announcement, January

16th, to May 30th, when the Department of Energy dropped its plan to create a waste site.

Coders read each story to identify the extent and type of enabling information. Enabling information could be "complete," "partial," or nonexistent. The sample of stories numbered 374, with a total of 2,398 instances of enabling information—about 6.4 per story. Editors of the newspapers were interviewed about their level of concern for the issue and their perception of their audience's concern.

Rossow and Dunwoody (1991) reported that the data partially supported their hypothesis that newspapers in low-pluralism settings would provide enabling information in greater quantity and detail than newspapers in high-pluralism settings. The hypothesis that editors' personal concerns about the repository would be related to the occurrence of enabling information was also supported. In other words, "The availability of useful detail varied by both the structure of the community . . . and by . . . differences in editors' personal concerns and perceptions of readers' concerns about the issue" (Rossow and Dunwoody, 1991, 99).

Every content analysis must report a reliability test, which tells whether the counting can be trusted. In the Rossow and Dunwoody study, reliability ranged from a perfect 1.0 to as low as .33. The latter coefficient was extremely low, but it was not clear in the article which items held low reliability. That information could be important. It also was not clear how the researchers "repaired" coding disagreements between the two coders. This issue is addressed in detail in the section on reliability, below.

This research was of considerable interest. It helped to explain the relationship between the kind of news that one reads and the kind of community in which one lives. It is far more than a simple description of a communication; it is a contribution to the theory of community structure or community news.

STARTING FROM SCRATCH: A HYPOTHETICAL CONTENT ANALYSIS

The topic that we will work with in this chapter is "violence on television." This idea is not new; Gerbner for several years produced an annual violence index, and in fact he has tried to draw a relationship between the violence on television and the perceptions of violence by the TV audience (Gerbner et al., 1977, 171–180; 1979, 177–196). But for present purposes the topic has certain advantages. First, it exemplifies the definitional problems with which content analysts must work; second, it lends itself to the development of theory; and third, it gives you a good excuse if needed, to combine work with play (i.e., watching television). And despite Gerbner's annual report, the jury is still out on both the level of violence on television and its relation to the audience's perceptions of violence in their communities.

The research questions are: What is the level of violence on television as indicated by the frequency of violent instances per half hour, both by type of program and across all types? How is the level of violence on television related to TV users' perceptions about the level of violence they personally are likely to encounter?

Now a question for you: How can these research questions contribute to the development of communication theory? Here is one answer. Researchers have long believed that people learn things from fiction presented as entertainment. That was the point as far back as the 1920s, when the Payne Fund supported studies of the effects of motion pictures on the youthful audience. In the mid-1960s, DeFleur (1970) articulated the proposition in his "cultural norms theory." He said that fictional scenes shown repeatedly in entertainment influenced the viewer's perception of normality. In other words, if people—especially young people—repeatedly saw nontraditional behaviors presented as routine, they were more likely to think those behaviors "normal" and to adopt them as their own.

A little later, Gerbner (Gerbner et al., 1977, 1979) developed a very similar idea: that television was helping to shape the viewers' version of "reality." He said television had become "the storyteller of our time," providing the cultural lore once provided by elders, and *cultivating* the viewers' perception of reality. In other words, people were relying increasingly on television for their notion of "reality." One result of this, Gerbner said, was that individuals who saw a great deal of violence on television developed an exaggerated estimate of the amount of violence in society. He called this the "mean world syndrome."

The notion certainly captures the imagination. How could a person watch 6 to 12 hours of television *each day* and not learn something? And if the person learned something, what was it? If the person learned to expect a "mean world," could it be surprising when so much of what entertains us is violent? But what else did the person learn? Interpersonal behaviors, such as how to get along or not get along with others? Values? Morals? Is our dramatic entertainment (especially stories of crime, violence, and horror) in any way related to crime and violence in American society? Clearly, these are important questions, and they are not resolved.

If the study is limited to a count of the acts of violence on television, we will have a descriptive study. If we can relate the violence to behavior, we will have a contribution to theory. The theory (which Gerbner called "cultivation theory" because television seemed to "cultivate" a perception of reality) is that personal behavior is at least partly explained by the kind and amount of television that a person watches.

In effect, the topic that we have selected has two research parts; one involves content analysis, and the other a cross-sectional survey. To carry this out, we would first have to study the level and frequency of violence on television, and then survey a sample of people to learn (a) which programs people watch, (b) how much violence they see, and (c) their perceptions of the level of violence in society.

Selecting the Sample

Some Generalities. Sampling is as important for content analysis as it is for survey research. The intent of any content analysis is to represent a textual whole, just as a sample is expected to represent a whole population. A biased sample cannot represent the whole. But how does the content analyst draw the sample in a way most likely to avoid bias? One possibility is to use a table of random numbers (TON). The analyst can number every page, program, story, day, or anything else, and rely on the table to distribute the choices.

In some cases, the researcher can be more directive. For example, if the researcher is looking for the average number of *newspaper stories* about the economy, then he or she has to be very careful about the newspaper editions that are reviewed because many stories are cyclical; for example, stories about economics probably occur more frequently at the turn of the fiscal year, at quarterly reporting times, at budget times, or during periods of stock market fluctuation. We might do well to make sure that all parts of the week, month, and quarter are represented.

One sampling device used to overcome this problem is the "composite" week or month. It is formed by taking, for example, a Monday from one week, a Tuesday from another, and so on, until the period is filled. This minimizes the dominance of a single story or the cyclical story. A similar approach can be taken in longitudinal research. For example, if you were studying the evolution of news photography, you might want to study news photos from about 1890 forward. That's a lot of photography, and some sampling would have to be done. A systematic interval might work: Starting with year 1, you could select each 5th, or 10th, or *n*th year to get a representative sample across the decades. The size of the sample would depend partly on the amount of labor that could be devoted to the project. But keep in mind that, just as in people-sampling, after the sample reaches a persuasive size, there is little to be gained from further work (see Stempel, 1955, 449–455).

But how can we get a sample to represent "violence on television"? Several decisions will have to be made. Will we study *all* of television, or only prime time? Should we include the cable channels, or limit the study to the commercial networks? Should we include the Saturday morning cartoon period? An incomplete sample will give us an incomplete answer to our principal research question. And, how will we define *violence?* If we define it loosely, we will have to include the Saturday morning cartoons. That mischievous Road Runner could give us trouble.

How many shows must we screen if we are to have a representative sample? If we had the resources, we could simply view each program in the TV schedule for, say, a week. But then we would have to see more than one of each, because any one might not be a good representation of the series. So, how many programs would we have to watch? The answer is not very clear. Probably the best answer is that we would have to watch enough programs to be persuasive. A very small number might not suffice if does not cover the range of possibilities. One yardstick would be to view programs until the coding is clearly repetitious and predictable (i.e., when there appears little to gain by continuing).

If this hypothetical project were carried out, this would be a massive project. Just taping the programs would take a great deal of planning and labor. (Tapes are required because coders often need to see a scene more than once.) And then the actual coding would be very slow; when scenes unfold quickly, the coder would need to stop, tabulate, and view again. The time required for coding might be several times longer than the length of the program that is being coded. The job would be highly labor-intensive.

The Hypothetical Study.   With adequate resources, we could study programs of *all* hours and all days; but realistically, and for purposes of illustration, we will study only *entertainment fiction on prime-time television*. That means we will exclude political speeches, sporting events, documentaries, magazine formats, exposés, and news, even if they sometimes portray scenes of violence; we will also exclude daytime programs and weekend programs. If cartoons occur during prime time, they will be included. *Prime time* will be defined as 7 to 11 P.M., although some would dispute that.

You can see that the definition of what will be studied is itself very important. A documentary may contain violence; sporting events certainly do—but are they germane to the point of the research? A good point could be made either way, but a decision has to be made; for our purposes they will be excluded.

But saying we will examine fiction programs during prime time is not enough: Which episodes? Over what period of time? The longer the time period we can study, the better our study will be, because time will help account for changes in program content during the season. If there are X-number of fresh episodes in the typical TV series in a season, we could select a systematic interval (e.g., each fourth episode, after a random start). This assumes it is not really necessary to study *every* episode, and that a sample will be an adequate representation of the whole.

In the belief that a small sample will be sufficient, we will plan to analyze three of the new episodes in a season for each fiction program. Even this size sample—three weeks of prime-time commercial television—will require very large amounts of time and labor.

Creating Definitions

Having selected a topic and decided the nature of the sample, we need to create some definitions. First, what constitutes "violence?" Although we are not attempting specifically to replicate Gerbner's work, it is convenient for purposes of illustration to use the same definition:

> Violence is defined as the overt expression of physical force, with or without a weapon, against self or other, compelling action against one's will on pain of being hurt or killed, or actually hurting or killing. (Gerbner et al., 1979, 178)

We will say that each separate and distinct act of violence is a reportable unit. For example, a gun fight is an act of violence; if the fight takes five minutes, it is still one instance, not a new instance for every bullet fired. But if there are three separate gun fights, each will be counted as a separate event. Right away, this introduces some complexities: If one event takes five minutes of program time, is it *reasonable* to consider it a single episode? It could easily be the centerpiece of a drama, yet be counted singly just as would any small, separate event. That does not seem right, yet there is no better alternative; such a scene could not be accurately reduced to its smallest parts.

This illustrates the immense difficulty of content analysis. It requires individual judgment, and there is likely to be a moderate level of error. We simply must do the best we can to keep the error level low. If it is too large, as indicated by a reliability test, we must abandon the coding and perhaps try some new definitions. Remember, the intent of the study is to represent the whole accurately, or at least as accurately as possible, not to be immobilized by minor imperfections.

To see further the fragility of the definition, we need only to conjure scenes of

TV violence and apply the definition to them. If someone *merely threatens* another person, is that violence? Is slapstick comedy violent (like the fellow with a mop on his shoulder whose quick change of directions throws the mop into the face of his buddy)? Are cartoons violent? Must the violence be human-to-human? For example, is it violence when the skier is caught in a *natural* disaster such as an avalanche? If Trapper John fights a grizzly, is that violence? You can see that *violence* is a difficult concept.

Gerbner's definition, of course, is not the only one that could be used. The following definition seems simpler, but perhaps is more inclusive: *by a human ?*

> Violence is any physical pain or injury inflicted on any individual, or damage to property, regardless of source.

The difference between the definitions points up the peculiarities of the method and the project. Kidnapping would be an act of violence under Gerbner's definition, but not as defined above, unless it involved injury. And Gerbner's definition accounts for coercion, whereas the briefer definition does not. But the alternative definition would include a landslide, a physical attack, or an attack by a mechanical source (e.g., missile, robot, or machine). It would *not* include *threat of violence,* or violence to a person's property. For example, if a thug threatened to break the leg of our hero, the threat would not count until it was carried out. If a villain were killed in a burning building, the death would be counted, but not the damage to the building, unless the latter constituted the central act of violence.

This is sticky: If the movie commando were to blow up a bridge, would that meet the Gerbner definition? What about a car chase in which the car careened into a stand of veggies, then crashed into 15 police cars, all with no known personal injuries?

Unfortunately, the issue of violence-as-humor also remains problematical. Is the comedian who nudges Mr. Pompous off the pier and into the river being violent? When one of the Three Stooges bonks another on the nose, is that violence?

There is also the definition of *injury.* What constitutes pain and injury? A shooting or a fight is clearly painful and injurious, but often the nature of the injury is ambiguous. We can instruct our coders: Count it as an injury if the action causes pain and suffering. (A bullet wound would be presumed to cause pain and suffering even if the victim were not shown writhing in agony.) Inevitably, there will be some disputes of judgment. That is one of the weaknesses of the system. In practice, a certain amount of error is inevitable; however, every effort must be made to minimize it.

Constructing Categories

In any content analysis, the categories in which items are counted must be both exhaustive and exclusive. *Exhaustive* implies that, in a count of behaviors, every behavior must be classifiable. For example, a conversation between adults might be applied to one of the following categories: (a) friendly, (b) neutral, (c) hostile, or (d) other. If every conversation cannot be categorized in one and only one category, or if too many counts fall into the "other" (i.e., undefined) category, then the categories are faulty.

The second requirement of category construction is that every category must be *exclusive.* If an item can be categorized in two places, then the categories are poor. Look back at the example in the preceding paragraph: Can every adult conversation be described by only one of four categories? Which category would you use for an intense business discussion? Categories must be constructed to make the most efficient and accurate classifications of the units.

How many categories are needed? There is no specific rule, but experience dictates a small number. When the number of categories is too great, cell frequency is small and analysis is difficult. Two to six categories are usually sufficient.

CC F Creating a Coding Form

Creation of the coding form precedes the counting. This will be one of the hardest parts of the analysis, because it requires very clear thinking about what is to be accomplished. As Kenny Rogers sings, "There'll be time enough for counting, when the dealing's done." We might add that, when the counting's done, we must have counted the right elements.

The coding form is a record whose layout and content varies with the nature of the research. It permits the researcher to document the items counted. The coding form is simply a page that includes information such as coding categories, dates, and coder name—all of which is useful in tabulation and analysis. For most content analyses, one form is needed for every item examined.

What would a coding form look like if we were to code instances of violence on television? Figure 15.2 is a good example. The coding form specifies the number of the item being counted, both within a program and across all programs, so that we can keep a running count of the instances of violence. Borrowing Lasswell's famous communication model, the coding form tells us "who did what to whom with what force and with what effect." All of these things will be helpful when we get to the point of making sense of the data, and ferreting out its implications.

Training Coders

Armed with a stack of coding forms, and presumably supported by a sophisticated videotaping system, we have to recruit and train coders. They can be students, faculty members, nonuniversity adults, or others, but they must be mature, capable, and responsible. They must be able to make reasonable judgments on the basis of given definitions.

Sources of Error in Coding

3 sources: system (1) Coder error. Unit (2) V unit definition error (3) Random error

There are <u>three sources</u> of error in coding. One is the coder; some coders are better than others because of qualities such as maturity, perspective, and experience. "Better" coders are likely to make judgments that would be reinforced by many or

CODING FORM

INSTRUCTIONS FOR CODING VIOLENCE IN PRIME-TIME TV. COMPLETE ONE FORM FOR EACH IN-
STANCE OF VIOLENCE; KEEP THESE SEPARATE BY PROGRAM. IN OTHER WORDS, WHEN THE PRO-
GRAM HAS BEEN REVIEWED, YOU SHOULD BE ABLE TO COUNT THE INCIDENTS OF CRIME AND
VIOLENCE FOR THAT PROGRAM.

Column
Number

Coder name: _____   _____

TV program name: _____   _____

Air date: _____   _____

Program length: 30   60   90   120   _____

Program Type: Sitcom
                Mystery (e.g., "Murder She Wrote")   _____
                Movie (not VCR)   _____
                Soap opera (serial)   _____
                Action (serial)   _____
                Other (identify) _____   _____

Perpetrator of violent episode: hero   _____   _____
                            villain   _____
                            other   _____
Approximate duration of violence: (in minutes and seconds)   _____   _____

Kind of pain or injury: death   _____
                    physical trauma   _____
                    psychological/emotional   _____
                    property only   _____
                    other   _____

Brief description of violence: _____

_____

Number of individuals involved in violence: _____   _____

Gender of perpetrator:	M	F	unknown	_____
Gender of recipient:	M	F	unknown	_____
Race of perpetrator:	White African American	Other		
Weapons used (check all that apply):	firearms		_____	_____
	blades		_____	
	bombs		_____	
	machinery		_____	
	martial arts		_____	
	other (explain)		_____	

Incident number (within program)   _____   _____

Incident number (across programs):   _____   _____

FIGURE 15.2   Sample Coding Form for the Hypothetical Analysis of Violence on Television

why not Race of Recipient?

293

most others of the culture. Another source of error is the definition of the unit being coded. An effective definition must be unambiguous and comprehensive enough to allow useful categorization of all items. Errors attributable to the coder or the definitions can be thought of as *systematic* errors because they are attributable to known causes. The third source of error, *random error*, includes everything not explained by coder or definition error. It might include working conditions or fatigue.

Wouldn't this coder error?

If two judges examine a codable element and disagree on its categorization, the fault could lie in any of the three sources of error. The author once assigned three graduate students a difficult coding task; and discovered that the coding performance by two of them was highly similar, but that of the third was consistently different. Hence, the coders were retrained, and the coding was resumed, but with no improvement. Only then did the author conclude that one of the coders should be replaced.

Who cares?!

It is important that the definitions be good enough to ensure compatible judgments among several coders; but this does not mean penalizing, retraining, or browbeating the aberrant judge or judges until conformity is achieved. Conformity is not the point; the reasonableness of the definition is. If reasonable people, after proper thought and training, can't agree on the use of a definition, then the definition might be the problem.

From time to time, the author has seen research in which coders were encouraged to *negotiate* difficult judgments. This is a doubtful practice. If multiple coders have to negotiate the proper categorization of a unit, have they demonstrated the usefulness of the definition, and have they contributed to the validity of the analysis? Or have they merely succumbed to the pressures of the situation? Probably the best strategy would be to rely on the definitions, and let the reliability fall where it will. After all, the analysis is not aimed at assessing the agreeability of coders; it is aimed at classifying text units.

Collecting Data

Typically, the coder uses one coding form for each unit being studied. For example, to code violence on television, we would need one coding form for each distinct act of violence. It is not permissible to skip countable but difficult units; instead the coder should examine a unit as many times as necessary, then change a coding decision if judgment dictates.

RELIABILITY

Reliability is near the heart of content analysis; if the coding is not reliable, the analysis cannot be trusted. You may recall from Chapter 3 that reliability takes several forms (e.g., test–retest, split half, Cronbach's alpha). But in content analysis, reliability is different. It refers to *intercoder reliability*, or the extent or degree of agreement among coders.

The Holsti Formula

— for 2 coders?

Holsti (1969) offered a popular measure of intercoder reliability:

Is This correct?

$$\text{Reliability} = 2M/(N_1 + N_2) \quad \text{or} \quad ? \quad \frac{2M}{(N_1 + N_2 + \cdots N_n)}$$

I = NO!

where M = coding decisions for which coders were in agreement
$N_1 + N_2$ = the total number of coding decisions   (Formula 15.1)

This formula yields a simple percentage of agreement between two coders. For example, if two coders examined 100 units, and agreed on the categorization in $^{75}\!/\!100$ instances, they would have a 75-percent reliability score ($[2 \times 75]/[N_1 = 100]$ + $[N_2 = 100]$ = .75). More simply, 75 agreements divided by 100 opportunities = 75-percent agreement.

But there is a serious flaw in the use of a simple percentage to estimate the reliability of two coders: The reliability check has the intent of confirming the usefulness of the definition that is used, but some of the agreement may be attributable to chance, not to the quality of a definition. In other words, when two coders put items into either category A or category B, they might select the same category occasionally *just by chance.* Thus, the percentage formula can give an inflated estimate of the quality of the definitions.

Scott's Pi

To account for this element of chance in coder agreement, Scott suggested "an improved method" of calculating reliability, which has become known as *Scott's pi* (Scott, 1969, 321–325):

$$\text{Pi} = \frac{\text{percent agreement observed} - \text{percent agreement expected}}{1 - \text{percent agreement expected}}$$

Percent agreement observed is calculated in the manner of Holsti's formula; it is the percentage of agreement between two coders. *Percent agreement expected* is the sum of the square of the percentage of each category.

For example, suppose you knew, a priori, that in a set of 100 news stories, 50 were of "hard news" and 50 were of "feature news," and you wanted to test the ability of coders to identify the types of news properly. In that case, the percentage expected would be 50. If the percentage observed were also 50, then agreement among coders, according to Scott's pi, would be a perfect 1 (i.e., $^{50}\!/\!50 = 1$). But if the percentage observed were any number less than 50, Scott's pi would be a decimal fraction of 1. The greater the departure from 1, the nearer the quotient to zero, and the less agreement there would be among coders.

But, suppose you *didn't* know the number of items that would fall into each category; what then would be the percentage expected? Scott's pi formula assumes that the best estimate of what *should* have happened (i.e., the expected frequency) is what *did* happen. Let's say two coders were to sort items into any of four categories. And let's say that they were in agreement on 80 percent of their categorizations. Further, in regard to items about which they agreed, they put 50 percent into category 1, 35 percent into category 2, 10 percent into category 3, and 5 percent into category 4. To find the percentage expected, we square each percentage as follows:

$$
\begin{aligned}
(.50 \times .50) &= .250 \\
(.35 \times .35) &= .123 \\
(.10 \times .10) &= .010 \\
(.05 \times .05) &= .003
\end{aligned}
$$

Total Expected = .386

Since the agreement observed was said to be 80 percent (or .80), we now have the numbers to work the formula of Scott's pi:

$$
\begin{aligned}
Pi &= .80 - .386 \ / \ 1 - .386 \\
&= .414 \ / \ .614 \\
&= .674
\end{aligned}
$$

(Formula 15.2)

You can see that the obtained reliability estimate of .67 is less than the .80 (or 80 percent) that was given by a simple percentage. The formula has corrected for chance agreements. In other words, when chance is considered, the agreement between coders possibly was less strong than might have seemed at first glance.

But what is the substantive interpretation of a pi reliability measure of .67? Is it good, bad, or moderate? The consensus seems to be that a pi greater than .70 represents an acceptable level of agreement. A pi of .60 to .70 probably would be considered marginal, at best; and a pi below .60 most likely is unsatisfactory (Landis and Koch, 1977, 363–374).

Craig's Kappa — *most effective*

Unfortunately, Scott's pi also has a weakness, although not in its math. The weakness is that it applies only to *two* coders and content analysis often involves multiple coders. Craig (1981, 260–264) and Fleiss (1971, 378–382) have generalized Scott's pi to multiple coders. Craig created the measure *kappa*, which extends Scott's pi to agreement among three coders. Fleiss carried the notion to "many raters." For anyone engaged in publishable content analysis, these are important studies to consult for the details of calculation.

In our hypothetical study of TV violence, we would have to compute a reliability score for each major coding unit. These would be percentages corrected for

chance agreements. Any score that failed to achieve a satisfactory (persuasive) level would have to be discussed forthrightly, or perhaps simply eliminated.

One aspect of coding error not addressed directly by measures such as Scott's pi is sample error. Any analysis that relies on a sample risks it. As with survey research, the larger the number of items examined, *assuming a random sample,* the smaller the expected sample error; hence an argument for large samples. However, no matter how large the sample, if it is biased, there is no correction. In the end, the sample simply must be "persuasive," irrespective of quantitative measures.[1]

LEARN BY DOING

Read Study Question 2 of Chapter 15; then propose a content analysis. For example, select a popular daily soap opera and watch an episode. What kinds of *behaviors* or interactions characterize the program? What *themes* are apparent? What portion of the dialogue is given to *despair?* What *social values* are implicit or explicit?

The point of content analysis is to convert text to numbers so that occurrences can be seen more clearly. As you watch the soap opera, begin to formulate a *coding form* in your own mind. If you are to make any generalities about the program, you will have to watch it more than once; you will have to describe and justify your *sample.*

When you have decided what you want to *code,* be careful to *define* the elements clearly. Your count is only as good as your definitions. As you *code* elements, make marginal notations that will help to justify your coding. For example, if you describe an interpersonal interaction as "hostile," you should be able to describe it so that a reader could agree or disagree with you.

If you work alone, you will not be able to estimate the *reliability* of your coding; if possible, team with another person on the same soap opera, but work independently, and check each other's work.

When you write up your results, describe your sample, the coding form, and the purpose of the research; discuss the reliability; and report the results. What generalities can you make? Would the results have credibility for others?

Validity

Content analysis, like any other research, must be assessed for validity. however, there are no specific guidelines for that assessment. Rather, validity depends on the quality of the definitions and the persuasiveness of the data, as well as on the basic concept of the research. A content analysis may be highly reliable, but if it is based on a false premise, it has little or no validity.

Suppose I wanted to study what I thought was the similarity between presidents Andrew Jackson (1829–1837) and Ronald Reagan (1981–1989). Both were colorful and somewhat charismatic leaders. It may be excessive to say both were ideologues, but both at least had a clear view of what they wanted to accomplish and they pursued it relentlessly. Furthermore, their unambiguous political positions won public favor. Wouldn't it be interesting to study their political positions, via the language of their speeches and writings, to identify their points of similarity and dissimilarity? Could it be that they were highly similar, separated only by 150 years?

We could expect several problems in such an analysis, but one stands out. It pertains to the evolution of language: If President Reagan used the word *conservative*, would it have meant the same to President Jackson? If President Jackson was interested in issues of American economics, were his concerns in any way comparable to those suggested by today's system and market that in his wildest dreams he would not have conjured? Would it be reasonable to compare "reality" then and now?

Consider another example: Suppose we were studying song lyrics of the 1940s and 1990s, and we needed to code the expression, "Give me your love." The 1940s version probably suggested loyalty, commitment, or perhaps hand-holding; the 1990s version probably suggests greater intimacy, and possibly less commitment. These are serious language differences that would threaten the validity of the research.

The nature of the sample can also threaten validity. Clearly, a poor sample of text cannot adequately represent the whole text.

Jackson and Reagan were decisive leaders; they were relatively unambiguous, and they played politics from a position of political and military strength. Undoubtedly they were similar in some regards; the difficulty is in subtracting the difference that is the result of 150 years, from the differences between the two presidents.

COMPUTER ANALYSIS OF TEXT

The potential for computer analysis of text is tremendous. That makes it the more remarkable in this computer age how little use of the computer has been made in content analysis.

The General Inquirer

One of the first computer programs for content analysis, written in the mid-1960s, was called *The General Inquirer* (Stone et al., 1966). It has been cited often in surveys of content analysis, but usually in the context of what is possible, not what has been done (Weber, 1990). In fact, it has been used relatively little, possibly because of the complexity of its documentation and its computer language. Even now, content analysis programs are seldom prominent in the literature.

The great potential of computer analysis is in its ability to process huge chunks of text at electric speed. The difficulties have been in inputting the data and defining useful elements to code. A few years ago, it would have been necessary to input data a word at the time, adding hugely to the cost of the research. Today, inputting is less of a problem, however, because character readers can accurately read most typefaces. In some cases, as with news wire services, copy can be captured directly on disk. This enables the analyst to study many thousands of words of newspaper copy daily for broad patterns in the news.

But of course the computer can do only what it is told, and so if it is programmed to detect the key word *collar*, it will count both "gets the collar white" and "white collar crime." It is up to the analyst to detect the difference. One helpful strategy is to program the computer to print several words on either side of the key word. This is called "key words in context" because it lets the analyst see the word in its own context.

Computer content analysis probably would be of little value in our study of TV violence because the computer can't decode nonverbal content; but it could be useful if we were studying the authorship of several unsigned Federalist Papers. In fact, that topic represented an interesting and important early use of content analysis. That particular analysis was done by hand, not computer (Mosteller and Wallace, 1963, 275–309). If we, 30 years later, were to input the disputed papers plus other papers whose authorship was known, then our comparison would be fairly quick.

In the original work, though, the quickness of the study was not crucial; it was the *idea* of how to detect authorship that was crucial. Researchers first looked for stylistic devices in language and structure, but found this unproductive. Finally, they fell upon what they called "insignificant" words (Paisley, 1963, 219–237)—words such as the articles *a, an,* and *the,* some prepositions, and conjunctions. Because language structure permits variable use of such words, different authors use different quantities of them. The authors of the Federalist Papers used characteristic quantities of these structural words, a kind of stylistic signature, and so it was possible to identify the authorship of the unsigned papers (Mosteller and Wallace, 1963; Paisley, 1963).

Computer Content Analysis: A Case Study

Brigitte Nacos and five colleagues (1991, 111–128) made an interesting comparison of computer-assisted content analysis and human coding. The objective of the research was to examine the reliability and validity of computer coding. They concluded, "The performance of the computer program was not completely satisfactory, [but] its successes and pitfalls encourage us to conclude that large-scale computer-assisted content analysis can make significant contributions to social science research" (Nacos et al., 1991, 112).

The subject of the analysis was news reporting in times of crisis: the Cuban missile crisis, the Dominican Republican invasion, and so on. Nacos (1990) had earlier conducted a manual analysis of three newspapers, the *New York Times*, the *Washington Post,* and the *Chicago Tribune.* She categorized news reports as supportive, probably supportive, neutral/ambiguous, or against/probably against presidential policy in the crisis. The test was to see if the computer would reach some of the same counts that she did. For some analyses, two categories such as supportive, probably supportive, were collapsed into one.

Coding for this type of analysis is difficult. Here are some examples of the distinctions Nacos had to make: In regard to the Grenada invasion, it was reported that Senator Malcolm Wallop said, "We are seeing an increasing level of Soviet adventuring all over the world." Nacos coded this as "supportive/probably supportive" of presidential policy. Senator Daniel Patrick Moynihan, on the other hand, called the invasion "an act of war." Nacos coded his statement as "against/probably against."

Can the computer be expected to make such judgments? Investigating coverage of Grenada, the computer analysis was initiated with a search of the Nexis data base for stories in the *Times* and the *Post*. The time period was Jan. 1983 to Nov. 25, 1983. The data base provided 1,174 stories with the word *Grenada*, but apparently 1,000 were used in the analysis—roughly the same number for the two newspapers. The program pulled "the text within 50 words" of the key word, *Grenada*. This provided a context for the discussion of Grenada. When *Grenada* referred to "Grenada Avenue," or any other irrelevant object, the reference was discarded.

Content Dictionaries

The next step was construction of a *dictionary* of terms to help the computer in its work. For example, if the researchers wanted to count the references to elements *hostile* to the U.S. action in Grenada, the machine was programmed to find words such as *Cuba* and *Cuban*. To count references *favorable* to the U.S. action, it was programmed to find words such as *rescue, liberated, moral,* and *legitimate.* The scoring of such word occurrences also was complex. The researchers had 34 rules; for example if the word *rescued* occurred within 30 spaces of *Grenada,* it was scored as favoring U.S. policy.

Nacos and her associates searched the reporting of two crises in this way. In the reportage of Grenada, the machine counts were satisfactorily close to the manual counts. But in the reportage of the Three-Mile Island nuclear accident, the comparison "was clearly a failure" (Nacos et al., 1991, 121). The computer count was markedly different from the manual count in some aspects of the coding. The difference, apparently, was that whereas Grenada was a rather static, one-dimensional matter, Three-Mile Island was ongoing, long-term, and changing. The computer had only one set of rules, and they apparently did not meet the subtle changes in the context.

The authors concluded: "The limitations that we found in the computer-assisted method are not trivial. [The] computer does not recognize ambiguities or problems as an attentive human coder would." Despite the mixed success of the head-to-head comparison, they said: "Our analysis has convinced us that the use of computer-assisted methods offers very promising possibilities for quantitative media research" (Nacos et al., 1991, 125).

Data Analysis

For the most part, the analysis of text involves frequencies and percentages, rather than statistical tests (Stempel and Westley, 1989, 137). This is partly because often the analyst is working with a complete collection rather than a sample, which renders statistical testing inappropriate. For example, if a whole book is being analyzed, it is not a sample; it is a *universe,* a whole. Statistical tests are designed to account for sample variation, but in the case of a universe there is none.

In the event of sampling, the most likely statistical test will be *chi-square,* a test of the difference between what was observed and what was expected. But Stempel and Westley (1989, 144) have pointed out that t-tests and factor analysis can also be appropriate. The kind of statistical analysis depends not only on sampling, but also on the nature of the data that are collected. For example, frequency data are appropriate for nonparametric tests, and interval data are suited to parametric tests.

Like the categories that make up the analysis, to some extent the statistical treatment depends on the ingenuity of the analyst. For example, one analyst might examine a text for the *frequency* of certain verbs; but another might attempt to measure the *intensity* (Dollard and Mowrer, 1947, 3–32) or *strength* of the verbs. Measures of intensity or strength no doubt would lend themselves to sophisticated parametric analysis.

Returning to our hypothetical study of TV violence, our first calculations would be frequencies and percentages; we would be reporting the number of acts of violence per program, per hour, and per prime-time cycle. As Gerbner did, we probably would use tests such as correlation or t-test to learn whether individuals who see the violence on television tend to overestimate the occurrence of violence in their own environment.

The second part of our hypothetical project would be to survey the TV audience to learn the amount of television watched. Because there is a great deal of violence in TV fiction, we might assume that the more people watch, the more violence they will be exposed to. But is that a reasonable assumption? Probably not. For example, a person could watch long hours of family situation comedies such as "Andy Griffith" and "Gilligan's Island" and not really see much violence. Conversely, a person could watch just a few programs, but concentrate on the most violent.

To pursue the notion that the observation of violence is related to a person's perception of a "mean world," we would have to measure (a) the extent to which the person feels threatened, and (b) the level of violence to which the person is exposed. These two elements would make use of principles discussed in the earlier chapters on sampling, measurement, and questionnaire design (chapters 4, 5, and 7); they will not be developed further here. But you can see the value of content analysis for this research: Without carefully documented estimates of the level of violence, we would have no way to sort out the question of whether a person's perception of violence is influenced by television or something else, such as one's personal environment. That is the problem that arose in the Gerbner cultivation research (Gerbner et al., 1977, 1979); critics said Gerbner's cultivation effects tended to disappear when rival independent variables were controlled.

SOME FINAL THOUGHTS

Content analysis as a formal research tool has been available for some 50 years or more. It has much to offer. In fact, it is limited only by the ingenuity of the user. Does it live up to its potential? Probably many researchers would think not. But that is the fault of the researcher, not the method. The key to good content analysis is clear thinking and deep thinking about the relationship among variables. Depth and clarity are not things that can be taught; they come from within.

SUMMARY

"Content analysis is a technique for the objective, systematic, and quantitative description of the manifest content of communication" (Berelson, 1952, 18). It is a method of reducing text to numbers so that the frequency of selected qualities can be learned. Virtually any communication can be analyzed by counting. The method typically involves nine steps or procedures. There are three principal sources of error: the coder, the definitions that are used, and other sources called random errors. Content analysis must be judged for reliability. If an analysis is not sufficiently reliable, its conclusion cannot be trusted. Statistical reporting in content analysis typically is limited to frequencies and percentages, but some projects employ parametric and multivariate methods.

STUDY QUESTIONS AND EXERCISES

1. The classical definition of content analysis stipulates that meanings are *manifest*, yet the text argues that meanings also can be *latent*; explain the distinction.

2. Propose a content analysis; it could involve any print medium or any visual medium. How would you create a sample? How would you construct coding categories? Outline the steps you would follow in conducting this research.

3. Explain why Scott's pi might be a better estimator of intercoder reliability than Holsti's percentage formula.

NOTE

1. The author wishes to thank Dr. Edward Blick and Dr. Nicholas DeBonis, formerly doctoral students at the University of Tennessee, for assistance in compiling the following suggested readings on reliability and validity in content analysis: Kassarjian, H. H. 1977. Content Analysis in Consumer Research. *Journal of Consumer Research* 4:8–18; Stempel, Guido H., III. 1955. Increasing Reliability in Content Analysis. *Journalism Quarterly* 32:449–455; Windhauser, J. W., and Guido H. Stempel, III. 1979. Reliability of Six Techniques for Content Analysis of Local Coverage. *Journalism Quarterly* 56:148–152; Danielson, Wayne A., and J. J. Mullen. 1965. A Basic Space Unit for Newspaper Content Analysis. *Journalism Quarterly* 42:108–109; Carney, T. F. 1972. *Content Analysis: A Technique for Systematic Inference from Communications.* Winnipeg: University of Manitoba Press; Janis, I. L., R. H. Fadner, and M. Janowitz. 1943. The Reliability of a Content Analysis Technique. *Public Opinion Quarterly* 7(2):293–296; Davis, F. J., and L. W. Turner. 1941. Sample Efficiency in Quantitative Newspaper Content Analysis. *Public Opinion Quarterly* 15(4):762–763; Coats, W. J., and S. W. Mulkey. 1940. A Study in Newspaper Sampling. *Public Opinion Quarterly* 14(3):533–546; Schutz, W. A. 1947. On Categorizing Qualitative Data in Content Analysis. *Public Opinion Quarterly* 22(4):503–515; Jones, R. L., and R. E. Carter, Jr. 1948. Some Procedures for Estimating "Newshole" in Content Analysis. *Pub-*

lic Opinion Quarterly 23(3):399–403; Haskins, J. H. 1966. Headline-and-Lead Scanning vs. Whole Item Reading in Content Analysis. *Journalism Quarterly* 43(3):333–335.

SOURCES

Albrecht, Milton C. 1956. Does Literature Reflect Common Values? *American Sociological Review* 21:722–729.

Berelson, Bernard. 1952. *Content Analysis in Communication Research.* New York: Free Press.

Craig, Robert. 1981. Generalization of Scott's Index of Intercoder Agreement. *Public Opinion Quarterly* 45:260–264.

DeFleur, Melvin. 1970. *Theories of Mass Communication.* 2d ed. New York: David McKay.

Dollard, John, and O. Hobart Mowrer. 1947. Measuring Tension in Written Documents. *Journal of Abnormal and Social Psychology* 42:3–32.

Fleiss, J. L. 1971. Measuring Nominal Scale Agreement Among Many Raters. *Psychological Bulletin* 76:378–382.

Gerbner, George, Larry Gross, Michael F. Eleey, Marilyn Jackson-Beeck, Suzanne Jeffries-Fox, and Nancy Signorelli. 1977. TV Violence Profile No. 8: The Highlights. *Journal of Communication* 27:171–180.

Gerbner, George, Larry Gross, Nancy Signorelli, Michael Morgan, and Marilyn Jackson-Beeck. 1979. The Demonstration of Power: Violence Profile No. 10. *Journal of Communication* 29(3):177–196.

Holsti, Ole R. 1969. *Content Analysis for the Social Sciences and Humanities.* Reading, Mass.: Addison-Wesley.

Krippendorff, Klaus. 1980. *Content Analysis: An Introduction to Its Methodology.* Beverly Hills, Calif.: Sage.

Landis, J. R., and G. G. Koch. 1977. An Application of Hierarchical Kappa-Type Statistics in the Assessment of Majority Agreement Among Multiple Observers. *Biometrics* 33:363–374.

Luebke, Barbara F. 1992. No More Content Analyses (Commentary). *Newspaper Research Journal* 13(1 and 2):2–9.

Martin, Helen. 1930. Nationalism in Children's Literature. *The Library Quarterly* 6:405–418.

McDiarmid, John. 1937. Presidential Inaugural Addresses: A Study in Verbal Symbols. *The Public Opinion Quarterly* July:79–82.

Mosteller, F., and D. L. Wallace. 1963. Inference in an Authorship Problem. *Journal of the American Statistical Association* 58:275–309.

Nacos, Brigitte L. 1990. *The Press, Presidents, and Crises.* New York: Columbia University Press.

Nacos, Brigitte L., Robert Y. Chapiro, John T. Young, David P. Fan, Torsten Kjellstrand, Craig McCaa. 1991. Content Analysis of News Reports: Comparing Human Coding and a Computer-Assisted Method. *Communication* 12:111–128.

Olien, C. M., G. A. Donohue, and P. J. Tichenor. 1978. Community Structure and Media Use. *Journalism Quarterly* 55(2):445–455.

Paisley, William J. 1963. Identifying the Unknown Communicator in Painting, Literature and Music: The Significance of Minor Encoding Habits. *Journal of Communication* 14:219–237.

Rosengren, Karl Erik, ed. 1981. Advances in Content Analysis. Vol. 9. In *Sage Annual Reviews of Communication Research.* Beverly Hills, Calif.: Sage.

Rossow, Marshel D., and Sharon Dunwoody. 1991. Inclusion of "Useful" Detail in Newspaper Coverage of a High-Level Nuclear Waste Siting Controversy. *Journalism Quarterly* 68(1–2):86–100.

Scott, William A. 1969. Reliability of Content Analysis: The Case of Nominal Scale Coding. *Public Opinion Quarterly* 19:321–325.

Seggar, John F., Jeffrey K. Hafen, and Helena Hannonen-Gladden. 1981. Television's Portrayals of Minorities and Women in Drama and Comedy Drama 1971–80. *Journal of Broadcasting* 25:3, 277–288.

Stempel, Guido H., III. 1955. Increasing Reliability in Content Analysis. *Journalism Quarterly* 32:449–455.

Stempel, Guido H., III, and Bruce H. Westley. 1989. *Research Methods in Mass Communications.* 2d ed. Englewood Cliffs, N.J.: Prentice-Hall.

Stone, Phillip J., D. C. Dunphy, M. S. Smith, and D. M. Ogilvie. 1966. *The General Inquirer: A Computer Approach to Content Analysis.* Cambridge, Mass.: MIT Press.

Weber, Robert Philip. 1990. *Basic Content Analysis.* Beverly Hills, Calif.: Sage.

Applying Research Methods to Mass Media

16

Fundamentals of Print Media Research

Many of the current technological barriers to information seeking . . . should dissolve with the advent of the new communication media. Video cassettes, cable television and computerized home communication centers each promise that a wealth of material now packaged for disparate media will become available in a single medium that is receiver-controlled. Prime time can be individually determined. It will depend on the schedule of each individual and when he wishes to use mass communication.

Maxwell E. McCombs, 1972

□

OBJECTIVES

After studying this chapter, you should be able to:

1. Calculate readership in terms of cost-per-thousand.

2. Generally describe psychographic and life-style research.

3. Calculate several measures of readability.

4. Describe studies of readership and graphic design.

5. Discuss some uses and gratifications of print media.

To this point, the text has attempted to prepare you broadly in the fundamentals of social science research. The material covered applies to *all* studies of mass communication. But researchers who service the media industry have adapted and extended these fundamentals to fit the special needs of their clients. This chapter and the three that follow will focus on the kinds of research and the methods of research that are of special interest to mass media clients.

INTRODUCTION

By far the most likely print media research is *applied research,* especially audience studies. Media managers and sponsors want to know the nature of their audience: its characteristics, preferences, and life-styles. Such research has a very understandable goal: to enable the medium to compete among media, and to deliver an audience to an advertiser.

Delivering the Audience

"Delivering" an audience to an advertiser might seem an odd conception, but if there is no audience or if the audience is overly small, advertising is pointless. When the mass media manager is able to attract a sufficient audience, the sale of advertising time becomes feasible. And so we try to deliver an audience.

Matching the Audience to the Message

Another goal of the media manager is to match the audience to the message or product being offered by the sponsor. That means some of the people delivered to the advertiser should be willing and able to respond favorably to the commodity offered, whether it is product or image. For example, a large audience of children will be of little value to the advertiser of stocks and bonds. Similarly, an advertisement for hair curlers might find a better outlet than the sports page of the newspapers. If the character of the audience is known, as represented by demographics, the sponsor can select the audience that is most likely to be interested in the product advertised.

To attract an audience, the media manager must offer something attractive: it could be a popular TV show, an insightful magazine article, a newspaper feature, or a special radio format. Keep in mind, however, that offering something attractive is no guarantee of an audience, because another medium may already have offered something attractive to the same audience. But it is a start.

How is the media manager to predict the power of the media product to attract an audience? Must he or she wait until the product scores big, or dies on the vine? Will intuition suffice? Can the medium or the sponsor afford the risk? Research can help provide answers to these questions.

But even if the audience is matched to the product, the message itself can defeat the intended response. That seems to have happened recently when advertisements introducing a luxury automobile failed to reveal its appearance. The advertisement did not present the image of the automobile. The intent might have been to create an elite mystique, but the tactic was seen by some as pretentious. It generated a great deal of discussion among viewers, and even in the newspapers, but might not have worked much to the advantage of the automaker.

MEDIA COMPETITION

Dividing the Pie

As grows the number of media clamoring for a portion of the public's attention, competition among media also grows. At one time, the three commercial networks had the TV industry virtually to themselves. That has changed. They now compete with dozens if not hundreds of channels on satellites and community antenna systems; with videocassette recorders (VCRs), pay systems, movie channels, sports channels, religious channels, health channels, and more. They also compete with national magazines and national newspapers for national advertising.

Radio also has become more competitive. Where radio once was dominated by AM signals, the dial is now crowded with FM as well. Each outlet—radio, television, print media—is scrambling for its share of the market. Each calculates its audience and the benefits of its product, and competes for advertisers.

Maxwell E. McCombs, whose monograph was quoted at the beginning of this chapter, spoke of this competition for the media "pie" in the context of the "principle of relative constancy." The principle suggested that the amount of money and time that people spend on mass media is rather constant and small. From 1929 through 1968, American households spent between 2 percent and 3 percent of their annual income on mass media (McCombs, 1972, 68).

Updating the principle, Wood and O'Hare (1991, 27) agreed: "Mass media spending as a fraction of income is remarkably stable over sixty years, a period including a depression, a world war, and rapid changes in technology." However, they found that spending can also vary by decade, and that it appeared to have increased significantly with the development of new technology during the 1970s. They said that consumers' willingness to spend more on media in 1978–1979 "prevented major losses by print and conventional audiovisual media."

And so, although the principle may not hold in a specific period, many new media are competing for pieces of a relatively small pie, the mass media audience. Mass media managers will have to work harder than ever to preserve or expand their portion of the market.

Costs

The costs of advertising vary dramatically. A 30-second spot for a 5-kilowatt radio station in a small town might cost $15 to $20; on a 100-kilowatt FM station with a 500,000 metropolitan area, $75 to $150; on a VHF TV station in the 25th market, $1,800 to $2,500; on a network weekday prime-time show, negotiable, but probably $65,000 to $150,000; on a network during the 1992 "Superbowl" special, about $850,000.

For print media, costs are estimated per column inch of space. A conventional newspaper page, for instance, has six columns, each with about 21.5 inches of usable space. As with broadcast audiences, the smaller the newspaper circulation, the lower the cost of a column inch. For example, a community newspaper of about 7,000 circulation might have a column-inch rate of $5.50 to $6.50, or a page cost of roughly $710 to $839. (To calculate page cost, multiply the number of column inches, usually 129, by the cost per inch.)

By comparison, a newspaper with 100,000 circulation might have a column-inch rate of about $30, or a page rate of roughly $4,000. A major metropolitan newspaper of 200,000 circulation might have a column-inch rate of $150 to $160, or a page rate of roughly $20,000. But these figures might be reduced by discounts and incentives; often, the newspaper receives only 75 to 80 percent of the maximum rate.

The stakes obviously are high; media struggle to attract the audience, and sponsors expect results for their money. But how would the client know whether the cost of advertising was competitive and efficient? One good indicator is *cost per thousand* (CPM), the dollar amount associated with each thousand members of the audience exposed to the advertisement. To calculate CPM, divide the cost of the advertisement by the number of thousands of audience members. For example, $710 divided by 7 (i.e., 7,000-member audience) equals $101.40 CPM; $20,000 divided by 200 (i.e., 200,000-member audience) equals $100 CPM.

But the client cannot limit an analysis to CPM; as Wimmer and Dominick (1991) pointed out, CPM can be more effectively estimated with a *revised* CPM estimate that includes *number of readers,* not just circulation, and *number of readers who are potential users of the product that is being advertised.* This means that the newspaper with the lowest column-inch rate is not necessarily the best buy.

or CPM (general)

CUSTOMIZED RESEARCH FOR PRINT MEDIA

Research conducted for media clients can be described as *customized* (tailored to the needs of the client) or *syndicated* (a single report purchased by numerous users). An audience survey for a local station is a customized study. The A. C. Nielsen TV ratings are a syndicated service. Each of the mass media is serviced by both syndicated and customized research.

Two Types of Research Services
Readership
Audience

For print media, the two principal types of research services are studies of the *readership* and studies of the *audience.* Studies of readership ask, among other things: Who subscribes? Who reads? What do they read? Where do they read (home, office, client office)? How much time do they spend at it? Do they notice the advertisements? and What are the characteristics of the reader?

Characteristics of the reader include demographics that form an audience *profile* (a description of the audience), as well as life-style and psychographic characteristics. Those are important research topics partly because they help identify the wishes of the audience, but also partly because they provide useful data to meet the competition for readers and advertisers.

Who Subscribes? There are several issues here. One is the definition of *subscribers*. Is a regular reader who buys from the newsstand a subscriber? Is a person who reads the paper at the office a subscriber? Is the number of copies *circulated* a better estimate? Circulation is calculated by the Audit Bureau of Circulation (ABC); it does not tell the *whole* story of readership, but it is a start.

The ABC circulation figure provides a first-impression estimate of the importance of a publication for advertising purposes. But it does not tell the extent to which readership exceeds subscribership. For example, a publication might count 100,000 *subscribers,* but 185,000 *readers,* or 1.85 readers per circulated copy. Some publications count *several* readers per subscriber, and so the advertiser can have far more potential exposures (or *impressions*) than would be suggested by circulation. This can be very important for purposes of sales and advertising effectiveness.

How to Increase Circulation? Newspapers are struggling with this question now, as new media encroach on what once was their territory. They estimate that young people are not reading much, although this probably always has been so. (It is later, when this group develops a heavier personal investment in the community, that they find reading a newspaper to be in their interest.)

Another problem for print media is that reading is a little more taxing than listening or viewing. The person who listens to the news on radio or television can *simultaneously* clean house, study, dine, exercise, or play with the dog. Not so for newspapers. To offset whatever the disadvantage, the newspaper must be especially attractive. Newspapers try to meet this challenge with attractive layouts, typefaces, photography, color, other graphics, and evolving story types.

For example, page one of today's newspaper is increasingly likely to include stories about nutrition, leisure, and life—stories that once would have been seen only on inside pages. And whereas page-one photos once might have shown spot news from home or abroad, today they are more likely artistic, colorful, and featurish. Newspapers try to anticipate and adapt to the needs of their readership.

Print's News Advantage. The news advantage that print media have over broadcasting is in regard to "depth" in the news; it is said that a 30-minute TV news show has only about as many words as a single newspaper page. A large metro Sunday newspaper might publish 100 pages or more in a single day. But there is some evidence that the audience does not have a great demand for "depth." Often—but it depends on the topic—they want only the briefer treatment of a story. *USA Today* might have reached that conclusion with its short-story approach to the news.[1]

All of this may have given you the impression that print media are in trouble; it is probably safer to say only that the early-warning lights are lit. With 59 million or more daily circulation, daily newspapers are far from dead; but they are feeling the heat of competition, and many are using research to stem the erosion, or to regain lost ground. Would-be prophets routinely predict the eventual failure of the newspaper industry; but so it was that they predicted educational television would transform education. It did not happen, except in small measure. To paraphrase Mark Twain, reports of the newspapers' death are greatly exaggerated.

For example, John Mennenga (1992, 45, 52), a newspaper marketing research consultant, called the exaggeration of the newspapers' condition a result of "misunderstanding of how newspaper readership information should be collected, calculated, and trended." Crucial is the difference between newspaper *subscribers* and *readers*. Mennenga said that if 2.2 persons *read* every newspaper, then the readership should be much higher than the 59 million that we usually hear. He added that many Americans read *more than one* newspaper per day.

Mennenga said the *measurement* of readership also contributed to the perception of newspaper decline. For example, when readership is measured in terms of "read every day," readership ranges from 33 to 50 percent, but when it is measured in terms of read "yesterday," the readership rate climbs to about 65 percent. Mennenga said that use of the word *every* presents an unrealistic standard that few can meet. Still, he conceded that in the 1960s, the *yesterday* readership rate was in the high 70s.

More than any loss of interest on the part of readers, a big threat to newspapers today is that advertisers might find more economical ways to reach an audience—for example, direct mail and newspaper *inserts*. If they are cheaper, even if they *accompany the delivered newspaper*, they will cut down on the space the newspaper can devote to news, further eroding the base of the newspaper as a product. Because of such developments, the fate of the newspapers is not easily predicted.

Researchers over the years have spent a good deal of effort identifying the characteristics of subscribers. In general, readership increases with age, then eventually declines. Readership often is related to community involvement, such as membership in civic organizations or participation in community activities. Readership also probably is related to home ownership; homeowners are clearly less likely transient, more likely concerned about their community and their government, hence more likely to want to keep up with public affairs. A newspaper also is more easily delivered to a home than a 10th-floor apartment. Whether these considerations apply equally to magazines is uncertain but likely.

Within the issue of readership is the question of which portions of the newspaper appeal to which members of the audience. In other words, who reads what? Does the reader read *all* of a story, or just a little of it? What portion of the readership appreciates the living section, the comics, the obituaries? About how much time does a reader spend with the newspaper? Is the reader interested enough in the product to be at least incidentally exposed to the advertiser's message?

To study readership, the researcher might use any of several techniques. One would be to mail the subscriber a copy of the paper, and ask the subscriber to check all of the stories and all of the ads that the person recalled having seen. This can be valuable information, but the return rate can be poor. An alternative is for the researcher to carry a copy of the paper to the home, and interview the subscriber first-hand. Since most subscribers work during the day, interviews would have to be at night; data would be slow and expensive to obtain. The alternative is a telephone interview. The researcher might invite the subscriber to recall the important stories of the day, or to bring the newspaper to the telephone so that readership of specific stories and advertisements could be assessed.

Who Reads? When a periodical goes to a home, is it read by one person, several, or none? If the circulation is 100,000, but the average readership is 3 persons per subscription, then the total readership is about 300,000—an important number. Is the periodical likely to be read in barber shops, physicians' offices, and the like, where readership will also be high? Furthermore, what is the likely age group to which the periodical appeals? Is it the age group that has the most discretionary money to spend?

What Do They Read? A metro daily can offer hundreds of pages of news and advertising on a given day, and so it is unlikely that all readers read all items; but then who reads what? Survey researchers have found, as you probably would expect, sex differences: Although it is not universal, men are more likely to read page one and the sports page; women the lifestyle and other sections. But careful analysis of circulation will show other points as well: For example, letters to the editor and obituary columns often have strong readership; special features such as advice columns also are popular. The informed publisher will have detailed research information about the readership of a newspaper.

How Much Time Do They Spend with the Newspaper? The reader who merely glances at page one and tosses the newspaper aside is not of great value to the advertiser. Better is the reader who scans or reads each page, thus being exposed to the advertiser's message as well as the important public affairs of the day. Best is the reader who, in addition to news, wants a product and searches the ads for the suggestion of a good deal.

Reading time can vary from none to a few seconds to lengthy reading. Researchers recognize that a reader's self-report of reading time will be error-prone; who keeps a stop-watch with their newspaper? But reading time usually is *estimated* in minutes, or in categories (e.g., none, up to 5 minutes, 15, 30, 45 minutes); the reader selects the best approximation. The reader's estimate can then be studied in relation to demographic data and whether the reader saw the commercial advertisements.

Why Do They Read? If you asked a person, "Why do you read the newspaper?" or "Why do you watch TV news?", you likely would be told: "To learn the news." But that is hardly the whole story. Actually, people have many different reasons or gratifications for buying into the news, and not all are readily articulated. Think about it: Why would a reader be interested in a bus wreck in some far off place that killed a dozen people? Or if the news is about a torrid debate in Washington, can the local person have any influence over it? The fact is, of course, that most of the national news is far removed from us, but we watch and read anyway. Why?

One theory (Haskins, 1987) is that hearing or reading about disasters and dissension keeps us alert to the dangers about us. In other words, news that arouses our interest might help protect us from the "beasts," real or imagined, around us.

Another idea is that we get a lot of positive gratification from the media. For example, we use the media for purposes of "social utility" (i.e., to have something to talk about with others). Often we hear someone say, "Did you read about [so-and-so] in the newspaper?" The person finds gratification in being able to recount the tale. Young people often use media for purposes of dating; they watch television together, and they share the fads that sweep the population by means of the media. In fact, careful analysis might reveal 25 to 50 different gratifications of media use. Here a few:

habit/ritual
convenience   *method (of gratification)*
escape
advice
vicarious experience
sexual gratification
courtship
tactile gratification
social orientation
babysitting
reference
history in progress
entertainment
relaxation
security
parasocial interaction
reduce loneliness
political knowledge
environmental surveillance
value reinforcement
financial information
shopping
fashion
spiritual enrichment
personal identity

We choose the media we use partly on the basis of habit and convenience. We do what we're accustomed to doing, and what is easy. In fact, when two things are otherwise equal, people tend to choose whichever is easier. But aside from habit and ease, we use media with a variety of purposes in mind. We want to be informed, to know what's going on in the world. We also want to be entertained. Information (such as news and documentaries) can be entertaining, but some materials (publications and programs) are specially created as entertainment. They encourage vicarious experience, relaxation, escapism, and just plain fun.

Most of us use the media for advice. For example, newspaper columns are dedicated to issues of romance, health, politics, the workplace, finances, physical fitness, manners, hobbies, and sex. Television also offers many programs of special interest, such as financial reports, home restoration, and public affairs.

Use of media for "tactile" gratification might seem strange, and it does need clarification. It does not suggest gratification in the sense of fetish, but rather in the sense of comfort. It is comforting to hold a publication in hand, and thus be in full control of it. There is a great difference between having a newspaper in your lap, or with your morning coffee, and viewing news on the tube. On the other hand, viewing news on the tube has its own gratifications.

We also use the media for social orientation. To understand this, you have to recall that our social experience is *regulated* by our customs, and the individual has to find self in the social structure. "Who am I," we ask, "and how do I fit in with these other people and these institutions?" The media help to tell us whether our own behavior is within bounds of acceptance.

Of course, we also use the media for reference purposes, as the source of important information, and sometimes for seeing history in progress. We watched raptly when the "tall ships" celebrated the U.S. Bicentennial, and when the Communist control of the Soviet Union began to collapse. The media bring us history in progress.

We use the media to learn that the world around us is or is not safe. Sometimes, we use it to reduce loneliness; some of us form a kind of bond with TV characters, others with the political and social leaders of the day. Other obvious uses of media are for shopping and for fashion. Finally, although not exhaustively, some of us use the media for spiritual enrichment. All of these gratifications and all of our concerns about readership can be addressed in *customized research*—studies that are tailored to the specific needs of the client rather than to the needs of the field as a whole.

LIFE-STYLE AND PSYCHOGRAPHICS RESEARCH

Demographics — *Who (characteristics)*

Audience research always includes the collection of *demographic data* such as age, education, income, home ownership, occupation, and number of children in family. But, Fletcher and Bowers point out, demographics alone are not always adequate: "For example, just because a male is between 18 and 34 years of age, has a high school education, and is a blue-collar worker, he is not necessarily a potential customer of a particular brand of cigarettes, although studies may indicate that he should be" (1991, 22). They warn the demographics may not reveal the individual's *motivation* in regard to the product or the *psychological* basis of the person's thinking.

Psychographic Research — *Why (motivation) attitudes behavior*

Psychographic research starts with the assumption that, although each of us is unique, we can be broadly classified as one or another type of consumer. The classification is accomplished by analysis of people's responses to a set of attitude or behavior statements. Naturally, attitudes and behaviors differ from person to person. But there are only so many possibilities, and so some us *share* attitude and behavioral proclivities. We also share goals and outlooks. For example, some of us are motivated by achievement, others by thrill, and others by security. Advertisers are interested in using these interpersonal similarities to sharpen their messages— to reach the most likely set of buyers with the most likely appreciated message.

One research firm, SRI International, developed a typology of consumers called the VALS 2 segmentation system (Fletcher and Bowers, 1991, 23). The two-dimensional system is based the variables "self-image" and "personal resources." A person's self-image is expected to interact with the person's resources in such a way as to characterize groups or types of consumers. For example, a person who can be described as a struggler, striver, achiever, or actualizer can also be described as driven by principle, status, or a need for action. The eight or so categories of respondents suggested by this approach can help advertisers target their audience.

You can imagine that if consumers can be typed in this way, advertisers should be able to structure their campaigns in such a way as to appeal to the types. Zeigler and Howard (1979, 158) pointed out that "broad psychographic character-istics may aid creative teams in developing long-range campaign themes and ideas." They said that advertisements for a fabric softener, "soft as a kitten's fur," for example, could be directed toward people identified as animal lovers. Similarly, people typed as "interested in foreign affairs" could be communicated to "in designs that communicate in any language." The psychographic concept encour-ages publishers and advertisers to identify the relevant commonalities of their au-diences and to gear their sales to those markets.

Life-Style Research

The concept of *life-style* is related to psychographics. Respondents typically are asked a wide range of questions about their activities, interests, and opinions. Dif-ferences are then detected in the analysis. Some of us are outgoing, and others are reserved; some are conservative, and others take risks; some of us avoid change, and others welcome it.

The benefit of the research hinges on the accuracy of the measures. Unfortu-nately, most of the measures are self-reports, and often these are riddled with error. For example, how accurate can you be in assessing your own willingness to take a risk? Although measurement errors tend to defeat the value of the research, life-style and psychographic research remain very important today as advertisers and publishers search for ways to direct their messages to their desired audiences.

Syndicated Research

The Audit Bureau of Circulation (ABC), mentioned earlier in the chapter, offers a syn-dicated research service to which periodicals and advertisers can subscribe. It pro-vides a standard in the sense that ABC is an objective auditor; ABC decides the accuracy of circulation figures and publishes the data for all of its subscribers to see. This avoids the problem of publishers inflating their circulation for the benefit of advertising sales. ABC circulation is *certified* to be accurate.

Another syndicated service, the Simmons Market Research Bureau (SMRB), provides demographic information on the readers of leading magazines and national newspapers such as *USA Today*. Typically it provides the race, age, sex, occupation, education, marital status, number of children, and income of the readers—plus information such as whether the readers own or rent their home and the geographic region where they live. SMRB also provides demographic information about listeners of various radio formats, viewers of specific TV programs, and users of various consumer products.

RESEARCH IN GRAPHIC DESIGN

Does the Audience Notice?

In their effort to attract and maintain a loyal following, and to attract new readers, newspaper publishers are always on the alert for innovations in graphic design that can make publications more appealing. These might involve a new typeface, a different type size, a new page layout, or a different photo orientation. Although it sometimes seems that the audience does not give these adjustments the importance that the publishers do, graphic design clearly is important. If the publication fails to respond to popular taste, for example, it risks being perceived as antique or otherwise unattractive—regardless of the content itself.

Graphic Design as Evolution

It's interesting to think of the *evolution* of graphic design. In the early years of printing, stories were set in single columns; a story continued down a column until necessity pushed it to the top of the next column. Pages had a *vertical appearance;* the flow of the page was from top to bottom in vertical columns. The pages by today's standards were dull. In the mid- to late-nineteenth century, newspapers began using multiple-column stories and more visuals. The visual flow of the page changed from purely vertical to a mix of vertical and horizontal.

Modular and Brace Layout. The mix of horizontal and vertical layout led to page formats called modular and brace. The *modular format* amounted to filling the page with more or less rectangular sections so that, for example, the upper half of the page had a separate appearance. The *brace format* tucked one story below and beside another so that one story was figuratively propped by another. The visual effect was a slope; the flow was not vertical, but not horizontal either. This kind of layout was most common until perhaps 15 or 20 years ago, when newspaper layout became increasingly horizontal (Moen, 1984).

Horizontal Layout. The modern page layout is described as horizontal because news items very often are spread across multiple columns, sometimes all the way across the page. The lead story in a daily newspaper today might be a feature about a new diet, laid out in six columns across page one, with a one-line head. The story is rather timeless; it certainly is not spot news. Below the story would be the newspaper nameplate and then some of the breaking news of the day. The story at the bottom of the page also might be spread widely across the page. And so, although some stories inevitably are set vertically, the predominant layout is horizontal. Does the audience notice? Not likely on the level of articulation; yet if the paper appeared outdated, readers would certainly grumble.

A related recent development is the use of a feature in the banner news spot (an important news position at the top of the page). As the press primps to please the audience, its editors are primping its stories as well, trying to put forth information that will sell. Urgent news will sell without help; but when there is no urgent news, the pressure remains on editors to sell their publication anyway. So editors search for items that today's generation will find satisfying, and to do this they must rely on research to keep up with their readers.

And so publishers must be attuned to the psychology of the audience, for purposes of both advertising and circulation, and must make adjustments to keep the audience happy, even if the adjustments seem minor.

Research on publication graphics usually includes surveys and experiments. Survey measures usually entail some measure of audience *satisfaction* (e.g., satisfaction with readability, satisfaction with the appearance of the publication, and satisfaction with headlines, photos, boxes, maps, and advertisements). Of course, satisfaction is relative, and so the publisher would need some standard, perhaps an earlier survey, for comparison. A before-and-after survey might accompany a major remake of the graphic design of a newspaper to gauge the impact of the changes.

How does the audience feel about changes in the appearance of their newspaper? Experiments can help find out. For example, suppose the publisher wanted to know whether a given typeface was a good choice. In a simple experiment, a researcher could expose comparable samples of readers to one of several typefaces. The samples could then be measured for satisfaction in any number of areas (e.g., legibility, strength, modernity, or friendliness).

STUDIES OF READABILITY

Students of communication research have a clear need to know the techniques and the rationale of readability measures. The writer or publisher, for example, who is uninformed on readability and how it is measured could easily write beyond the comfort level of the reading audience. Unchecked, that could become a serious problem.

Writing Above the Audience

The point of *readability* is to match the writing to the reading level of the audience. Editors have recognized this need for many years. The first studies of readability were published in the 1920s and 1930s (see Severin and Tankard, 1984, for a review). In general, early studies focused on the unique characteristics of language (e.g., abstractions, number of different words, and number of nouns or structural words used). The researchers hoped to build formulas that would permit easy, accurate assessment of difficulty level.

The best-known researcher in the measurement of readability is Rudolf Flesch, whose *The Art of Readable Writing,* a second book to grow out of his doctoral dissertation, was published in 1949. Therein he outlined the *Flesch formula* for "reading ease" (adapted from Flesch, 1949, 213):

1. Pick a number of paragraphs to represent the text.
2. Select one or more samples of 100 words.
3. Calculate the average sentence length (SL). (SL equals the number of words divided by the number of sentences)
4. Calculate the number of syllables per 100 words (SYLL).
5. Apply the following formula:

$$\text{Reading ease} = 206.835 - 0.846(\text{SYLL}) - 1.015\ (\text{SL}) \quad (\text{Formula 16.1})$$

6. Compare the score to Flesch's chart to estimate the difficulty of the reading. (Flesch, 1949).

Generally, the larger the reading ease score, the easier the reading. A score of zero means that the text is virtually unreadable; a score of 100 means it is very easy to read. A score between 60 and 70 was called "standard."

However, for the reading ease score really to have meaning, its validity must be assessed. The assessment could be on the level of intuition, or perhaps face validity. For example, if a text passage scored very difficult, but was reported by readers to be very easy, you would have reason to suspect invalidity. Another measure of validity would be to apply more than one measure of readability to the same sample of text. There are several other popular measures.

One was developed by Robert Gunning in 1952. It has the advantage of being much easier to apply than the Flesch formula, which is based on regression. Gunning's formula is called the *Fog index*. The researcher selects one or more samples of 100 words and calculates an average sentence length (ASL). Next, the researcher counts the number of words with more than two syllables (SYLL). Finally, add the SYLL count to the ASL and multiply the total by 0.4; the result is the estimated grade level of the text.

Another formula, developed by McLaughlin (1969), is called the *SMOG index*. The researcher is expected to select 30 sentences, 10 each from the beginning, middle, and end of the text. With those sentences, add each word of more than two syllables and find the square root. The result is the estimated grade level of the text.

A final method takes a different tack. Taylor's (1953) *Cloze procedure* involves deleting each *n*th word from a sample of text and asking the readers to try to guess the missing words. The degree of difficulty is calculated from the percentage of correct guesses.

These measures provide *rough estimates* of readability; still, every publisher should use them to encourage successful communication.

LEARN BY DOING

A Comparison of Three Measures of Readability

In order to appreciate the technique and the variability of readability measures, conduct a readability study of this text. Select a sample from any section of the text, and compute the Flesch, Gunning, and McLaughlin readability scores.

Flesch Formula

Average sentence length (ASL) = number of words divided by number of sentences: _____

Number of syllables per 100 words (SYLL) = number of syllables divided by 100: _____

Flesch formula: 206.835 − 0.846(SYLL) − 1.015(SL) Reading ease = _____

Gunning's Fog Index

Average sentence length (ASL) = number of words divided by number of sentences: _____

Number of words of more than two syllables: _____
Add ASL and number of words of more than two syllables: _____
Multiply the sum by 0.4: _____
Fog readability = _____

McLaughlin's SMOG Index

Count all words greater than two syllables: _____
Take the square root of the count: _____
SMOG grade level = _____

Questions: How closely matched are the three readability scores? Do the scores match your *intuitive* measure of reading difficulty? What might explain the differences in the three scores?

A CASE STUDY OF NEWSPAPER RESEARCH

The publisher of a daily newspaper of under-25,000 circulation telephoned a researcher for assistance in conducting an audience survey. The publisher wanted to learn several things about the newspaper readers: How satisfied are they? What parts of the newspaper do they like to read? How much time do they spend at it? Do they see the display advertisements? the classifieds? Is the newspaper "fair" in its treatment of people and issues in the news? How "good" a newspaper is it? But especially, would the audience support a Sunday edition of the newspaper? This latter point was the major purpose of the survey; the other questions were useful but mainly advisory.

The researcher met with the publisher and his staff to firm up the purposes, methods, and scope of the research, then submitted a proposed budget. The sample of 1,600 would be drawn from telephone numbers in the principal circulation area. It was expected that only about one in four numbers randomly dialed would result in a completed survey. In fact, the completed sample numbered 403, even with callbacks. For a sample of this size, the error margin was estimated as plus-or-minus 5 percent (rounded off). Because the publisher was contemplating spending a large amount of cash in the startup of a Sunday paper, the error level was very important. It constituted one of the decision points on whether to go forward with the management plan.

Moving quickly, the researcher in the next few days prepared the questionnaire and planned for its administration. But rather than hiring and training interviewers, he proposed to subcontract the interviewing. He felt it would speed and professionalize the service. (Some research firms offer the special services of sampling and interviewing. They have a ready plan for sampling, and they are equipped with telephones and computers. They have a reliable stable of trained telephone interviewers.) The researcher calculated the cost of the subcontract and included that in the budget.

The interviews opened with two questions about where the respondent gets his or her local or national/international news:

> From what source are you most likely to learn what's happening in the nation and world—from television, newspapers, magazines, friends, or where?
>
> From what source are you most likely to learn what's happening in your local area—from television, newspapers, magazines, friends, or where?

The next several questions asked whether or to what extent the audience relied on radio and television and cable for news, and whether they already subscribe to a Sunday newspaper (from a nearby competing daily). And then, the crucial question:

> Do you feel the need for a Sunday edition of the [name local newspaper]?

The decision to start or not start a Sunday edition would depend largely on two issues: circulation and advertising. The interviewers therefore asked several questions about readers' use of advertising and shopping centers; their shopping preferences; and their awareness of advertising inserts and direct mail advertising. Readers then were asked about readership of each of the following:

> front page
> local news
> news about other areas of the state/region
> national news
> editorials
> letters to the editor
> political columns on editorial page
> bridal news
> news of local clubs, organizations, churches
> columns from county communities
> news about celebrities
> obituaries

weather
local sports
regional sports
national sports
sports statistics
[name of local columnist] stories
[name of other local columnist] stories
local "gossip" column
25–50 years ago column
Love is . . .
Dear Abby
horoscope
crossword puzzle
TV premiere
Focus pages
Weekender
Mini-page
comics
display advertisements
classified advertisements
agricultural page
student news
Business Beat
religion page
Lads and Lasses
news on men and women in armed forces
Billy Graham
Bible verses
Today's Chuckle
It Happened Here (police report)
Erma Bombeck

It is an impressive list, especially for the small price of a newspaper, but since the newspaper had an investment in every item, it needed to gauge audience approval of every item. Similarly, readers were asked about readership of seven political columns and 12 comic strips. Finally, after asking about reading convenience (e.g., stories that "jump" to an inside page), and demographics (including home ownership and recent major purchases), the interviewers asked readers to judge whether the newspaper was excellent, good, fair, or poor.

The instrument was very long—six pages, 8½-by-11-inches—but the variety and scope of the information was beneficial. Measures were predominantly Likert-type and categorical, never open-ended. The researcher arranged for the coding and inputting of data and the software program that would generate the frequencies and tables for the client. Output included the number of respondents and the percentage for each response, and occasional cross-tabulations with chi-square statistical tests of relationship.

Data showed that the newspaper was well liked by its audience; that respondents read it carefully (many even read the classified advertisements); that the special features and comics were well liked; and that, in fact, a majority thought the paper should publish a Sunday edition. But a slightly smaller number said they would buy a Sunday paper. Since "would buy" is *hypothetical,* there was the possibility the actual number of supporters of a Sunday edition might have been even less than reported. The publisher did not divulge the "critical mass" that would *i.e. break even* have been required to venture into the Sunday edition, but apparently it was not reached. The demand for the edition was too slight. The publisher accepted the data as given, within a range explained by sample variation, and declined to go forward with plans for a Sunday edition. Nevertheless, the publisher had a much better picture of his readers and their perceptions of the newspaper.

That the research indicated insufficient interest in a Sunday newspaper does not mean that the research failed. The research uncovered the facts as they existed, and the publisher used the information to make his decision. Without the research he might or might not have launched an expensive project that could have been financially unsound. In a crowded and complicated market, publishers probably will rely increasingly on research to advise them of their competitive status and to chart the way toward improved community and advertising services.

SUMMARY

Most print media research is applied research, and it takes several forms: audience analysis, product evaluation, psychographic/life-style analysis, readership, readability, and graphic design. Applied research has become more important as increasing numbers of media compete for the audience. Advertisers also support applied research because they hope to target the audience to the product.

STUDY QUESTIONS AND EXERCISES

1. Explain and comment on research by McCombs (1972) and Wood and O'Hare (1991) in regard to "the principle of relative constancy" that was discussed in this chapter. Draw a picture of the media "pie" that existed in 1965 and the one that exists today. What do the pictures suggest? Are the circles the same size and are the slices the same thickness in both periods?

2. What is the future of the printed newspaper? Will it be eclipsed by electronic information? Will future generations awake to drink their morning coffee over their personal computer news menus? Identify the strengths and weaknesses of printed publications vis-à-vis electronic communication.

3. Ask a friend or two, without telling them your purpose, why they read a newspaper or watch TV news. They will probably tell you they read or view "to find

out what's going on." But is that the whole reason? What are some other functions the news has for a person? Describe the uses a person makes of the news and the gratifications associated with it.

4. If possible, turn to a recent Standard Rate and Data Service (SRDS), which is a newspaper data service for buyers and advertisers, volume of newspaper rates and data and identify one each of three towns that would be classified small, medium, or large. The SRDS reports the per-inch cost of advertising, the number of column inches per page, and the newspaper circulation. For each selection, multiply the column-inch cost by the number of inches per page to obtain a full-page cost. Example: $10.53 \times 129 = \$1,358.37$. Keep in mind that costs often are softened by discounts and repeat contracts. Divide the page cost by the number of thousands reported as ABC circulation. Example: Divide the page cost, $1,358.37, by the circulation, 7,500; or, $\$1,358.37 \div 7.55$ (the decimal expression of the number of thousands of readers) = $179.92 CPM. To calculate the per subscriber cost, divide the page cost by the total circulation. To see the relation between advertising cost and circulation, compare the data for three newspapers—small, medium, and large. Discuss the relative benefits and liabilities of the three would-be purchases.

NOTE

1. At the time of this writing, *USA Today*, the Gannett national newspaper, was using short paragraphs and short stories—a conscious effort to make the paper attractive and useful to its readers.

SOURCES

Flesch, Rudolf. 1949. *The Art of Readable Writing.* New York: Harper & Row.

Fletcher, Alan D., and Thomas A. Bowers. 1991. *Fundamentals of Advertising Research.* 4th ed. Belmont, Calif.: Wadsworth.

Gunning, Robert. 1952. *The Technique of Clear Writing.* New York: McGraw-Hill.

Haskins, Jack B. 1987. Toward a Psycho-Biological Theory of News Reading. Mss., School of Journalism, University of Tennessee, Knoxville.

McCombs, Maxwell E. 1972. Mass Media in the Marketplace. *Journalism Monographs* August (No. 24).

McLaughlin, H. 1969. SMOG Grading: A New Readability Formula. *Journal of Reading* 22(4):639–646.

Mennenga, John T. 1922. Shop Talk at Thirty: Decline in Newspaper Readership Should not Be Overestimated. *Editor and Publisher*, February 15:45, 52.

Moen, Daryl R. 1984. *Newspaper Layout and Design.* Ames: Iowa State University Press.

Severin, Werner J., and James W. Tankard, Jr. 1984. *Communication Theories: Origins, Methods, Uses.* White Plains, N.Y.: Longman.

Taylor, W. 1953. Cloze Procedure: A New Tool for Measuring Readability. *Journalism Quarterly* 30(4):415–433.

Wimmer, Roger D., and Joseph R. Dominick. 1991. *Mass Media Research: An Introduction.* Belmont, Calif.: Wadsworth.

Wood, William C., and Sharon L. O'Hare. 1991. Paying for the Video Revolution: Consumer Spending on the Mass Media. *Journal of Communication* 41(1):24–30.

CHAPTER

17

Broadcast Media Research

HERBERT H. HOWARD
University of Tennessee, Knoxville

□
OBJECTIVES

After reading this chapter, you should be able to:

1. Understand how audience measurement studies are conducted.

2. Understand why sample audience data (randomly derived) can be projected to the larger universe from which they have been drawn.

3. Understand how respondents are selected for a broadcast audience survey.

4. Understand the strengths and weaknesses of the various techniques used to collect audience data, including diaries, telephone surveys, personal interviews, focus groups, and metering devices.

5. Understand the terms used in reporting audience research information, including rating and share, households using television (HUT), audience composition, and others.

6. Compute ratings from audience share and HUT data.

7. Interpret analytical measures such as cumulative audience data, gross audience, and reach and frequency.

8. Compute gross rating points, time spent listening, cost per thousand, and cost per point.

9. Understand which types of audience research are provided by each of the major research organizations.

Broadcasters and radio and TV advertisers require extensive audience research to plan and conduct their activities. Radio and TV advertising is priced and sold according to the size and demographic characteristics of audiences served by networks and stations. Advertisers and their agencies buy time for commercial messages on the basis of audience research data that tell them what programs, times, and stations or networks reach their desired demographic audiences most effectively and efficiently. Radio and TV broadcasters and cable operators also rely on audience research data when making programming decisions. Usually, those decisions are intended to maximize the station's audience size in order to make the station attractive to advertisers. Few businesses are researched as extensively as are the broadcast media.

The need for high-quality research into audience behavior and program popularity has increased dramatically in recent decades. Today, with more than 98 percent of all households owning and using radio and TV sets on a regular basis, the broadcast programming and advertising industries represent billions of dollars of economic activity and sales opportunities each year.

Knowing the size and composition of audiences throughout the broadcast day is vitally important to advertisers, their agencies, program producers and syndicators, networks and stations, broadcast sales representatives, and other related organizations.

Today's audience research is a far cry from the earliest attempts at analyzing radio listenership during the 1925–1935 era, when audience measurement generally consisted of counting fan mail attracted by various programs. Contemporary audience measurement, which resembles public opinion polling, has been raised to the scientific level, relying on procedures such as statistical sampling, electronic data gathering, and computerized processing. In the interest of cost-effectiveness, modern marketing techniques also require that advertisers deliver their selling messages to specific **target audiences** of potential customers rather than to undifferentiated mass audiences.

Two major research organizations and a number of other firms gather and produce broadcast audience research data. Nielsen Media Research (A. C. Nielsen Co.) provides both national network and local market TV audience studies on a regular basis. It is well known for its weekly network ratings and its "overnight" audience reports conducted in some of the largest markets. The Arbitron Company produces market-by-market studies for both television and radio. Both Nielsen and Arbitron conduct concurrent individual market studies, known as national *sweeps*, when viewing in local markets is surveyed across the country.

AUDIENCE MEASUREMENT TECHNIQUES

Modern audience measurement is based on the concept of *statistical inference*, which allows researchers to estimate the characteristics of a total population (e.g., all TV-equipped households in an area) from information obtained through random sampling. Although some variations exist among the research firms, all audience measurement involves three distinct phases: (1) selecting the sample, (2) gathering the data, and (3) processing the results.

Sampling Procedures

Ideally, a perfect research study would include information from every possible person or household in a broadcast market. However, economic and logistical limitations make such a census impractical. Instead, audience research firms obtain data from sample households that are scientifically selected to represent the entire population being measured.

Although unbelievers may criticize survey research because it uses relatively small samples, evidence strongly supports the usefulness and reliability of sampling techniques. For example, statistical projections on voting intentions derived from public opinion polls usually compare quite closely with actual vote counts. In many other ways, too, we base everyday decisions on sampling procedures. Don't chefs taste a small sample of the food they prepare to determine if the seasoning is adequate? Farmers engage in soil sampling to test the nutrients in their fields, and doctors take blood samples for diagnostic purposes.

To permit the projection of sample data to a larger population, a sample must reflect with a high degree of accuracy the universe it purports to represent. Lists commonly used to select a sample include telephone directories, the U.S. Census data on housing, and household mailing lists. The usefulness of any such catalog depends on how accurately and completely it lists the population it purports to include. Because of inherent limitations in telephone directory listings (e.g., unlisted numbers, homes without telephones, numbers added since publication), researchers sometimes choose a sample frame through random digit dialing rather than from the directory itself. Tables of random numbers also may be used to gain access to all telephone households, including those not listed in directories.

Selection of respondents may be done randomly or through structured quota samples. In *random selection,* each household within a universe has an equal and independent chance of being chosen. This procedure usually produces an acceptably representative sample, within determinable statistical limitations. *Quota samples* differ from pure random samples in that they prescribe representative proportions of people in each important category, such as age, sex, race, education, urban/rural/suburban residency, and socioeconomic status. Specific individuals within such structured quotas, however, may still be selected through random process. The main advantage of the quota system is the assurance that all significant elements within a population are represented proportionately in the sample.

Whereas sample representation is a function of sampling procedure, the precision of the results depends largely on sample size. Below a certain sample size, results become highly subject to error; above a certain size, cost-effectiveness is compromised. Researchers must decide how much sampling error they are willing to tolerate in view of the costs and the need for precise results. (See Chapter 4 for a more thorough discussion of sample sizes.)

Data Gathering

Procedures employed to gather data on viewing and listening from sample households are among the most critical factors in producing reliable audience research. Each of the four methods commonly used—the diary method, telephone interviews, personal interviews, and metering devices—has advantages and disadvantages.

In the **diary** method, researchers place one or more diaries (viewing or listening logs) in a sample of households in which members have agreed to write down all TV or radio programs seen or heard. Diaries are very useful for obtaining data on audience demographics, as well as raw information needed to calculate program ratings, audience shares, and the total size of media audiences. This method is reasonably fast and economical.

However, diary research has certain disadvantages. Reliability may be questioned because of uneven diary-keeping by respondents. Some respondents put it off until the end of the logging period, when memory of specific viewing has dimmed. In some households, there is uncertainty as to who fills out the diary. There is also the chance that respondents will become unduly conscious of their media behavior and, consequently, may alter their usual viewing or listening patterns.

The *telephone survey* method, pioneered in the 1930s by the C. E. Hooper Company ("Hooperratings") is especially useful for obtaining data on viewing and listening being done at the time of the call. Information collected on a coincidental basis is presumed to contain fewer errors than data collected from recall. In addition to coincidental telephone surveys, telephone interviews can be used to obtain recalled information about viewing or listening during a recent period, usually the past 24 hours.

Telephone interviewing is a highly cost-effective method of gathering audience data for computing ratings, shares, and the demographic composition of the audience. Except during early morning and late evening hours, it is an appropriate means for gathering both coincidental and recalled viewing and listening data. It is also a means by which to measure the automobile radio audience. A problem with telephone surveys is a growing reluctance among the public to give answers to unknown interviewers, especially if they probe into matters such as family characteristics.

Personal interviews, usually conducted in the homes of respondents, are especially useful for obtaining detailed information on viewing and listening, including the use of out-of-home receiving sets (e.g., car radios). This method offers great flexibility because it permits interviewers to probe in some depth for opinions and other qualitative information on programs and talent. Usually, interviewers use an **aided recall** approach, whereby respondents are shown a list of available programs (or stations) and are asked to indicate which ones they have watched or heard.

One advantage of personal interviewing is that the interviewer can verify the representativeness of the sample population for characteristics such as age, sex, race, ethnic group, or socioeconomics. However, personal interviewing is costly, and the problem of maintaining security for interviewers in many residential areas has deterred this form of research in recent years. In fact, at this time, none of the major audience research firms use the personal interview technique on a residential basis.

A variation on personal interviewing is **focus group research,** in which a group of selected individuals is brought together at some designated location to answer questions about their TV or radio experience and preferences. Because participants are interviewed in a group situation, individuals interact with one another as the interviewer probes for qualitative information.

Focus group research is not used by Nielsen or Arbitron, which concentrate on pure numerical data in a highly structured format. However, it is used extensively by news and programming consultants and by station management personnel as a means of seeking underlying qualitative information as to why people watch what they do or what might entice them to watch a particular program or station. Focus group research also is used to help identify issues or concerns that later may be explored more fully through survey research.

Perfecting a **metering device** that could avoid all of the problems of human error has been a longtime goal of media researchers. The earliest devices were attached to TV or radio receivers to record set usage by time and station in a constant sample of homes. Early mechanical recorders produced film or punched-tape records of viewing information, which respondents then mailed to the research firm. More recently, electronic monitoring devices were connected by special telephone circuits to a central computer that dialed each device periodically, retrieved the stored data, and then tabulated the results. Several problems existed with the meters. First, it was possible to obtain data only on the time and channel to which a television set was tuned. Thus, research firms had to supplement this data with demographic information obtained from household or individual diaries. Additional problems were created for diary keepers by the expansion of cable networks and the strange and inconsistent channel assignments given to broadcast TV stations by cable operators. As a result, the A. C. Nielsen Company began to experiment with individual metering devices, or *People Meters*, in 1978. Nielsen introduced the device on an operational basis during the late 1980s, and now Nielsen Media Research uses it to gather data for national TV audience measurement.

The heart of the People Meter is a device smaller than a cigar box that is connected to each TV set in a sample household. An accompanying remote control unit enables participants to make electronic entries from anywhere in the room. Each member of the sample household is assigned a personal viewing button on the unit. People Meters record when the set is turned on, who is viewing, which channel is being watched, when the channel is changed, and when the set is turned off. The data are stored in the in-home metering system until retrieval by the company's computer. Through this system, more accurate viewing information is said to be possible for various demographic groups.

Despite the advantages of the People Meter system, it is not without problems. Viewing by young children may not be properly reported because of their inability to operate the activation equipment; and there is no way to know whether viewers remain in the room with the TV set after turning it on.

Data Processing

The final step in producing quality audience research requires careful tabulation and processing of raw viewing and listening data to its final form. Data contained in diaries must first be edited for authenticity and procedural accuracy, then coded for computer entry and processing.

Data obtained from People Meters and other electronic devices are retrieved daily by a central computer, which accesses the storage unit of the in-home device through a telephone connection. The meter and computer system must be checked periodically for technical malfunctions. Once entered into the computer, data may be tabulated and analyzed in many different ways to discern patterns of audience behavior.

The final report is a highly detailed set of data on viewing or listening in a market during every period of the broadcast week. Clients may obtain this report both in hard copy and on computer tape, at prices that vary according to the size of the market area being studied. Annual costs for audience measurement services per client may range into six figures.

The major audience research services work with industry representatives on a continuing basis to improve their methodology. For example, further efforts to refine the People Meter may enable it to record individual viewing with no effort by the individual. Minimum standards for broadcast and cable research have been established by the Electronic Media Rating Council (EMRC), the agency that audits and accredits rating services.[1]

LEARN BY DOING

To gain firsthand experience in performing research, divide the class into teams of five students each. Each team is responsible (a) for developing a questionnaire and (after the best questionnaire has been selected, or compiled from the initial efforts) (b) for conducting a telephone survey to determine the media habits of local residents. Each team should collect and tabulate 100 survey forms.

By pooling your efforts on designing the questionnaire and compiling the data, your class will better understand media use in your community.

TERMS USED IN AUDIENCE RESEARCH

In order to interpret the data produced by audience research organizations, it is necessary first to understand the terminology used in viewing and listening studies. These terms define survey areas geographically; express audience size; and describe ways in which audience data may be analyzed. Although each rating service has its own terms and definitions, the variations are only slight.

Survey Area Terminology

Audience measurement studies are conducted both nationally and for individual markets. National program ratings, such as those produced for network television by the Nielsen Television Index (NTI) service, are based on sampling throughout the 48 contiguous states. The geographical designations commonly used to designate local broadcast markets are *Metropolitan Statistical Areas* (*MSAs*); *TV market areas* (Areas of Dominant Influence [ADI] and Designated Market Areas [DMAs]);

and *total survey areas* (*TSAs*). These types of markets are shown in map form in Figure 17.1.

Metropolitan Areas

The U.S. Office of Management and Budget (OMB) defines a *metropolitan area* as a population center composed of a central city and the urban area that surrounds it. Officially designated as **Metropolitan Statistical Areas** (**MSAs**), these urban concentrations consist of at least one city of 50,000 population or more, or two or more nearby cities with at least 25,000 population each. The MSA also includes the entire county in which the major city (or cities) is situated, plus adjacent counties that are socially and economically integrated with the central community into an urban complex. Markets with at least one million population that contain two or more primary MSAs are identified as *Consolidated Metropolitan Statistical Areas* (*CMSAs*).

Because most important TV stations and many of the largest radio stations are located in metropolitan areas, an MSA, or *metro area,* is regarded as the heart of a broadcast market. It is an important geographical area for advertisers because the customers for many businesses are concentrated there. For that reason, published audience studies usually include metro viewing or listening data. For many purposes, however, metro area information is too limited; hence, data on two larger zones, television market areas and total survey areas, also are usually found in audience reports.

Television Market Areas

TV stations normally provide regional coverage, with signals that may be received up to 100 airline miles from the transmitter. Because these signals usually reach far beyond urban centers into the surrounding region, the metro designation is generally inadequate to describe a total TV market area.

The two major TV research services, Nielsen and Arbitron, have defined *TV market areas* as exclusive geographical regions based on the preponderance of viewing in each of the counties in the entire country. Thus, under Arbitron's **Areas of Dominant Influence** (**ADI**), or Nielsen's **Designated Market Areas (DMAs),** each market is specified as the area (counties) in which most viewing is directed to the TV stations of the designated city.

For example, the Columbus, Ohio, market includes all of the counties in which viewers tend to watch Columbus's TV stations more than those from any other city. Sometimes, because of the allocation of TV channels by the Federal Communications Commission (FCC), TV markets contain the names of two or more cities that are the primary sources of television for their **hyphenated market.** Examples include the Raleigh-Durham market in North Carolina, the Dallas-Fort Worth market in Texas, and the Sacramento-Stockton market in California.

As with metro areas, audience research firms provide both *rating* and *share* data (explained below), as well as demographic information, for these TV market areas.

Arbitron also uses its ADI as the geographical market areas for measuring

Knoxville

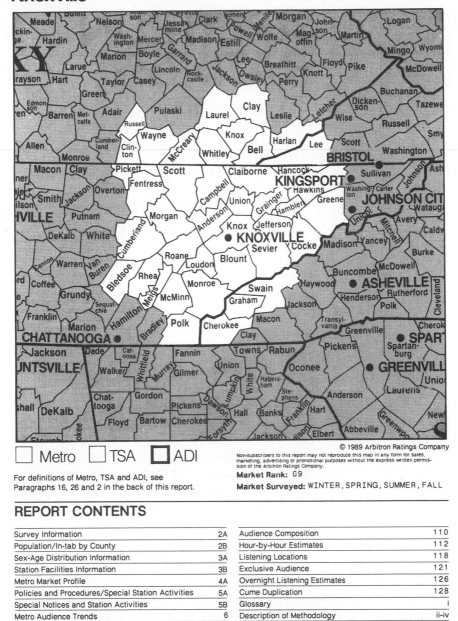

☐ Metro ☐ TSA ☐ ADI

For definitions of Metro, TSA and ADI, see
Paragraphs 16, 26 and 2 in the back of this report.

© 1989 Arbitron Ratings Company

Market Rank: 69

Market Surveyed: WINTER, SPRING, SUMMER, FALL

REPORT CONTENTS

ARBITRON RATINGS

2A

FIGURE 17.1 Illustration of a Broadcast Market: Metro, TSA, and ADI (*Source:* Copyright ©
1989 The Arbitron Company. Reprinted by permission.)

radio listenership. In addition to radio data based on metro-area listening habits, these reports provide listening information for larger regions whose parameters coincide with TV market boundaries.

Total Survey Area

Although the ADI and DMA market arrangement works well in most respects, it tends to discredit (disallow) viewing to stations that have some viewership in adjoining ADI or DMA markets. Normally such out-of-market viewing does not show up in the rating and share columns for an adjoining TV market because viewing isn't intense enough across the entire market to meet minimum reporting criteria. This problem results from the fact that each county is assigned to one and only one TV market, even though TV signals extend across county lines. Both Arbitron and Nielsen handle this problem by counting *total viewership* among households and persons (not ratings and shares) in the *total survey area (TSA)* for stations wherever viewership is reported. Thus, stations receive credit for viewing in counties both inside and outside the home ADI or DMA market area.

TSA data, found in both Arbitron and Nielsen studies, include total households reached, total persons reached, and estimates for each program on the basis of age and gender *wherever the research finds viewership to a station's programs.*

AUDIENCE DATA TERMINOLOGY

The size of audiences for various networks, stations, and programs involves another whole set of audience measurement terms. These terms include *potential audience, households using television (HUT), persons using ratio (PUR), share of audience,* and *program (station) rating.* Broadcast audiences are usually analyzed by *demographic composition* and *demographic ratings,* as well as by *cumulative (unduplicated) ratings.* Common radio terms include *average quarter-hour (AQH) persons, AQH ratings,* and *AQH share.* All numbers used to designate **shares** or **ratings** must be interpreted as percentages.

Potential Audience

unit = household

The *potential audience* for any station includes all households equipped with the appropriate TV or radio set in the sampling area (i.e., metro, ADI/DMA, or TSA). For the 1993–1994 season, the national TV audience potential was approximately 93 million households. Potential audiences for local broadcast markets vary with their populations and the extent of TV set saturation. The New York City ADI alone, with 6,750,000 TV households, accounts for 7.7 percent of all U.S. TV households; and the top-10 markets combined contain 31.4 percent of all of the nation's TV households. Knoxville, Tennessee, the 62nd market, contains 420,900 households, or about 0.46 percent.

Households Using Television

The term **households using television (HUT)** provides an estimate of the percentage of households with one or more sets turned on during any given period. Thus, HUT represents the total *actual* audience at any specific time.

HUT is given as a percentage of the *total number of television households* (*TVHH*) in a survey area—the nation, a metro area, an ADI, or a DMA. For example, as illustrated in Figure 17.2, if a market includes 500,000 TV households and 250,000 of them have their sets in use, the HUT figure is 50 percent. The number of TV-equipped households varies from market to market. Also, the HUT level varies with time of day and with season. It normally is highest during evening prime time, and during the winter.

Persons Using Radio

Persons using radio (PUR) is used precisely as HUT is used for television; it represents the estimated number of people listening to radio for five minutes or more in an *average quarter-hour* in any specified *daypart*. PUR and HUT provide an indication of how widely radio and television are used at a given time in a given market.

Share of Audience

To understand share of audience, remember that at any given time the actual audience specifically consists of those individuals or households actually using their TV sets or radios. (Others not using them are not part of the *actual audience* [HUT or PUR] at that time, even though they are part of the *potential audience*.) Therefore, *share of audience* represents the percentage of the *actual audience* that is tuned to a specific program or station.

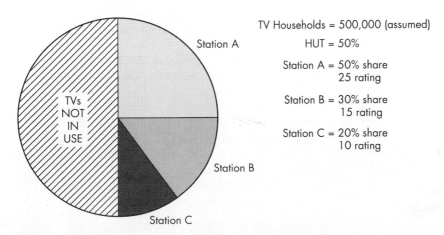

FIGURE 17.2 Rating and Share Relationship

If half of the households in that market of 500,000 TV households (Figure 17.2) are using television, the HUT level is 50 percent, or 250,000. Then, if half of those 250,000 households are watching station A, that station has a 50-percent *share* or 125,000 households watching. Stations B and C have 30- and 20-percent shares, respectively.

In major markets such as New York, Los Angeles, and Chicago, network-affiliated TV stations generally receive sign-on to sign-off shares of 15 to 20 percent, while major independent stations average 10 to 15 percent in the same markets. Cable networks usually achieve shares of 1 percent or less. In contrast, leading radio stations in those markets usually attain overall average quarter-hour shares (listeners age 12 or older) ranging from 4 to 9 percent. In smaller markets with fewer stations from which to choose, audience shares are usually higher.

Share-of-audience percentages are useful in comparing the popularity of all programs broadcast *at the same time*. However, because the size of the available audience (HUT or PUR level) fluctuates widely throughout the day, it is erroneous to attempt to compare audiences of programs broadcast at *different times* on the basis of their audience *shares*.

To illustrate this problem, let's assume that in our hypothetical market of 500,000 TV households, the HUT for 9 P.M. is 60 percent. The available audience, therefore, consists of 300,000 households (500,000 × .60). If station A has a 40-percent share, its reach is an estimated 120,000 households (300,000 × .40). Now, assume that the station has an identical 40-percent share of the audience at noon when the typical HUT is about 10 percent. In this case, station A attracts 40 percent of an *available* audience of only 50,000 households (500,000 × .10), or only 20,000 households (50,000 × .40), which is merely one-sixth of the 40-percent audience share in the first instance. Although share-of-audience data are useful for comparing programs within a specific time period, a better measure is required for comparing programs across time periods within the same market.

Program and Station Ratings

The problem just described has been overcome through program and station ratings. By definition, a *program rating* or *station rating* is the estimated percentage of the total *potential audience* (all households equipped with TV sets or radios in the survey area) that is tuned to a specific program or station. Because the potential audience is constant, there is comparability between ratings for programs regardless of the time of broadcast, provided they come from the same survey of the same market. For example, if two network shows both achieved ratings of 20 in a national survey, we can safely infer that about 20 of every 100 households viewed each program. Their respective shares and audience demographics may have differed, but the numerical size of the estimated audiences for the two programs would be approximately the same.

A convenient formula for computing ratings is

$$\text{Rating} = \text{share} \times \text{HUT}$$

Applying this formula to the example given in Figure 17.2, station A's 50-percent share with a HUT of 50 percent results in a 25.0 rating. This is confirmed by that station's audience depicted as one-fourth of the total potential audience in the pie chart.

Since each rating point represents 1 percent of all TV households, one national rating point is worth approximately 930,000 TV homes (93 million × .01). A one-rating point differential between networks is immensely significant in terms of potential advertising revenues, because advertising rates are based on the size and demographics of the audience. With cable networks, even a 0.1-point difference can translate into a huge difference annually in the amount of money and network can generate from advertisers.

In a local broadcast market, the number of households represented by each rating point is determined by multiplying the number of potential viewing households in the market by 0.01.

Rating points within various demographic groups also are valuable because they focus specifically on target groups desired by programmers and advertisers. For example, a demographic rating of 10 within the 25-to-54 age group—male, female, or both—indicates that 10 percent of that demographic group's total number were counted in the program's estimated audience.

Television rating and share data are provided by Nielsen and Arbitron in their audience studies for both MSA and ADI or DMA markets for all time periods of the broadcast week. In addition, ratings and share averages are summarized for various *dayparts* (e.g., 6 to 10 A.M., 10 A.M. to 4 P.M., or 4 to 7 P.M.). Rating and share data for radio listening are presented on an average-quarter-hour basis within dayparts, rather than for specific times. Arbitron radio reports also provide *average person* estimates, indicating the estimated number of people listening to a radio station during an average quarter-hour within each daypart.

Audience Composition. Programming decision makers and station or network sales managers use demographic information about audiences attracted to various programs to aid in strategic program scheduling and to solicit advertising. The rating services provide a full range of demographic data for network and local TV programs and, in major markets, for radio also. These data include estimated numbers of viewers and listeners, as well as demographic ratings.

ANALYTICAL TERMS

Several other audience-related terms are widely used in analyzing broadcast audiences. These include *cumulative audience, gross audience, reach* and *frequency, gross rating points, time spent listening, cost per thousand*, and *cost per point*.

Cumulative audience data, or "*cumes*," indicate the estimated number of different households or people who tuned to a specific program or station at least once during a stated period of time. *Cume ratings* indicate the cumulative number of people (*unduplicated audience*) reached by a station as a percentage of the total population in the survey area. For example, if a radio station as a *cume reach* of 200,000 persons out of a potential of 500,000 persons, its *cume rating* is 40.

In television, a *cume audience* might be an estimate of the number of different households that watched a five-day-a-week program, such as a serial drama or a newscast, at least once during the week. In radio, it might indicate the number of different people who listened to a station at least once during a specified time, usually a week.

Gross audience refers to the total number of households (or people) reached over a period of time, counting each one *every time* it is included in an audience. For example, a program's *gross audience* represents the total number of viewers, duplicated and unduplicated, for a five-day-a-week program.

It is useful in broadcast advertising to know both the cume audience and the gross audience, since advertisers' goals vary. The *cume* indicates the reach, whereas *gross audience* reveals the total number of impressions delivered by a campaign. Both terms are important in the advertising concepts of *reach* and *frequency*.

Reach is used in broadcast advertising to indicate the number of different households or people exposed to campaign messages. A viewer needs to watch only once to be counted in the estimated reach for a program or campaign. In essence, *reach* and *cume audience* are synonymous.

Frequency refers to the average number of times each viewer or listener is reached or exposed to an advertiser's message within a given period of time. The procedure for computing frequency is

$$\text{Frequency} = \frac{\text{gross audience (impressions)}}{\text{reach (cumulative audience)}}$$

For example, assume the following data represent viewing to WWWW-TV's five-nights-per-wek "Evening News":

Average household audience	120,000
Cumulative audience/reach	250,000
Advertising messages *(period)*	5
Gross audience (impressions) (5 × 120,000)	600,000
Frequency = 600,000/250,000	
= 2.4	

The significance of reach and frequency lies in the fact that advertising needs differ from one situation to another. Some advertisers require high levels of repetition (*frequency*) as constant reminders of brand names and images. Other clients need less repetition, but broader audience exposure (*reach*). Advertising campaigns may be planned strategically to emphasize either reach or frequency within a given number of rating points and a specified budget.

In broadcast advertising, the term **gross rating points** (**GRP**) represents the overall reach of a campaign expressed in *gross ratings* (the sum of ratings for all advertising insertions) instead of numbers of viewers or viewing households. Since each rating point represents 1 percent of the potential audience, a campaign's GRPs indicate the weight of the campaign schedule with respect to the total potential audience. Theoretically, a schedule consisting of 100 GRPs is equivalent to reaching the total potential audience. In practice, however, the audience delivered in a 100 GRP campaign is not quite 100 percent of the population because of reach and frequency variations. Some people or households are reached more than once, and others are not reached at all. GRPs also may be calculated for demographic audiences.

Like *gross audience,* GRP is an analytical measure used to determine the extent to which an advertising campaign blankets a broadcast market. Often the number of commercials purchased is based on a predetermined number of GRPs theoretically needed to provide the desired level of advertising exposure. For example, at least 100 weekly GRPs are needed for a low-level saturation campaign intended to maintain brand awareness; and 200 weekly GRPs may be needed for a high-level saturation schedule to launch a new product.

Time spent listening (TSL) is an estimate of the average length of time each listener stays tuned to a particular radio station. TSL may be calculated from average quarter-hour audience and cume audience data and is a measure of audience loyalty and satisfaction with station programming. The formula for calculating TSL is as follows:

$$TSL = \frac{\text{average quarter-hour audience} \times \text{number of quarter hours}}{\text{cume audience}}$$

Advertisers who use the broadcast media place their schedules with the expectation of attaining their sales objectives as efficiently as possible. The most common measure of cost efficiency is **cost per thousand (CPM)**, defined as the expenditure needed for each 1,000 households or people with an advertising message or an entire campaign. The formula for calculating CPM for either a single spot or for a campaign is as follows:

$$CPM = \frac{\text{cost of advertising} \times 1,000}{\text{audience}}$$

For example, if WWWW-TV's "Evening News" delivers an average audience of 120,000 households and the price for a single 30-second spot is $600, then the household CPM can be computed:

$$CPM = \$600,000 / 120,000 = \$5.00$$

If a schedule of prime-time spots delivers a gross audience of 800,000 households and the total price for the schedule is $8,500, the household CPM for the entire schedule can be computed:

$$CPM = \$8,500,000 / 800,000 = \$10.62$$

Just as advertisers evaluate the efficiency of broadcast advertising on a CPM basis, they also consider the cost for reaching each rating point in their schedules. In computing *cost per point* (CPP), media buyers and sellers must remember that the value of a rating point varies from one market to another. The formula for CPP is as follows:

CPP = total cost/number of rating points achieved

Like the CPM, the CPP can be calculated on the basis of household ratings or on a demographic rating point basis. In the newscast example given earlier, suppose the program's rating is 24 and the cost remains at $600. The CPP can be calculated as follows:

CPP = $600 divided by 24 rating points = $25.00

LEARN BY DOING

1. Assume that your TV market has 350,000 TV households and a population of 1,200,000 people over two years of age. How many households must have a TV set turned on to attain a HUT level of 25 percent? 40 percent? 50 percent?
2. If the HUT level is 40 percent for the early evening (6 P.M.) news period, and station A has a share of 40 percent, how many households are watching station A's news? What is the rating of station A's newscast?
3. If the HUT level is 60 percent at 9 P.M. and station A has a 40-percent share of that audience, how much larger is its audience at 9 P.M. than at 6 P.M.? What would the station's rating be at 9 P.M.?
4. Assume that the nightly news on station A has an average audience of 65,000 households and a cumulative audience of 200,000. What frequency would result for a client that schedules one announcement each day for a week during the newscast?
5. In question 4, what is the CPM if the station charges $275 per spot?
6. What is the CPP?

AUDIENCE MEASUREMENT SERVICES

Radio audience measurement began on a systematic basis in the 1930s through the efforts of the Cooperative Analysis of Broadcasting (CAB) and Clark-Hooper, Inc. CAB was established by the American Association of Advertising Agencies and the Association of National Advertisers as an industry-supported organization to provide audience information on the new medium. Clark-Hooper and its successor, C. E. Hooper, Inc., provided the famous "Hooperratings," which pioneered the use of telephone coincidental research.

Nielsen Media Research and the Arbitron Company now produce program ratings on a regular basis. The following sections describe the research products of these two leading research organizations. In addition, a number of other firms specialize in customized and usually proprietary research work.

Nielsen Media Research

Nielsen Media Research, a division of the A. C. Nielsen Company, maintains two broadcast research units: the *Nielsen Television Index* (*NTI*) and the *Nielsen Station Index* (*NSI*). NTI uses People Meters to produce network program ratings and other national TV viewership data. NSI provides ratings, shares, and audience demographic data for local TV markets through a combination of metering devices and diaries. Nielsen, headquartered in New York City, also monitors viewing of pay cable television and in-home use of videocassette recorders (VCRs).

NTI obtains data for its *household audience estimates* from People Meters, which are placed in a representative sample of U.S. TV households. These devices record the tuning behavior of individuals within the sample households and allow Nielsen to project both the total number of viewing households and *audience composition estimates.*

NTI uses the area probability sampling technique to select sample households from a data base that includes all households in the United States. Actual samples include all types of households and neighborhoods in cities, towns, and rural areas, with and without telephones, geographically dispersed in more than 600 counties. The People Meter's operational sample includes more than 4,000 homes. Each participating household remains in the sample for about two years, long enough to provide continuity of information.

NTI's best-known publication is the *Nielsen National TV Ratings,* popularly known as "The Pocketpiece" among industry workers. This weekly publication, which fits neatly into a vest pocket, gives information about the national TV audience such as the following:

1. Household audience estimates and shares for network programs.
2. Audience composition estimates for a large number of demographic characteristics.
3. Season-to-date and quarter-to-date averages of program audiences.
4. Average audience estimates for major types of programs.
5. Overall TV-set usage data, compared with the previous year.
6. TV-set usage data by time periods.
7. Average audience and shares for "other" viewing sources, such as independent stations, public stations, cable originated programs, and pay services.

NSI provides individual stations and media buyers with a *local* audience measurement service similar to NTI's national service. NSI conducts TV audience surveys in more than 200 markets, providing three to seven audience studies (based on four-week periods) per year. These reports, called *Viewers in Profile,* include both metro and Designated Market Area (DMA) ratings, total audiences, cumulative reach, and estimates of viewing over a wide range of demographic groups.

As noted earlier, NSI is essentially diary-based, except in roughly 30 of the nation's largest markets where a combination of metered and diary-gathered data is obtained. NSI uses a random selection of sample households from telephone directories, except in some of the largest markets where the *total telephone frame* (all telephones, listed and unlisted) is used as the base.

In addition, NSI uses the NTI area probability samples in the 25 largest cities, where the data gathering is accomplished by a combination of monitoring devices and diaries. In other markets, participating households are asked to keep a TV viewing diary for one week.

After basic data from sample homes reaches Nielsen's offices, diaries and data tapes are examined closely to ensure accuracy throughout the processing and production operation. After passing inspection, the diary data are keyed directly into computers (which already contain viewing data). A final inspection is conducted on the completed data for internal consistency and verification of any unusual trends. The entire process, from receipt of raw data to finished reports, is almost completely automatic. A sample page from a local "Viewers in Profile" is shown in Figure 17.3. Special customized audience studies also may be ordered for local markets from NSI.

The Arbitron Company

The Arbitron Company, a subsidiary of Control Data Corporation, provides network and local research for both television and radio. Arbitron, headquartered in New York City, has its operations center at Beltsville, Maryland. It uses diaries for gathering local market data and an electronic monitoring device for overnight ratings of network prime-time programs in some of the largest TV markets.

In addition, Arbitron offers a variety of other reports and custom services, including overnight telephone coincidental surveys. Arbitron also has launched its ScanAmerica People Meter service to gather consumer purchasing data on viewers of various TV programs.

To conduct its local market studies, Arbitron has divided the entire United States into geographic sampling units, which usually consist of one county each. Diaries are placed in each sampling unit on the basis of population and expected rate of return of diaries. Arbitron's sample households are computer selected from lists of all households, using an interval selection process.

Separate samples are generated for each week of the four-week rating period, and each cooperating household keeps its diary for seven days. Special interviewing techniques are used in some markets to help obtain data from households

ST. LOUIS, MO

WK1 10/30–11/05 WK2 11/06–11/12 WK3 11/13–11/19 WK4 11/20–11/26

PROGRAM AVERAGES

METRO HH RTG	METRO HH SHR	STATION	DAY	PROGRAM	DMA HH RATINGS WEEKS 1	2	3	4	MULTI-WEEK AVG. RTG	SHR	SHARE TREND ¤ OCT '86	MAY '86	FEB '86	NOV '85	HUT	PERSONS 2+	18+	12-34	18-34	18-49	25-54	WOMEN 18+	18-34	18-49	25-49	25-54	WKG	FEM 12-24	PER 12-24	MEN 18+	18-34	18-49	25-49	25-54	TNS 12-17	CHILD 2-11	6-11
1	2				3	4	5	6	7	8	9	10	11	12	13	14	15	16	17	18	19	20	21	22	23	24	25	26	27	28	29	30	31	32	33	34	35
2				*R.S.E. THRESHOLDS 25+%*	*7*	*7*	*7*	*7*	*2*							*1*	*1*	*3*	*3*	*2*	*2*	*2*	*5*	*3*	*3*	*3*	*4*	*7*	*5*	*2*	*6*	*3*	*4*	*3*	*10*	*7*	*10*
1				*(1 S.E.) 4 WK AVG 50+%*	*2*	*2*	*2*	*2*	*LT*							*LT*	*LT*	*1*	*1*	*1*	*LT*	*LT*	*1*	*1*	*1*	*1*	*1*	*2*	*1*	*1*	*2*	*1*	*1*	*1*	*3*	*2*	*3*
				5.30PM																																	
8	15	KTVI	MON	ABC-WORLD NWS	9	11	9	5	9	15	16	17X	18	20	58	4	5	2	2	4	5	6	3	4	5	5	5			5	2	4	5	5	1		1
9	17		TUE	ABC-WORLD NWS	8	9	11	6	9	16	18	18X	18	20	56	4	5	2	3	4	4	6	3	4	5	5	6	2	2	5	2	3	3	3	1	1	1
8	15		WED	ABC-WORLD NWS	8	9	8	5	8	14	25	19X	17	19	54	4	5	2	3	3	4	5	3	3	4	4	4	1	1	5	3	3	4	4	1		
10	17		THU	ABC-WORLD NWS	10	10	10	9	10	17	19	20X	17	20	59	6	7	4	5	5	6	7	4	5	6	6	6	1	2	7	5	5	6	6		1	2
8	16		FRI	ABC-WORLD NWS	8	10	8	6	8	16	19	22X	17	18	51	4	5	2	3	3	4	5	2	3	3	4	4	1		6	3	4	5	5			
9	*16*		*AVS*	*ABC-WORLD NWS*	*9*	*10*	*9*	*6*	*9*	*15*	*19*	*19X*	*17*	*19*	*55*	*4*	*6*	*3*	*3*	*4*	*5*	*6*	*3*	*4*	*5*	*5*	*5*	*1*	*1*	*6*	*3*	*4*	*5*	*5*	*1*	*1*	*1*
2	5		SUN	TURNABOUT	3	2	2	4	2	5	17	6	9	13	46	1	2	1	1	1	2	2	1	1	1	2	2	1		2	1	1	2	2			1
				5.45PM																																	
3	8	KMOV	SAT	CBS CLLG-POST2			3		3	7	18	21	18	15	35	2	2	1	2	2	2	1	1	1	1	1	2			3	3	3	5	4		1	
4	11	KTVI	SAT	CFA-PSTGME-ABC	5	4	4		4	11					37	2	2	2	2	2	2	1	2	1	1	1	1	1	2	4	3	3	3	3	1	1	1
5	*12*		*NOR*	*CFA-PSTGME-ABC*	*5*	*4*	*4*		*4*	*11*	*12*	*17*	*18*	*7*	*37*	*2*	*2*	*2*	*3*	*2*	*2*	*1*	*2*	*1*	*1*	*1*	*1*	*2*	*2*	*4*	*4*	*4*	*4*	*4*	*1*	*1*	*1*
				6.00PM																																	
4	7	KDNL	MON	GIMME A BREAK	4	3	4	3	4	6	8	14	13	13	60	3	2	4	3	2	1	3	5	4	2	2	3	9	6	1	1	1	1	1	7	6	6
5	8		TUE	GIMME A BREAK	5	3	4	4	4	7	7	16	15	14	58	3	1	3	2	2	1	2	3	2	2	1	2	4	4	1	1	1	1	1	5	7	9
5	9		WED	GIMME A BREAK	4	3	4	4	4	7	7	10	15	13	56	3	2	4	3	2	2	3	5	4	3	2	2	9	6	1	1	1	1	1	7	6	6
5	8		THU	GIMME A BREAK	5	5	4	3	4	7	9	13	14	14	64	3	2	4	3	3	2	3	5	4	2	2	3	9	6	2	2	2	2	2	6	5	7
4	8		FRI	GIMME A BREAK	3	4	4	3	4	6	9	14	16	14	55	3	2	3	3	2	2	3	4	4	2	2	3	6	5	1	1	1	1	1	4	5	5
5	*8*		*AVS*	*GIMME A BREAK*	*4*	*4*	*4*	*3*	*4*	*7*	*8*	*13*	*14*	*14*	*59*	*3*	*2*	*4*	*3*	*2*	*2*	*3*	*4*	*4*	*2*	*2*	*3*	*7*	*5*	*1*	*1*	*1*	*1*	*1*	*6*	*6*	*7*
4	8		SAT	ONE BIG FAMILY	3	3	2	5	3	7	4	6	8	9	44	2	2	2	2	2	2	2	3	3	2	2	2	2	2	1	1	1	1	1	3	2	3
1	1		SUN	KDNL SUN-SPCLS	1	1		<<	1	1	1	4	5	5	63						1									1	1	1	1	1			
2	3		SUN	WACKY WRL-SPTS			2		2	3	2	5	5	5	57	1	1	1	1	1	1	2	2	2	3	2				1						1	
9	16	KMOV	MON	NWS 4 ST L 6	7	7	6	15	9	15	23	20	20	17	60	5	6	3	3	4	6	7	4	5	6	6	6	3	2	5	2	3	4	5	3	1	1
9	15		TUE	NWS 4 ST L 6	8	7	4	14	8	14	20	20	20	17	58	5	6	3	4	5	5	7	5	6	6	7	7	3	3	5	3	3	4	4	2	1	1
10	17		WED	NWS 4 ST L 6	8	10	6	15	10	17	18	22	19	17	56	6	7	4	4	5	6	7	4	6	7	7	6	2	2	7	5	4	5	5	2	1	2
13	20		THU	NWS 4 ST L 6	11	10	12	18	13	20	20	20	19	18	64	8	10	5	6	7	8	11	8	9	9	10	10	6	4	8	4	5	6	7	3		
10	18		FRI	NWS 4 ST L 6	8	10	9	12	10	18	21	20	20	18	55	6	8	4	4	5	6	9	6	7	6	7	8	6	4	6	3	4	4	4	3	3	2
10	*17*		*AVS*	*NWS 4 ST L 6*	*9*	*9*	*7*	*15*	*10*	*17*	*20*	*20*	*20*	*17*	*59*	*6*	*7*	*4*	*4*	*5*	*6*	*8*	*5*	*7*	*7*	*7*	*7*	*4*	*3*	*6*	*3*	*4*	*5*	*5*	*2*	*1*	*1*
6	13		SAT	NWS 4 ST L 6	5	7	4	6	6	12	15	22	18	16	44	4	5	2	3	3	3	4	2	2	2	2	3	2	3	5	4	4	3	3	1	2	2
31	50		SUN	60 MINUTES	33	27	27	29	29	47					62	18	23	9	10	14	18	24	10	15	16	18	20	7	7	22	10	14	16	18	4	3	4
30	*51*		*NOR*	*60 MINUTES*	*33*	*27*	*27*	*28*	*29*	*48*	*44*	*48*	*44*	*42*	*61*	*18*	*23*	*9*	*11*	*15*	*18*	*23*	*10*	*15*	*16*	*17*	*21*	*7*	*7*	*22*	*11*	*15*	*17*	*19*	*4*	*3*	*3*
9	*17*		*AV6*	*NWS 4 ST L 6*	*8*	*8*	*7*	*13*	*9*	*16*	*20*	*21*	*19*	*17*	*56*	*6*	*7*	*4*	*4*	*5*	*6*	*8*	*5*	*6*	*6*	*7*	*7*	*4*	*3*	*6*	*4*	*4*	*4*	*5*	*2*	*1*	*1*
10	17	KPLR	MON	FACTS OF LIFE	11	12	10	9	10	17	12	9	12	11	60	7	4	9	6	5	5	4	6	6	6	5	5	11	11	4	7	5	4	4	17	15	18
9	15		TUE	FACTS OF LIFE	6	11	8	9	8	14	13	8	10	11	58	5	4	8	7	5	4	4	7	6	6	6	4	12	10	3	6	4	3	3	13	8	10
8	15		WED	FACTS OF LIFE	7	10	7	9	8	14	11	9	10	10	56	6	4	7	5	5	4	4	5	5	5	5	5	11	10	3	5	4	3	3	14	12	14
10	16		THU	FACTS OF LIFE	8	11	8	11	10	15	13	7	12	9	64	7	4	9	6	5	5	5	8	6	6	6	6	15	12	3	5	4	4	4	19	15	19
7	14		FRI	FACTS OF LIFE	4	10	8	8	8	14	12	7	9	8	55	6	4	8	6	6	5	5	8	7	6	5	6	12	10	3	5	4	4	4	14	10	12
9	*15*		*AVS*	*FACTS OF LIFE*	*7*	*11*	*8*	*9*	*9*	*15*	*12*	*8*	*11*	*10*	*59*	*6*	*4*	*8*	*6*	*5*	*5*	*4*	*7*	*6*	*6*	*5*	*5*	*12*	*11*	*3*	*5*	*4*	*4*	*4*	*15*	*12*	*15*
4	6		SAT	BLUES HCKY				3	3	6	16	7	10	9	55	3	1	5	3	2	2	1	2	2	1	1	1	5	6	1	3	2	2	2	10	5	
7	16		SAT	PUTTIN ON HITS	9	7	5		7	16	17	13	21	20	43	5	3	5	4	3	4	4	5	5	4	5	5	8	7	2	2	2	2	3	11	7	11
4	6		SUN	STAR SEARCH	4	3	4	1	3	6	8	4X	7	5	61	2	2	3	2	2	2	3	3	3	2	3	4	6	4	2	1	1	1	2	5	1	2
24	41	KSDK	MON	6PM EYEWIT NWS	26	25	23	21	24	39	35	35X	36	35	60	14	17	7	8	10	12	18	8	10	11	12	14	5	5	17	9	10	10	12	3	3	4
24	42		TUE	6PM EYEWIT NWS	22	29	21	23	24	41	34	33X	34	34	58	14	18	7	7	10	12	19	8	11	14	14	13	4	4	16	7	8	10	11	5	3	3
22	40		WED	6PM EYEWIT NWS	22	26	22	18	22	39	30	36X	34	36	56	13	17	5	6	8	11	17	6	8	9	11	11	2	3	16	7	8	9	11	1	2	3
25	39		THU	6PM EYEWIT NWS	25	25	21	25	24	37	35	37X	35	35	64	14	18	5	6	9	12	19	6	10	12	13	14	3	3	17	6	9	10	11	3	4	5
21	38		FRI	6PM EYEWIT NWS	16	25	22	18	20	36	34	34X	33	35	55	12	14	6	7	9	11	16	8	10	12	12	10	5	4	13	6	8	9	10	3	4	6
23	*40*		*AVS*	*6PM EYEWIT NWS*	*22*	*26*	*22*	*21*	*23*	*38*	*34*	*35X*	*34*	*35*	*59*	*14*	*17*	*6*	*7*	*9*	*12*	*18*	*7*	*10*	*12*	*12*	*13*	*4*	*4*	*16*	*7*	*9*	*10*	*11*	*3*	*3*	*4*
18	41		SAT	EYEWIT NWS SAT	18	16	16	19	17	39	36	27	28	33	44	11	13	4	4	7	9	14	4	6	8	9	9	1	2	13	5	7	8	9	2	3	3
13	22		SUN	OUR HOUSE	13	10	14	18	14	22					62	11	10	12	12	11	10	11	14	13	12	12	12	13	12	9	10	9	8	8	10	12	12
13	*21*		*NOR*	*OUR HOUSE*	*13*	*10*		*18*	*14*	*22*	*23*	*15*	*17*	*19*	*63*	*11*	*11*	*12*	*11*	*11*	*10*	*13*	*14*	*13*	*13*	*12*	*13*	*13*	*12*	*9*	*9*	*8*	*8*	*8*	*12*	*12*	*13*
10	17	KTVI	MON	CH 2 NWS-6.00	8	11	8	9	9	15	16	14X	15	18	60	5	6	3	3	4	5	7	4	5	6	6	6	1	1	5	2	4	5	5	1		
9	15		TUE	CH 2 NWS-6.00	9	8	10	6	8	14	18	15X	15	17	58	4	5	3	3	4	5	6	4	5	5	5	7	3	2	5	3	4	5	5	2	1	1
8	14		WED	CH 2 NWS-6.00	7	9	6	6	7	12	24	14X	15	16	56	4	5	3	4	4	5	5	4	4	5	5	5	1	1	5	3	4	5	4			1
9	14		THU	CH 2 NWS-6.00	7	11	9	8	9	14	16	15X	16	18	64	5	6	4	5	5	6	6	5	6	6	6	6	3	3	6	5	5	5	5	2	2	2
9	16		FRI	CH 2 NWS-6.00	9	9	7	8	8	15	15	18X	16	16	55	4	5	3	3	4	5	6	4	4	4	5	6	2	2	5	2	4	4	4	1	1	
9	*15*		*AVS*	*CH 2 NWS-6.00*	*8*	*10*	*8*	*7*	*8*	*14*	*18*	*15X*	*15*	*17*	*59*	*4*	*6*	*3*	*4*	*4*	*5*	*6*	*4*	*5*	*5*	*5*	*6*	*2*	*2*	*5*	*3*	*4*	*5*	*5*	*1*	*1*	*1*
6	14		SAT	CH2 WKND NWS	5	5	6	5	5	12	16	14X	15	11	44	3	4	2	2	2	3	3	1	2	2	2	3	1	1	4	2	3	3	3	1		
13	21		SUN	DISNEY SUN MOV	10	12	13	15	13	20	19	21	21	24	62	12	8	11	10	10	12	9	10	11	13	12	10	9	10	8	9	9	12	11	16	25	27
				6.30PM																																	
3	6	KDNL	MON	BENSON	2	4	2	4	3	5	5	11	10	11	62	2	1	2	1	2	1	2	2	2	2	2	3	4	3	1		1		1	3	5	5
3	5		TUE	BENSON	3	2	3	2	3	4	6	12	11	12	58	2	1	1	1	1	1	1	1	1	1	1	2	2	2	1		1	1	1	3	5	5
3	6		WED	BENSON	3	2	3	4	3	5	5	8	10	11	58	2	1	2	2	1	1	2	2	2	1	1	1	5	4	1	1	1	1	1	5	3	4
4	6		THU	BENSON	3	3	4	3	3	5	6	10	11	11	67	2	2	3	2	2	2	2	2	2	2	2	2	4	4	2	2	2	1	2	4	4	4
3	5		FRI	BENSON	2	2	2	2	2	4	4	12	12	10	55	1	1	1	1	1	1	1	1	2	1	1	2	1	1	1	1	1			1	3	4
3	*5*		*AVS*	*BENSON*	*2*	*3*	*3*	*3*	*3*	*5*	*5*	*10*	*10*	*11*	*60*	*2*	*1*	*2*	*1*	*1*	*1*	*1*	*2*	*2*	*1*	*1*	*2*	*3*	*3*	*1*	*1*	*1*	*1*	*1*	*3*	*4*	*4*
2	5		SAT	DANCE FEVER	3	2	2	2	2	4	3	4	8	9	50	1	1	1	1	1	2	2	1	2	2	2	2		1	1	1	1	2	2	1	1	2
1	2		SUN	STEAMERS SOCCR			1		1	2	2	4	4	3	59	1	1	1	1	1	1		1	1	1	1	1		1	1	1	1	1	1		1	
11	18	KMOV	MON	NW NEWLYWED GM	9	13	10	13	11	18	21	22X	23	21	62	8	8	7	6	7	7	9	8	8	7	7	7	12	9	7	5	6	6	6	10	6	8
10	17		TUE	NW NEWLYWED GM	8	12	7	13	10	17	22	18X	25	24	58	6	7	6	6	6	7	7	7	7	8	8	5	7	5	6	5	5	7	7	7	4	7
10	17		WED	NW NEWLYWED GM	9	12	7	10	10	17	18	23X	26	21	58	7	7	6	6	6	6	7	7	7	7	7	7	7	7	7	5	6	6	6	8	6	7
13	19		THU	NW NEWLYWED GM	11	11	14	13	12	18	20	20X	24	23	67	8	9	6	7	7	8	11	10	10	9	9	9	10	6	8	4	5	6	7	6	4	6
10	18		FRI	NW NEWLYWED GM	10	11	8	13	10	19	21	20X	25	24	55	7	7	7	7	7	7	8	8	8	8	8	7	9	7	6	5	6	7	6	8	6	8
11	*18*		*AVS*	*NW NEWLYWED GM*	*9*	*12*	*9*	*12*	*11*	*18*	*20*	*21X*	*25*	*23*	*60*	*7*	*8*	*7*	*6*	*7*	*7*	*8*	*8*	*8*	*8*	*8*	*7*	*9*	*7*	*7*	*5*	*5*	*6*	*6*	*8*	*5*	*7*
4	7		SAT	WHAT A COUNTRY	1	3	3	6	3	7	8	13	14	14	50	2	3	1	2	2	2	3	2	2	2	2	3	2	1	2	2	2	2	2	1	1	1
1	2				3	4	5	6	7	8	9	10	11	12	13	14	15	16	17	18	19	20	21	22	23	24	25	26	27	28	29	30	31	32	33	34	35

NOVEMBER 1986

See Program Index for complete details of program start time, duration and weeks of telecast.
¤ 4-Week Time Period Averages.

24

FIGURE 17.3 *Viewers in Profile* 1986 (*Source:* Copyright © 1986 Nielsen Media Research. Reprinted by permission.)

whose members may have language or literacy problems and who otherwise might not be fully represented in the sample. Average weekly program ratings and share data are computed from the combined multiweekly samples, following a careful screening of diaries for accuracy.

Arbitron TV Market Reports are produced for more than 200 U.S. TV markets. Each market is surveyed three to eight times per year. The following categories are included in the reports: Area of Dominant Influence (ADI) market data; daypart audience summary; network program averages; weekly program and time-period averages; program averages; and ADI ratings trends. The reports closely resemble those of Nielsen, including rating and share data for the metro area and the larger ADI. Audience totals and demographic data also are provided for the Total Survey Area (TSA), which includes viewership within and beyond the ADIs. Each report includes viewing data for each program broadcast in the market, as well as daypart summaries. A sample page from a local *Arbitron TV Market Report* is shown in Figure 17.4.

Arbitron Radio conducts audience surveys up to four times annually in about 200 markets. These reports, covering 12-week periods, provide data on listening, at home and away, for metro and ADI areas. Arbitron uses the same ADI areas for both television and radio, in order to provide geographically comparable data to clients. Figure 17.5 (page 346) shows Arbitron's format for presenting average-quarter-hour and cumulative radio audience data.

Arbitron Radio also conducts national studies of the audiences of the radio networks. Its special *Ethnic Reports* detail the radio listening habits of the African American and Hispanic segments of the population in several large cities.

Other Audience Measurement Services

Several additional research services provide more specialized audience measurement for broadcast stations, advertisers, and other clients. The Simmons Market Research Bureau, of New York, specializes in audience profile information. Its reports provide demographic/psychographic data and buying behavior information on audiences for various types of TV programs and radio formats.

The audience of the radio networks is measured twice a year by Statistical Research, Inc., of Westwood, N.J. Popularly known as RADAR (for "Radio's All Dimension Audience Research"), this research is based on telephone interview data from more than 8,000 respondents over 12 years of age.

Other prominent research organizations that measure viewing behavior and program and personality preferences include the Trendex, TvQ, and Videodex services. Much of their research seeks qualitative information about audience preferences used in making decisions about programs and on-air talent. Some lesser known research firms, news consultants, and university-related research centers also offer "on-demand" audience and public opinion studies, including surveys of nonmetropolitan radio markets.

The *Broadcasting/Cable Yearbook* and *Television/Cable Factbook* contain annual published listings of research firms.

Time Period Estimates

DAY AND TIME / STATION PROGRAM	JUL 05	JUL 12	JUL 19	JUL 26	RTG	SHR	MAY 89	FEB 89	NOV 88	JUL 88	M-RTG	M-SHR	2+	18+	12-24	12-34	18-34	18-49	21-49	25-54	35+	35-64	50+	W18+	W18-24	W12-34	W18-34	W21-49	W25-49	W25-54	WW	M18+	M18-34	M21-49	M25-49	M25-54
col #	1	2	3	4	5	6	59	60	61	62	8	9	11	12	13	14	15	16	17	18	19	20	21	22	23	24	25	26	27	28		30	31	32	33	34	35
RELATIVE STD-ERR 25% THRESHOLDS (1σ) 50%	6 / 1	6 / 1	6 / 1	6 / 1	1 / –						3 / –		1 / –	3 / 1	1 / –	2 / 1	1 / –	2 / 1	1 / –	1 / –	1 / –	1 / –	1 / –	9 / 2	4 / 1	2 / –	2 / 1	2 / –	3 / 1	2 / –	4 / 1		5 / 2	5 / –	2 / –	3 / 1	2 / 1

MON-FRI

2:30P– 3:00P

Station Program	1	2	3	4	5	6	59	60	61	62	8	9	2+	18+	12-24	12-34	18-34	18-49	21-49	25-54	35+	35-64	50+	W18+	W18-24	W12-34	W18-34	W21-49	W25-49	W25-54	M18+	M18-34	M21-49	M25-49	M25-54
WATE LIFE TO LIVE	4	4	5	2	4	14	12	10	20	11	3	13	2	2	3	3	3	3	2	2	2	3	3	4	4	4	4	3	2	1	1	1	1	2	2
WKXT AS WRLD TRNS	4	4	10	6	6	23	27	39	25	23	7	27	3	3	4	4	3	3	3	3	2	2	3	4	8	6	5	5	5	4	2	1	1	1	1
WBIR ANOTHER WRL<	10				10	41					10	43	5	6	7	6	7	6	6	6	5	5	8	10		10	10		8		3		1	1	1
ANOTHER WRLD		4	8	9	7	26					8	32	4	4	7	5	4	3	3	3	3	3	5	6	11	6	6	5	4	3	2	1	1	1	1
--4 WK AVG--			8		8	29	29	21	27	42	9	35	4	4	7	5	5	4	4	3	4	4	6	7	11	8	7	7	5	5	2	1	1	1	1
WKCH DENIS ANIMTD	3	1	2	2	2	8					2	9	2		1									1		1									
DENIS ANIMTD‡		1			1	4					2	8	1		1		1	1	1	1				1		1		1	1	1					1
--4 WK AVG--					2	7	4	3	3	5	2	9	2		1									1											
WSJK PTV	–		–	–						**																									
HUT/PVT/TOT	25	24	31	26	27		23	29	24	27	25		15	14	19	17	15	13	13	12	11	14		19	29	23	20	20	19	18	14	8	7	6	6	6

3:00P– 3:30P

Station Program	1	2	3	4	5	6	59	60	61	62	8	9	2+	18+	12-24	12-34	18-34	18-49	21-49	25-54	35+	35-64	50+	W18+	W18-24	W12-34	W18-34	W21-49	W25-49	W25-54	M18+	M18-34	M21-49	M25-49	M25-54
WATE GEN HOSPITAL	6	6	5	5	5	19	14	11	20	11	4	16	3	3	4	4	5	3	3	3	2	3	5	6	8	6	5	5	4	5	2	1	1	1	1
WKXT GUIDING LGHT	5	6	9	7	7	25	28	37	23	20	8	31	4	4	5	4	4	4	4	3	3	3	4	5	10	7	6	6	5	5	2	1	1	1	1
WBIR SANTA BARBR<	6				6	24					6	27	3	4	5	4	4	4	2	4	3	6	7	7		6	6		3		2		1	1	1
SANTA BARBRA		4	6	6	5	19					7	26	3	3	4	4	3	3	3	3	3	3	4	5		6	6		3		2		1	1	1
--4 WK AVG--					6	20	22	18	21	37	7	26	3	3	6	4	4	3	3	3	3	3	3	5	10	6	5	5	4	4	2	1	1	1	1
WKCH WOODY WDPCKR	3	1	2	2	2	7	5	6	7	5	2	10	2		1		1						1	1		1									
WSJK PTV	1	–		1	1	2	3			**	1	2	1																						
HUT/PVT/TOT	26	27	29	28	28		27	31	25	26	26		16	15	22	19	17	14	14	12	13	11	15	21	34	27	22	22	19	18	16	8	7	6	6	6

3:30P– 4:00P

Station Program	1	2	3	4	5	6	59	60	61	62	8	9	2+	18+	12-24	12-34	18-34	18-49	21-49	25-54	35+	35-64	50+	W18+	W18-24	W12-34	W18-34	W21-49	W25-49	W25-54	M18+	M18-34	M21-49	M25-49	M25-54
WATE GEN HOSPITAL	6	6	5	5	5	19	14	11	20	11	4	16	3	3	4	4	5	3	3	3	3	3	5	6	8	6	5	5	5	5	2	1	1	1	1
WKXT GUIDING LGHT	5	6	9	7	7	24	27	36	23	19	8	29	4	4	5	4	4	4	4	3	3	3	3	6	9	7	6	6	5	5	2	1	1	1	1
WBIR SANTA BARBR<	6				6	24					7	26	3	4	5	4	4	4	2	4	3	6	6	6		6	6		3		2		1	1	1
SANTA BARBRA		4	6	6	5	18					7	24	3	3	6	4	3	2	3	2	3	3	3	4		7	5		3		3		1	1	1
--4 WK AVG--					6	20	22	18	20	36	7	25	3	3	5	4	3	3	3	3	3	3	3	4	9	7	5	5	4	3	2	1	1	1	1
WKCH ALVN CHPMK-S	3	2	2	2	2	8	4	6	8	4	3	11	2		1							1				1									
WSJK PTV	1	1	–	1	1	2	3			**	1	4	2																						
HUT/PVT/TOT	27	29	29	29	28		29	32	25	27	27		16	15	21	18	17	14	14	12	13	11	15	21	33	27	22	22	19	18	17	8	7	6	6	6

4:00P– 4:30P

Station Program	1	2	3	4	5	6	59	60	61	62	8	9	2+	18+	12-24	12-34	18-34	18-49	21-49	25-54	35+	35-64	50+	W18+	W18-24	W12-34	W18-34	W21-49	W25-49	W25-54	M18+	M18-34	M21-49	M25-49	M25-54
WATE DIVORC COURT	8	6	7	8	7	25	22	23	19	21	6	22	5	5	5	4	4	4	4	6	4	8	7	7	6	6	6	5	5	5	4	3	2	3	2
WKXT KATE ALLIE-S	3	2	4	6	4	13	10	12	10	10	4	16	2	2	5	4	3	2	2	2	1	1	3	9	4	3	3	2	2	4	1	2	1	1	1
WBIR OPRAH WINFR<	8				8	29					7	27	4	4	3	4	4	4	4	2	5	7	7	8	8		6	6		6		3		3	2
OPRAH WINFRY		6	6	7	7	22					9	32	3	4	3	3	4	3	3	3	3	4	5	5	5	4	4	4	4	3	3	2	2	2	2
--4 WK AVG--		6	6	7	7	24	28	33	35	37	9	30	3	4	3	3	4	3	3	3	3	4	5	6	5	5	5	4	4	3	3	2	2	2	2
WKCH REAL GHSTBST	3	1	4	1	2	8	7	5	10	7	3	10	2	1	2	1	1	1	1	1			1	1		1	1	1	1	1	1	1	1	1	1
WSJK PTV	–	1	–		1		4	2		**	1		1																						
HUT/PVT/TOT	29	26	31	31	29		30	37	34	38	28		17	16	21	18	17	14	14	13	16	13	19	21	30	23	20	19	17	16	15	11	11	9	9	9

4:30P– 5:00P

Station Program	1	2	3	4	5	6	59	60	61	62	8	9	2+	18+	12-24	12-34	18-34	18-49	21-49	25-54	35+	35-64	50+	W18+	W18-24	W12-34	W18-34	W21-49	W25-49	W25-54	M18+	M18-34	M21-49	M25-49	M25-54
WATE SUPERIOR CRT	7	6	8	8	7	25	22	24	22	20	6	23	5	5	4	4	4	4	4	6	4	8	7	6	6	6	6	5	5	5	4	3	3	3	3
WKXT FAMLY TIES-S	3	2	3	6	4	12	9	11	10	10	5	17	2	2	5	3	2	2	2	1	2	2	3	8	4	3	3	2	2	4	1	2	1	1	1
WBIR OPRAH WINFR<	9				9	30					8	29	4	4	3	4	4	4	4	2	7	6	8	8		6	5		6		3		2	2
OPRAH WINFRY		6	6	7	6	22					8	30	3	4	3	3	4	3	4	3	3	4	5	5	5	4	4	4	3	3	2	2	2	2	2
--4 WK AVG--					7	24	29	33	33	36	8	29	3	4	3	3	4	3	3	3	3	4	5	6	5	5	4	4	4	4	2	2	2	2	2
WKCH DUCK TALES	3	1	4	1	2	8	6	11	11	3	10	2	2	1	2	1	1	1	1	1			1	1		1	1	1	1	1					
WSJK PTV	–	–	–				3	2		**	1	2																							
HUT/PVT/TOT	29	26	30	32	29		31	37	32	31	28		18	16	24	16	16	14	13	16	13	19		20	31	23	19	18	16	16		12	11	10	10	10

5:00P– 5:30P

Station Program	1	2	3	4	5	6	59	60	61	62	8	9	2+	18+	12-24	12-34	18-34	18-49	21-49	25-54	35+	35-64	50+	W18+	W18-24	W12-34	W18-34	W21-49	W25-49	W25-54	M18+	M18-34	M21-49	M25-49	M25-54
WATE PEOPLES CRT	8	7	7	7	7	23	23	20	14	23	7	24	5	4	4	4	4	4	4	6	5	8	6	5	5	4	4	4	4	5	5	2	3	3	3
WKXT NGHT COURT-S	4	3	6	8	5	17	13	11	14	9	7	23	3	3	6	5	4	3	3	2	3	2	3	7	4	4	4	3	3	4	3	3	2	3	2
WBIR THREES CMPNY	9	5	8	8	8	24	27	31	35	32	7	24	4	4	5	5	3	3	2	5	3	8	6	5	4	3	4	3	4	3	4	3	2	2	1
WKCH BRADY BUNCH	2	1	4	3	2	8	5	7	6	8	3	10	2	1	2	2	1	1	1	1			1	1	3	1	1	1	1	1					
WSJK PTV	–	–	–					2		**																								
HUT/PVT/TOT	30	27	32	36	31		32	38	31	30	29		19	18	23	20	18	16	15	14	18	16	23	21	30	23	20	19	17	17	19	15	13	12	11	12

5:30P– 6:00P

Station Program	1	2	3	4	5	6	59	60	61	62	8	9	2+	18+	12-24	12-34	18-34	18-49	21-49	25-54	35+	35-64	50+	W18+	W18-24	W12-34	W18-34	W21-49	W25-49	W25-54	M18+	M18-34	M21-49	M25-49	M25-54
WATE A GRIFFITH	8	5	9	12	9	25	19	21	17	20	9	26	6	6	6	7	6	6	6	5	6	6	9	9	7	7	6	6	6	6	7	5	6	6	6
WKXT NWS FIRST NW	3	4	4	4	4	12	12	14	10	12	4	12	3	3	1	1	3	3	3	4	3	3	4	3	1	1	1	3	4	3	3	2	2	2	3
WBIR JEOPARDY	13	11	12	13	12	35	35	31	43	38	13	37	7	8	6	5	5	5	5	4	10	7	15	10	8	7	7	5	6	9	6	3	2	2	3
WKCH SILVR SPNS-S	3	1	4	2	2	7	5	6	6	7	3	9	2	1	3	2	1	1	1	1	1		1	2	4	2	1	1	1	1	1	1	1	1	1
WSJK PTV	–	–	–				5			**																								
HUT/PVT/TOT	34	31	35	41	35		36	44	37	34	35		21	22	20	20	19	19	19	24	21	29	26	29	25	23	23	21	22	24	19	15	14	15	16

6:00P– 6:30P

Station Program	1	2	3	4	5	6	59	60	61	62	8	9	2+	18+	12-24	12-34	18-34	18-49	21-49	25-54	35+	35-64	50+	W18+	W18-24	W12-34	W18-34	W21-49	W25-49	W25-54	M18+	M18-34	M21-49	M25-49	M25-54
WATE EYWTNS NWS 6	16	12	15	20	15	30	26	29	29	27	18	33	10	12	5	8	9	9	9	10	13	11	17	13	5	10	9	10	11	11	11	8	9	9	10
WKXT NW8 FIRST NW	4	3	3	4	3	7	8	8	6	5	9		3	3	1	1	2	2	2	3	3	2	3	3	2	2	3	3	2	2	4	2	2	2	2
WBIR ACTN NWS 6PM	26	18	23	21	22	43	45	43	43	50	25	45	13	16	7	9	9	10	11	20	16	28	19	10	11	12	12	13	15	13	6	7	7	7	8
WKCH HPY DAYS AGN	3	1	3	4	2	5	3	4	3	3	3		2	1	4	3	2	2	1	1	1		2	5	4	2	1	1	1	1	1	1	1	1	1
WSJK PTV	–	–	–					2		**																								
HUT/PVT/TOT	55	45	52	55	52		52	63	57	53	54		32	37	21	24	26	28	29	31	43	37	53	41	27	31	32	33	32	34	35	32	22	24	25	28

6:30P– 7:00P

Station Program	1	2	3	4	5	6	59	60	61	62	8	9	2+	18+	12-24	12-34	18-34	18-49	21-49	25-54	35+	35-64	50+	W18+	W18-24	W12-34	W18-34	W21-49	W25-49	W25-54	M18+	M18-34	M21-49	M25-49	M25-54
WATE ABC WRLD NWS	13	13	13	15	13	28	24	25	27	25	15	30	8	10	4	7	8	8	9	11	9	13	10	9	5	8	9	9	8	8	9	9	8	9	9
WKXT CBS EVE NEWS	3	3	2	4	3	7	9	11	10	8	8	10	2	3	1	1	2	2	2	4	3	3	3	3	1	2	3	3	3	1	2	2	2	2	2
WBIR NBC NGHT NWS	21	15	20	17	18	39	39	40	38	46	21	41	10	13	6	7	7	7	8	16	13	23	15	7	8	9	9	10	13	11	11	5	5	5	7
WKCH CHRLS N CHRG	3	1	4	3	3	6	5	3	4		3		2	1	3	2	1	1	1	1	1		2	6	3	2	2	2	2	2		1	1	1	1
WSJK PTV	–	–	–					2		**																								
HUT/PVT/TOT	50	43	48	47	47		48	59	54	47	50		28	32	20	21	23	25	25	27	38	32	46	35	25	28	28	27	29	30	29	20	22	23	25

7:00P– 7:30P

Station Program	1	2	3	4	5	6	59	60	61	62	8	9	2+	18+	12-24	12-34	18-34	18-49	21-49	25-54	35+	35-64	50+	W18+	W18-24	W12-34	W18-34	W21-49	W25-49	W25-54	M18+	M18-34	M21-49	M25-49	M25-54
WATE ENTRTNMT TON	6	5	9	7	7	15	17	20	18	18	7	15	4	4	5	5	5	5	4	4	4	4	5	5	4	4	4	4	4	4	4	4	4	4	4
WKXT CURRENT AFFR	8	5	6	9	7	16	20	17	13	8	9	19	6	6	4	5	5	5	5	4	6	6	7	6	2	4	5	5	4	4	5	4	3	4	4
WBIR WHEEL OF FOR	17	14	19	13	16	36	34	32	38	41	18	39	9	11	5	6	7	6	7	14	9	22	13	7	8	7	7	6	7	10	9	4	4	4	4
WKCH MORK MINDY-S	2	1	3	3	2	5	3	3	3	4	2		1	1	2	2	1	1	1	1	1		1	2	4	2	1	1	1	1	1	1	1	1	1
WSJK PTV	1		1		1		1	2		**	1												1												
HUT/PVT/TOT	45	40	47	45	44		51	63	58	47	50		27	30	21	22	23	25	26	34	30	40	33	26	20	28	28	28	30	30	26	20	21	22	23

7:30P– 8:00P

Station Program	1	2	3	4	5	6	59	60	61	62	8	9	2+	18+	12-24	12-34	18-34	18-49	21-49	25-54	35+	35-64	50+	W18+	W18-24	W12-34	W18-34	W21-49	W25-49	W25-54	M18+	M18-34	M21-49	M25-49	M25-54
WATE COSBY SHOW-S	10	8	11	13	10	23	21	16	25	19	12	26	7	9	8	7	7	7	7	7	7	7	9	10	10	9	9	10	9	5	5	5	5	5	5
WKXT MASH-S	7	5	5		6	13					6	14	3	4	4	4	3	3	4	4	4	4	4	2	6	6	6				5	4	5	5	5
MASH-S <			6	6	14					8	18	4	3	4	4	3	4	4	6	5	6	4	4	6	6				4	4	4	5	4
--4 WK AVG--					6	13	15	15	13	14	7	15	3	4	4	4	3	3	4	4	4	4	4	3	6	6	5				4	4	4	5	4
WBIR FAMLY FEUD-S	15	14	16	12	14	32	34	34	32	28	15	33	8	10	5	6	6	6	6	12	8	18	12	7	8	8	7	8	10	7	4	3	4	4	4
WKCH SLEDGE HAMMR	1	1	3	3	2	5	3	4	2	4	1		2	1	1	1	1	1	1	1			1	1	3	1	1	1	1						
WSJK PTV	1	–	–	1	1	2	2	3		**	1	1									1	1													
HUT/PVT/TOT	44	43	45	44	44		50	60	57	41	45		29	30	25	25	24	26	26	27	33	30	38	34	29	29	30	30	31	31	26	21	22	23	24
col #	1	2	3	4	5	6	59	60	61	62	8	9	11	12	13	14	15	16	17	18	19	20	21	22	23	24	25	26	27	28	30	31	32	33	34	35

* SAMPLE BELOW MINIMUM FOR WEEKLY REPORTING
** SHARE/HUT TRENDS NOT AVAILABLE
– DID NOT ACHIEVE A REPORTABLE WEEKLY RATING
‡ TECHNICAL DIFFICULTY
< M-F PROGRAM AIRED LESS THAN FIVE DAYS
+ COMBINED PARENT/SATELLITE
▲ SEE TABLE ON PAGE v

FIGURE 17.4 *Arbitron TV Market Report* 1989 (*Source:* Copyright © 1989 The Arbitron Company. Reprinted by permission.)

Metro Audience Trends*
PERSONS 12+

	MONDAY-FRIDAY 7PM-MID					WEEKEND 6AM-MID				
	FALL 87	WINTER 88	SPRING 88	SUMMER 88	FALL 88	FALL 87	WINTER 88	SPRING 88	SUMMER 88	FALL 88
WEZK										
SHARE	8.2	14.9	11.1	7.6	8.7	8.5	11.8	9.1	8.1	8.2
AQH(00)	38	53	44	33	33	61	78	62	55	56
CUME RTG	6.4	7.6	6.2	4.9	6.1	12.5	13.0	11.4	10.9	11.7
WGAP										
SHARE	1.7	.8	.5	.7	2.1	1.8	1.4	2.6	1.0	2.8
AQH(00)	8	3	2	3	8	13	9	18	7	19
CUME RTG	1.2	.8	.7	1.1	1.2	2.9	2.8	2.8	3.1	2.9
WIMZ										
SHARE	.4	.3	.8	.2		.8	.2	.7	.1	.1
AQH(00)	2	1	3	1		6	1	5	1	1
CUME RTG	.4	.4	.7	.3	.1	1.4	.7	.7	.5	.2
WIMZ-FM										
SHARE	17.3	12.4	16.3	14.7	17.6	10.6	9.5	15.2	12.2	12.8
AQH(00)	80	44	65	64	67	76	63	104	83	87
CUME RTG	11.4	9.8	10.5	10.3	11.3	14.6	13.3	18.1	16.2	17.3
WIVK										
SHARE					2.9	5.3	3.5	4.2	3.8	4.3
AQH(00)					11	38	23	29	26	29
CUME RTG					2.0	5.2	3.2	4.5	4.2	5.2
WIVK-FM										
SHARE	30.3	20.3	27.9	27.0	22.8	29.9	28.8	29.8	34.2	29.7
AQH(00)	140	72	111	117	87	214	191	204	233	202
CUME RTG	17.6	14.6	16.4	20.1	15.9	32.5	29.8	29.4	30.3	34.8
+WKGN										
SHARE	1.5	1.7	.8	1.8	.8	1.0	2.0	1.0	1.2	.9
AQH(00)	7	6	3	8	3	7	13	7	8	6
CUME RTG	1.5	1.2	1.3	.6	.5	1.6	2.1	1.5	1.2	1.4
WKNF										
SHARE	1.1	.8	2.0	.7	1.0	.7	.8	1.0	1.2	1.3
AQH(00)	5	3	8	3	4	5	5	7	8	9
CUME RTG	.8	.7	1.3	1.1	1.7	2.1	1.4	1.5	2.4	2.6
WMYU										
SHARE	10.4	9.0	7.3	9.9	14.7	13.3	10.9	8.5	10.7	12.8
AQH(00)	48	32	29	43	56	95	72	58	73	87
CUME RTG	11.1	9.1	8.2	10.4	10.5	19.4	16.6	13.0	17.3	21.6
+WNOX										
SHARE	.6		**	**	.5	.1	.3	**	**	
AQH(00)	3		**	**	2	1	2	**	**	
CUME RTG	.6	.3	**	**	.8	.5	.7	**	**	.8
WOKI										
SHARE	8.9	20.8	12.1	15.9	14.7	7.1	11.2	9.2	10.9	10.9
AQH(00)	41	74	48	69	56	51	74	63	74	74
CUME RTG	6.7	9.2	8.2	8.0	10.3	12.2	13.5	12.7	11.3	16.1
+WQBB										
SHARE			.5			.8	.9	1.3	.7	2.3
AQH(00)			2			6	6	9	5	16
CUME RTG			.3	.1		.8	1.4	1.0	1.0	1.4
WRJZ										
SHARE	1.5	2.5	1.0	2.1	.3	1.5	1.7	1.3	.6	.1
AQH(00)	7	9	4	9	1	11	11	9	4	1
CUME RTG	1.5	1.2	1.4	2.0	1.2	2.8	2.1	2.8	2.6	1.5
WSEV										
SHARE				**		1.1	1.4	1.5	**	1.0
AQH(00)				**		8	9	10	**	7
CUME RTG				**		2.1	2.2	.8	**	1.3
TOTALS										
AQH RTG	9.1	7.0	7.8	8.6	7.5	14.1	13.1	13.5	13.4	13.4
AQH(00)	462	355	398	434	381	715	663	685	681	681
CUME RTG	53.5	49.5	52.3	51.3	52.8	82.9	81.1	80.7	77.0	84.1

Footnote Symbols: ** Station(s) not reported this survey.   + Station(s) reported with different call letters in prior surveys - see Page 5B.

ARBITRON RATINGS
8

KNOXVILLE   **FALL 1988**

*See page iv Restrictions On Use Of Report for restrictions on the use of Trends data.

FIGURE 17.5 Sample Arbitron Radio Report Page (*Source:* Copyright © 1988 The Arbitron Company. Reprinted by permission.)

OTHER APPROACHES
TO BROADCAST RESEARCH

Audience rating studies represent a quantitative approach to describing broadcast audiences. Although these studies are valuable in making programming and advertising decisions, they cannot explain *why* viewers and listeners prefer and tune-in to certain programs for performers, or why they avoid others. Ideally, therefore, ratings should be supplemented with additional types of research that can provide insight into viewing and listening motivations.

Many broadcasters conduct or commission special research intended to get at reasons why the audience prefers certain air personalities, certain types of music, and certain programs over others. *Focus group research* is particularly useful, because well-selected participants can provide great insight into the choices listeners and viewers make. Some radio stations use *call-out* research via the telephone to determine trends in music preferences and to seek understanding of the underlying reasons for the audience behavior revealed by the ratings.

Another approach toward understanding audiences is psychographic research. Whereas traditional research studies reveal the size and demographic composition of audiences, the goal of psychographic research is to determine the presence of social and cultural variations within audience segments. In short, *psychographic research* seeks to learn about the life-styles of the audience and to match life-styles to both product preferences and listening and viewing choices. A leading source of psychographic information is the *Simmons Target Group Index*, published by Simmons Market Research Bureau, of New York.

SUMMARY

Millions of dollars are spent each year to produce audience research that quantifies the listening and viewing activities of the American public. Following accepted statistical and survey procedures, these audience measurement studies, despite some limitations, serve as a basis for media decision-making.

Efforts are made constantly to improve the methods for gathering data on broadcast audiences. Even though audience research is less than a perfect science, the wide acceptance of the ratings confirms that this system is the most effective and efficient means devised thus far for learning the details of viewing and listening behavior. Hence, station and program ratings play a very prominent role in the management of the electronic media.

Audience research is a principal tool for decision-making in broadcast programming and advertising. Although the ratings can only describe audience behavior at a specified time, they remain the primary means for predictive analysis of audience trends. Despite their inherent limitations, audience measurement provides useful insight into the public's use of the broadcast media.

DISCUSSION QUESTIONS AND EXERCISES

1. Which audience research method provides the most accurate information on listening/viewing patterns? Explain your choice in terms of strengths and weaknesses. How might this method be improved?

2. The confidence level in survey research and the cost of research increase with the size of the sample drawn from the survey population. Total accuracy, if attainable, would require a complete census of the population. Typical surveys have confidence intervals of plus-or-minus 1 to 4 percent. How accurate does the measurement of a broadcast audience need to be for the research purpose?

3. Discuss how the development of cable television has complicated the task of measuring the TV audience.

4. Compare and contrast the research needs of cable networks and broadcast TV networks. Should the confidence interval for cable networks be larger, smaller, or the same as that for broadcast television? Why?

5. Arbitron and Nielsen overlap in some of their ratings functions, resulting in duplication of effort. Is this wasteful of media resources, or is it desirable to have more than one rating service? Explain your reasoning.

6. What new trends do you foresee in audience measurement?

NOTE

1. The EMRC is headquartered at 420 Lexington Avenue, New York, NY 10017.

SOURCES AND SUGGESTED READINGS

A Guide to Understanding and Using Radio Audience Estimates. New York: Arbitron. Published annually.

A Guide to Understanding and Using TV Audience Estimates. New York: Arbitron. Published annually.

Beville, H. M., Jr. 1985. *Audience Ratings: Radio, Television, and Cable.* Hillsdale, N.J.: Lawrence Erlbaum.

Beyond the Ratings. New York: Arbitron. Published monthly.

Duncan, J. H., Jr. *American Radio.* Indianapolis: Duncan's American Radio. Published semi-annually.

Everything You've Always Wanted to Know about TV Ratings. New York: Nielsen Media Research.

Fletcher, J. E., ed. 1981. *Handbook of Radio and TV Broadcasting: Research Procedures in Audience, Program, and Revenues.* New York: Van Nostrand Reinhold.

Hall, R. W. 1991. *Media Math.* Lincolnwood, Ill.: NTC Business Books.

Nielsen Report on Television. New York: Nielsen Media Research. Published annually.

Zeigler, S. K., and H. Howard. 1991. *Broadcast Advertising.* 3rd ed. Ames: Iowa State University Press.

18

Public Relations Research

SUSAN LUCARELLI

University of Tennessee, Knoxville

□
OBJECTIVES

After studying this chapter, you should be able to:

1. Use the PROBE formula to define a public relations problem or analyze a public relations opportunity.

2. Incorporate research into each phase of the PROBE process.

3. Identify and describe some award-winning contemporary public relations campaigns.

4. Recognize the range of public relations activities that are necessary to service clients.

5. Describe the common methods of research in public relations.

INTRODUCTION

The use of research to guide public relations programs has grown during the past decade, and that trend is expected to continue. James Grunig, one of the most prominent researchers in the public relations field, predicts that public relations "will be based more on research and become more of a managerial discipline than a technical one" (*PR Reporter*, April 8, 1991).

In an effort to assess the extent to which research is incorporated into the public relations process, researcher Walter K. Lindenmann, of Ketchum Public Relations, conducted a nationwide survey of practitioners at the nation's largest corporations, at nonprofit organizations, at counseling firms, and in academia (Lindenmann, 1990, 3–16). The 53-item, self-administered mail questionnaire drew a 27-percent response rate in 1988. Among the findings was that research was assuming increasing importance among public relations professionals; more than half of the respondents were allocating research funds in their budget. The four most often cited research techniques were literature searches and information retrieval projects; publicity tracking or media monitoring; surveys by mail or telephone; and focus groups (see Table 18.1).

Furthermore, large public relations firms such as Ketchum Public Relations are encouraging the acquisition of research skills by graduate students. For example, the "SMART" grant, Scientific Management and Research Techniques, is coordinated by the Institute for Public Relations Research and Education and is underwritten by Ketchum.

A comparison of evaluation methods used to analyze the results of a campaign effort indicated that practitioners were becoming "more oriented toward or-

TABLE 18.1 Research Techniques Respondents Claimed They Used Most Frequently

	Total (253)	Corporate Execs (148)	Association Execs (14)	Nonprofit Execs (25)	Counselors (37)	Academicians (18)
Literature searches/information retrieval	33.6%	28.4%	28.6%	8.0%	64.9%	55.6%
Publicity tracking	29.6	25.7	57.1	40.0	35.1	11.1
Telephone/mail surveys with simple cross-tabs	26.9	21.6	28.6	20.0	51.4	38.9
Focus groups	20.2	22.3	7.1	26.0	27.0	5.6
PR/communications audits	16.2	9.5	—	12.0	56.8	11.1
Secondary analysis studies	16.2	10.1	7.1	12.0	35.1	33.3
Consumer inquiry analysis	15.0	18.9	7.1	20.0	5.4	5.6
Depth interviews with opinion leaders	13.8	9.5	7.1	12.0	35.1	16.7
Readership/readability study	12.3	10.8	14.3	12.0	13.5	22.2
Pre and post tests (before-and-after polls)	8.3	8.8	21.4	—	5.4	16.7
Sophisticated techniques (conjoint/factor analysis)	7.1	7.4	7.1	—	2.7	27.8
Psychographic analysis	6.3	8.1	—	—	8.1	5.6
Mall intercept/shopping center studies	5.9	6.8	7.1	4.0	5.4	5.6
Content analysis studies	4.7	2.7	—	4.0	10.8	16.7
Experimental Designs	4.3	4.1	—	8.0	5.4	5.6
Unobtrusive measures (role playing, observation, participation)	2.0	2.0	—	—	—	11.1
Model building	1.6	1.4	—	—	2.7	5.6

SOURCE Lindermann, Walter K. 1990. Research, Evaluation and Measurement: A National Perspective. *Public Relations Review* 16(2): 10.

ganizational goal achievement" (Bissland, 1990, 25–35). As the 1990s began, practitioners were recognizing the importance of evaluation methods that examined the goal of the public relations program rather than only the amount of media coverage or its effects on targeted audiences (see Table 18.2).

Another trend in public relations research is the use of technology that will make "real-time decision-making" possible. The time delay between data collection and data analysis will decrease with the diffusion of technology that keeps relevant information about an individual or household in a single database. "In packaged goods the revolution is driven by scanner technology. In media, by people meters, especially passive people meters. In services, by database marketing systems" (*PR Reporter*, 1992).

Before launching into the specific research methods used in public relations programs it is important to understand current thought on the practice of Public Relations research. The Public Relations Society of America formally adopted the following definition in 1988: "Public relations helps an organization and its publics adapt mutually to each other" (*PRSA Foundation Monograph Series*, 1991, 2. Another

TABLE 18.2 Evaluation Methods Preferred by Silver Anvil Winners: 1980–1981 and 1988–1989 Compared

Methods	1980–1981	1988–1989	Change, Significance
Output Measures			
Messages produced	25.0	15.3	–9.7 n.s.
Contacts by media	8.3	4.2	–4.1 n.s.
Media coverage	70.0	79.2	9.2 n.s.
Inferred audiences	31.7	36.1	4.4 n.s.
Financial measures	10.0	15.3	5.3 n.s.
Measures of Intermediate Effects			
Actual audiences	28.3	41.7	13.4 n.s.
Audience feedback	31.7	31.9	0.2 n.s.
Praise	43.3	34.7	–8.6 n.s.
Continuation	20.0	23.6	3.6 n.s.
Behavioral science measures	25.0	44.4	19.4*
Measures of Organizational Goal Achievement			
Inferred Achievement	53.3	87.5	34.2***
Substantiated Achievement	13.3	43.3	29.8***
Probability of Chance, According to Chi-Square			

*p < .05
***p < .001
N.S. Not Significant

Percentages of all winners for the respective columns: 1980–1981 (60 winners) and 1988–1989 (72 winners)
SOURCE Lindermann, Walter K. 1990. Research Evaluation and Measurement: A National Perspective. *Public Relations Review* 16(2): 32.

widely accepted definition is that by Grunig: Public relations is "the management of communication between an organization and its publics" (Grunig and Hunt, 1984). Both James and Larissa Grunig, editors of the *Journal of Public Relations Research*, and others have been instrumental in arguing that public relations is a management function and that public relations practitioners belong near by top of an organization's decision making structure. Managing communication requires a variety of skills, which the Public Relations Society of America outlined in 1982 (PRSA Foundation, 1991, 5):

- Anticipating, analyzing and interpreting public opinion, attitudes, and issues that might impact, for good or ill, the operations and plans of the organization.
- Counseling management at all levels in the organization with regard to policy decisions, courses of action, and communication, taking into account their public ramifications and the organization's social or citizenship responsibilities.
- Researching, conducting, and evaluating, on a continuing basis, programs of action and communication to achieve the informed public understanding necessary to the success of an organization's aims.
- Planning and implementing the organization's efforts to influence or change public policy.
- Setting objectives, planning, budgeting, recruiting, and training staff, developing facilities, in short, *managing* the resources needed to perform all of the above. [Emphasis in the original]

The research skills necessary for managing communication, therefore, encompass a broad range of activities. Although less formal research skills will suffice for activities such as sending out press releases or organizing a press conference, formal research abilities are increasingly in demand for planning and executing public relations programs and campaigns.

There are several models for approaching a public relations problem or opportunity, and each uses research techniques early in the planning process. One of the first models was offered by John Marston in 1979. Marston's RACE formula—research, action, communication, evaluation—demonstrates the premiere place research holds in public relations planning and encourages formal research in the evaluation phase as well (Marston, 1984, 104). The popular formula offered by Jerry Hendrix—research, objectives, programming, evaluation—also stresses initial research activities and the use of evaluation measures at the end of the campaign. Hendrix emphasizes the need for research in three areas initially: the client, the public relations opportunity or problem, and the target audience (Hendrix, 1992, 64–80).

These two formulas share a focus on initial research and postevaluation. Making research a separate step relegates research to a certain point in time and discourages continuous monitoring of a program; yet both formal and informal research could be used to monitor a public relations program. Broom and Dozier (1990) have refined the basic ideas of the Marston and Hendrix formulas to incorporate research at crucial junctures throughout a public relations program—planning, monitoring, and evaluating. It seems appropriate to offer a formula that incorporates research as a continuous activity, not as one step of many or at junctures. Research, assessment, and application of research results are important *throughout* the public relations process. Research is not just a step in the process—*it is the process.*

PROBE FORMULA

The PROBE formula, offered as an alternative, builds research into *each phase* of public relations planning, programming, execution, and evaluation. It includes what other formulas do not: *a re-evaluation* step that allows an organization to adjust its goals and responsibilities in light of new problems and new opportunities. The five steps of the PROBE formula are:

Probe Formula Step	**Appropriate Research**
1. Problem definition/opportunity analysis	a. Communication audit using content analysis and survey research to improve external or internal communication. b. Focus groups c. Attitudinal or awareness surveys. d. Network analysis. e. Psychographic and demographic analysis of active, aware, or latent public. f. Situation analysis of public. g. Environmental monitoring studies or issue-tracking project.
2. Re-evaluate organizational goals/responsibilities	a. Social audit to measure social performance. b. Issues management. c. In-depth interviews with managerial staff. d. Examine mission statement; content analysis sample of annual reports during previous decade. e. Update legislative, regulatory impact statements. f. Determine public perception of organization's responsibilities via focus groups then surveys.
3. Operationalize objectives	a. Map communication flow from controlled media; map communication flow from uncontrolled media. b. Determine cost efficiency of each medium vehicle.

c. Determine message content, format, vehicle.
d. Copy-test messages, slogans, jingles.
e. Develop media lists, including trade journals.
f. Allocate resources, budget, staff.

4. Build relationships
    a. Match communication source with audience target.

5. Evaluate relationships
    a. Measure output or products.
    b. Measure outcomes or results.

The PROBE formula starts with a *problem definition* or *opportunity analysis*. A certain set of research activities, commonly done at this point, are described in the list. Other research activities are possible, but these are some of the more common ones. Next there is the re-evaluation phase, followed by research that allows objectives to be put into action. Building relationships and evaluating the building effort are the fourth and fifth steps. As you can see from the list, research activities are appropriate at each phase of the public relations process.

All public relations efforts are aimed at building or maintaining relationships with an organization's publics (constituencies). Too often, evaluation centers on counting the number of media references to the organization and calculating reach and frequency, but *that* says Kitty Ward (of K. Ladd Ward and Company, Hingham, Mass.), "should never be considered a substitute for evaluating outcomes." Ward confirms that the most important questions in evaluating *outcomes* as opposed to *outputs,* (outputs are important but not the all of evaluation), is to ask: "Did [the program] tangibly build and strengthen relationships with customers and other constituencies important to the organization's bottom-line success?" (*PR Reporter,* 1991).

In order to illustrate the public relations research process, and the PROBE formula, examples of actual public relations programs and campaigns are described on the following pages. Many of the examples are Silver Anvil public relations campaigns for 1989 and 1990. Silver Anvils are annual awards that recognize outstanding public relations programs; they are meant to "provide instructive models to other professionals" (Bissland, 1990, 20–25). The awards are made by the Public Relations Society of America.

PROBE FORMULA STEP 1: PROBLEM DEFINITION/ OPPORTUNITY ANALYSIS, COMMUNICATION AUDIT, AND THE UMCOM STUDY

The communication audit is designed to evaluate the response to an organization's communication efforts. The audit is helpful in detecting breakdowns in communication, and makes it possible to head off potential problems. In addition, the audit is useful in identifying the strengths of an organization's communication efforts. It can be used to evaluate responses to both external and internal communication strategies.

Both survey research and content analysis were used in an internal communication audit for United Methodist Communications (UMCom) in 1989. UMCom's mission was to help the church tell its story. It had 140 employees nationwide, most of whom worked at UMCom's Nashville headquarters. In addition to distributing thousands of print media annually, UMCom had a public media division that produced a weekly half-hour TV program distributed nationwide (Caudill, 1989).

Research for the UMCom communication audit commenced with an analysis of the organization's internal communication goals and mission statement. The audit analyzed the match between these goals and the attitudes of employees toward the four principal routes of internal communication and the content of the two internal newsletters.

A readership survey was designed to determine whether and how often employees had seen each of the two internal newsletters. It sought information about levels of satisfaction, usefulness, and interest in each newsletter's delivery and content. Several open-ended questions allowed employees to make general comments about and suggest improvements for each newsletter. One series of questions also permitted employees to rate the ability of each newsletter to meet several of the stated goals of the UMCom internal communication program. Another series of questions helped analyze the effectiveness and usefulness of bimonthly meetings with the executive director and of employees' use of a suggestion box. The response rate for the self-administered mail questionnaire was 50.4 percent. (A census of all 123 employees at its Nashville headquarters was attempted.)

To determine whether the stated goals were being incorporated into printed material distributed to employees, an analysis of the actual content of the two internal newsletters was conducted. The general purposes of *content analysis* are to compare variable characteristics, to analyze trends, and to determine the intent of various messages. It is particularly useful in a *communication audit*, for isolating and analyzing significant words, phrases, and symbols and then comparing their use in different printed or visual media.

The content analysis for UMCom involved coding 11 issues of "Keeping You Posted," published between August 1988 and August 1989, and six issues of "UMCommunity" of the same time period. The intercoder reliability was 77 percent. The results of the content analysis were compared with the readership survey results to develop a fuller picture of employees' responses to UMCom's internal communication efforts (see Table 18.3 A–C).

TABLE 18.3A   Use of Personal Pronouns as Distance Indicators (average number of mentions)

	"Keeping You Posted"	"UMCommunity"
Our/We/Us	10.1	18.3
I	2.4	2.7
He/She	6.0	9.7

TABLE 18.3B   Second References—First Name versus Last Name (average number of mentions)

	"Keeping You Posted"	"UMCommunity"
First name	2.0	10
Last name	2.1	0.5

TABLE 18.3C Organizational References (average number of mentions)

	"Keeping You Posted"	"UMCommunity"
UMCom as UMCom	11	11.6
UMCom in third person	1.4	0.6
UMCom with our/your	2.8	2.0
UMCom with family	0	0.8

The categories constructed for the content analysis concentrated on the goals outlined in UMCom's mission statement:

1. Enhance employees' and retirees' sense of importance to the agency and its goals.
2. Keep employees and retireees abreast of the latest information about UMCom projects, products, policies, changes, and events as they affect employees and retirees.
3. Promote caring and sharing to encourage a family atmosphere and trust through UMCom publications.
4. Nurture employees' and retirees' feelings that UMCom is a friendly place that has talented, creative, and caring people who are glad they work at UMCom.

Indicators of employee importance, informational content, the promotion of a family atmosphere, and nurturing of friendly feeling toward UMCom were constructed. For example, the use of personal pronouns such as *our, we, us* were compared with *I, me, he/she*. The use of *he/she* or *I* is psychologically more distant than the use of *our, we,* or *us,* which carry overtones of team spirit and familial bonds. Another indicator of psychological distance was the use of first names versus last names upon second reference to an individual in the newsletters. Using the first name indicates a greater degree of familiarity and closeness than use of the last name. A third indicator was linkage of the UMCom name with *our, your,* and *family*.

A measure of employees' access to the newsletters was constructed by monitoring the number of articles with bylines versus the number of articles written by the editor. In general, the more employees feel that they have access to newsletters, the more they tend to think of the newsletter as theirs.

Pictorial categories were constructed to assess the impact of visuals. The number of different employees and departments mentioned also was monitored

TABLE 18.4 Employees Mentioned versus Nonemployees/Retirees (average number of mentions)

	"Keeping You Posted"	"UMCommunity"
Employees	32.8	74.2
Nonemployees	14.1	10.7
Retirees	3.0	8.7
Affiliation unclear	1.0	4.3

(see Table 18.4). Conventional wisdom holds that the more that people are in photos, and the more that they are mentioned, the more they will read or pay attention to the medium—if only out of self-interest.

Analysis of the manifest content of the two major printed means of internal communication at UMCom, and readers' reactions to them, indicated (a) that considerable effort was being made to meet the objectives of the mission statement and (b) that readers appreciated that effort. Several recommendations were made based on the original research, among them:

1. More consistent and frequent distribution of "UMCommunity."
2. More photographs in both newsletters.
3. More personal stories in both newsletters.
4. More personal involvement in both newsletters.
5. More "Ask the General Secretary" meetings.
6. The Suggestion Box is not needed.

FOCUS GROUPS: NEW PRODUCT LAUNCH

Gemstar Development Corporation

An example of how a problem can become a public relations opportunity, and of how research can make communicating the solution easier, is Gemstar Development Corporation's launch of VCR Plus+ with the help of Rogers and Associates, a Los Angeles public relations firm (New Product Launch of VCR Plus , 1990). The problem was that although 70 million Americans owned videocassette recorders (VCRs), the vast majority did not know how to program them to tape movies and TV shows. Gemstar developed a remote-control instant programming device, VCR Plus+, that uses numerical codes printed in newspapers (*PlusCodes*) to help people program VCRs in one step.

Focus group research during April and May 1990 and secondary research from the Nielsen Home Video Index and industry trade publications identified the following constraints on VCR buying and VCR use, and the potential for a simplified programming device such as the one Gemstar manufactured:

Obstacles

- Taping programs on a VCR was a major source of consumer frustration.
- The majority of VCR owners did not tape TV shows but would do so if the process were simpler.
- A low-cost device that simplified taping would have enormous consumer appeal if the technology were proven and reliable.
- Although there was no current competitive product, several large companies were pursuing alternate programming systems—Gemstar had an opportunity to create and own a new consumer electronics product category.
- Retail sales of VCRs and other video-related products were flat.
- Newspapers were losing subscribers to television; however, consumers would buy a publication for the sole purpose of receiving programming codes. (New Product Launch of VCR Plus+, 1990, 1)

	Wanted* Score (N = 47)
1. High fidelity picture quality.	8.83
2. Feature that lets you bypass the cable box and in one step record different cable shows on more than one channel.	8.65**
3. A VCR that quickly locates a segment on your recorded tape for play-back or editing.	8.34
4. You can program your VCR in seconds to record the T.V. shows you want to record while you watch them or when you are away from home.	8.23
5. Mistake-proof VCR programming that eliminates the chance of your recording the wrong program.	8.19
6. Instant programmer for your VCR to record any T.V. program as easily as dialing a telephone number.	8.15
7. "One-step" procedure for recording any T.V. show you want to watch later.	8.04
8. High fidelity audio quality from your tape recordings.	7.57
9. When you make a mistake in programming your VCR to record a show, you do not need to repeat the entire programming procedure to correct the error.	7.55
10. Clear, sharp "stop action" still pictures.	7.19
11. VCR tape editing feature that removes any blank spaces on your tape recordings.	7.06
12. VCR that tells you how much tape you need to record the T.V. program you have selected to record.	7.06
13. "On-screen display" describes T.V. program recording steps.	7.00

* 1 = Not at all   **Cable box users only
   10 = Extremely

FIGURE 18.1   VCR Plus+ New Product Launch: Benefits/Features Wanted (10 point scale*) (*Source:* Reprinted by permission of Rogers & Associates, Los Angeles, California.)

Three focus groups were conducted in Torrance and Whittier, California, near Los Angeles; and two were conducted in Oakbrook, Illinois, near Chicago. Respondents were selected on the basis of whether they owned a VCR and were responsible for the buying decision. Two focus groups included respondents who had cable box TV service, noncable TV service, and cable (nonbox) service (Focus Groups, i). All three focus groups were used to evaluate Gemstar's new instant programmer. Each session lasted two hours, and a total of 48 people participated.

According to the focus group transcripts, "Most of the spontaneous comments on problems and improvements centered on simplified programming and a way to quickly identify the beginning and the end of a recorded segment on the tape" (p. 5). Some of the actual comments about programming programs were as follows:

Transcript Results

I couldn't get the programming to go on when you are not home and you want something to come on at one o'clock and then turn off at three o'clock. I just couldn't get that for love or money. I kept on trying to set it and program it and doing back to the manual and I just couldn't get it to work.

I just had a hard time recording because of all the instructions on how to hook it up and what buttons to push. I don't even move the furniture because I would have to unplug it. You know it just scares me.

> I was going to say the same thing, that it's complicated. Sometimes you know
> with all the buttons you don't know exactly what you are doing unless you
> had the experience of using it several times (p. 6).

Rating scales were constructed of the benefits or features focus group respondents wanted from their VCRs. Among the highest rated features were high-fidelity picture quality and mistake-proof VCR programming (see Figure 18.1). A separate scale rated the overall evaluation of the respondent's current VCR and the new VCR with instant programmer (see Figure 18.2).

Focus groups also were used to evaluate trade names for the new instant programmer. Seventy-four percent chose VCR Plus+ over other names such as "Showtime," "Zipcoder," "Tracker," and "Wiz" (New Product Launch, 33). Seventy-seven percent of the focus group respondents actually bought or ordered the instant programmer.

ATTITUDE/AWARENESS SURVEYS

Baltimore Archdiocese

Although there is a definite shift toward creating more public realtions opportunities, most practitioners are still problem solvers. For example, to reverse a 20-percent enrollment decline, the Baltimore archdiocese of the Catholic Church hired the Adams Sandlar firm to survey perceptions of the adult public about Catholic education. The firm also conducted an attitudinal survey of administrators, teachers, parents, and clergy; analyzed the content of press coverage about Catholic education; analyzed enrollment statistics, demographics, and trends; and interviewed administrators and principals to get their point of view on the problem (*PR Reporter*, 1991). The archdiocese and the Sandlar firm won the Public Relations Society of America 1991 Silver Anvil Award for marketing communications by a nonprofit organization.

Geneva Steel

Survey research was the backbone of another Silver Anvil award-winning campaign. Geneva Steel was the largest integrated steel mill west of the Mississippi River. It had been purchased by a group of private investors from U.S. Steel in 1987 after sitting idle for most of 1986. Environmentalists in Orem, Utah, recently gained widespread media attention by attacking Geneva Steel's air-pollution control record. State air-quality officials also were critical (Geneva Steel $2 Bill Campaign, 1989). The company contended that it was in compliance with "every health-based air emission standard" at the time of these attacks.

During the problem definition step, Geneva Steel commissioned simple random-sample telephone surveys from Dan Jones and Associates of Salt Lake City in February and April 1989. The surveys showed that clean air advocates were

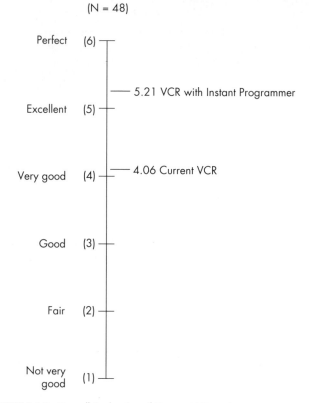

OVERALL EVALUATION OF CURRENT VCR
AND NEW VCR WITH INSTANT PROGRAMMER

(N = 48)

FIGURE 18.2 Overall Evaluation of Current VCR and New VCR with Instant Programmer (*Source:* Reprinted by permission of Rogers & Associates, Los Angeles, California.)

having a negative impact on Geneva Steel. In February 1989, 80 percent of respondents said they wanted to see Geneva Steel remain open, but by April 71 percent expressed that opinion. According to survey research in April, 71 percent of Utah County residents said that Geneva Steel was somewhat important or very important to the *local* economy, and 71 percent said that it was somewhat important or very important to the *state* economy.

The research showed a statistical correlation between understanding Geneva Steel's economic impact and having a favorable attitude toward the company. Therefore, the corporate communications department set a goal of improving public attitudes toward the company by demonstrating Geneva's Steel's importance to the economy. Employees were given part of their profit-sharing checks that year in $2 bills; and merchants were encouraged to participate in the "Two-Buck Bonanza" by offering $2-bill specials, discounts, and coupons. By pumping thousands of $2 bills into the local economy, Geneva Steel reminded employees and merchants of its importance nearly every time money changed hands.

A follow-up survey was conducted in December 1989 as part of the evaluation process. Ninety percent of those surveyed said that Geneva Steel was somewhat important or very important to the local economy, and 77 percent said it was somewhat important or very important to the state economy. Seventy-five percent said they thought Geneva Steel should remain open.

Other measures of effectiveness included use of a clipping service to track three days of news coverage from newspapers, radio, and television, and focus group research. In addition to using survey findings to plan the campaign objective, the corporate communications staff used survey findings to determine which of its executives made favorable or unfavorable impressions on respondents from the random sample. The survey also asked respondents to rate the credibility of organizations making statements about Geneva Steel. Surprisingly, 78 percent of the respondents thought that the current management of Geneva Steel was somewhat credible or very credible, but 89 percent thought that state air-quality officials made credible statements about Geneva, too (see Figure 18.3).

In summary, formal survey research was used to define the public relations problem; suggest an attitude change strategy consistent with solving the problem; find credible communicators; and evaluate the success of the program. This was accomplished by assessing attitude change, which shifted more favorably toward the company in terms of (a) perceptions about its importance to the local and state economy and (b) attitudes toward having the company stay open.

PSYCHOGRAPHIC ANALYSIS

Ordway Music Theatre

The grand opening of the Ordway Music Theatre in Saint Paul, Minnesota, in 1985 was guided by marketing research using the values, attitudes, and life-styles (VALS) typology developed by SRI International. Padilla and Speer, of Minneapolis helped Ordway Theatre planners target potential theater goers by analyzing (a) what types of acts each group ("Achievers," "Societally Conscious," "Experientials," and "Integrateds") preferred, (b) what obstacles existed to attending the theater, and (c) in what proportion each VALS type attended theater acts. Also analyzed were the media sources each type used to find out about theatre news (Hendrix, 1992, 65) Research indicated that the primary target group should be "Achievers," and that the message to this group should be "the experience of going to the theater" (see Figure 18.4, page 363).

SITUATION ANALYSIS

James Grunig developed a situational theory of publics that uses three independent variables—problem recognition, constraint recognition, and level of involvement—to explain how groups of people coalesce around an issue, such as

If the following organizations were to make statements about Geneva Steel, how credible (believable) would you find them:

(Rotate)	Very Credible	Somewhat Credible	Not too Credible	Not Credible at all	Don't Know	Mean
74) Current management of Geneva:	20%	58%	14%	4%	5%	2.01
75) Coalition to save Geneva:	13%	54%	20%	3%	10%	2.14
76) Utah Valley Citizens for clean air:	21%	53%	17%	4%	6%	2.03
77) League of Women Voters:	16%	56%	12%	3%	14%	2.03
78) Provo/Orem Chamber of Commerce:	28%	52%	10%	2%	8%	1.84
79) University Professors:	35%	44%	10%	4%	7%	1.62
89) Geneva Wives Association:	10%	49%	24%	4%	13%	2.26
81) State Air Quality Officials:	45%	44%	5%	2%	4%	1.62
82) US Steel Executives:	17%	55%	16%	4%	8%	2.08

NOW, I WOULD LIKE TO READ YOU A BRIEF LIST OF NAMES AND HAVE YOU TELL ME, FOR EACH ONE, FIRST IF YOU HAVE HEARD OF THE PERSON; THEN, IF SO, WHETHER YOU HAVE A FAVORABLE OR UNFAVORABLE IMPRESSION OF THAT PERSON: (INTERVIEWERS: <u>ROTATE ALL NAMES</u>)

Rotate	Very Favorable	Somewhat Favorable	Somewhat Unfavorable	Very Unfavorable	Heard of, No Opinion	Never Heard of	DK	Mean
83) Joe Cannon	10%	28%	10%	4%	18%	29%	0%	2.16
84) Chase Peterson	16%	18%	2%	1%	13%	50%	0%	1.67
85) Jeffrey Holland	51%	19%	1%	0%	7%	20%	1%	1.30
86) Chris Cannon	6%	25%	7%	2%	16%	43%	1%	2.13
87) Steve Densley	5%	16%	1%	1%	11%	65%	1%	1.95
88) Joe Jenkins	12%	32%	3%	4%	13%	35%	1%	1.97
89) Jim Ferguson	15%	33%	2%	2%	16%	31%	1%	1.81
90) Brent Morris	7%	16%	3%	6%	13%	54%	1%	2.27

91) Would you rather have the Geneva Steel plant remain open or should it be closed?

Open 80%
Closed 12%
Don't know 2%
Depends (VOL) 5%

FIGURE 18.3 Geneva Steel $2 Bill Campaign (*Source:* Reprinted by permission of Geneva Steel Corporation, Provo, Utah.)

pollution, hiring practices, or plant closings (Grunig and Hunt, 1984, 104). Application of the theory allows publics to be classified as active, aware, latent, or non-existent.

Generally speaking an *active public* is a group of people who recognize that a problem exists, and are willing to discuss the issue and organize to do something about it. An *aware public* recognizes that a problem exists but may not be ready to

Marketing Ordway Music Theatre Using SRI International's VALS Typologies

Memorandum

TO: OMT Operations Staff
FROM: Jane Cooper
RE: Sneaking up on marketing acts booked for opening season
DATE: August 26, 1984

The Initial Question: how best to spread acts across 4 columns?

#1	Sub-question:	What types of acts do 4 VALS typologies prefer?
#2	Sub-question:	In what proportion do VALS types attend any acts?
#3	Sub-question:	What OMT-booked acts are preferred by each VALS type?
#4	Sub-question:	Can we spread achiever-preferred acts (etc.) across the 4 columns evenly so each VALS type has plenty to select from?
#5	Sub-question:	What media placements are implied by the categorizing of booked acts according to VALS type?
#6	Sub-question:	What advertising costs must be incurred for each act and for the overall season promotion?

#1 What types of acts do 4 VALS typologies prefer?

Achievers	Societally Conscious	Experientials	Integrateds
Generally popular	classics	popular	popular
modern contemporary	modern contemporary	modern contemporary	classics
classics	popular	classics	modern contemporary

FIGURE 18.4   Using VALS to Help Identify Publics (*Source:* Hendrix, Jerry A. 1992. *Public Relations Cases.* 2nd ed. Belmont, Calif.: Wadsworth.)

discuss it or get involved. Whether or not the aware public becomes active depends on its level of involvement and recognition of constraints to being involved. A *latent public* faces a problem created by an organization but does not see it as a problem. An example might be a chemical manufacturer that has been storing hazardous waste on-site while the surrounding community is unaware that the waste has contaminated its groundwater. A *nonpublic* neither has consequences on an organization nor is subject to organization consequences (Grunig and Hunt, 1984, 145).

LEARN BY DOING

Take each company or organization discussed in this chapter; formulate a list of publics according to the Grunig typology on page 361; and classify publics for each company or organization. Discuss what communication strategies might be appropriate for transforming a latent public to an aware public, and from an aware public to an active public.

PROBE FORMULA STEP 2:
RE-EVALUATE ORGANIZATIONAL
GOALS AND RESPONSIBILITIES

National Association of Secondary School Principals

A decade of survey and secondary research showed the National Association of Secondary School Principals (NASSP) that American high school principals were not doing a good job of communicating with parents and other community members (Education Hotline, 1989). Many principals were not perceived as leaders, and the principals themselves indicated that they disliked contact with parents.

The NASSP decided to use a two-way communication approach to bring principals into contact with people who had serious questions about the state of American education. NASSP and the nationwide newspaper *USA Today* combined resources to set up a telephone hotline on education during the 1989 and 1990 NASSP national conventions. Principals and assistant principals from across the United States answered calls from more than 1,500 people during the 1989 convention alone.

The NASSP public relations staff recruited 120 principals and their assistants and equipped them with background materials prepared after a LEXIS (electronic data bases) search of the character and coverage of *USA Today* hotlines. The NASSP staff also reviewed three major newspapers to determine what education issues were current, and they interviewed *USA Today* staff members in order to work out the details of the education hotline. Formal evaluation of the education hotline was made through a survey of participants and tabulation of press clippings.

Organizations can better re-evaluate their goals and responsibilities if they anticipate social, political, and economic issues that will have an impact on them. This is why issues management has become one of the growth areas for public relations people. *Issues management* "is a management process with goals to help preserve markets, reduce risk, create opportunities and manage image as an organizational asset" (*PR Reporter*, 1992). It requires the ability to use the survey results, content analyses of media, and in-depth interviewing of business and opinion leaders to anticipate and assess the impact of issues on organizations. Of at least 150 different kinds of forecasting techniques, only nine are commonly used (Newsom, Scott, and Turk, 1989). These include computer modeling of likely trends and written scenarios of likely outcomes for an organization.

Examine and Update: Archive Corporation

Past research reports, financial documents, and annual reports were valuable sources of information for a new investor relations program for Archive Corporation, a manufacturer and supplier of computer products useful for data storage and backup.

Robert E. Maples, vice president of Hill and Knowlton, of Newport Beach, Calif., helped Archive analyze its strengths and weaknesses to position it better with target audiences. Target audiences were identified by developing a computerized database of analysts and media that included 1,800 people. The first step in the internal communication audit was to review annual reports and documents prepared for the Securities and Exchange Commission; annual and quarterly reports for itself and its competitors; press releases; brochures; and advertising. Analysis of their contents indicated that "Archive was performing above average financially, but was having trouble distinguishing itself in the financial community" (Archive Investor Relations, 1989, 9).

In 1988, a communication survey of the financial community was conducted. Participants were seven security analysts, seven institutional analysts, and three portfolio managers from 15 organizations. Designed to elicit perceptions of Archive as an investment, and its strengths and weaknesses, the main survey contained 15 open-ended questions. The results showed that there were "concerns over management's capabilities to control its growth both internally and externally" and "doubts about the Company's long-term strategy" (Archive Investor Relations, 1989, 11). The identified strengths and weaknesses of the company were:

Strengths

- Leadership in technology of tape drives
- Leadership in supplying tape drives to workstations and PC environments
- Good profitability relative to industry
- Reputation for quality
- Satisfied, quality customer base
- Sound balance sheet

Weaknesses

- History of negative surprises
- Exposure to PS/2 tape machines
- Participation in an industry that is little understood, or misunderstood

Because research showed that Archive lacked recognition in the financial community, an objective was to depict Archive as a "sleeper" for alert investors. Other objectives included building awareness of Archive as a good investment.

PROBE FORMULA STEP 3: OPERATIONALIZE OBJECTIVES

Sybron Chemicals

A series of chemical spills, gaseous emissions, and a plant fire that seriously injured two workers at Sybron Chemicals in New Jersey spurred the hiring of a public affairs and communication firm to take charge of a badly shaken community in the latter half of 1988 (Sybron Chemicals, 1989).

The public affairs firm of Holt, Ross and Yulish was commissioned to do a door-to-door survey to assess the extent of Sybron Chemical's loss of trust and credibility, and to establish a line of communication. The company was considering a telephone hotline, an alert system, and a neighborhood advisory council; therefore, it used the survey process to gather feedback about the desirability of such initiatives and to offer its Prompt Inquiry and Notification System (PINS), which would become operational in five months.

A census of all homes within 1.5 miles of the plant was sought in 1988. Postcards with interview times were sent out and several attempts were made to interview all households. As a result, 45 percent of the households granted a 45-minute, face-to-face interview.

Eighty-seven percent of interview respondents wanted to be notified when there was a problem at the plant, such as an accidental emission. By 1989, fifty-nine percent of the respondents wanted to be notified of "serious accidents" only; but a significant other group, 40 percent, wanted to know "about any incidents that release 'significant' odors even though 'they pose no health or safety threat'" (Sybron Chemicals, 1989, 14). Sybron Chemicals responded by operationalizing a key community relations objective: "To assure or reassure the neighbors around our plant that we do care about the effect that we have on them" (Sybron Chemicals, 1989, 7).

Because Sybron Chemicals ranked households within 1.5 miles of its plant as a priority public, and because research showed that those residents were fearful of not knowing what was happening at the plant, a logical objective was to establish a permanent two-way communication channel. Research showed that messages could be channeled most efficiently and in a controlled manner from plant to community via telephone lines enhanced with communication software.

The operationalization came in the form of PINS, a computerized, two-way hotline that permitted the plant to dial its 300 subscribers electronically and notify them about conditions at the plant. It also was made available 24 hours a day for subscribers and nonsubscribers to call and hear a recording about the status of the plant. Messages could be left if questions remained unanswered.

Beef Industry Council

Another example of *operationalizing objectives* to tailor messages to targeted publics involved the Beef Industry Council. Focus groups were used to find the "hot buttons" for messages pitched to ethnic groups and to the health conscious (Beef Industry Council, 1990). Simmons Market Research Bureau data indicated that the appropriate priority publics for the Beef Industry Council were restaurant and hotel dining establishments. A random telephone survey indicated that only 23 percent of the priority public restaurateurs said that their new menu introductions included beef; many were shifting to chicken and fish because these were perceived to be healthier. These and other survey findings led to the objective "to maintain beef's dominance in the foodservice marketplace by increasing operator awareness that beef is suited to new, contemporary menu items." The single key message was that "beef is the leading ingredient for healthful menu creativity because it adapts to contemporary eating styles."

USE OF A MEDIA AUDIT: PITCHING THE RIGHT ANGLE

Sylvan Learning Centers

A media audit conducted for Sylvan Learning Centers found little recognition or awareness of the centers as America's largest supplemental education services company. The audit indicated that an appropriate strategy would be to target editors and reporters likely to be interested in education issues, build a media list, and develop newsworthy angles to pitch stories. For example, with the help of Ketchum Public Relations, Sylvan Learning Centers established a news hook by writing and producing two pamphlets, "The Guide to Good Studying" and "How to Talk to Your School Counselor" and placed write-in offers for them in *USA Today* and other newspapers around the country (Teaching America about Supplemental Education, 1990).

Ketchum Public Relations also obtained personal media briefings with education and parenting editors at *Parents Magazine, Family Circle, Time, Newsweek, Ladies' Home Journal, Working Mother, USA Today, Education Week,* CNN, ABC, CBS, and NBC. In addition, it placed a feature article, "Warning Signs: Could Your Child Be a Dropout," in the Associated Press Annual Back-To-School Package, which opened the way for the article to be published in more than 250 newspapers (Teaching America, 1990, 2).

PROBE FORMULA STEP 4: BUILD RELATIONSHIPS

Creating a Coalition: Trout Unlimited

[handwritten annotation: advocacy group]

An opposition group called Trout Unlimited was successful in reversing favorable public opinion toward the proposed Two Forks Dam near Denver, Colorado. The group claimed that the dam would "flood 30 miles of prime wild trout habitat on a river categorized by the U.S. Fish and Wildlife Service as 'unique, irreplaceable and of national significance'" (Why Two Forks? 1989).

Trout Unlimited secured the unpaid services of Russell, Karsh and Hagan of Englewood, Colorado, and used polling data being provided to the *Denver Post* and "Channel 4 News" to establish baseline and tracking data to "refine and hammer on target themes" (Why Two Forks? 1989, 3). The polling data included 600 telephone interviews with registered voters. (A random sample of 600 has an error margin of plus or minus 4 percentage points.) The data showed that 50 percent of responsents favored building Two Forks, and 31 percent were opposed.

Trout Unlimited and its public relations firm began primary research shortly thereafter in order to (a) identify groups and individuals with a stake in the dam project; (b) identify problems with proponents' statements about the dam project; and (c) develop a network of contacts in policy-making, environmental, and community service groups. Research results were used to "locate possible coalitions against Two Forks" (Why Two Forks? 1989, 4).

Research results also were used to develop a plan for identifying target publics by community, age, sex, ethnicity, and occupation—and by organizational affiliations, including recreation businesses and groups, general businesses, government, and environmental groups (Why Two Forks? 1989, 13, 14). The results helped to identify issues and strategies for each targeted segment. For example, Trout Unlimited created negative publicity by showing targeted demographic groups—Colorado taxpayers, suburban and city homeowners, Denver residents who didn't need the water, fishermen, the elderly, low-income and minority residents, the environmentally concerned—what each would lose if the Two Forks dam were built.

Polling over the course of the three-year opposition program shifted public sentiment from favorable to unfavorable. "By the time the EPA review administrator announced the veto decision [against the dam] in August, 1989, public opinion stood at a solid 42 percent opposed to the dam and 31 percent for it" (Why Two Forks? 1989, 7).

Expanding a Relationship: Wendy's International

Wendy's International found itself in fourth place behind industry leader McDonald's and its two tagalongs in the fast food industry, Burger King and Hardee's, after having held the number-three position for some time. The public relations firm of Hill and Knowlton was retained to re-establish Wendy's as "the quality leader in the fast food industry" (Dave Thomas Platform, 1990).

Confidential tracking studies, a NEXIS/LEXIS (database) search of all available articles on the fast-food industry, and a Gallup Survey called the "Fast Food IQ Test" indicated that Wendy's was perceived as having the highest quality and best-tasting food among its competitors. The content analysis of articles on the industry indicated that a recurring media "hot button" was nutrition.

Hill and Knowlton capitalized on the quality image and the media concern over nutrition in the fast-food industry by surveying registered dieticians at the 1990 American Dietetic Association convention in Denver. The survey was used to build a relationship with an organization that had expertise in nutrition and whose membership viewed Wendy's products as being nutritious. Survey results determined the message content of a news release sent to major media. This news release was part of Hill and Knowlton's objective of generating 250 million impressions in consumer media (600 million impressions actually were created).

Strengthening a Relationship: McDonald's

Although McDonald's was a leader in instituting recycling programs in its restaurants and in buying recycled products, it could not shake the image of contributing to a throwaway society. McDonald's decided to strengthen its relationship with consumers and environmentalists by "closing the recycling loop," according to Holt, Ross and Yulish, a New Jersey public affairs and communication firm that helped the fast-food giant set up the McRecycle USA program (McDonald's McRecycle USA Program, 1990).

The program was designed to stimulate the market for recycled products, and McDonald's committed itself to purchasing $100 million-worth of recycled materials. As part of the program, more than 350 suppliers and manufacturers of recycled products registered with the toll-free McRecycle USA Registry Service. Other businesses were permitted to use the registry to find businesses specializing in recycled products.

Secondary research and in-depth interviewing led McDonald's and its consultant, Holt, Ross and Yulish, to the decision to implement the McRecycle program. Assessment of a 1989 solid waste study by the U.S. Office of Technology Assessment convinced company officials that long-term recycling programs could survive only if there were markets for recycled materials. In-depth interviewing with company officials, solid waste personnel, and environmentalists indicated that McDonald's was being blamed for excessive packaging, destruction of the rain forests, depletion of the ozone layer, and litter.

Both the toll-free registry and the McRecycle USA Information Center (an office at McDonald's headquarters to meet with suppliers and manufacturers of recycled products) were a result of that research. McRecycle is illustrative of the need for continuous monitoring of previous efforts to build a relationship with important publics. Those previous efforts, including a pilot polystyrene recycling program in 450 of its restaurants in New England, had fallen short of the mark; but without additional research, McDonald's would not have known that further building and strengthening of its relationships was needed.

PROBE FORMULA STEP 5: EVALUATE RELATIONSHIPS

Measuring Output: Sylvan Learning Centers

An example of measuring outcomes or products is the public relations program conducted by Sylvan Learning Centers mentioned earlier. Only 30 percent of respondents to nationwide survey recognized the company as a supplemental education provider in unaided recall testing (Teaching America, 1990). Five objectives were planned on the basis of survey results indicating low name recognition and awarness. The five objectives were as follows:

1. Deliver print and broadcast media coverage consistently over 12 months.
2. Secure one or more Sylvan name references per article.
3. Measure publicity impact through a reader response vehicle.
4. Generate direct-response prospect inquiries.
5. Deliver 150 or more prospect inquiries per every 10 Sylvan Learning Center locations and, by extension, help increase annual revenues and inquiry-to-conversion rates.

Evaluation research on the first objective through media monitoring and clipping services showed that 645 newspaper and magazine articles resulted from the awareness campaign. Output was measured in terms of reach, 21.6 million audience impressions in 1,500 markets; and placement, 54 articles per month on the average.

A content analysis of the 645 articles and a morning news program showed that the Sylvan name was referred to one or more times per article. Publicity was measured through a reader-response mechanism in 65 percent of all media placements. Evaluation research for the fourth objective entailed keeping track of sales inquiries. Ketchum Public Relations claimed that the print and broadcast publicity generated 7,953 inquiries, "three times the volume of paid advertising generated leads." Finally, Ketchum evaluated the fifth objective in terms of the number of inquiries at every tenth Sylvan Learning Center and conversion of inquiries to actual enrollment. Both figures increased significantly.

Measuring Outcomes

Cobb Community Transit. Three other public relations programs demonstrate the process of evaluation in terms of outcomes. A 1989 awareness campaign to promote the Cobb Community Transit (CCT) system in Cobb County just outside of Atlanta, Georgia, used ridership figures to evaluate the outcome of the new public transportation system. The CCT had just been approved by a narrow margin, and one of the objectives was to meet monthly and annual ridership goals. The prestart projection for riders during the first month of operation was 4,500; the actual count was 7,625 in the first four days. The higher-than-projected ridership count continued in the first year, with an average of 4,600 riders daily. Original projections had been that the CCT would handle one million riders after three years of operation (Cobb Is Going Places with CCT, 1989).

Athens and Clarke County. A second example of using outcomes to measure the effectiveness of a public relations program involved helping to pass a referendum that would consolidate city and county governments in Athens and Clarke County, Georgia. The program objective was to secure 51 percent of the votes in target precincts in Clarke County and 51 percent in targeted precincts in Athens as required by Georgia law (Unification: The Better Way, 1989). Outcomes were measured in terms of voter turnout, which was 42 percent of all registered voters, and the vote returns. The referendum passed by 59.2 percent of the vote.

Public Schools of Albuquerque. A third example of measuring outcomes also involved analysis of vote totals. In the case of a mil levy campaign for public schools in Albuquerque, New Mexico, voters had turned down a mil increase by a margin of two to one. Without additional funding, the school district would have no money for capital improvements. The levy was a tough sell in 1990 because of a series of controversial decisions that redrew attendance boundaries and reassessed property valuations. Furthermore, in October 1989, just three months before the election, a furor erupted over the showing of *The Last Temptation of Christ* to two senior honors world history classes. Groups opposed to the film showing threatened to defeat the levy if the film was not banned. However, by skillful cultivation of editors, and endorsements from influential groups such as the local chamber of commerce and the League of Women Voters, the levy passed by a five-to-one margin (APS Mil Levy Campaign, 1990).

LEARN BY DOING

Develop a research design that would help an organization build public support for a proposed alternative high school in your area. The alternative high school would serve students either who have dropped out of a regular high school in the area, or who have been unable to graduate for one reason or another. Use the PROBE formula to suggest appropriate research at the various stages in campaign planning. Be very specific about your suggestions. If you suggest survey research, for example, you should (a) determine the population from which you wish to sample, the sample size, and the survey method; and (b) develop a prototype survey instrument. Suggest the appropriate statistics for analysis of survey results. If you suggest the use of a focus group, give a rationale for choosing the participants, determine the number and size of focus groups to be used, and develop a schedule of questions that will be used by the discussant.

SUMMARY

Most of the cases used to illustrate public relations research were Silver Anvil Award winners. Survey research, content analysis, focus groups, and use of secondary research are all represented.

Public relations research has steadily made progress toward expanding the variety of methods used to create, plan, monitor, and execute programs to communicate with various publics. The trend is toward using more sophisticated techniques to support program planning decisions and to provide evidence that public relations programs contribute to the bottom line. Although progress has been made in making research the foundation for planning, increasing emphasis will be placed on quantifying the evaluation process to measure success. Appropriately, measures to evaluate the success of the entire public relations program—that is, the public relations process—are receiving increasing emphasis.

STUDY QUESTIONS AND EXERCISES

1. Is research a step in the public relations process or should it be part of the entire process? How can this be done?

2. How could psychographic analysis be applied to provide more feedback about the publics associated with Sybron Chemical?

3. Distinguish between building a relationship, expanding a relationship, and strengthening a relationship. Use examples from the chapter and from current events to demonstrate the distinctions.

4. What is the difference between defining a public relations problem and defining a public relations opportunity? How might research methods differ depending on whether a problem or an opportunity is involved?

SOURCES

APS Mil Levy Campaign. 1990. Albuquerque Public Schools. Silver Anvil Award.

Archive Investor Relations. 1989. Archive Corporation. Silver Anvil Award.

Beef Industry Council Marketing Communications Program. 1990. Beef Industry Council with Ketchum Public Relations. Silver Anvil Award.

Bissland, James H. 1990. Accountability Gap: Evaluation Practices Show Improvement. *Public Relations Review* 16(2):25–35.

Broom, Glen, and Dave Dozier. 1990. *Using Research in Public Relations: Applications to Program Management.* Englewood Cliffs, N.J.: Prentice-Hall.

Cobb Is Going Places with CCT. 1989. Cobb Community Transit with Ketchum Public Relations. Silver Anvil Award.

Dave Thomas Platform. 1990. Wendy's International with Hill and Knowlton Public Relations. Silver Anvil Award.

Education Hotline—An Event which Helped People. National Association of Secondary School Principals. Silver Anvil Award.

Geneva Steel $2 Bill Campaign. 1989. Public Relations Society of America. Silver Anvil Award.

Grunig, James A., and Todd Hunt. 1984. *Managing Public Relations.* New York: Holt, Rinehart & Winston.

Hendrix, Jerry A. 1992. *Public Relations Cases.* 2d ed. Belmont, Calif.: Wadsworth.

Lindenmann, Walter K. 1990. Research, Evaluation and Measurement: A National Perspective. *Public Relations Review* 16(2): 3–16.

Lucarelli-Caudill, Susan M. L. 1989. Communications Audit for United Methodist Communications. Nashville.

Marston, John E. 1984. *Managing Public Relations.* New York: Holt, Rinehart & Winston.

McDonald's McRecycle USA Program. 1990. McDonald's Corporation with Holt, Ross and Yulish. Silver Anvil Award.

New Product Launch of VCR Plus+. 1990. Gemstar Development Corporation with Rogers and Associates. Silver Anvil Award.

Newsom, Doug, Alan Scott, and Judy Vanslyke Turk. 1989. *This Is PR: The Realities of Public Relations.* 4th ed. Belmont, Calif.: Wadsworth.

PR Reporter. 1991. 37(14):1.

PR Reporter. 1991. 34(16):1.

PR Reporter. 1992. 35(4):1.

PR Reporter. 1992. 35(5):1.

PRSA Foundation Monograph Series. 1991. *Public Relations: An Overview.*

Sybron Chemicals Inc.—A Case Study in Community Relations. 1989. Sybron Chemicals with Holt, Ross and Yulish. Silver Anvil Award.

Teaching America about Supplemental Education. 1990. Sylvan Learning Centers with Ketchum Public Relations. Silver Anvil Award.

Unification: The Better Way. 1989. A Campaign for City-County Government Consolidation with Ketchum Public Relations. Silver Anvil Award.

Ward, Kitty. 1991. *PR Reporter* 29(6):1.

Why Two Forks? 1989. Colorado Trout Unlimited with Russell, Karsh and Hagan Public Relations. Silver Anvil Award.

CHAPTER

19

Advertising Research

MICHAEL J. STANKEY AND MARIEA GRUBBS HOY
University of Tennessee, Knoxville

□

OBJECTIVES

After studying this chapter, you should be able to:

1. Understand how research fills the need for information in five important areas of advertising knowledge.

2. Locate and use 10 key sources of advertising information.

3. Identify meaningful differences in product and media consumption data.

4. Understand how meaningful differences in data affect advertising decisions.

5. Understand when secondary and primary research or custom research is necessary in advertising planning.

On the surface, planning an advertising campaign would seem to be a fairly straightforward task. Simply take a product that offers a consumer benefit, identify a consumer group most likely to respond to the benefit, prepare a message communicating the benefit to the group members in their own terms, and place the message in media vehicles that the targeted group are most likely to use. Unfortunately, executing the task is not nearly as easy as describing it. For each of these dimensions, there are multiple options to consider. Many products offer several benefits, both objective and subjective. Which is best? Consumers can be divided into groups according to multitude of criteria. Which is most appropriate? Messages can be constructed using a vast array of pictures, words, music, and situations. Which is most effective? Hundreds of media vehicles are available for carrying the message to consumers. Which best serves the purpose?

Advertising research helps the planner answer these questions. To the extent that advertising *planning* is characterized by the evaluation of multiple options, advertising *research* is characterized by the search for meaningful differences—differences that provide the planner with a foundation for choosing one course of action over another.

In his classic work, *How to Become an Advertising Man,* James Webb Young (1979) outlined seven categories of knowledge that are specifically related to the skills, techniques, and processes of advertising. Of these seven, five categories are particularly relevant to advertising research: (1) knowledge of the specific situation, (2) knowledge of markets, (3) knowledge of message carriers, (4) knowledge of propositions, and (5) knowledge of messages. These organizational criteria are as relevant today as they were in the early 1960s when Young was delivering lectures to students at the University of Chicago and to trainees at the J. Walter Thompson advertising agency. What has changed over the years is not the categories of advertising knowledge, but the resources and technology for generating and retrieving useful information about the categories.

The purpose of this chapter is to acquaint you with some of the current sources and uses of advertising information and to illustrate how meaningful differences within this information can help the advertising planner make decisions.

A CASE HISTORY

Dr. Raymond Specks is an independent optometrist who offers a full range of vision services, from performing eye examinations, to fitting contact lenses, to selling designer eyeglass frames and lenses. Although Dr. Specks regularly advertises in newspapers, telephone yellow pages, church directories, and through direct mail, he is unsure who his customers are and why they choose him. Furthermore, Dr. Specks has moved his office closer to the large university in town and has expanded his collection of eyeglass frames. He can handle more business than he is currently getting and wonders if his advertising is as effective as it could be.

The case of Dr. Specks is not unlike that of any advertiser, small or large. Every advertiser needs to know who its customers are, understand what benefits they are seeking, and how to reach them through messages placed in advertising media. Let's see how Dr. Specks can get a clearer understanding of how well his advertising is working by doing research in five of Young's categories of advertising knowledge.

Knowledge of the Specific Situation

Young (1979, 74–77) likens advertising planning to military planning. Much in the way military students learn to prepare an "appreciation of the situation" before formulating a plan of attack, so too must advertising planners gain an appreciation of what they are up against before running the first ad.

The purpose of the *situation analysis* is to identify problems and opportunities that need to be considered when making key advertising decisions. Young (1979, 74) noted that good advertising agencies use a formal process for gathering information. This process may involve using a checklist of all the types of information an agency needs about an advertiser's business: its organization, products, markets, capabilities and resources, and competition. Company records are a good place to start learning about an advertiser's products and capabilities; but the library is a good place to start learning about the broader contexts of markets and competition and the trends that affect them.

Of the many resources available at your university or city library, nine are particularly reliable and commonly available. It would be very unusual to make a complete check of these sources without finding something useful about an advertiser's situation.

- *Standard and Poor's Industry Surveys* is a two-volume publication that contains excellent in-depth analysis of 22 broad industries. It includes current and future prospects, financial information on competitors, and industry-related publications.

- The *Value Line Investment Survey* provides less detailed, but more timely, analysis of 1,600 companies in 90 industries, with emphasis on factors affecting operating performance and stock price in both the short and long run.

- The *U.S. Industrial Outlook* analyzes the prospects for more than 350 manufacturing and service industries defined by the Standard Industrial Classification (SIC) system of the U.S. Office of Management and Budget.

- The *New York Times Index* and the *Wall Street Journal Index* document articles in these highly credible and widely available newspapers—often with detailed abstracts, and always with publication date, section, and page number.

- The *Predicasts Basebook,* an outstanding source of quantitative trend data, provides 28,000 14-year series of data on population, employment, and industries arranged by SIC code.

- The *Statistical Abstract of the United States* is an excellent summary of statistics on the social, political, and economic organization of the United States. It is a useful starting point for accessing the wealth of information generated by the U.S. government.

- The *U.S. Bureau of Census* conducts censuses of population and housing every 10 years and censuses of economic activity every 5 years. It offers specific publications on retail trade, wholesale trade, service industries, manufacturing, construction industries, and transportation.

- The *Leading National Advertisers (LNA) Ad $ Summary* lists nine media-advertising expenditures for national advertisers arranged by industry classification and by brand name.

Although much valuable information can be gained from company records and the sources described above, additional information may still be required before the advertising planner can attain a solid appreciation for the situation. Custom research may be necessary to tap into the minds of consumers or trade channel members. Certainly firsthand observation of the advertiser's product or service as compared with that of competitors would generate useful insight. Regardless of the sources used, the planner should leave this first stage of research with a good sense of the advertiser's capabilities in overcoming key problems and exploiting available opportunities.

LEARN BY DOING

In this section, nine sources of information have been discussed as being valuable for gaining knowledge of the specific advertising situation. Gain some firsthand experience with these sources by doing the following exercises.

1. Find out which of the nine sources are available at your university or community library and locate where they are shelved.
2. The product categories listed below are ones that college graduates are at least 50 percent more likely than average to consume. For each product category, determine the extent of information available in each of the nine sources. (For the *New York Times Index* and *Wall Street Journal Index,* identify how many articles have appeared in the past three years.) Prepare a chart to summarize your findings: List the product categories across the top and the nine sources down the side.

   airline travel
   hardcover books
   car rental
   compact discs
   35-mm color film
   domestic and imported wine

Case History

Standard and Poor's, Value Line, and *U.S. Industrial Outlook* failed to produce much analysis on the optical goods industry, but the remaining suggested sources provided useful information to help paint a clear picture of the competitive forces facing Dr. Specks. The *New York Times* and *Wall Street Journal* indexes for 1988–1990 listed 137 articles on eyes, eyesight, and eyeglasses. A single *New York Times* article provided excellent background on the increased demand for eyeglasses and the subsequent rise in competition (Deutsch, 1989, III-4). The article stated that the first wave of baby boomers had hit middle age and many were buying multiple pairs of glasses to use as fashion accessories. These two factors had helped to create an $11 billion market for eyewear in 1988. The growing demand plus the high markup on frames and lenses (often as high as 250 percent) had attracted large chains of eyewear stores, which were squeezing small independents like Dr. Specks out of business. Figures 19.1–19.4 further document this situation.

Figure 19.1 shows data from *Predicasts Basebook* on the growth in consumer spending on ophthalmic goods compared with the growth in the U.S. population. The population grew by 14.1 percent from 1976 to 1989, but consumer spending on

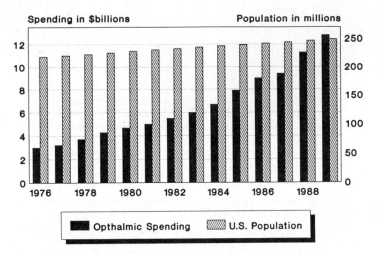

FIGURE 19.1   Consumer Spending on Ophthalmic Goods (*Source:* 1991 *Predicasts Basebook.*)

ophthalmic goods during the same period grew by 326.7 percent. *Predicasts Basebook* reports that growth is expected to continue at the annual rate of 11.8 percent.

Figure 19.2 shows data from the *Census of Retail Trade* for 1982 and 1987, which illustrates the extent to which large firms are pushing smaller firms out of business. During the five-year period covered, the number of optical goods stores with annual sales of less than $100,000 declined by one-fourth, while the number of stores with annual sales of $250,000 or more almost tripled. Similar results for offices of optometrists were found by examining the *Census of Service Industries* for the same years.

Table 19.1 pairs information from the *New York Times* article (Deutsch, 1989)

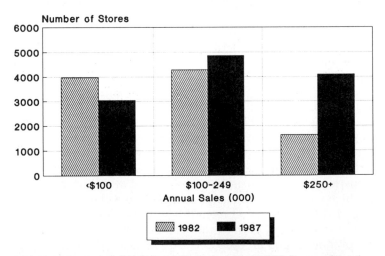

FIGURE 19.2   Optical Goods Stores (*Source:* 1982/1987 *Census of Retail Trade.*)

TABLE 19.1 Top-Ten Eyewear Retailers in 1989

Retailer	Sales (in $ millions)	Advertising (in millions)
Pearle	599	43.7
LensCrafters	489	37.6
Cole Vision	311	—
Sterling Optical	120	3.0
Royal International	101	0.4
D&K Optical	75	—
Eye Care Centers	73	—
Benson Optical	70	0.1
NuVision	58	0.8
Eckerd Vision	57	31.5 (drug)

SOURCE *New York Times,* November 26, 1989; 1990 *LNA AD $ Summary.*

with advertising spending data gathered from the *LNA Ad $ Summary.* Pearle and Lenscrafters appear to be the major players in the eyewear industry, especially in terms of advertising spending: Combined spending by the two chains in 1990 was $81.3 million.

This scenario means both good and bad news for Dr. Specks. The good news is that demand for optical services has and will continue to grow at a healthy pace. The bad news is that national chains armed with big promotional budgets threaten to put the squeeze on his operation. But these are national trends. What about conditions in Dr. Specks's local market?

A check of the local telephone yellow pages revealed 43 listings under the heading "Optometrists," with five Pearle locations, three SuperX drugstore locations, two Lenscrafters locations, and six other competitors within the same three-digit telephone exchange as Dr. Specks. Figure 19.3 shows the partial results of a telephone survey conducted among patients of Dr. Specks. Although 42 percent of Dr. Specks's patients also bought their eyeglasses from him, nearly half of the "defector" patients bought their glasses at Lenscrafters and Andes Optical (a local independent with the same telephone exchange as Dr. Specks). Surprisingly, the national leader, Pearle, with its five locations filled the eyeglass prescriptions of less than 5 percent of Specks's patients.

Firsthand observation of the Lenscrafters locations and Dr. Specks's revealed an interesting finding. Lenscrafters had a vast selection of frames on display, but many were duplicates of the same style. Dr. Specks had fewer total frames in his collection, but only one frame per style was displayed and catalogs were available for special ordering frames not on display. This could be a meaningful difference to promote in advertising.

Knowledge of Markets

Young (1979, 22) described *markets* as congeries of people having some common denominator when it comes to the consumption of a particular product category. This common denominator may be quantitatively expressed in demographic

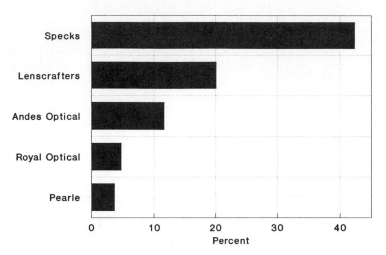

FIGURE 19.3 Where Patients Bought Last Eyeglasses (*Source:* Survey of Dr. Specks's Patients.)

terms such as age, education, or income; or qualitatively expressed in terms such as tastes, interests, or life-styles. Given the many criteria available for dividing consumers into groups, the advertising planner must attempt to discover which of the available criteria best differentiates product users from nonusers.

The standard source of information on markets is the *Simmons Study of Media and Markets*—based on a national sample projectable to adults 18 or older living in the continental United States and published annually as 13 media volumes and 30 product volumes. It cross-tabulates product consumption levels with several sets of demographic criteria, including sex, age, education, employment, occupation, marital status, race, census region, marketing region, county size, city type, area of dominant influence (ADI), household income, household size, presence of children, and home ownership. These data allow the planner to identify the groups of consumers who are more likely to consume a product or service and to identify the size of those groups.

Case History

Figure 19.4 shows a partial page taken from *Simmons Study of Media and Markets* (Volume P-25), which details consumption of prescription eyeglasses and contact lenses by various demographic criteria. The top row shows that 56.2 percent (101,851,000) of the total U.S. adult population (181,131,000) currently wear prescription eyeglasses or contact lenses. The question facing the planner is whether certain groups are more likely than this average to wear prescription glasses. Is there a common denominator that clearly differentiates users from nonusers? This is a critical question for Dr. Specks because scarce advertising dollars will have greater impact if they can be directed at consumers who are more likely to need and buy eyeglasses.

Figure 19.4 further shows that 11,495,000 (column A) adults ages 18 to 24 currently wear eyeglasses or contact lenses. This number represents 11.3 percent (col-

	TOTAL U.S. '000	CURRENTLY WEAR PRES. EYEGLASSES OR CONTACT LENSES				WEAR PRES. EYEGLASSES (SUN, TINTED, REGULAR)				WEAR CONTACT LENSES				SOFT NON-TINTED			
		A '000	B % DOWN	C % ACROSS	D INDX	A '000	B % DOWN	C % ACROSS	D INDX	A '000	B % DOWN	C % ACROSS	D INDX	A '000	B % DOWN	C % ACROSS	D INDX
TOTAL ADULTS	181131	101851	100.0	56.2	100	92669	100.0	51.2	100	17418	100.0	9.6	100	7040	100.0	3.9	100
MALES	86476	44446	43.6	51.4	91	40569	43.8	46.9	92	6420	36.9	7.4	77	2510	35.7	2.9	75
FEMALES	94655	57405	56.4	60.6	108	52100	56.2	55.0	108	10998	63.1	11.6	121	4530	64.3	4.8	123
18 – 24	25507	11495	11.3	45.1	80	10029	10.8	39.3	77	3317	19.0	13.0	135	1536	21.8	6.0	155
25 – 34	43858	20009	19.6	45.6	81	17389	18.8	39.6	77	6419	36.9	14.6	152	2784	39.5	6.3	163
35 – 44	36206	19025	18.7	52.5	93	17168	18.5	47.4	93	4139	23.8	11.4	119	1387	19.7	3.8	99
45 – 54	24795	16190	15.9	65.3	116	15001	16.2	60.5	118	1832	10.5	7.4	77	699	9.9	2.8	73
55 – 64	21496	14753	14.5	68.6	122	13800	14.9	64.2	125	1018	5.8	4.7	49	*375	5.3	1.7	45
65 OR OLDER	29268	20381	20.0	69.6	124	19281	20.8	65.9	129	694	4.0	2.4	25	*259	3.7	0.9	23
18 – 34	69365	31503	30.9	45.4	81	27419	29.6	39.5	77	9735	55.9	14.0	146	4320	61.4	6.2	160
18 – 49	119427	59258	58.2	49.6	88	52506	56.7	44.0	86	15172	87.1	12.7	132	6292	89.4	5.3	136
25 – 54	104859	55223	54.2	52.7	94	49559	53.5	47.3	92	12390	71.1	11.8	123	4870	69.2	4.6	119
35 – 49	50062	27754	27.2	55.4	99	25087	27.1	50.1	98	5436	31.2	10.9	113	1972	28.0	3.9	101
50 OR OLDER	61704	42594	41.8	69.0	123	40163	43.3	65.1	127	2246	12.9	3.6	38	748	10.6	1.2	31
GRADUATED COLLEGE	34578	22366	22.0	64.7	115	19725	21.3	57.0	112	5904	33.9	17.1	178	2578	36.6	7.5	192
ATTENDED COLLEGE	33812	19855	19.5	58.7	104	17709	19.1	52.4	102	4641	26.6	13.7	143	1884	26.8	5.6	143
GRADUATED HIGH SCHOOL	71180	38628	37.9	54.3	97	35646	38.5	50.1	98	5574	32.0	7.8	81	2150	30.5	3.0	78
DID NOT GRADUATE HIGH SCHOOL	41560	21003	20.6	50.5	90	19589	21.1	47.1	92	1298	7.5	3.1	32	*428	6.1	1.0	26
EMPLOYED MALES	66051	32767	32.2	49.6	88	29617	32.0	44.8	88	5755	33.0	8.7	91	2260	32.1	3.4	88
EMPLOYED FEMALES	54108	32369	31.8	59.8	106	28488	30.7	52.7	103	8617	49.5	15.9	166	3538	50.3	6.5	168
EMPLOYED FULL-TIME	108437	58196	57.1	53.7	95	52044	56.2	48.0	94	12745	73.2	11.8	122	5160	73.3	4.8	122
EMPLOYED PART-TIME	11721	6940	6.8	59.2	105	6061	6.5	51.7	101	1628	9.3	13.9	144	*638	9.1	5.4	140
NOT EMPLOYED	60972	36716	36.0	60.2	107	34564	37.3	56.7	111	3046	17.5	5.0	52	1242	17.6	2.0	52
PROFESSIONAL/MANAGER	31879	20400	20.0	64.0	114	17887	19.3	56.1	110	5477	31.4	17.2	179	2428	34.5	7.6	196
TECH/CLERICAL/SALES	37678	21349	21.0	56.7	101	19079	20.6	50.6	99	5039	28.9	13.4	139	2036	28.9	5.4	139
PRECISION/CRAFT	14826	7254	7.1	48.9	87	6333	6.8	42.7	83	1349	7.7	9.1	95	*337	4.8	2.3	58
OTHER EMPLOYED	35775	16133	15.8	45.1	80	14806	16.0	41.4	81	2507	14.4	7.0	73	997	14.2	2.8	72
SINGLE	39788	18697	18.4	47.0	84	16504	17.8	41.5	81	4651	26.7	11.7	122	2189	31.1	5.5	142
MARRIED	108473	64474	63.3	59.4	106	59071	63.7	54.5	106	10508	60.3	9.7	101	3958	56.2	3.6	94
DIVORCED/SEPARATED/WIDOWED	32870	18680	18.3	56.8	101	17094	18.4	52.0	102	2259	13.0	6.9	71	892	12.7	2.7	70
PARENTS	60843	30034	29.5	49.4	88	26608	28.7	43.7	85	7121	40.9	11.7	122	2705	38.4	4.4	114
WHITE	155331	90606	89.0	58.3	104	82407	88.9	53.1	104	15920	91.4	10.2	107	6488	92.2	4.2	107
BLACK	20477	8688	8.5	42.4	75	7853	8.5	38.4	75	1051	6.0	5.1	53	*333	4.7	1.6	62
OTHER	5322	2557	2.5	48.0	85	2408	2.6	45.2	88	*447	2.6	8.4	87	**219	3.1	4.1	106

FIGURE 19.4 Sample Data from *Simmons Study of Media and Markets* (*Source:* From Simmons Market Research Bureau, Inc., 1990 *Study of Media and Markets.* Copyright 1990 Simmons Market Research Bureau, Inc. Reprinted by permission.)

umn B) of the 101,851,000 total adults currently wearing eyeglasses or contact lenses and accounts for 45.1 percent (column C) of the 25,507,000 total adults ages 18 to 24. Comparing the percentage of 18- to 24-year-olds wearing eyeglasses (45.1) with the percentage of all adults wearing eyeglasses (56.2) yields an index of 80 in column D (45.1 ÷ 56.2 × 100 = 80). With an index of 100 representing average, this means that 18- to 24-year-olds are 20 percent *less* likely than average (80 − 100 = −20) to wear eyeglasses. By contrast, adults age 65 or older represent 20.0 percent (column B) of all adults wearing eyeglasses and are 24 percent *more* likely than average (124 − 100 = 24) to wear eyeglasses.

Figure 19.5 illustrates the preceding index analysis for all six age categories. The bar graph shows a clear relationship between age and use of eyeglasses. Adults ages 18–24, 25–34, and 35–44 are 20 percent, 19 percent, and 7 percent less likely than average to wear glasses. Adults ages 45–54, 55–64, and 65 or older are 16 percent, 22 percent, and 24 percent more likely to wear glasses. Furthermore, adults age 65 or older are 44 percent more likely than adults ages 18–24 to wear eyeglasses (124 − 80 = 44). A similar analysis on the remaining *Simmons* criteria reveals that age makes the biggest difference in separating users and nonusers of eyeglasses and contact lenses.

With this knowledge in hand, the survey of patients results reported in Figure 19.3 can be re-analyzed for any meaningful differences resulting from age. Figure 19.6 shows that patients of Dr. Specks who also buy their eyeglasses from him are only slightly more likely to be age 45 or older. Roughly 42 percent of younger patients and 45 percent of older patients bought their eyeglasses from Dr. Specks.

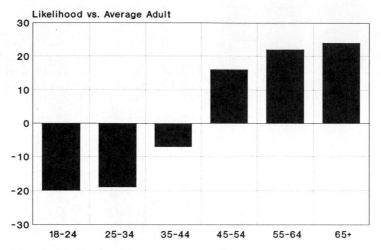

FIGURE 19.5   Eyeglass/Contact Lens Wearers by Age (*Source:* From Simmons Market Research Bureau, Inc., 1990 Study of Media and Markets. Copyright 1990 *Simmons Market Research Bureau,* Inc. Reprinted by permission.)

The big differences due to age occurred with the "defectors." Almost 25 percent of younger defectors bought their glasses at Lenscrafters, compared with only 12 percent of older defectors. By contrast, 18 percent of older defectors bought their glasses at Andes Optical, compared with only 8 percent of younger defectors. This means that although Dr. Specks seems to appeal equally to young and old patients, he is likely to lose the eyeglass business of younger patients to Lenscrafters and of older patients to Andes Optical.

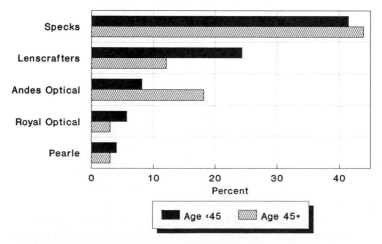

FIGURE 19.6   Where Patients Bought Last Eyeglasses by Age (*Source:* Survey of Specks's Patients.)

LEARN BY DOING

In the last Learn by Doing exercise, the compact disc was identified as one category in which college graduates are at least 50 percent more likely than average to make purchases. The source for making this claim is the *Simmons Study of Media and Markets* discussed in this section. Practice using this source by doing the following exercises:

1. Reprinted in Figure 19.7 is a partial page from *Simmons* dealing with compact disc consumption. The 168 appearing for "graduated college" in column D of "bought in last 12 months" means that adults who have graduated college are 68 percent more likely than average to have bought a compact disc in the last 12 months (168 index − 100 average index = 68). Which three segments are *most* likely to be heavy users of compact discs? Which three segments are *least* likely to be heavy users of compact discs? Which group of segments (e.g., age, education) seems best to differentiate the most likely from the least likely *heavy* users?

2. Relate your knowledge of the product category with your consumption findings. What is it about compact discs that makes the first three segments you identified consume them heavily? What is it about compact discs that makes the second three segments not consume them heavily? What is it about compact discs that makes the group of segments you identified best differentiate heavy users?

	TOTAL U.S. '000	BOUGHT IN LAST 12 MONTHS				HEAVY FIVE OR MORE				LIGHT ONE-FOUR			
		A '000	B % DOWN	C % ACROSS	D INDX	A '000	B % DOWN	C % ACROSS	D INDX	A '000	B % DOWN	C % ACROSS	D INDX
TOTAL ADULTS	181131	16867	100.0	9.3	100	10829	100.0	6.0	100	6038	100.0	3.3	100
MALES	86476	9551	56.6	11.0	119	6874	63.5	7.9	133	2677	44.3	3.1	93
FEMALES	94655	7316	43.4	7.7	83	3955	36.5	4.2	70	3362	55.7	3.6	107
18 − 24	25507	3361	19.9	13.2	142	2434	22.5	9.5	160	928	15.4	3.6	109
25 − 34	43858	5774	34.2	13.2	141	3616	33.4	8.2	138	2158	35.7	4.9	148
35 − 44	36206	3495	20.7	9.7	104	2304	21.3	6.4	106	1191	19.7	3.3	99
45 − 54	24795	2011	11.9	8.1	87	1213	11.2	4.9	82	797	13.2	3.2	96
55 − 64	21496	1266	7.5	5.9	63	751	6.9	3.5	58	*514	8.5	2.4	72
65 OR OLDER	29268	960	5.7	3.3	35	511	4.7	1.7	29	450	7.5	1.5	46
18 − 34	69365	9135	54.2	13.2	141	6049	55.9	8.7	146	3086	51.1	4.4	133
18 − 49	119427	13917	82.5	11.7	125	9057	83.6	7.6	127	4860	80.5	4.1	122
25 − 54	104859	11280	66.9	10.8	116	7134	65.9	6.8	114	4146	68.7	4.0	119
35 − 49	50062	4781	28.3	9.6	103	3008	27.8	6.0	101	1774	29.4	3.5	106
50 OR OLDER	61704	2951	17.5	4.8	51	1772	16.4	2.9	48	1179	19.5	1.9	57
GRADUATED COLLEGE	34578	5402	32.0	15.6	168	3416	31.5	9.9	165	1986	32.9	5.7	172
ATTENDED COLLEGE	33812	4127	24.5	12.2	131	2616	24.2	7.7	129	1511	25.0	4.5	134
GRADUATED HIGH SCHOOL	71180	5892	34.9	8.3	89	4006	37.0	5.6	94	1886	31.2	2.6	79
DID NOT GRADUATE HIGH SCHOOL	41560	1446	8.6	3.5	37	791	7.3	1.9	32	*655	10.8	1.6	47
EMPLOYED MALES	66051	8492	50.3	12.9	138	6098	56.3	9.2	154	2395	39.7	3.6	109
EMPLOYED FEMALES	54108	5333	31.6	9.9	106	2969	27.4	5.5	92	2364	39.2	4.4	131
EMPLOYED FULL−TIME	108437	12738	75.5	11.7	126	8433	77.9	7.8	130	4305	71.3	4.0	119
EMPLOYED PART−TIME	11721	1087	6.4	9.3	100	*634	5.9	5.4	90	*454	7.5	3.9	116
NOT EMPLOYED	60972	3042	18.0	5.0	54	1762	16.3	2.9	48	1280	21.2	2.1	63
PROFESSIONAL/MANAGER	31879	4920	29.2	15.4	166	3198	29.5	10.0	168	1722	28.5	5.4	162
TECH/CLERICAL/SALES	37678	4575	27.1	12.1	130	2951	27.3	7.8	131	1624	26.9	4.3	129
PRECISION/CRAFT	14826	1437	8.5	9.7	104	948	8.8	6.4	107	*488	8.1	3.3	99
OTHER EMPLOYED	35775	2894	17.2	8.1	87	1969	18.2	5.5	92	925	15.3	2.6	78
SINGLE	39788	6016	35.7	15.1	162	4270	39.4	10.7	180	1745	28.9	4.4	132
MARRIED	108473	9228	54.7	8.5	91	5656	52.2	5.2	87	3573	59.2	3.3	99
DIVORCED/SEPARATED/WIDOWED	32870	1623	9.6	4.9	53	903	8.3	2.7	46	720	11.9	2.2	66
PARENTS	60843	4847	28.7	8.0	86	2929	27.0	4.8	81	1919	31.8	3.2	95
WHITE	155331	15214	90.2	9.8	105	9801	90.5	6.3	106	5414	89.7	3.5	105
BLACK	20477	1141	6.8	5.6	60	739	6.8	3.6	60	*402	6.7	2.0	59
OTHER	5322	*512	3.0	9.6	103	**289	2.7	5.4	91	**223	3.7	4.2	126

FIGURE 19.7 (*Source:* From Simmons Market Research Bureau, Inc., 1990 *Study of Media and Markets.* Copyright 1990 Simmons Market Research Bureau, Inc. Reprinted by permission.)

KNOWLEDGE OF MESSAGE CARRIERS

Young (1979, 37) referred to advertising media as "carriers" to underscore their function of transporting the advertising message from advertiser to consumer. Much as there are multiple types of carriers in the transportation business (e.g., railroad, airplane, boat, truck), each with advantages and disadvantages in serving particular destinations, there are also multiple carriers in the advertising business (e.g., television, radio, magazines, newspapers), each with advantages and disadvantages in serving particular markets. The advertising planner must sort through numerous options and decide first which types of media to use and second which specific carriers to use within each type.

It should come as no surprise that one of the standard sources of information about carriers of advertising is the same source used to analyze destinations. The *Simmons Study of Media and Markets* provides a wealth of information about consumer use of media types and specific vehicles within types. Media usage is cross-tabulated both by product consumption and by demographic categories.

One of the more useful items provided by *Simmons* is a quintile breakdown of media class consumption. For each of the major media classes (e.g., television, radio, magazines, newspapers), *Simmons* divides the population into five relatively equal-sized groups called *quintiles* based on consumption of the media class. Quintile 1 represents the 20 percent of the population that is the heaviest consumer of the media class. Quintile 5 is the 20 percent of the population that is the lightest consumer of the media class. On average across all media classes, quintiles 1, 2, and 3 combine to account for about 90 percent of all media consumed. *Simmons* defines a *dual user* as someone who falls into quintiles 1, 2, or 3 for each of two media classes.

The advertising planner would prefer to run advertising messages in media types that are used heavily by the targeted group of consumers. The planner can use *Simmons* to identify not only which single media types are likely to be used heavily, but also which *pairs* of media are likely to be used heavily. This information can be used in conjunction with competitor spending data from the *LNA Ad $ Summary* to pinpoint the appropriate advertising media strategy.

Case History

Let's assume that Dr. Specks wants to reduce the defection of his older patients to Andes Optical. The 45-or-older age group was found to be more likely than average to wear prescription eyeglasses, and this age group is growing faster than the overall population. These two factors make it attractive for current and future advertising efforts. The question at hand is: Which media types is this age group more likely to use heavily?

Figure 19.8 illustrates the *Simmons* dual media usage data for adults age 45 or older. The same index analysis used in the previous section is used here to identify the pairs of media most likely to be used heavily by the target group. The bar graph shows that adults ages 45 or older are 22 percent more likely than average to be heavy users of both newspapers and television (*N-T*), but less likely than average

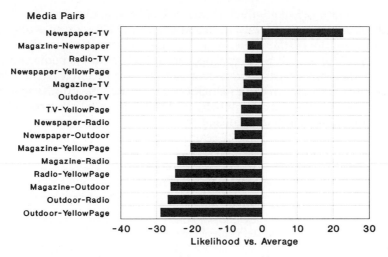

FIGURE 19.8 Dual Media Use by Adults Ages 45 or Older (*Source:* From Simmons Market Research Bureau, Inc., 1990 *Study of Media and Markets.* Copyright 1990 Simmons Market Research Bureau, Inc. Reprinted by permission.)

to use all other combinations. A person of this age group is only 4 percent less likely than average to be a dual user of magazines and newspapers (*M-N*), but is almost 30 percent less likely than average to be a dual user of outdoor and yellow pages (*O-YP*). Assuming that the adults age 45 or older in Dr. Specks's local market are similar to the same group nationwide, newspapers and television would appear to be good media choices.

Figure 19.9 shows the media spending patterns of optical goods advertisers compared with the spending patterns of all advertisers as derived from the *LNA Ad $ Summary.* The bar graph shows that national optical goods advertisers are

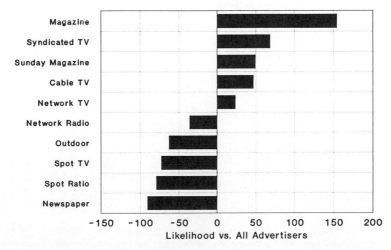

FIGURE 19.9 Optical Goods Relative Ad Spending (*Source:* 1991 *LNA Ad $ Summary,* January to September.)

over 150 percent more likely than average to use magazines and between 70 percent and 23 percent more likely to use syndicated, cable, or network television. These data, paired with the audience media-use information from Figure 19.8 confirm that television would be an appropriate and competitive media choice. On the other hand, national optical goods advertisers are 90 percent less likely than average to use newspapers. This gives Dr. Specks a unique opportunity to advertise in a medium known to be used heavily by adults 45 or older that is relatively free of advertising from the national chains.

LEARN BY DOING

Earlier, you used *Simmons Study of Media and Markets* to find differences in consumption of compact discs among segments of the adult population. The exercises below will give you experience at identifying media consumption differences among population segments using the same source.

1. Reprinted in Figure 19.10 is a partial page from *Simmons* showing magazine readership by educational level among adults. For each educational level, identify the three individual magazine titles most likely to be read (do not include magazine groups identified with [GROSS] or [GRS] following their titles).

2. Do the magazines you identified for each educational level make sense? What insight can you gain into the life-styles or interests of adults based on their educational level and magazine readership? Develop a short biographical sketch of a typical adult who might fit your educational and readership findings.

	TOTAL U.S. '000	GRADUATED COLLEGE				ATTENDED COLLEGE (1-3 YRS.)				GRADUATED HIGH SCHOOL				ATTENDED HIGH SCHOOL (1-3 YRS.)			
		A '000	B % DOWN	C % ACROSS	D INDX	A '000	B % DOWN	C % ACROSS	D INDX	A '000	B % DOWN	C % ACROSS	D INDX	A '000	B % DOWN	C % ACROSS	D INDX
TOTAL	181131	34578	100.0	19.1	100	33812	100.0	18.7	100	71180	100.0	39.3	100	22598	100.0	12.5	100
AMERICAN BABY	2466	646	1.9	26.2	137	547	1.6	22.2	119	1071	1.5	43.4	111	•161	0.7	6.5	52
AMERICAN HEALTH	2167	509	1.5	23.5	123	653	1.9	30.1	161	766	1.1	35.3	90	•134	0.6	6.2	50
ARCHITECTURAL DIGEST	2101	1069	3.1	50.9	267	572	1.7	27.2	146	440	0.6	20.9	53	••12	0.1	0.6	5
BABY TALK	1803	•279	0.8	15.5	81	357	1.1	19.8	106	805	1.1	44.6	114	•295	1.3	16.4	131
BARRON'S	1338	863	2.5	64.5	338	193	0.6	14.4	77	214	0.3	16.0	41	••25	0.1	1.9	15
BETTER HOMES & GARDENS	22312	4756	13.8	21.3	112	4668	13.8	20.9	112	9520	13.4	42.7	109	2010	8.9	9.0	72
BON APPETIT	3631	1254	3.6	34.5	181	915	2.7	25.2	135	1291	1.8	35.6	90	105	0.5	2.9	23
BRIDE'S	3357	415	1.2	12.4	65	851	2.5	25.4	136	1407	2.0	41.9	107	569	2.5	16.9	136
BUSINESS WEEK	6751	3194	9.2	47.3	248	1446	4.3	21.4	115	1757	2.5	26.0	66	•251	1.1	3.7	30
THE CABLE GUIDE	8958	1403	4.1	15.7	82	2427	7.2	27.1	145	3643	5.1	40.7	103	1166	5.2	13.0	104
CAPPER'S GRIT (GROSS)	1784	•209	0.6	11.7	61	268	0.8	15.0	80	619	0.9	34.7	88	392	1.7	22.0	176
CAR AND DRIVER	5110	901	2.6	17.6	92	1301	3.8	25.5	136	2115	3.0	41.4	105	665	2.9	13.0	104
CHANGING TIMES	2077	891	2.6	42.9	225	457	1.4	22.0	118	566	0.8	27.3	69	••116	0.5	5.6	45
COLONIAL HOMES	1859	645	1.9	34.7	182	493	1.5	26.5	142	596	0.8	32.1	82	••48	0.2	2.6	21
CONDE NAST LIMITED (GROSS)	17993	5183	15.0	28.8	151	4894	14.5	27.2	146	6216	8.7	34.5	88	1248	5.5	6.9	56
CONDE NAST PKG. WOMEN (GRS)	24380	4719	13.6	19.4	101	6785	20.1	27.8	149	9507	13.4	39.0	99	2811	12.4	11.5	92
CONDE NAST TRAVELER	1345	491	1.4	36.5	191	405	1.2	30.1	161	355	0.5	26.4	67	••76	0.3	5.7	45
CONSUMERS DIGEST	3287	951	2.8	28.9	152	861	2.5	26.2	140	1284	1.8	39.1	99	•123	0.5	3.7	30
COSMOPOLITAN	11299	2070	6.0	18.3	96	3011	8.9	26.6	143	4907	6.9	43.4	111	1127	5.0	10.0	80
COUNTRY HOME	2704	657	1.9	24.3	127	728	2.2	26.9	144	995	1.4	36.8	94	••195	0.9	7.2	58
COUNTRY LIVING	6707	1533	4.4	22.9	120	1792	5.3	26.7	143	2643	3.7	39.4	100	519	2.3	7.7	62
CYCLE	1901	•190	0.5	10.0	52	376	1.1	19.8	106	835	1.2	43.9	112	450	2.0	23.7	190
CYCLE WORLD	2028	•232	0.7	11.4	60	408	1.2	20.1	108	882	1.2	43.5	111	444	2.0	21.9	175
DIAMANDIS MAG NETWORK (GRS)	19778	4064	11.8	20.5	108	4629	13.7	23.4	125	8081	11.4	40.9	104	2450	10.8	12.4	99
DIAMANDIS MTRCYCL GRP (GRS)	3929	423	1.2	10.8	56	784	2.3	20.0	107	1718	2.4	43.7	111	894	4.0	22.8	182
DISCOVER	3714	1055	3.1	28.4	149	845	2.5	22.8	122	1464	2.1	39.4	100	•256	1.1	6.9	55
EBONY	8684	1240	3.6	14.3	75	1929	5.7	22.2	119	3351	4.7	38.6	98	1500	6.6	17.3	138
ELLE	2132	494	1.4	23.2	121	624	1.8	29.3	157	761	1.1	35.7	91	••164	0.7	7.7	62
ESQUIRE	2612	696	2.0	26.6	140	693	2.0	26.5	142	830	1.2	31.8	81	•217	1.0	8.3	67
ESSENCE	4070	697	2.0	17.1	90	971	2.9	23.9	128	1663	2.3	40.9	104	570	2.5	14.0	112
FAMILY CIRCLE	17066	2767	8.0	16.2	85	3580	10.6	21.0	112	7994	11.2	46.8	119	1496	6.6	8.8	70
FAMILY CIRCLE/MCCALL'S (GRS)	31428	4949	14.3	15.7	82	6505	19.2	20.7	111	14713	20.7	46.8	119	3013	13.3	9.6	77
THE FAMILY HANDYMAN	3416	571	1.7	16.7	88	749	2.2	21.9	117	1567	2.2	45.9	117	•327	1.4	9.6	77
FIELD & STREAM	10730	1342	3.9	12.5	66	2249	6.7	21.0	112	4900	6.9	45.7	116	1354	6.0	12.6	101
FINANCIAL WORLD	1416	682	2.0	48.2	252	359	1.1	25.4	136	325	0.5	23.0	58	••39	0.2	2.8	22

FIGURE 19.10 (*Source:* From Simmons Market Research Bureau, Inc., 1990 *Study of Media and Markets.* Copyright 1990 Simmons Market Research Bureau, Inc. Reprinted by permission.)

KNOWLEDGE OF PROPOSITIONS

According to Young (1979, 19), the *proposition* made to the audience is the most important single element in any advertisement. The proposition is the quid pro quo—the benefit the audience member will receive for what the advertiser asks him or her to do. Years of copytesting research have demonstrated that a change in proposition can have a dramatic effect on the response rate to an advertisement. So important is the proposition that Young recommended that the planner be crystal clear in his or her mind as to what the proposition is, and have good reason to believe that it is appealing to the audience being addressed, before he or she sits down to prepare an ad.

Two levels of propositions are relevant to the advertising planner. The first level contains propositions with broad cultural or social roots that cut across many product categories. Protecting the environment or saving time are examples of broad-based concerns that often show up as appeals in advertising. The second level includes propositions that are more specific with respect to the product category being advertised. Getting better gas mileage or taking better pictures are examples of product-specific appeals around which advertising might be built. Although regular exposure to the popular media will help the advertising planner keep abreast of general cultural and societal concerns, custom research is generally required to learn more about product-specific propositions and their selling power.

Case History

The telephone survey of Dr. Specks's patients mentioned in earlier sections included questions about factors that affected respondents' purchase of eyeglasses. Figure 19.11 illustrates the top five factors broken down by age. Generally, *location* was reported as being the most important factor affecting purchase (among 31 per-

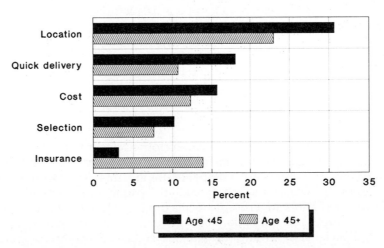

FIGURE 19.11   Factors Affecting Purchase of Eyeglasses (*Source:* Survey of Dr. Specks's Patients.)

cent of patients under age 45 and 23 percent of patients over 45). For younger patients, this was followed in order by quick delivery (18 percent), cost, selection, and insurance. Older patients, however, reported a different set of priorities: After location, they cited insurance (14 percent) and cost (12 percent).

These findings suggest that the proposition used in Dr. Specks's advertising should vary depending on the audience being addressed, keeping in mind that whatever benefit is promised must be delivered. It would make little sense to stress quick delivery if indeed consumers could get faster delivery elsewhere. If the goal is to keep younger patients from defecting to Lenscrafters, Dr. Specks may need to establish a cost or selection advantage in his advertising, since Lenscrafters may have the edge in location and speed of delivery. If the goal is to keep older patients from defecting to Andes Optical, Dr. Specks may need to elaborate on insurance claim processing or senior discounts that may be superior to Andes Optical. In either case, additional competitor analysis is required before the best proposition can be developed.

KNOWLEDGE OF MESSAGES

articulating the proposition

Young (1979, 29) described the advertising message itself as the heart of the whole advertising operation—where the advertiser and the planner win or lose. The advertisement itself is where the proposition is presented to audience members in terms that they can understand and with which they can relate. The trick, of course, is for the planner to learn to think and feel like a member of the group being addressed, and this is not always easy. It is difficult to climb out of one's own experience and mindset to see with someone else's eyes and hear with someone else's ears. Yet the task of preparing a meaningful message demands exactly that.

Given the difficulties of seeing the world through the eyes of others and given the infinite possible combinations of words, pictures, and sounds that can be used to present the proposition, advertising research at the message level is critical in terms of separating effective advertisements from ineffective ones. Custom research is almost always required to fill this need.

Case History

Recall that Dr. Specks has recently moved his office closer to the local university and he regularly advertises in the university's daily newspaper. Two-thirds of his patients who read the university newspaper are less than 45 years old. Let's suppose that Dr. Specks wants to appeal more to the younger orientation of the paper and wants to stress in his advertisements his unique selection of frames and close proximity to campus. The situation analysis presented earlier revealed that although Dr. Specks has fewer total frames in his collection compared with Lenscrafters, there are no duplicates and so the selection is actually pretty good.

The question is which of several advertisement options best communicates the idea to members of the university community. A separate copytesting study was conducted to answer this question.

Two sets of ads were developed to test against the ad Dr. Specks has been running in the newspaper. Figure 19.12 shows examples of the two new ad series tested. The original ad is not shown. The "Get Crazy" series highlights a different frame in each ad, accompanied by a bold and catchy headline. The "Snowflakes" series illustrates concepts unique in nature, such as snowflakes or fingerprints, and parallels that uniqueness to Dr. Specks's collection. Before the test was conducted, it was felt that the "Get Crazy" series would outperform the other two sets.

After being presented with a test ad, survey respondents were asked to report what they felt was the main idea of the ad and to evaluate Dr. Specks's busi-

FIGURE 19.12 Sample Advertisements Tested

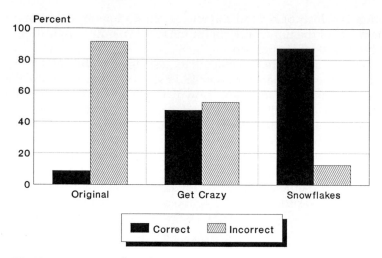

FIGURE 19.13 Main Selling Idea (*Source:* Survey of university audience.)

ness on the factors identified previously to be important to the younger audience. Figure 19.13 shows how well the main idea was communicated by each of the three sets of ads. Clearly, the original ad failed to communicate the idea of selection, because less than 10 percent of respondents cited the idea correctly. By contrast, almost 90 percent of respondents got the selection idea with the "Snowflakes" series. The "Get Crazy" series fell in the middle, with just less than half the respondents correctly reporting the intended selling idea. These results were surprising given the original gut feeling about the superiority of the "Get Crazy" series.

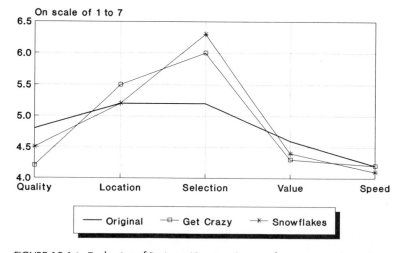

FIGURE 19.14 Evaluation of Business (*Source:* Survey of university audience.)

Figure 19.14 illustrates the response across five purchase-relevant factors (i.e., quality, location, selection, value, and speed). The original ad proved to be the most ambiguous, having recorded moderate responses across the board. Both the "Get Crazy" and "Snowflakes" series outperformed the original ad in terms of influencing the evaluation of selection. A paired-comparison test revealed that the large differences between the original ad and both of the test series were indeed statistically significant ($p < .01$), not due to chance. The slight differences in selection evaluation between the two test series was not statistically significant.

The copytest results suggest that the "Snowflakes" series of ads might be best at communicating the selection idea quickly and with little confusion. The "Get Crazy" series did not vary significantly from the "Snowflakes" series in terms of the five selling criteria evaluated, but if used may require more repetition to convey the main selling idea. It appears that either series of ads would be better than the original ad in communicating the unique selection of frames available from Dr. Specks.

SUMMARY

Advertising research can reveal meaningful differences to help advertising planners make better decisions. Several sources offer useful information on specific situations, markets, and message carriers; and custom research is appropriate for gaining insight into specific situations, propositions, and messages.

In the case of Dr. Raymond Specks, advertising research revealed many interesting findings that suggested ways to help him better target his advertising efforts. Adults aged 45 or older were found to be more likely than average to wear prescription eyeglasses or contact lenses. Dr. Specks was most likely to lose patients in that age group to another local independent, Andes Optical. Younger patients were most likely to defect to the national chain Lenscrafters. The priorities of older patients were found to be different from the priorities of younger patients. Older patients valued location, insurance, cost, and quick delivery. Younger patients were concerned with location, quick delivery, cost, and selection. Adults 45 and older were found to be likely heavy users of newspapers and television. Two sets of test ads were found to communicate the idea of selection much better than the ad used by Dr. Specks.

STUDY QUESTIONS AND EXERCISES

1. For each of the five areas of advertising knowledge discussed in this chapter, summarize the information needed and the likely means of obtaining the information. In which areas are secondary sources of information most appropriate? In which areas are primary sources most fitting?

2. In analyzing data, especially data obtained from sample surveys, it is important to determine whether or not apparent differences are statistically significant. In other words, the differences found must not be due to chance or peculiarities of the sample chosen. The chi-square statistic is often used to test for differences between percentages. Using a chi-square table from any standard statistics text found in your library and the information listed below, determine which of the apparent differences by age in figures 19.7 and 19.11 are statistically significant at a confidence level of .10 or better.

For Figure 19.7:

	df	χ^2
Specks	1	0.08
Lenscrafters	1	4.06
Andes Optical	1	4.70
Royal Optical	1	0.79
Pearle	1	0.16

For Figure 19.11:

	df	χ^2
Location	1	1.16
Quick Delivery	1	1.94
Cost	1	0.43
Selection	1	0.39
Insurance	1	9.45

Would your findings affect the conclusions drawn in the text regarding these figures? If so, how?

3. One of the assumptions made in advertising planning is that the population segments most likely to consume a product category would be receptive to being exposed to advertisements about brands within the category. A *Newsweek* article (February 5, 1990, p. 46) suggests that this assumption is not always valid. At issue is the marketing of malt liquor and cigarettes to African Americans and Hispanics. The *Simmons* data reprinted in Figure 19.15 illustrate that "blacks" are 212 percent more likely than average to be "top half users" of malt liquor and that "others" (the *Simmons* category that includes Hispanics) are 84 percent more likely than average to be "top half users." The same data are the type that would have malt liquor makers target African Americans and Hispanics to receive advertisements about new and existing products.

   a. Besides "black" and "other," which three segments are most likely to be "top half users" of malt liquor? Which three segments are least likely to be "top half users"? Which group of segments seems to differentiate best between most likely and least likely "top half users"?

   b. Locate and read the *Newsweek* article mentioned above. Where do you stand on the issue? What other product categories might provoke a similar defensive reaction among members of targeted segments?

	TOTAL U.S. '000	ALL USERS A '000	B % DOWN	C % ACROSS	D INDX	TOP HALF USERS THREE OR MORE A '000	B % DOWN	C % ACROSS	D INDX	BOTTOM HALF USERS TWO OR LESS A '000	B % DOWN	C % ACROSS	D INDX
TOTAL ADULTS	181131	8903	100.0	4.9	100	3932	100.0	2.2	100	4971	100.0	2.7	100
MALES	86476	5888	66.1	6.8	139	2816	71.6	3.3	150	3072	61.8	3.6	129
FEMALES	94655	3016	33.9	3.2	65	1117	28.4	1.2	54	1899	38.2	2.0	73
18 - 24	25507	1701	19.1	6.7	136	999	25.4	3.9	180	703	14.1	2.8	100
25 - 34	43858	2602	29.2	5.9	121	1120	28.5	2.6	118	1483	29.8	3.4	123
35 - 44	36206	1830	20.6	5.1	103	747	19.0	2.1	95	1083	21.8	3.0	109
45 - 54	24795	1066	12.0	4.3	87	*431	11.0	1.7	80	635	12.8	2.6	93
55 - 64	21496	788	8.9	3.7	75	*365	9.3	1.7	78	*424	8.5	2.0	72
65 OR OLDER	29268	916	10.3	3.1	64	271	6.9	0.9	43	645	13.0	2.2	80
18 - 34	69365	4304	48.3	6.2	126	2118	53.9	3.1	141	2185	44.0	3.2	115
18 - 49	119427	6735	75.6	5.6	115	3135	79.7	2.6	121	3599	72.4	3.0	110
25 - 54	104859	5497	61.7	5.2	107	2298	58.4	2.2	101	3200	64.4	3.1	111
35 - 49	50062	2431	27.3	4.9	99	1017	25.9	2.0	94	1414	28.4	2.8	103
50 OR OLDER	61704.	2169	24.4	3.5	72	797	20.3	1.3	60	1372	27.6	2.2	81
GRADUATED COLLEGE	34578	1364	15.3	3.9	80	*399	10.1	1.2	53	965	19.4	2.8	102
ATTENDED COLLEGE	33812	1475	16.6	4.4	89	633	16.1	1.9	86	843	17.0	2.5	91
GRADUATED HIGH SCHOOL	71180	3351	37.6	4.7	96	1429	36.3	2.0	92	1922	38.7	2.7	98
DID NOT GRADUATE HIGH SCHOOL	41560	2714	30.5	6.5	133	1472	37.4	3.5	163	1242	25.0	3.0	109
EMPLOYED MALES	66051	4452	50.0	6.7	137	1999	50.8	3.0	139	2453	49.3	3.7	135
EMPLOYED FEMALES	54108	1703	19.1	3.1	64	*599	15.2	1.1	51	1104	22.2	2.0	74
EMPLOYED FULL-TIME	108437	5748	64.6	5.3	108	2394	60.9	2.2	102	3354	67.5	3.1	113
EMPLOYED PART-TIME	11721	*407	4.6	3.5	71	**204	5.2	1.7	80	**203	4.1	1.7	63
NOT EMPLOYED	60972	2749	30.9	4.5	92	1334	33.9	2.2	101	1414	28.4	2.3	85
PROFESSIONAL/MANAGER	31879	1117	12.5	3.5	71	*348	8.9	1.1	50	769	15.5	2.4	88
TECH/CLERICAL/SALES	37678	1322	14.8	3.5	71	*396	10.1	1.1	48	925	18.6	2.5	89
PRECISION/CRAFT	14826	1043	11.7	7.0	143	*550	14.0	3.7	171	*494	9.9	3.3	121
OTHER EMPLOYED	35775	2673	30.0	7.5	152	1304	33.2	3.6	168	1369	27.5	3.8	139
SINGLE	39788	3358	37.7	8.4	172	1924	48.9	4.8	223	1434	28.8	3.6	131
MARRIED	108473	3979	44.7	3.7	75	1366	34.7	1.3	58	2614	52.6	2.4	88
DIVORCED/SEPARATED/WIDOWED	32870	1566	17.6	4.8	97	643	16.4	2.0	90	923	18.6	2.8	102
PARENTS	60843	3005	33.8	4.9	100	1051	26.7	1.7	80	1954	39.3	3.2	117
WHITE	155331	6031	67.7	3.9	79	2332	59.3	1.5	69	3699	74.4	2.4	87
BLACK	20477	2424	27.2	11.8	241	1389	35.3	6.8	312	1035	20.8	5.1	184
OTHER	5322	*449	5.0	8.4	172	**212	5.4	4.0	184	**237	4.8	4.5	162

FIGURE 19.15 (*Source:* From Simmons Market Research Bureau, Inc., 1990 *Study of Media and Markets.* Copyright 1990 Simmons Market Research Bureau, Inc. Reprinted by permission.)

SOURCES

Deutsch, Claudia H. 1989. The Battle over Eyewear. *New York Times,* November 26, III-4.
Young, James Webb. 1979. *How to Become an Advertising Man.* Chicago: Crain.

The Research Literature

- Chapter 20: Libraries and Mass Communication Research. This chapter introduces the vast resources of a major university library. Emphasis is on computer applications and good use of existing databases.

CHAPTER

20

Libraries and Mass Communication Research

JANE S. ROW
University of Tennessee, Knoxville

□
OBJECTIVES

After studying this chapter, you should be able to:

1. Find research material using a library catalog.

2. Plan and implement a search strategy.

3. Describe some of the resources found in most major libraries relevant to mass communication.

4. Define a database and explain its advantages for the researcher.

5. Explain computer searching and Boolean logic; plan an on-line search.

6. Identify, find, and use primary data files and public opinion research available via computer.

INFORMATION AND SOCIETY

In the past two decades we have been bombarded with articles on the information society and information proliferation. Alvin Toffler in his book, *The Third Wave,* created a wonderful image of the problem: "An information bomb is exploding in

---

our midst, showering us with a shrapnel of images and drastically changing the way each of us perceives and acts upon our private world." (Toffler, 1981, 156).

The amount of published information is mind boggling. It is estimated that the number of items published worldwide is close to 600,000 per year, and some are predicting the figure will reach one million by the year 2000 (Getz, 1990). Clearly, the information explosion allows us access to more information than we can use or handle. The challenge for all of us is to learn how to find, evaluate, and use appropriate amounts of information effectively.

Consider the words of John Perry, a former newspaper editor:

> True, to be a journalist you must know how to read, write, and spell, and think logically. It helps also to have mastered the basic tricks of the trade, such as writing a lead or focusing a camera. But what is needed even more than that is a knowledge of this fascinating world: geography, biology, economics, philosophy, sociology, music, law, sports, agriculture, political science, literature, mathematics, religion. You name it, and as a journalist you will have to be explaining it someday to an audience that depends on you to give it more than "just the facts." (quoted in Newton, 1984, 3–4)

Although Perry was addressing journalists, his comments are applicable to all disciplines in mass communication. We must find the "facts" and then make sense of them.

How do libraries fit into all of this? Libraries play a crucial role in our information society because they are responsible for collecting, organizing, managing, and providing access points to information resources. In addition, modern libraries are also playing a vital role in integrating new computing technology with traditional information formats. Not to use or understand them is to ignore a valuable asset in our society. How well you are able to manipulate a library's resources may mean the difference between success or failure on a job assignment, a research paper, or a business decision.

The rest of this chapter will be devoted to introducing you to modern libraries, the resources they offer, and the research process involved in using resources effectively. You will also learn about basic on-line searching techniques needed to access computer databases.

LIBRARIES: AN OVERVIEW

America's past paints an image of libraries as quiet places, older buildings, book stacks, and study time. It is important to recognize that today's research libraries are in many ways quite different from the Carnegie libraries of another era. Libraries do more than "mark and park books." Instead they are concerned about collecting information in a variety of formats. Hence we see them, in addition to providing services centering around traditional print formats, collecting materials in microforms, compact discs, magnetic tape, video and audio tape, and interactive video.

America's libraries are active places staffed by highly trained information specialists who are interested in providing the information services needed in our changing society. Knowing what resources to consult and how to find those resources are challenges for the researcher.

Stepping into a large, modern library can be intimidating for the unfamiliar. Generally libraries are organized by function: circulation services, periodicals, microforms, audiovisual services, government documents, interlibrary loan, and reference services. Although all are important, it is vital to the mass communication researcher to know about the department that offers research assistance: the reference department. You will find a noncirculating collection of materials such as encyclopedias, almanacs, handbooks, and indexes; these are the tools necessary for answering questions and finding materials. The personnel in the reference department, particularly the reference librarian, can be critical to your research. These highly trained professionals with masters degrees in library and information science are available to answer questions about the collection, help you develop a research strategy, and help you find materials. The best place to start, when trying to understand the particular library you are using, is to visit this department.

CLASSIFICATION SYSTEMS

In order to use libraries effectively, it is important to know the basis of the arrangement of materials, known as the *classification system.* The two most commonly used systems in this country are the Dewey decimal system and the Library of Congress classification. They are the systematic and logical arrangement of materials—systems that bring material on the same subject together in one place.

Although there is not enough space in this chapter for an extensive discussion of the two systems, a basic overview of the Library of Congress classification may be helpful. This system, developed during the latter nineteenth century for the use of the Library of Congress, has gradually been adopted by most academic libraries. It is a combination of letters and numbers, with 21 primary classes and numerous subdivisions. Each primary class is designated by a single letter. Because the Library of Congress classification uses letters and numbers, it is considered to have broader application and greater flexibility than the Dewey decimal system. There is also more room for adding new fields of knowledge.

The general classes in the Library of Congress classification are listed in Figure 20.1. An example of further breakdown for the letter *P* appears in Figure 20.2. Although it is not necessary for you to remember all 21 classes, it is helpful to know the class for your area of interest and its breakdowns. Knowing where to go in the library for general browsing is productive and interesting. A complete list of classes and subclasses can be found in *LC Classification Outline* (Washington, D.C.: Library of Congress, Subject Cataloging Division).

Understanding how libraries organize materials through a classification scheme is only one part of the puzzle. Another very important aspect is how to locate material using a card or on-line catalog. The *library catalog* is the index to the cataloged materials of a library. On a typical card you will find the *call number* (the classification number needed to locate the book on the shelf), the author, title, place of publication, date of publication, biographical notes, *tracings* (additional subject

```
A  —  GENERAL WORKS—(.e.g, encyclopedias, newspapers, periodicals)
B  —  PHILOSOPHY
C  —  HISTORY AND AUXILIARY SCIENCES
D  —  UNIVERSLA AND OLD WORLD HISTORY—(except America)
E-F—  HISTORY, THE AMERICAS
G  —  GEOGRAPHY, ANTHROPOLOGY—(including folklore and sports)
H  —  SOCIAL SCIENCES—(e.g., economics, sociology, business)
J  —  POLITICAL SCIENCE
K  —  LAW
L  —  EDUCATION
M  —  MUSIC
N  —  FINE ARTS
P  —  LANGUAGE AND LITERATURE
Q  —  SCIENCE—(.e.g, mathematics, physics, and biology)
R  —  MEDICINE—(.e.g, encyclopedias, newspapers, periodicals)
S  —  AGRICULTURE, PLANT, AND ANIMAL INDUSTRY
T  —  TECHNOLOGY—(.e.g, engineering, manufacturing)
U  —  MILITARY SCIENCE
V  —  NAVAL SCIENCE
Z  —  BIBLIOGRAPHY AND LIBRARY SCIENCE
```

FIGURE 20.1   General Classes of the Library of Congress Classification

headings under which the book is listed), and *International Standard Book Number (ISBN;* the unique identification number assigned to each book, a social security number for books so to speak).

It is quite likely that the library you use has an *on-line catalog* (computer catalog). More and more libraries are converting to computer access for their cataloged materials. The information available in an on-line catalog is essentially the same as that in a card catalog, but the means of access may be different.

On-line catalogs offer several advantages over manual card catalogs. The obvious is *speed* of access. It is also possible to have more access points than author, title, and subject. It is not uncommon to look for material by type of format, language, call number, and key word. Many systems also have acquisition and cataloging modules, which make it possible to tell whether or not material is on order and which assist in the cataloging process. Frequently, on-line tutorials are part of the system and easy-to- read instructions are kept near each terminal.

Using either catalog can be straightforward if you know the author or title of

```
P  —  LANGUAGE AND LITERATURE
        PN  —  Literature (general)
              PN1990-1992.92  —  Broadcasting
              PN1991-1991.9   —  Radio Broadcasting
              PN4699-5650     —  Journalism
              PN4735-4748     —  Relations to the State/Government
                                 and the Press; Liberty of the Press
```

FIGURE 20.2   Breakdown of the Letter *P*

the material you want. But if you don't have an author or title, and are interested in finding information on a specific subject, the catalog can be more complex. Let's take a look at the catalog card for the book entitled *Ripoff: A Look at Corruption in America,* shown in Figure 20.3.

At the bottom of the card is a series of assigned subject headings, referred to as the *tracings section* of the card. As you can see, this title can be found under five different subject headings: "United States—Moral conditions," "Business ethics," "Corruption (in politics)—United States," "Corporations—United States—Corrupt practices," and "Judicial corruption—United States."

Often, the subject that comes to mind does not yield the results expected. For example, you may be looking for material on "oil slicks" in the on-line catalog or look for that term in the card catalog, and discover you can't find that topic. How do you resolve the problem? To search the library catalog you can rely on your own knowledge, synonyms, or inverting word order (e.g., advertising-political or politics-advertising). But the most helpful resource you can use is the *Library of Congress Subject Headings (LCSH).* This four-volume set is a list of subject headings used by the Library of Congress and is the standard terminology in most academic libraries. *LCSH* identifies the correct words and phrases to use, as well as the terms not to use. It will give you a list of related headings, and pull you from narrower terms to broader terms. A sample section is shown in Figure 20.4.

Learning to consult the *LCSH* will save you time by telling you under what headings a given subject may be found. It directs you to other headings and other useful aspects of a subject. It also breaks down subjects into several parts, thus aiding researchers in limiting their subjects. Linking the *LCSH* to the efficient use of the catalog is essential. Without it, the researcher may miss valuable information.

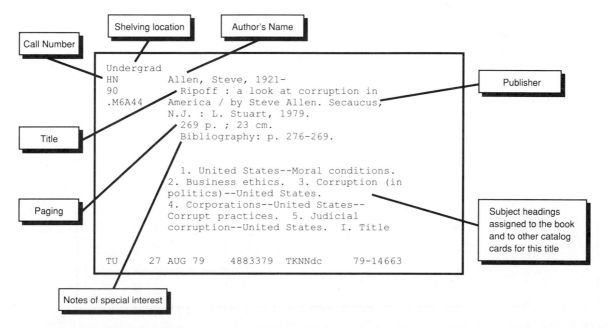

FIGURE 20.3 Sample Catalog Card

Oil pools
USE Oil fields
Oil poppy
USE Opium poppy
Oil printing (Photography)
USE Photography—Printing processes—Oil
Oil process (Photography)
USE Photography—Printing processes—Oil
Oil properties valuation
USE Oil fields—Valuation
Oil reclamation
USE Petroleum waste—Recycling
Oil recovery, Thermal
USE Thermal oil recovery
Oil refineries
USE Petroleum refineries
Oil removal (Sewage purification)
USE Sewage—Purification—Oil removal
Oil reserves
USE Petroleum—Reserves
Oil reservoir engineering
[TN871]
BT Petroleum engineering
NT Oil fields—Production methods
Oil saturation in reservoirs
Oil rigs
USE Oil well drilling rigs
Oil royalties
USE Oil and gas leases
Oil sands (*May Subd Geog*)
UF Bituminous sand
Oil-bearing sands
Tar sand
BT Oil-shales
Petroleum—Geology
—**Law and legislation** (*May Subd Geog*)
BT Petroleum law and legislation
—**Permeability**
NT Formation damage (Petroleum engineering)
Oil sands extraction plants
(*May Subd Geog*)
BT Oil sands industry
Petroleum refineries
Oil sands industry (*May Subd Geog*)
BT Petroleum industry and trade
NT Oil sands extraction plants
—**Canada**
Oil sardine, Indian
USE Sardinella longiceps
Oil saturation in reservoirs
UF Reservoir oil saturation
Residual oil saturation in reservoirs
Saturation of oil in reservoirs
BT Oil reservoir engineering
Secondary recovery of oil
Oil seed plants
USE Oilseed plants
Oil seeds
USE Oilseeds
Oil seep
USE Oil seepage
Oil seepage (*May Subd Geog*)
UF Oil seep
BT Oil fields
Petroleum
Seepage
Oil separators
UF Oil skimmers
Oil-water separators
Separators, Oil
BT Oil pollution of water
Separators (Machines)
Water—Purification
NT Oil spill booms
Oil-shale industry (*May Subd Geog*)
BT Petroleum industry and trade
NT Shale oils—Refining
—**Equipment and supplies**
[TP699]

Oil shale reserves
USE Oil-shales—Reserves
Oil-shales (*May Subd Geog*)
[TN858-TN859]
UF Kerogen shales
Shales, Kerogen
Shales, Oil
BT Energy minerals
Shale
NT Kerogen
Oil sands
Sapropelites
—**Reserves**
UF Oil shale reserves
Reserves of oil-shale
Oil silk
[TS1669]
UF Oilsilk
Silk, Oiled
BT Silk
Waterproofing of fabrics
Oil skimmers
USE Oil separators
Oil slick containment booms
USE Oil spill booms
Oil spill booms (*May Subd Geog*)
UF Booms, Oil spill
Oil slick containment booms
BT Oil separators
Oil spill damages, Liability for
USE Liability for oil pollution damage[s]
Oil spills (*May Subd Geog*)
BT Waste spills
RT Oil pollution of rivers, harbors, et[c.]
Oil pollution of the sea
SA *subdivision* Effect of oil spills on
individual animals and group[s ...]
animals, e.g. Fishes—Effect o[...]
spills on
NT Oil pollution of water
—**Claims**
UF Claims against oil spill dama[ge]
RT Liability for oil pollution dam[ages]
—**Environmental aspects**
(*May Subd Geog*)
NT Oil spills and wildlife
—**Law and legislation** (*May Subd Ge[og]*)
BT Environmental law
Petroleum law and legislation
NT Liability for oil pollution dam[ages]
Oil spills and wildlife (*May Subd Geog*)
UF Wildlife and oil spills
BT Oil spills—Environmental aspect[s]
Wildlife conservation
Oil spray pesticides
USE Oil as pesticide
Oil storage tanks
[TP692.5]
BT Petroleum—Storage
Storage tanks
RT Petroleum—Offshore storage
—**Evaporation control**
[TP692.5]
BT Evaporation control
—**Insulation**
BT Insulation (Heat)
Oil stoves
USE Stoves, Oil
Oil tagging (*May Subd Geog*)
[TD427.P4]
BT Oil inspection
Petroleum products—Analysis
Oil tankers
USE Tankers
Oil-water separators
USE Oil separators
Oil well blowouts
USE Oil wells—Blowouts
Oil well boring
USE Oil well drilling

Oil well casing
UF Casing, Oil well
BT Oil well drilling
Oil wells—Equipment and supplies
NT Casinghead gas
—**Cathodic protection**
BT Cathodic protection
—**Welding**
Oil well cementing
UF Oil well plugging
BT Oil well drilling
Oil wells—Maintenance and repair

Petroleum engineering
Petroleum in submerged lands
NT Drilling platforms
Offshore support vessels
Riser pipe
—**Law and legislation** (*May Subd Geog*)
BT Offshore structures (International law)
Petroleum law and legislation
Oil well drilling fluids
USE Drilling muds
Oil well drilling muds
USE Drilling muds
Oil well drilling rigs (*May Subd Geog*)
[TN871.5]

Oil slick containment booms
USE Oil spill booms
Oil spill booms (*May Subd Geog*)
UF Booms, Oil spill
Oil slick containment booms
BT Oil separators
Oil spill damages, Liability for
USE Liability for oil pollution damages
Oil spills (*May Subd Geog*)
BT Waste spills
RT Oil pollution of rivers, harbors, etc.
Oil pollution of the sea
SA *subdivision* Effect of oil spills on *under*
individual animals and groups of
animals, e.g. Fishes—Effect of oil
spills on
NT Oil pollution of water
— **Claims**
UF Claims against oil spill damage
RT Liability for oil pollution damages
— **Environmental aspects**
(*May Subd Geog*)
NT Oil spills and wildlife
— **Law and legislation** (*May Subd Geog*)
BT Environmental law
Petroleum law and legislation
NT Liability for oil pollution damages
Oil spills and wildlife (*May Subd Geog*)
UF Wildlife and oil spills
BT Oil spills—Environmental aspects
Wildlife conservation

FIGURE 20.4 Sample Section from the *Library of Congress Subject Headings*

RESEARCH STRATEGIES

Perhaps the most overlooked aspect of library research is the preparation time needed before you even enter the library. In essence, a research strategy equates to developing a plan for the efficient use of your time. Look at the following example of a research problem and analyze what you would need to do:

> Congratulations! You have been asked by the National Geographic Society to do a feature on the war for independence in Eritrea, the northernmost province in Ethiopia, and its implications on the future of Ethiopia. You are also to assess the problems of famine. In addition you will be meeting with the official Ethiopian People's Liberation Front, a Marxist rebel organization. This is a perfect opportunity to combine your interests in history, political science, geography, and agriculture with your skills in research and writing. This is one of your first international assignments and you expect to plan carefully. With the society paying all of your expenses, plus a salary, you want to impress the editors with your wise use of time and careful organization. You will select a team to join you on this three-week expedition to Ethiopia. What information will you need before you depart? How will you organize your search?

The first step is to analyze the topic's dimensions and limitations. What information do you need to find? In this example, the dimensions include world famine, the number of starving people, Ethiopia (its culture, religion, population, economy, and government), Eritrea, and the general political situation in the area. One of the limitations you might consider is time. Are you interested in the famine occurring this year, or do you want to look at famine in Ethiopia over a longer time?

The second step is to identify and clarify subject terms. At this time you would want to consult the *LCSH* and start keeping a list of the terms you could use to find information on your topic (i.e., famine, Africa, Ethiopia, Marxist groups, Eritrea).

The third step is to consider the need for primary or secondary sources. *Primary sources* include firsthand material that hasn't been interpreted by anyone. Perhaps you could get the transcripts of Ethiopians interviewed on the CNN newscasts, or the personal journals of doctors and other visitors to the country. *Secondary sources* are interpretations of primary sources done by someone else. Books about Ethiopia, encyclopedia articles, and news accounts would be examples.

The fourth step is to estimate the quantity of material you need. If you are doing a 500-word story for your local paper, you know you don't need a great deal. If on the other hand, you are doing a 15-page story for *The Atlantic* or *The National Geographic* you need considerably more. This is a judgment call for the researcher.

The fifth step in your planning process is to determine the quality of the information needed. Do you need popular material such as articles from *Time* magazine, or do you need more scholarly material as would appear in *Foreign Affairs*? Be prepared to evaluate the credibility of your sources. Are the points of view presented with objectivity, or is there a clear bias?

The sixth step is to determine how current your information must be. Do you need yesterday's news, or will material written over the past 10 years suffice? Do you need factual information, analytical information, or a combination of both?

Other important issues include deciding which information formats might be useful (Do you want to find videotape, audio cassettes, books, or periodicals?) and how to budget your time. Identifying the sources and then locating the material can take considerable time. Checking with a reference librarian about the complexity of your research may help you to forecast how much time you will need.

When you have gone through all of these steps, you will be ready to think about finding the resources you need.

SELECTED RESOURCES FOR MASS COMMUNICATION

Because of the interdisciplinary nature of mass communication, the resources available are vast. This chapter cannot cover all of them, but it will provide an introduction to types of sources. The selected titles represent a sampling of the more important information tools. These sources, which will answer factual questions and lead you to additional information, can usually be found in the reference section of the library.

Reference materials are kept in a separate area of the library and do not circulate. There are two basic categories of materials. The first is *general reference material*, which covers wide ranges of information on different topics. The second is *subject reference material*, which is specific to one subject area. Within these two broad categories are two additional types, direct access sources and indirect access material. *Direct access sources* give specific information. Examples include:

Dictionaries
Encyclopedias
Directories
Handbooks
Almanacs
Gazetteers
Guide books
Biographical dictionaries
Atlases
Manuals
Yearbooks

Indirect access materials help you to identify other sources for information. Examples include bibliographies, indexes, and abstracts.

Encyclopedias

Encyclopedias are sometimes overused and abused by students. They can, however, be a very important first step in the research process, particularly if you are looking for an overview article that organizes and synthesizes a topic. This type of article can help put a topic into perspective and give you help organizing your thoughts on what aspect to develop. Many encyclopedias have signed, in-depth articles with excellent bibliographies that can lead you to important material on the topic. Encyclopedias are usually divided into two categories: general and subject related. A *general encyclopedia* is a general compilation of information on a wide range of topics. Examples of typical general encyclopedias are *The Encyclopaedia Britannica* (Chicago: Encyclopedia Britannica) and *Encyclopedia Americana* (Danbury, Conn.: Grolier). A *subject-related encyclopedia* focuses on a specific discipline or area of study. Examples of this type are *The Encyclopedia of Psychology* (New York: Wiley) and the *McGraw-Hill Encyclopedia of Science and Technology* (New York: McGraw-Hill).

There is an amazing number of subject encyclopedias. To find one in a subject area of interest, consult one of two useful reference guides: *ARBA Guide to Subject Encyclopedias* (Littleton, Colo.: Libraries Unlimited) or *First Stop: The Master Index to Subject Encyclopedias* (Phoenix: Oryx).

One important subject encyclopedia for mass communication is the *International Encyclopedia of Communications* (New York: Oxford University Press). This four-volume set contains approximately 550 articles covering most aspects of communication, ranging from advertising and public relations, to communication research, government regulation, international communication, journalism, political communication, and theorists. It has a detailed subject index and is a good starting point for many areas of mass communication research.

The following list is just a sampling of the variety of subject encyclopedias:

Encyclopedia of American Political History
Encyclopedia of Banking and Finance
Encyclopedia of Bioethics
Encyclopedia of Crime and Justice
Encyclopedia of Education
Encyclopedia of Religion
Encyclopedia of Philosophy
Encyclopedia of Judaica
Encyclopedia of Islam
Encyclopedia of The Third World
Cassell's Encyclopedia of World Literature
Grzimek's Animal Life Encyclopedia
New Catholic Encyclopedia
Medical and Health Encyclopedia
New York Times Encyclopedia of Film
WorldMark Encyclopedia of the Nations

Dictionaries

Dictionaries contain information about words, spelling, pronunciation, etymology, and usage. *Unabridged dictionaries* include all words in the language with their definitions; *abridged dictionaries* are shorter versions.

Dictionaries, like encyclopedias, can be specialized by subject area; so it is possible to find dictionaries for almost all disciplines (e.g., psychology, religion, politics, business, mathematics, and biology). There are several dictionaries for mass communication. Two of the more important are the *Longman Dictionary of Mass Media and Communications* (New York: Longman) and *The Communication Handbook: A Dictionary* (New York: Harper & Row). These two titles cover many of the same terms, but *The Longman Dictionary* is unique in that a subfield is identified with each entry (e.g., advertising, broadcasting, newspaper journalism, photojournalism, publishing, film). If a term has a special meaning to the subfield, that meaning is noted. *The Communication Handbook's* strength is that in addition to definitions, essays are provided on certain terms.

Specialized dictionaries within the field of mass communication also exist. *The Broadcast Communications Dictionary* (New York: Greenwood Press), for example, contains more than 6,000 technical, common, and slang terms used by broadcast communicators. Another title of interest is the *Dictionary of Advertising* (Lincolnwood, Ill.: NTC Business Books). It concentrates on words used in marketing, copyrighting, art direction, graphics, media planning, research analysis, and consumer research.

Almanacs, Yearbooks, and Handbooks

These are usually one-volume, easy-to-use works that provide concise factual information on a great many topics: current and historical events, people, countries and governments, organizations, and statistical trends. They summarize events and data; and for that reason, they often provide the quick answer that doesn't need a lot of detail. If you are interested in finding out the name of a president of a foreign country, the number of deaths due to drunk driving, or the names of the *Challenger* crew, you will likely find the answer in this kind of resource.

The following list of selected "high-use" titles will probably be very helpful to you as a researcher:

Demographic Yearbook   (New York: Department of Economic and Social Affairs, Statistical Office, United Nations), published by the United Nations, is a comprehensive collection of international demographic statistics. It gives world population data, with statistics on related subjects such as mortality, population, marriage, and divorce rates.

Europa World Yearbook   (London: Europa Publications Limited) is a source of interesting information on the mass media of countries around the world (not just Europe). Along with detailed information on the political, economic, and commercial institutions of a country, you will find information on the number of newspapers, TV stations, and radio receivers. The names and addresses of news agencies, newspapers, and electronic media are given.

Municipal Yearbook   (Washington, D.C.: International City Management Association) provides statistical information on U.S. cities and counties and addresses questions and issues associated with government. It is a good source for financial data on topics such as municipal salaries and expenditures. Names, addresses, and telephone numbers of government officials are included.

The World Almanac and Book of Facts (New York: Scripps-Howard) is perhaps the best handbook for miscellaneous factual information. It includes such diverse subjects as copyright law, the environment, presidential elections, social security, weights and measures, taxes, food and nutrition, and flags of the world. It also has the year's 10 top news stories.

The Statistical Abstract of the United States (Washington, D.C.: U.S. Bureau of the Census) is the first place to look for U.S. statistical information. It has been published annually since 1878 and provides social, political, and economic data. The source for each table is cited, so the researcher can track down the original data.

Directories

Mass communication specialists are frequently interested in finding basic information such as data about television and radio stations, the names of individuals responsible for the public relations for a firm, or the target audience of a periodical and its cost of advertising. All of this information can be found in directories. These resources lead you to people, organizations, institutions, and information about them. The following list is of directories important for the mass communication specialist:

Directories in Print (Detroit: Gale) will help you identify the existence of a directory in a subject area of interest. The newest edition contains more than 10,000 entries indexed by subject categories such as business, finance, advertising, marketing, public relations, publishing, broadcast media, medicine, community services, and social concerns.

Editor and Publisher International Yearbook (New York: Editor and Publisher) is useful for both statistical and directory information on American, Canadian, and foreign journalism. It lists U.S. and Canadian dailies, syndicates, wire services, advertising agencies, schools of journalism, foreign correspondents, and directors of foreign press associations.

Editor and Publisher Market Guide (New York: Editor and Publisher) is a guide to U.S. and Canadian markets that publish a daily newspaper. The market information includes data on transportation systems, population, financial institutions, climate, retailing centers, principal industries, and newspapers.

Gale Directory of Publications and Broadcast Media (Detroit: Gale) lists daily and weekly newspapers and periodicals published in the United States and Canada. It has a geographical arrangement and includes information on frequency, subscription rate, circulation, and key personnel. Radio station entries list owner, operating hours, wattage, and format (e.g., classic rock).

Standard Rate and Data Service (Wilmette, Ill.) publishes a series of directories covering the media. The titles in the series are:
> *Business Publications Press and Data*
> *Canadian Advertising Rates and Data*
> *Consumer Magazines and Agri-Media Rates and Data*
> *Newspaper Rates and Data*

> *Print Media Rates and Data*
> *Spot Radio Rates and Data*
> *Spot Television Rates and Data*

In most cases, the directories provide an editorial profile, information on rate policies, specific advertising rates, circulation, and audience statistics.

The Standard Periodical Directory (New York: Oxbridge) is one of several comprehensive guides to periodicals published in the United States and Canada. Periodicals can be accessed by subject and by title. Entries also usually include the publisher, address, and circulation.

The Working Press of the Nation (Chicago: National Research Bureau) is a five-volume directory of U.S. newspapers, magazines, TV and radio feature writers, photographers, international publications of U.S.-based companies, government agencies, clubs, and associations. Each entry provides detailed information, including personnel, circulation, frequency, and address.

O'Dwyer's Directory of Public Relations Firms (New York: J. R. O'Dwyer) provides information about people and firms in the field of public relations. Address, telephone number, personnel, and a brief description of functions are typically included with each entry.

Biographical Sources

There are a multitude of sources for information about people. Checking the standards of admission to these sources can be very enlightening. If the people listed submit their own biographical information, then it is possible a certain bias will exist.

The Biography and Genealogy Master Index (Detroit: Gale) is probably the best place to start hunting for information on people. Over 8 million entries from over 350 biographical sources are indexed in this multivolume set. Each entry contains a source code that leads the user to the titles indexed. Some of the better known sources indexed in this title are:

> *The Biography Index* (New York: H. W. Wilson)
> *Current Biography* (New York: H. W. Wilson)
> *International Who's Who* (London: Europa Publications)
> *Who's Who in America* (Wilmette, Illinois: Marquis Who's Who)

Like many other types of reference sources, there are special biographical sources for various subject areas. If you are looking for biographical information on a journalist, a scientist, or a politician, there is probably, in addition to the general biographical sources, a special subject-related source that will discuss the individual. Examples include the following:

American Men and Women of Science (New York: R. R. Bowker) lists 290,000 prominent scientists in the physical and life sciences, all of whom have made significant contributions to scientific work. Standard biographical data is given, along with a current mailing address.

Biographical Dictionary of American Journalism (New York: Greenwood Press) provides sketches of American journalism from 1690 to 1989 in a one-volume reference book. There are more than 500 entries from newspapers, magazines, radio, television, and various occupations related to mass communication. Reporters, editors, publishers, correspondents, cartoonists, illustrators, and photographers are all represented. This alphabetical listing summarizes the significant contributions of each individual.

Politics in America (Washington, D.C.: Congressional Quarterly) will take you beyond the basic biographical data. An editorial biography for each national legislator, including a photograph, is given. A description of the congressional district or state the individual represents, a brief financial campaign report, a report on the legislative activity of the individual, and key voting statistics are included.

Atlases, Gazetteers, and Guidebooks

An *atlas* is a book designed primarily to provide maps. The maps can range in subject content; for example, they can be political, economic, geographic, or demographic. A *gazetteer* is a dictionary of geographic places, usually without maps. A gazetteer can give historical, cultural, and statistical information about a place. A *guidebook,* in addition to providing maps and other facts, often includes information on things such as restaurants, hotel accommodations, and unique things to do and see in a specific place. Examples include:

Rand McNally Commercial Atlas and Marketing Guide (Chicago: Rand McNally) leads you to business and commercial data. The large maps for each state are detailed. More than 128,000 principal cities, towns, and inhabited places are indexed. Each entry includes information on population, elevation, zip code, and transportation systems.

Webster's New Geographical Dictionary (Springfield, Mass.: G. & C. Merriam) contains 50,000 entries, some maps, and a list of administrative divisions of major counties and U.S. states—making it extremely useful for U.S. geographic information.

Indexes and Abstracts

Most of the library catalogs you will encounter will not include access to periodical literature or chapters in books. Therefore, it is important to become familiar with the variety of indexes and abstracts that will be the key to finding this kind of material. Very few of them deal exclusively with mass communication topics. Yet, mass communication is covered in many of the general and specialized indexes of other fields. As is true of the other reference materials we have talked about, these indexes and abstracts also can be divided into general sources and subject-related ones. Again, it is impossible to include all of the indexes and abstracts that are important. The ones in this chapter should give you a sense of the variety and type of coverage available. It is a good idea to check with the reference librarian to see if there is an index you ought to be consulting for your research.

General Indexes

Reader's Guide to Periodical Literature (New York: H. W. Wilson) is the general index with which most people are familiar. It tends to cover the popular newsstand magazines such as *Time* and *Newsweek.* It is a very useful index for researching current topics, and its subject index is easy to use.

InfoTrac (CD ROM. Foster City, Calif.: Information Access Company) is a quick way to get much of the same kind of information found in *Reader's Guide* by using a microcomputer. The Information Access Company has merged optical disc and microcomputer technology to produce a series of databases that index general periodicals and major city newspapers. More and more public libraries and most academic libraries have this technology in their reference rooms.

Specialized Indexes

ABC News Index (Woodbridge, Conn.: Research Publications) provides access to the complete transcripts for TV programs such as "Nightline," "ABC News Special," "Business World," "20/20," and "This Week with David Brinkley." The index can be searched by subject, program title, or names of personalities. Access is to a microfiche collection of transcripts. Accompanying each entry is a short abstract.

Alternative Press Index (Baltimore: Alternative Press Center) captures the underground and radical press. Access is by either subject or author. It is an invaluable resource for gaining access to points of view not in the mainstream press.

Art Index (New York: H. W. Wilson) covers 200 domestic and foreign art periodicals on subjects such as architecture, archeology, art history, arts and crafts, city planning, fine arts, graphic arts, industrial design, photography, and film. There is excellent coverage of photojournalism.

Business Periodicals Index (New York: H. W. Wilson) provides indexing of more than 300 magazines and journals in accounting, advertising, marketing, banking, communication, economics, finance and investment, insurance, labor, management, and public relations. There are many subject headings related to media management.

The National Newspaper Index (Belmont, Calif.: Information Access) puts together in one system the indexes to the *New York Times, Wall Street Journal, Christian Science Monitor, Chicago Tribune,* and *Los Angeles Times.* It is available on-line, on CD ROM, and on microfiche.

NewsBank Index (New Cannan, Conn.: NewsBank) selectively indexes more than 450 U.S. newspapers. The subject index leads to a microfiche collection of full text articles. This is an excellent source for getting a survey of the American regional press.

The New York Times Index (New York: New York Times) dates back to 1851, making it an excellent source to verify historical dates. Abstracts accompany most of the subject headings. Each entry provides the date, section, page, and column of the paper in which the article is found.

PAIS International in Print (New York: Public Affairs Information Service) focuses on issues surrounding public policy. Periodicals, books, government documents, and reports are indexed. The coverage is international and draws from literature in almost all social science fields.

Resources in Education (RIE) (Washington, D.C.: U.S. Government Printing Office) is part of the Educational Resources Information Center (ERIC) system, a national system of clearinghouses, funded by the U.S. Office of Education. The *Current Index to Journals in Education (CIJE)* is the second part. *RIE* indexes and abstracts research reports, bibliographies, curriculum materials, and conference papers. *CIJE* indexes approximately 800 periodicals in the field of education.

Social Sciences Index (New York: H. W. Wilson) indexes approximately 350 interdisciplinary periodicals from fields such as political science, public administration, law, sociology, and anthropology. It has both author and subject indexes.

Abstracts. Abstracts not only give basic bibliographic information needed to locate material, but also provide a short summary of the article or book. This kind of index is extremely valuable in helping researchers identify relevant sources without actually having first to retrieve them. Several abstracting services are available in a variety of subject areas. Some that might be particularly important to the area of mass communication are listed here:

Communications Abstracts (Newbury Park, Calif.: Sage) comes out on a bimonthly basis and indexes more than 200 periodicals, along with books and research reports. There are both subject and author indexes. The subject headings include advertising, broadcasting, communication theory, consumer behavior, group communication, interpersonal communication, communication law, media effects, political communication, public opinion, and research.

Journalism Abstracts (Columbia, S.C.: Association for Education in Journalism and Mass Communication) is the place to look for doctoral dissertations and masters' theses from major research institutions in the United States and Canada. There are author, subject, and institution indexes.

Psychological Abstracts (Arlington, Va.: American Psychological Association) is important for searching psychological literature. Books, periodicals, dissertations, and conference papers are included. To access the appropriate subject heading it is important to consult the *Thesaurus of Psychological Index Terms*. (This is a one-volume list of the subject headings found in the index.) *Psychological Abstracts* is available on-line, and in CD ROM format.

Citation Indexes. Citation indexes are based on the assumption that when an author cites the work of another author, the two works are related in subject matter. A *citation index* identifies and groups together all newly published articles that have cited the same earlier publication. The earlier publication then becomes an indexing term for current articles that deal with the same subject. At present, there are three different citation indexes produced by the Institute for Scientific Information (ISI). They include the *Science Citation Index*, the *Social Sciences Citation Index*, and the *Arts and Humanities Citation Index*.

Science Citation Index (SCI) covers the literature of the medical and life sciences, physical and chemical sciences, behavioral sciences, engineering, technology, applied sciences, and agricultural, biological, and environmental sciences. Approximately 5,000 of the most prominent scientific journals are indexed.

Social Sciences Citation Index (SSCI) provides interdisciplinary indexing to the social sciences, covering areas such as anthropology, business and finance, education, political science, psychology, and social work. Over 120,000 new journal articles and close to 5,000 items from books are indexed each year.

Arts and Humanities Citation Index (A&HCI) covers literature, music, religion, philosophy, art, dance, and history. Approximately 1,000 prominent journals in the humanities and more than 124 books are indexed each year.

Bibliographies and Guides to the Literature

Bibliographies and guides to the literature are valuable research aids that list sources of information. Often they are descriptive, and lead to the basic works considered important in a field. Guides to the literature are particularly useful if you are unfamiliar with a subject area, because they help you to determine the essential material to review. Some of the better known bibliographic guides to the literature in mass communication include:

Basic Books in the Mass Media (Urbana, Ill.: Urbana Press) has more than 1,900 entries. All aspects of mass communication literature are covered. Subject areas include theory, structure, film, print media, broadcast media, book publishing, advertising, and others. Several bibliographies are cited. Its author and title indexes are good.

A Guide to Mass Communications Sources (Lexington, Ky.: Journalism Monographs) is now over 10 years old (1981), but the classic titles important to mass communication are covered here, as well as the fundamental journal titles a researcher needs to consult. Each citation is annotated, making this a very helpful bibliography.

Journalism: A Guide to the Reference Literature (Englewood, Colo.: Libraries Unlimited) is a comprehensive guide to references works in print and broadcast journalism. Chapters are organized by type of material (e.g., directories, yearbooks, handbooks). The detailed subject and title indexes will lead you to more than 700 sources.

Statistical Resources

The U.S. government is probably the most important statistics-gathering agency in the world. For finding basic factual information, several titles are available. Some of the most important are:

American Statistical Index (ASI) (Bethesda, Md.: Congressional Information Service) is a master guide and index to statistical publications of the U.S. government. Publications may be found by title, subject, or category (e.g., race, country, sex). The index leads you to a microfiche full text version of the original document.

The Statistical Abstract of the United States (Washington, D.C.: U.S. Government Printing Office), previously mentioned, summarizes statistical data from most government and some nongovernment agencies. It is the best place to go for the most-asked-about statistics related to the social, political, and economic conditions of the United States.

Statistical Reference Index (SRI) (Washington, D.C.: U.S. Congressional Information Service) is the companion guide to the *American Statistical Index (ASI)*. This index leads you to data produced by non–U.S. government sources, such as state and local governments, business organizations, and private agencies. This index, like *ASI,* leads you to a microfiche collection of full text articles.

STATISTICS AND THE U.S. BUREAU OF THE CENSUS

Of all the statistics generated by the U.S. government, those of the Census Bureau are probably the best known and perhaps the most important. Census numbers determine not only how our political boundaries are drawn, but also how federal funds are distributed to communities. Private business sector and community planning decisions are often based on census results.

The Census Bureau gathers data on subjects such as population, housing, business, agriculture, government finances, and foreign trade. Since the first U.S. Census was taken in 1790, the Census Bureau has regularly counted the American people, their activities, products, and possessions.

Although the U.S. Constitution (Article 1, Section 2) requires that a population census be conducted every 10 years, it is important to know that the Census Bureau issues hundreds of reports that come out more frequently. For example, other censuses are taken and issued on a five-year schedule. The Economic Census (composed of sections for retail trade, wholesale trade, service industries, construction, manufacturing, mineral industries, and transportation) falls into this category; it comes out in years ending in 2 and 7 (e.g., 1982, 1987, 1992, 1997). A variety of data reports are issued quarterly, monthly, and yearly. Some of the special series publications over the past few years have included detailed data reports on topics such as child support and alimony, fertility, labor force status and other characteristics of persons with a work disability, and computer use in this country.

Data are issued in traditional print format, as well as on magnetic tape, diskettes, and CD ROM. An on-line database that provides access to the most current information issued from the Census Bureau is called CENDATA. It is available through Compuserve and Dialog Search Services, which are two private companies that provide software technology to access the database.

Information about Census Bureau publications is available in *The Bureau of Census Catalog.* This annual catalog provides bibliographic data, abstracts, and ordering information. "Data User News," a monthly newsletter, provides information about current censuses, surveys, products, and programs, including computer tape files. The names of key contact people and their telephone numbers are also listed.

LEARN BY DOING

Census Data reveal a lot about who we are, what we do, and how we live. As an exercise in learning to use the Census, visit a library that collects census material and look at a title called *The General Population Characteristics.* Pick the volume for the state where you are presently living and answer the following questions:

Using Census Data

1. How many women, 18 years and over are in your state?
2. What is the median age for all males in the county where you live?
3. How many persons per household are there in your city?
4. What is the number of Spanish origin families in your city?

Government Documents

U.S. government documents cover a wide range of topics aimed at many different audiences. The official definition from the *U.S. Code* is "informational matter which is published as an individual document at government expense, or as required by law" (44 U.S.C. 1901). They can be some of the most important and valuable resources available to you. You will find firsthand reports of government activities, for example, reports of the Watergate scandal, the *Challenger* disaster, and the Supreme Court nominations of Robert Bork, Clarence Thomas, and Ruth Bader Ginsberg. Because almost every aspect of human activity is of concern to our government, you can almost always be assured that government publications have addressed your research topic. Whether the issue is groundwater contamination, child care, the homeless, or unemployment, there will be a government document on the topic. A couple of the more important tracking sources for government documents are the following:

Monthly Catalog to U.S. Government Publications (Washington, D.C.: Government Printing Office) is the primary source for identifying publications of the U.S. government. Approximately 20,000 titles are indexed each year. Many libraries now have this available on a CD ROM title, MARCIVE.

Congressional Information Service Index (CIS Index) (Washington, D.C.: Congressional Information Service) is an indexing and abstracting service that will lead you to Congressional hearings, committee prints, House and Senate documents, reports, miscellaneous publications, and Senate executive reports and documents. Testimony of witnesses at hearings is summarized. This is an invaluable source for tracing legislative histories.

Again, these titles represent only a few of the many available to the researcher in mass communication. Consultation with reference librarians and the basic guides to the literature will reveal a great deal more worthwhile material.

COMPUTER DATABASES AND LIBRARIES

Starting in the early 1980s libraries began to be a part of the microcomputer revolution. It is now commonplace for libraries to have multiple microcomputer workstations. Some will provide access to the automated catalog; others will be CD ROM products that allow users to search for information in special databases; and still others will be connected to on-line systems that provide access to databases on a mainframe computer at a remote site. All of this technology creates new information literacy challenges. To have a basic understanding of how technological access to information works is important to the mass communication researcher. It is quite likely that we are approaching a time when every person will have the capability to sit at his or her own workstation and access a great variety of databases in order to search for information.

What is a database? A *database* is a collection of information on a common theme or subject. Databases are produced by organizations or companies that collect and organize information. For example, the *PsycInfo Database,* produced by the American Psychological Association, is essentially the computerized form of the paper index *Psychological Abstracts.* The database producers sell their databases to companies that develop the software to access the information. These companies are called *vendors.* Think of them as middlemen. There are several companies that provide database services. Some of the best known are DIALOG (owned by Knight Ridder, it provides access to over 350 databases), BRS (owned by Bibliographic Retrieval Services; over 150 databases), Wilsonline (owned by H. W. Wilson; approximately 20 databases), and Nexis (owned by Mead; over 120 databases).

Libraries pay a subscription rate to tap into the vendor's bank of databases. Every time a particular database is used a fee is charged, part of it going to the vendor and part going to the database producer.

There are basically three kinds of databases: bibliographic, numeric, and full text. The *bibliographic database* corresponds to the periodical indexes and abstracts. It leads to references to journal or newspaper articles, technical reports, conference papers, dissertations, or books. A reference or *citation* includes the information you need to locate the source document, such as author, title, journal name, and publication date. The *numeric database* applies to statistical data and tables. *The Census of Population and Housing* produced by the U.S. government is an example. *Full text databases* allow you to pull out the complete text of an article. The "Papers" database produced by Knight-Ridder is an example; it allows you to tap into several different newspapers and retrieve the complete text of articles.

Libraries usually offer two services connected with computerized searching. One is called *mediated searching.* In this situation, an appointment is made with a librarian who is highly skilled at database searching. The librarian will conduct an informal interview with the client to make sure both parties have a clear understanding of what information is needed. After the interview, the librarian will perform the search.

The other service is *end-user searching*, in which the library user often is asked to take a tutorial and then proceeds alone to use specially designated systems.

On-Line Searching

On-line searching is an interaction with a computer, via a telecommunications system, in which data are transmitted and processed immediately. Depending on the system you are using, you could be sitting at a terminal in Houston, talking to a computer in California or New York. The advantage of going on-line to search for information is that you can save time because information access is much faster and efficient. Another powerful asset of computer searching is that often the database has multiple access points that allow for greater flexibility in searching. You are not limited to author, title, and subject searching, but can look for information in other ways (e.g., through type of material, language, or keyword). Updates are also likely to be more current than they would be with the printed copy.

Despite the many advantages of on-line searching, there are some reasons why it might not be appropriate. First, the database is only as good as its producer. So, if the database is not well done, the search can end up being a costly unproductive venture. On-line systems cost money. You will pay telephone line connect time and a fee for every minute you are searching the database. In addition, some databases will charge you a certain amount for every citation you retrieve. Costs vary considerably with each database, ranging from as little as $15 per hour to well over $100 per hour. Another possible disadvantage to on-line searching is limited time coverage. If the database covers material from 1988 to present, and you are looking for articles written in the 1970s, you will not find what you want.

Search Preparation and Boolean Logic

Although different companies may use different syntax or protocols for their systems, they all rely on the same basic logic—and all work best when the researcher takes time to plan a search strategy. This holds true whether you are using an end-user system and doing your own search, or have made an appointment with an experienced librarian to do a mediated search. The basic logic and search preparation are the same.

The first step in preparing for a search is to write a sentence or two describing your topic: for example, "What role has the mass media played in terrorist activities such as hostage taking?"

The next step is to identify the major concepts in your statement. The concepts in the above sentence would look like this:

Concept A   Concept B
Mass Media   Terrorism

Boolean Logic

After completing a written statement and identifying the key concepts, it is important to try to pick possible databases that might contain appropriate information. Vendors publish catalogs containing descriptions of available databases, and these catalogs should be available to you in the database search services area of the library. If you are participating in a mediated search, the librarian will make recommendations to you.

The next step is to develop a list of synonyms, key words, or phrases that describe each of your concepts. In many cases, the database producer will publish a thesaurus for you to consult. A *database thesaurus* is a list of indexing terms (commonly called *controlled vocabulary*) that are unique to the database. Using these terms should guarantee a better result. If a thesaurus is not available, using a dictionary or the print version of the index can be very helpful.

For the example we are using (the role of the mass media in terrorist activities), we will use the *PAIS International* (Public Affairs Information Service, Inc) database. Although there are probably others that might be useful, this one was chosen because of its interdisciplinary coverage and its strength in public policy, government, and international issues.

Consulting the *PAIS* thesaurus we might find the following terms to describe our key concepts:

CONCEPT A	CONCEPT B
MASS MEDIA	*TERRORISM*
Mass Media	Terrorism
Broadcast Journalism	Hostages

Once appropriate terms have been identified for the topic, it is time to apply Boolean logic to the search. *Boolean logic* is what makes computer searching so powerful. Named after the nineteenth-century mathematician and philosopher George Boole, this technique is based on his "algebra of logic." Fortunately, Boolean logic is not difficult to understand because it makes use of three familiar terms: *and, or, not.* These terms are known as *logical operators;* they perform the tasks of informational retrieval as the database is searched.

The *or* operator broadens a search. It is the linking term used to connect similar words that describe the topic (see Figure 20.5). In our example, we want to look for information not only on the term *terrorism,* but also on the term *hostages.* Therefore, we will link these two terms together with the word *or.*

The *and* operator is used to narrow the search. Using this term we can link different concepts (see Figures 20.6 and 20.7, page 419). For our search we want articles that contain information on terms that relate to both terrorism and the mass media. All of our terms need to be present in the article.

The *not* operator is used to exclude articles that contain a certain term. Suppose you were retrieving articles that discussed radio coverage and you did not want to look at that aspect of mass media. You could conceivably enter "mass media not radio" as a search expression. However, the *not* operator needs to be used with caution, because if used incorrectly it can eliminate relevant information.

Use of Boolean Operator "OR"

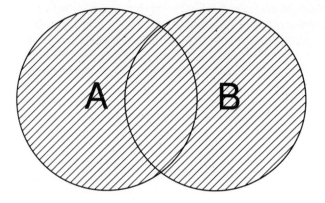

Result is citations to all documents
with either "A" OR "B" OR both.

FIGURE 20.5   Use of the Boolean Operator *or*

Use of Boolean Operator "AND"

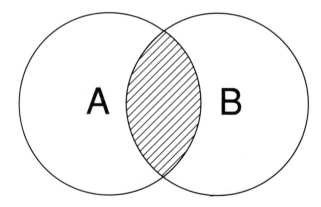

Result is citations to all documents
with index terms "A" AND "B."

FIGURE 20.6   Use of the Boolean Operator *and*

Use of the Boolean Operator "NOT"

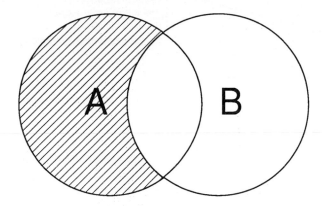

Only the shaded items will be retrieved.

FIGURE 20.7   Use of the Boolean Operator *not*

If we were actually taping into the *PAIS International* database on the Dialog system, a very simple search strategy might be the one shown in Figure 20.8.

PUBLIC OPINION DATA FILES AND SURVEY RESEARCH

Although there may be some disagreement about which term to use (the academic community preferring *survey research* and the media preferring *polls*), there is little disagreement that survey research yields a unique and valuable type of information. Modern public opinion and survey research dates back to the late 1930s with the work of George Gallup, Elmo Roper, and Archibald Crossley. Since then there have been tens of thousands of surveys conducted and probably hundreds of thousands of questions asked. Through the use of scientifically developed methodologies, survey research allows one to identify and perhaps explain values, attitudes, beliefs, and behavior of a large segment of the population by administering questions to a much smaller segment. This data has proved to be accurate and reliable (Smith and Weil, 1990, 609–626).

In their book *Search Strategies in Mass Communication*, Jean Ward and Kathleen Hansen (1992, 207) delineate some common uses of polls and surveys:

1. Provide editorial and news content for the mass media.
2. Form the basis of marketing or advertising media research.
3. Measure public opinion for public relations, governmental, or political uses.
4. Build social science theory.

There are a variety of ways of accessing this information, and consulting a reference librarian will get you to the appropriate source. Although a great number of paper indexes cover this kind of information, electronic access presents some of

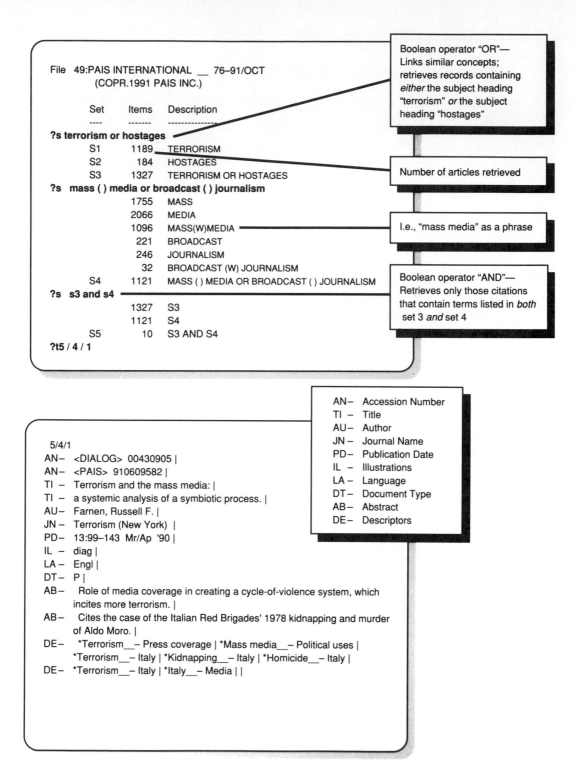

File 49:PAIS INTERNATIONAL __ 76–91/OCT
        (COPR.1991 PAIS INC.)

        Set   Items   Description
        ----   ------- --------------

?s terrorism or hostages

        S1   1189   TERRORISM
        S2   184   HOSTAGES
        S3   1327   TERRORISM OR HOSTAGES

?s   mass ( ) media or broadcast ( ) journalism

                1755   MASS
                2066   MEDIA
                1096   MASS(W)MEDIA
                 221   BROADCAST
                 246   JOURNALISM
                  32   BROADCAST (W) JOURNALISM
        S4   1121   MASS ( ) MEDIA OR BROADCAST ( ) JOURNALISM

?s   s3 and s4

                1327   S3
                1121   S4
        S5   10   S3 AND S4

?t5 / 4 / 1

> Boolean operator "OR"—Links similar concepts; retrieves records containing *either* the subject heading "terrorism" *or* the subject heading "hostages"

> Number of articles retrieved

> I.e., "mass media" as a phrase

> Boolean operator "AND"—Retrieves only those citations that contain terms listed in *both* set 3 *and* set 4

5/4/1
AN–   <DIALOG> 00430905 |
AN–   <PAIS> 910609582 |
TI – Terrorism and the mass media: |
TI – a systemic analysis of a symbiotic process. |
AU– Farnen, Russell F. |
JN – Terrorism (New York) |
PD– 13:99–143 Mr/Ap '90 |
IL – diag |
LA – Engl |
DT– P |
AB–   Role of media coverage in creating a cycle-of-violence system, which
       incites more terrorism. |
AB–   Cites the case of the Italian Red Brigades' 1978 kidnapping and murder
       of Aldo Moro. |
DE–   *Terrorism__– Press coverage | *Mass media__– Political uses |
      *Terrorism__– Italy | *Kidnapping__– Italy | *Homicide__– Italy |
DE–   *Terrorism__– Italy | *Italy__– Media | |

AN–   Accession Number
TI –   Title
AU–   Author
JN –   Journal Name
PD–   Publication Date
IL –   Illustrations
LA –   Language
DT–   Document Type
AB–   Abstract
DE–   Descriptors

FIGURE 20.8   Sample Search from *PAIS International* Database (*Source:* Dialog Search Services. Copyright ©
1991 PAIS Inc. Reprinted by permission of Public Affairs International.)

the most interesting and efficient ways to find the information. *Public Opinion Online (POLL),* a database produced by the Roper Center for Public Opinion Research, is a full text collection of public opinion surveys that have been conducted by major U.S. polling firms (these would include Gallup, Harris, Roper, Yankleovich, National Opinion Research Center, and various media organizations). POLL is available through Dialog Search Services.

LEARN BY DOING

As a practice exercise use the database worksheet to develop a strategy for searching. Use the Boolean operators to link your concepts. Your practice exercise is the following problem:

You are a local news anchor hosting a special TV production on terrorism. You will lead a panel discussion of local experts, so it is important that you find background information on the topic. For your research, your local librarian has suggested that you use the ERIC (Educational Resources Information Center) CD ROM database. The librarian has reminded you that it is important to consult the ERIC thesaurus to pick the appropriate terms. Go to your local library and actually experiment with the database. After doing this exercise, stop by the reference desk and ask the librarian to discuss your search strategy with you.

Database Search Worksheet

1. In a sentence, describe your topic.
   For example, "What role has the media played in terrorist activities?"
2. Identify the major concepts in the above statement.
   For example:
   Concept A: Mass Media   Concept B: Terrorism
3. List the databases you think are possible choices for this search.
4. If the database has a thesaurus, match your concepts with the terms listed in the thesaurus. If a thesaurus is not available, identify synonyms or related terms for your concepts.

	Concept A	AND		Concept B	AND		Concept C
OR			OR			OR	
OR			OR			OR	
OR			OR			OR	

5. List any search restrictions:
   Abstracts (if available)
   English language only
   Publication years
   Dissertations
   Book reviews
   Age group

A sample search from the POLL database appears in Figure 20.9. In this example, we are looking for questions that the Gallup organization might have asked

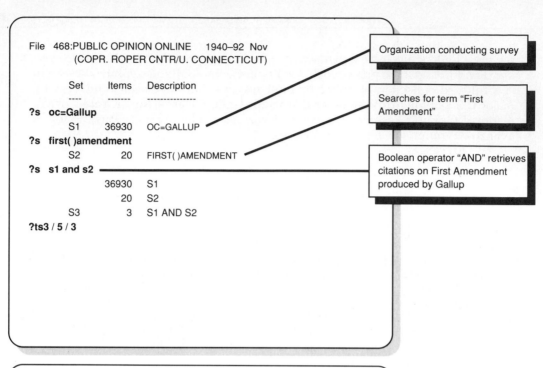

File 468:PUBLIC OPINION ONLINE   1940–92 Nov
    (COPR. ROPER CNTR/U. CONNECTICUT)

	Set	Items	Description
	----	-------	---------------
?s oc=Gallup			
	S1	36930	OC=GALLUP
?s first( )amendment			
	S2	20	FIRST( )AMENDMENT
?s s1 and s2			
		36930	S1
		20	S2
	S3	3	S1 AND S2
?ts3 / 5 / 3			

Organization conducting survey

Searches for term "First Amendment"

Boolean operator "AND" retrieves citations on First Amendment produced by Gallup

---

3/5/3
00028805   QUESTION ID: USGALLUP.1145 Q06A

010   Do you happen to know what the First Amendment to the U.S. (United States) Constitution is, or what it deals with?

Freedom of religion	3 %
Freedom of speech	21
Freedom of the press	4
Freedom of assembly	1
Bill of Rights	1
Freedom (unspecified – It insures the basic freedoms	1
Constitution – something to do with Constitution	*
Miscellaneous	6
Don't Know	70

ORGANIZATION CONDUCTING SURVEY:	GALLUP ORGANIZATION (GALLUP)
SOURCE:	GALLUP POLL–AIPO
SURVEY BEGINNING DATE:	12 / 07 / 79
SURVEY ENDING DATE:	12 / 10 / 79
SURVEY RELEASE DATE:	12 / 10 / 79
INTERVIEW METHOD:	Personal
NO. OF RESPONDENTS:	1522
SURVEY POPULATION:	National adult
DESCRIPTORS:	DEMOCRACY; RIGHTS

FIGURE 20.9   A Sample Search from the POLL Database (*Source:* Copyright © 1991 PAIS Inc. Reprinted by permission of Public Affairs International.)

on the First Amendment. If we pick the question asked in 1979, the results are interesting and perhaps somewhat depressing when we see that 70 percent of the respondents didn't know what the First Amendment was about. Although much information is given in this on-line database, the researcher does not gain access to the primary data of the survey (e.g., age, sex, educational attainment). To access that data, one would have to ask for the data from the originating group. It is important to recognize that much research conducted by private groups is considered proprietary. Groups may not share their data, or if they do, they may put severe restrictions on it.

The Institute for Research in the Social Sciences (IRSS) at the University of North Carolina at Chapel Hill maintains a large collection of national and statewide polls. The *Public Opinion Item Index* is a database they have created that allows researchers using a microcomputer to search specific survey questions using keywords.

The Louis Harris Data Center Holdings is another electronic source, housed at the Institute for Research in the Social Sciences, and containing survey data conducted by Louis Harris and Associates. A researcher with a microcomputer with telnet capability (a computer protocol for accessing other computers) can tap into this database. (For information on how to connect and the cost, contact the Institute for Research in the Social Sciences, Manning Hall, University of North Carolina, Chapel Hill.)

Researchers associated with major academic institutions that belong to the Inter-University Consortium for Political and Social Research (ICPSR) will find that they have access to the world's largest depository of machine-readable datafiles in the social sciences. ICPSR is located at the University of Michigan at Ann Arbor, and houses more than 25,000 data files. *The Guide to Resources and Services* (Ann Arbor, Mich.: Inter-University Consortium for Political and Social Research) will aid in identifying an appropriate datatape. A wide range of data sets are available, including titles such as the "General Social Survey," the "National Election Studies," and the "U.S. Census." These data files allow for secondary data analysis. Procedures for acquiring the data vary from institution to institution. Often, the library will acquire and catalog the tape and code book. The actual tape will be sent to the computing center for storage and retrieval. Successful access to this kind of information is, in many cases, the result of collaborative efforts between the libraries and the computing centers.

EVALUATING THE SOURCES

Mass communication researchers, by the nature of their training, are usually cognizant of the importance of evaluating information. Just as your face-to-face interview may or may not be credible, so too may the printed or nonprinted word.

The following questions are important ones to ask as you use sources: Does the language in the document carry an emotional tone? Is it objective? Is the article a signed article by a credible source? Is the publisher respected? Are opposing views presented? What has been left out? Remember, experts can be wrong. There are, of course, other critical and evaluative questions you can ask. What is important is that you learn how to consume information and make critical judgments on its worth.

SUMMARY

The information explosion is likely to continue. The challenge for all of us is to learn to cope with the mass of resources and the technological changes going on around us. Libraries, as an integral part of the information society, may be the best possible link you have to making the most productive use of your time and the many resources available to you.

Modern libraries are being revolutionized by the computer. Today we find, store, and use information in ways not possible a decade ago. As libraries continue to operate in a rapidly changing environment, the researcher is gaining wonderful opportunities to access needed materials with speed and ease. Whether it be print, on-line, CD ROM, or some technology not conceived of today, we are in the information age and libraries are a significant part of the twenty- first century.

STUDY QUESTIONS AND EXERCISES

1. Using the example of the search strategy described for the trip to Ethiopia (see page 403), develop a realistic information task for a journalistic, advertising, or public relations assignment you might encounter. Develop a plan for resolving the information needed for your assignment.

2. Name the broad headings of reference materials that are available to you in a typical reference department.

3. Describe what a database is.

4. Define on-line searching.

5. Name the three Boolean operators.

SOURCES

Getz, Malcolm. 1990. *Annual Report of Emory University Libraries.* Atlanta: Emory University Libraries.

Newton, Ray. 1984. *The Impact of New and High Technology Upon University Instruction in Mass Communication.* ERIC ED 251 836.

Smith, Tom W., and Frederick D. Weil. 1990. A Report: Finding Public Opinion Data: A Guide to Sources. *Public Opinion Quarterly* 54(4):609–626.

Toffler, Alvin. 1981. *Third Wave.* New York: Bantam Books.

Ward, Jean, and Kathleen Hansen. 1993. *Search Strategies in Mass Communication.* 2d ed. New York: Longman.

The Environmental Survey
Data Set and Program

```
data list fixed/id 1-3 example 4 biodgrad 5 overstat 6 notacomp 7
   involve 8 pesticid 9 sinflgov 10 writreps 11 recycle 12 safeenv 13
   envpgmra 14 nuclgood 15 boycott 16 imakdiff 17 ireadmag 18 ibuyprod 19
   myhealth 20 nocrisis 21 newtechs 22 campus 23 joinprot 24 uninhabt 25
   iusetv 26 ccouncil 27 fitefire 28 seppikup 29 nsprinfo 30
   goodwatr 31 natlnews 32 dump 33 speakout 34 buyrecyc 35 priority 36
   nucgener 37 conserve 38 pbsonenv 39 deadlife 40 library 41 bothsids 42
   buycrecy 43 dreswarm 44 sex 45 age 46-47 party 48 leaning 49 income 50
   hompopul 51 USpollut 52 TNpollut 53 rhealth 54 rhomless 55 rjobopps 56
   rpollutn 57 rpopulat 58 group 59.
variable labels sex 'sex of respondent'/party 'political affiliation'/
   leaning 'respondents political leaning'/income 'your family income'/
   hompopul 'population of your hometown'/
   USpollut 'severity of pollution in the United States'/
   TNpollut 'severity of pollution in E TN region'/
   rhealth 'importance of health care for all'/
   rhomless 'importance of homelessness'/
   rjobopps 'priority of employment as an issue'/
   rpollutn 'priority of pollution as an issue'/
   rpopulat 'priority population control as an issue'.
value labels sex 1 'male' 2 'female'
   /party 1 'republican' 2 'democrat' 3 'independent' 4 'other' 5 'none'
   /leaning 1 'very liberal' 2 'moderately liberal' 3 'moderate'
    4 'moderately conservative' 5 'very conservative'
   /income 1 'less than 25k' 2 '25k to to 49,999' 3 '50k to 100k' 4 '>100k'
   /hompopul 1 'greater than 300k' 2 '150k to 299,999' 3 '50k to 149,999'
    4 '10k to 49,999' 5 'less than 10k'
   /USpollut 1 'mild' 4 'moderate' 7 'severe'
   /TNpollut 1 'mild' 4 'moderate' 7 'severe'.
begin data.

001 5464254554464445533454211446342455524352119132267423151
002 5434455335544333444314321431356444133311111221432561324512451
003 5464456664344335453324444345525362772536312415313441531
004 717664672455666611545553655353523522555555220 12144214351
005 4522264444545352744344545324475544442554622122226632514
006762353555216661653423654164527556265636652223334652314
007 6237457753277477143476637573416747375772185313653142451
008 7426274674777477154677417475717717474777221241474214351
009775517657733177577313773717573527717374776221223175324151
010 7336655345466367132545636365726646552565221141366341251
011 5435564661555145342155566151645733155141120134354352411
012534554353535 63665465463535354635353565341231344562314
013772465247514671472521373276616346462134212113245442135
014 52234565222762674434656463526266262436562212211562431
015662466557224642775464756435354377272426741201424553521
016762362276157465771722666176522447776341351255421773512
017775535256635435666341245614545355636753656123143165351
018 5326356631427176141252216525327527541175223142246341251
019 6557666716777567732272327262377777672436133124177534121
020 4444453533226554456655455435554655551201321443124
021 5464653555444536444355344453555554454451222331543214
022 7453772242165165521156216575635635141555221222143231451
023 5555444546555555555445455555555444545455221133133312451
024 5335616651176167161577467171736717172766121143354312451
025 6334653531446245333536531634255333535143222122214332145
026 6226656624666566635663636664224213276214351
027 3553463331552123335125124453533331213241201443233215
028 443455553244434544454543535355444524334322023234431254
029772167777251775761426756573747177165656672253213641432512
```

```
030 62364356454572672 1445714545226535553556221332455321541
151 7517677734437475163695627545517736555577222423356214351
152771167777121772771226777475557177717272774222133377134251
153424565324516521347221262152445444541324451202331442315 41
154762555665422775772562776273525466373737562193524673124 51
155524644435114411654433473345535426751417422181424553124 51
156541436646114611564411475153634355271415112211544661234 51
157 624644 64655637524227651657364563456435622122316632145 1
158 72176675324573776426667175646177264524451225124672143 51
159 7117655713376177114666617421726726362666224332374431251
160771275677174764765355677275645262721614631251214653214 51
161 714775654527747714147741747472741774477722153347734512 1
162 62565 3711175154341116117263537713111146118143454542311
163564365556415661663411555165667266453536331181244544213 51
164565246756726652452612776762655456462625711182334531243 51
170 75566355444762664543454345556577554636771251341654231 51
171 64466456333764576445354535425644 65543512113115413524 1

173 71176656333352664443443254545366354556642211 3 454143251
176 7337665634446476444454517565457766446674221 2 3 355254131
177 71377776361775771134757173756166166766662213221 77254311
178652456555325532562322263265532652325225322232465521341
179 5427164714127127254114716364777623161614221131167134251
180662476746153775661356445177555536636666672212222353241351
391672274577111662761124746473553267155643441195225672451 32
392771177775351777771117747774547177124747762193232772341 52
393672275365171765771424755176767267267766641211222763541 22
39467525566631477276111373615557527746114273118344444 321 2
395656475557162455666441355175646566566476512113426432415 2
396666331376565564676614245646566466547556542353128122672314 52
397742553345644554551633757134556167375747661191334553412 52
398673474256325741462411776575617667543615551181434564213 52
399547467463234243543544312647463543457577467571191333453154 12 42
400773276757153774771632775177625367463735571181242754132 52
401762276577153575771555757575757167275656662181334653241 52
402643173437411151654541541174641466172517651201333643512 42
403762476677641576771114244174747177476547771373217477452 132
404773444567267747764612644175734277775631751182332545412 32
405772232447413751671411747174557157565777751185332673421 52
406773555657557755773624557575655577777667772183431744123 52
407762174564534764771147727744655772657377411814256554231 2
408771377465617361761524577175724167375625621181423554321 52
409555344535326452564552532252526365552245411914264514232
410536775331216661472471777167616347651616441182354523145 2
41151376151171114116311155644454741411151111814354421435 2
412653562544635771552521662764546657264211421171425534213 52
413445553426354543343454322424643264453452242411913344345132 2
414 15434412615241147421561542226547444131111119133242132452
415772374564114774771742773144644177314466475119332377153242
416771375275122772661325646175535157264637461181345652143 52
417756774447521517177466167117161747767321154119332454241352
418751577 17115515777551177557171777717771757120332 34  1  2
419655774534234624664522654263665566466656762195412451253 42
420671141141141414147111117117141516726155556120 22 566123452
51176336454243445235443355314545424514563235222223454152342
51277546457657776576712334671677772675677276722154255741 2352
51376446766743665367664664417474626757753277220244465241 352
51465566654543444545655445655546455454453454121232365521 342
51577237554312426367253347517262755435626632203344651342 52
51675227676635477367273667277274716717571756218133467214 352
```

```
517 4677473221411114331111417111471546131115135142162132542
518755164555565664465544464353733266665535532182335542143 52
519754255576455474752341477576456167564545672202334664231 52
520654146655134761471556767652717157154 7 754119133464351242
521762564645323652773553563274547175363737572191334542341 52
522766676567677677777655555575766177245576622212 3565134252
523555533321314231133661253162615344243111121211325423512 42
524531175521424572275371777147372747714471473219133544341252
525361242422327562474412731424 2 72 47437124722111354524135 2
526634264667636663772556475176767265354526652211331643124 52
527772276543412461463311362162527557153415422202332672143 52
528774367576515651661412465273512654565164322033366442315 2
529662266657422161662324766166727156271617552191 3 154234152
530771245677131767761213737572717167574727662213345752513 42
531 71373133127771777314674175717377772715772225345651345 22
532663454547431654553543564454545453545355512 0 3 456124352
533656275666335575661324555165664256466657652213223641234 52
534562455646345535352534455556453653552212231561452 3 2
535663565544363445265242155466354434544453445221221 65134252
536656475542614772455615712171717456771316672221 4 365423152
537646374532514661453611561175267255422317551211 4 165421352
538 65365551414551453621576354445537354416451221441423214 52
539642752557453343543212452154454164476427642231433645312 42
540545772267132131573111347165556475461316762212423542315 42
031 351555663225616526322552755536543523255522132254134251
032565353547244646611411474171776654554515562191432542134 51
033 665555465444 3371 44453 34454321567466661242432441342 51
034553154665253762553525556565563625666465353121333244421 351
035776465556531446276333456515353546536563263220321254214 351
036636232562226662553522653535351225233352221211432333214 51
037555535544555116515716146744546171662615176512013236542 1351
038663166576251775571527567775757157655525322123334421435 1
039765765557746461671511266173553567761453651253244564132 51
040671677454235774454335654364546557364632541195214763452 11
041 5556464643455365543145326543556645342335121141243231451
042762364556544661471512557177757154454725572191434753124 51
043 6227636641437756241145717175716756664567219333454542351
044445532544346344544345452744443624545543421201433425214 31
045776556665715277576125775717555715627464576222213176412 351
046776663555741117167436626616655725716244567219212375421 351
047554535664455665455453344544445445554344412115415443125 1
048675652447514664663255146155557255354553571221321644132 51
049 775445574166625544254236565656756442556119143455132451
050674566131113731371416654176737556721513212211235514235 1
051534351312214543354331453145544354553431341235231442314 51
052 71217677571764671324676273747177176717652193233752451 31
053 642645564246526666523263173635256363526431181222543241 51
054653445535454553572534576376677167562626552212332543125 41
055 653535463553444655446216553544435563453422122244412435 1
056562456675347264666717167166717167375615261211234553214 1
057 44244627417661142411452265254224461442471221332543214 51
058763355554226552562434564155567345551612641211442554231 51
059554274355314751553434555165535257361315441181333533241 51
060 543454252145616434212331534343644333325121951435321345 1
361415156121111731165421267211717534561314312205432543214 52
362661715131114441271511772174547767117111122201434472514 32
363643644412114551445211411114141536446131243220524453 1 2
364557453625314551557541361145233345551315531201525443214 52
365577115717714177477151777175727471771777567722632137743 5212
366675252156416571771341652165667265355316362201434543251 42
```

```
367555464544114561564411364452537264251516442202325652 41352
368473615545214621756211332277673467451437561223233612 51432
369434274654434474444443424355653464444 3446 213233544 52312
370 63375454 1677167141477724261526757161667227222165132452
371671166576134772763217657174666166372426542202133356213452
372662467756 14651 5454145516574655444361321221333266215432
373672364376311761661424643174546257153526572191231661 34252
374217521311517244233711315121632316542121121183535222 41352
375 74146773424771661632436273734146755447341172 3  477    12
376 735775572467767713146251726271674776466714034346735 2142
377673475767311441775462757175757357262653561181434543 51242
378565277547232672261234643775546167463734551183341552 51342
379 564633261245525423215461534453555445354511914215552 1342
38067375574151776136341136113761544535151645118143543143522
381656375751113671671622724152627166351725461185221543 14252
382565375357243674662443637264346376465544652185224563 52142
38356257527511741576413767172527167141414665123 1234 52
38455454353631656156562123225353645755132654118143456341252
38575126667746277577152675617575617727674577218323467543212
386544574327317661677422676477743676555177611852244243 2152
387761374577171774771156777176657177365747771203321764 32152
388 4736474121734157774114412414146674114111117342555 321452
389653455233214351241311265741217435341512331181335555 312452
390643167666214765672434654176 6 6167564546772182222665 41232
481676266777242776763416657174676266266746671212234644 13252
482771367444614475567121575717566446645575475122213165 231452
483 611246777745765767336641765571675677366522023116453 1422
4847611747773617 4771127765174747167167765752192121654 15232
485 7514663532646275144457516544627737663772211232541 23452
486 5257774111175157641547757755667551756225223255245 1352
487763274754334563652333467275457255253637562212232541 34252
48877417566712177477135234117163715464254646222233464 321452
489442376351114671563312365172725355231621112232321773 21452
490752255475422651673435635163544267462632252222212551 32452
491 6426772342245134316113117371635635241662221133254 421352
492 443544412145211256214414322442324423255531143241 352
493 624534555424626534345671765562753735576722213346 4142352
494745574336224727361511553674446155464227551233324641 42352
495565345443332444145242233415531534444141342223132554 124352
496675567555534552674455573756565564635375622121315432 1452
497675355535353533555535533535553535535555355522113416 5123452
498773567365446673574423355175763567436155422112446621 3452
499 71437336127721672543743775757467754646612155447754 3122
500777575524326672755531471274643346452514762211334453 21452
501 531555574155516715374771757671764736176422114415431 2452
50267117777774477714713127777173714177356615441332421542 43152
50336715755655435647723233535666652656757567722313217532 1452
504676656667735467367152253317354417557564676227222266 214352
505766156657675655777656765557577517546775777220234167 134252
506775475644617772775621145162736277671427451212334342 41352
5077751177777115771777171777771757171773777177522522147 7243152
508 5727711722163256121136715461755517353424233531544 123452
509544266666653356225443435446464444646453636219252164 312452
51055225547472146525714117676757572561517155212113356424 1452
061776566577234555652331455173556475476553672211124663 41251
062 4355636335635333433336365563535623433536221132156321451
063 625546651253516724216561636362554363333512114415354 2311
064675267665326662665622665266756277666525572221233653 41251
065772675544232654664521651122727277173711772213222754 13251
06635634177732511337665744321223 473 56352361191441542 31541
```

```
067665655436544536754344466556677565546445641211341541    1 1
068 4355636335635353354336465563 43455366     221312156321451
069 6457376534546477152476747675556447662357121144331    342151
070 7227677755277577655776757676727627775777712312321    143251
071 66664746 16531675532674376667465262534652172332      234151
072 6566576422565527745347753767664652546236612212241    352741
073 7764575322435266553467646556665535261456220233331    342151
074 552645554536635532335341754342563555324512422435534512
075 721 75455247737177776677676717717673676220222175213451
076 6325153532565165344224465354467555221   12152 354315241
0777672667625613635635315322636371671465664612322245435127 1
0787643666663246646623257265636361774656556622033256432415 1
079 7226645552476677241662436252627745555566221243365345121
080 631327775247727746357566637341775565325611932316732415 1
081772266547233662663433764175534354355522572192231644132 51
082 62235665227764771135766665557255275725571211241551453 21
0835722746532226626622446556565573355546425722224146521435 1
084 722746633327627622457555665554456546435622113235432514 1
085 611757622257736743457666666675555536337711914335412543 1
086 535453322112215443113311454576641414125322012344421543 1
087776275557674776674555666466527167475735662281214761342 51
088 72365666254663663332666175656254656565221133 5542513 1
089652264341344 525623345652526243463534275622153325412   1
090 722775772417777715157574746471771767377722521126732415 1
331 462432246567524635621462634673766424226422014335734125 2
332764374567114773671424576563427567565615661201   46641325 2
33376647675774413217177167311242753545171147121122477154322
334664574232313661672414631534654646252423119533155213452
33556515544321147246245475415545744527464457119 43 354241352
336 665776675666646626135671776562763775277622813326521345 2
33766364573621433156464144613461645726141766219142353321452
3386437765322133714716415611442175564516115411914336525134 2
339345472611517511375631573161411617741517151261533541243 52
340622171456217761777175777175354177775717571201341644153 22
34161617562472777266141122627464224675622447127141233451232
34266427565651457156251355616161536755151375119132563341252
343634553464422642461622175162524256465534551191431544521 32
344772563377547746771414747175752277774447771222315551432 52
345655536444544235355244455335453434525563645220232365142352
346 176747114177711176211221422421457271511112015323 1     2

348463672346124331575451241174536 56 46564776119143166142352
349556566624332442156433166416461555745662351241414552513 42
35073567566741747465751175515443535755452157118 54 45232145 2
35164336353511 75136241263717222334747521332122 13 177251342
352633263234113452472311767135456465264737471191323761423 52
353 332545463567536635227524547444575767366612353214435124 2
35462572626211771473117441667463512617114612115356643125 2
355542144326524451562451473252715265453523522192341653124 52
356575577411714731576111775173717657374411471275422643214 52
357762374554426772462411663163727357546613311193535643142 52
358775661164314751473112217171744457774116261191515552134 52
359751144375317764571421747175575267576747551212332634521 32
360 454355573445425656125541645445451434214512113445321435 2
211 254533354254412355432522323233544212162421912214423154 1
212 725562674527637614265171715572753755667711922346621345 1
213672457676272762666232443427464727725766677221212167124351
214 4536466624562655621657172624266562311561371413662413 51
215772455666251774771325756575757256255737772205221663541 21
216762166666147764671656666166667267175666762285213644351 21
```

```
21756653556454365535565332652652653536675522343121142143231541
21864236565633355465242555526552327647434375127131166241351
219 6115217252273246171462776252214722252221123132465135421
220 6417776612276237441365316554755615562532219222364123451
221 7227664424666365121366437666327776652345127332256245311
222 7226527727375277652372637262517656565577133311266345211
223635275552127671662515376274637176757513762251432545411231
224 6355537461776177576257537771527774462664221222164531241
225 645536435 646656571456526373627676252676123142134143251
226 7115656557566466164675615566517766756253120334477143251
227 5325557635255456145465636353616636563655219232466324151
228 7546434555345456434435517555647555452464121542475211  341
229  3366657117761672611274173537257555514451181534643542111
230 5425364741455146151247417541625663151246118142453413151
231 6354455535277557632117633777355715442736120144135423511
232 5767644523543455325145445644455545151353221143454431251
233 4357645672335633645317536245535775231747122234143142351
234 535526314463526755325644677425465 7557571193532534211351
235 4762223411543145543147143341554444151745219234133314251
091 6427555743677157131374737543756457361345220333254451231
092 53465556154554663444667475746646475657661211322654311251
093671475464114763562214757172517467457511611203241662431511
094 41163143135741472 2167412372733747261237122531562      1
095765656666745477457452476677766734645464566219233177123451
096767557466363777674746567175751167776656712122247725143111
097 4436564342455155225245224366223424641141221223454312541
098 6634564462762757711444777776767476477477621912235521345111
099566176555144461676753474176657666453721641211441543214511
100 711777771 17777717177277727271771777677712051237734521111
101 7127766527476266241575647262616716772367121523277435211
102 356257525176215576117211262556251621215435445132111
103 5533666562653265446242521526245564525225721914426621345111
104 7227646522266276641676417542766717361466124411365214351
105766254466743467477741476515466411774765377722232316432415111
106 6236676341276157731266747262736546352353124242255231451
107 425654 6656566554666565344545567564465451211312774351211
108 5434543434545454334454345434541233244254311
109 6756365465664566554655465645665664455645122232365521431
110 6455346454554654564544533454544546544545126141354312451
111 62234557232553662354654262635353563656255522032146624531111
112 5324535722655667215463426543534736553555122222366451231
113 231336553117513725316561723252571743223321934135532145111
114 42454343 3164156551447545161724525241111220222155231451
115 665532532336737635635652566666566233535622203421654132511
116 6226666734576477245576546467676475634661213313672534111
117 53574454 22742672415754163547257264654571243312643142511
118 573717775225727776623757172722267666626541203344534532111
1196622655674247767544157371726271774764656522153415623415111
```

```
181655646677464662571421453174454155262515462200 3245342351111
182 7346577715657676616377267574627727462563119133256425131
183 7456456626446676445445525545426446645361219222355423151
184672376556223563671264667165237456276625562212413532531411
185666645555655565555555555565555655565555546662204314553124511
186 353635575275526535332654775654676663534613114245634125111
187 4563252562733243663226212535555575322133125142354251341
188 6225666753276677143564567667727626775676223213266324151
189 53353546526531435552463255345455664232233221143154132451
190 5243553741554267351157227655756654443762222334664312511
191 56362756216651662213765151745534455311552221434543421511
```

```
192 5677246334656543711115463372777553131153122133443241351
193 7217777713447176121466616574726625572573121223365143251

195 5347475621447166211157527151766635221154122133442241351
196 67347456732277366345254767757727636564676221432254143251
197 55536347512474267431223475672626647222647222151244231451
198 2767274641766153771111115255544275316454124151423421531
199 65346534621356256245475526443436636252555135332465513241
200 66237667712277275231145747674717627232477224152255142351
202 7752775677214771771412764163217166172767772211 466413251
203 7554656556776375112345676567766567661177120534147312451
204 76757445555476776765556434445577657665667122222155153241
205 7723772447741774771415753275765267565725661222213 76514321
206 5436356343755255643256316563515777544667120142442341251
207 3455354522435235353246315563545535252635220143164124351
208 3625763311265137241217515563737616212132219153245213451
209 6563466623465365363435626355535635353556218153444421351
210 6457434514455457155465714545714666575554120132466341251
421 6317474311376145352177517656644734162744119533363321452
422 5422733151124215462513411335145663131652218132144213452
423 56327676335557167344276615244635745673445119332464351242
424 66437364551666165451166426241535756121751118143154431252
425 554654374266425564433462645453465443556118333244541322
426 5477524122476226256665335474566627771473221211534451232
427 6622646553465626667436745627562554116441181341554321452
428 7723566672555 5577131676717363657775775776118532356425132
429 76477466513577457654476417554757777574666220232477423152
430 7515751761113714713117751737171451517155521952265253412
431 53566512344632315311435225314354745541124220333241231452
432 53474263531515156151175416444615555141556128122453213452
433 5437235551564126355215617554625555211644118142253412352
434 67245435733274277154345617474546637344375219223466143252
435 76347656742466167321144747461737775141546125135367342152
437 3361113116215744767511471614163174224352218234332     2
438 1723214641755126543126215111156777111757119241543421352
439 77136676577577777151676717661716746776451218232165214352
440 54777466577477466773113544452624727332767218143332251342
441 57457257742775157364657715464417544651555122142355412352
442 76135557717656377153345517574617536764774218233376231452
443 64466224241534134255146116445644334621343119331143231452
444 55441764474213716725414442424215715441755218144454451322
445 65325433532355245413155335254424535242242120132345134252
446 75226564435126175372463417575423616453646118333445431252
447 4331364657611713427713462123371242626626121332145321452
448 53356663533 6624666 176557221535746351746218424264251342
449 7564356564416116745447675651475756675656119215412352
241 77667776673366177667114711246644713133111118222345132451
242 57766433434115512344322454455754335712111119232464431251
243 6661767766127635654235661646766761411416321923255412531
244 6635664645345535533222661544754763543553220143254413251
245 5555554546534565456342346635546425432144255121142467124351
246 7116577632477577156576317265717717373377220223475314251
247 7535444731575177645475417171737766354356219323554541321
248 634543534 354533434534354444334535343434219112165514231
249 53533153413551554412554453334335525141552219133455542131
250 7717777744166177544734174743442647145122252365345121
121 322665622226256222266626565626625233255123241165231451
122 6226665753266266342567456565525716661756125222376213451
123 543656555334426544224642425354573165431655222233265123451
124 6316447753276366443545456355425736352755121322366124351
```

```
125 6246555652455265462226526455636635352545123133376321451
126 2517666722726166262226262222666666222642220322466132451
127 7216453213465147233174316552635625273633120211465214351
128 4337124553625445565255415563535765443354120132 44132451
129 6666776615666467161476717666616716674377121542 477325141
130 5234313242455155143176316372534737672756120343454432151
131 6236425541352256442176626573636646572666121142454342151
132 5365633644343177654137417564737757353777121322266452131
133 7326777736766666732667757464627646775777222321266413251
134 5455655666565456623256656455636567566666234122155312451
135 7227777735277566633567667464627736765677123311256421351
136 5365545721565267141177216473277774657761213332266421351
137 6643565473154515577411745643445345414132412221326431425
138 7632656472155515521445656566561654647254412033337542135
139 7651767552255557711435766777562774737155312413247443215
140 6652666654522772562544476365666156755627562211342641354
141 5532751151517746613777576636751371646325721922225412435
142 7753775361417346647 5451675777147363742541221331663143
143 5554336333253223576513215343553523343323121142265224351
144 7722672662626756625776557567626726665367220323177314251
145 6623763622424636544257543644763463556534612132216521435
146 6255452114452553521555175526354241515442211322644312
147 5642765574245656534323551756573644545466622014325454123
148 6733666565344526665317541636573664532266521922346441532
149 7711777717177577112777272777717774742192233772325141
150 6226655726456256245245517563546626342665219131454312451
300 7731744271244315445113672776274664633136623013554513245
301 6317656744247466143434447573517747454666220232566412352
302 3446335521343165232146424424346536541763222222356321452
303 4455563463113761461663755155437175135633422193221652134
304 6612566665525646625354551544551564554565623113247634125
305 6523652557325572671242747154647166564737772191 4 54553142
```

```
307 7733765774547777716177575242462771747477521 9 23376423152
308 5655564643424651554452563265554453462533532192325433214
309 6612666673256656712646741746362763557467722123415523415
310 5111711711127451541121413132117273111417752205247752134
311 673666 47214662661565757167736365563525662191334543214
312 5635655541246615744326641646442334425142221921326521345
313 6662655474136747714213311746541774764477721933323332154
314 7724572571247646712347544647574771747377721912346514325
315 567373646216671366712647234577267665317361223324 53 21  2
316 6654635442153715543116645443135354511174112013315321435
317 4336463422426137342156316555466452414542194432143145
318 7776667774117547617322671635471671766576722114326434125
319 4447437473142144541144414454224574131124120112554541322
320 7711757773447757713167451747441675647466511952226543125
321 5212536662177717737112651627211647765175311914345352143
322 5124653411274177252167613474757626544747228222465241352
324 5737754553226415713152671179533355241352
325 6577745161111715716311651565671551557254721935447725134
326 7712132374117617713147374414551471767547512333416745321
327 7367743474146422617513521311615775415122411914357534125
328 7662651771317737752277271727271771757326612131136635421
329 5534666531156635713225662636361552656365612015157614235
330 7662455655443426655315471646435545555461201435541234
451 6525655373334546735215642545563774735445512022335641235
452 5421736774756556742145471645453555645165613122235724135
453 6644746564367665421234452445332467443245721832325442315
454 5642767674136717756247461767471752726377421822315432145
```

```
4555557777751151537775175362717151777717757711831413132145 2
4566713643573177617771511355775716355173756671181431654312 52
4577622767362117612773114774627242572716116412014436432154 2
4586536564542546155534555625444436656121545119332464142352
4595733755524177716523225361736361557316165411814335412534 2
4606634666572444636435242552646653665645466321814255624135 2
4617471556451444614775146761316144775567175111913214645123 2
4626434455463224313743122563534164574525153311813245432145 2
4636756724574175217527213571777175775424147511832415354132 2
4646445747533425526654311543447566572522265411923245513245 2
4657533743415756714713146666645423462646134512423256532145 2
4666423435216266312623116562735464463546212311914155512345 2
4676521645561317526622545652754472571655456621822326643215 2
4685543665454553635635454332635455563632266622214125513245 2
4694633466652126614632635726354635635314144221834344521345 2
4706341734242146416544224541423243643515264612014335643125 2
471 7357543764463136241177147274764767452644120133264534122
4721753766611337746764647741144464663235113322534466451232
4736533752556646654556125336164636266376556451201434664513 22
4746521654651425736627322453645542653744264721913235313245 2
4755622755661435735614345671765675556165537552195424554312 52
4767623736772617767622266373735371771666277712122327534521 2
4777635757774436637622235476757572774475377712033316445231 2
4785654564631636467616147661775445672327644322322326653124 2
47956334674421 7615664226471735172363231156220322355231452
4806611756575125716725245771726271571556151522013336413245 2
237 7237417712266567252475716545767756673767222142267321451
238 2535456361255125541455445562656725131756122142354312451
239 6116767756177677222676726141717717556765223143376134251
240 5663213551562145651157211411555553141422119222242142531
1656543655663347635725545553745452563554554611933256532145 1
end data.
t-test groups = group (1,2)
  /variables = USpollut TNpollut
  /options = 2.
```

B

An Introduction to Computers for Data Analysts

S. PAUL WRIGHT
University of Tennessee, Knoxville

1. What Is a Computer?

A *computer* is simply a device for processing information. These days, computers are mostly electronic devices, but they can also be mechanical, as in the case of the abacus or of the mechanical adding machines that preceded electronic computers. What does a computer do? It takes existing information and "processes" it to produce new information (or, if not new, then at least rearranged and enhanced). In *computerese*—the technical language of computing—the existing information that goes into the computer is called *input*, and the new information that comes out is called (surprise!) *output*.

An important point to remember is this: When computers are used for statistical data analysis, there are two kinds of input and two kinds of output. In order to do data analysis, you must have data and you must decide what to do with the data. Therefore, the two kinds of input are (1) data and (2) instructions on how to analyze the data. Instructions are commonly called *commands*, and a series of instructions is commonly called a *program*. The two kinds of output are (1) the results of the analysis and (2) miscellaneous messages, including error messages, warnings, and computer usage statistics.

Computers come in all sizes, but traditionally a computer is thought of as belonging to one of three size categories. The largest and fastest computers, which usually serve many computer users simultaneously, are usually called *mainframe* computers. The University of Tennessee Computing Center (UTCC), for example, operates several mainframe computers for faculty and student use. Some of these are from IBM, and some are VAXes from Digital

Equipment Corporation. At the other extreme, the smallest computers, which are usually used by only one person at a time, are called *microcomputers.* These include personal computers (PCs) or home computers, such as the IBM PC and its clones and the Apple Macintosh computers. In between are *minicomputers.* But the boundaries between these size categories are not clearcut. For example, the VAX computers have traditionally been considered minicomputers, but the newer and bigger VAXes would probably be called mainframes. And on the other hand, there are the super-microcomputers, often called *workstations,* which are actually somewhere between a "micro" and a "mini."

2. The Parts of a Computer

All computers, no matter what size, have the same basic construction. I find it helpful to think of a computer as consisting of these five parts: (1) input devices, (2) output devices, (3) the central processing unit, or CPU, (4) external storage devices, and (5) software. The first four parts make up the physical machinery of the computer and are called the computer's *hardware. Software* refers to a program containing instructions for carrying out some tasks on the computer. I will discuss the parts one at a time.

An *input device* is a piece of equipment used to get information (data and/or instructions) into the computer. The primary input device for most computers is a typewriter-like keyboard. Other input devices, which tend to be used more with microcomputers than with mainframes, include the mouse, trackball, joy stick, scanner, and light pen. If you know what these are, fine; if not, don't worry about it.

An *output device* is used to get information (messages and/or results) out of the computer. The two most common output devices are a *terminal screen* (or CRT for cathode ray tube, or VDT for video display tube) and some type of printer (impact printers, dot-matrix printers, laser printers, etc.). Other output devices include *plotters* (for producing high-resolution graphs on paper) and *speakers* (for audio output).

The "heart" of the computer is the *central processing unit,* or *CPU;* it is the part that does most of the real computing. Within the CPU are circuits for controlling the flow of information, circuits for doing the actual computations, and the computer's *memory.* Despite the name, the information in the computer's memory is *not* "remembered"; that's what external storage devices are for. Computer memory is actually *temporary* internal storage space. Memory is where information is held (temporarily) in the computer while it is being processed. Once the processing is done, the computer's memory is erased!

An *external storage device* is a piece of equipment used to store information electronically for later use by the computer. It is "permanent" storage (at least until you erase it—intentionally or accidentally!). External storage can be used for both input and output; that is, you can store data and instructions for later input into the computer, and you can store the messages and results that come out. External storage actually has two components: (1) the storage *medium* on which the stored information resides and (2) the storage *device* that transfers the information between the storage medium and the computer. For example, some microcomputers allow information to be stored on audiocassette tapes. The cassette tape is the storage medium, and the cassette recorder/player is the storage device. A more common storage medium for microcomputers is the *floppy disk,* which comes in 3.5-inch and 5.25-inch sizes, with its accompanying storage device, the *floppy disk drive.* The next step up in computer storage is the hard disk. A *hard disk* can hold more information than a floppy disk, and it can transfer its information to and from the computer faster; it also costs more. In many hard disks, the storage medium is permanently mounted in the storage device, and the whole unit is simply a relatively small (for microcomputers) to relatively large (for mainframes) box. Hard disks with removable media are available, too. In some computers, a hard disk may be installed inside the cabinet with the CPU, so that it does not appear to be a separate part of the computer. Though disk storage is the most common form of storage these days—on mainframes, minis and micros—there are other alternatives. As mentioned above, ordinary cassette tapes can be used for storage on some computers. There are also other forms of magnetic tape storage that hold more information and are more reliable. Another more recent form of computer storage is optical storage on a compact disk.

The four parts of the computer discussed above make up the computer's *hardware.* The CPU actually does the computing, and in honor of its central role in the computer, the other three parts making up the hardware are called *peripherals.*

The final part of the computer is the *software.* Many would not classify software as part of the computer since it is not part of the machinery. I include it as part of the computer because the computer is incomplete without it. The software is what makes the computer work. That is, the software tells the hardware what to do. To be more precise, *you* tell the software what you want the computer to do, and the software translates your request into "machine language" that the hardware can understand. Software is usually thought of as existing on two different levels: (1) the operating system and (2) applications software.

The *operating system* (or simply *OS*) provides the basic interface between you and the computer. It is a lot like a receptionist in an office. The OS takes your request and either handles it on the spot or passes the request along to the appropriate specialist. (The applications software packages are the specialists.) Here are the names of some of the operating systems you may run across. For example, currently there are two IBM mainframes operated by UTCC for faculty and student use. One runs the MVS operating system, used mostly for research requiring substantial computing power. It also runs an interactive system called TSO. The other IBM mainframe runs CMS, a relatively "user friendly" system used by many faculty and graduate student researchers and in some classes. The VAX "mainframe" system (actually a cluster of several VAX computers), which is used extensively in classes as well as by faculty and student researchers, runs the VMS system. UTCC's multi-user Sun workstations use the UNIX operating system. Students and faculty members at UTK also have access to microcomputers maintained by UTCC. These include IBM PCs and Apple Macintosh computers. (Of course, many departments and many individual faculty members and students have their own personal computers as well.) A widely used IBM PC operating system is called DOS (for disk operating system). A newer IBM PC operating system that should eventually replace DOS is OS/2.

Applications software packages are the "specialists" mentioned above. There are too many types of software to mention them all, so I'll just name a few types that should be of most interest to data analysts. Perhaps the most essential type of software on any computer is the *editor,* which is used to enter all kinds of information (data, programs, letters, papers, etc.) to be stored "on the computer" (i.e., on the computer's external storage device). It is also used to modify or "edit" information that was previously stored. On some computer systems, an editor may be referred to as a "word processing package." Different computer systems have different editors, and many systems have several different editors to choose from. (One notable exception is WordPerfect, which runs on IBM PC, Macintosh, IBM CMS, and VAX VMS. This is not an endorsement of WordPerfect, simply a statement of fact. I'm not a WordPerfect user myself.)

One other type of application software package of interest to data analysts is, of course, the data analysis software package (or statistical software package). Again, there are many to choose from. Some run on only one computer system; others run on several different computer systems. I'll list (in alphabetical order) some of the packages I have used, just so you can have some examples: BMDP, Data Desk, JMP, Minitab, SAS, SPSS, Statgraphics, Systat. (This is obviously a very selective list; if I have omitted your favorite, I apologize.)

3. Measuring Computing Power

When people talk about how "powerful" their computers are, they usually refer to two things: (1) how fast they are and (2) how much storage capacity they have. Storage capacity includes both the amount of memory in the CPU and the amount of external storage (sometimes disk storage—most often hard disk storage).

Computing speed can be measured in several ways. One way is to state the basic *clock speed* of the CPU. Roughly speaking, this is how fast the processor "ticks"—the faster it ticks, the faster your instructions get carried out. Clock speed is usually stated in *megahertz, or MHz* for short; one MHz is one million cycles (clock ticks) per second. For example, top-of-the-line microcomputers have processors that runs at up to around 50 MHz. Mainframes usually run much faster. Another way to measure speed is in terms of the number of instructions the computer can process per second. Two common units of measurement are *MIPS* (millions of instructions per second) and megaflops or *MFLOPS* (millions of floating point operations per second—see below for more about "floating point"). For example, the current generation of microcomputers are capable of as much as 5 to 10 MIPS and around 0.5 MFLOPS. At the other extreme, UTCC's most powerful mainframe computer is capable (theoretically, under ideal circumstances) of 50 MIPS and 100 MFLOPS. Of course, these numbers will probably be obsolete by the time you read this because of continuing improvements in computer technology.

Storage capacity, both in memory and in external storage, is measured in the number of characters of information that can be stored. On a computer, one *character* (i.e., one alphabetic letter, one numeric digit, one punctuation mark) takes up one *byte* of storage. So computer storage is measured in bytes, *kilobytes or KB* (roughly a thousand bytes), and *megabytes or MB* (roughly a million bytes). The amount of memory on microcomputers has gradually crept up from a few KB to a few MB. Mainframes tend to have a few tens of MB of memory. Floppy disk capacities have grown from a few hundred KB to between one and two MB. Microcomputer hard disks have gone from about 5 MB up to a couple hundred MB. Mainframe hard disks usually have capacities in the hundreds, or even thousands, of MB. (A thousand megabytes, which is roughly one billion bytes, is called a *gigabyte*.) Compact disk storage systems also have capacities in the hundreds or thousands of MB.

4. How Is Information Stored in a Computer?

First of all, there are two distinct types of computers. The computers that I have been discussing (and will continue to discuss) are *digital* computers. The other type of computer, about which I will say nothing except the name so that you will have heard of it, is the *analog* computer. On a digital computer all information is stored (usually electronically or magnetically) on devices or materials that can exist in one of two states. The two states could be called "on" and "off," or "true" and "false," or "up" and "down," but they are most often represented numerically with the digits 1 and 0. Thus, all information in the computer is represented by strings of *1*s and *0*s. Because there are only two digits in this system, it is called a *binary* (or base 2) number system. The smallest unit of information on a digital computer, then, is a single *binary digit* (a 1 or 0), or *bit*.

The more commonly used unit for measuring information, referred to in the previous section, is the *byte*, which is a string of *eight bits*. As you already know, a byte represents a single character. That is, each character of text that is entered into a computer is converted to a string of eight *0*s and *1*s. As a mathematically minded person would quickly realize, this means there are 256 (2 to the 8th power) possible characters in the computer's alphabet. Why so many? Though we think of our alphabet as having 26 letters, there's actually much more to it than that. First of all, there are two different versions of each letter, lowercase and uppercase. Then there are the 10 numeric digits of our decimal (base 10) number system. Then there are all the special symbols for punctuation, mathematical operations, etc. On top of that, the computer includes in its alphabet a number of "invisible" characters having special functions. Two of the least esoteric examples of invisible characters are the characters produced by striking the carriage return key or the tab key. Even with all these, there are only about 128 "standard" characters that everyone agrees on, leaving lots of room for future expansion.

At some point in time, someone had to decide what string of eight 0s and 1s should be used to represent each character. For better or worse, two such systems are in wide use. The standard system, used by nearly everyone, is called *ASCII* (pronounced "ask-ee"), which stands for American Standard Code for Information Interchange. The other, "nonstandard" system, which is used only on IBM mainframes (but not on IBM PCs) is *EBCDIC* (pronounced "ebb-see-dick"), which stands for Extended Binary Coded Decimal Interchange Code. For your entertainment, I've included a few examples of ASCII and EBCDIC codes in the table below.

	ASCII			EBCDIC		
character	binary	hex	decimal	binary	hex	decimal
A	0100 0001	41	65	1100 0001	C1	193
a	0110 0001	61	97	1000 0001	81	129
b	0110 0010	62	98	1000 0010	82	130
c	0110 0010	63	99	1000 0011	83	131
z	0111 1010	7A	122	1010 1001	A9	169
1	0011 0001	31	49	1111 0001	F1	241
2	0011 0010	32	50	1111 0010	F2	242
9	0011 1001	39	57	1111 1001	F9	249
.	0010 1110	2E	46	0100 1011	4B	75
?	0011 1111	3F	63	0110 1111	6F	111
+	0010 1011	2B	43	0100 1110	4E	78
return	0000 1101	0D	13	0000 1101	0D	13

This needs some explanation: What do the *hex* and *decimal* columns represent? They are two different commonly used shorthand notations for the binary codes; it's simply easier to write 65 or 41 than to write 01000001. First the easy one. The decimal column tells the position of the character within the alphabet. Thus, the uppercase *A* is, roughly speaking, the 65th letter of the ASCII alphabet. (For the mathematically minded, 65 is the value in the decimal number system that corresponds to the value 01000001 in the binary number system.) The hex column is the corresponding value in the *hexadecimal* (base 16) number system. It turns out (because 16 is 2 to the 4th power) that every string of 4 binary digits corresponds to a single hexadecimal character, so the hexadecimal representation is only one-fourth as long as the binary representation. This shorthand is especially useful with large binary numbers as the example in the next paragraph shows. It's really not important to know how to convert between binary, decimal, and hexadecimal (unless you're a computer scientist), and I include it here only because *hexadecimal* is one of those words (like *byte* and *ASCII*) that you need to have at least heard, even if you don't fully understand them.

ASCII and EBCDIC are only part of the story about how information is stored in the computer. *Essentially all information in external storage (e.g., disk storage) is stored using ASCII or EBCDIC codes;* but when the information goes into the computer's memory for processing, things change. At that point, it becomes necessary to distinguish between two fundamentally different types of information: (1) *numeric* information and (2) *character* information. Character information is stored in memory just as it is on disk, using ASCII or EBCDIC codes, one byte per character. That doesn't work for numbers. The thing that makes numbers different from other character strings is that arithmetic is done with numbers—addition, subtraction, division, etc. In order to do arithmetic with a number like, say, 13, the string of characters representing the decimal number must be converted, not into an arbitrary and numerically meaningless string of bits using ASCII or EBCDIC codes, but into the corresponding number in the binary number system. For example, the ASCII code for the two characters *1* and *3* is "00110001 00110011", but the numeric quantity represented by *13* in the decimal number system is 1101 in the binary number system. Thus the binary number for the *quantity 13* is quite different from the ASCII (or EBCDIC) representation of the *character string 13*.

If all numbers were small whole numbers, it would be sufficient to simply express them as binary numbers. But numbers can be integers or fractions, positive or negative, and very large or very small. To accommodate all this variety, computers use the binary equivalent of scientific notation, which is called the *floating point* representation of the number. For example, the decimal fraction 0.00000375 could be written, using scientific notation (also called exponential notation), as $.375 \times 10^7$ (.375 times 10 raised to the 7th power). The three parts of the number are the *fraction* (.375, also called the *mantissa*), the *base* (10), and the *exponent* (7, also called the *characteristic*).

Just how these parts are converted into a floating point number in the computer's memory depends on the computer system, but with most computer systems, floating point numbers come in two sizes. *Single precision* floating point numbers are 4 bytes (32 bits) long, and *double precision* floating point numbers are 8 bytes (64 bits) long. (Some computer systems also have *extended precision* numbers that are 16 bytes long.) Most calculations done in statistical software packages are done in double precision. Notice that every double precision number, no matter how large or small, takes up the same amount of memory in the computer: 8 bytes, or a string of 64 zeros and ones. Making all numbers the same size is necessary for doing arithmetic. Of the 64 bits, 1 bit is for the sign (usually 0 for positive and 1 for negative), 7 bits are commonly used for the exponent, and the remaining 56 bits contain the fraction. This scheme allows about 17 significant (decimal) digits of accuracy. Notice that the base doesn't have to be specified since, on any given computer system, it is always the same. (However, different computer systems use different bases.) The fraction and the exponent are expressed as binary numbers (though a little trickery is usually used to allow for a negative exponent). For example, on IBM mainframes, the decimal fraction 0.00000375 would be stored in memory as the binary string 0011110000111110111010100010000010011010101010100011101011010001 or, in hexadecimal shorthand, 3C3EEA209AAA3AD1. The same number on the VAX (VMS operating system) is 7B3782A8A86A46EB.

Incidentally, just because a number (like 0.00000375) can be expressed precisely in decimal, that doesn't mean it can be expressed precisely in binary. This is the case with many binary fractions; it's like trying to write *one-third* in decimal. So there are round-off errors in computer math. Using a more precise representation (double precision rather than single) reduces the error. Even so, when you see a computer printout with results printed to umpteen decimal places, you can be pretty sure that the last few decimal digits are inaccurate.

5. Giving Instructions to the Computer

Ultimately, if you want the computer to work for you, you have to communicate with it by way of instructions to the operating system and application software packages. Different software systems have different "styles" of communication. One important distinction is that some systems specialize in batch processing, and others are interactive. Another is that some systems are command driven and others are menu driven. On many modern computer systems, you get to choose the style of communication you prefer.

In *batch processing,* you draw up a list of things you want the computer to do (e.g., a series of data analysis procedures). That is, you prepare series of instructions for the computer; such a series of instructions is called a *program.* Then you submit the program to the computer, and you wait while the computer carries out the instructions and prepares a report of the results. If you made a mistake somewhere in your instructions, you revise your program and try again. By contrast, in *interactive processing,* you basically carry on a conversation with the computer (thus it is sometimes called *conversational* processing). You say something to the computer—that is, you give the computer a *command* (e.g., you ask it to do a certain data analysis procedure); and the computer says something back to you (it gives you the results, or it tells you why it couldn't obtain the results)—usually almost immediately. By doing things interactively, you are able to use the results from one command to help you decide what to have the computer do next. This is quite valuable in data analysis where, for example, you may want to check certain assumptions before you commit to a particular data analysis procedure. Another advantage of interactive processing is that you can usually correct your mistakes. If the computer misunderstands a command you give it, you can try again. In all fairness, batch processing also has its advantages. One such advantage is that once you have submitted your program to the computer, you are free to do other things while the computer is running your program. Also, batch processing is very useful in a production environment where the same program (often a very long program) is run repeatedly (e.g., monthly, weekly, or daily). Fortunately, on many computer systems (especially on mainframes) you have the best of both worlds: You can submit a program for batch processing using a command issued from an interactive processing session.

Another useful distinction is between command-driven and menu-driven systems. In a *command-driven system,* you issue commands or instructions to the computer in words. Since today's computers don't understand everyday English, you first have to take time to learn to speak the computer's language before you can begin to use it effectively. Typically, computer language commands are something like English, but very simplified, very limited in vocabulary, and frustratingly intolerant of misspellings and incorrect punctuation. In contrast, with a well-implemented *menu-driven system,* you are able to use the computer with almost no initial training. The computer presents you with a list of choices of things to do (a *menu*), and you simply choose from it. Each time the computer needs more information from you, it presents you with another list of choices. If you are uncertain about what choice to make, you can usually ask for help. There is no language to learn, so no initial training is required, provided you know enough about the application you are using to make sensible choices. (For example, you are unlikely to be able to use a menu-driven data analysis package if you know nothing about statistics.) In other words, menu-driven systems tend to be more "user friendly" than command driven systems. On the other hand, once you have learned the computer's language, you can usually get your work done faster using a command-driven system. (As an analogy, think how much faster it is to issue a string of commands, "Give me a burger with lettuce and tomato but no onion, a small order of fries, and a large coke," than to answer a series of questions one at a time, "Do you want tomato on that? what about lettuce? and onion? Would you like fries with that? large or small?" and so on.)

In the past, operating systems and applications tended to be either command driven or menu driven. Some people may have even chosen which computer to buy (e.g., IBM PC versus Macintosh) or which applications software to use (e.g., SAS versus Statgraphics) based on their preference for style of communication with the computer. However, this distinction is breaking down. Many systems now allow you to choose to use commands, or menus, or a combination of both.

Guidelines for the Public Use of Market and Opinion Research

This is an effort to state a professional consensus on how market and opinion research for public use should be assessed and what determines how useful, sound and credible particular research may be in such applications. The guidelines which follow outline the criteria which are important in the evaluation of the validity and reliability of research results and of the weight to be given to them.

It was written because research is being used increasingly for public purposes:

- as evidence in legal cases
- as evidence in testimony at government and other public hearings
- in support of advertising or publicity claims for products, candidates or causes
- as support for news stories and features which appear in the press and other media.

These public purposes can and do impact broadly on our lives and our institutions. They are creating a new role for research and a need for new ways to assess its soundness and value.

Research used for public purposes is different from internal or private research in its implications and in its quality requirements. *Research used internally* by companies, individuals or governments only has to meet the requirements of its sponsor, and while it is often done to exacting specifications, it may also be done to standards that are less demanding than those required for public research. It may be useful to its sponsors even though it is selective in its orientation, or based on very limited cases, tests or opinions.

For such research, the sponsor decides how the research will be used and how much credibility and weight to give the results. The sponsor can set the standards because the sponsor bears all the consequences of the research.

However, when research is put to a public purpose the situation is different. This research can affect the interests of people and organizations who have neither solicited nor supported it. Once it is published or reported it may come to be put to purposes for which it was not intended, and the public use may impute authority to the research not anticipated by those who designed and conducted it. It may lend an importance that the research itself does not warrant.

Given the potential fallout from research that is put to public use, it is essential that such research be conducted carefully and judged critically.

This is not to say that the standards for such research should be dogmatic or unrealistic. Few absolute standards of quality ever apply to market and opinion research. Decisions about what to do and how many cases to study, and what words to use to communicate what meaning are often pragmatic and, on occasion, somewhat arbitrary.

The realities of the field make compromise inevitable and perfection impossible. Nonetheless, when research is put to public use, it is essential that it be fairly and competently conducted and that it be honestly reported.

The guidelines that follow are intended to aid those who would use research publicly to reach well-considered judgments on the suitability of the research for that purpose.

In the final analysis, a number of factors affect the quality of research and all of them must be considered when the research is judged. The *Guidelines* group these factors into seven areas of evaluation:

A. ORIGIN—What is behind the research
B. DESIGN—The concept and the plan
C. EXECUTION—Collecting and handling the information
D. STABILITY—Sample size and reliability
E. APPLICABILITY—Generalizing the findings
F. MEANING—Interpretations and conclusions
G. CANDOR—Open reporting and disclosure

The guidelines for each of the areas identify major issues that must be considered, and state the research principles that should be applied. After each set of guidelines, two sets of questions are listed:

Key Questions: These questions are so basic that the usefulness of the research must be open to serious challenge if they cannot all be answered affirmatively from the information provided.
Quality Checkpoints: These questions are designed to provide further indications of the value of a piece of research for public use. Some of these questions may not apply or be of critical importance to a specific study. But, generally speaking, the more of these questions that can be answered affirmatively, the sounder the research and the better suited it is to public use.

Most of these questions can be judged by careful study of the research in question, without special technical knowledge, but in some cases, it may be necessary to get a professional research opinion.

A good deal of information is needed to assess how research results may legitimately be used. Those who do the research should provide whatever is needed to judge it. If needed information is not supplied, and the users of the research cannot secure it on their own inquiry and initiative, an assumption that the information would reflect negatively on the study is probably justified. In the final analysis, it is the responsibility of those who elect to put research to public use to demonstrate its soundness and value.

A. ORIGIN—What Is Behind the Research

Research should start with a clear statement of why it was conducted, who paid for it, and who was responsible for the way it was done.

Specific research can be judged best against an understanding of its intent and background. Misrepresenting the source or sponsorship of research or concealing its true purpose from its users distorts its value. Distortion can also occur with the public use of research that was not meant for and is not appropriate to such purpose.

Those who did the research and those who sponsored and designed it should acknowledge their responsibility for it and, when the research is reported, they should say whether or not they concur with the findings as presented.

Key Questions:

A-1. Does the report identify the organizations that initiated and that paid for the research?   _____

A-2. Is there a statement of the purpose of the research that says clearly what it was meant to accomplish?   _____

A-3. Are the organizations which designed and were responsible for conducting the research identified?   _____

Quality Checkpoints:

A-4. Is there a statement by the sponsors acknowledging their acceptance of the research and its reported findings?   _____

A-5. Is there a statement from the responsible researchers of their concurrence with the reported findings?   _____

A-6. Are the problems to which the research is directed distinguished from other related or broader problems that the research was not designed to address?   _____

A-7. Is the present use of the research the use for which it was designed?   _____

B. DESIGN—The Concept and the Plan

The research approach, the sample, and the analysis should be clearly described, and they should conform to the requirements of objective and scientific study, and to the purpose for which the research was conducted.

The universe—which is the population of people, facilities or occurrences to be studied—should be carefully specified, and the sample should be designed to represent that universe.

A plan for the research, covering the kinds of measurements to be made, the method of data collection and a proposal for analyzing the findings, should be set up and agreed to before the research is undertaken.

The research should be designed to produce fair measurements and honest information. It should not try to mislead its users. It should not pretend to an objectivity or a significance it does not merit.

In planning, the time, money and skills to be invested in the research should be balanced against the impact of the expected information. Important decisions ought not to be based on poorly conceived and grossly inadequate studies, nor should great efforts be invested to produce trivial data.

Key Questions:

B-1. Is there a full description, in non-technical language, of the research design, including a definition of what is measured and how the data are collected? _____

B-2. Is the design consistent with the stated purpose for which the research was conducted? _____

B-3. Is the design evenhanded, that is, is it free of leading questions and other bias; does it address questions of fact and opinion without inducing answers that unfairly benefit the study sponsors? _____

B-4. Have precautions been taken to avoid or equalize patterns of sequence or timing or other factors that might prejudice or distort the findings? _____

B-5. Does it address questions which respondents are capable of answering? _____

B-6. Is there a precise statement of the universe or population the research is meant to represent? _____

B-7. Does the sampling source or frame fairly represent the population under study? _____

B-8. Does the report specify the kind of sample used, and clearly describe the method of sample selection? _____

B-9. Does the report describe the plan for analysis of the data? _____

B-10. Are copies of all questionnaire forms, field and sampling instructions and other study materials available to anyone with a legitimate interest in the research? _____

Quality Checkpoints:

B-11. Does the study use a random sample—that is, one which gives every member of the sampling frame an equal or known chance of selection? _____

B-12. Does the research use procedures for the selection of respondents that are not subject to the orientation or convenience of the interviewers? _____

B-13. If the research calls for continuing panels or repeated studies, are there unbiased ways to update or rotate the original sample? _____

B-14. In field use, would the questionnaire hold the interest and attention of the respondents and the interviewer? _____

B-15. Is the information asked for limited to what people can supply and can reasonably be expected to give openly and accurately? _____

B-16. Are study or test conditions or responses relevant to the situation to which the findings are supposed to relate? _____

B-17. Where controls or other products are involved, are they the appropriate ones to be included? _____

B-18. Was the plan for analysis set up and agreed to before the data were collected? _____

C. EXECUTION—Collecting and Handling the Information

The integrity and value of research depends on the competence and honesty with which information is collected and processed. Care in performing these functions determines, in large measure, how good the data finally are.

A vigorous effort should be made to follow and complete the sampling plan. When substitutions are made, they should be explained and documented, whether they are made when the sample is drawn, or in the field, or in tabulation, or weighting. Any weighting or ascription that is employed should be explained in detail.

Data should be carefully gathered, by competent and conscientious people, using forms and methods that are appropriate to the problem. Continuing checks should be made to ensure that data collection procedures are followed and to provide objective evidence on how well the work is done.

Collected data should be processed and analyzed in ways that best preserve and present their meaning.

Departures from the research plan should be avoided, but if they become necessary, they should be disclosed and fully explained.

Key Questions:

C-1. Does the report specify the proportion of the designed sample from which information was collected and processed or say the proportion cannot be determined? _____

C-2. Is there an objective report on the care with which the data were collected? _____

C-3. Were those who collected data kept free of clues to the study sponsorship or the expected responses, or other leads or information that might condition or bias the information they obtained and recorded? _____

Quality Checkpoints:

C-4. Are the coding rules and procedures available for review? _____

C-5. If the data are weighted, is the range of the weights reported? _____

C-6. Is the basis for the weights described and evaluated? _____

C-7. Is the effect of the weights on the reliability of the final estimates reported? _____

C-8. Were there persistent efforts, through carefully scheduled callbacks, to interview designated respondents? _____

C-9. Is the rate of sample completion calculated on the basis of the total de-signed sample (including all eligible respondents, whether or not a contact was made or attempted)? _____

C-10. Were objective tests made to determine how completing the balance of the sample would have changed the results? _____

C-11. Does the report discuss any substitutions made for any parts of the se-lected sample, either in the field or when the sample was designed and drawn, or state that there were no substitutions? _____

C-12. Are problems which were encountered in the course of the data col-lection reported? _____

C-13. Were the interviewers carefully selected, trained, supervised and paid enough to ensure their positive attitude and cooperation? _____

C-14. Were the interviewers compensated on the basis of hours worked rather than on the basis of amount of work completed? _____

C-15. If the research was a continuing design, was the identity of respon-dents, interviewers and sampling locations protected to avoid possi-ble manipulation of reported behavior or other contamination of fu-ture findings? _____

C-16. Was data gathering limited to what was reported firsthand by respon-dents, or observed directly in the field? _____

C-17. Were there confidential validation checks of the field sampling and the data gathering by unbiased independent researchers with no fi-nancial stake in a positive validation? _____

C-18. Does the report give specific information on the results of the field validations? _____

C-19. Does the report give a full explanation of any unplanned or uncom-mon mathematical manipulation of the collected data? _____

C-20. To the extent that it can be checked, did the data processing preserve the meaning and the integrity of the collected information? _____

C-21. Were the operations of the research opened to objective professional inspection, with full disclosure of the results of such inspection? _____

D. STABILITY—Sample Size and Reliability

The sample size should be reported, and it should be large enough, given the sample design employed, to yield stable results for the selected population.

The reporting of data from sample surveys should carry understandable and correctly calculated information on the statistical reliability of the major findings, or a statement that the reliability cannot be computed.

Calculation of sampling error limits should take into account the nature of the sam-pling design as well as the size of the sample.

Sampling error limits should be stated without implying that the type of error they treat is the only one that may affect the findings. The discussions of data reliability should not obscure possible questions about the overall accuracy (including nonsampling as well as sampling errors).

In repetitive studies, it should be recognized that apparent differences can result simply from changes in time or place or in the test environment or other factors.

Key Questions:

D-1. Was the sample large enough to provide stable findings? _____

D-2. Are sampling error limits shown if they can be computed? _____

D-3. Are methods of calculating the sampling error described, or if the error cannot be computed, is this stated and explained? _____

D-4. Does the treatment of sampling error limits make clear that they do not cover nonsampling error? _____

D-5. For the major findings, are the reported error tolerances based on direct analysis of the variability of the collected data? _____

Quality Checkpoints:

D-6. Is the sample's reliability discussed in language that can be clearly understood without a technical knowledge of statistics? _____

D-7. Is the unweighted sample size reported both for the sample as a whole and for each subgroup for which data are analyzed? _____

D-8. If findings are reported for small numbers of respondents, are appropriate restrictions brought to the attention of the users of the research? _____

D-9. In balancing disproportionate sampling, were reasonable limits placed on the weights assigned to individual cases? _____

E. APPLICABILITY—Generalizing the Findings

Research is usually not relevant to everybody or forever. In reporting on research, there should be a statement of the population it represents and the conditions under which it applies.

Information should not be generalized if the results do not apply to a broader universe. Statistical projection of the results to a larger population implies that the results represent that population.

Research should not present information drawn largely from sources that are easy to contact or interested in the subject without noting that such persons may not be typical of other parts of the population.

If the source of data is not typical or is uncertain, the findings may have little or no general significance, and this should be acknowledged.

The time the data were collected should be specified, and if this influenced or may have influenced the results, a statement to that effect should be included. If the data are time sensitive, they must be viewed in the context of the particular time they were collected.

Key Questions:

E-1. Does the report specify when the data were collected? _____

E-2. Does the report say clearly whether its findings do or do not apply beyond the direct source of the data? _____

E-3. Is it clear who is underrepresented by the research, or not represented at all? _____

E-4. If the research has limited application, is there a statement covering who or what it represents and the times or conditions under which it applies? _____

Quality Checkpoints:

E-5. If the information comes from sources that are easy to contact or specifically interested in the subject, is it noted that this information may not be typical of other parts of the population? _____

E-6. Does the report comment on the presence or absence of any exceptional events that might be reflected in the reported data, noting, for example, any audience and circulation drives, brand deals, publicity and promotion, and other transient factors that could affect the results? _____

F. MEANING—Interpretations and Conclusions

The value of research depends directly on what, if anything, has to be assumed to use the research for its intended purpose. If the assumptions are not made clear, or if they are open to serious question, the research is, at best, of uncertain value.

All interpretations of the research should be forthright, and consistent with the factual findings. Small differences should not be exaggerated and large differences should not be ignored or disparaged.

For research put to public use, what is important is whether it is appropriate, in concept and execution, to the purpose to which it is being applied. Research should not be judged by its labels, its stated intention, by the reputation of the sponsor or the research organization, or by its conformity to common research practices. Rather, it should be judged by the nature and quality of the actual measurements, and the relevance of those measures to the conclusions the data are being used to support.

Two particularly complex issues in the interpretation of research findings are the determination of causation and the prediction of future behavior. In general, people have a limited understanding and ability to report on their own motivations or explain their actions. The reasons behind the differences and the correlations found in study data are always more complex than they seem on the surface. Statistical relationships, in themselves, do not prove cause and effect. The careful identification and study of a broad spectrum of known variables, and systematic tracking of changes over time add confidence, but not absolute certainty, to the analysis.

Analyzing and generalizing the meaning of tests and experimental approaches is similarly, a complex business. All tests are, in some degree, artificial. The nature and the intensity of the stimulus, its method of application, the timing and character of the measurement of response and the representativeness of the test sample are all potential issues that need serious consideration in generalizing beyond the specific set of observations.

Key Questions:

F-1. Are the measurements described in simple and direct language? _____

F-2. Does it make logical sense to use such measurements for the purpose to which they are being put? _____

F-3. Are the actual findings clearly differentiated from the interpretation of the findings? _____

F-4. Has rigorous objectivity and sound judgment been exercised in interpreting research findings as evidence of causation or as predictive of future behavior? _____

Quality Checkpoints:

F-5. Is there an effort to make explicit any important assumptions that must be made in drawing conclusions from the research? _____

F–6. Does the report treat realistically people's ability to give valid or unbiased or quantitative responses? _____

F–7. Does the report specifically qualify any data that depend on the respondents' memories over time or their ability to predict future behavior? _____

F–8. Are the effects of the data-gathering instruments and methods made clear? _____

G. CANDOR—Open Reporting and Disclosure

Research should be presented for what it is, stating clearly how it was done, what it measured and the findings it produced.

The presentation should be direct, simple, and free of exaggerations, distortions and unsupported conclusions. Implications, inferences and speculative findings should be identified as such and not intermingled with either the hard data or the conclusions derived directly from the data.

Release of research findings should be accompanied by a description of the procedures in enough detail that a good researcher could redo the study without further information.

All of the gathered information should be available for inspection. Suppression of information unfavorable to the sponsor, or embarrassing to the responsible researcher, destroys the credibility of reported findings.

Key Questions:

G-1. Is there a full and forthright disclosure of how the research was done? _____

G-2. Have all of the relevant findings been released, including any information potentially unfavorable to the sponsor or embarrassing to the responsible researcher? _____

G-3. Has the research been fairly presented? _____

Quality Checkpoints:

G-4. Are all definitions, classification rules, coding procedures, weights and terminology explained in clear and unambiguous language?   _____

G-5. Are the records of the research preserved and, with proper safeguard to the privacy of respondents, are they available to answer responsible inquiries about the collected data?   _____

G-6. Is the presentation free of bias, exaggeration and graphic or other distortions?   _____

G-7. Is there a statement on the limitations of the research and possible misinterpretations of the findings?   _____

Selected Terms:
A Glossary

ADI Area of Dominant Influence; also known as Designated Market Area. The counties in which most viewing is directed toward the TV stations of the city by which the market is designated.

Adjusted R-Squared A conservative estimate of the percentage of variance accounted for.

Aided Recall In news readership or advertising research, an interview technique in which the respondent is reminded of what was available and asked to recall whether it was observed.

Alternative Hypothesis Usually labeled H_1. It is the statement that says, for statistical hypothesis testing, the observed variation in a comparison is not likely attributable to chance; namely, that A does not equal B.

ANOVA Analysis of variance; a statistical procedure used in some multiple or multivariate comparisons that focuses on the variance within and among groups.

Applied Research Sometimes called *administrative* or *problem-solving research* because it is used for administrative purposes and for decision-making.

Area Probability Sample A sample in which elements are taken from increasingly small geographic areas; for example, a sample could be based on selected states, counties, metropolitan areas, neighborhoods (telephone exchanges or zip codes), blocks.

Attribute Control Also called *statistical control;* in statistical analysis, the study of variables A and B under conditions of C or D through N.

Average The sum of scores divided by the number of scores; the mean.

Balanced Response Options Having an equal number of response options above and below the midpoint of a scale.

Binary Code A numeric code in which all symbols are cast as sets of zeros and ones; each unique set has a distinct function in the computer.

Bounded Recall A survey question technique that provides respondents with a time frame so that responses are not overly inclusive.

Callbacks Telephone calls made by a survey research supervisor to confirm the occurrence and the accuracy of an interview.

Case Study A research method that focuses on individual cases rather than cross-sectional samples.

Census A survey of all members of a population.

Central Tendency A summary data point that helps to describe a distribution; for example, the mean, median, or mode.

Chi-Square A test of the independence of variables, or goodness of fit; a distribution-free test based on the difference between expected and observed outcomes.

Chips Tiny electronic conductors that replaced vacuum tubes.

Cluster Sample A sample that focuses on specific demographic characteristics.

Coding Form In content analysis, an instrument of data collection.

Cohort Survey A sample of people who have a shared characteristic, such as all who graduated from high school in 1991.

Computer Program A set of instructions; in data analysis, instruction that divides a problem into its logical parts and puts them in proper order.

Convenience Sample A sample chosen on the basis of convenience rather than external validity.

Construct An idea formed from a set of concepts.

Construct Validity Determination whether a construct is supported by evidence.

Content Analysis A research technique for the systematic analysis of text.

Contingency Coefficient A measure of the relationship between variables measured at the nominal level when cells number 2×3 or greater. (*See also* Phi Coefficient.)

Continuous Variable Any variable whose values can sensibly be expressed in decimal form.

Correlation A ratio of the variances of two or more groups as an estimate of the extent to which one variable is related positively or negatively to another; an estimate of the extent that variables vary together.

CPM Cost per thousand. A measure of cost efficiency; the cost of advertising multiplied by 1,000, divided by the average number of people in the audience.

Critical Research Research that interprets phenomena from the standpoint of political and economic influences.

Cronbach's Alpha A reliability estimate based on interitem correlation and the contribution of each item to the overall reliability of a measurement.

Cross-Sectional Survey A probability sample; a sample in which all elements of the population have a known probability of being selected.

Cross-Tabulation Also called *crossbreaks*; a table of the frequency of response options for two or more variables simultaneously.

Data-Searching Reviewing data for relationships between variables in advance of theory and hypotheses to support such relationships.

Degrees of Freedom Abbreviated *df*; the number of elements in a set that are free to vary (i.e., whose quantity is unknown); a correction that is used in statistical hypothesis testing.

Demand Characteristic The wording of an item such that a respondent would be encouraged to respond to the perceived expectations of the researcher.

Dependent Variable A variable influenced by another variable; for example, if frequency of newspaper reading depends on education level, frequency of newspaper reading is a dependent variable.

Diary In audience measurement, a chronological record of media use; a self-report.

Dimensionality In measurement, the nature of the components of concepts.

Dispersion A measure of the spread of data about the mean of a distribution; usually expressed as the *range, variance,* or *standard deviation.*

Double-Barreled Question A question with two parts, but only one set of response options.

Eigenvalue In factor analysis, the sum of the squared loadings on a factor.

Elaboration Modeling An early method of explaining a relationship between two variables by systematically adding other variables.

Empiricism A logical framework that deals with the nature of scientific evidence.

Environmental Control Assurance that respondents in all research conditions have similar accommodations.

EPSEM Equal probability of selection method; a sample in which every element has a known probability of inclusion.

Exit Poll A survey of individuals leaving the polling station.

Expected Values In the chi-square test, the criterion against which the observed outcome is judged.

Experimental Manipulation Increasing or decreasing the presence of a research variable.

Experimenter Bias Variance attributable to characteristics of the experimenter rather than to the experimental variable.

Ex-Post Hypothesizing Waiting until data are reviewed before hypothesizing relationships and their directions.

External Validity The extent to which a measure taken from a sample generalizes to the population.

Factor Analysis A statistical technique for discovering or confirming relationships among variables; involves identifying underlying mathematical relationships.

Factor Loading In factor analysis, a coefficient smaller than 1.0 that represents the extent to which a variable correlates with its factor.

F-Distribution A theoretical distribution against which the variation in multivariable studies are gauged.

Field Experiment Experimental research that is conducted in the field rather than in the laboratory.

Fixed Format A style of data input; for example, data are entered in a consistent sequence and in a consistent column number. (*See also* Free Format.)

Focus Group Research A survey method in which groups of six to nine people are brought together to discuss a concept or product.

Forced Choice Response A kind of response option; a questionnaire item with limited response options.

Free Format A style of data input; for example, data are entered in a fixed sequence, but not a fixed column. (*See also* Fixed Format.)

GRP Gross Rating Points. The overall reach of a campaign expressed in ratings (the sum of ratings for all ad insertions) instead of the numbers of viewers or viewing.

HUT Homes using television; a fraction of the number of homes capable of receiving a TV program.

Hyphenated Market The combination of two or more communities as a single market for audience research purposes.

Hypothesis A statement of the expected relationship among variables.

Hypothetical Question In survey research, a question posed in the form: "If _____ , then *would you* _____?"

Implicit Negative A survey item that can be perceived in a negative way even if negativity was not intended.

Independent Variable A variable that influences another variable; for example, if frequency of newspaper reading depends to some extent on education level, then education level is an independent variable.

In-Depth Interview A qualitative research method; typically open-ended and tape-recorded for later analysis.

Index Any combination of measures that, taken together, constitute a supportable measure of a variable.

Interval Measures Measures that not only distinguish responses by rank, but by equal intervals; not only is a 1 more or less than a 2, but the difference between 1 and 2 is the same as that between 2 and 3.

Internal Validity The extent to which an instrument measures what it was intended to measure.

Instrument Euphemism for a questionnaire or measuring device; the instrument by which data are collected.

Instrument Error Variance that is attributable to faulty measurement or administration of an instrument.

Kurtosis A description of the vertical shape of a distribution; usually with three descriptors: leptokurtic, mesokurtic, and platykurtic.

Landmarks A survey question technique that helps respondents reconstruct an attitude or event by providing cues that spur recollection.

Likert Scale Developed by Rensis Likert; a 5-point agree–disagree scale useful in establishing unidimensionality; also used in attitude measurement.

Lottery Method A probability sample in which any member of a population has an equal chance of being selected.

Magnitude Estimation Scaling A measurement technique in which respondents judge an object against an internal standard.

Mainframe A central computer for multiple users; usually quicker and more powerful than a desktop personal computer (PC).

Matching A sample technique in which comparison groups are matched on selected criteria rather than on the basis of random assignment.

Mean The sum of scores divided by the number of scores; the average.

Median In a distribution of scores from low to high, the score that falls in the middle.

Metering Device In video research, a device for recording program origin, program, and in some cases the demographic characteristics of the viewer.

Mode In a distribution of scores from low to high, the score that occurs most often.

MSA Metropolitan Survey Area; also known as Metro Area. A population center composed of a central city and the urban area that surrounds it.

Multiple-R The model correlation; the square root of the R-Square.

Multiple Regression A technique for assessing changes in Y, a dependent variable, as a function of more than one independent variable, $X \ldots N$.

Nominal Measures Instrument items whose response options are on the order of "naming"; for example, asking a respondent to name a preferred political party.

Non-Probability Sample A sample in which not every member of the population has a known probability of inclusion.

Normal Distribution A theoretical distribution with equal proportions on either side of the mean; usually described as a bell-shaped (symmetrical) curve.

Null Hypothesis Usually labelled H_o; the hypothesis that, for purposes of statistical hypothesis testing, $A = B$ (i.e., that A is not different from B).

Open-Ended Response A data-collection technique in which response options are not provided; response is not limited by space or time.

Operational Definition The definition of a concept by its operational terms (e.g., defining *voter* as persons who voted in a given election).

Ordinal Measures Measures that order or rank responses but not necessarily in equal intervals; for example, on an ordinal scale of 1 to 5, a 1 is more or less than a 2 by a whole number or by any part of a number.

Outliers Extreme scores—those that tend to lie alone in a distribution.

Oversampling Selecting a greater number of respondents in demographic groups than their proportion in the population; for example, if Italian Americans make up only 5 percent of a population, the researcher who is especially interested in Italian American responses might use a sample in which that group is represented in greater proportion.

Panel A sample of people interviewed on more than one occasion.

Parameters Sample statistics that are used to describe a population.

Participant Observation A research technique in which the researcher enters the research site and joins the activities there while gathering data for analysis.

"Person-on-the-Street" Sample A non-probability sample that is limited to people who are able to be in a given place at a given time.

Phi Coefficient A measure of association between variables measured at the nominal level when cells number 2 × 2. (*See also* Contingency Coefficient.)

Pilot Study An exploratory or preliminary study.

Population All of the elements from which a sample can be drawn; the whole of which the sample is a subset.

Population Distribution A description of the responses to variables by members of a population.

PRE Proportional reduction in error; if the introduction of new variables improves the prediction in the relationship between two variables, the improvement can be computed as a ratio of the error in one predictor variable to another.

Predictive Validity Estimate of the usefulness of one variable in predicting another.

Private Research Research methods applied for proprietary or nonpublication purposes.

Prestige Bias The wording of an instrument item such that a respondent might be encouraged to select what would be presumed the more prestigious response option.

Pretest In experimental methods, a baseline on which the effect of a manipulation is estimated. In survey methods, a test of the utility of the instrument.

Probability Sample Also known as *equal probability of selection method* or *EPSEM;* a sample in which every element has a known probability of inclusion.

Proprietary Research Research that is conducted for the purposes of the sponsor, not for purposes of science.

Public Research Research that is open to review, replication, and cumulation.

Purposive Sample A sample chosen because its members have certain characteristics.

Qualitative Research Any investigation that attempts to understand the meanings that things have for individuals from their own perspective.

Quota Sample A sample with special representation given to members of selected demographic groups.

Random Having no predictable outcome; a random sample from a population has no predictable combination of elements.

Range In a distribution of scores, the difference between the highest and the lowest.

Rating In TV audience research, the percentage viewing as a fraction of the number of homes with television.

Ratio Measure Having the same properties of an interval measure, but with the added property of an absolute zero; for example, the thermometer.

Regression Analysis An extension of correlation, fundamentally related to analysis of variance (ANOVA); it estimates the changes in *Y,* a dependent variable, with changes in *X,* an independent variable.

Regression Sum of Squares Variation in the model that can be attributed to regression.

Reliability The extent to which an instrument produces the same outcome in repeated uses.

Replication Repetition of a previous study.

Research Design A plan for research.

Research Hypothesis A formal statement of the relationship among variables.

Residual Sum of Squares Variation in a model that is not explained.

Rotated Factor Matrix Columns of loadings representing the factors identified by rotation.

Rotation In factor analysis, a statistical procedure designed to improve the identification of subsets of variables.

R-Squared An estimate of the percentage of variance accounted for.

Sample A subset or a fraction of a population.

Sample Distribution How persons responded to variables; a description or plot of the responses of a sample.

Sampling Distribution A theoretical distribution of the means of many samples from a population.

Sampling Error The extent to which a sample parameter deviates from a population parameter.

Science A method of knowing things; derived from the Latin *scire,* meaning "having knowledge."

Semantic Differential A scale developed in the 1950s to measure the components of meaning; a set of opposite adjectives separated by seven response options; useful in attitude research.

Serendipity Interesting things found by chance.

Share In TV audience research, the percentage of homes watching a given program as a fraction of the number of homes using television.

Significance A measure of whether a sample statistic exceeds what could reasonably be attributed to chance; in statistical hypothesis testing, a decimal number that estimates the likelihood of wrongly accepting a hypothesis; usually stated as a p-value between 0 and 1, where the smaller the decimal, the greater the significance.

Simple Random Sample A probability sample in which every member of a population has a known and equal chance of being selected.

Simple Regression Used in predicting one score on the basis of another.

Skewness A description of the horizontal shape of a distribution; usually presented as positive or negative skew.

Snowball Samples See Sociometric Sample.

Social Science Application of systematic, objective methods in the study of human behavior.

Sociometric Design Same as Socio-sample; a research design in which respondents are asked to identify others who could contribute meaningfully to the survey.

Socio-Sample Formed by having respondents identify others who they believe could contribute meaningfully to the survey.

Standard Deviation In a distribution, an estimate of the dispersion of scores about the mean; it is different from variance in that its coefficient is stated as a square root.

Statistical Control See Attribute Control.

Statistical Model A combination of measurements intended to provide the optimum variance-accounted-for in relation to a dependent variable.

Statistical Package Computer program for the analysis of data.

Stratified Sample Usually a probability sample proportional to strata within the population; for example, a stratified sample of college students could be proportional to the class standing (strata) of the respondents.

Survey Research The collection of data from multiple respondents.

Systematic Interval Sample Also called *systematic random sample;* a probability sample in which elements are drawn from a preset interval in a sample frame; for example, a sample taken systematically from a telephone directory.

Target Audience People in a cross-sectional audience, who are expected to be most receptive to the message or product of the sponsor.

T-Distribution An extension of the Z-distribution; a distribution that accounts for the number of elements in a sample.

Telephone Call-Ins A nonscientific survey method in which people are encouraged to telephone their "vote" on a popular issue.

Theoretical Research Research aimed at understanding and predicting communication behavior; explores relationships among variables; sometimes called *pure* or *basic research.*

Trend Survey A survey that traces responses of different samples over time.

Unidimensionality Having a single dimension.

Variance In a distribution, an estimate of the dispersion of the scores around the mean; it is larger than the standard deviation (SD) because the coefficient is stated in terms of squared scores.

Weighting Multiplying a survey response by a number calculated to correct for discrepancies between the makeup of the population and the makeup of the sample.

Working Hypothesis A hypothesis that guides a research project; the working hypothesis broadly states an expected relationship between variables.

Z-Distribution A distribution that converts every point in a sampling distribution and population distribution to a standard score.

Index